THE
CAMBRIDGE EDITION OF
THE LETTERS AND WORKS OF
D. H. LAWRENCE

THE LETTERS OF D. H. LAWRENCE

*Vol. I: September 1901 – May 1913
James T. Boulton

*Vol. II: June 1913 – October 1916
George J. Zytaruk and James T. Boulton

*Vol. III: October 1916 – June 1921
James T. Boulton and Andrew Robertson

Vol. IV: June 1921 – March 1924
Warren Roberts, James T. Boulton and Elizabeth Mansfield

Vol. V: 1924 – 1927
James T. Boulton and Lindeth Vasey

Vol. VI: 1927 – 1928
James T. Boulton and Gerald M. Lacy

Vol. VII: 1928 – 1930
Keith Sagar and James T. Boulton

* Already published

THE LETTERS OF D. H. LAWRENCE

GENERAL EDITOR
James T. Boulton
Professor of English Studies, University of Birmingham

EDITORIAL BOARD
Gerald Lacy, *Angelo State University, Texas*
Elizabeth Mansfield, *Cornell University*
Warren Roberts, *University of Texas at Austin*
Andrew Robertson, *University of Birmingham*
Keith Sagar, *University of Manchester*
Lindeth Vasey, *Cambridge University Press*
George Zytaruk, *Nipissing University College, Ontario*

THE LETTERS OF
D. H. LAWRENCE,

VOLUME IV
June 1921 – March 1924

EDITED BY
WARREN ROBERTS
JAMES T. BOULTON
AND
ELIZABETH MANSFIELD

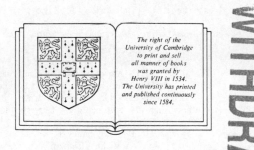

*The right of the
University of Cambridge
to print and sell
all manner of books
was granted by
Henry VIII in 1534.
The University has printed
and published continuously
since 1584.*

CAMBRIDGE UNIVERSITY PRESS
CAMBRIDGE
LONDON   NEW YORK   NEW ROCHELLE
MELBOURNE   SYDNEY

Published by the Press Syndicate of the University of Cambridge
The Pitt Building, Trumpington Street, Cambridge CB2 1RP
32 East 57th Street, New York, NY 10022, USA
10 Stamford Road, Oakleigh, Melbourne 3166, Australia

First published 1987

Printed in Great Britain at
the University Press, Cambridge

Library of Congress cataloguing in publication data

Lawrence, D. H. (David Herbert), 1885–1930.
The letters of D. H. Lawrence.
(The Cambridge edition of the letters and works of
D. H. Lawrence)
Includes indexes.
v. 4. June 1921–March 1924
edited by Warren Roberts, James T. Boulton and Elizabeth Mansfield
1. Lawrence, D. H. (David Herbert), 1885–1930–
Correspondence.   2. Authors, English–20th century–
Corrrespondence.   I. Boulton, James T.   II. Zytaruk,
George J.   III. Robertson, Andrew, 1945– .
IV. Title.   V. Series: Lawrence, D. H. (David Herbert),
1885–1930. Works.   1979.
PR6023.A93Z53   1979   823'.9'12 [B]   78-7531

British Library cataloguing in publication data

Lawrence, D. H.
The Letters of D. H. Lawrence.
Vol. 4: June 1921 – March 1924 (The Cambridge
edition of the letters and works of D. H. Lawrence)
1. Lawrence, D. H. – Correspondence
2. Authors, English – 20th century – Correspondence
I. Title   II. Roberts, Warren
III. Boulton, James T.
IV. Mansfield, Elizabeth

ISBN 0 521 22147 1 (v.1)
    0 521 23113 2 (v. 4)

SE

CONTENTS

ILLUSTRATIONS

Between pages 260 and 261

ACKNOWLEDGEMENTS

The Editorial Board offers its thanks to those owners of manuscripts whose holdings have been made available for the present volume. The relevant list of cue-titles identifies the owners in question.

The volume editors are grateful to fellow members of the Editorial Board, as well as to Mr Michael Black and his editorial staff at the Press, for advice and practical assistance. They particularly acknowledge the value of the meticulous scrutiny of their typescript by Dr Lindeth Vasey.

The following institutions and libraries generously facilitated the editors' work: Beinecke Rare Books and Manuscripts Library, Yale University; the Berg Collection at the New York Public Library; the British Library; Emory University; the Harwood Foundation of the University of New Mexico; the Houghton Library, Harvard University; Humanities Research Center, University of Texas at Austin; Middlebury College; University of Birmingham; and the University of Nottingham.

The editors are indebted to many individuals who have freely responded to requests for guidance and information. These include: Ms Jean Cook Barkhorn; Mr Jack Boyer; Mr Edmund R. Brill; Ms Marie Byrne; Mr John Carswell; Professor L. D. Clark; Professor Nicholas R. Clifford; Mr Louis Cottam; Professor Paul M. Cubeta; Mr H. C. Davis; Professor A. E. Douglas; Mrs Marian Eames; Dr P. Eggert; Mr Frank Farrell; Mr N. Furbank; Mr R. Garnett; Mrs E. Goodband; Professor J. Grenville; Mr John Grover; Mrs Rachel Hawk; Mr Colin Haycraft; Ms Daphne Hellman; Mr Frederick Jeffrey; Mr S. J. Jenkins; Mrs Olivia Rolfe Johnson; Mr Jan Juta; Dr Mara Kalnins; Mr Clark Kimball; Mrs Carolyn Law; Professor D. Lomax; Ms Bernadette Lujan; Mr Thomas McCarthy; Ms Ginny Machann; Professor P. McNair; Ms Rowena Martinez; Ms Margaret Medcalf; Dr V. Melikian; Professor Thomas Moisan; Mr C. Noall; Mrs Harwood B. Picard; Mrs Edgar L. Rossin; Mr John Ruffells; Mrs Idella Purnell Stone; Ms Jacqueline Stone; Mr Malin Wilson; Mr David Witt; Dr John Worthen; Mr C. Zuccaro. Special thanks are due to Dr Frank K. Robinson for his translations of letters written in German; Mrs Anne Buckley for her secretarial skills; Mrs Elma Forbes for compiling the index in its final form; Mrs Margaret Boulton and Mrs Pat Roberts for their tolerance and invaluable assistance at all times.

For permission to use copyright material in the annotation, gratitude is expressed to: Messrs Chatto & Windus (for a letter relating to the publication of *Look! We Have Come Through!*); Mrs Sylvia Secker (for letters written by

Martin Secker); the University of Illinois (for use of the Secker Letter-Books); and the Viking Press (for an agreement concerning *The Rainbow*).

Illustrations in this volume have been made available through the courtesy of: Ms Marianne von Eckardt; the Harwood Foundation of the University of New Mexico; Humanities Research Center, University of Texas at Austin; Mr Jan Juta and Mrs Janos Scholz; Professor Gerald Lacy; Mrs Alexandra Lee Levin; Miss Nancy Lutton, the Library Board of Western Australia; New York Public Library; Mrs Harwood B. Picard; Dr Warren Roberts; William Siebenhaar Collection in the Battye Library; Mrs Idella Purnell Stone; Dr John Worthen.

NOTE ON THE TEXT

A full statement of the 'Rules of Transcription' and an explanation of the 'Editorial Apparatus' are provided in Volume I, pp. xviii–xx. The reader may, however, like to be reminded that the following symbols are used:

[   ]   indicates a defect in the MS making it impossible even to conjecture what Lawrence had written. Where a reconstruction can be hazarded or a fault corrected, the conjecture or correction is shown within the square brackets.

[. . .]   indicates a deletion which cannot be deciphered or a postmark which is wholly or partly illegible.

TMS =   typed manuscript

TMSC =   typed manuscript copy

TSCC =   typescript carbon copy

Maps are provided to show the location of places which Lawrence visited for the first time during the period covered by this volume. No attempt has been made fully to repeat information given on the maps in Volumes I, II and III.

CUE-TITLES

Cue-titles are employed both for manuscript locations and for printed works. The following appear in this volume.

A. Manuscript locations

Ascherman	Mrs Lois Ascherman
BL	British Library
BPL	Boston Public Library
Brill	Mr Edmund R. Brill
BucU	Bucknell University
Carswell	Mr John Carswell
Clarke	Mr W. H. Clarke
Cockburn	Dr Andrew Cockburn
Cotterell	Mrs Hilda Cotterell
Cushman	Professor Keith Cushman
Forster	Mr W. Forster
Garnett, R	Mr Richard Garnett

Grover	Mr John Grover
GSArchiv	Goethe–und Schiller-Archiv, Weimar
Harrison	Mr R. Austin Harrison
Heinemann	Messrs W. Heinemann
Holahan	Mr Michael Holahan
HU	Harvard University
Hubrecht	Dr A. V. M. Hubrecht
Jeffrey	Mr Frederick Jeffrey
KCC	King's College, Cambridge
King	Miss Joan King
Lacy	Professor Gerald M. Lacy
Lawlor	Mrs Pat Lawlor
Lazarus	Mr George Lazarus
LC	Library of Congress
Moore	Mrs Beatrice Moore
NCL	Nottinghamshire County Libraries
Needham	Mrs Margaret Needham
NWU	Northwestern University
NYPL	New York Public Library
NZNL	National Library of New Zealand
Pepper	Mr James Pepper
PU	Princeton University
Ritzi	Ms Elizabeth Ritzi
SIU	Southern Illinois University
Smith	Charles H. Smith Collection, University of Indiana
SNMuseum	Schiller-Nationalmuseum
SVerlag	Suhrkamp Verlag
Throssell	Mr R. P. Throssell
UCB	University of California at Berkeley
UChi	University of Chicago
UCin	University of Cincinnati
UCLA	University of California at Los Angeles
UInd	University of Indiana
UN	University of Nottingham
UNCCH	University of North Carolina at Chapel Hill
UNYB	State University of New York at Buffalo
UT	University of Texas at Austin
UTul	University of Tulsa
WAPL	Western Australia Public Library
YU	Yale University

B. Printed works
(The place of publication, here and throughout, is London unless otherwise stated.)

Brewster   Earl Brewster and Achsah Brewster. *D. H. Lawrence: Reminiscences and Correspondence.* Secker, 1934

Bynner   Witter Bynner. *Journey with Genius: Recollections and Reflections Concerning the D. H. Lawrences.* New York: Day, 1951

Carswell   Catherine Carswell. *The Savage Pilgrimage: A Narrative of D. H. Lawrence.* Chatto and Windus, 1932

Damon   S. Foster Damon. *Amy Lowell: A Chronicle.* New York: Houghton Mifflin, 1935

DHL Review   *The D. H. Lawrence Review.* Fayetteville: University of Arkansas, 1968–

Draper   R. P. Draper, ed. *D. H. Lawrence: The Critical Heritage.* Routledge & Kegan Paul, 1970

Frieda Lawrence   Frieda Lawrence. *"Not I, But the Wind . . .".* Santa Fe: Rydal Press, 1934

Gransden   K. W. Gransden, 'Rananim: D. H. Lawrence's Letters to S. S. Koteliansky', *Twentieth Century*, clix (January–June, 1956), 22–32

Huxley   Aldous Huxley, ed. *The Letters of D. H. Lawrence.* Heinemann, 1932

Irvine, Brett   Peter L. Irvine and Anne Kiley, eds. 'D. H. Lawrence and Frieda Lawrence: Letters to Dorothy Brett', *D. H. Lawrence Review*, ix (Fayetteville, Spring 1976), 1–116

Lacy, *Seltzer*   Gerald M. Lacy, ed. *D. H. Lawrence: Letters to Thomas and Adele Seltzer.* Santa Barbara: Black Sparrow Press, 1976

Lawrence–Gelder Ada Lawrence and G. Stuart Gelder. *Young Lorenzo: Early Life of D. H. Lawrence.* Florence: G. Orioli [1931]

Letters, i.   James T. Boulton, ed. *The Letters of D. H. Lawrence*, Volume I, September 1901–May 1913. Cambridge: Cambridge University Press, 1979

Letters, ii.   George J. Zytaruk and James T. Boulton, eds. *The Letters of D. H. Lawrence*, Volume II, June 1913–October 1916. Cambridge: Cambridge University Press, 1981.

Letters, iii.	James T. Boulton and Andrew Robertson, eds. *The Letters of D. H. Lawrence*, Volume III, October 1916–June 1921. Cambridge: Cambridge University Press, 1984
Luhan	Mabel Dodge Luhan. *Lorenzo in Taos*. New York: Knopf, 1932
Merrild	Knud Merrild. *A Poet and Two Painters: A Memoir of D. H. Lawrence*. Routledge & Kegan Paul, 1938
Moore, *Intelligent Heart*	Harry T. Moore. *The Intelligent Heart: The Story of D. H. Lawrence*. New York: Farrar, Straus, and Young, 1954
Moore, *Poste Restante*	Harry T. Moore. *Poste Restante: A Lawrence Travel Calendar*. Berkeley and Los Angeles: University of California Press, 1956
Moore	Harry T. Moore, ed. *The Collected Letters of D. H. Lawrence*. 2 volumes. Heinemann, 1962
Murry, *New Adelphi*	John Middleton Murry, 'Reminiscences of D. H. Lawrence I–VII', *New Adelphi*, iii (June–August 1930–March 1931)
Nehls	Edward Nehls, ed. *D. H. Lawrence: A Composite Biography*. 3 volumes. Madison: University of Wisconsin Press, 1957–9
Roberts	Warren Roberts. *A Bibliography of D. H. Lawrence*, 2nd edition. Cambridge: Cambridge University Press, 1982
Secker	Martin Secker, ed. *Letters from D. H. Lawrence to Martin Secker 1911–1930*. [Bridgefoot, Iver] 1970
Tedlock, *Lawrence MSS*	E. W. Tedlock. *The Frieda Lawrence Collection of D. H. Lawrence Manuscripts: A Descriptive Bibliography*. Albuquerque: University of New Mexico, 1948
Zytaruk	George J. Zytaruk, ed. *The Quest for Rananim: D. H. Lawrence's Letters to S. S. Koteliansky 1914 to 1930*. Montreal: McGill–Queen's University Press, 1970

MONETARY TERMS

tanner = sixpence (6d) = 2½p.
bob = one shilling (1/-) = 5p.
half-a-crown = 2/6 = 12½p.
quid = £1.
guinea = £1/1/- = £1.05.

LAWRENCE: A CHRONOLOGY, 1921–1924

27 April–10 July 1921	At Hôtel Krone, Ebersteinberg, Baden-Baden
1 June 1921	Finishes *Aaron's Rod*; begins *Fantasia*
10 June 1921	First trade edition of *Women in Love* published in England by Martin Secker
July 1921	'Mosquito' in *Bookman*, 'Snake' in *Dial*
5–c. 27 July 1921	Robert Mountsier visits Lawrences
10–18 July 1921	To Zell-am-See via Konstanz and Bregenz, Austria
20 July–25 August 1921	At Villa Alpensee, Thumersbach, Zell-am-See
23 July 1921	'Whitman' in *Nation and Athenaeum*
August 1921	'Wintry Peacock' in *Metropolitan*
7 August 1921	Receives TS of *Aaron's Rod* from Curtis Brown
13–16 August 1921	Mountsier at Zell-am-See; then leaves for Paris
14 August 1921	Receives TS of *Mr Noon* from Curtis Brown
post 14 August 1921	'Pomegranate' and 'Medlars and Sorb Apples' in *English Review* (August)
21 August 1921	'Whitman' in *New York Call*
25 August 1921	To 32 Via dei Bardi, Florence
30 August 1921	Mary Cannan visits
2 September 1921	Philip Heseltine threatens libel action in response to *Women in Love* (settled on 15 November 1921)
c. 11–17 September 1921	Catherine and Donald Carswell visit
12 September 1921	Percy and Irene Whittley visit
19 September 1921	First batch of proofs for German translation of *The Rainbow* from Dr Anton Kippenberg
20–2 September 1921	To Siena (21 September) and Rome (c. 22 September) with Whittleys
c. 23–7 September 1921	Visits Earl and Achsah Brewster in Capri
28 September 1921–20 February 1922	At Fontana Vecchia, Taormina, Sicily

October 1921	'The Revolutionary' in *English Review*; extract from *Sea and Sardinia* in *Dial*; 'Snake' in *London Mercury*
	TS of *Aaron's Rod* to Seltzer; begins reading Giovanni Verga
22 October 1921	Sends MS of *Fantasia of the Unconscious* to Seltzer
November 1921	Extract from *Sea and Sardinia* in *Dial*; 'Fanny and Annie' in *Hutchinson's Story Magazine*
5 November 1921	Begins correspondence with Mabel Dodge Sterne who invites him to New Mexico
23 November 1921	Sends TS of *Aaron's Rod* to Curtis Brown for Secker
7 December 1921	Sends MSS for eight of the *England, My England* stories to Curtis Brown
9 December 1921	*Tortoises* published in USA by Seltzer; acknowledges James Tait Black Memorial Prize for *The Lost Girl*
12 December 1921	*Sea and Sardinia* published in USA by Seltzer
21 December 1921	Finishes 'The Ladybird' and 'England, My England'
January 1922	'The Gentleman from San Francisco' in *Dial*; begins translation of Verga's *Mastro-don Gesualdo*
9 January 1922	'The Ladybird' and 'England, My England' typescripts to Curtis Brown and Mountsier
26 January 1922	MS of 'Dregs' (later published as *Memoirs of the Foreign Legion*) and 'Magnus Memoir' to Mountsier
February 1922	'An Episode' (from *Aaron's Rod*) in *Dial*; 'Almond Blossom' in *English Review*
18 February 1922	MS of *Studies in Classic American Literature* to Curtis Brown
20–6 February 1922	To Naples via Palermo
26 February 1922	Leaves Naples for Ceylon aboard *R.M.S. Osterley*
2 March 1922	Port Said
13 March 1922	Met by Earl Brewster at Colombo, Ceylon
14 March–c. 23 April 1922	At Ardnaree, Lake View Estate, Kandy, Ceylon with Brewsters

23 March 1922	Sees Prince of Wales at Perahera in Kandy
April 1922	Begins translating Giovanni Verga's *Novelle Rusticane* (*Little Novels of Sicily*)
3 April 1922	Sends last of *Mastro-don Gesualdo* MS to Mountsier
11 April 1922	Receives proofs of 'The Horse-Dealer's Daughter' (published in *English Review*, April 1922)
14 April 1922	*Aaron's Rod* published in USA by Seltzer
22 April 1922	First part of *Novelle Rusticane* MS to Mountsier
c. 23 April 1922	Visits Judge and Mrs Ennis at 'Braemore', Bullers Road, Colombo, Ceylon
24 April–4 May 1922	To West Australia on *R.M.S. Orsova*
May 1922	Last of *Novelle Rusticane* MS to Mountsier; 'The Fox I' in *Dial* (II–IV, June–August); *The Gentleman from San Francisco* published in England by Hogarth Press; 'The Shadow in the Rose Garden' in *Georgian Stories 1922*
4–6 May 1922	Savoy Hotel, Perth, West Australia
6–18 May 1922	At 'Leithdale', Darlington, West Australia; meets Mary Louisa ('Mollie') Skinner and William Siebenhaar
18 May 1922	To Sydney on *S.S. Malwa* via Adelaide (22 May) and Melbourne
27–8 May 1922	Sydney, New South Wales
29 May–10 August 1922	At 'Wyewurk', Thirroul, New South Wales
June 1922	Fifty signed copies of *Women in Love* published in England by Secker from sheets of the first American edition; 'Fish' in *English Review*; *Aaron's Rod* published in England by Secker
3 June 1922	Has begun *Kangaroo*
15 June 1922	'Wintry Peacock' in *New Decameron III*
21 June 1922	*Kangaroo* half finished
15 July 1922	Finishes *Kangaroo*; posts MS to Mountsier on 20 July
August 1922	'Monkey Nuts' in *Sovereign*
9 August 1922	To Thirroul for Sydney
11 August 1922	En route to San Francisco on *R.M.S. Tahiti*

15 August 1922	Wellington, New Zealand
20 August 1922	Rarotonga, Cook Islands
22–3 August 1922	Papeete, Tahiti, Society Islands
4–8 September 1922	Palace Hotel, San Francisco
8–10 September 1922	To Lamy, New Mexico; meets Mabel Dodge Sterne and Tony Luhan. Meets Willard ('Spud') Johnson and Alice Corbin Henderson at Witter Bynner's home in Santa Fe
11 September–1 December 1922	At Taos
12 September 1922	Case against Seltzer for publication of *Women in Love* dismissed
14–18 September 1922	To Jicarilla Apache Indian Reservation with Tony Luhan and Bessie Freeman
25 September 1922	Receives first part of Siebenhaar's translation of *Max Havelaar*
c. October 1922	Meets Walter Ufer, Knud Merrild and Kai Götzsche
12 October 1922	Sends Spud Johnson review of Ben Hecht's *Fantazius Mallare*
16 October 1922	Finishes revision of TS of *Kangaroo*; posts to Mountsier on 25 October
23 October 1922	*Fantasia of the Unconscious* published in USA by Seltzer (in England by Secker, September 1923)
24 October 1922	*England, My England* published in USA by Seltzer (in England by Secker, January 1924)
31 October 1922	Sends Bursum Bill article to Scofield Thayer of the *Dial*; visits Mabel Dodge Sterne's ranch which she later gives to Frieda
November 1922	'Bat' and 'Baby Tortoise' in *English Review*; 'The Evening Land' and 'Turkey-Cock' in *Poetry*
6 November 1922	Receives copies of *Fantasia of the Unconscious*, *England, My England* and *Women in Love* from Seltzer
1 December 1922–18 March 1923	At William Hawk's Del Monte Ranch; Merrild and Götzsche occupy a cabin nearby

25 December 1922–c. 2 January 1923	Seltzers in Taos
30 December 1922	Mountsier arrives in Taos
January 1923	Lawrence's portrait painted by Götzsche
4 January 1923	Last page of *Kangaroo* sent to Seltzer
February 1923	'Indians and an Englishman' in *Dial*
2 February 1923	Learns of Katherine Mansfield's death, 9 January at Fontainebleau
3 February 1923	Severs business connection with Mountsier
10 February 1923	Sends MS of *Birds, Beasts and Flowers* to Seltzer
11 February 1923	Telegram to Seltzer, regarding Judge John Ford's objection to *Women in Love*, in *New York Times*
17 February 1923	Proofs of *Ladybird* to Seltzer
March 1923	'Taos' in *Dial*; *The Ladybird* published in England by Secker (in USA by Seltzer, 21 April 1923, as *The Captain's Doll*)
18–21 March 1923	En route to El Paso via Taos and Santa Fe
21–3 March 1923	En route from El Paso to Mexico City
24 March–27 April 1923	At Hotel Monte Carlo, Avenida Uruguay 69, Mexico D. F.
26 March 1923	Bynner and Johnson arrive in Mexico City
April 1923	'Elephant' in *English Review*; 'The Future of the Novel' ('Surgery for the Novel – Or a Bomb') in *Literary Digest International Book Review*; 'St Matthew' in *Poetry*; *Sea and Sardinia* published in England by Secker
1 April 1923	Attends bullfight in Mexico City
3 April 1923	Visits San Juan Teotihuacán pyramids
5 April 1923	Visits Cuernavaca
13–21 April 1923	Visits Puebla, Tehuacan and Orizaba
ante 27 April 1923	Learns of Mabel Dodge Sterne's marriage to Tony Luhan
29 April–1 May 1923	At Hotel Arzopalo, Chapala
May 1923	'Model Americans', a review of Stuart Sherman's *Americans*, in *Dial*; John Middleton Murry begins publication of *Adelphi*
1 May 1923	'Resurrection' in *The New Poetry*

ante 2 May 1923	Meets Idella Purnell, editor of *Palms*, in Guadalajara
2 May–9 July 1923	At Calle Zaragoza 4, Chapala
c. 10 May 1923	Bynner and Johnson arrive in Chapala; begins *The Plumed Serpent*
June 1923	'Trees and Babies and Papas and Mamas', a chapter from *Fantasia of the Unconscious*, in *Adelphi*
15–18 June 1923	Reads Frederick Carter's 'Dragon' MS (published as *The Dragon of the Alchemist*, 1926)
25–7 June 1923	Travels on Lake Chapala to Ocotlan and Tirzapan
July 1923	*Psychoanalysis and the Unconscious* published in England by Secker; 'Education and Sex', a chapter from *Fantasia of the Unconscious*, in *Adelphi*; 'Nostalgia' in *Palms*
4–7 July 1923	Travels with Bynner, Johnson and Idella Purnell on Lake Chapala
9–19 July 1923	Leaves Chapala for New York via Laredo and San Antonio, New Orleans and Washington D.C.
19 July 1923	Arrives New York City
20 July–21 August 1923	At 'Birkindele' (Seltzer's cottage), Union Hill, Morris Plains, New Jersey
c. 20 July–7 August 1923	Reads proofs for *Kangaroo*; *Birds, Beasts and Flowers*; and *Mastro-don Gesualdo*
26 July 1923	Corrected galley proofs of *Kangaroo* sent to Curtis Brown
2 August 1923	Lunch with editors of the *Nation*
18 August 1923	Frieda to England on *R.M.S. Orbita*
20 August 1923	'An Interview with DHL' in *New York Evening Post*
22–7 August 1923	Visits Bessie Freeman in Buffalo
25 August 1923	Visits Niagara Falls, Canada
27 August 1923	*Studies in Classic American Literature* published in USA by Seltzer; leaves New York
27–30 August 1923	En route from Buffalo to Los Angeles via Chicago and Omaha, to stay with Merrild

31 August 1923	Leaves Los Angeles for Santa Monica; stays until 12 September
September 1923	*Kangaroo* published in England by Secker (in USA by Seltzer on 17 September); 'St Joseph's Ass' in *Adelphi*
2 September 1923	Begins to 'make a book' of Mollie Skinner's 'The House of Ellis' (later *The Boy in the Bush*, 1924)
9 September 1923	To Santa Barbara with Merrild, Götzsche, and Harry and Olivia Johnson
10 September 1923	To Lompoc to observe eclipse
12–25 September 1923	Los Angeles
25–7 September 1923	To Guaymas, Sonora, Mexico via Palm Springs with Götzsche
29 September 1923	'A Spiritual Record', a review of *A Second Contemporary Verse Anthology*, in *New York Evening Post Literary Review*
Autumn 1923	'Autumn in New Mexico' in *Palms*
October 1923	'Cypresses', 'Saint Matthew', 'Spirits Summoned West' in *Adelphi*
1 October 1923	To Navojoa, Sonora
c. 3–4 October 1923	Visits Minas Nuevas near Alamos, Sonora
5 October 1923	To Mazatlan, Sinaloa
7 October 1923	Arrives Mazatlan
9 October 1923	*Birds, Beasts and Flowers* published in USA by Seltzer (in England by Secker in November)
10 October 1923	At Tepic, Nayarit; 'Peace', 'Bare Almond Trees', 'Tropic' in *Nation* (New York)
13 October 1923	*Mastro-don Gesualdo* published in USA by Seltzer
14–17 October 1923	En route to Guadalajara via Ixtlan, La Quemada and Etzatlan
17 October–17 November 1923	Hotel Garcia, Guadalajara
21 October 1923	Visits Chapala
3 November 1923	Receives copies of *Mastro-don Gesualdo* and *Birds, Beasts and Flowers* from Seltzer
15 November 1923	Finishes *The Boy in the Bush* and sends last of MS to Curtis Brown

17–22 November 1923	To Mexico City and Vera Cruz (21–2 November)
22 November–12 December 1923	Sails with Götzsche, via Havana (25 November), for Plymouth, England, on the *S.S. Toledo*
December 1923	'The Proper Study' in *Adelphi*; 'Au Revoir U.S.A.' in *Laughing Horse*
14 December 1923–23 January 1924	At 110 Heath Street, Hampstead, London
Christmas 1923	'A Britisher Has a Word With an Editor' in *Palms*
31 December 1923–3 January 1924	Nottingham and Derby for family visit
3–5 January 1924	To Pontesbury, Shropshire, to visit Frederick Carter
23 January–6 February 1924	At Hotel de Versailles, 60 Blvd Montparnasse, Paris
February 1924	'On Being Religious' in *Adelphi*
4 February 1924	Meets Sylvia Beach at Shakespeare and Company
6 February 1924	En route for Baden-Baden via Strasbourg
7–20 February 1924	In Baden-Baden
19 February 1924	Sends review of *Book of Revelation* by John Oman to Murry for *Adelphi*
20 February 1924	En route for Paris via Strasbourg
21–5 February 1924	At Hotel de Versailles, 60 Blvd Montparnasse, Paris
22 February 1924	Visits Versailles
24 February 1924	Visits Chartres
26 February–5 March 1924	At Garland's Hotel, Suffolk Street, Pall Mall, London
March 1924	'On Human Destiny' in *Adelphi*
5 March 1924	Sails from Southampton for New York on *R.M.S. Aquitania*
11 March 1924	Arrives New York

Europe (c. 1921–4)

The World

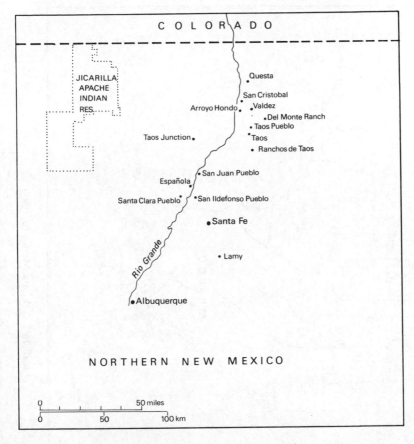

Northern New Mexico (c. 1922–3)

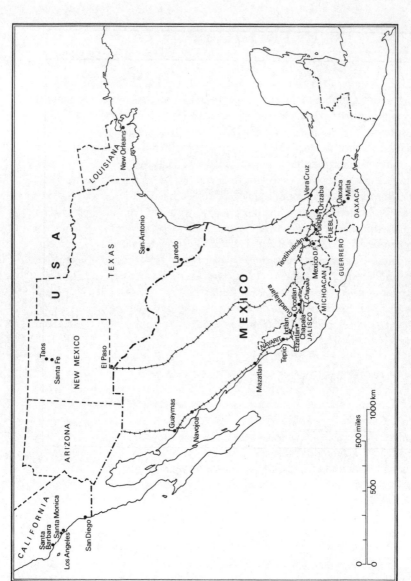

Southern U.S.A. and Mexico (c. 1923)

INTRODUCTION

'In a man's letters his soul lies naked.' This remark by Samuel Johnson applies with undoubted relevance to D. H. Lawrence, who revealed himself and recorded the events of his life and his world more vividly in his correspondence than any writer of his day. As a literary genre the letter was a métier in which Lawrence excelled, and in these letters we have not only a biography of the artist, but a portrait of the time as well.

The early twenties were especially important to Lawrence as a professional writer. For him it was a time of change, a change motivated largely by his long interest in America and a disillusionment with the old Europe, which culminated in his departure from Taormina in February 1922. It is not an exaggeration to say that travel in the new world provided the most significant experience of Lawrence's mature life. Australia, and particularly the United States and Mexico, offered entirely new and exciting materials which he was to exploit in the years following his departure from Europe. He explored Australia and America, made new friends and acquaintances and found himself growing more distant from some with whom he had corresponded frequently in the past.

In spite of his many difficulties with agents and publishers, Lawrence managed to establish an enduring relationship with Curtis Brown who became his agent for England in mid-1921 and continued to represent him there, and in the United States as well, after Lawrence severed his connection with Robert Mountsier in February 1923. Laurence Pollinger who dealt with Lawrence matters as a member of the Curtis Brown firm, later founded his own agency, Laurence Pollinger Ltd, which continues to represent the Lawrence estate today.

However, the most important change for Lawrence as a writer was an increasing dependence on the United States as the primary publishing outlet for his work. In Thomas Seltzer he found a new publisher and continued to use Robert Mountsier as his American agent, although he eventually broke with both. Mountsier and Seltzer became major correspondents for Lawrence; of the more than eight hundred letters in this volume, about a quarter were written to Adele and Thomas Seltzer and Mountsier. Lawrence had met Mountsier in Cornwall in 1916, and by 1921 he was Lawrence's sole literary agent in the United States. As with Seltzer the relationship at first was not merely a business one. For several months Mountsier and Lawrence collaborated in an effort to find a yacht in which they could sail away from Europe, but they were unsuccessful. Mountsier visited the Lawrences in

Baden-Baden and accompanied them to Zell-am-See in Austria; he was later in Taos with them at the same time as the Seltzers, during Christmas 1922. By then Lawrence had begun to tire of Mountsier. Seltzer and Mountsier were unable to work together amicably and this annoyed Lawrence considerably.

Seltzer's first Lawrence book was *Touch and Go* published in June 1920 soon after Seltzer dissolved his partnership with Temple Scott and began to publish under his own name. It was Seltzer who published the privately printed first edition of *Women in Love* in New York in November 1920, after English publishers had refused to touch the manuscript as a result of the difficulty Methuen had experienced with *The Rainbow*.[1] Altogether, twenty of Lawrence's books appeared with the Seltzer imprint, and of eight major works published between May 1921 and March 1923 only one was published first in England.

An important consequence of Lawrence's closer relationship with America was the increased income he received from his American publishers. This significantly altered life for him and Frieda; for the first time in his life as a professional writer, they were free from the constant worry about money which had made Lawrence so miserable during the war years in England.

In June 1921 Lawrence and Frieda were staying at the Hôtel Krone in Ebersteinberg near Baden-Baden, where Frieda could be close to her mother who was ill. The Baroness von Richthofen lived in the Ludwig Wilhelmstift, a retirement home which Frieda described in *"Not I, But the Wind . . ."* In her book Frieda devotes a chapter to Lawrence's relationship with her mother. Lawrence and his mother-in-law were genuinely fond of one another, and he wrote to her often as he and Frieda travelled about. Lawrence's kindness to Frieda's family reveals an aspect of his character often overlooked by his critics. Life in post-war Germany was difficult, and Lawrence helped them whenever he could. He instructed Anton Kippenberg of the Insel Verlag to send the money due to him for the German edition of *The Rainbow* to his mother-in-law, and when Germany was experiencing disastrous inflation after the war, he frequently sent money or clothing, remembering especially the children.

Lawrence was always sensitive to the people and social conditions around him. He wrote to Lady Cynthia Asquith about the situation in Germany, 'Germany very *still* . . . very little money. Yet not poor . . . Everything so *clean* – quite a shock after Italy – and nobody begging and parasiting'. He

---

[1] In November 1915 the Bow Street Magistrate's Court ordered all copies of *The Rainbow* seized under an Obscene Publications Act passed in 1857. Subsequently the books were ordered to be destroyed.

spoke contemptuously of 'profiteers' whom he called 'money hogs in motorcars'.[2] In February of 1924 he was to write his very perceptive 'Letter from Germany' in which he uncannily describes the emerging ambience of Nazi Germany.[3] In this he was indeed a prophet.

However he was restless. No person and no place pleased him for long; to Catherine Carswell[4] and others he dwelt constantly on the malaise he felt for Europe. Although he seemed never to be sure about his plans for the future, the one pervading theme which continued to appear in his letters was a determination to leave the old world. In July he wrote to Marie Hubrecht, whom he had known in Taormina, that if he went back to the Fontana Vecchia for 'this one winter, I don't think I shall return next year'.[5] Meanwhile he grew irritable in Ebersteinberg and later in Zell-am-See, where he and Frieda went to visit her sister Johanna von Schreibershofen. To Catherine Carswell he wrote: 'Perhaps it is one can't live with people any more – en ménage. Anyhow there it is. Frieda loves it and is quite bitter that I say I want to go away. But there it is – I do.'[6]

By August, just before their departure for Florence, he had written desperately to Rosalind Baynes, 'impossible to work in this country: no wits left, all gone loose and scattered. I shan't be sorry to come back to Italy again: but feel Europe is a bit empty altogether. Only the States are worse, I'm sure.' A few days in Zell with Mountsier had given him a strong distaste for 'Yankees'; he continued, 'I suppose I shall go one day – because one chafes so here in Europe, and that seems the only way out.'[7]

In mid-September Lawrence and Frieda hurried from Florence to Capri to visit Earl and Achsah Brewster who were about to leave Italy for India. Lawrence had met the Brewsters a few weeks earlier in Capri on the way from Taormina to Baden-Baden, and learned that they had once lived in Fontana Vecchia, the villa where the Lawrences made their home in Taormina. The Brewsters were American painters who lived in Europe. Earl Brewster was a student of oriental philosophy, and he, his wife Achsah and their young daughter Harwood became close friends of the Lawrences. The Brewsters were among the very few of Lawrence's friends who never turned on him or against whom he never felt anger or disappointment. Their book about

---

[2] Letter 2253
[3] Addressed to the Editor of *New Statesman and Nation* and conjecturally dated 19 February 1924, the article (in the form of a letter) was not published in that journal until 13 October 1934 (see E. D. McDonald, ed , *Phoenix*, 1936, pp. 107–10).
[4] Catherine Carswell, a friend of Lawrence since 1914, wrote *The Savage Pilgrimage* (1932) after his death, an impassioned defence of the man and his work. She was discharged from the *Glasgow Herald* for writing a favourable review of *The Rainbow*.
[5] Letter 2277   [6] Letter 2301   [7] Letter 2305

Lawrence, *Reminiscences and Correspondence*, is exceptional in the picture it gives of a gentle, friendly man. When Lawrence and Frieda eventually left Europe, it was to follow the Brewsters to Ceylon.

Immediately after his return to Fontana Vecchia from Capri, Lawrence wrote to Earl Brewster a troubled letter filled with disturbing news about the reception of his work in England. There was a denunciation of *Women in Love* by *John Bull*, a solicitor's advice that a libel action threatened the novel and a 'very cold letter' from his agent that *Aaron's Rod* could not be accepted.[8] The difficulties in England and Brewster's impending departure for Ceylon seemingly threw into sharp focus the discontent he felt for the old world and reinforced his determination to leave Europe. Nevertheless after a few days in the Sicilian sun Lawrence was more content. He wrote to Amy Lowell in October of his pleasure in being back at Fontana Vecchia,

. . . we are both so glad to be back here, in silence and peace and sunshine. It is lovely weather . . . I love the Ionian sea. It is open like a great blue opening in front of us, so delicate and self-contained. The hibiscus flowers are coming again in the garden. I am so thankful to come south.[9]

Still he thought about accompanying the Brewsters to Ceylon but could not bring himself to the point of actually leaving Taormina. He temporised by saying that he would eventually go East, 'ultimately to go west'. His feeling for the old Europe was summed up in the letter to Brewster: 'But my heart – and my soul are broken, in Europe. It's no use, the threads are broken.'[10]

During the following months he continued to vacillate between a desire to follow the Brewsters to Ceylon and a decision to go directly to the United States. In November 1921 he wrote to Earl Brewster, 'I feel at the moment I don't care where I live . . . But if you tempt me one little bit I'll splash my way to Ceylon.'[11] This same month brought the invitation from Mabel Dodge Sterne to visit Taos, New Mexico. Mabel Dodge Sterne, later Mabel Dodge Luhan, can be described succinctly as a wealthy patroness of the arts, but she was much more than that. Born Mabel Ganson of wealthy parents in Buffalo, New York, she was a woman of many marriages, the last being to Tony Luhan, a Pueblo Indian with whom she was living when the Lawrences arrived in Taos. She and her second husband, Edwin Dodge, a Boston architect, had lived in Europe before the first World War. During the war and for a few years afterward she maintained a Greenwich Village apartment where she became famous for her Wednesday evenings for avant garde writers, artists and radical intellectuals. She became the mistress of John Reed, the young American who wrote *Ten Days That Shook the World* and worked for the bolshevist

⁸ Letter 2344   ⁹ Letter 2352   ¹⁰ Letter 2344   ¹¹ Letter 2362

revolution in Russia. When Greenwich Village bohemian life began to pall, Mabel went to New Mexico for the avowed purpose of reviving ancient crafts and skills among the Pueblo Indians. She lived there until her death in 1962. Her friendship with Lawrence was a turbulent one, although they wrote letters to each other as long as he lived.

Almost the incarnation of Lawrence's intellectual wilful woman, Mabel Dodge Sterne exerted a powerful influence on those around her and was easily the most significant person to touch Lawrence's life during the period covered by this volume of letters. She first wrote to him because his descriptions of Sardinia led her to believe that he was the one writer who could do justice to the starkly beautiful landscape of New Mexico. For a while he thought more about going to America; Mabel's invitation excited him and he was intrigued by her description of the country and the Indians.

Leo Stein and his sister Gertrude had stayed with Mabel Dodge at the Villa Curonia in Florence, and probably at Mabel's request Leo wrote an enthusiastic letter to Lawrence extolling the virtues and the beauties of New Mexico. In Florence, Lawrence had also learned something more of New Mexico through the paintings of Maurice Sterne, Mabel's third husband, who had spent some time in Taos.

But as usual Lawrence could not make a decision. Although he responded to Mabel's letters that he intended to come to America at once and assured her in December that he would definitely depart for New Mexico in January 1922, he summed up the real state of his mind in a letter to Mountsier: 'Suddenly that I am on the point of coming to America I feel I *can't* come. Not yet. It is something almost stronger than I am. I would rather go to Ceylon, and come to America later, from the east.'[12]

It was almost as if he had a premonition that his association with Mabel Dodge Sterne was to be one of his most frustrating and explosive friendships. In any case he did decide to delay his visit to America, sailing from Naples on 26 February 1922 on the *R.M.S. Osterley* for Ceylon.

In spite of the restlessness and indecision Lawrence exhibited during the months before his departure, he managed to accomplish a considerable amount of work. In early June he wrote to Seltzer asking if it were worth while to go on with the second volume of his theory of the unconscious; the first draft was finished in the same month and revised in October at Fontana Vecchia and finally published as *Fantasia of the Unconscious* by Seltzer in October of the following year. He contacted printers in Germany to get prices and specifications for the colour reproductions of Jan Juta's illustrations for *Sea*

and Sardinia, and he began to plan a children's 'History of Italian Painting'
for the Medici Society in London, a project which was soon abandoned.
Aaron's Rod was finished at Ebersteinberg and the manuscript sent to Curtis
Brown for typing. Later at Zell-am-See in August he worked at revising the
typescript, and on the way home to Taormina they stopped briefly in Florence
where he received from the Leipzig publishing house, Insel Verlag, the first
pages of the proofs of Else Jaffe's German translation of *The Rainbow*. Else
Jaffe was Frieda's older sister to whom Lawrence wrote many letters; she was
one of the first women students at Heidelberg and translated several of
Lawrence's books.

From Fontana Vecchia in early October 1921 he wrote to Amy Lowell that
once he had gathered himself 'together' he wanted to get to work, and
complained that he had done only two poems, 'Fish' and 'Bat', during the
summer.[13] However, he still wrote steadily. Although fuming with anger at
Philip Heseltine for the threatened libel action against *Women in Love*, he
forwarded the altered pages describing Halliday's (Heseltine's) mistress and
their apartment to Secker on 8 October. In November and December
Lawrence wrote 'The Captain's Doll', revised 'The Fox' and finished 'The
Ladybird' as the third of the three long short-stories published in England as
The Ladybird and in the United States as *The Captain's Doll*, and by the first of
December he had sent to Mountsier a collection of short fiction which was to
provide material for *England, My England* – two rather considerable volumes.
His final major undertaking before leaving Italy was the 'Introduction' for
Maurice Magnus' *Memoirs of the Foreign Legion*[14] which he posted to
Mountsier in January 1922. Seldom idle, he wrote to Mary Cannan in mid-
February while they awaited berths on the *R.M.S. Osterley*, that he was
'filling in' his time translating Giovanni Verga's *Mastro-don Gesualdo*. He
had begun reading Verga soon after his return to Fontana Vecchia in
September and continued with the translation as the *Osterley* made its way to
Ceylon.

Meanwhile Lawrence's writing continued to appear in periodicals on both

---

[13] Letter 2352
[14] Lawrence met Maurice Magnus, a somewhat mysterious American, in 1919 at Florence in
company with Norman Douglas. Lawrence, who lived economically, was vexed when Magnus
refused to forgo his gentlemanly standard of living. Magnus committed suicide at Malta in
1920 owing money to several people. After some difficulty Lawrence arranged for the
publication of Magnus' manuscript, 'Dregs', under the title *Memoirs of the Foreign Legion* for
which he wrote a long introduction. Subsequently Lawrence found himself engaged in a lively
quarrel with Norman Douglas, Magnus' literary executor. See Lawrence's letter, 'The Late
Mr. Maurice Magnus', in the *New Statesman* for 20 February 1926 (*Phoenix* 806–7) and *D. H.
Lawrence and Maurice Magnus* by Norman Douglas, published privately by the author at
Florence in 1924.

sides of the Atlantic. The *Dial* published poetry and excerpts from *Sea and Sardinia* and *Aaron's Rod*, and in January the outcome of collaboration with S. S. Koteliansky, 'The Gentleman from San Francisco'.[15] The *English Review* published poetry which later appeared in *Birds, Beasts and Flowers*; 'Wintry Peacock' came out in *Metropolitan*. The essay on Whitman appeared in the *New York Call* and in *Nation and Athenaeum*. The first trade edition of *Women in Love* was published in London by Secker in June 1921, and Seltzer brought out *Sea and Sardinia* and *Tortoises* in New York six months later. Lawrence's career did not falter no matter how much he himself appeared to be at odds with the world. There was one bit of encouragement; in December he received word that he had been awarded the James Tait Black Prize for *The Lost Girl*. He responded to the news that he was very pleased, 'especially pleased at having at last some spark of friendly recognition out of Britain. It has been mostly abuse.'[16]

Aboard the *Osterley* Lawrence wrote to Lady Cynthia Asquith describing the sight of Etna disappearing behind the ship as it sailed eastward, 'I nearly wept, of course, but hardened my heart . . .'[17] Despite his lingering nostalgia for Italy, Lawrence became excited about the sights and sounds of his new surroundings. He wrote enthusiastically to Koteliansky about Port Said, '. . . it is still just like *Arabian Nights*, with water-sellers and scribes in the street'[18] and was impressed with the passage through the Suez Canal. The tone of his letters changed almost immediately. To Rosalind Baynes he wrote after little more than a week aboard the *Osterley*:

Being at sea is so queer – it sort of dissolves for the time being all the connections with the land, and one feels a bit like a sea-bird must feel. – It is my opinion that once beyond the Red Sea one does not feel any more that tension and pressure one suffers from in England – in Europe altogether – even in America I believe – perhaps worse there. I feel so glad I have come out . . .[19]

Very soon after their arrival at Colombo Lawrence was recording his impressions of Ceylon in his correspondence. To his sister Emily he wrote entertainingly of their situation:

We have been in the bungalow a week. It is about a mile or mile and a half from Kandy, looking down on the lake: very lovely . . . We sit on the verandahs and watch the chipmunks and chameleons and lizards and tropical birds among the trees and bamboos . . .[20]

But to other correspondents he was already indicating his unrest and desire to be away: 'It is very hot. – lovely to look at – but I doubt if I shall stay very long

[15] A translation of the story by Ivan Bunin.   [16] Letter 2391
[17] Letter 2467   [18] Letter 2469   [19] Letter 2472   [20] Letter 2476

in Ceylon.' Later in the same letter to Mountsier: 'I don't believe I shall write
a line in Ceylon – at least not here in the hot part.'[21] On Thursday, 23 March,
the Prince of Wales' visit to Ceylon was celebrated with an extravagant
Perahera at Kandy. Lawrence was impressed with the magnificence of the
display, but sympathised with the young Prince who was quite obviously
weary and uncomfortable. The poem 'Elephant' contains Lawrence's fullest
description of the Perahera and his impressions of the Prince. He wrote to
Catherine Carswell: 'The Prince of Wales was here on Thursday – looks worn
out and nervy, poor thing – the Perahera in the evening with a hundred
elephants was lovely – But I don't believe I shall ever work here.'[22]

By the end of March 1922 Lawrence had already had enough of the East and
was writing to Robert Pratt Barlow, an acquaintance in Taormina, about his
rediscovery of virtue in Europe and especially in England for Englishmen, 'I
really think that the most living clue of life is in us Englishmen in England.'[23]
The visit to Ceylon was not a successful venture, and Lawrence summed up a
multitude of complaints about the East in a letter to Mabel Dodge Sterne in
April:

> . . . the thick, choky feel of tropical forest . . . the horrid noises of the birds and
> creatures . . . the nauseous tropical fruits; the nasty faces and yellow robes of the
> Buddhist monks, the little vulgar dens of the temples . . . all this I cannot bear.[24]

Later, en route to Sydney from Melbourne, he recorded more of his
impressions of India and the East in a pertinent observation to Mountsier:

> . . . India will fall into chaos once the British let go. The religions are so antagonistic –
> Hindu and Mahommedan – and then Buddha . . . all this 'nationalism' and 'self-
> government' and 'liberty' are all tripe. They've no more notion of liberty than a jackal
> has.[25]

The stay in Ceylon was not productive. Apart from the poem 'Elephant'
apparently Lawrence worked only on his translations of Verga, sending the
last of *Mastro-don Gesualdo* to Mountsier in early April, and by the end of the
month he had forwarded the first of the short stories to be published later as
Little Novels of Sicily. In April, while the Lawrences were in Ceylon, *Aaron's
Rod* was published in New York and 'The Horse-Dealer's Daughter'
appeared in the *English Review*. But all this was far away; the heat was making
Lawrence irritable and uncomfortable, and it must have been with considerable relief that he and Frieda sailed from Colombo on 24 April 1922 for
Fremantle, West Australia.

When the Lawrences reached West Australia they were welcomed by Mrs
Anna Jenkins, who had been a fellow traveller aboard the *Osterley* from

[21] Letter 2475   [22] Letter 2478   [23] Letter 2480   [24] Letter 2493   [25] Letter 2523

Naples. She met the ship in Fremantle, entertained them in Perth and arranged accommodation in 'Leithdale', a guest house in Darlington, some sixteen miles from Perth in the Australian bush. It was here that Lawrence met Mollie Skinner, one of the proprietors of the guest house, with whom he was to collaborate on *The Boy in the Bush*. Mollie Skinner had been a nurse during the war and published *Letters of a V. A. D.* about her experiences. Lawrence read this and a manuscript later to be published as *Black Swans*. He talked with her about her writing and suggested that she write about the early settlers in Western Australia, the resulting manuscript being re-written as *The Boy in the Bush*. Apparently Lawrence was on his best behaviour in Western Australia. Mollie Skinner remarked on his pleasant nature and quoted Frieda's reaction to his even tempered way at 'Leithdale': 'He is so gentle and kind . . . since we arrived here . . . you stupid people do not know him as he is, so cantankerous, so passionate and disconsolate.'[26]

Lawrence enjoyed being something of a literary lion in Perth. He visited a bookstore, the Booklovers' Library, a gathering place for persons interested in books and literature, and was pleased to find his own books on sale there and a copy of the banned *Rainbow* in the library of the local Mechanics' Institute. In Perth he met William Siebenhaar who brought some of his poems for Lawrence to read. Lawrence was not impressed by them but later helped Siebenhaar find a publisher for his translation of E. D. Dekker's (Multatuli) *Max Havelaar*, and wrote an introduction for the book when it was published by Knopf in 1927. Although Lawrence stayed in Western Australia only a fortnight, he made a vivid impression on the people he met there. His Australian experience, like the major novel *Kangaroo* which resulted from it, has been perhaps the least understood and appreciated period of his life.

From the letters written during the comparatively few weeks Lawrence and Frieda lived at Thirroul near Sydney in New South Wales, one might suppose that they saw no one and did little if any travelling about. Lawrence seems to go out of his way to emphasise their isolation from Australian society; 'there isn't a soul on this side of Australia knows I am here, or knows who I am.'[27] Although he writes in these terms repeatedly, obviously he must have visited Sydney and certainly was his usual observant self with respect to the social and political life of the country. Australian critics mistakenly condemned *Kangaroo* for its superficiality and lack of understanding of Australia; Professor A. D. Hope specifically takes Lawrence to task for his 'hopelessly unreal' account of Australian politics.[28] However, in 1965 John Alexander, an Australian schoolmaster who has written an unpublished book about

---

[26] Nehls, ii. 137–8.   [27] Letter 2537
[28] See Robert Darroch, *D. H. Lawrence in Australia* (Melbourne, 1981), p. 24.

Lawrence entitled 'An Antipodean Study of D. H. Lawrence', noted that the newspaper headlines quoted in *Kangaroo* were taken directly from contemporary issues of the Sydney *Bulletin*. Lawrence must at least have read the *Bulletin* with unusual care. In 1981 Robert Darroch demonstrated in his book *D. H. Lawrence in Australia* that Lawrence had a much more serious involvement with Australian social and political life than his correspondence indicates. That part of *Kangaroo* dealing with the protofascist party of Benjamin Cooley has been seen as exclusively the product of Lawrence's imagination, but Darroch argues convincingly that the novel is based on actual situations and persons, in much the same way as Lawrence's other writings.

The superficial aspect of Lawrence's stay in Australia is quickly told. He and Frieda left Fremantle on 18 May and after calling at Adelaide and Melbourne arrived at Sydney on Saturday 27 May. After one or two days in Sydney they moved into 'Wyewurk', a cottage in Thirroul, a seaside resort and mining town some 48 miles south of Sydney. The decision to stay in Australia for a while was partly due to economic reasons, because they had to wait for Mountsier to send money before they could move on. Lawrence's reaction to Australia was mixed. He had written from Darlington: 'We are here about 16 miles out of Perth – bush all round – marvellous air, marvellous sun and sky – strange, vast empty country – hoary unending "bush" with a pre-primeval ghost in it . . . but – But – BUT – Well, it's always an anticlimax of buts. – I just don't want to stay, that's all.'[29] On board the *Malwa* en route to Sydney he wrote to Mountsier, 'Australia is liberty gone senile – gone almost imbecile. The human life seems to me very barren: one could never make a novel out of these people, they haven't got any insides to them, to write about.'[30] In Sydney his negative feeling about Australia and the Australians became intensified. 'I don't really like it, it is so raw – so crude. The people are so crude in their feelings . . . The aristocracy are the people who own big shops – and there is no respect for anything else.'[31]

Almost as soon as they were settled in 'Wyewurk' Lawrence began to consider the sailings of various ships by which they could proceed to San Francisco. On 3 June he wrote to Mabel Dodge Sterne listing several possible sailings, but saying, 'I have started a novel and if I can go on with it I shall stay till I've finished it – till about end of august.'[32] The novel was *Kangaroo* which, combined with the lack of funds and Frieda's desire to stay in one place for a while, kept them in Thirroul until the second week in August.

Not very much of Lawrence's work was published while they were in Australia. In America the *Dial* published 'The Fox'. He had two short stories

[29] Letter 2514   [30] Letter 2523   [31] Letter 2527   [32] Letter 2529

in anthologies in England, 'The Shadow in the Rose Garden' in *Georgian Stories* and 'Wintry Peacock' in the *New Decameron III*. One poem, 'Fish', appeared in the *English Review*. In June Secker issued the special 50 signed copies of *Women in Love* made up in London from the sheets of the privately printed Seltzer edition.

Apparently all of Lawrence's creative efforts in Australia went into the writing of *Kangaroo*; he wrote only one other piece, a poem which he also called 'Kangaroo'. The writing of the novel was a remarkable tour de force. He reported that he was more than half finished with the novel on 21 June and had only two more chapters to do on 7 July. The manuscript was posted to Mountsier in America via the *S. S. Makura* on 20 July. It was Lawrence's intention to leave on the next ship to sail for San Francisco, the *Tahiti*. Fortunately the sailing of the *Tahiti* was delayed long enough for Lawrence to receive the funds from Mountsier which enabled him and Frieda to leave, barely fourteen weeks after their arrival at Fremantle, West Australia.

Although Lawrence still had reservations about the United States and had admitted to a 'Heimweh' for the old Europe, he maintained a steady correspondence with Mabel Dodge Sterne assuring her of his eventual arrival in Taos. He had written to her from Ceylon expressing some of his continuing doubts about America and Taos:

I still of course mistrust Taos very much, chiefly on account of the artists. I feel I never want to see an artist again while I live . . . I wish I could come to America without meeting the awful 'cultured' Americans with their limited self-righteous ideals and their mechanical love-motion and their bullying, detestable negative creed of liberty and democracy.[33]

Lawrence then went on to explain himself, perhaps more fully than he intended: 'Naturally I find myself in diametric opposition to every American – and everybody else, besides American – whom I come across.' The voyage from Sydney to San Francisco was uneventful. The ship called at Wellington, New Zealand, Rarotonga and Tahiti. In Wellington he thought of Katherine Mansfield and sent her a postcard with the last word she was ever to receive from him, 'Ricordi'.[34] Lawrence wrote to Mountsier that San Francisco was pleasant but not 'overwhelming'; however, he was somewhat intimidated by the constant 'noise of *iron*' and the terrifying 'black, glossy streets with steel rails in ribbons like the path of death itself'. He was glad to be away toward New Mexico on 8 September where he hoped for a 'bit of quiet'.[35]

Lawrence's reaction to his initial experience of New Mexico was more intense than any other of the many impressions he recorded from his travels.

[33] Letter 2493   [34] Letter 2565   [35] Letters 2583, 2589

His own words from the essay 'New Mexico' bear witness to the power of his feelings.

But the moment I saw the brilliant, proud morning shine high up over the deserts of Santa Fe, something stood still in my soul, and I started to attend. There was a certain magnificence in the high-up day, a certain eagle-like royalty, so different from the equally pure, equally pristine and lovely morning of Australia, which is so soft, so utterly pure in its softness . . . In the magnificent fierce morning of New Mexico one sprang awake, a new part of the soul woke up suddenly, and the old world gave way to a new.[36]

This was, however, written many years afterward, and although his letters and much that he wrote about the American Southwest support the validity of this description of the way he felt about New Mexico and the desert, he was not always happy with either the people there or his experiences.

After their long train ride from San Francisco the Lawrences were met at Lamy, the station for Santa Fe, by Mabel Sterne and Tony Luhan who had come from Taos by automobile. The trip from Taos was long and arduous in 1922, making it necessary for the traveller to stay overnight in Santa Fe. Mabel had neglected to reserve accommodation in Santa Fe so she had to arrange for Lawrence and Frieda to spend the night at the home of Witter Bynner, the American poet. Here they met Willard ('Spud') Johnson who acted as Bynner's secretary, and Alice Corbin Henderson and her family. The Hendersons were important members of the literary and artistic colony in Santa Fe. William Penhallow Henderson was a painter and designer; his wife Alice Corbin Henderson was a poet who with Harriet Monroe had founded *Poetry* in Chicago before coming to New Mexico.

The next day Lawrence and Frieda were taken to Taos where they were installed in a special adobe house prepared for them. In her book about Lawrence, *Lorenzo in Taos*, written in the form of a letter to Robinson Jeffers, Mabel Luhan tells of their first night in New Mexico and gives her version of the uneven relationship which followed. The special house had been built for Tony on Indian land, and the Lawrences were the first ones to live in it.

Although Mabel Sterne was right about Lawrence's ability to portray vividly the New Mexico she loved, she was unsuccessful in establishing a satisfactory rapport with the man she had 'willed' to come to America. Lawrence was wary of her efforts on his behalf, and was soon in open revolt against her as patroness and hostess. Frieda did not encourage a project which involved a collaboration between Mabel and Lawrence on an autobiographical novel of her life with Tony. This led to strained relations and by the end of

[36] *Phoenix* 142.

September Lawrence was writing, 'I am settling down a bit better here, and Mabel Sterne is learning to leave us alone, and *not* to be a padrona.' By mid-November the break was inevitable and at the beginning of December the Lawrences moved for the winter to Del Monte Ranch, owned by the Hawk family, in the foothills above Taos. Soon afterward Lawrence wrote from Del Monte ranch to Frieda's mother, responding to her inquiry about Mabel Dodge Sterne:

You asked about Mabel Dodge: American – rich – only child – from Buffalo, on Lake Erie – bankers – 42 years old – short, stout – looks young – has had three husbands – an Evans (dead), a Dodge (divorced), and a Maurice Sterne (Jew, Russian, painter, young) (also divorced). Has now an Indian, Tony, a fat fellow. Has lived much in Europe – Paris, Nice, Florence – is rather famous in New York, and little loved – very clever for a female – another culture-bearer – likes to play the 'patroness' – hates the white world, and loves the Indians out of hate – is very 'noble', wants to be very 'good', and is very wicked – has a terrible will to power – woman power, you know – wanted to become a witch, and, at the same time, a Mary of Bethany at Jesus's feet – a stout white crow, a cooing raven of misfortune, a little buffalo.[37]

The winter of 1922–3 which the Lawrences spent in the mountains above Taos must have been one of the happiest periods of his travels, perhaps because he was busy doing the ordinary things of life, cutting wood, baking bread, taking care of the ranch animals as well as doing enough writing to satisfy his creative being. At the ranch they had the two Danish artists Kai Götzsche and Knud Merrild for company, which pleased Lawrence. Götzsche and Merrild had come to the United States the year before and travelled from New York to New Mexico in a Model T Ford car, bearing a letter of introduction to Walter Ufer, the doyen of the artist colony in Taos. They became friends with Lawrence and accepted his invitation to live in a cabin near the Lawrences on the Hawk ranch during the winter of 1922–3. While they were there Kai Götzsche painted a major portrait of Lawrence sitting before the fireplace in the cabin. Originally given to Adele Seltzer, the portrait is now at the University of Texas. Götzsche accompanied Lawrence on his trip to Mexico in September 1923 while Frieda was in England. Later Knud Merrild wrote one of the more rewarding books of Lawrence memoirs, *A Poet and Two Painters*, published in 1938.

Lawrence was more content away from Taos, where he suffered 'too much Mabel Sterne and suppers and motor drives and people dropping in'.[38] In December he described life on the ranch with enthusiasm:

We have come 17 miles from Taos: are now settled in an old log cabin, 5 rooms, on this ranch on the foothills: mountain forest and white snow behind – desert, like a great

[37] Letters 2618, 2669   [38] Letter 2682

dim pool below – and other mountains, west, far away . . . We cut down a great balsam pine, and tomorrow are going to haul it in. We all go riding – the country is quite wild –[39]

Later he was to have his own ranch in the mountains, and Taos came closer to being a home for the Lawrences than any of the places they lived before his death in 1930. Nevertheless the old Lawrence demon was still there; he began thinking about leaving in January, 'I don't know which way to go – whether to go east, and via Greenland to Russia – or else south, and perhaps via Palm Springs to Old Mexico, and so to Europe.'[40]

By the middle of March 1923 when they actually left for Mexico, Lawrence had done a considerable amount of writing. There were several essays about the Indians and the Southwest. 'Indians and an Englishman' and 'Taos' were both published in the *Dial*, and political activists enlisted his services in support of their fight against the Bursum Bill affecting Indian lands. This resulted in 'Certain Americans and an Englishman' in the *New York Times Magazine*. More important work included his revision of the typescript of *Kangaroo* in October and *Studies in Classic American Literature* in November and December. He had also revised *Little Novels of Sicily* by January 1923. During this period he wrote the first of his American poems, 'Autumn in Taos', 'Eagle in New Mexico' and 'American Eagle', and some of the other poems in *Birds, Beasts and Flowers* which he finished putting together for Seltzer in February. *Fantasia of the Unconscious* and *England, My England* were published by Seltzer in October 1922 and *The Ladybird* appeared in London the following March.

Lawrence reported a fairly substantial income for 1922, $5,439.67 for the United States alone, which was approximately $34,000 in 1980s purchasing power. His success in America was due largely to the efforts of Thomas Seltzer, whose list included some of the most distinguished writers of the time; Anton Chekhov, Henry James, Marcel Proust and Arthur Schnitzler among others. Seltzer defended *Women in Love* against the Society for the Suppression of Vice and won, the case being dismissed by a New York magistrate in September 1922. By December Lawrence reported that 10,000 copies of the cheap edition of *Women in Love* had been sold, with 3,000 copies of the more expensive edition. The publicity concerning the case and the wide distribution of *Women in Love* helped spread Lawrence's reputation in the United States. He rather off-handedly acknowledged the importance of America to his career later in December to Catherine Carswell: 'I seem to have a fair sale over here – *Women in Love* going now into 15,000. Why do they read me? But anyhow, they *do* read me – which is more than England does.'[41]

[39] Letter 2670   [40] Letter 2699   [41] Letter 2682

Nevertheless his business affairs at the beginning of 1923 were chaotic. As usual Lawrence's relations with his publishers and agents were constantly changing, especially when the association became too close geographically. Lawrence had grown tired of Mountsier in Zell-am-See, and when both the Seltzers and Mountsier visited the Lawrences at Christmas 1922 at Del Monte Ranch, the situation soon became tense and uncomfortable. Seltzer and Mountsier could not agree about matters involving Lawrence. Adele and Thomas Seltzer left after Christmas, but Mountsier stayed on in Taos. Lawrence finally dispensed with Mountsier's services in early February 1923, telling Seltzer that he agreed with him about Mountsier.

Lawrence then proceeded to act for himself. A lawsuit on his behalf was pending in New York for the purpose of retrieving publishing rights from Benjamin Huebsch and Mitchell Kennerley. He was attempting to coordinate English and American publishing schedules, writing to both Secker and Curtis Brown at the same time, frequently cautioning Secker not to let Curtis Brown know that he was writing to him about business matters. Meanwhile more of his American interests were left to Seltzer. It was difficult for Lawrence to manage these business affairs while travelling about, and confusion resulted. To complicate matters further, Seltzer, although a discerning publisher, was not a good business man. Lawrence, with some cause, reiterated the complaint that he was not kept informed, and wrote repeatedly asking for proofs and information about publishing dates and sales figures.

Frieda and Lawrence arrived in Mexico City on 24 March 1923 and were soon joined by Witter Bynner and Willard ('Spud') Johnson. Much of their time in Mexico was spent in sightseeing. They all went to a bull fight in Mexico City which provided material for the vivid first chapter of *The Plumed Serpent*. The Lawrences saw the pyramids of Teotihuacán, visited Cuernavaca and Guadalajara and finally set up house in Chapala, a small village about thirty miles from Guadalajara. Lawrence was not without his usual indecision about their future movements. On 21 April he wrote to a number of people saying that they were about to sail for New York and would be in England by June, but instead he began to work on his Mexico novel, then called 'Quetzalcoatl'. On 9 May he told Seltzer that he had made two false starts on a novel, but by 10 June he could write that it was two-thirds done. The first draft of 'Quetzalcoatl' was finished, or nearly so, by the end of June.

While Lawrence was in Mexico, Martin Secker published *Sea and Sardinia* and *Psychology and the Unconscious* in England. Excerpts from *Fantasia of the Unconscious* appeared in the *Adelphi*. Only a few poems were published; 'Elephant' in the *English Review* and 'St Matthew' in *Poetry*. In April the biting essay on the modern novel, 'Surgery for the Novel – Or a Bomb', was published in the *Literary Digest International Book Review*; in May the *Dial* contained Lawrence's review of Stuart Sherman's *Americans*.

In mid-July the Lawrences finally departed overland for New York to visit the Seltzers, so that Lawrence could correct the proofs which had been piling up while they were in Mexico. After ten days on the road they reached New York to spend what must have been a hectic month. They stayed in a country cottage owned by the Seltzers near Dover, New Jersey, where Lawrence kept busy at various literary labours. He read proofs for *Kangaroo*, *Birds, Beasts and Flowers* and *Mastro-don Gesualdo*. Mollie Skinner's manuscript of her novel 'The House of Ellis', eventually to become *The Boy in the Bush*, was forwarded to him by Mountsier. Lawrence corrected the translation of Maxim Gorky's *Reminiscences of Leonid Andreyev* for Koteliansky which had been submitted to the *Dial*, and he was asked by Henry Seidel Canby to review *A Second Contemporary Verse Anthology* for the *New York Evening Post*.

In spite of the proofs which awaited him and his dislike for the 'furious mechanical life' of the city, Lawrence and Frieda did not spend all of their time at the New Jersey cottage. The Seltzers gave a dinner party for eight at the Algonquin Hotel, a favourite meeting place for artists and writers. Seltzer invited literary notables for lunch to meet Lawrence, on one occasion Henry Seidel Canby, Christopher Morley and William Rose Benét. He also met John Macy, Lewis Gannet, Franklin P. Adams and Oswald Garrison Villard, editor of the *Nation*.

Perhaps his acceptance by literary and publishing circles in New York softened Lawrence's attitude toward writers and America in general, for he gave a rare interview to the *New York Evening Post* before leaving. He explained his fundamental notion about America and the reason for his 'travel about the world'. Said Lawrence: 'There has got to be a thread which carries through from our Western civilization – a fundamental belief in our present civilization [which] could live through the destruction of its mechanical machinery. This thread would supply the spark kept alive to kindle the civilization of the future when this over-mechanized civilization of ours crashes to the ground.' He went on to say, 'I feel it more in America than anywhere else . . . it seems to be down in the center where the mountains are.'[42]

As the end of their New York visit drew near, Frieda urged Lawrence to go on to England as they had been planning for months, but he refused. He told Koteliansky early in August: 'I feel I cant come yet to England – though I came here on purpose. But it's no good, I shall have to put it off.'[43] Frieda

[42] *New York Evening Post*, 20 August 1923.   [43] Letter 2880

sailed alone for Southampton on the *R.M.S. Orbita* on 18 August, and a few days later Lawrence left New York for Los Angeles. The parting was not a happy one; Catherine Carswell reported that Lawrence and Frieda parted in anger after the worst quarrel ('perhaps the very worst') of their life together.[44]

Without Frieda, Lawrence travelled restlessly, working very little, going from place to place down the west coast of Mexico, then across to Guadalajara and Chapala trying to recapture some of the satisfaction he had experienced during the previous stay in Mexico. He arrived in Los Angeles on 30 August, by way of Chicago, on the 'Los Angeles Limited', where he was met by Knud Merrild and Kai Götzsche in the tin Lizzie in which they had come to Taos. It was a happy reunion. Lawrence lived in Santa Monica until the middle of September, near the Danes who were working on a mural.

As usual Lawrence could not remain still or be happy in one place for long. By the last week in September he had persuaded Götzsche to accompany him to Mexico. They left on 25 September and arrived at Guaymas, Sonora, two days later. They went on, visiting Navojoa and Mazatlan, reaching Tepic, Nayarit on 10 October. From Tepic they had to travel a difficult way by car and mules to Etzatlan where they could take a train to Guadalajara. Here they stayed for a month, and Lawrence renewed his acquaintance with Dr George Purnell and his daughter, Idella, who published the little poetry magazine *Palms* to which Lawrence contributed.

During their travels Lawrence reported his experiences to his family and friends. He wrote to the Seltzers, John Middleton Murry, Koteliansky and Merrild; he even resumed his correspondence with Mabel, now Mabel Luhan, Mrs Sterne having married Tony during the past spring. With Mabel he negotiated an uneasy truce but did not neglect to give advice about the conduct of her life, writing in one letter: 'One day I will come to you and take your submission: when you are ready.'[45] One suspects that there may still have been a lack of complete mutual understanding.

Of the letters he may have written to Frieda, only one survives from the period of their separation which was perhaps the nearest they ever came to an open break. In late September he wrote to Bessie Freeman, 'Frieda will be coming out soon',[46] and in October from Navojoa to Witter Bynner: 'Where F[rieda] is I don't know . . . She may be in America again by now.'[47] Apparently a letter from Frieda awaited him at Guadalajara, because he reported immediately afterward that Frieda did not want to return to the

[44] Carswell 190.   [45] Letter 2954
[46] Letter 2925. Lawrence met Bessie Freeman, a girlhood friend of Mabel Dodge Sterne, at Taos in September 1922. He subsequently visited her in Buffalo, New York, in August 1923.
[47] Letter 2927

United States or Mexico but wanted him to come to England. Lawrence still hoped that Frieda would join him in Mexico for the winter, but by the end of the month he had decided to return to Europe, and when Frieda cabled the one word 'come' in early November he began to look for a ship to England. In the one letter to Frieda, dated 10 November, he wrote of his efforts to find passage home. He and Götzsche sailed on the *S.S. Toledo* for Plymouth, England, on 22 November, and by 14 December 1923 he was writing from 110 Heath Street, Hampstead, London. The Lawrences occupied a flat taken by Frieda in the house where Donald and Catherine Carswell lived.

It was during the period in Mexico that Lawrence rewrote Mollie Skinner's 'House of Ellis' as *The Boy in the Bush*; he also did some minor revision of Frederick Carter's manuscript of *The Dragon of the Alchemists* which had reached him in Mexico and which eventually resulted in the posthumously published *Apocalypse*. Apparently his only other work was a series of essays including 'The Proper Study', 'Au Revoir U.S.A.' and some of the essays beginning with the word 'On': 'On Human Destiny', 'On Being a Man', etc.

Lawrence had earned a respite from writing; never before or afterwards were so many Lawrence books published within so short a time. Seltzer published *Studies in Classic American Literature* in August 1923, and September saw the publication of *Kangaroo* and *Fantasia of the Unconscious* by Secker in London. Seltzer published *Kangaroo* in September and in October *Birds, Beasts and Flowers* and *Mastro-don Gesualdo*. Then in November Secker brought out *Birds, Beasts and Flowers* in London, and Seltzer published *The Captain's Doll* in New York.

Lawrence came home to find more of his books in print and available than had ever been the case before, but there is little or no reflection of this triumph in his correspondence. He and Frieda were in Europe for almost three months, and it was a wretched time for Lawrence. He was ill with a cold and writing to Seltzer within a week of his arrival, ' Am here – loathe London – hate England – feel like an animal in a trap', and a few days later, ' I *loathe* every minute of it here . . . I can't stand this side . . . God get me out of here.'[48] Apparently Seltzer was not forthcoming with the information about affairs in the United States which he expected, and Lawrence became impatient with him. On 18 February 1924 he wrote to Curtis Brown that he had had no word from Seltzer for six weeks, and the last letter to Seltzer before the departure for New York was cold and business-like in contrast to the usual friendly tone of his previous correspondence: '. . . once I am fixed up with Curtis Brown I needn't bother about the business end of our relationship any more'.[49]

---

[48] Letters 2977, 2980   [49] Letter 3068

After spending New Year 1924 with his family in Nottingham and Derbyshire, Lawrence went directly to Shropshire where he met Frederick Carter to discuss the manuscript of Carter's *Dragon of the Alchemists*. Carter was a painter and etcher who corresponded with Lawrence about the symbolism in the New Testament book, 'Revelation of St John the Divine'. They planned a collaboration on a book about the apocalyptic writings for which Lawrence would write the introduction. A short piece entitled 'Introduction for Frederick Carter's "Revelation of St. John the Divine"' was published in the *London Mercury* in the summer of 1930 shortly after Lawrence's death, but a later version was published by Orioli as *Apocalypse* in the Lungarno Series in 1931. Carter's own work, *The Dragon of the Revelation*, appeared the same year in London with the Desmond Harmsworth imprint. In the preface, Carter discussed the proposed collaboration which resulted in an independent work by each. His more extensive comment on Lawrence, *D. H. Lawrence and the Body Mystical*, contains an etched portrait of Lawrence.

At the end of January, Frieda and Lawrence went to Paris where they remained through the first week in February. Here Lawrence met Sylvia Beach and visited her bookshop, Shakespeare and Company, and sent postcards of all of the usual tourist monuments to his correspondents. It is interesting to speculate about his visit to Shakespeare and Company. Sylvia Beach and her Paris bookshop appear in almost every literary memoir of the period, and she was justly famous as the courageous publisher of James Joyce's *Ulysses* in February 1922. Although Lawrence himself had little to do with the literary coteries of his day, during the preceding winter in Taos he had asked Seltzer for a copy of Beach's edition of James Joyce's novel. *Ulysses* suffered from the Society for the Suppression of Vice as did Lawrence's own *Women in Love*, and Lawrence was curious, saying to Seltzer, 'I read it is the last thing in novels: I'd best look at it.' Returning the book Lawrence wrote:

I am sorry, but I am one of the people who can't read *Ulysses*. Only bits. But I am glad I have seen the book, since in Europe they usually mention us together – James Joyce and D. H. Lawrence – and I feel I ought to know in what company I creep to immortality. I guess Joyce would look as much askance on me as I on him.[50]

Although Lawrence was later to become quite angry when Sylvia Beach refused to publish *Lady Chatterley's Lover* in Paris, after this first visit he wrote to Seltzer asking that a photograph of himself be sent to Shakespeare and Company which he noted, 'is quite a famous little modern library: sells

[50] Letters 2610, 2654

my books'.[51] From Paris the Lawrences went to Baden-Baden to see Frieda's mother. After a short visit they left on Wednesday 20 February for England via Paris, where they stayed for the week-end. Returning to London on the following Tuesday, they remained at Garland's Hotel in Pall Mall until they left for New York early in March.

The time in Europe was too disturbed for Lawrence to do much writing. He continued the series of essays begun in Guadalajara, publishing several of them in the *Adelphi*. He wrote the Paris and London 'Letters' for Spud Johnson's *Laughing Horse* and a similar letter on Germany, published posthumously in the *New Statesman and Nation* in 1934. His interest in Frederick Carter's writing led him to collaborate with Carter on an article for the *Adelphi*, and the *Adelphi* also published his review of John Oman's *Book of Revelation*. Lawrence told Koteliansky in January 1924 that he was working on a 'couple of stories', which probably included 'Jimmy and the Desperate Woman', 'The Last Laugh' and 'The Border Line'; all three were sent to Curtis Brown in April. Both 'The Border Line' and 'Jimmy and the Desperate Woman' are supposed to contain portraits of John Middleton Murry. 'The Border Line' is especially significant for its portrayal of the relationship between Murry, Frieda and Lawrence. The story can be interpreted as a prediction that Murry and Frieda would marry after Lawrence's death when Murry would be cuckolded by Lawrence who would return as a ghost. It is a bitter but amusing comment on his estrangement from Frieda and his unhappy experiences with Murry.

The unfortunate climax of the whole European visit was the infamous dinner party at the Café Royal given by the Lawrences; the guest list was a roster of possible recruits for Lawrence's New World Rananim: the Carswells, John Middleton Murry, Koteliansky, Mary Cannan, Mark Gertler and the Honourable Dorothy Brett. After drinking a considerable amount of wine, Lawrence invited each guest in turn to accompany him to New Mexico. The results of his invitation were ambiguous, and the evening ended in complete disaster; Lawrence had to be carried home by Koteliansky and Murry.

Lawrence had seen his friends, visited his family, travelled in France and Germany and dealt with business matters as best he could in London. He was tired of the climate and depressed by England; more than ready to return to America and Taos. He wanted to discuss business affairs with Seltzer in New York and get on to New Mexico as soon as possible. He and Frieda sailed on the *Aquitania* on 5 March 1924 from Southampton, accompanied by Dorothy Brett, the only volunteer for his New World Rananim.

---

[51] Letter 3032

As the *Aquitania* neared New York, Lawrence's letters revealed a change in mood. To Mark Gertler he wrote: 'Now we are off America there is a strong north wind, the sea smoking its spray, and dark grey waves, and this big ship rolling . . . I rather like it.' And to Murry: 'it's good to get away from the doom of Europe'.[52]   F.W.R.

[52] Letters 3089, 3090

THE LETTERS

2243. To S. S. Koteliansky, [4 June 1921]
Text: MS BL; PC v. [Woman spinning]; Postmark, Baden-Baden 4 6 21; Zytaruk 220.

[Ludwig-Wilhelmstift, Baden-Baden]
[4 June 1921]

[1]Tell me how many words in the story,[2] and which publisher you think to offer it to.
Alas that your gay desires can't take effect!

DHL

Lend me, or send me, a simple book on Einstein's Relativity – and I'll return it, or pay for it.

Am sending you my *Psychoanalysis and Unconscious*.[3] But don't let anybody see it in London yet. I want them to wait till it is published. Barbara etc.[4] They shan't begin pecking at me beforehand.

I shall tell my friend Robert Mountsier to see you.[5] He is my New York agent, is in London, and is coming here, presumably.

Greet Sonia[6]   DHL

R. Mountsier. 36 Guilford St. WC 1.

---

[1] DHL's correspondent, Samuel Solomonovich Koteliansky ('Kot') (1880–1955), was Russian-born but naturalised British. He produced over 30 translations of Russian works, some of them with DHL acting as 'editor'. Kot was a close friend and correspondent of DHL's, 1914–30. See *Letters*, ii. 205 n. 4.

[2] 'The Gentleman from San Francisco' by Ivan Alekseyevich Bunin (1870–1953) appeared in the *Dial*, January 1922. It was collected in *The Gentleman from San Francisco and Other Stories* (1922); the title page listed the translators as Leonard Woolf and S. S. Koteliansky, but an errata slip gives DHL as Kot's collaborator on the title-story and notes that his name was omitted in error.

[3] *Psychoanalysis and the Unconscious*, first published in New York by Thomas Seltzer on 10 May 1921; English publication (by Martin Secker) was delayed until July 1923.

[4] Barbara Low (1877–1955), aunt of Ivy Litvinov (1889–1977), and the sister-in-law of Dr David Eder (1865–1936), an early Freudian psychoanalyst; she was a pioneer in psychoanalysis in England; she published *Psycho-Analysis: A Brief Outline of the Freudian Theory* (1920). See *Letters*, ii. 279 n. 6.

[5] Robert Mountsier (1888–1972), an American journalist, functioned as DHL's agent in New York until 1923. See *Letters*, iii. 24 n. 4.

[6] Sonia Farbman, wife of a Russian journalist, Michael ('Grisha') Farbman, who took the house at 5 Acacia Road, St John's Wood, from Katherine Mansfield (1888–1923) in 1915. Kot lived with the Farbmans and eventually took over the house. See *Letters*, ii. 570 n. 3.

23

2244. To Robert Mountsier, [4 June 1921]
Text: MS Smith; PC v. Ebersteinburg bei Baden-Baden; Postmark, Baden-Baden 4 6 21;
Unpublished.

[Ebersteinburg bei Baden-Baden]
[4 June 1921]

Your little letter yesterday – Very well, I will write Capt. Short.[1] I like him
too, very much, always did. – Did you call and see Nigel de Grey about the
Picture book.[2] Do. Seems to be going to be rather a lot of work. S. Koteliansky,
friend, Russian, wrote would I 'English' a translation he has made of a
Russian story. Call and see Koteliansky, he is interesting – an old Jew friend –
not old in years – about 38 or 39.

       S. Koteliansky, 5 Acacia Road, St Johns Wood, N. W. 8.

He's on the telephone under *Bourse Gazette* – a Russian newspaper. The
house is Michael Farbman's, the Russian journalist. – Then let the boat wait a
bit.[3] Don't decide anything till we've talked together properly. – If you come
bring 1 lb tea – good tea – they let you bring a pound.

DHL

    Ebersteinburg is much nicer than this p.c.

2245. To Jan Juta, 7 June 1921
Text: MS UT; Unpublished.

Ludwig Wilhelmstift, *BadenBaden*, Germania
7 June 1921

Dear Jannie[4]

    Had your espresso[5] from Sardinia today. So glad you enjoyed it. Yes, let us
go later. – Am very keen to see the pictures. – London publishers jumping for
fright at the thought of color:[6] expense! But to hell with them – They just *must*.
And Curtis Brown must make them. You know he is now my agent.[7]

---

[1] John Tregerthen Short (1849–1930), formerly the captain of a steamship and later a shipowner,
had retired to St Ives, his family home. He owned Higher Tregerthen in Cornwall, where the
Lawrences lived from March 1916 to October 1917. See *Letters*, ii. 575 n. 2.

[2] Nigel de Grey (1886–1951), a director of the Medici Society Ltd which, in conjunction with
Oxford University Press, proposed to publish a book of 'Art Pictures for Children' (*Letters*, iii.
714, 723). O.U.P. had invited DHL to provide the text for the book.

[3] Mountsier was keen to buy a boat jointly with DHL (see *Letters*, iii. 684); DHL had eagerly
sought advice from Capt. Short; but he was now beginning to lose his initial enthusiasm for
Mountsier's proposal (see *Letters*, iii. 730).

[4] Jan Juta (1897–   ), South African painter, had met DHL in January 1920 when studying at
the British School in Rome. The two men were collaborating on *Sea and Sardinia*.

[5] Express letter.

[6] The eight colour paintings Juta had done as illustrations for *Sea and Sardinia*.

[7] Albert Curtis Brown (1866–1945), managing director of Curtis Brown Ltd, became DHL's
English literary agent in April 1921. See *Letters*, iii. 566, 700.

Let me know as soon as you're ready, and we will meet. Would you like to go to Zell am See, near Salzburg, Austrian Tyrol, where F[rieda]'s sister Johanna has a *Gut?*[1] Not far from Innsbruck.

I have nearly decided to do a 'Child's Book on Art' for the Medici Society. Pictures from Giotto to Constable: sort of history of art – and culture – for children. *Might* go to Florence to do it.

We are still in our Gasthaus Krone, about 3 miles out of Baden – black and white village – old castle above – Rhine plain, and Vosges, far beyond – and round us steep hills all forest, firs and beech woods. Very lovely and still – and cheap. Everybody very friendly. And a feeling, like Sardinia, of being out of the world. Somehow Germany is cut off. And that's what I like. – Beautiful orchestra in Kurhaus.[2]

Next week F's mother – much better in health – comes here too.[3] On 1st. July Else with three children.[4] Else's husband Prof Jaffé died at Whitsun, so she is a widow. – But the world is very quiet here: poor, but not poverty: and plenty of everything, and cheap for us.

Mountsier in London – Coming here soon. Mad on having a little *ship*. It will probably come off. He has got about £1000. He nearly bought a boat in Cornwall. Now we are trying Hamburg. In the autumn we may be sailing for the Pacific – for Fontana Vecchia en route.[5] Would you like to come, with Burr?[6]

But you might come with her to Zell in July or August. Let us see how things go.

I finished *Aaron's Rod* here.[7] I go off by myself into the woods and write each morning. I find a forest such a strange stimulus – the trees are like living company, they seem to give off something dynamic and secret, and anti human – or non-human. Especially fir-trees. We've had hot weather for five weeks – *very* hot. I wrote all *Aaron* out of doors. But you won't like it. I am now doing the sequel little psychoanalysis book, in my interim.[8] If Burr wants a copy I'll send her one: of the *Psychoanalysis and the Unconscious.*

---

[1] Johanna ('Nusch') von Schreibershofen, née von Richthofen (1882–1971) and her husband Max (1864–1944) had a villa on the lake. See *Letters*, i. 391 n. 4.   [2] 'Spa hotel'.
[3] Baroness Anna von Richthofen (1851–1930).
[4] Else Jaffe, née von Richthofen (1874–1973), Frieda's older sister, was the widow of Edgar Jaffe (1866–1921), Professor of Social Economics at the University of Heidelberg. Her children were: Friedrich ('Friedel') (b. 1903), Marianne (b. 1905) and Hans (b. 1909). A fourth child, Peter, died in 1915.
[5] The Lawrences' home in Taormina, Sicily, since March 1920.
[6] Nickname for Elizabeth Humes, Juta's American fiancée. 'Burr' refers to the rolling 'r' in her Southern accent.
[7] *Aaron's Rod* was published in April 1922 in America by Seltzer and in June 1922 in England by Secker.
[8] The sequel was *Fantasia of the Unconscious*, published by Seltzer in October 1922 and Secker in September 1923.

I believe *Women in Love* is out in England this week.[1] Curse them all: – But England is in a bad way. How do you feel Italy now? Here seems so far off. – Have you heard from Alan and his *doormouse* and his cherryblossom?[2] And Violet![3]

Shall keep you informed of news. Am *very keen* to see the sketches.

D. H. Lawrence

2246. To Curtis Brown, 7 June 1921
Text: MS UT; Unpublished.

Ludwig Wilhelmstift, *Baden Baden.*

7 June 1921

Dear Curtis Brown

I wrote to Secker only what I wrote you:[4] that I had finished *Aaron's Rod*, and that probably he would prefer to publish this full length novel before starting on *Mr Noon*.[5] Nothing else. Whatever I write to Secker I will tell you exactly.

Mr de Grey of the Medici Society, with Ely, of the Oxford Press,[6] asked me about this Child's Book on Art, which they are publishing between them. It will contain about 20[7] Medici Society illustrations, and I am to do 80,000 words for letter press. Terms – 10% royalty up to 3,500, 15½% – after. Advance £50. Price of book 10/6 to 15/-. Time allowed – till December. De Grey sent me a batch of pictures. I wrote him for further details, and to ask him if he and Ely would supply me with reference books, so that I need *not* go to Florence. I wait his answer. When I hear I shall decide, and then tell him to make the agreement with you. – Half American royalties I am to have – and I forget about the Colonial editions. Write me any suggestion by return – I will then decide finally if I shall do the book. It would quite amuse me. You will make the agreement.

Mountsier says Secker turned down the little Psychoanalysis book. Of

[1] Secker published the first trade edition of *Women in Love* on 10 June 1921.
[2] Alan Insole, Welsh painter and friend of Juta's. DHL's other references cannot be explained.
[3] Alan Insole's sister Violet (she lived in Cheyne Walk).
[4] Martin Secker (1882–1978), London publisher. *New Poems* (1918) was the first of DHL's books to appear under his imprint; Secker continued as his publisher throughout DHL's lifetime and beyond. m., 1921, Caterina Maria ('Rina') Capellero (1896–1969). See *Letters*, i. 275 and n. 1.
[5] The MS of this novel remained unfinished after DHL put it aside in January 1921. Secker and Seltzer had considered publishing Part I of *Mr Noon* separately but decided to await the novel's completion. That part eventually appeared in *A Modern Lover* (Secker, 1934); for the whole (though incomplete) text see *Mr Noon*, ed. Lindeth Vasey (Cambridge University Press, 1984).
[6] Herbert Ely was responsible for the Juvenile and Elementary Schools Department of Oxford University Press. DHL had dealt with him over *Movements in European History* (see *Letters*, iii. 276).   [7] 20] 80

course Secker is not the man to take it, anyhow. I think myself Secker is useless, save for novels or library books. Heinemann publishes works on Psychoanalysis: so does Fisher Unwin.

And then, as I wrote before – did you get that letter? – I don't want Secker to have the *Sardinia* book. It would fall dead flat. It may be no publisher will be very keen on it. But let us see. It is an exact and *real* travel book: no stunt. Time will come when people will want such: when they're sick of stunts and showing off. – My friend Jan Juta has just left Sardinia where he has done a set of flat color designs of costumes etc – and pictures of landscape. I want these – or some of them – included. I want a publisher who will make a color book – John Lane or Heinemann or Blackie – and not funk it. I am willing to have very small royalty if cost of production is so alarming to the poor souls. Juta will make any little agreement he likes with me: nothing official. – If nobody wants to do the color, then let the MS. wait, and we'll try America first. – There is also a portrait sketch of me, done by Juta.[1] I'll send you a photograph of it.

I must get *Aaron's Rod* typed. But I await Mountsier, who has first part of MS.

Hope all this is clear and satisfactory.

D. H. Lawrence

I believe Fisher Unwin sold really a lot of Barbara Low's little *Introduction to Psychoanalysis*. The subject is in the air now.

2247. To Robert Mountsier, 7 June 1921
Text: MS Smith; Postmark, Baden-Baden 7. 6. 21; Unpublished.

Baden Baden.
Tuesday. 7 June 1921

Dear M[ountsier]
  I have your letter of Saturday.
1. Curtis B[rown] has no cause to grumble. The few words I wrote to Secker I wrote identically to CB.: viz, that I would rather *Mr Noon I.* waited till after *Aaron* was out. Let agents not be fussy.
2. I told you what the Medici Press offered: royalty of 10% up to 3,500, then 15%: advance of £50. I have got a selection of the pictures. If de Grey will *send* me books for reference, I shall do the book. I await his letter – Then shall write CB. to make agreement. This kind of business I must do alone. How does an agent know *what* I want to do?
3. CB is an idiot to offer Secker the *Psy[choanalysis] and Uncon[scious]* and *Sardinia*. Secker is absolutely *useless* as a publisher, save of novels or library

---

[1] Now at UT (the portrait from it, in oils, is in the National Portrait Gallery).

books. I could have done better myself: unless CB. is just acting up to
Secker Contract. – Heinemann or Unwin must do the *Psy. and Unc.*
 Juta has done flat color sketches for *Sardinia*, and I want them included
if possible. I don't want Secker to think of the book. John Lane might. I
don't have any financial arrangement with Juta. He won't care anyhow.
4. *Aaron* won't serialise. – Wish I had a machine, I'd type it myself.
5. Am writing my sister about coat.[1]
6. My mother-in-law is coming up here next week – On July 1st. my sister-in-
   law from Munich with three children.[2] I'm sure you won't like it then –
   You'd better defer your coming here till end July. Then we could either
   meet in Florence or Zell-am-See or even Paris, to talk things over.
7. I still hear nothing satisfactory about German ships – but enquiries are
   going on.
8. I am doing the new psychoanalysis book, because it is in my head. Expect it
   wont take a month. Picture book will take more than a month.
9. Shall probably make a little tour in Black Forest next week with F[rieda].
   Hope you'll like Ireland. I've got a friend there – Gordon Campbell. –
C H G. Campbell in Dublin, Barrister, son of Sir James Campbell, Lord
chief something or other.[3] I give you a note to him.

D. H. Lawrence

You can get Campbell's address – from
S. Kotiliansky, 5 Acacia Rd, St. Johns Wood N.W.8
if not in Dublin.
 Have you got the first part of *Aaron's Rod* from Miss Monk?[4] If so, since our
meeting is perhaps indefinite, would you post me the typescript, you keeping
the manuscript.

DHL

[1] Plans had been tentatively made for Mountsier to bring DHL's sister Lettice Ada Clarke
(1887–1948) to visit the Lawrences in Ebersteinburg. He was also asked to bring cloth to be
made into a coat for Frieda. See *Letters*, iii. 723–4, 731.   [2] See p. 25 n. 4.
[3] Charles Henry Gordon Campbell (1885–1963), later 2nd Baron Glenavy of Milltown, was,
1919–22, Secretary of the Irish Department, Ministry of Labour. His father, Sir James Henry
Mussen Campbell (1851–1931), had been Lord Chief Justice of Ireland (1916–18) and was now
Lord Chancellor of Ireland (1918–21). In 1921, he became Baron Glenavy of Milltown, Co.
Dublin. See *Letters*, ii. 51 n. 1.
[4] Violet Monk knew DHL during the War, when she and her cousin Cecily Lambert lived at
Grimsbury Farm (the setting for DHL's 'The Fox'), close to the Lawrences' cottage in
Hermitage. She was typing *Aaron's Rod* (see *Letters*, iii. 724).

2248. To Gordon Campbell, 7 June 1921
Text: MS Smith; Unpublished.

Ludwig-Wilhelmstift, *BadenBaden*, Germany
7 June 1921

Dear Campbell

Have thought of you so often, in all this newspaper – Ireland.[1] Send me a line.

The bearer of this note, Robert Mountsier, is a friend: an American journalist: does my business in New York: and is coming out here to see me. So if you feel like sending me all your kindest regards by him, you must see him and tell him so.

Frieda and I send many regards to you and Beatrice.[2] How are the children? Come and see us in Taormina in the late autumn, wont you? Or meet us in Florence in September. Fun that would be.

D. H. Lawrence

Don't know your address.

2249. To S. S. Koteliansky, 9 June 1921
Text: MS BL; Postmark, Baden-B[aden] 9 6 2[. . .]; Zytaruk 221–2.

Hotel Krone, Ebersteinburg, bei BadenBaden.
9 June 1921

My dear Kot.

Send the two stories along and I will have a shot at them now immediately.[3] I am doing nothing in particular at the moment. Then you can offer them if you like to Woolf,[4] and if that is no go, we will make Curtis Brown do something with them (if you like): and Mountsier in America. You know Curtis B. is now my agent: not very exciting, but more obedient than the impudent Pinker.[5] – Mountsier I hear has[6] gone to Ireland. See him when he comes back.

I couldn't send the *Psycho.* book: the damned Authorities sent it back and said I must get an Erlaubnis[7] to send it out of the country. So I have written to Karlsruhe for the said Erlaubnis.

---

[1] Newspapers carried daily reports of violence in Ireland, attacks on British troops and civilians, arson etc, contemporary with the debate on Home Rule.

[2] Beatrice Moss Campbell, née Elvery (d. 1970), m. Gordon Campbell 1912.

[3] It appears that Koteliansky sent only one, 'The Gentleman from San Francisco' (see Letter 2258).

[4] Leonard Sidney Woolf (1880–1969) and Virginia Woolf (1882–1941), the novelist, ran the Hogarth Press. See *Letters*, iii. 198 and n. 1.

[5] James Brand Pinker (1863–1922) was DHL's literary agent 1914–20; their confidence in one another deteriorated sharply towards the end of their relationship. See *Letters*, iii. 14–16.

[6] has] had   [7] 'Permit'.

I am sure Sophie Issayevna's[1] head will be better out of London. London is bad for one. Perhaps she will come to Baden. There is such a nice little house to let here for eight months. – And here in Ebersteinburg, 3 miles from Baden, higher, cooler, among the woods, one pays only 35 M. a day. Tell Sonia if she stays in Germany to come to Baden.

My mother-in-law is coming here next week – so please write to this address.

And look, I have broken my pen. It is a *Swan* but the nib I got in Italy. Perhaps the nib too is no good – Ask them. The rest of the pen I have all right – only this section has the bit broken which goes up the back of the nib. Ask

Mabie Todds, 79 High Holborn,

if they will mend this, or if I need a new section or if I had just as well have a new pen entirely. I send only this section because they would make me get permissions for the rest.

As soon as Einstein comes[2] I will send you a cheque for it and this pen. But read the Einstein first.

Will send *Psycho.* as soon as I get permit.

Many greetings to Sonia and Ghita.[3]

I shall depart into the woods to write the stories when they come.

DHL

The nib is bent.

You may send what you like *into* Germany.

2250. To Alfred Sutro, [c. 9 June 1921]
Text: Alfred Sutro, *Celebrities and Simple Souls* (1933), p.100.

[Hotel Krone, Ebersteinburg, bei Baden-Baden]
[c. 9 June 1921][4]

There is at least one thing of which you may be certain, your women will be more chaste than mine.

---

[1] Sonia Farbman's maiden name, Sonia being a diminutive of Sophia.
[2] Albert Einstein, *Relativity: the special and the general theory. A popular exposition*, trans. R. W. Lawson (1920).   [3] Ghita was the Farbmans' daughter.
[4] Alfred Sutro (1863–1933), playwright, published a series of 'duologues' under the title *Women in Love: Eight Studies in Sentiment* in 1902. Possibly as a result of the *TLS* review of *Women in Love*, 9 June 1921, Sutro told DHL that the title had been used before but that the matter was of no consequence since his book had been long out of print. Sutro had been generous to DHL on an earlier occasion: see *Letters*, ii. 213, 224–5 n. 4.

2251. To Michael Sadleir, [10 June 1921]
Text: MS UNCCH; Unpublished.

Hotel Krone, *Ebersteinburg, BadenBaden,* Germany
10 June.
Dear Sadler[1]
Your letter today.[2] Alas, all my MSS are in Taormina. The 'Wintry Peacock' story was published in America, and is quite free for England. I think *The Metropolitan* did it. But my Amer. agent,
Robert Mountsier, 36 Guilford St., W. C. I –
is at this moment in England. He will get you a copy of the story. I write him now. He may be in Ireland this instant – and is coming here almost immediately. Nail him at once, and get this story.[3] I should be happy to have £20. – and willing, out of justice then, to give back the £10. I had from you via Milford.[4] Am poor as ever: publish, but am not paid: at least £200 per annum.

Yes, I'm glad Secker did *Women in Love.* And I hope there's no loss for him.

Yes, take 'Wintry Peacock' for your *Decameron,* if you like and can: sale outright as you say.

Yrs   D. H. Lawrence

---

[1] Michael Thomas Harvey Sadleir (1888–1957); his family name was 'Sadler' but he modified the spelling in 1919 to distinguish himself from his father Sir Michael Sadler. He was a distinguished bibliophile and bibliographer, as well as a novelist; with Cyril Beaumont he edited *New Paths* (1918) to which DHL contributed; and he was to publish *The New Decameron,* Vol. III (15 June 1922) in which DHL's 'Wintry Peacock' was reprinted. The story first appeared in *Metropolitan,* August 1921. See *Letters,* iii. 202 n. 1.

[2] Sadleir had written on 5 June (MS Smith):

Dear D. H. Lawrence,
   Have you yet disposed in England or tied up that story you sent for an ill-fated magazine – the one Milford paid for when we couldn't use it? I ask, because I am deputed to collect collaborators for a third volume of a thing called "The New Decameron" – a series of books in each of which ten characters each tell a story. The publisher wants a more distinguished caste and I am asking Beresford, Rose Macaulay and Norman Davey as a start. I should like that story of yours and I think Blackwell would pay £20 for it – outright payment. I put this up to you personally. Would you let me know if you like the idea, assuming the others come in, and what sort of payment you think fair. 5000 words is about the length. We cant have too slight stuff because its a *book* not a magazine. That fine thing you sent before would do admirably.
   I have just bought "Women in Love" in Secker's edition. May it prosper. I think it very sporting of him to bring it out.

Yours sincerely

[3] Sadleir wrote to Mountsier on 17 June 1921 (TMS Smith) requesting a copy of the *Metropolitan* text.

[4] In February 1920 Sadleir had invited DHL to contribute a story to a new review to be published by Oxford University Press; Humphrey Milford (1877–1952), Publisher to O.U.P., had clearly paid DHL a fee of £10 for the story; but the review never appeared (see *Letters,* iii. 474 and n. 1).

2252. To J. B. Pinker, 11 June 1921
Text: MS UNYB; Unpublished.

Ludwig-Wilhelmstift, *Baden-Baden*, Germany
11. June 1921

Dear Pinker

Thank you for the cheque for nine guineas received today on acc. of the 'Blind Man' story from the *English Review*.[1]

Yrs D. H. Lawrence

2253. To Lady Cynthia Asquith, [11 June 1921]
Text: MS UT; Postmark, Baden-Baden 13 6 21; Unpublished.

per Adr. Frau Baronin von Richthofen, Ludwig-Wilhelmstift,
Baden-Baden, Germany.

June 11th

I haven't heard from you[2] for at least ten months, till your note today via Secker. He sent you, I presume, a copy of *Women in Love*, addressed to Stanway[3] – as I ordered him to do. If not, let me know.

F[rieda]'s mother was ill. So she F came here in March. I arrived at the end of April.[4] We are not in the 'Stift' with my mother-in-law, but out at Ebersteinburg in a village in a small hotel where we live for seven shillings a day for the pair of us: or eight shillings, including wine: Of course it's a rough Village hotel, but very nice – 3 miles from Baden Baden. Why not come?

I'd make your fortune if I could. Anyhow I'll tell my friend Robt. Mountsier – who is my American agent – and who is in London at the moment – or Ireland – to send you forthwith a certain story called 'Fanny and Annie'. – 'You', being, by euphemism, Hutchinson and Co.[5] Are Hutchinsons friendly to me? – I've got Curtis Brown for an agent.

Suppose Adelphi Terrace House is Barrie.[6] Mary C[annan] told me of her flight to London[7] – and buzz-buzz back again, as fast as you can 'plane. –

[1] The story appeared in *English Review*, xxxi (July 1920), 22–41.
[2] DHL's correspondent, Lady Cynthia Asquith, née Charteris (1887–1960), met DHL in July 1913 (see *Letters*, ii. 48); they frequently exchanged letters thereafter. Her husband, Herbert ('Beb') Asquith (1881–1947), the son of the former Prime Minister, Herbert Henry Asquith (1852–1928), was a barrister but also poet and novelist.
[3] Stanway House, Gloucestershire, where Lady Cynthia grew up.   [4] April] February
[5] 'Fanny and Annie' appeared in *Hutchinson's Magazine*, 21 November 1921. (Herbert Asquith was working for Hutchinson & Co in 1921.)
[6] Sir James Matthew Barrie (1860–1937), novelist and dramatist to whom Lady Cynthia was secretary 1918–37.
[7] Mary Cannan, née Ansell (1867–1950), m. (1) Sir James Barrie, (2) Gilbert Cannan (1884–1955), novelist and playwright. Mary Cannan was a neighbour and became a friend of the

Then J[ohn] M[iddleton Murry]'s 'abject apologies'.[1]
I've still got the house in Taormina. Ought to go back to it about Sept.
Welcome you there if ever you feel like it.

Ott[oline] was in Rome.[2] Didn't see her, but heard all – and enough.

Nice here: F's room looks far away across Rhine plain to Vosges: mine on
the black and white Dorf and the pine woods. The Black Forest's last dark
skirts round us. I hie forth and hide myself under the trees and write,
mornings. – Germany very *still*: feels life-empty: very little money. Yet not
poor: great blank of young men, a blank in the life stream: Schiebers enough,
profiteers, pesce carne,[3] money hogs in motorcars, mostly Jews: man[y] of
people poor but so *scrupulous*, neat and nice and all. Everything so *clean* – quite
a shock after Italy – and nobody begging and parasiting: terrible relief after
Sicily. – It's a wonderful *big* country – big landscape. And amazing law-
abiding people: incredible. Because there's really *no*[4] authority that has any
force: no uniforms at all, save tram and post: policemen; two wistful fathers
looking apologetic in their trousers. This is all the 'force' Baden boasts. Yet
such order, everything to the minute. Queer psyche.

Don't know how long we shall be here. F's sister Johanna has a *Gut* near
Salzburg, Austrian Tyrol: on a *See* among mts. Invites us there for rest of
summer. May go. Then perhaps Taormina in Sept. Don't know.

Mountsier dying to buy a tiny yacht for about £1000 and sail round world
with us. Do you know anybody to sell – or *hire* – such a yacht? *Do think*. It
would be such fun.

We are as usual, financially. I don't care. I've got about £75 in the bank, and
to hell with everybody. Who'll tread on the tails of my coat?

Should like to see you. But the thought of England is so sterilising.

No, you never even acknowledged the receipt of *The Lost Girl*?[5] And Secker
sent it. Bad manners. – Nor did Eddie Marsh.[6] V. bad manners. And I know I
paid Secker 8/6 per copy. Die Welt ist Kaput.[7]

Foxgloves out here – wild strawberries, and Heidelbeern.[8]

Lawrences when they lived near Chesham, Bucks., in 1914–15; their friendship had been
renewed in Capri and then in Sicily, in early 1920.
[1] John Middleton Murry (1889–1957), journalist and critic. m. Katherine Mansfield, 1918. The
relationship between the Murrys and the Lawrences had been storm-ridden since its inception
in 1913; DHL broke it off in January/February 1920 (see *Letters*, iii. 467–8).
[2] Lady Ottoline Violet Anne Morrell (1873–1938), a well-known hostess and patroness of the arts
whose close friendship with DHL was ruptured in 1917 after she learned of her portrayal as
Hermione Roddice in *Women in Love*. See *Letters*, ii. 253 n. 3.
[3] 'Profiteers . . . fish meat'.   [4] *no*] now   [5] Published by Secker, November 1920.
[6] Sir Edward Howard Marsh (1872–1953), writer and civil servant. In 1912, Marsh requested a
poem from DHL for *Georgian Poetry 1911–1912*; from that time he became friendly and often
acted with great generosity towards the Lawrences (see *Letters*, ii. 2–3).
[7] 'The world is finished'.   [8] 'Bilberries'.

Have finished a novel called *Aaron's Rod*, which never buds even.
How are your children?[1]
Should like to see you again.
F. sends love.
Hope your husband enjoys it. Damn it, it's a come-down. It's all a
comedown. Why don't you seduce a Jewish millionaire. Pah – ! Only, why
should one have to do jobs.

                                                          Wiedersehn   D. H. Lawrence
    Tell J. M. what I think of him.

2254. To Curtis Brown, [12 June 1921]
Text: MS UT; Huxley 517–8.

                                    Hotel Krone,[2] *Ebersteinburg, Baden Baden*
                                                                    Sunday 12 June
Dear Curtis Brown
    Please write to this address.
    I write today to[3] Secker, that if he cared for the *Sardinia* book, and if he
could see his way to do the color illustrations, I would try and accommodate
him with regard to royalty and advance – Juta would not ask anything, (unless
a small royalty on sales or as you suggest here over 2,000.) – And if you think it
is no good bothering about periodicals, then let Secker see *Sardinia* as soon as
he likes. The illustrations would be mostly people-scenes: like the eggs in
Cagliari – not landscape: and in flat color wash easy to reproduce. Tell Secker
to say how many he could put in, if any. – And I could make any arrangement
with[4] Juta privately, for payment. He won't mind anyhow. But I simply dont
want to leave him in the lurch, if I think his illustrations are good.
    Mountsier has first part of *Aarons*[5] *Rod*. I must wait for him, and revise,
before I can let you have MS. – It is quite finished.
    I hear that Hutchinsons are friendly to me – if that is any use to you: and I
ask Mountsier to turn over to you for them[6] a short story 'Fanny and Annie',
of which I have no copy. All my loose MSS in Taormina, alas. – Mountsier has
a complete understanding with you, I know: so he will tell you if he has the
MS. – I want to tell de Grey: to make out the Medici agreement with you, as
soon as I have your letter of advice.

                                                          Yrs   D. H. Lawrence

[1] Lady Cynthia had three children – John (1911–37), Michael (b. 1914), Simon (b. 1919) – but
   DHL had shown a particular concern for the first who was autistic. See *Letters*, ii. 335–7; iii.
   201.   [2] Hotel Krone] Ludwig Wilhelm   [3] write today to] wrote
   [4] with] for   [5] *Aarons*] Luck   [6] you for them] them

2255. To Martin Secker, [12 June 1921]
Text: MS UInd; Secker 42.

Hotel Krone, *Ebersteinburg, BadenBaden*
Sunday 12 June
Dear Secker
Your letter today. Thanks for sending out eight copies *Women in Love*. I drank a bottle of beautiful Moselle to its luck: and dreamed of huge blue prosecution papers: so it is quite safe. – Send out at your discretion to the damned papers. –¹ Thank you for paying in to my bank the remainder of the £100.² Oh God, what a sweat of a life. – *Aarons Rod* quite finished: not at all impossible. I only await Mountsier with the first part, which was typed in England. – – I will finish 'Lucky Noon' before Christmas, God being with me.³ But it will be rather impossible, only funny – It is 3-parts done, nearly the first two vols – up to 1913. Sec. part ends 1914. Third part ends 1919. But third part not yet begun. Part I you have seen. Part II, which is 3 times as long – or more – is about ½ done. MS in Palermo. Will get it here.

For the Lord's Sake, don't let Curtis Brown imagine I write you any business. It is high treason in his eyes.

As for *Sardinia*, have only the one – copy – and don't believe you'd care for it. Also Jan Juta has just sweated away a month in Sardinia, doing flat-color sketches for it. 1 can't leave him in the lurch. If his sketches are good – haven't seen them yet – I'd rather *Sardinia* were never published at all, than minus his contribution. – He won't want money. And if you could rise to a few color illustrations, I'd try and accommodate you in royalty or advance. Oh God! – But doubt if you'll like *Sardinia*. I'll tell CB to let you see it without more ado, *if you think the color illustrations possible*. Myself I think *Sardinia* rather a marvel of veracity. But this is not what people want. I give you leave to cut it *ad lib*. Let me know and I'll write CB at once to give you the MS to read. But *don't* tell him I wrote you this.

Let me know news of *Women in Love*. Am grateful to you for doing this book, and *Rainbow* in future. If I don't feel keen for you to do *Sardinia*, it is also because I feel you won't like it. – Of course you are quite right not to bother with the little *Psychoanalysis* book.

¹ Secker had been very apprehensive about publishing *Women in Love* and had at one time considered not distributing review-copies in order to avoid undue publicity. DHL once shared this view: see *Letters*, iii. 638.
² Secker had paid £50 of the advance royalties in May, promising the remaining £50 not later than 10 June 1921 (see [Martin Secker] *Letters from a Publisher*, 1970, p. 13).
³ DHL started referring to *Mr Noon* as 'Lucky Noon' when he began to write what would become Part II. Noon becomes 'lucky' when he meets Johanna (modelled on Frieda).

I might go to Paris. If so, Herm. Poor Monty.[1] Damn pigs.

D. H. Lawrence

2256. To Robert Mountsier, [12 June 1921]

Text: MS Smith; Postmark, Baden-Baden 13 6 21; Unpublished.

Krone,[2] Baden Baden
Sunday. 12. June

Dear M[ountsier]

Send, procure by some means 'Wintry Peacock', the story published last fall in New York by, I believe, *The Metropolitan*, to Michael Sadler, whose address I enclose. *Don't* consult Curtis B[rown] yet, as I sold this story to Sadler last July and had £10. for it. It's a more or less shut bargain. But any surplus I'll take from Blackwell.[3]

Also, a letter from Cynthia Asquith – Her husband is with Hutchinsons, the publishers: and they'd very much like to see a story. Where is 'Fanny and Annie'? – did you ever send it to that swine Squire?[4] Tell Curtis B. that Hutchinsons are friendly.

A letter from Hamburg. Very many difficulties in way of a German boat. But still trying.

Think of going to Zell am See in July. If you don't want to come, will meet you in Paris and discuss and settle all we can. Then I'll go to Austria.

Hear from Miss Monk she has sent you *Aaron's* first part. I must see it: and then I must send this Conclusion to be typed.

Hope you enjoy Ireland.

D. H. Lawrence

Give 'F[anny] and A[nnie]' story to CB. for *Hutchinsons*, of course.[5]

2257. To S. S. Koteliansky, 15 June 1921

Text: MS BL; PC; Postmark, Baden-Baden 15 6 21; Zytaruk 223.

[Hotel Krone, Ebersteinburg, bei Baden-Baden]
15 June 1921

Today came the Einstein – very many thanks. When you send me the pen, I

[1] Their mutual friend, the novelist (Sir) Edward Montague Compton Mackenzie (1883–1972) whom DHL had met on Capri in December 1919. In 1920 Mackenzie had become tenant of the Channel Islands, Herm and Jethou. See *Letters*, ii. 212 n. 1.
[2] Krone] Ludwig Wilhelmstift
[3] See p. 31 nn. 2 and 4. (*The New Decameron* was published by Basil Blackwell.)
[4] (Sir) John Collings Squire (1884–1958), pseudonym Solomon Eagle, poet, journalist, founder and editor of the *London Mercury* (1919–34).
[5] The postscript was written on the verso of the envelope.

shall send cheque. – Today also I have posted to you four copies of *Psychoan[alysis] and the Unconscious.* Will you give Barbara two copies, one for herself, one for Eder. I wrote Eder's name in one. Keep one for yourself – I wrote your name – and let the other one lie for a while, I may ask you to send it to somebody else. I trouble you so far because of the bother of getting permissions here.

Write to me
Hotel Krone, Ebersteinburg, bei BadenBaden.

I wait to hear about the stories.

DHL

2258. To S. S. Koteliansky, 16 June 1921
Text: MS BL; Postmark, Baden-Baden 16 6 21; Moore 656–7.

[Hotel Krone, Ebersteinburg, bei Baden-Baden][1]
16 June 1921

My dear Kot

Yesterday the 'Gent[leman] from S[an] Francisco' and the pen: very many thanks. Have read the 'Gent'. – and in spite of its lugubriousness, grin with joy. Was Bunin one of the Gorki-Capri crowd?[2] – or only a visitor? But it is screamingly good of Naples and Capri: so comically like the reality: only just a trifle too earnest about it. I will soon get it written over: don't think your text needs much altering. I love a 'little curved peeled-off dog' – it is too good to alter.[3]

For the pen many thanks. I write this with it.

I will send you Einstein when I leave Germany. Can't face another permission-form the size of a wall-poster just yet.

Havent heard from Mountsier for two weeks. He was going to Ireland to journalise. Send him a p.c. to 36 Guilford St. – and to hell if he is fidgetty. But he's not fidgetty – you'll like him. And I really think *The Dial* might print 'The Gent'. And if so, we get at least 100 dollars. Good for us!

Einstein isn't so metaphysically marvellous, but I like him for taking out the pin which fixed down our fluttering little physical universe.

Greet Sonia vielmal.[4]

DHL

---

[1] For this letter – together with 2260, 2262, 2263, 2265, 2267 and 2270 – DHL used the hotel's headed notepaper.
[2] The Russian writer Maxim Gorky (1868–1936) lived on Capri 1906–13.
[3] This phrase was changed to 'a tiny cringing peeled-off dog' when 'The Gentleman from San Francisco' appeared in the *Dial*, and to 'a tiny, cringing, hairless little dog' in *The Gentleman from San Francisco and Other Stories.*   [4] 'many times'.

Don't know what *Einstein* cost: but send 7/- and don't cavil with me about it. – What was poor Ott[oline']s nose out of joint for, I wonder: didn't the *Times* say that Hermione was a grand-sincere figure, among a nest of perverse puppies?¹ So the wet flea has hopped to Switzerland – which Kurort?² What is Campbell's address?

2259. To Ada Russell, [16 June 1921]
Text: Moore, *Intelligent Heart* 280–1.

[Hotel Krone, Ebersteinburg, bei Baden-Baden]
[16 June 1921]

³We came to Germany two months ago, because my mother-in-law was very ill. [But she is better and will soon travel to Ebersteinburg which is] very lovely really – a little black and white village, with the big woods all round, the edge of the Black Forest and the Rhine away beyond, in the plain below, and then the Vosges dim beyond the plain. [And Germany seems] so big and so *still*: strange and hushed: so very different from before the war. It is nice to be in a country where people are not so disgustingly full of money as they are everywhere else. Nobody has any money any more except the profiteers, chiefly Jews, with which Baden Baden is swarming.

2260. To Robert Mountsier, 20 June 1921
Text: MS Smith; Postmark, Baden-Baden 20. 6. 21; Unpublished.

[Hotel Krone, Ebersteinburg, bei Baden-Baden]
20n Juni 1921

Dear M[ountsier]
Your note from Aran Isles today. – You must please yourself about coming here. My mother-in-law here – and on 1st July comes my sister-in-law from Munich: but speaks good English. I think of staying till about 10th. July: then walking across Black Forest to Lake Constance: then either to Munich for a week, or direct to Zell-am-See via Innsbruck. I think to stay in Zell-am-See,

¹ Edmund Blunden, the reviewer in *TLS*, 9 June 1921, had commented: 'The satirically treated figure of Hermione stands out as, probably, the one thing in the whole work which was worth Mr Lawrence's powers and time or the reader's. . . . there is something of immense dignity in her . . . She, in the midst of all her artificiality, in all her masks and postures, is sincere. Most of the other characters . . . are little better than "shadows of life and artificial flowers".'
² DHL's reference is to Murry who had gone to join Katherine Mansfield whose 'health resort' was now Sierre in Switzerland.
³ DHL's correspondent was Ada (Dwyer) Russell (b. 1863), American actress, Amy Lowell's life-long friend and companion. She had known the Lawrences since August 1914.

in Austrian Tyrol, till September. Then if nothing better happens, to Italy. If you feel like it, then you can come too. Otherwise we will just talk things over here, or I would even come to Paris for a few days.

Please see Koteliansky,

5 Acacia Rd. St Johns Wood –

telephone *Bourse Gazette*, same address. I am just writing over for him a Russian story which the *Dial* surely would print.

Please bring the overcoat. My sister says she thinks it will be all right. I don't want to bother her further.

Please bring *tea*, and two or three tubes of *Kolynos* tooth-paste, for all of which I will pay when I see you. Nothing else.

If you come here, leave your big trunk in Paris, and bring only valises and typewriter.

A ship in Hamburg almost impossible. We must talk it over. – A letter from a friend in Japan.[1] He loves Japan. He might join us in the ship: is rich.

I have nearly done the Second book of the *Unconscious*. Hope to finish in eight days. Interests me.

Bring MS of *Aaron* which lies at American Express.

Have agreed to do the Picture book, and await agreement from Curtis B[rown]. He, CB, will tell you about the Sardinia book and Juta's illustrations. I am enquiring cost of making color-illustrations here, in Stuttgart. Want Medici Press to send me some books for reference for the Picture Book.

I don't really want to go back to Taormina this winter. But shall do so if nothing else turns up.

I have written you two letters before.

Wiedersehn DHL

If you come here, let me know as soon as possible, to engage room.

2261. To Martin Secker, [23 June 1921]
Text: MS UInd; PC; Postmark, Baden-Baden 23 6 21; Secker 43.

Hotel Krone, Ebersteinburg, bei BadenBaden
23 June

Dear Secker

Will you please send a copy of *Women in Love* to

Frau Frieda Gross,[2] Ascona, Locarno, Switzerland.

Write to me here. – I saw the *Times* notice.

D. H. Lawrence

---

[1] Alan Insole (see Letters 2265 and 2272).
[2] The widow of Dr Otto Gross (1877–1919) (see *Letters*, i. 395 n. 1).

2262. To Dr Anton Kippenberg, 23 June 1921
Text: MS SNMuseum; *Die Insel* Eine Ausstellung zur Geschichte des Verlags unter Anton und
Katharina Kippenberg (Marbach, 1965), p. 214.

[Hotel Krone, Ebersteinburg, bei Baden-Baden]
23 June 1921

Dear Dr Kippenberg[1]

I had your very kind letter a while ago: and also the *Contes Drolatiques* and
the *Nibelung Song*.[2] The latter I can't read, the German is so difficult. – Now I
suppose these new sanctions will prevent your exporting these. I sent my sister
a cuckoo clock: 250 Mark: and in England they made her pay £1. – which is
now 260 Mark – for the Sanctions tax. This makes me so angry. England
deserves to have her coal strike.[3]

I sent you *Women in Love* from Seckers edition. I think it the best of my
books. But of course *The Times* says it is only filthy and false and tedious. I
hate them all. – I shall send you a little book which Seltzer published in
America:[4] *Psychoanalysis and the Unconscious*. It is not about psychoanalysis
particularly – but a first attempt at establishing something definite in place of
the vague Freudian Unconscious. It may bore you.

I too am sorry we cannot meet. But I feel it is not destined, just yet. I have a
friend in Grimma-Sachsen – and perhaps next year I shall come and see him.[5]
Then I shall come also to Leipsig. But if you come to Italy, be sure and let me
know. I can usually find you rooms or a little Wohnung[6] that would be less
expensive than an hotel.

I think in about a fortnight's time we shall leave for Munich, where I have a
sister-in-law – Frau Professor Else Jaffe. – then on to the Austrian Tyrol – and
in the early autumn back to Italy. I didn't go to England after all, because my
native land makes me so angry at present: so stupid, so meaningless. I am
afraid the coal-strike will develop into something very serious: probably a
labour government and a republic in the end. But anything better than the
helpless nothingness and smallness which it is now: England.

I feel that Germany is strong enough inwardly – she is in no real danger. She

---

[1] Dr Anton Kippenberg (1874–1950) was the head of Insel Verlag in Leipzig, the publishing
house which produced the German translation of *The Rainbow* (by Franz Franzius), 1922.
Kippenberg had been interested in DHL's writings by Douglas Goldring in 1919 (see
Letters, iii. 7).
[2] Insel Verlag published Balzac's *Les Contes Drolatiques* and *Der Nibelunge Not-Kudrun*, both in
1921.
[3] The miners' strike began with the support of the railwaymen and transport workers; on 15 April
1921 (known as 'Black Friday'), they lost this support; and on 1 July, they finally reached a
settlement with the employers.
[4] Thomas Seltzer (1875–1943) was DHL's chief American publisher in the 1920s. See Lacy,
Seltzer 171ff.   [5] Unidentified.   [6] 'House or flat'.

has an almost feminine power of passive resistance and stubbornness. I have been quite happy here: everybody very nice with me. And I have been very happy away in the woods: the great trees, the power of the tree life, the power of the forest. I have done quite a lot of work, out in the woods, sitting at the foot of a tree well out of sight. So, the tree-life stimulates one, and one gets away from people-life.

The Ludwig Wilhelmstift address will always find me.

Best of wishes, and many thanks for the books.

Yours   D. H. Lawrence

2263. To Robert Mountsier, 23 June 1921
Text: MS Smith; Postmark, Baden-Baden 23 6 21; Unpublished.

[Hotel Krone, Ebersteinburg, bei Baden-Baden]

23 June 1921

Dear M[ountsier]

I have decided to go to Florence for a month at least to do the book for the Medici: leave here about 3rd. July – go to Innsbruck direct – call for two days at Zell-am-See: and so arrive in Florence about July 7th.

You will choose whether to come with us, or go direct from Paris to Florence. If the latter, stay at Berchiellis' Hotel, on the Lungarno: or at Nardini's, in the Cathedral Square – Piazza del Duomo. When we come we hope to have the flat 32 Via de' Bardi. – if you are there before us call at the British Institute, Via dei Conti, Florence – and see Deane Perceval, who is arranging the flat for us.[1] I'll tell him you're coming.

Haste   D. H. Lawrence

2264. To Robert Mountsier, [23 June 1921]
Text: MS Smith; PC; Postmark, Baden-Baden 23 6 21; Unpublished.

Ebersteinburg.

23 June

Dear M[ountsier]

I have decided to go to Florence to write the Medici book – leave here about July 3rd go via Innsbruck, call for two days at Zell am See – arrive Florence about July 7th.

---

[1] Deane Perceval was the first Secretary of the British Institute in Florence, 1919–22. (He spent a month in Taormina in mid-1920; see *Letters*, iii. 575.) See p. 48 n. 4.

Have written you to Librairie Terquem – you may not get this p.c. –
Perhaps you may prefer to go direct to Florence from Paris.

DHL

2265. To Jan Juta, 23–4 June 1921
Text: MS UT; Unpublished.

[Hotel Krone, Ebersteinburg, bei Baden-Baden]
23 June 1921

Dear Johnnie

The pictures just come: I like them *very* much, and Frieda is enraptured. I
am sending them at once to Stuttgart to ask.[1] The question apparently would
be the evading of the Sanctions, which are awful. I sent my sister a clock, cost
250 Marks (£1.) and she had to pay again £1. – sanctions duty. We'd have to
smuggle somehow. I like them *very* much. How much do you think they ought
to be reduced?

Friday 24th June.

I left off this, waiting for your letter. – The pictures have gone to Stuttgart:
and now we'll see what the Herr Hofrath Max Schreiber says about the cost. I
have thought about it last evening and this morning: think it is a great pity to
have the pictures *reduced* in size – or *bound in* to a book. Because you know they
are not book-illustrations. They just aren't. I shall contrive if possible that
they be printed unreduced, the size they now are,[2] and sold as a separate loose
folio[3] with a foreword from me, but *in conjunction* with my book: that is, 12/6
for book and folio together, and book 7/6, pictures 7/6 apart. Something like
that, if it can possibly be managed. Publisher must bear all cost. – I don't like
the printing *under* the picture: would prefer it on the back. It interrupts the
picture. Also you haven't *signed* them. We must attend to this. Don't like the
title 'Path of the Righteous' – I would rather it were exact and local – 'Sunday
Morning' – or 'Church-Goers', 'Terranova' – also 'New Laid Eggs' – rather
'Egg Market' – and 'The Gathering of the Tribe' something different. So
that it is all just *real*. Perhaps you'll let me suggest titles.[4] – I am keen to see the
other three.

If only we can circumvent those bloody sanctions. We must try and work
officials in England, if nothing else: or smuggle into Italy. Prepare your wits.
If we can get the goods landed in England sanctionless – there is no import

---

[1] To the printer, Max Schreiber (see Letter 2271).
[2] unreduced, the size they now are,] the same size   [3] folio] foreword
[4] In the published book a title appeared below each picture, together with Juta's name. The titles
finally selected were: 'Orosei', ' Isili', 'Tonara', 'Sorgono', 'Fonni', 'Gavoi', 'Nuoro' and
'Terranova'.

duty – then I can work a publisher. And we want the thing out if possible by 1st November.

I may come to Florence in about a fortnight's time, for a month, to do that book for the Medici Society. Shall decide next week, then let you know. And then we'll do something for August.

I wrote Réné. What a blow for her![1]

Heard from Alan: rapturising over the sweetness of Jap. brothels and gardens. Hope the whale won't swallow him. I can see the Japs are gently pulling his leg, poor dear.

My mother-in-law liked 'Path of Righteous' best. F[rieda] liked 'Nuoro' and 'Orosei' – and I like 'Nuoro', 'Gavoi', and 'Fonni' best. – If in connection with book, order would have to be reversed. You remember I *started* at Cagliari and *left off* at Terranova.

If we come to Florence we shall probably call at Zell-am-See and prospect. If you came in Aug. with us there we could probably have the Pamm – the farmhouse – to ourselves – and live for 10 Liras a day easily. Journey not dear – you take ticket straight from Rome to the frontier – near Innsbruck – for about 160 Liras. And from Innsbruck to Zell about 20 Liras only. But would Burr like a peasant farm on a hill? Not too rough? – Anyhow we'll see.

DHL

2266. To Robert Mountsier, [26 June 1921]
Text: MS Smith; Telegram; Unpublished.

[Baden-Baden]
[26 June 1921]

Robert Mountsier
Come direct here Florence doubtful.

Lawrence

2267. To Robert Mountsier, 27 June 1921
Text: MS Smith; Unpublished.

[Hotel Krone, Ebersteinburg, bei Baden-Baden]
27 June 1921

Dear M[ountsier]
Your letter this morning. I shall go down to Baden and telegraph after lunch.[2]

---

[1] Réné, Jan Juta's sister, m. Luke Hansard. (See Letter 2272.)
[2] An envelope to Mountsier survives (MS Smith), postmarked 26 June 1921. (On the verso DHL wrote: 'Have letters of yours forwarded from Florence'.) It may suggest that DHL misdated this letter; if so, then the telegram to which he refers here is Letter 2266.

I still don't hear from Florence about the flat. But I hear that Italy is *very* hot and uncomfortable. So doubt going there.

But leave your trunk in the care of the American Express in Paris, and then it can be sent to Italy when you like. It will come quite quickly. Or the Whittleys can bring it on if they come in Sept.[1]

The woods are *very* lovely. I propose to send all the goods on to Constance from here – about July 7th. – walk across Schwarzwald to Constance then cross the Lake to the Austrian frontier Bregenz – and so to Zell. I felt you didn't want to come to Germany and Austria. But if you think you will enjoy it, come along and let us go together. Come as soon as possible, so we can fix things up before we set off – perhaps I can do a bit of typing.

If you'd rather *bring* the trunk, then do so. – Perhaps it is best to hang on to one's stuff. Yes, *bring it*. Final decision.

I will meet you at Baden–O'os, where you change. It is only 10 minutes from Baden. Or if the trains dont fit, I will be at BadenBaden station. I presume you come via Strassburg by the night train, arrive BadenBaden about 10.30 a.m.

Have received *Aaron* MS.

Hope this gets you.

DHL

2268. To Emily King, [c. 28 June 1921]
Text: MS Needham; PC v. [Bavarian farmhouse]; Postmark, [. . .]; Unpublished.

[Hotel Krone, Ebersteinburg, bei Baden-Baden]
[c. 28 June 1921][2]

I hope by now you have got your parcel and that they haven't made you pay any Sanction. Let me know if they have, the brutes, and I'll send it you again. And let me know if everything is there. – My mother in law has been with us for ten days, but now is seedy again, so must go back to BadenBaden: very disappointing. On Friday comes Else from Munich here to this hotel. We shall stay about another fortnight – then to Constance, and over the lake to Austria. I do hope Sam is well again.[3] Beautiful weather here.

Love   DHL

---

[1] Irene Tregerthen Whittley (b. 1887), daughter of DHL's landlord in Cornwall, Capt. Short, and her husband Percy W. Whittley. They had been friends of the Lawrences since March 1916 and, in August 1920, had joined DHL for a walking-tour in northern Italy. They visited the Lawrences and accompanied them to Siena and Rome in September 1921. See *Letters*, ii. 590 n. 1.

[2] This date takes account of DHL's departure from Baden-Baden in 'about another fortnight' – he left on 9 July; and of Else Jaffe's arrival 'on Friday' – and she arrived on 1 July.

[3] Samuel Taylor King (1880–1965), m. DHL's elder sister Emily Una (1882–1962), 5 November 1904.

2269. To Jan Juta, 29 June 1921
Text: MS UT; Unpublished.

Hotel Krone, *Ebersteinburg*, BadenBaden

29 June 1921

Dear Johnnie

Today the answer from the printer: cheap. Marks 4.50 per square centimetre: that is, for a picture about the size we want it – exactly *half* your picture, each way – which is 13 × 10 cm. – the cost of *engraving the plate* for *four-colour* process would be 600 Marks. The exchange is now 260 or 265 M. to the £1. So that the engraving of the block would cost about £2··5··0. I enquired in England from the Medici press – 6/6 per square inch, for *3-color* process: which would amount to about £5. for the same picture-block. So here we gain. I calculate £18. would make us the eight blocks, and the size exactly *half* your picture each way 13 × 10 instead of 26 × 20. The biggest picture is 28 × 20, the smallest 24 × 20.

The Herr Hofrath writes that the pictures *must* be reproduced – that they will come out beautifully, that they will lose nothing by being reduced, and that the colour is admirable for engraving, and that they are very original. – 'Sie sind hoch-originell und treffen das Localcolorit ganz ausgezeichnet. . – Die Bilder müssen in vierfachen Farbdruck hergestellt werden – .' – Which means – 'They are highly original and strike the local-coloring quite extraordinarily. – They must be printed in the four-fold color-printing – ' Only he says nothing about the damned sanctions.

I write now to ask the cost of 2,000 printed copies of each.

I expect Mountsier the end of the week. Then we will force the hands of the publishers. Seltzer and Secker between them ought joyfully to pay *all costs* and you a small royalty into the bargain. I'm not going to let them off.

The bigger the size, the increase in cost is so enormous that we'll stick to this size, ½ yours, more or less, and bind them in the book.

I really think next week we shall leave for Austria – walk from Freiburg to Constance – cross the lake to Bregenz – then via Innsbruck to Zell.

I look forward to the arrival of the remaining three designs. We must cut out the titles. Consider carefully the appearance of the sheet. I think we might put just the place name – Orosei – Terranova – rather small, under the right hand corner. Then your signature on the pictures – what about it.

DHL

2270. To Robert Mountsier, 30 June 1921
Text: MS Smith; Postmark, Baden-Baden 1 7 21; Unpublished.

[Hotel Krone, Ebersteinburg, bei Baden-Baden]
30 June 1921

Dear M[ountsier]

I have your letter of 28th. June. I am sorry if my postcard made you prepare for North Italy. There is already a letter at Paris containing my plans.

I intend to leave here next Thursday – July 7th. – for Freiburg: to walk across the Feldberg to Constance: to cross the lake to Bregenz, the Austrian frontier: and then to proceed by rail via Innsbruck to Zell. If we like Zell, I intend to stay there through the heat – perhaps till end August. If we don't like it, I shall move South to Italy. Today I have an answer – after a very long interval – that the flat in Florence is at my disposal if I want it. – But that everybody is leaving, and it is very hot.

Please don't trouble about cloth or drawers. Just tea and toothpaste, if these are no trouble.

Don't forget that you have been saying you were coming here ever since May 10th. – and that we have had a room constantly waiting. You have small cause to complain of *my* change of plans. As for the expense of England, I haven't kept you there.

I am not staying here any longer than Thursday or Friday. One can have enough of relations at close quarters.

If you are going with us from Freiburg to Austria, then don't arrive later than July 7th here, or we shall be gone. If you arrive on Monday or Tuesday, as you say, then we will leave all your goods at the station, and *walk* up here. So bring night things in a small handbag that we can carry. Or you can stay in BadenBaden the two nights, as you prefer. – We shall do our passports for Austria in Constance. It is sure to be possible. – Lawrence, Krone, Ebersteinburg, BadenBaden is sufficient telegraphic address.

DHL

I have not written again to London because you said you were leaving Tues. or Wed. for Paris.

2271. To Curtis Brown, 2 July 1921
Text: MS UT; Huxley 517–18.

Hotel Krone, Ebersteinburg, BadenBaden
2 July 1921

Dear Curtis Brown

Today your letter and Medici agreement: for both many thanks: I think the latter quite satisfactory. One must give and take. But I do regret loss of American rights.

Only I have written to de Grey that I want title altering to 'A History of Italian Painting for Children'. I don't see how *one* Dürer can represent Germany, and Chardin or Lancret, France, and the awful Rembrandts, the mere Terborch and Van der Goes, Holland.[1] And I won't say a word about pictures which are not included. The supply of illustrations is too unsatisfactory for a child's hist[ory] of painting. Whereas there is a fair representation of Italy. And the subject is quite big enough.

I return agreement, with word 'Italian' inserted by me. I feel that it would prove just unsatisfactory to go out of Italy.

I shall want very few books – about four. But I'll write de Grey.

I have five Juta drawings for the Sardinia book: they are very good, in flat brilliant color, excellent. I expect three more from Juta: making eight. I sent these five to a man in Stuttgart, to enquire cost of color-reproduction. He says, the cost of engraving plates for the 4-color process, size 13 × 10 cm., is 600 Mark. The Mark today is at 272. I asked de Grey for a quotation. Same plate in England costs just about £5. More than double. I have asked Max Schreiber now for the cost of 2,000 printed copies, from one plate. When he replies I'll tell you at once. He – the color-printer, quite a famous one – said the pictures were most original and perfect for reproduction. Now it seems to me we ought to be able to raise enough money for these – between England and New York. I wrote Seltzer yesterday. If there should be a magazine chance, the pictures could be printed on pages to fit. For a book, the size should be about 22 × 14 cm., book-page; – picture 13 × 10 cm. I want this to be managed.[2]

I expect Mountsier Tuesday – and we shall probably leave end of next week, for Constance and Innsbruck. Will let you know immediately Mountsier arrives and we decide.

One difficulty about importing pictures from Germany is the new Sanctions impost. Must think of it.

Scheme the pictures for me. They are really very *new* and good.

Yrs D. H. Lawrence

P.S. On second thoughts I will keep the agreement till I have an answer

[1] The painters were: Albrecht Dürer (1471–1528); Jean-Baptiste-Siméon Chardin (1699–1779); Nicholas Lancret (1690–1743); Rembrandt Harmensz van Rijn (1606–69); Gerard Terborch (1617–81); and Hugo van der Goes (c. 1440–82).

[2] A MS in the Curtis Brown archive (UT) indicates that Juta sent to Brown the (undated) estimate DHL received from Schreiber. In an unknown hand the following instruction was written at the end of the printer's estimate: 'It must be made plain to any English publisher that he cannot hold the Juta pictures longer than Aug. 1, because they absolutely must go to America soon for book, and possibly magazine, publication.'

from you and de Grey. I would *much rather* have the book in my own name, if
de Grey will agree.[1] He can use it in full if he likes.

David Herbert Lawrence

I would like *ten* presentation copies – ask for that.

2272. To Mary Cannan, 4 July 1921
Text: MS Lazarus; Moore 658–9.

Hotel Krone, Ebersteinburg, BadenBaden
4 Juli 1921

My dear Mary

We had your note after your second trip to England. No, I hadn't heard of
the boy's drowning. What was he doing to get drowned?[2] J. M. [Barrie] has a
fatal touch for those he loves. They die.[3]

We are still here, but I am in rags of impatience now to leave. I think we
shall go on Thursday – leave for Freiburg, and from there walk across the
Black Forest to Constance – cross the lake to Bregenz, in Austria, and go over
Innsbruck to Zell-am-See, in the Austrian Tyrol – Frieda's sister's place. If
we like it, stay some weeks. If not, move south over the Brenner – via Cortina
and the Dolomites if I can afford it – to Florence. Miss Morrison will let us
have a lovely flat, across the river from the Uffizi, in Florence.[4] – But on the
way down I should like to see if there is any place where I would wish to live. I
don't want to go to Taormina for another winter. The house is paid until
September. If I find another place I shall fetch away the things. When we are
in Florence you must come there.

There is no news. I finished *Aaron's Rod* here. You will like it in bits only.
Juta has done really clever illustrations for the *Sardinia* book, but the
publishers are wailing about costs. So I am trying to get the pictures[5] color-
reproduced here in Germany. They are costume-decorations, brilliant flat
color – eight of them.

My mother-in-law was here, but wasn't so well, so had to be taken back to

[1] De Grey may have suggested that the book be published under a pseudonym such as the
'Lawrence H. Davison' used for *Movements in European History* (Oxford, 1921).
[2] Michael Llewelyn Davies (1900–21) was drowned in Sandford Pool, near Oxford, in May 1921,
while bathing with another undergraduate. It was for the Davies boys that Barrie invented the
story of Peter Pan.
[3] A number of people close to Barrie had suffered sudden or accidental death: 1867, his brother
David from a fall on the ice; 1892, the Rev. James Winter, his friend and fiancé of his sister
Maggie; 1895, his sister Jane Ann and, two days later, his mother.
[4] Nellie Morrison, the daughter of a Scottish Presbyterian doctor, lived at 32 Via dei Bardi,
Florence (where the Lawrences stayed in late August 1921). She had recently introduced DHL
to Earl and Achsah Brewster (see *Letters*, iii. 720).   [5] the pictures] them

the Stift. My sister in law is here from Munich, with two children. They are nice – but relatives are a mistake, and that's the end of it. One should never see one's relations – or anybody else's.

We've been in this hotel-place ten weeks, so you may imagine I am fed up. Tomorrow is due to arrive Robert Mountsier, the American who looks after my affairs in New York. He is perfectly crazy to have a small yacht and go round the world. Probably in the end we'll bring it off. He has got £1000 – and a perfect little yacht only costs £2000. He has looked at every ship in England, I should think. We should need only a captain and one competent man – preferably educated, friendly – who would come more or less for fun. It is quite feasible. When we bring it off, you can come for a trip, if you aren't scared. Frieda is scared, she says. I am not. I would like to break out of Europe. It has been like a bad meal of various courses – Europe – and one has got indigestion from every course. – Insole writes from Japan that it is perfectly fascinating. I should like to see it – also Siam. Something more velvety than Europe.

I am supposed to write 'A History of Italian Painting, for Children' – for the Medici Press. Don't know whether I shall ever get it done.

Woods here are full of raspberries and bilberries. If only they were near one's home, to make jam. I feel it is a lovely opportunity lost.

Réné Hansard has had to go to her farm.[1] She says Lukey muddled the banking accounts, and she has had to sell her Chelsea house and all in it, to get straight. It has been a bitter blow to her. Still, she says they will have a motorcar at their farm near Cannes. I never understand.

The Ludwig-Wilhelmstift address always finds us.

Hope all goes well.

DHL

2273. To Emily King, [5 July 1921]
Text: MS Needham; PC v. H. Hoffmann, 'Schönmünzach, Murgtal'; Postmark, Baden-Baden 6 7 21; Unpublished.

[Hotel Krone, Ebersteinburg, bei Baden-Baden]
July 5th

I am sorry the glass was broken: I'll bet the Customs did it. Mountsier arrived here today. We are leaving on Saturday for Freiburg – shall walk across the Black Forest to Constance – cross Lake Constance to the Austrian side – and so to F[rieda]'s younger sister. Address

---

[1] The Hansard farm was in Mougins, Alpes Maritimes, France.

c/o Frau von Schreibershofen, Tumersbach, *Zell-am-See*, bei Salzburg, Austria.
Would it be a nuisance to you to send us two pounds of tea there – as *Gift*. I will pay. Will write later.

Love DHL

2274. To Ada Clarke, [5 July 1921]
Text: MS Clarke; PC v. Sonntag-Morgen im Frühling; Postmark, [. . .]; Unpublished.

[Hotel Krone, Ebersteinburg, bei Baden-Baden]
– July 5th.

Your letter today – also today arrives Mountsier with the coat, which fits very well, except a wee bit big round the collar. But nothing. Frieda's blue serge has made a whole long travelling coat, and a skirt: very nice. – I shan't tell you which cloth I like until you tell me *how much* a suit-length costs in England. We leave here on Saturday for Freiburg: walk over the Black Forest to Constance – cross the lake and on to Zell. – Address
c/o Frau von Schreibershofen, Tumersbach, *Zell-am-See*, bei Salzburg, Austria.
We shall be there about July 16th.

Love. DHL

2275. To Thomas Seltzer, [8 July 1921]
Text: MS UT; PC; Postmark, Baden-Baden 8[?] 7 21; Lacy, *Seltzer* 21.

[Hotel Krone, Ebersteinburg, bei Baden-Baden]
8 Juli.

Mountsier here – we leave in two days – address
c/o Frau von Schreibershofen, Tumersbach, *Zell-am-See*, bei Salzburg, Austria.
Hope to send *Aarons Rod* soon – we'll type it out at Zell – as soon as possible.

D. H. Lawrence

2276. To Martin Secker, 8 July 1921
Text: MS UInd; PC; Postmark, Baden-Baden 8 7 21; Secker 43.

[Hotel Krone, Ebersteinburg, bei Baden-Baden]
8. Juli 1921

Dear Secker
    We are leaving here tomorrow – new address

c/o Frau von Schreibershofen, Tumersbach, *Zell-am-See, bei Salzburg.*
Austria.
Hope all is well.

D. H. Lawrence[1]

2277. **To Marie Hubrecht, 9 July 1921**
Text: MS Hubrecht; Unpublished.

Hotel Krone, Ebersteinburg, Baden Baden
9 July 1921

Dear Miss Hubrecht[2]

It was so nice of you to invite me to Doorn. But I felt I hadn't the energy to go to more consuls and take more journeys. I begin absolutely to hate travelling from country to country. So also I have not gone to England.

We leave here tomorrow – going via Konstanz to the Austrian Tyrol, to stay about a month with my wife's younger sister. The address is

c/o Frau von Schreibershofen, Tumersbach, *Zell-am-See*, bei Salzburg,
Austria.

There my sister-in-law has a farm and a villa on the lake. We think to stay there about a month, then move south to Italy.

I have enjoyed being in Germany, in the quiet of this village, and with the Black Forest trees for company. I shall always remember Ebersteinburg gratefully. Nobody swindles, the little children never beg, and it is not sordid. Really, Sicily is humanly too degraded and degrading. If I go back for this one winter, I don't think I shall return next year. I would rather find a place where no tourists come, and where no 'artists' and no 'Ducas' have their villas.[3]

I have worked quite hard here: but now am at an end for the time being. The boxes are packed, and we have that uneasy feeling of the eve of departure. I feel as if I were moving back, away from the main centres of this European activity. And that is what I want to do.

---

[1] Secker replied on 12 July (Secker Letter-Book, UIll): '. . . All well here. No prosecution papers. Sales [of *Women in Love*] to date amount to 1123 copies. Rebecca West had three columns about the book in last Saturday's "New Statesman". The only other reviews were in the "Westminster Gazette" and "Time and Tide", both written by Rose Macaulay.
I am anxious to receive the typescript of "Aaron's Rod".'

[2] Marie ('Tuttie') Hubrecht (1865–1950), a painter, had once owned Fontana Vecchia, the Lawrences' home in Taormina; she retained an elegant studio, Rocca Forte, in the town; but her home was at the Witte Huis, Doorn, 20 km s e. of Utrecht in Holland. Her portrait-drawing of DHL is reproduced in *Letters*, iii.

[3] DHL alludes to Hon. Alexander Nelson Hood (1854–1937), who was generally known as the 'Duca' with respect to his title as Duke of Bronte, Sicily. He had a sizable estate at Castello di Maniace, Bronte, and a villa, La Falconara, in Taormina. See *Letters*, iii. 491 n. 2.

Will you come to Taormina for the winter, and live in your studio? I feel you are like me, and don't want to live much in Sicily any more.

My wife sends her warm regards, I mine.

D. H. Lawrence

2278. To Curtis Brown, 9 July 1921
Text: MS UT; Unpublished.

per Adr. Frau Baronin von Richthofen, Ludwig-Wilhelmstift,
Baden Baden
9 July 1921

Dear Curtis Brown

I send you here the eight pictures of Sardinia which Juta forwarded me from Rome. Mountsier has written about them today. Juta's address is:

Sig. Jan Juta, *Anticoli-Corrada*, Prov. di Roma, Italy.

Let me know at once if you receive them safely.

Yours sincerely   D. H. Lawrence

2279. To Margaret King, [15 July 1921]
Text: MS Forster; PC v. Konstanz, Konziliumsgebäude; Postmark, [. . .]; Unpublished.

Constance.
15 July.

[1]We walked across the Black Forest – got here last night. Fearfully hot. Waiting here for passports from Berlin – then by steamer to Austria. – This is the famous Council House,[2] just by the harbour. Have you begun your holidays yet? – and where are you going?

Love   DHL

2280. To Catherine Carswell, [16 July 1921]
Text: MS YU; PC v. Konstanz, Rheintarturm mit Lesehalle; Postmark, Konstanz 16 7 21; cited in Moore, *Poste Restante* 63.

Constance.
16 July

[3]We are on our way to the Austrian Tyrol – hope to cross this lake Monday – the address

[1] DHL's correspondent was his niece, Margaret ('Peg' or 'Peggy') Emily King (b. 1909).
[2] In 1414, a Council of the Church met at Constance and ended the Great Schism, electing one pope in place of the three who had each been claiming supreme authority.
[3] DHL's correspondent, Catherine Roxburgh Carswell (1879–1946), was a novelist, biographer and journalist. Her first novel, *Open the Door!* appeared in 1920; her second, *The Camomile: An*

Villa Alpensee, Tumersbach, *Zell-am-See* bei Salzburg, Austria.
I suppose we shall be in Zell for a month – then Italy. Let us know what are
your plans. Very hot here.

DHL

2281. To Ada Clarke, [18 July 1921]
Text: MS Clarke; PC v. Leontopodium alpinum; Postmark, [. . .]; Unpublished.

Bregenz –
18 July

We have just got into Austria after much wrath spent on passport officials –
travel through the night now to Innsbruck – Zell tomorrow or Wed. – write a
line there. – This is a picture of edelweiss growing wild on the mountains here.
Terrific thunderstorm.

love DHL

2282. To Margaret King, [18 July 1921]
Text: MS Forster; PC v. Leontopodium alpinum; Postmark, [. . .]21; Unpublished.

Bregenz.
18 Juli

We have just crossed into Austria – not without a lot of bother with passports,
and in the midst of a thunderstorm. – This is a color-photograph of the
edelweiss growing wild up the mountains here – will send you another later.
Arrive Zell tomorrow or Wednesday. Write there.

DHL

2283. To Gertrude Cooper, [18 July 1921]
Text: MS Clarke; PC v. Primula auricula, Gentiana acaulis; Postmark, [. . .]; Unpublished.

Bregenz
18 July.

¹I am wondering what you are doing for the holidays – where are you going?
Somehow the fates didn't let me come to England this summer. But we are all
in the same world. – This is a picture of gentian and the little Alpine primulus.
– Another night of travelling in front of us.

Love. DHL

Invention was to be published in April 1922. She and her husband, Donald Carswell (1882–
1940), who was a barrister and journalist, had been friends of the Lawrences since 1914. See
Letters, ii. 187 n. 5.
¹ The addressee, Gertrude ('Grit' or 'Gertie') Cooper (1885–1942), was a childhood friend of
DHL at Lynn Croft, Eastwood. Since 1919 she had lived with his sister, Ada Clarke. See
Letters, i. 23 n. 1.

2284. To Emily King, [21 July 1921]
Text: MS Needham; PC v. Leontopodium alpinum; Postmark, [. . .] Unpublished.

Villa Alpensee, Thumersbach, *Zell-am-See*, bei Salzburg, Austria
21 July

Arrived here yesterday – quite lovely, on a small lake, with snow mountains opposite. Shall stay till August at least. Much cooler here.

Love. DHL

2285. To Curtis Brown, 21 July 1921
Text: MS UT; Unpublished.

Villa Alpensee, Thumersbach, *Zell-am-See*, bei Salzburg
21 July 1921

Dear Curtis Brown

This is the remainder of *Aarons Rod*. I had planned to type it myself, but find no type-writing machine available. Have it done as quick as possible, then send it back to me for revision – true copy and carbon copy both. I have the first 143 pages here ready typed.[1] But I want to do a lot of revision on the typescript.

Hope this post is quick.

Mountsier writes about Secker. I want to go *warily* with him – S. – but *not* to be unfriendly – I want to be always fair to him.

D. H. Lawrence

2286. To J. Ellingham Brooks, [21 July 1921]
Text: MS BucU; PC v. Leontopodium alpinum; Postmark, [. . .] 24 7 [. . .]; Unpublished.

Villa Alpensee, Thumersbach – *Zell-am-See*, bei Salzburg.
21 July.

Your letter came on here.[2] Do you mean to say you did not receive *W[omen] in Love*? That scoundrel S[ecker] charged me for it – also for copies to Douglas, who likewise has received nothing.[3] It is Sec. who is jewing us. I'll have a go at him, and will write you later. – We are here in the Tyrol for a week or two – may see you as we come south.

more anon.

DHL

---

[1] See p. 28 n. 4.
[2] John Ellingham Brooks (1863–1929), a homosexual who left England after the Wilde trial and lived in Capri for the rest of his life. DHL met him there in January 1920 (see *Letters*, iii. 443 and n. 2).
[3] George Norman Douglas (1868–1952), novelist and essayist, whom DHL first met when Douglas was Assistant Editor of the *English Review* in 1913 (see *Letters*, ii. 31 and n. 4). He had settled in Italy and Capri. DHL portrayed him as James Argyle in *Aaron's Rod*.

2287. To Curtis Brown, 25 July 1921
Text: MS UT; Huxley 521.

Villa Alpensee, Thumersbach, *Zell-am-See*, bei Salzburg,
Austria
25 July 1921

Dear Curtis Brown

Mountsier has just read me a list of poems and *Studies in Classic Amer[ican] Literature* etc that you have been sending out to the various papers.[1] Now I hate the thought of these things being trotted round to Austin Harrison[2] and *Country Life* and so on, and being sent back by a lot of little people. Will you please tell your magazine man to go slowly: not to send out anything unless it seems really likely to suit the miserable periodicals. I know what the English weeklies and monthlies are, and have no hopes of ever selling more than an odd thing now and then. Therefore I would rather sell *nothing* than have the goods hawked round and cheapened in the eyes of a lot of little people. I don't really like *The English Review* at all. – So as the things come back, please don't send them out again unless you think it really wise.

I posted you part of the MS. of *Aarons Rod*, to get it typed for me. I hope you have received it safely.

And as I said before, while I want to keep a fairly close hand on Secker, I don't want to let him down or be mean to him in any way.

Yours   D. H. Lawrence

2288. To Catherine Carswell, [26 July 1921]
Text: MS YU; PC v. Zell-am-See; Postmark, [. . .]; Unpublished.

[Villa Alpensee, Thumersbach, Zell-am-See, bei Salzburg]
Tuesday.[3]

Your letter today. It is very lovely here – am not *sure* how long we stay, but maybe throughout August. Be careful to get every necessary sort of *visé* on your passport, and the Ein-und-*Ausreise* from Germany[4] – one can have such

[1] Of the twelve essays collected in *Studies in Classic American Literature* (Seltzer, 1923) eight had already appeared in periodicals ('Whitman' only two days before this letter, in *Nation and Athenæum*). The two essays on Melville, the one on Dana and 'Hawthorne's "Blithedale Romance"' were never placed with magazine editors before the book was published.

[2] Austin Harrison (1873–1928), editor of the *English Review* since 1909, had published seven of the American essays (see Roberts C55–8, 60–1, 64). *English Review* had printed DHL's writings frequently since November 1909.

[3] This letter, dated 'Tuesday' by DHL, was written before Letter 2298, dated 'Sunday'. The only appropriate dates for a Tuesday and a following Sunday after DHL's arrival in Zell-am-See and before his letter of 3 August to Catherine Carswell are 26 and 31 July.

[4] 'Entry-and-exit *permit*'.

tiresome bothers. Hotels here 600 Kronen per day. – Do another thing for me. Could Don get passport forms from Cooks or Passport office, and fill in the necessary part, and send them or bring them. We must both have our passports renewed. – Railway cheap here – and one can get all one wants. Be sure and write, and tell me if you want to know anything.

DHL

2289. To Baroness Anna von Richthofen, [30 July 1921]
Text: MS UCB; PC v. Tummersbach bei Zell am See; Postmark, Zell [. . .] 30 [. . .];
Unpublished.

[Villa Alpensee, Thumersbach, Zell-am-See, bei Salzburg]
Samstag

– Hier siehst du den Villa. Die Frieda hat den kleinen Balcon, oben. Wir waren gestern mit dem Wagen in Bad Fusch – dann zu Fuss nach Ferleiten, unter dem Gletscher: alles klar und wunderschön, der grosse Gletscher lehnend zum Thal, und glänzend weiss: und das Wasser so laut, so stark und schnell. Heute ist kühler: Gott sei dank du kannst dieses heisses Wetter dauern. Aber hier ist es nie *zu* heiss. – Ich hatte deinen Brief gestern. Die Bucher sind auch angekommen, heut.

Love. DHL

[– Here you see the villa. Frieda has the little balcony, upstairs. We were yesterday with the trap in Bad Fusch – then on foot to Ferleiten, under the glacier: everything clear and marvellously beautiful, the great glacier leaning towards the valley, and gleaming white: and the water so loud, so strong and fast. Today is cooler: thank God you can endure this hot weather. But here it is never *too* hot. – I had your letter yesterday. The books arrived too, today.

Love. DHL]

2290. To Amy Lowell, [30 July 1921]
Text: MS HU; PC v. Zell-am-See; Postmark, [. . .]; Moore, *Intelligent Heart* 281.

Thumersbach. Zell-am-See
30 July.

Today has come the copy of *Legends*,[1] forwarded from Baden Baden: for which many thanks. I shall read it this evening. We are here in Austria, in the Tyrol among the mountains for a while – very pleasant to see the snow looking fierce, and to hear the water roaring once more savage and unquenched. In

---

[1] *Legends*, a book of poems (published in May 1921) by the American Imagist poet Amy Lowell (1874–1925). DHL met her in 1914 and corresponded with her frequently after that time. See *Letters*, ii. 203 n. 2.

Sicily water expires so soon. Here it is rampant and full of lust. – I hope you are better from all operations,[1] and enjoying the launch abroad of *Legends*. Frieda sends many greetings, with mine. Remember us to Miss Russell. The Baden address is always safe.

D. H. Lawrence

2291. To Michael Sadleir, 30 July 1921
Text: MS UT; Unpublished.

Villa Alpensee, Thumersbach, *Zell-am-See*, bei Salzburg,
Austria
30 July 1921
Dear Sadler

I have at last managed to get hold of 'Wintry Peacock'. It is due to appear in the American *Metropolitan* in August, so I am told.[2]

Let me know if you receive it, and if anything is being done with it. If you do print it, you reserve[3] me, I presume, the right to include it later on in a book of my collected short stories. That is my wish.

Greetings   D. H. Lawrence

2292. To Thomas Seltzer, 30 July 1921
Text: MS UT; Lacy, *Seltzer* 23.

Villa Alpensee, Thumersbach, *Zell-am-See*, bei Salzburg,
Austria
30 July 1921
Dear Seltzer

Your letter of 15 July today. I had your cable in Baden. – I had to send 2nd half of *Aaron's Rod* to England to be typed after all. Expect it back next week. Then shall post it to you. I shall post your copy two weeks sooner than Secker's. He hasn't seen the book yet. Mountsier read the first half and didn't like it: takes upon himself to lecture me about it. Says it will be unpopular. Can't help it. It is what I mean, for the moment. It isn't 'improper' at all: only it never turns the other cheek, and spits on ecstasy. I like it, because it kicks against the pricks.[4] I'll send it the first possible moment.

Mountsier loathes me because I will develop my *Unconscious* ideas. But I have written the second book, and know it good. In about three years time I'll write the third book, and then – fertig.[5] If you send me the criticisms, I'll answer them in a nice peppery introduction.

---

[1] She had her fourth hernia operation on 17 May.   [2] See p. 31 n. 1.
[3] reserve] allow   [4] Cf. Acts ix. 5 (A.V.).   [5] 'finished'.

Somehow my compass will not point to America. We'll probably go to Italy in September.

Austria is Kaput[1] and doesn't seem to care a bit.

Curtis Brown will have sent you the Juta pictures. I do hope you'll like them and have them reproduced. And I do hope Thayer will print one or two articles from *Sea and Sardinia* in the *Dial*, and so help to pay for the pictures.[2] Let me know.

Perhaps when I am cajoled into a good mood, I will write you a Tyrol story – short novel – like 'Wintry Peacock'. Life is long.

Pleasant here – my sister in law's summer villa – with lake, boats, carriage, and snowy mountains. You can buy anything you like, with enough Krone.

Don't know anything about *Hearsts*.[3] Gruesome sounding sort of name. But then it's all one boat.

                                                    Yrs   D. H. Lawrence
Very many thanks for sending the 'Wintry Peacock' proofs.

2293. To Scofield Thayer, 30 July 1921
Text: MS YU; Nicholas Joost and Alvin Sullivan, *D. H. Lawrence and 'The Dial'* (Carbondale, 1970), p. 42.

                    Villa Alpensee, Thumersbach, *Zell-am-See*, bei Salzburg,
                                                                        Austria
                                                                    30 July 1921
Dear Thayer
    I asked Miss Monk to post to you, c/o Brown Shipley, after she had typed it out, a copy of a story: 'The Gentleman from San Francisco': translated from the Russian of S. Bunin by my friend S[amuel] Koteliansky, and by me rubbed up into readable English.[4] – Having experience of Naples and Capri, I find the story extremely good as a presentation of the unpleasant side of the picture. It is extraordinarily *it*. You may like to print it in *The Dial*. If so let me know. If you wanted any information about Bunin, you could write to:

    S. Koteliansky. 5. Acacia Rd. St. Johns Wood. London N. W. 8.
I would rather my name didn't appear: but make no serious objection if it would be of use to you. If you don't want the story, do you think anyone else in America might consider it? I want to help Koteliansky if I can.

    Then I suppose Seltzer or Mountsier will send you the *Sardinia* travel book. You won't like it, probably, because, as somebody said, it lacks the quality of ecstasy which is usual in Mr Lawrence's work. But I think it is pretty

---

[1] 'Finished'.   [2] Scofield Thayer was editor of the *Dial*.
[3] The magazine *Hearst's International*. (See also Letters 2600, 2603 and 2697.)
[4] See p. 23 n. 2.

vivid as a flash-light travel-book. I hope Seltzer will do the colored illustrations by Jan Juta. They are good. You'll like *them*. How long are you going to be in Europe?[1] And are you ever coming this way? – or Italy? I should like to meet you. Probably we shall go to Florence end of August – then later to Taormina. – I hate the word 'probably'. I didn't answer you about Apostolic Beasts. Of course I knew it should be Evangelic Beasts – But then I loathe the word Evangel, and prefer the Apostolic sense of the animals.[2] What a cross, irritable paper *The Dial* is! Yet you all insist I shall be ecstatic. – I'm glad Rémy de Gourmont's Sparrowdust is settled.[3] It was rubbish. Otherwise the *Dial* is fun.

Yrs D. H. Lawrence

2294. To Ada Clarke, [30 July 1921]
Text: MS Clarke; PC v. Thumersbach – Hotel Belle Vue; Postmark, [. . .]; Lawrence–Gelder 169–70.

[Villa Alpensee, Thumersbach, Zell-am-See, bei Salzburg]
Saturday.

– This is the villa – and our boathouse. It has been hot also here – so we bathe twice a day. We have four boats – must row across to Zell for everything. Drove yesterday with the pony to Ferleiten, under the glacier very beautiful, the great sloping white mass. The flowers a bit higher up are really lovely. – When do you go to Llandudno? Send F[rieda] the stuff as soon as you can. Hope you are having a good time.

Love. DHL

2295. To Robert Mountsier, [30 July 1921]
Text: MS Smith; PC v. Zell am See; Postmark, Zell [. . .] 30 VII 21; Unpublished.

[Villa Alpensee, Thumersbach, Zell-am-See, bei Salzburg]
Saturday

– Have your letter – your things are all right. Let us know in time when you think of returning – place very full, people begging us for a room every day. No

---

[1] Thayer was in Europe (principally living in Vienna), July 1921–September 1923
[2] DHL's three poems – 'Saint Mark', 'Saint Luke', 'Saint John' – appeared in the *Dial*, April 1921, under the title 'Apostolic Beasts'. When they were collected in *Birds, Beasts and Flowers* (Seltzer, 1923), the title for these poems (together with 'Saint Matthew') was 'Evangelistic Beasts'.
[3] Remy de Gourmont (1858–1915), 'Dust for Sparrows', trans. Ezra Pound, appeared in the *Dial*, 1920–1.

news except Curtis B[rown] has received the pictures[1] and is sending them
straight to Seltzer. One letter only for you. We are undecided about Salzburg.
Weather not too hot.

                                                                    DHL

2296. To Gertrude Cooper, [30? July 1921]
Text: MS Clarke; PC v. Fuschertal; Postmark, [. . .]; Unpublished.
                [Villa Alpensee, Thumersbach, Zell-am-See, bei Salzburg]
                                                                Saturday.

Pamela[2] says you are looking thin – this dry hot summer! Where are you
spending your holiday? – and are you still busy with your job? – This is how
one climbs on to the snow. But this year it is very dangerous, because the ice is
rotten owing to the heat. The snow was all melted, only the curious glacier-ice
showing – but now much more snow than ever. – I do hope everything goes
nicely with you.

                                                            Love. DHL

2297. To Margaret King, [30 July 1921]
Text: MS Clarke; PC v. Zell am See mit dem Hundstein; Postmark, [. . .]; Unpublished.
                [Villa Alpensee, Thumersbach, Zell-am-See, bei Salzburg]
                                                                Saturday.

I am wondering if you have gone away for the holiday – and where. I have not
had a line from you or your mother since we are here. You have the address –
        Villa Alpensee, Thumersbach, *Zell-am-See*, bei Salzburg. Austria
This villa is across the lake from Zell – just out of sight on this postcard. It lies
on the edge of the lake, so we bathe every day from the boathouse. We have
four boats, to go back and forth in – and a horse and a little carriage to drive up
the Valleys. On Tuesday we climbed the Hundstein – twice as high as
Snowdon – and the snowy peaks all round. Yesterday we drove and walked to
the big glacier at Ferleiten – or rather under it. The water roars down like
thunder. Pity you can't all be here – it is never *too* hot. Send a line.

                                                            Love. DHL

---

[1] Juta's illustrations for *Sea and Sardinia*.
[2] A family nickname for DHL's sister Emily King.

2298. To Catherine Carswell, [31 July 1921]
Text: MS YU; PC v. Tauern (Salzburg); Postmark, [. . .]; Unpublished.
[Villa Alpensee, Thumersbach, Zell-am-See, bei Salzburg]
Sunday.

Your p.c. just now. I only want Don to get the two application forms (which I must have, and they cost nothing) – fill in *his* part (and the names if he likes) – and send them to me. Then either in Vienna or Rome I can get the passports. But I need these application forms filled in and *certified*, as you know.[1] And neither here nor in Italy do I know any doctors or clergymen etc.

It is hot again. If I can bring myself to patience I will stay on. Otherwise to *Florence*: see you there. If you come here, then Paris-Zurich-Innsbruck, or Hook of Holland-Munich-Salzburg – as you prefer. I'll get you rooms in 'Lohninghof' hotel. German route cheaper. There is a through carriage from Paris to Zell – the Vienna carriage. Bring 1 lb tea – that is free. I shall let you know quickly what I do.

DHL

2299. To Amy Lowell, 31 July 1921
Text: MS HU; Damon 569–70.
Villa Alpensee, Thumersbach, *Zell-am-See*, bei Salzburg, Austria
31 July 1921
Dear Amy

I had your letter and the eight dollars yesterday. I had much rather you had had the fuchsia tree.[2] There are lovely ones here.

Very many thanks for looking after my poems so kindly. Mountsier is over here just now. He is rather overbearing, I fancy. I had understood that you had said, of the poems, that 'The Mosquito' was the only one worth printing.[3]

I do hope the operation was successful and final and that you can live your own life freely.

I read *Legends* last night, – and again this morning. I like them the best of all your poems. You have always written of the existence and magic of *things* –

---

[1] Donald Carswell, as a barrister, could certify the passport applications.
[2] In a letter, 6 July 1921 (Damon 567–8), Amy Lowell had thanked DHL for offering to buy her a pot of fuchsias with his share of the royalties from the anthologies, *Some Imagist Poets* (Boston and New York, 1915–17).
[3] Amy Lowell did not place the poems DHL had sent most recently, because Mountsier considered this his job. However, she told the editor of the *Bookman* to take 'Mosquito' (July 1921). (See unpublished letter from Amy Lowell, 6 July 1921, MS HU.) In a later letter to DHL (7 September 1921) she denied saying that 'Mosquito' was the only one worth printing (Damon 573).

porcelain and rain: and of *things* you catch an essence: even cannon and ships. But in this book it is life and death superseding things. So I like this book the best.

I like best 'Many Swans' which I have read twice and which I feel really speaks inside my unexplained soul. I should not like to try to explain it, because of the deep fear and danger that is in it. But it isn't a myth of the sun. It is something else. All the better that we can't say offhand what. That means it is true. It rings a note in my soul. Then I like 'Blackbird'[1] and 'Witch Woman.' But I doubt if you quite get her – the Witch Woman.

Those three, for me, are much the best, and the best of all your poems.

'The Statue' is very amusing and nicely done – only Julius got off too lightly. His *things* should have pinched him a bit more excruciatingly. She should have flung her leaden arms round his neck in the lake, and nothing but bubbles to tell the tale.[2] I must read 'Yucca and Passion Vine' again. I don't quite get it. But it is most *interesting*, after 'Swans'. 'Porcelain' is lovely as things.[3]

I hope you'll have as much pleasure as you wish out of the public reception of the book.

Wonder what you'll do next.

D. H. Lawrence

2300. To Baroness Anna von Richthofen, [31 July 1921]
Text: MS UT; Postmark, Zell [. . .] 2 viii 21; Unpublished.

[Villa Alpensee, Thumersbach, Zell-am-See, bei Salzburg]
Sontag. 31 Juli.
Liebeste und einigste Schwiegermutter,

Die Frauen schimpfen, aber ich muss doch sagen, du bist gescheiter wie deine Töchter alle.

Wir haben 4 Hähnchen gefressen, 4 Liter Pfirrsichbohle gesaufen, und jetzt fangen wir an zu kämpfen. Also, hilf mir, dein Schwiegersöhnle.

D. H. Lawrence

[Absender:] alle Alpenseeliger.
[Frieda Lawrence begins]
Der Pamtauer Frieda im Urzustand –

---

[1] I.e. 'Funeral Song for the Indian Chief Blackbird'.
[2] Julian is a writer and owner of the garden statue (in lead) which he found in an antique shop. The 'things' are the objects in his house, which come alive and threaten him. He escapes from the 'things' and the statue by jumping into the lake and swimming to the village.
[3] 'Memorandum Confided by a Yucca to a Passion-Vine' and 'A Legend of Porcelain'.

[Hadubrand begins]
   der lieben Alten im stillen Kämmerlein die innigsten Grüsse
                                                                    Hadu
[Anita begins]
   Mir ist schlecht
                                                          Herzl.   Anita

[Dearest and only Schwiegermutter,
   The women grumble, but I really must say, you are cleverer than all your
daughters.
   We have gobbled 4 chickens, guzzled 4 litres of peach-punch, and now we
begin to fight. So, help me, your little son-in-law.
                                                             D. H. Lawrence

[Sender:] All Alpine-lake-blissful-ones.
[Frieda Lawrence begins]
   To the Pamtau Frieda in original condition –
[Hadubrand begins]
   To you, dear Old One in your calm little retreat, the most heartfelt greetings
                                                                    Hadu

[Anita begins]
   I feel sick
                                                  Affect[ionately].   Anita][1]

2301. To Catherine Carswell, 3 August 1921
Text: MS YU; cited in Carswell 145.
                        Villa Alpensee, Tumersbach, *Zell-am-See*, bei Salzburg, Austria
                                                                 3 August. 1921
My dear Catherine
   I have been waiting to see whether I could really stay on here. You know we
are with Frieda's younger sister Johanna, her husband, son and daughter. The
villa is on the edge of the lake, we bathe and boat and go excursions into the
mountains. The snow isn't far. And the Schreibershofens are really *very* nice
with us. And yet, I feel I can't breathe. Everything is free and perfectly easy.

---

[1] The messages and the state of the MS cast doubt on the sobriety of the Baroness's
correspondents. In addition to DHL and Frieda they were Anita (b. 1901) and Hadubrand
(b. 1905), children of Frieda's younger sister Johanna ('Nusch'). Johanna was probably one of
the inebriated company.

And still I feel I can't breathe. Perhaps it is one can't live with people any more – en ménage. Anyhow there it is. Frieda loves it and is quite bitter that I say I want to go away. But there it is – I do.

There is a very nice flat we can have in Florence, for not very much. Only this terrific heat when it is going to end? But anyhow I shall leave here about 12th August. If it keeps so hot I shall stay somewhere near Meran for a while, and perhaps look round and see if I might like to live there. I don't much want to go back to Taormina again. If the weather breaks, and it rains, I shall go to Florence. We should see you there anyway. We'll write more about that.

It is quite beautiful here. There is a very pleasant, largish peasant hotel which you would like:

'Lohningshof', Thumersbach, Zell-am-See.

It is on this side the lake: across from Zell. And you eat à la carte, which is much more satisfactory in this part of the world. The ordinary inexpensive hotel here costs 600 Krone a day – mounts up to about 700. You can buy almost anything, with enough Krone. But the shops are empty – the land financially and commercially just ruined. There is very good white bread – but the food is monotonous. Still, you'd never know you were in a ruined land. The Austrians are as amiable as ever. Travelling is cheap, and quite easy, and the people honest and pleasant. September is a lovely month too, here. But when I have stayed out my month, I feel I shall have to go.

I hope Don didn't mind my asking him to get the passport forms and fill up his part. Frieda's passport is so full, I don't know how she is going to get into Italy. And both the passes expire end of September. We must get new ones in Rome.

I was very glad to hear the book was done: shall be interested to see it.[1] You will probably now get into the real swing for writing.

I shall let you know my movements. We might even meet in Meran or Bozen. That is Italy now; but full Tyrol. – It is never *too* hot here – but it must be pretty bad in town.

au revoir   D. H. Lawrence

2302. To Catherine Carswell, [4 August 1921]
Text: MS YU; PC v. [Flowers]; Postmark, [. . .]; cited in Moore, *Intelligent Heart* 282.

[Villa Alpensee, Thumersbach, Zell-am-See, bei Salzburg]
4 Aug.

Dear C[atherine],

My sister has a dress-length of thin stuff for Frieda. Do you think you might smuggle it in? The post is *so* risky. The address is

Mrs L A Clarke, Grosvenor Rd, *Ripley nr. Derby.*

---

[1] Catherine Carswell's second novel: see p. 52 n. 3.

Yet if you are going to struggle all round Austria and Germany, it will be a curse. It has begun to rain – pouring all day. If it continues we shall go to Florence next week – about 12th or 14th. We can have a very nice flat there. I have not been to Siena and Perugia – we might go together.

DHL

Nothing so awful as Alps when it rains.

2303. To Emily King, [4? August 1921]
Text: MS Needham; PC v. Thumersbach – Hotel Belle Vue; Postmark, [. . .]; Unpublished.

[Villa Alpensee, Thumersbach, Zell-am-See, bei Salzburg]
Thursday

I have doubts about the post here. Your bit of tea has not come. Will you please *not* send the two pounds of tea here at all: send it, about the 16th. of this month to:
Herrn Major Max von Schreibershofen, Dahlmannstr. 5. *Berlin. Geschenk.*[1]
This is our villa and boathouse – the farm is up the slope behind the hotel.

DHL

2304. To Curtis Brown, [7 August 1921]
Text: MS UT; Huxley 520–1.

Villa Alpensee, Thumersbach, *Zell-am-See, bei Salzburg.*
Austria
7 July 1921[2]

Dear Curtis Brown
I was very glad to get the two copies of *Aaron's Rod* this morning – beautifully typed and bound. Very many thanks. I was just beginning to be uneasy, having had no word from you.
Tell me please what the cost is, so that I can compare with what I pay in Italy.
I will return the whole MS. directly. But *please* see that Seckers date of publication does not precede Seltzers.
About the pictures. I am afraid I let myself be a little too much influenced by Mountsier: who, of course, quite rightly takes the purely American point of view. We must, however, keep our own point. I understand the pictures have gone to Seltzer. He will keep you fully informed of what he is doing. If Secker will buy sheets and pictures from Seltzer, well and good. If not, let us make an

[1] 'Gift'.
[2] It is assumed that DHL should have written 7 August: on 7 July he was not at Zell-am-See but at Baden-Baden; furthermore Curtis Brown's office stamp recorded the letter's arrival on 13 August.

agreement with the Medici Society, if they are willing. You will see to that, and I won't interfere. Perhaps we can manage that *The Mercury*[1] and *The Dial* print an extract[2] with two or three pictures. That also I leave to you. We must not have the English side of the business subordinated too much to the American.

About magazines – I can't help feeling a hatred of their ways and means and all that. But still am grateful to you and your magazine manager for all the trouble you have taken. Somebody told me there was part of the 'Whitman' essay in *The Nation*.[3]

About the Medici Society – I was sorry to have to make that sudden change.[4] But I couldn't know what lay before me till I had really started to plan the book. And when I had dimly made my plan, I found that the Medici supply of pictures for Holland, Germany, France and Spain was just quite hopelessly inadequate. One *can't* write about pictures unless the pictures are there. I know it must have annoyed de Grey – who was in all things very nice and considerate. So I was sorry. But it is as I say.

I am not sure how long we stay here. The weather is hot again – Florence would be intolerable. Yet I want to go south.

Mountsier dislikes *Aarons Rod*, and says it will be unpopular. That will be as it will be.

                                                        Yrs   D. H. Lawrence

2305. To Rosalind Baynes, 9 August 1921
Text: MS UN; Nehls, ii. 68.

                Villa Alpensee, Thumersbach, *Zell-am-See*, bei Salzburg, Austria
                                                                9 Aug 1921

Dear Rosalind[5]

Your letter from Rifredi here. We have been in the north since April – in Baden Baden and then here, with Frieda's sister. Very nice here – lake, snow mountains etc. We shall stay, I suppose, while the heat lasts.

No, I didn't know you had been in Switzerland. Bridget's *morale* must be more Jungian than Swiss, I think. But Zurich is a dreary-souled city. Austria is quite without morale – of that sort. – Mary Cannan wrote that Godwin was getting his divorce – is that so?

[1] *The Mercury*] Squire   [2] extract] article   [3] See p. 55 n. 1.
[4] See p. 24 n. 2.
[5] Rosalind Baynes (1891–1973), the divorced wife of Helton Godwin Baynes (1882–1943). Baynes was Jung's assistant in Zurich, 1919–22; he edited and translated Jung's *Psychological Types* (1921), etc; and presumably Rosalind had taken her daughter Bridget to visit her father. DHL was apparently unaware that the Baynes had been divorced in April (see *Times*, 27 April 1921). (See *Letters*, i. 475 n. 3; iii. 478 n. 2.)

What are you doing for the winter? – staying in Florence?[1] I suppose we shall go back to Taormina in October. I will let you know when we go through Florence – stay there I don't know how long.

No work doing here: impossible to work in this country: no wits left, all gone loose and scattered. I shan't be sorry to come back to Italy again: but feel Europe is a bit empty altogether. Only the States are worse, I'm sure. We had a friend here – Robert Mountsier – from New York. He badly wanted us to go there for the winter: me lecture. But I got such a strong distaste for Yankees, seeing him every day, that at the moment wild horses wouldn't drag me. I suppose I shall go one day – because one chafes so here in Europe, and that seems the only way out. But it's a *pis aller*.

We might come to Florence for a month – in September. But not if it's going to be awfully hot. Here is very pleasant – we have our own boats and bathing and pony carriage and all very easy. Too easy. Too pleasant. Austria is *very* cheap, reckoning the exchange – and you can get everything with enough Krone. The Krone is now 3,000 to £1. It was before the war about 23. But here in the country nobody is poor.

Is Godwin going to marry the lady? and did you see her?[2] He is only a fool.

What's the news of Joan, Bertie, the children, Eleanor, Alexander, and everybody?[3] I have heard nothing for such a long time. I intended to go to England – but didn't want to, when I got near enough. I liked Germany – we were near BadenBaden, in the Black Forest, in a peasant inn for 3 months. I loved the forest – the great landscape – so big – and the stillness. It made a big impression on me. Everybody very pleasant.

F[rieda] sends greetings.

DHL

2306. To Michael Sadleir, [9 August 1921]
Text: MS UNCCH; Unpublished.

Villa Alpensee, Thumersbach, *Zell-am-See*, bei Salzburg, Austria
9 Aug.

Dear Sadler

I return story herewith – with all the alterations to fit.[4]

---

[1] Rosalind Baynes occupied the Villa Canovaia, San Gervasio, Florence for a period from January 1920; DHL had stayed there 3–28 September 1920.

[2] Baynes re-married in 1922; his second wife was Hilda Davidson; she may be referred to here.

[3] The people mentioned here were: Rosalind Baynes' brother-in-law and sister, Herbert ('Bertie') (1887–1945) and Joan (1889–) Farjeon; their children, Annabel, Gervase and Joscelyn; Herbert's sister, the writer Eleanor Farjeon (1881–1965); and the pianist and composer, Arthur Alexander (1891–1969). DHL first met Rosalind Baynes in the Farjeons' house at Buckleberry Common, Berks; it is possible that he met Alexander there too when he visited the Farjeons from Hermitage, 1918–19. [4] See Letter 2291.

I quite agree that the story should not re-appear for some time after the *Decameron* is out. But at any rate I dont want to collect my short stories yet – certainly not within the next twelve months – and dont mind making it longer – not before the year 1923.

Curtis Brown is acting as my agent. But as this arrangement between us is a sequel to the previous Milford arrangement, I shall consider it unnecessary to refer the matter to Curtis Brown: unless you would rather it went through his hands.

When does Blackwell think to bring out the book?

Yours   D. H. Lawrence

2307. To Thomas Seltzer, [12 August 1921]
Text: MS UT; Telegram; Unpublished.

[Villa Alpensee, Thumersbach, Zell-am-See, bei Salzburg]

[12 August 1921]

[Seltzer begins] Cable authorisation to sell second serial rights *Lost Girl*.

Seltzer

[DHL begins] Answer: Authorise sale serial rights.

Lawrence[1]

2308. To Thomas Seltzer, 12 August 1921
Text: MS NWU; PC v. Zell am See, Kitzsteinhorn; Postmark, 12 VIII 21; Lacy, *Seltzer* 25.

[Villa Alpensee, Thumersbach, Zell-am-See, bei Salzburg]

12 August 1921

Have your cable 'Cable authorisation to sell second serial rights *Lost Girl*.' Mountsier is in Vienna at the moment, so I reply 'Authorise sale serial rights – Lawrence.' – Don't quite know what second serial rights are – hope you'll tell me.[2]

D. H. Lawrence

Anyhow I hope it's something nice, and authorise sale in hopes.

DHL

---

[1] DHL drafted his reply on the telegram he received from Seltzer.

[2] On 20 August 1921 Seltzer wrote to Mountsier (Lacy, *Seltzer* 214): 'About ten days ago the assistant managing editor of the Brooklyn Eagle called me up and told me he wanted to run *The Lost Girl* serially in the Brooklyn Eagle. I immediately cabled to Lawrence. As I have had no reply I suppose the cable did not reach him. I am sorry. . . . I don't think we can get much money for the second serial rights. They don't pay much as a rule, but the Brooklyn Eagle is a good, old, conservative organ and it would mean a great deal to us in the matter of publicity.'

2309. To Robert Mountsier, [12 August 1921]
Text: MS Smith; Postmark, Zell am See 12 VIII 21; Unpublished.

Villa Alpensee, Zell-am-See
Friday 1.0 p.m.

Dear M[ountsier]

Just got your letter from Salzburg – this may get you. I have got you a room again in Belle Vue: Lohninghof nothing – Will meet 6.0 train tomorrow evening.

Various letters for you, and a telegram.

I wrote to Wïen a p.c. – immediately I had your Budapest letter: Saturday, I believe.

More tomorrow.

DHL

2310. To Curtis Brown, 14 August 1921
Text: MS UT; Unpublished.

Villa Alpensee, Thumersbach, *Zell-am-See*, bei Salzburg,
Austria
14 August 1921.

Dear Curtis Brown

Herewith the proofs for the *English Review*, which Mountsier has just given me.[1]

I may be some time sending the *Aaron* MSS: must go through it carefully. Surely it is just as well also if Secker publishes it next Spring: is there really any hurry? Please answer.

I want Seltzer to hurry up with *Sardinia*: that I want out this autumn. Have you spoken of it to Secker.

I want to leave for Florence quite soon: it is no longer warm here. But shall let you know.

Yrs D. H. Lawrence

Write next time

32 Via dei Bardi. Florence.[2]

I shall be there probably by the 23r[d.][3]

MS. *Mr Noon* just come.[4]

---

[1] The proofs were of two poems in *English Review*, August 1921: 'Medlars and Sorb Apples' and 'Pomegranate'.   [2] See p. 48 n. 4.   [3] MS torn.

[4] Curtis Brown replied on 26 August 1921 (TMS Smith):

Dear Lawrence

Yours of August 14 is at hand. I'm much relieved to hear "MR. NOON" got to you safely. Secker isn't very sure he can make any profit on the Sardinia book, and is dead certain he can't afford to make the colour plates. But if he can get them reasonably from Seltzer that will probably alter his view. It would be a pity to publish the book over here without the

2311. To Catherine Carswell, [15 August 1921]
Text: MS YU; PC v. Austrian scene; Postmark, [. . .]; cited in Moore, *Poste Restante* 63.

[Villa Alpensee, Thumersbach, Zell-am-See, bei Salzburg]
15 August

We are leaving here at the end of this week – shall be in Florence early next week – address
32 Via dei Bardi.
Weather wet and cold – I want to go to Italy. You go straight there and come back this way.

DHL

2312. To Ada Clarke, [15 August 1921]
Text: MS Clarke; PC v. Gross Venediger 3660 m. [With roadside shrine]; Postmark, [. . .]; Unpublished.

[Villa Alpensee, Thumersbach, Zell-am-See, bei Salzburg]
15 Aug.

We leave at the end of the week for Florence – arrive there about 24th – write
32 Via dei Bardi – Florence.
Hope the stuff for me won't take long – I shall be so glad to have it for a birthday present – raining here and quite chilly – hope Jack's cough is better[1] – Haven't heard again from Cath[erine] Carswell – write to Florence.

DHL

2313. To Martin Secker, [15 August 1921]
Text: MS UInd; PC v. Gross Venediger 3660 m. [With roadside shrine]; Postmark, [. . .]; Unpublished.

[Villa Alpensee, Thumersbach, Zell-am-See, bei Salzburg]
15 August.

Am leaving Austria this week – going to Florence – address
32 Via dei Bardi.
Expect to be there till end October – then Taormina.
Hope all goes well.

DHL

illustrations, so it seems to be wise to let the matter rest until we or you can hear from Seltzer. If we can show Secker proofs of the illustrations, and quote good terms, I believe all will be well.
Next Spring will be all right for "AARON'S ROD". In fact I believe it would be better, unless the book can be put in hand instantly, for it isn't a Christmas book.

Yours sincerely

[1] John Lawrence Clarke (1915–42), DHL's nephew.

2314. To Thomas Seltzer, 15 August 1921
Text: Cited in American Art Association, *First Editions and Autograph Letters and Manuscripts by Famous Modern Authors*, 29–30, January 1936, p. 116, Item No. 378.

Thumersbach, Zell-am-See
15 August 1921

Probably you won't like it; probably it won't sell. Yet it is what I want it to be. I am satisfied with it. It is the end of the *Rainbow–Women in Love* novels: and my last word. I enclosed a little Foreword to it, which you print or not, as you like.[1]

2315. To Harry Leggett, [16 August 1921]
Text: MS UT; Unpublished.

Thumersbach
16 August

Dear Mr Leggett[2]

I enclose proof of 'The Revolutionary', which came this morning.[3] Proof of the other *English Review* poems I returned two days ago.

I am leaving here at the end of this week. Will you please address me at
32 Via dei Bardi, *Florence*. Italy.

Yrs   D. H. Lawrence

2316. To Dr Anton Kippenberg, 16 August 1921
Text: MS GSArchiv; Unpublished.

Thumersbach, *Zell-am-See*, b/Salzburg
16 August 1921

Dear Dr Kippenberg,

I have not heard from you for a very long time, and should like to have some news. How is the *Rainbow* progressing? – Could you send me proofs? – and when do you think to publish the book?[4]

The summer is over, so we are going back to Italy. I have been so happy these three months in Germany, and one month in Austria. But now I want to go south again.

Will you write to me
32 Via dei Bardi, *Florence*.
I shall be there till about 1st. October, then back to Taormina.

Next year I hope we may meet, either in Germany or in Italy.

Yours Sincerely   D. H. Lawrence

---

[1] The letter accompanied DHL's MS 'Foreword to *Aaron's Rod*'; the MS (sold in New York in 1936) has not been located, nor has the letter (sold with it).
[2] He was an employee in the London Office of Curtis Brown.
[3] 'The Revolutionary' appeared in *English Review*, xxxiii (September 1921), 169–71.
[4] See p. 40 n. 1.

2317. To Baroness Anna von Richthofen, 17 August 1921
Text: MS UCB; Unpublished.

Thumersbach, *Zell-am-See*, Österreich
17 August 1921

Meine liebe Schwiegermutter

I have not written to you for quite a long time. But the days slip past, and nothing remarkable happens, there is nothing to tell.

The hot weather is gone: much snow has fallen on the Kitsteinhorn, and the air is never hot any more. This afternoon we went the way you went last year, over the hill and meadows to Bruck. We drank Kaffee in the Gasthaus, and came home as the sun sank behind the hills opposite. It was very pleasant. But what a long walk for you, last year!

Mountsier has gone: he left yesterday for Innsbruck and Luzern and Interlaken, on his way to Paris. Thank goodness we shall not be troubled with him in Italy.

We too are leaving either on Saturday or on Monday, 22nd. It has been so very nice here: but now I want to move on. The real summer is over, and I must go south. I feel a Sehnsucht nach Italien.[1] So, this time next week we shall probably be in Florence. We shall have the flat to ourselves, and I shall be glad to be alone again. Nusch and everybody here have been *so* nice all the time. But then one wants to be alone again. The address will be

32 Via dei Bardi, *Florence.*

Write to us there.

I have not heard from the Insel Verlag – so I shall write to Kippenberg and ask him what he is doing. Then I will let you know. – I asked Emil to send you the few Marks that were left over after the passports were paid for.

I am glad you will not have the great heat any longer: you will feel much better now it is cooler. – I have such friendly remembrances of Ebersteinburg and BadenBaden and the Stift. Remember me to Fräulein Bader.[2]

Best of good wishes to you.

D. H. Lawrence

2318. To Scofield Thayer, 17 August 1921
Text: MS YU; Joost and Sullivan, *D. H. Lawrence and 'The Dial'*, pp. 45–6.

Villa Alpensee, Thumersbach, Zell-am-See, bei Salzburg
17 August 1921

Dear Thayer

Ach no. Vielen Dank[3] – but the North Sea, a storm, a cross editor at the end

[1] 'Longing for Italy'.
[2] Fräulein Bader, formerly a teacher, was a neighbour of the Baroness.
[3] 'Oh no. Many thanks'.

of an endless railway journey: ach nein, süsser Herrgott, was hab'ich dann getan? Jeh o Jeh, warum soll ich so gestraft werden! Nimmer, nein: aber tausendmal Dank.[1]

No. It snowed on the mountains here and seven people fell down a glacier for ever and I foreswore the north. I loathe the smell of snow in my nostrils. I loathe the accursed white element grinning under heaven. I shall die if I don't eat yellow figs within a fortnight. I am going south. Yea, I am going imperially over the Brenner. I am going south. Gott sei dank, ich reise fort. Ich habe genug – satt – satt: bin schon vier Monat hier in der teutonischen Welt ertrunken; jetzt schwimm'ich heraus, kletter wie ein Meerneckar über Stein und Fels aus, heraus, weg.[2] I am going south. No more snow.

But why don't you make a detour? Go to Augsburg on your way to Wien, and come to Florence on your way back to Paris. Come to Florence. I shall be there certainly till October 1st, and will stay on a bit if you are appearing. We leave here next Monday.

> 32 Via dei Bardi, Florence.

Send a line there. – Or we'll meet in the spring.

Mountsier said he thought you had seen *Sardinia* and didn't like it. Well, you probably *won't* like it. Yet it was partly your asking for travel sketches à la *Twilight in Italy*[3] which made me write it: half an eye on *The Dial*. So live up to your responsibility.

> 'And then he took a Dial from his poke
> And looking on it with lacklustre eye
> Said very wisely: "Tis now ten oclock."'[4]

'The Gent. from San Francisco' will probably have reached you. If I can wring the English MS. of *Sea and Sardinia* out of

> Curtis Brown, 6 Henrietta St, London W.C. 2

– you shall have it. Send him a line yourself and ask him for it, if you wish.

I shall go to Taormina for the winter: then, if I have enough dollars to my name, so that I can face New York with calm equanimity, knowing I can leave it on the next train for anywhere if I like, then in the spring I too shall come to AMERICA. Needless to say my knees lose their brassy strength, and feel like chocolate fondants at the thought.

D. H. Lawrence

[1] 'Oh no, sweet Lord God, whatever have I done? Lord oh Lord, why should I be punished so! Never, no: but a thousand thanks.'

[2] 'Thank God, I'm leaving. I have enough – full – full: have drowned four months already here in the Teutonic world; now I am going to swim out, clamber out like a water sprite over boulder and cliff, forth, away.'

[3] DHL's first travel-book, published in 1916.

[4] *As You Like It* III. vii. 20–2 ['. . . he drew a dial . . . Says . . . It is ten o'clock'].

2319. To Robert Mountsier, [17 August 1921]
Text: MS Smith; PC v. Zell am See mit Hohe Tauern; Postmark, [. . .[; Unpublished.

[Villa Alpensee, Thumersbach, Zell-am-See, bei Salzburg]
17 Aug.

– I just had a letter from Thayer inviting me to Westerland–Sylt on the North
Sea (Germany): Says he has *not* seen *Sardinia,* and would like to: his
permanent address
c/o Brown, Shipley and Co, 1 Pall Mall W.
His address now is
Haus Miramar, *Westerland-Sylt,* Deutschland, Nordsee.
He leaves Sept 2nd for Berlin – later Wien – stay there winter – Paris early
spring. He invites me to Sylt now, he pay all expenses. But no – I must go
south. Write him.

DHL

Wonder if Curtis B[rown] could show him English MS of *S[ea] and
S[ardinia]*.

2320. To Robert Mountsier, [18? August 1921]
Text: MS Smith; Unpublished.

Thumersbach
Thursday

Dear M[ountsier]
I shall send you today the MS. of *Aaron's Rod.* Write to Florence, will you,
32 Via dei Bardi.
We shall be there by the end of the month, and whether we have the flat or not
Windeam[1] will always give me the letters. I don't know whether it is any good
thinking of trying any bit of *Aaron* for *The Dial:* the Florence part, if any: or
the Sir William Franks part.[2]
Thanks for your p.c. from Innsbruck. You didn't stay long. I must try if I
can't get my visas and away in two hours.
I didn't send the cable to Seltzer after all: somehow didn't want to: don't
like the idea of pressing him. I wrote him however.
No further news through the post. – I shall not be sorry to leave Austria.
Don't write any more here: better to Florence.

More anon   DHL

---

[1] Unidentified.
[2] The last six chapters of *Aaron's Rod* are set in Florence; chaps XII and XIII are 'the Sir William
Franks part'. The *Dial* for February 1922 contained selections from chap. XIV ('XX
Settembre') under the title 'An Episode'.

2321. To Baroness Anna von Richthofen, [19 August 1921]
Text: MS UCB; Unpublished.

Zell-am-See.
Freitag

Liebe Schwiegermutter

Der langweiliger, der Mountsier verlangt noch etwas. Er will zwei von den Porzellan-figuren '*Chardin*', die in den Lauben in der nähe vom Kurhaus zu verkaufen sind. Er will wissen was es kosten würde, zwei Figuren, *gut* gepackt, nach Berlin geschickt und in Berlin bezahlt zu haben. Die Figuren die er verlangt sind:

1. Der rote Bub der geschimpft ist von seiner Mutter.
2. Die kleine Familie zu Tisch, mit dem kleinen Mädchen die das Tischgebet macht.

Er will Geld schicken nach Berlin zu einem Freund, der wird den Briefträger zahlen.

Kannst du ihm vielleicht ein Wort schreiben, um ihm die Kosten zu sagen, wann du die weisst.

Mr. Robert Mountsier, c/o American Express Co. 11. rue Scribe, *Paris*, Frankreich.

Mir kannst du's auch sagen.

Wir reisen Montag früh weg: um ½ 5. Ich hoffe am Dienstag sind wir schon in Florenz: 32 Via dei Bardi. Schreibe wieder da.

Ich hatte deinen Brief gestern. Gott sie dank dass es dir so gut geht. Hier ist nichts neues: sonst das die Frauen haben alle neue Bauenröcke. Die Anita wartet und wartet, um vom Hinke zu hören, wan er kommen wird. Aber er sagt nimmer. Sie hoffen sehr das die Verheiratung vor den 11[1] September sein kann. Jetzt ist es aber kaum möglich. Max and Hardu reisen fort am 11.[2]

Hier ist es immer wunderbar schön – Frieda und ich gehen morgen mit dem Auto nach Moserboden. Sie sagt sie[3] will auf einem Gletscher treten. Es ist viel Schnee gefallen daroben – Morgens und Abends ist es scharf kühl. Der Gletscher sollte wunderschön aussehen.

Der arme Onkel – er ist aber dumm, dass er fangt wieder an eine Geschäft aufzubauen. Sie könnten, die zwei, still und ruhig leben mit dem Geld das sie noch haben, und er könnte seinen beliebten Arabisch fuhren. Aber nein – Geld – immer noch Geld. Es ist eine Krankheit.

Hier geht es alle gut.

Tausendmal Grusse von uns zwei.

D. H. Lawrence

---

[1] 11] 1st   [2] 11] 1st   [3] sie] she

[Zell-am-See
Friday[1]

Dear Schwiegermutter

That bore, Mountsier, asks for something more. He wants two of the porcelain figurines '*Chardin*', which are for sale in the arcades near the Kurhaus. He wants to know what it would cost to have two figurines, *well* packed, sent to Berlin and paid for in Berlin. The figurines he asks for are:

1. The red boy being scolded by his mother.
2. The little family at table, with the little girl saying grace.

He wants to send money to Berlin to a friend, who will pay the postman.

Can you perhaps write him a word to tell him the costs, when you know them:

Mr Robert Mountsier, c/o American Express Co. 11. rue Scribe, *Paris*, France.

You can tell me too.

We leave early Monday: at 4:30. I hope on Tuesday we'll already be in Florence: 32 Via dei Bardi. Write again there.

I had your letter yesterday. Thank God you are so well. Here there's no news: except that the women all have new peasant skirts. Anita waits and waits to hear from Hinke, when he will come.[2] But he never says. They hope very much that the wedding can be before 1st September. But now it is hardly possible. Max and Hadu leave the 1st.

Here it is always wonderfully beautiful – Frieda and I go tomorrow by motorcar to Moserboden. She says she wants to set foot on a glacier. Much snow has fallen up there – mornings and evenings it is sharply cool. The glacier should look marvellous.

Poor Uncle – he's quite foolish, to begin again to build up a business.[3] They could, the two, live quietly and peacefully with the money they have left, and he could pursue his beloved Arabic. But no – money – always money. It's a sickness.

---

[1] DHL obviously wrote this letter toward the end of his stay in Zell-am-See and after Mountsier had left for Paris on 16 August. DHL wrote to Mountsier on Monday 22 August (Letter 2324), telling him that he had written to the Baroness von Richthofen about the Chardin figures. The only Friday between these two dates was 19 August.

[2] Anita von Schreibershofen, m., 1922, Ernest von Hinke. He had served in the Germany army, had lost his estate by 1918 and, after considerable effort, qualified as an engineer.

[3] DHL's uncle Fritz Johann Heinrich Krenkow (1872–1953), b. Schönberg, Mecklenburg; came to England, 1894; m. DHL's mother's sister, Ada Rose Beardsall; naturalised, 1911. From 1921, Krenkow devoted himself to the study of Arabic poetry and to lexicographical scholarship. Associated with a hosiery firm from 1899, Krenkow may have considered going into business for himself. See *Letters*, i. 77 n. 1.

Here all are well.
A thousand greetings from us two

D. H. Lawrence]

2322. To Amy Lowell, [21? August 1921]
Text: MS HU; PC v. Gentiana brachyphylla, Potentilla frigida; Postmark, [. . .]; cited in
Moore, Poste Restante 64.

[Villa Alpensee, Thumersbach, Zell-am-See, bei Salzburg]
[21? August 1921]

We are leaving here this week for Florence –
32 Via dei Bardi.
Suppose we shall stay there till end of September, then to Taormina again for
the winter. Hope you are getting strong and feeling well, and having a good
time with *Legends* notices.

Yrs.   D. H. Lawrence

2323. To Percy Whittley, [21 August 1921]
Text: MS UT; Unpublished.

Villa Alpensee, Thumersbach, *Zell-am-See*, bei Salzburg,
Austria
21 August

Dear Whittley
    I ought to have written you sooner. – but waited and waited to see what we
were really going to do for September. It is decided. We leave here tomorrow
for Innsbruck on our way to Florence. Write to me there:
32 Via dei Bardi, *Florence*.
and say what you are doing. I expect we shall stay in Florence till end of
September – then to Taormina. Will find you rooms and arrange all for you, if
you write. I expect to be at 32 Via dei Bardi by the 24th.
    It is very nice here – you would have liked it better here, I know: a lake to
bathe in, boats, snowy mountains, lovely excursions, and a glacier within
reach. But then the German language, of course: though in Zell in the shop
and bank they speak English and are *very* friendly. If you think you would like
here you could write to
    Hotel Belle Vue, Thumersbach, *Zell-am-See* b[ei] Salzburg.

The cost is about 700 or 800 Kronen a day – very pleasant everything – and you know what the exchange is. The Paris train to Vienna stops in Zell: Paris to Zell without changing. There are already English people in the Belle Vue. But if Italy, then write me at once to Florence.

Best of wishes from us both to both.

D. H. Lawrence

The route is Paris-Basel-Zurich-Innsbruck-Zell or Hook of Holland-Cologne-Munich-Salzburg-Zell.

Also, even nicer *Hotel Lohninghof* – same address – but don't know if they speak English.

2324. To Robert Mountsier, [22 August 1921]
Text: MS Smith; PC v. [Alpine flowers]; Postmark, Thumersbach 23 VIII 21; Unpublished.

[Villa Alpensee, Thumersbach, Zell-am-See, bei Salzburg]
Monday

I wrote to Baden Baden about your Chardin groups – asked my m[other]-in-law to write direct to you. No news here – leaving for Innsbruck week-end.

DHL

2325. To S. S. Koteliansky, [25 August 1921]
Text: MS BL; PC v. S. Geisler's Krimmler Tauernhaus. [Alpine scene]; Postmark, [. . .]; Zytaruk 225.

Villa Alpensee, Zell-am-See, Austria
25 Aug

I sent the 'Gentleman' to Miss Monk – she has typed it and is posting one copy to Thayer of the *Dial*, one to you.[1] I wrote to Thayer – he is in Paris – but have only his London address

c/o Brown Shipley and Co, 1. Pall Mall. W.

Hope he will put the thing through. We leave directly for Florence – – address
32 Via dei Bardi, Florence.

Write there.

DHL

---

[1] See Letter 2293.

2326. To S. S. Koteliansky, [26 August 1921]
Text: MS BL; PC v. École de Raphael, Étude; Postmark, Firenze 26 VIII 1921;
Zytaruk 226.

32 Via dei Bardi, Florence
[26 August 1921]

Got here yesterday – found your letter – Miss Monk, *Grimsbury Farm, Long Lane near Newbury* – is a Hermitage friend, and ought to have sent you that MS by now. I have written her about it. You can write also if you don't get it soon. As for little J[ohn] M[iddleton] M[urry], he is too rotten to kick. I do hope Thayer will take the 'Gent[leman]'. You must find it dreary in No. 5.[1]

DHL

2327. To Percy Whittley, [29 August 1921]
Text: MS UT; PC v. Messina, Corso Vittorio Emanuele col Nettuno; Postmark, Firenze 29 VIII 1921; Unpublished.

32 Via dei Bardi. Florence
29 Aug.

Had your letter today – also Mrs Whittleys, forwarded here. Glad you will be turning up: will get you a room when you fix your date – as soon as possible – and meet you when you arrive. Weather lovely here. Mountsier is in Paris – c/o Amer[ican] Express, 11 rue Scribe.
Just possible he will come here with you. Perceval is here: Florence very nice. You can easily get to Rome from here. I'll think if there's any little thing I want you to bring.

Au revoir. DHL

2328. To Curtis Brown, 29 August 1921
Text: MS UT; PC; Postmark, Firenze 29 8 21; Unpublished.

32 Via dei Bardi. Florence.
29 August 1921

Many thanks for the cheque for £7-11-2, from the *Nation* for 'Whitman', which I have received today.

D. H. Lawrence

---

[1] I.e. No. 5 Acacia Road, St John's Wood.

2329. To Dr Anton Kippenberg, 29 August 1921
Text: MS GSArchiv; Unpublished.

32 Via dei Bardi, *Firenze*, Italien
29 August 1921

Dear Dr Kippenberg

Thank you for your letter of 19 August, with the enclosed proof-page. But I think you must have made a mistake, and sent me a page from another book, for I can find nothing of *The Rainbow* here.

I shall be very much interested to see the whole proof of the translation: am anxious to know how the book reads in German. Please don't forget to send me the Satizprobe[1] as soon as it is ready.

And believe me.

Very Sincerely Yours   D. H. Lawrence

2330. To Robert Mountsier, 29 August 1921
Text: MS Smith; Postmark, Firenze 29 VIII 1921; Unpublished.

32 Via dei Bardi, *Florence*
29 August 1921

Dear M[ountsier]

I found your letter here – also these two letters at Cooks. Again automatically I opened one, but didn't read more than four words.

I am feeling tired and seedy after the north – and not able to take in anything. Thankful to be in the flat by ourselves, rather dark and cool. Have hardly been out yet. – The Whittleys are coming to Florence on Sept 12th. They want to go to Rome too. I shall get them a room in Berchiellis' hotel. Would it amuse you to come with them for a trip – or are you tired of tripping? I am dead tired – feel I don't want to travel another yard.

Mary Cannan is coming tomorrow – staying in the Lucchesi – cross because we wouldn't go to Montecarlo. I won't go anywhere.

I've had no letters – save this from Curtis.

While I am here I shall have a shot at writing six or seven Italian Stories that would make a book by itself: two Venice, one Verona, one Florence, one Rome, one Anticoli, one Capri, one Sicily. Do you think it is a nice idea? How long ought they to be? does it matter if they are rather long? I do want to make money this winter, to cross the seas in the early spring. I want to leave Europe. Even Italy means nothing to me, though I prefer it to the north.

Hope we'll hear before long from Seltzer.

Yrs   DHL

---

[1] 'Proofs'.

2331. To Nelly Morrison, 1 September 1921
Text: TMSC NWU; Huxley 523–4.

32, Via dei Bardi, Firenze
1 Sept. 1921.

Dear Nelly Morrison,

I had your letter yesterday. Everything goes well with us: we like your flat more every day: have all our meals on the terrace, when the wind isn't too strong. I find it lovely and cool, and am writing a story about Venice.[1] Later I want to write one about Florence and this house: modern of course.

Is Venice very lovely just now? Writing about it makes me realise how beautiful it is.

Peggy is pretty well, I think. She's not going to die of a broken heart, whatever else she dies of. So don't flatter yourself. Yesterday Tina gave her a bath on the terrace here, in the red trough. She trembled and looked pathetic, but loved all the notice taken of her.

Poor Tina has trouble with her teeth, bad inflamation of the lower gums: looks a wretch and feels it: but is rather better now, after certain lotions etc. from the dentist.

I tried Casanova, but he smells.[2] One can be immoral if one likes, but one must not be a creeping, itching, fingering inferior being, led on chiefly by a dirty sniffing kind of curiosity, without pride or clearness of soul. For me, a man must have pride, good natural inward pride. Without that, cleverness only stinks. But I will treat the battered volumes as gingerly as such *crotter*[3] deserves.

Two days ago, Mrs. Gilbert Cannan arrived from France. She is an old friend. She was here when Tina was bathing Peggy, and drying the same Peggy in the shut-up bedroom – next the salotta here: Mrs. Cannan immediately began pining to come and stay in it for a week or two. She made me promise to write and ask you if you would let it to her for three weeks or a month, and she would engage to vacate it at once if you should need it or want it. She would have her meals with us, but I am not sure if I want a permanent guest. But do as you wish.

The plants are watered very regularly, and seem quite well.

Juta is due to arrive tomorrow in Florence.

Greet Gino,[4] and be greeted yourself by us both.

Yrs, D.H. Lawrence

---

[1] This story (which DHL later seems to have considered expanding into a novel) was discontinued and no manuscript is known to exist for it. See Letters 2348 and 2368.

[2] Giacomo Casanova de Seingalt (1725–98), an Italian adventurer, author of *Mémoires Ecrits par Lui-Même* (12 vols., Paris, 1826–38). DHL 'tried' Casanova on two previous occasions: see *Letters*, ii. 42, 100.   [3] 'dirt'.   [4] Unidentified.

2332. To Percy Whittley, [6 September 1921]
Text: MS UT; Unpublished.

.32 Via dei Bardi, *Florence*, 3⁰ Piano – 3rd Floor
Tuesday.[1]

Dear Whittley

Your letter this morning. As far as I make out you arrive at Pisa at 3.0 oclock on Monday morning – in the small hours. You must change there – wait three hours. If it's light enough go out and look at the cathedral and the leaning tower. If you like, stay a few hours longer in Pisa. The first train leaves at 6.0.

Pisa –	6.0	8.35	13.5	15.35	20.50
Firenze	8.28	11.5	15.25	17.15	23.25
	your train				

I shall get you a room at the Pensione Lucchesi, Lung'arno della Zecca, Zecca. I shall meet the 8.28 Monday morning, all being well. If you are coming by another train, wire me. If I don't meet you, drive straight to the Lucchesi. In Pisa the trains run from the station to the cathedral – the Duomo.

au revoir   DHL

2333. To Robert Mountsier, 9 September 1921
Text: MS Smith; Postmark, Firenze 10. 9. 21; Unpublished.

32 Via dei Bardi, *Firenze*.
9 September 1921.

Dear M[ountsier].

I had a letter from Seltzer too – he didn't mention prices or anything. If I could find it I'd send it – but nothing in it. If *Sardinia* is going to cost him a great deal – but there, let the damned public pay. I don't say anything about business to him.

I am having the second *Psychoanalysis* typed here. Shall I call it 'Child Consciousness'?[2] When I get the *crit*[*icism*]*s* I'll answer them in an introduction: feel like kicking somebody.

I am going to write to Huebsch about *The Rainbow*, and ask him for a copy.[3]

---

[1] It is apparent from Letter 2335 that the Whittleys were to arrive on 12 September. The date of this letter – written on the preceding Tuesday – must therefore be 6 September.

[2] *Fantasia of the Unconscious* focuses upon children; in chap. XIII DHL states: 'this is an essay on Child Consciousness'.

[3] Benjamin W. Huebsch (1876–1964), a New York publisher whose firm merged with the Viking Press in 1925. Huebsch published an expurgated version of *The Rainbow* on 30 November 1915. See *Letters*, ii. 479–80.

Yes, I agree to Seltzer's terms for the *History*.[1]
The Whittleys arrive on Monday. — Like you, I feel tired and sick of travel
and Europe is lost on me. Even Florence wearies me — I feel I just want to get
away from its infernal noise. Taormina is at any rate quiet. — I shan't stay long
in Europe.
I began the Venice story — interesting idea I have — but I can't work here. — I
only wrote 'Fish' — which I enclose. And I want to do 'Bat'.[2]
I am not sending *Aaron's Rod* to England until you advise me.
Poor Erzberger![3]

                                                              Belli Saluti   DHL

2334. To Baroness Anna von Richthofen, 10 September 1921
Text: MS UCB; Unpublished.

                                                    32 Via dei Bardi, *Florenz*
                                                    10 September 1921.

Meine liebe Schwiegermutter

Der schlimmer Kippenberg spricht nimmer kein Wort von Geld — sagt nur
dass er schicht gleich einen Drucksatzt, und dass das Buch wird wahrscheinlich dieses Jahr erschcinen. Hoffen wir immer. Hier ist zehn Pfund,
besser wie nichts.

Immer wunderschön hier. Vorgestern war ein Feierabend — gestern
Maria's Geburtstag. Auf dem Arno viele Boote mit grossen schönen
Lanternen — und Lanternen durch die Strassen. Es war hübsch — der Abend
so warm. Die Sonne ist noch heiss, aber die Luft frisch. Wir waren auf der
Höhe in Fiesole — man sieht weit, weit, die Appeninen und das grossen Tal,
mit dem Arno, der Flus, der kommt von der Ferne sowie die Treppen
hinunter — grade so wie Treppen hinunter. — Die Trauben hangen immer
noch schwarz, geheimnisvoll schwarz unter den Blättern, und Pfirrsiche so rot
und gold. Es ist so schön, wenn man weit, weit sehen kann, und auf dem Ebene
die Stadt so allein, so weiblich, und auf den Hügeln die Villas weiss oder
rosefarbe, und immer wieder die Zipressen, wie schwarze Schattenflammen
die zusammen drängen. Dies ist Toskana, und nirgendwo sind die Zipressen
so schön und stolz, wie Schwarz-flammen aus der Urzeit, vor die Römer
gekommen sind, als die Etruskaner immer hier waren, schlank und fein und
• still und mit nakten Elegance, schwarz-haarig, mit schmalen Füssen.

[1] *Movements in European History* (1921) was never published in USA despite Seltzer's twice-
expressed willingness to produce an American edition 'under Lawrence's own name' (see
Tacy, *Seltzer* 208, 216).
[2] 'Fish' appeared in *English Review*, xxxiv (June 1922), 505–10; 'Bat', in xxxv (November 1922),
381–2. Both were collected in *Birds, Beasts and Flowers*.
[3] Matthias Erzberger (1875–1921), a leading moderate politician of the Catholic Centre party in
Germany, was killed by members of a nationalist organization on 26 August 1921.

Wir sitzen auf dem Terrasse. Es ist abend, die Sonne sinkt hinter den Carrarabergen, die Hügeln werden dunkel. Auf dem Ponte Vecchio die Fenster von den kleinen Haüschen scheinen gelb, und machen goldenen Punkten auf dem Wasser. Jetzt muss ich die electrishe Tischlampe anzünden, um zu schreiben. Wir essen Abendessen hier draussen.

Sonntag fahren wir fort an den Castello Ruggero, etwas 10 Kilometer – Wir haben Freunde da – Es soll schön sein – ein altes Italienisches Schloss. – Am 15n. fängt die Dante festa an, hier. Sie machen etwas schön – ein Prozession kommt aus dem Land, und es soll genau so sein als wann die Florentiner mit Dante heimkehrten vom Schlacht von Campodino – etwa in 1260. Sie haben alle die alte Tracht und alte Waffen und Rüstung, und kommen in einem Menge durch die Porta Romana, Ritter, Knechte, und alle.

Die Schwalben waren tausende – und sind schon wieder fort, nach Sizilien. Man sagt, es wird kalt sein. – Denke nicht zu viel an die Deutsche Valuta – die kluge Deutsche Finanzier haben einen Finger in jenem Spiel.

Viele schone Grüsse. – Dein Schwiegersohn

DHL

[My dear Schwiegermutter

That wretched Kippenberg says never a word about money – says only that he is sending a proof directly, and that the book will probably appear this year. Let's keep hoping. Here is ten pounds, better than nothing.

Always very beautiful here. Day before yesterday was a holiday – yesterday Mary's birthday.[1] On the Arno many boats with great lovely lanterns – and lanterns through the streets. It was pretty – the evening so warm. The sun is still hot, but the air fresh. We were on the height in Fiesole – one sees far, far, the Appenines and the great valley, with the Arno, the river, which comes down from the distance just like the steps – down exactly like steps. – The grapes still hang black, mysteriously black beneath the leaves, and peaches so red and gold. It's so lovely, when one can see far, far, and on the plain the city so alone, so feminine, and on the hills the villas, white or pink, and again and again the cypresses, like black shadowflames crowding together. This is Tuscany, and nowhere are the cypresses so beautiful and proud, like black-flames from primeval times, before the Romans had come, when the Etruscans were still here, slender and fine and still and with naked elegance, black haired, with narrow feet.

We are sitting on the terrace. It is evening, the sun sinks behind the Carrara mountains, the hills grow dark. On the Ponte Vecchio the windows of the little

---

[1] The birthday of the Blessed Virgin Mary is celebrated on 8 September.

houses shine yellow, and make golden points on the water. Now I must light the electric table-lamp to write. We are eating supper out here.

Sunday we go to Castello Ruggero, about 10 kilometres – We have friends there – It's supposed to be beautiful – an old Italian castle – On the 15th the Dante festa begins here. They're doing something lovely – a procession is coming from the country, and it is supposed to be exactly as when the Florentines with Dante returned home from the Battle of Campodino – in about 1260.[1] They'll all have the old local costume and old weapons and armour, and come in a throng through the Porta Romana, knights, grooms, and all.

The swallows were in their thousands – and are already gone to Sicily. They say it's going to be cold. – Don't think too much about the German exchange – the clever German financiers have a finger in that game.

Many kind greetings. – Your son-in-law

DHL]

2335. To Robert Mountsier, 12 September 1921
Text: MS Smith; Postmark, Firenze 12. IX 1921; Unpublished.

32 Via dei Bardi, *Florence*
Monday 12 Sept 1921

My dear M[ountsier],

Your letter of Sept 8th. this morning. Why are you going to London, and how long are you stopping?

I wrote you a letter to Paris, and enclosed poem 'Fish', which you said you missed from *Beasts*. I shall send you 'Bat' tomorrow or next day.

I think better withold *Aaron* till spring: but I leave the final decision to you. I shall not post my MS. to Curtis until you tell me to. – I doubt if England would publish parts: in magazines.

I think the 'Novara' chapters – leaving out that long Aaron-introspect bit about his wife: i.e., just the chapters about the Sir Wm Franks place – would do for magazines: also the Florence chapters: also the Milan incident: all separate.[2] But I am not very keen on English magazines' doing the book, really. I *don't want it hawked around*. – Curtis has a duplicate of the latter half – all that is any way fit for serial. He could correct this from your copy, if he wanted. *But don't let him go raggedly around with bits of the novel in England.*

I don't care one bit whether England does *Psychoanalysis*. The whole thing

---

[1] Cf. *Movements in European History*, chap. XIII.   [2] See p. 74 n. 2.

is written for America, and I shant even give Curtis the MS of Part II until
Seltzer has got it out and well started. Let England wait.

I met the Whittleys at the station at 8.30 this morning: tired, but pleased at
being abroad: very disappointed at missing you in Paris. Whittley has a lot of
new information for you about that ship[1] – the price down to £1,000 – and
could be got lower still. But he will write.

I think to leave here in about eight or nine day's time, for Taormina. So
unless anything urgent occurs, write to Fontana Vecchia, Taormina. The
Whittleys are going to Rome – probably along with us.

I will get him to add a note to this.

DHL

Have you got the Chardins? – at what cost?[2]

Ship *James and Edward* price now £1000.

Whittley will send you a letter from Tresidder of St Ives who will be in
London and would like to see you[3] – write to Tresidder and fix an
appointment if you wish, because he, T, is now quite anxious to help you:
because he wants to recover his own £200 out of the boat.

2336. To Thomas Seltzer, [15 September 1921]
Text: MS UT; PC v. Firenze, Palazzo Vecchio; Postmark, Firenze 15. IX 1921; Lacy,
Seltzer 26.

Florence.

15 Sept.

I had the press cuttings of *Psychoanalysis* today – will answer them – they are
quite amusing.[4] The book – the second part – is being typed here. I leave for
Siena and Rome next week. Write to Taormina.

D. H. Lawrence

---

[1] See p. 24 n. 3.   [2] See Letter 2321.
[3] W. J. Tressider was a marine engineer at Porthgwidden, St Ives.
[4] DHL is referring to the 'Foreword to *Fantasia of the Unconscious*'. Twelve of its sixteen pages
     consist of quotations from reviews of *Psychoanalysis* and DHL's comments on them. When the
     'Foreword' was printed these pages were omitted. See also p. 93 n. 1.

2337. To Martin Secker, 15 September 1921
Text: MS UInd; Postmark, Firenze 15. IX 1921; Secker 43.

32 Via de' Bardi, *Firenze*
15 Sept 1921

Dear Secker

Heseltine trying to make himself important.[1] Ma andiamo lemme lemme![2]
Send me the book to *Taormina* – shall be there by the 25th. – and I will
consider the alterations: – if they are necessary.
But we'll go softly.

Yrs   D. H. Lawrence

How many have you sold, of *Women in Love? Please* send a copy to
Miss Marie Hubrecht, Witte Huis, *Doorn*, bei Utrecht, Holland.

2338. To S. S. Koteliansky, [16 September 1921]
Text: MS BL; PC v. Firenze, Chiesa di Or. S. Michele; Postmark, Firenze, 16 IX 1921;
Zytaruk 226.

[32 Via dei Bardi, Florence]
Sept. 16

– Your letter today. I heard from Miss Monk that she had sent a copy of
'Gentleman' to Thayer of *The Dial*, and a copy to you. I wait to hear from
Thayer. We leave next week – going to Taormina. Write to Fontana Vecchia –
I didn't want you to pay *anything* for the typing – please cash the 15/-. – You
are not trying Squire. – I want my new novel postponed till spring[3] – Florence
wildly festivating Dante – such a row. Greet Sonia and Grisha and Ghita.

DHL

2339. To Emily King, [16 September 1921]
Text: MS Needham; PC v. Firenze, Piazza e Chiesa di S. Maria Novella; Postmark, Firenze
16 [. . .]; Unpublished.

[32 Via dei Bardi, Florence]
16 Sept

I sent Peg a letter and a number of stereoscope photographs some time back –

---

[1] Philip Arnold Heseltine (1894–1930), pseudonym Peter Warlock; composer, writer on music,
and editor of old English airs. Heseltine threatened to sue DHL for libel unless alterations were
made in the descriptions of Halliday and Pussum in *Women in Love*. (It is clear from a letter, 7
September 1921, from Secker's office, that Heseltine's solicitors – Messrs Clifford Webster,
Emmet & Coote – had written to the publisher on 2 September. Secker had agreed not to
circulate further copies of *Women in Love* until the matter was settled.)
[2] 'But let us go very slowly, very slowly!'   [3] *Aaron's Rod*.

hope they arrived: I have no word from you for a long time. We leave next week for Taormina. Write there. Florence in the thick of the Dante Festival.

DHL

2340. To Curtis Brown, 17 September 1921
Text: MS UT; Huxley 524.

32 Via de' Bardi, *Florence*
17 Sept 1921

Dear Curtis Brown

Will you put these three poems with *Birds Beasts and Flowers*: among the Beasts.[1]

We leave here on Tuesday. Please write henceforth to Fontana Vecchia, *Taormina*, Sicily. I hear Secker is having trouble with *Women in Love*.

I hope you had a good holiday and are feeling well.

Yrs   D. H. Lawrence

Poems are 'Fish', 'Bat', 'Man and Bat'.

2341. To Robert Mountsier, [17 September 1921]
Text: MS Smith; Postmark, Firenze 17 IX 1921; Unpublished.

32 Via de' Bardi, *Florence*
Saturday

My dear M[ountsier]

Secker writes that a man called Philip Heseltine is proposing a libel action for *W[omen] in Love* – wants me to alter text. Another letter from Secker I enclose.[2]

I enclose 'Bat', and 'Man and Bat'. I will send copies to Curtis. – Don't lose these, will you.

I have got reviews from Seltzer of *Psychoanalysis*. Shall answer them in Taormina.[3]

---

[1] 'Fish', 'Bat' and 'Man and Bat' appear among 'Creatures' in the published text.

[2] Secker's letter, 14 September 1921 (MS Smith), reads as follows:

Dear Lawrence

No more blue prosecution papers, but *John Bull* are now, in this week's issue, calling on the police to intervene. I do not attach much importance to this: I think Heseltine is more serious.

I have bought from Seltzer 50 copies of the American edition [of *Women in Love*]. If I print a special page for binding in will you autograph 50? I think I should have no difficulty in selling a signed edition and will credit you with 10% of the proceeds.

Yours sincerely   Martin Secker

What about *Aaron's Rod*?

In his letter Secker is referring to the article in *John Bull* by the magazine's assistant editor, Charles Pilley: 'A Book the Police Should Ban'.   [3] Taormina] Capri

Juta is here: will be in London about 28th or 30th. Shall give him your address if you like to see him.

We leave with the Whittleys next Tuesday for Siena. Write to Taormina. Tell me what you think of Seckers 10%. – You might see Secker and speak about the Heseltine affair. I believe the thing to do is to go quietly and let Heseltine get tired. He's a half imbecile fool.

Hope you had my letter from Paris with 'Fish'.

DHL

What are you doing in London? How long there?

2342. To Dr Anton Kippenberg, 19 September 1921
Text: MS GSArchiv; Unpublished.

32 Via dei Bardi, Florence
19 Sept 1921

Dear Dr Kippenberg
Today I received *Homer* and *Dante*,[1] and also the first pages of the proof of *The Rainbow*. For all of which many thanks.

I am leaving Florence tomorrow on my way to Sicily. Will you please address me at

Fontana Vecchia, *Taormina*, Sicilia.

Yours Sincerely   D. H. Lawrence

2343. To Catherine Carswell, [21 September 1921]
Text: MS YU; PC; Postmark, Fir[enze] 21 IX [. . .] 92 [. . .]; cited in Carswell 154.

Siena.
Wednesday

This in case you shouldn't get the note at the Banca Commerciale. – We must leave tonight – must get to Capri to see the Brewsters[2] who are leaving for India. Very sorry to miss you.

I left you a parcel, six plates, which I wish you would take to England for my sister. Do hope you won't hate it.

I feel you will soon be coming to Italy to live. Want to hear all your news. Shall write fully from Taormina. Greet Don.

DHL

No sign yet of the cloth from Zell. Perhaps you might enquire in London.

DHL

---

[1] Insel Verlag published *Homers Odyssee* (1911) and *Dante: Vita Nuova* (1920).
[2] Earl Henry Brewster (1878–1957) and Achsah Barlow Brewster (1878–1945), American painters. DHL met them on Capri in April 1921. See *Letters*, iii. 711 n. 1.

2344. To Earl and Achsah Brewster, [29 September 1921]
Text: MS UT; Brewster 27.

Fontana Vecchia
Wednesday[1]

Dear Brewster – and Achsah Brewster

Got here in the dark and rain of last night. – But how lovely it is here! I'm sure you've forgotten: the great window of the eastern sky, seaward. I like it *much* the best of any place in Italy: and adore Fontana Vecchia.

But my heart – and my soul are broken, in Europe. It's no use, the threads are broken. I will go east, intending ultimately to go west, as soon as I can get a ship: that is, before March. I would come in January for sure, if one could be sure of ships. I had better wait for my tramp steamer, because I should have to go *very* gently, monetarily.

My post contained nothing but a would-be official denunciation of *Women in Love* from *John Bull*. – I am all things evil: a tremble from my publishers: a very cold letter from my agent, that *Aaron's Rod* can't be accepted: and a solicitors information about *W. in Love*, that a libel action is impending. – Sweets to the sweet.[2] – Yet I wouldn't call it *sorrow* – merde! Mille fois merde![3]

I am so glad we came to Capri. Let us pitch our tents side by side in the howling wilderness[4] of these christian countries. Let us go from the Sodom of angels like Lot and Abraham, before the fire falls.[5]

No, but seriously, let us agree to take a way together into the future. If only you were going in January, I would come along. As it is, I will follow in January or in February: not long.

Very many thanks to you and Achsah Brewster for all your hospitality, and to Alpha Barlow for her kindness in burnoosing me.[6]

I will write again soon. Let us have the faith and courage to move together on this slippery ball of quick-silver of a dissolving world.

DHL

Together we go! Divided we straggle!

Am sending you my *Psychoanalysis*. Think you can keep it – think I can get another from London.

---

[1] The Lawrences arrived in Taormina on Wednesday 28 September 1921; as the contents indicate, this letter was written on the following day.
[2] *Hamlet* V. i. 230.   [3] 'shit! A thousand times shit!'
[4] Deuteronomy xxxii. 10.   [5] See Genesis xix. 1–29.
[6] Alpha Barlow was visiting her sister, Achsah Brewster, when DHL visited the Brewsters in Capri. The Brewsters were fond of wearing Arab capes, called burnooses.

2345. To Catherine Carswell, [29 September 1921]
Text: MS YU; PC v. Firenze, Cortile del Palazzo Vecchio; Postmark, Taormina 30 SET 21; Carswell 154.

Taormina.
29 Sept.

We got home last night in a whirlwind and rain – but so glad to come to rest, I can't tell you – still like this place best – the sea open to the east, to the heart of the east, away from Europe. – I had your letter – it seemed only a moment we saw you – but the sympathy is there. You must come here. – The cloth has arrived in Austria, so all well.

Love   DHL

Did you take the plates for me from Haskards?[1]

2346. To S. S. Koteliansky, [30 September 1921]
Text: MS BL; Postmark, Taormina 30 SET 21; Zytaruk 227.

Fontana Vecchia, Taormina,
Friday

My dear Kot

We got here last night. I pick up the first bit of paper I find, in a medley of unpacking, to tell you that Thayer will publish 'The Gentleman', but that *page 5* is missing from his Manuscript. Can you see to that? His address is

Hotel Adlon, Unter den Linden, *Berlin*

I have no word from Thayer himself; my letter was from Robert Mountsier, 142 Marylebone Rd. He will tell you anything you may want to know.

I am so glad to be back – *so* tired of Europe – every new place one sees makes one more sick.

Greet everybody

DHL

2347. To Irene Whittley, [30 September 1921]
Text: MS UT; Unpublished.

Fontana Vecchia, *Taormina*, Sicilia
Friday

We got home on Wednesday night – two hours late – and after having been turned out of the train twice in the pouring rain with all the bags: once the

---

[1] Haskard & Co. Ltd were DHL's bankers in Florence (see *Letters*, iii. 482). Letter 2343 was addressed to Catherine Carswell c/o Haskard & Co., Palazzo Antinori, Firenze.

carriage-axles had run hot – they always do – once they decided to discard the coach we were in. Brutes! It rained and blew like a madness. – It rains here now.

But we are so thankful to be back, to be still. The very silence is heaven, after all the turmoil. Never again will I dash about as we dashed this year. I feel worn to ribbons. As for you, I am terrified lest you are still collapsed. Today – this mortal afternoon – almost at this very hour – you should be arriving in Rome. I'll bet it's raining there too. The autumn rains have set in a week or more too soon. I shall be glad to hear that you are safe and sound. Poor Whittley has had a bad time, I know.

We still love Taormina, and our house particularly. I like it here better than any of the other places. I love the sea open to the east, in the full sunrise. – The trouble is there is so little food: no milk now for the next six weeks, till the goats have their kids: no butter except tinned: rather bad bread. However, they have just arrived with my barrel of wine. I expect Brewster left you the two little pictures at Naples. I wanted

        Mrs King, 480 Main St, Carlton nr Nottingham

to have the Raphael Madonna – the one with the fruit frame: and

        Mrs Clarke, Grosvenor Rd, Ripley nr. Derby

to have the Botticelli: Madonna of the Pomegranate. But I hope Mrs Clarke will be coming to London, and that will save you any further bother packing them.

There is no news here: nothing but the rain and the silence. I hope soon to hear that you are safe and sound after a battering holiday. It has been strenuous for you: but you may really feel better later on, because of the absolute difference in the kind of strenuousness.

The Carswells did not *go to Siena* at all: I had a letter here. Good thing we didn't wait for them.

Well – au revoir, till next year.

                                    DHL

2348. To Thomas Seltzer, 8 October 1921
Text: MS UT; Postmark, Taormina 8 Ott 21; Lacy, *Seltzer* 26.

                      Fontana Vecchia, *Taormina*, Sicilia
                                 8 Ottobre 1921

Dear Seltzer

I hope Mountsier has sent you the MS of *Aarons Rod*. He emphatically dislikes the book, but then he is not responsible for it. I want you to write and tell me simply what you feel about it. It is the last of my serious English novels – the end of *The Rainbow*, *Women in Love* line. It had to be written – and had to come to such an end. If you wish, I will write a proper little explanatory foreword to it – not the one I sent from Zell am See. I want you to tell me if you consider it 'dangerous' – and what bit of it you think so – and if you'd like any small alteration made. If you would, please name the specific lines.

I have begun a proper *story* novel – in the Venetian lagoons: not pretty pretty – but no sex and no problems: no love, particularly. It wont go to England at all.

But I am held up at the moment going over the MS of 'The Child and the Unconscious' – which follows *Psychoanalysis and the Unconscious*. I like it much better than *Psy. and the Uncon*. It has about 52,000 words. I have written a foreword answering the critics: rather funny.[1] As soon as I have this ready – in a few days – I will send it you direct, introduction and all. The introduction you might perhaps offer to some periodical: it is really comical.

Friends[2] very much want me to go to Ceylon – about February. I don't know. I may. I will collect my short stories, for a volume, to have my MSS in order – if such a thing be possible. I am tired of Europe – it is somehow finished for me – finished with *Aaron's Rod*. Done. I wish I could find a ship that would carry me round the world and land me somewhere in the West – New Mexico or California – and I could have a little house and two goats, somewhere away by myself in the Rocky Mountains. I may manage that.

With all this the Venice story doesn't look like getting ahead very fast. Send me some news.

D. H. Lawrence

Do you like the title 'The Child and the Unconscious'? Or 'Child Consciousness'?

2349. To Martin Secker, [8 October 1921]
Text: MS UInd; Secker 44.

Fontana Vecchia, *Taormina*, Sicilia.
8 October

Dear Secker

I enclose the altered pages. The Pussum I have made a blue-eyed fair-haired little thing: Halliday black and swarthy: the manservant an Arab: the flat a house in St Johns Wood. For this last item, *please correct in a previous chapter*. Please go through it all carefully, to see there are no discrepancies.

I think it all perfect nonsense – as if there weren't dozens of little Pussums

---

[1] The 'Foreword' to *Fantasia of the Unconscious* is dated 'Taormina. 8 October 1921'. In the book when published, the 'Introduction' appears as chap. 1; here DHL appears to have in mind only the 'Foreword' which he hoped to publish separately (see also Letter 2358).

[2] Earl and Achsah Brewster.

about Chelsea, and dozens of Hallidays anywhere. But I do it since you wish it this way.

D. H. Lawrence[1]

[1] After receiving this letter and before he received Letter 2365, Secker wrote as follows to Heseltine's solicitors concerning the alleged libel of Heseltine as 'Halliday' and (his wife) Minnie Lucie Channing as 'Pussum' in *Women in Love* (Secker Letter-Book, UIll):

18th Oct. 1921

Dear Sirs,

I have to-day heard from Mr. Lawrence, in a letter dated October 8, and hasten to communicate with you. Mr. Lawrence is prepared to make the verbal changes shown on the marked pages which I send herewith, not as he says, that he considers the matter important, but in deference to my wish that no reasonable effort should be spared to remove any possible objections which your client may have. If your client agrees to the text as modified in this manner, I will undertake to carry out the alterations and to see that no further copies are issued in the original state. Will you please let me hear from you as soon as you have communicated with your client.

Yours faithfully

October 18, 1921

Dear Sirs,

I am much obliged for your letter. I quite appreciate my position in the matter, but I do not admit that your client has been grossly libelled in choosing to identify himself with a character in a work of fiction, nor do I consider that he is entitled to damages, substantial or otherwise. Both Mr Lawrence and myself have now done all we can. The author at my earnest desire to make every reasonable concession, suggested such alterations in the text in the future as to eliminate any fancied resemblance, and I have, in the meantime, suspended the circulation of the book at considerable pecuniary loss to us both. If your client is not satisfied with this I have no further proposal to offer, and he must now take such further steps in the matter as commend themselves to him.

Yours faithfully

November 4 1921

Dear Sirs,

In answer to your letter of October 27 I write to say that I am willing to agree to the terms you mention provided that your client will accept the alterations in the text suggested by the author, or with the addition of such verbal ones, or small excisions, which I could carry through without further reference to Mr Lawrence. If however your client insists on large sections of the book being removed, I must necessarily refer the matter again to Mr Lawrence, incurring more bother and delay. I am agreeing to the pecuniary part of the affair without reference to the author, simply to settle the matter as soon as possible, and I hope your client will reciprocate. If I am to write Mr Lawrence again a complete list of your client's requirements would be very useful.

Yours faithfully

8th November 1921

Dear Sirs,

I am much obliged for your letter of yesterday and note that your client will accept the alterations of the text of "Women in Love" as already submitted by Mr. Lawrence, with the addition of the substitution of the name "Minette" for "Pussum". I am at once putting in hand a new edition of the book, giving effect to these changes.

I am enclosing my cheque for £60.10., in settlement of Mr. Heseltine's claim and your costs.

Yours faithfully

For a full account of the textual changes in Secker's printings of the novel, see *Women in Love*, ed. David Farmer, Lindeth Vasey and John Worthen (Cambridge University Press, 1987).

2350. To Earl Brewster, 8 October 1921
Text: MS UT; Brewster 29.

Fontana Vecchia, *Taormina*, Sicilia
Sabato. 8 Ottobre 1921

Dear Brewster

I thought to have heard from you – but nothing. I wrote you the next morning after we were back. I forgot to send the Lire 100 – and here it is. I believe it should be a few Liras more, but leave it at the hundred.

My post has brought me nothing nice: no, not one single nice word since I am back. But that doesn't alter things. I am determined to sail away before next March. Where to depends largely on where I can get a ship to. I will hear what you have to say of Ceylon.

My plan is, ultimately, to get a little farm somewhere by myself, in Mexico, New Mexico, Rocky Mountains, or British Columbia. The desire to be away from the body of mankind – to be a bit of a hermit – is paramount. In the old world, even of Buddha, I have no deep hope.[1] But I would like to see it, too, and speak with it.

I would like you and Achsah Brewster and the child[2] to settle somewhere near. I would rather dig a little, and tend a few fruit trees with you, than meditate with you. I would rather we did a bit of quiet manual work together – and spent our days in our own solitude and labour.

There, I think that's the ultimate of what I want. – Tell me how you finally feel.

D. H. Lawrence

I would much rather approach America from the Pacific than from the Atlantic.

I sent you *Psychoanalysis and the Unconscious.* If you were near enough I would like you to read the MS of its sequel – I have it now.

2351. To Robert Mountsier, [8 October 1921]
Text: MS Smith; Unpublished.

Fontana Vecchia, *Taormina*, Sicily
8 October.

Dear M[ountsier]

We are back, thank goodness, and settled in the peace and quiet of our own house.

I had your two letters. About *Aaron's Rod*, I want Seltzer to have it as it stands, and to hear what he says, and I will write to him direct about literary

---

[1] Brewster was engaged in the study of oriental philosophy.
[2] The Brewsters' daughter, Harwood (1912–).

details of it. Whether Secker turns it down or not is all one to me. English publication no longer interests me much.

I am going over the MS. of the new 'Unconscious' book. Think I shall call it 'The Child and the Unconscious'. I have done the introduction – rather amusingly – but don't know if it is any good for magazines. It seems rather useless posting the MS to London first, so if it is all the same, I will send the whole thing direct to Seltzer. – There are about 50 or 52,000 words.

The next thing, I think I will collect my short stories for a book, ready, so that my MSS are in order.

The Brewsters, from Capri, sail for Ceylon in a fortnight. They very much want me to go. They will find me a place, and if it turns out nice, in their idea, I think I'll go, about February. I wish you would send me, please, an exact account of the moneys. Please deduct your own percentage. I wish to know exactly what I have available. Say what sum I ought in any case to leave deposited, for possible expenses occurred in America.

Your movements sound rather uncertain. In case you should go to Russia, or some far-off place, I suppose you will turn over my business to the Curtis Brown American dept. It seems you could hardly handle it from Moscow: and better someone should be on the spot. Let me know about this, please.

Probably you will have seen the Whittleys by now. I was so sorry – so much travelling was really too much for them both.

It is beautiful hot weather here, such a lovely sea, to the east. I feel like going really away.

No news, and nothing new. Frieda sends greetings.

                                                                    DHL

I wish you would post *Aaron* to Seltzer, if you have not yet done so. I will hear what he says before I try Secker at all.

2352. To Amy Lowell, 9 October 1921
Text: MS HU; Damon 576–7.

                                            Fontana Vecchia, *Taormina*, Sicilia
                                                              9 October 1921
My dear Amy

I had your letter forwarded from BadenBaden yesterday – also the cheque for six dollars.[1] I am so sorry you have had such a summer of illness. Have you really not been able to leave your room? I call that bitter. Can you go out now? Deve finire, questo guaio.[2]

---

[1] Amy Lowell had sent DHL a cheque for $6.13, his share of royalties from the anthologies *Some Imagist Poets* (1915–17).   [2] 'It must end, this misfortune'.

Yes, do quote anything you like from my letter, about *Legends*.[1] I said what I felt, for anybody to read or hear.

I agree with you, that American poetry today is better than English.[2] As for me, in direction I am more than half American. I always write really towards America: my listener is there. England has gone all thick and fuzzy in the head, and can't hear. tant pis pour elle![3]

After all the shifting about, we are both so glad to be back here, in silence and peace and sunshine. It is lovely weather. The sun rises day after day red and unhidden out of the sea, after the morning star, which is very bright before he comes. I watch the dawn every day from my bed: but when the suns rim makes the first bit of fire, we get up. – I love the Ionian sea. It is open like a great blue opening in front of us, so delicate and self-contained. The hibiscus flowers are coming again in the garden. I am so thankful to come south. The north just shatters one inside. Even as far as Naples. But south of Naples – from Amalfi – there is the pristine Mediterranean influence, never to be shattered. Such a lovely *morning* world: forever morning. I hate going north – and I hate snow grinning on the tops of mountains. Jamais plus.[4]

When I gather myself together I want to set to work. I only did two poems all the summer – 'Fish' and 'Bat'. But I did 'Harlequinade of the Unconscious.'[5]

Have you done your Chinese book?[6] I shall be interested to see that.

I am thankful to be at rest for the moment – but feel more than ever come loose from all moorings. I suppose I shall really leave Europe. But feel very mistrustful of the States. Wohin?[7] We shall see.

I do hope you will be better, and able to go about and taste the world. After all, one's writing is only for when there is nothing nicer to be done.

Do you have any feeling about Mexico? I have an idea I should like to go there – and have some little place in the country, with a goat and a bit of a garden. But my compass-needle is a shifty devil.

Greet Mrs Russell from us both. It must be sad for her too, if you can't go out. Be better – be on your feet, thats the chief.

saluti cari   D. H. Lawrence

---

[1] See Letter 2299.
[2] In her letter of 7 September, Amy Lowell said that contemporary American poetry was superior to the English, with the exception of DHL's own (Damon 574).
[3] 'So much the worse for her!' [4] 'Never again.'
[5] I.e. *Fantasia of the Unconscious.*
[6] *Fir-Flower Tablets* (New York, 1921), translations by Florence Ayscough and Amy Lowell of Chinese poems. [7] 'Whither?'

2353. To Violet Monk, 12 October 1921
Text: MS SIU; Nehls, ii. 79–81.

Fontana Vecchia, *Taormina*, Sicilia
12 October 1921

Dear Monk

I wanted to write sooner, of course. But we only got back about ten days ago, and then my cheque-book was empty and I had to write for a new one: which arrived yesterday. – Thank you so much for doing the 'Gentleman' and sending him off. If you think a pound is right, then I am sure it is. I am sorry I have been so long – but I waited from day to day, as one does.

I wonder what you have called your bungalow. Rome is too big. Call it Capricorn, the sign of the Goat – or The Triangle, for its three inmates – or call it after a tree, if it's got a nice tree – The Pear Tree, the Fir Tree, The Maple Tree: – or call it Coney Grey if it's got rabbits: or Thorny Croft, if it's got thorns; or Whin Meadows, if it's got gorse like the last: or Maiden Place if you want to make a joke on yourselves. Do call it Maiden Place.

We are so thankful to be back and settled down a bit – arrived so tired and battered after so many journeys. Another year I simply will not do it.

It is lovely here: brilliant sun all day long, and perfect warm nights with the moon just leaving the sea. It seems like July was, further north. No end to the summer this year. I am hoping really to do some work, but don't feel much like it.

I wish I could send you something for the new house. Only the post is such a curse. I suppose you have got furniture more than enough.

You sound a groggy couple[1] as far as health goes. You want somebody to make you both real cross, twice a day, and the sciatica and the rheumatism would go. But Berkshire is a dozy country. I feel my summer travels didn't do much more than put me in a perfect fury with everything. But then that's the effect most things have on me. The older I get, the angrier I become, generally. And Italy is a country to keep you in a temper from day to day: the people, I mean.

Here they are waiting for the rains, to plough and to sow the seeds and put in potatoes and everything. But luckily it rained a good deal in September, so we have spinach and cabbages and carrots. At the moment it doesn't look as if it would ever rain again. – We are eating the last figs and grapes and melons: and the first pomegranates. But the damned goats are all going to have kids, so there's no milk. And there's never any butter, except tinned, from Milan.

Well, I hope it is still summery at Hermitage. This is a lovely time there, when there are chestnuts and the woods are yellow. Do you remember

[1] See p. 28 n. 4.

when we went to Evie Burgess' for tea[1] – after finding rather little chestnuts? It seems so much darker and colder, even to think of it. – We don't dream of a fire yet: cook on just a handful of charcoal, which you fan with a fan to make it hot: and even that makes the kitchen too warm.

Greet the Lambert. Tell her she is not to look lamentable over her glasses. Greet also Miss Furlong, who is the only brisk one among you.[2] And don't you hobble about like a witch in gaiters.

D. H. Lawrence

2354. To Edward Garnett, 17 October 1921
Text: MS NYPL; Postmark, Taormina 18 OTT 21; Huxley 525–6.

Fontana Vecchia, *Taormina*. Sicily.

17 Oct. 1921

Dear Garnett[3]

We got back here two weeks ago, and found the book, *Grenzen der Seele*, and your letter.[4] I'm so sorry there are all these months of delay.

I think *Grenzen der Seele* is really very interesting. But you know I'm the last person in the world to judge as to what other people will like. Lucka's study of Grenz-leute – the border-line people – as contrasted with the middle-people seems to me very illuminating and fertile. The Grenzleute are those who are on the verge of human understanding, and who widen the frontiers of human knowledge all the time – and the frontiers of life. Strange, rather fascinating studies of Dostoevsky, Shakspeare, Goethe etc. Quite fascinating if you like to read such books. But I've no idea *what* England likes to read, really. – I won't write direct to Cape now[5] – it seems so late, and I don't want the guinea. – The only person Lucka really reverences at all is the genius, and reverences him the more according to the degree of purity of his genius, reverences him less according to the degree of his practicality. So he doesn't think very highly of Napoleon – a Mittelmensch[6] – and *very* highly of Shakspeare and Dostoevsky.

---

[1] Possibly either Evelyn Burgess of Hye or the wife of Ralph Burgess of Hermitage (see Nehls, ii. 466).

[2] 'The dancing and gym mistress at Hermitage who occasionally stayed with Miss Cecily Lambert and Miss Violet Monk at Grimsbury Farm' (Nehls, ii. 466).

[3] Edward Garnett (1868–1937), critic, essayist and dramatist; literary adviser to the publishing firm of Duckworth; and DHL's close friend and patron during his early years as a writer. (See *Letters*, i. 15–18, 297 n, 2; ii. 4–7.) m. 1889, Constance Black (1861–1946); she became a renowned translator of Russian literature.

[4] Emil Lucka (1877–1941) first published his *Grenzen der Seele* in 1916; it had recently been reissued (1920).   [5] The publisher Jonathan Cape Ltd.

[6] A term invented to mean 'mediocre genius' in contradistinction to the Nietzschean 'Übermensch' or 'superman'.

I was glad to hear from you again – wonder what you are doing – still looking after books, pruning them and re-potting them, I know.

I had heard about Bunny's shop, but his marriage, no.[1] So please write by return and say who she is and when the marriage took place and where the wedding was and is there a little Bunny by now and is Mrs Garnett pleased and are you and do you flirt with your daughter-in-law? If you don't, then something is seriously wrong. Because I always think of you when a hornet hovers round the jam pots after one has made jam. Only you're all Badger-grey instead of striped. But a humming wasp all the same.

I still feel battered after all the summer travels. Oh, travelling is hell – trains etc. And the north always makes me feel just weak and hopeless. It's a *dreadful* muddle. I'm so thankful to be back in the south beyond the Straits of Messina, in the shadow of Etna, and with the Ionian Sea in front: the lovely, lovely dawn-sea where the sun does nothing but rise. Somehow my heart seems to escape out into the open Ionian sea, towards Greece, in the morning – past, and towards the east. Thank heaven I need not look north, towards England or middle Europe.

I am collecting a book of short stories. *Do please* send me that 'Primrose Path' story, and anything else you have.[2] Or let them be typed out and send me the bill and the typed copies. I should be so much obliged. The 'Primrose Path' story has never been published, and is probably good for a hundred dollars in America. I'll share them with you when I get them.

Frieda sends many greetings. Will you ever come this way?

D. H. Lawrence

Greet Bunny from me – and all nice proper congratulations from us both.

I hear I am in worse odour than ever, for *Women in Love*. But pah, what do I care for all the canaille.

Tell me David's address, and I'll send him a little present, just to keep him in mind that such tiresome people as ourselves are still in the world with him.

DHL

[1] Edward Garnett's son, David ('Bunny') (1892–1981) had enjoyed a close relationship with DHL and Frieda. He was later novelist, editor and autobiographer (see *Letters*, i. 315 n. 1); shortly after the war he, with Francis ('Frankie') Birrell (1889–1935), had opened a bookshop in London (see *Flowers of the Forest*, 1955, pp. 202 ff). m. Rachel Marshall, March 1921.

[2] DHL had asked Garnett for the MS of 'Primrose Path' (later published in *England, My England and Other Stories*, New York, 1922) as long ago as December 1913 (see *Letters*, ii. 127, 133).

2355. To Achsah Brewster, [18? October 1921]
Text: MS UT; Brewster 31–3.

Taormina.
Tuesday

Dear Achsah Brewster
 Ach! ach Gott! – tiresome name to spell you've got. – I had your diminutive
letter, and thought it was a wedding-card. – Suppose you're feeling really
rather high and mighty, now you're actually off East.
 Well – your Taormina friends are storming over your departure. Miss
Fisher thinks it's *madness*, madness.[1] I say 'Why?' – and she replies
ambiguously: 'For Achsah! It may be all right for *him*, but for Achsah it's
madness.' – Again I say why – and all the answer is 'Has *she* got this Buddha-
business on the brain as well?' I say just a touch, whereupon Miss Fisher goes
ttt! – *madness*!! – She was in a great state in the train after having seen
Brewster: raging up and down – and I had all my work to prevent her getting
out at Battipaglia and places whose names even shouldn't be on the map, in the
night and the pouring rain, to come back to *Earl*. 'I can't go without seeing
Earl again – I can't, I simply can-NOT.' And brandishing her fist while the
Italians made goo-goo eyes.
 Ah well, she's dismissed it all again as *Madness* now. She came here one
evening: and my, how she grumbles about everything. It's really almost
funny. She also had a tea-party, Wood and Rosalie and us:[2] so of course
somebody underneath practised the pianoforte in a most rudimentary fashion
all the while. – 'Can you bear it *another* instant?' – 'What Miss Fisher?' – 'Why
that AW-ful noise! – Did you EVER! I hate the place. I simply HATE the
place. And I hate the PEOPLE – Oh my! – And the flies! Aren't the flies
simply AWful . . !'
 On Sunday Wood had a tea-party – with a now famous Taormina violinist
who has returned from the Chicago region, his wife having died. Everybody
was there – Bowdwin, Josephine May, Rosalie, Baron Stempel, the Ciccio
Atenasios and a whole crowd.[3] Wood's house is getting more gilded and
stuccoed every day. The Taormina 'artist' played 'The Rosary'! con
moltissimo espressione, till I thought his fiddle-strings were turning thick as

---

[1] Elizabeth ('Bessie') Fisher, a close friend of the Brewsters, described by Harwood Brewster
   Picard as 'very mannish in her dress and bearing (for those days)'.
[2] Wood was a rather impecunious American painter regarded as an amusing member of the
   expatriate community in Taormina; Rosalie Bull (d. 1922?), an Englishwoman and friend of the
   Brewsters, had founded a Theosophical Society in the town. See *Letters*, iii. 506 n. 5, 636 n. 1.
[3] Bowdwin (d. 1943?), a wealthy American who had studied in Italy, now lived in Rocca Bella
   which DHL knew well from the days when it was owned by Marie Hubrecht. Stempel, who
   originated in Baltic Russia, is remembered as a homosexual. The others named have not been
   identified. See *Letters*, iii. 506 n. 5, 637 n. 1.

salsiccia¹ with emotion. Poor darling, his wife has lately died. She used to accompany him on the piano, with so much *feeling*, said Giuseppina May, that, poor thing, she was nothing but a shadow. And now she isn't even that. – Well, it was awful. – Then poor Bowdwin in a pale yellow summer suit and a black vulcanite sort of port-hole over his left eye, through the window of which his poor murdered eye looks something awful: like a dreadful ghost of a one-eye, all discolored and scarred, looking through a window.

Frieda is now raging round me. We've got to go to tea to Rosalies. She's having a sort of 'welcome-all'. I'll write to Ceylon and tell you how it 'transpires'.

I shan't say anything about goodbyeing. But write soon and say how it is.

D. H. Lawrence

[Frieda Lawrence begins]

And I have never written and thanked you and told all the things I wanted to say, but we have talked of you and thought of you, with that gentle nut of a Miss Fisher, with her hard shell and sweet-kernel. Taormina is disturbed about your journey – and of course Lorenzo and I have packed up with you – We wanted to send you books but thought you would curse for more luggage – So here goes –

Frieda

2356. To Earl Brewster, [18? October 1921]
Text: MS UT; Brewster 30–1.

Fontana Vecchia, *Taormina*, Sicilia
Tuesday

Dear Brewster

Well, you are packed up, apparently, and on your way. I had your second letter just this minute – also Mrs Brewster's. Santa Lucia seems quite a long stride, really, if 4 Venti is *left* behind.² Ach Gott, that first stride of clearing out of one's house genuinely *costs*.

Here we sit: the rain has begun: and I feel rather gloomy. – Europe is my own continent, so I feel bad about it. I feel as if it was dying under my eyes. Maybe it isn't at all: but I get the feeling just the same, you see. It's almost precisely as if somebody were dying: one's mother, for example. One's unconscious simply bristles and listens for death. That is how Taormina, Italy, all affects me since summer. So when I leave Europe, I feel I want to go for ever.

¹ 'sausage'. ('The Rosary', a very popular song by the American composer, Ethelbert Nevin, 1862–1901, is excessively sentimental.)
² 'Torre dei Quattro Venti' was the house in which the Brewsters lived on the island of Capri, built by the American artist Elihu Vedder (1836–1923).

As a good omen, I was that very instant dreaming in my siesta dream that you had written from *Ceylon* and that it was lovely, lovely there – when the banging of the espresso boy on my door woke me. And I was just in some odd way seeing Ceylon myself. Let's hope we'll tie the broken end of the dream to reality.

I will write to you to Ceylon. I wish you had had time to read my *Fantasia of the Unconscious* before you went. I've just finished correcting it. – Write to me *quickly* from Ceylon, and tell me first impressions, and if one could live there cheaply enough. I'm sure upper Ceylon is lovely. – I'm rather inclined to think, myself, that people matter more than place. But the east seems to me the world to meditate in, Europe the world to *feel* in, America the world to act in.

But I don't feel very sure about anything.

I will write quite often.

D. H. Lawrence

2357. To Robert Mountsier, 18 October 1921
Text: MS Smith; Postmark, Taormina 19 OTT 21; Unpublished.

Fontana Vecchia, *Taormina*, Sicily
18 Oct 1921

Dear Mountsier

I don't know what has become of the little Charleroi cheques that you gave me:[1] I had them always safely with my passports, but now I cant find them at all. So will you check off their numbers and stop them at the bank. I shall also write to Mr Hastings now. We may as well be quite safe. – Stupid of me to have lost them – but there we are!

I want to get properly into touch with my American money, because I really want to sail away somewhere this winter – or early spring.

I haven't heard from you in answer to my last letter: the mail is very slow.

I have quite done the 'Unconscious' book – think of calling it *Fantasia of the Unconscious*. Seltzer can vary it if he likes.

I don't feel much like work. Am collecting short stories to make a book any time, and to get my MSS in order. Basil Blackwell of Oxford asked me if I couldn't give *him* a vol. of short stories. You know he is doing 'Wintry Peacock' in his *New Decameron* series[2] – in January presumably – and I engaged not to put this story into a volume for another year. – It is possible Blackwell might do *Psychoanalysis* – he is 49 Broad Street, Oxford.

[1] I.e. cheques drawn on the Charleroi Savings and Trust Co., Charleroi, Pennsylvania. 'Mr Hastings' mentioned later was an official of the bank. Letters written to Mr Hastings, and to the bank on 26 October 1921 (Tedlock, *Lawrence MSS* 93), have not survived.
[2] See p. 31 n. 1.

The autumn rains are just beginning. The residents are just coming back: teaparties in full swing this week.

I saw the *John Bull* attack. Don't give a fig for the canaille.

What are you really doing all the winter – Wonder if you are still in London, and if you have seen the Whittleys. I haven't heard from them since they are back and am a bit uneasy because we left her rather seedy in Naples.

F[rieda] sends greetings.

D. H. Lawrence

2358. To Thomas Seltzer, 22 October 1921
Text: MS UT; Postmark, Taormina 22 OTT 21; Lacy, *Seltzer* 27.

Fontana Vecchia, Taormina, Sicily.
22 October 1921

Dear Seltzer

I am sending you today the MS. of *Fantasia of the Unconscious*: also an introduction,[1] a reply to some critics of *Psychoanalysis and the Unconscious*; – and a small introduction to *Aaron's Rod*. – As for a title, I don't mind if you alter it to something else. – The introduction you might like to publish in some magazine – do as you think well. – I think, if any book of mine is going to make your fortune, this *Fantasia* will be the one. – You may think differently.

I hear from Mountsier that he is posting you *Aaron's Rod*. I hope you won't dislike it as much as he does. – But I want you to publish it about as it stands. I will make any small modification you wish. So write at once. You won't think of publishing it before spring. I don't want you to. – I promise you, it is the last of my 'serious' novels.

I haven't heard from you for a long time – about two months. Mountsier writes that book business is very bad in America, and that we're all going to the devil. Vogue la galère.[2]

Let me hear from you.

D. H. Lawrence

2359. To Catherine Carswell, [24 October 1921]
Text: MS YU; cited in Carswell 156.

Fontana Vecchia, Taormina, Sicilia
Monday. 25 October

My dear Catherine

So they don't like your *Camomile* at all![3] – It may be the name, you know. Perhaps if you called it Gingerbread they'd sup it up like anything. To hell with them all, anyhow. But tell me the latest about it. I am always interested. – Their wry faces make me want the more to read the MS. Why ever didn't you bring it along?

[1] DHL is referring to the 'Foreword': see p. 86 n. 4.   [2] 'Come what may.'
[3] See p. 52 n. 3.

I have had Secker very sick, over the *John Bull* article, and still worse, over a fellow who wants to bring a libel action because he says he's Halliday.[1] Don't know how it will all end. Snotty little lot of people.

I bet you were glad to get back. Travelling is peculiarly disheartening this year, I find. Not so much the inconveniences as the kind of slow poison one breathes in every new atmosphere. – I didn't like Siena a bit. We had rather a lovely day in Rome, drove far out on the Campagna. – I was sick in Capri. – And now the very sight of a train makes me jib. – Yet I wouldn't pretend to be serenely content. You wouldn't believe me if I did. Italy has for some reason gone a little rancid in my mouth. May be just my mouth. And probably Italy – or Sicily anyhow – is better than any other place even then. But I can't get the little taste of canker out of my mouth. The people – .

Here of course it is like a continual Mad Hatters tea-party. If you'll let it be, it is all teaparty – and you wonder who on earth is going head over heels into the teapot next. On Saturday we were summoned to a gathering of Britons to discuss the erection of an English church here, at the estimated cost of £25,000 sterling – signed Bronte: which means of course Alec Nelson Hood, Duca di Bronte.[2] I didn't go, fearing they might ask me for the £25000.

I am not very busy: just pottering with short stories. Think I may as well get the MSS together as far as possible. Feel like making my will also. Not that I'm going to die. But to give myself a nice sense of finality. – Ask Don which regiment of Scots wears the tight tartan trews: the quite tight ones: if they wear them still, and if not, when they left off: if they wore them at all in the wartime: and if the officers also had them. I want a man in those tight trews in a story.[3] – Also will you tell me *what* then was the secret of the Etruscans, which you saw written so plainly in the place you went to? Please dont forget to tell me, as they really do rather puzzle me, the Etruscans.

It is marvellous weather – I hear also in England. The place is very beautiful, and we go some rather fascinating walks into the country. But I don't really give a damn for any blooming thing. I haven't heard from my sister, so don't know if she has fetched her plates:[4] I hope so. Did you hate carrying them? – I never thanked that man for the Lady Gregory plays.[5] But do you know I *can't* read dear Lady Gregory: too much of an insipid old stew. I have only been reading Giovanni Verga lately. He exercises quite a fascination on me, and makes me feel quite sick at the end. But perhaps that is only if one

[1] See p. 87 n. 1.   [2] See p. 51 n. 3

[3] The story was 'The Captain's Doll' and the information Carswell provided may account for the fact that the regiment is not identified in the story, and for the statement in the Secker edition, chap. 11: 'none of the English officers, or rather Scottish, wear the close-fitting tartan trews any more – except for fancy dress' (p. 179).   [4] See Letter 2345.

[5] Augusta, Lady Gregory (1852–1932) wrote many plays for the Irish National Theatre, which she co-founded with William Butler Yeats (1865–1939).

knows Sicily. – Do you know if he is translated into English? – *I. Malavoglia* or *Mastro-don Gesualdo* – or *Novelle Rusticane* or the other short stories.¹ It would be fun to do him – his *language* is so fascinating.

Tell me about the *Camomile* – and I hope all is well and happy. Greet Don. I must say I quite frequently sympathise with his point of view. Answer me my questions, and say what you are doing.

D. H. Lawrence

2360. To Benjamin Huebsch, 28 October 1921
Text: MS UT; Unpublished.

Fontana Vecchia, Taormina, Sicily
28 October 1921

Dear Huebsch

I heard you had out a new edition of the *Rainbow*.² I wonder how it went. Will you tell me.

Will you also send me a couple of copies of the book here, if there is nothing to prevent your doing so?

Yours   D. H. Lawrence

2361. To Robert Mountsier, [31 October 1921]
Text: MS Smith; Postmark, Taormina 1 NOV 21; Unpublished.

Fontana Vecchia, Taormina, Sicilia
Monday 31 Oct.

Dear M[ountsier]

Your letter of 24th today. I will send this express and it may get you. – I am

---

¹ *I Malavoglia* (1881), *Mastro-don Gesualdo* (1889) and *Novelle Rusticane* (1883) by Giovanni Verga (1840–1922). DHL later published translations of Verga: *Mastro-don Gesualdo* (1923); *Little Novels of Sicily* (1925); *Cavalleria Rusticana and Other Stories* (1928).

² The first American edition (an expurgated text) was published by Huebsch in New York on 30 November 1915. The edition to which DHL is referring is clarified in Huebsch's reply (TMSC LC), 22 November 1921:

Dear Lawrence,
  Yours of October 28th has just come. Yes, I did issue another edition of "The Rainbow". I am pretty sure that I told Mr. Mountsier that I would do this.
  To reprint and distribute the book in the regular course of business would have been to invite suppression, because there is no doubt that our unofficial censors would welcome the opportunity to stamp out the book. Instead, therefore, I canvassed the trade and took subscriptions for about 1000 copies. . . .
  Owing to the fact that the edition was limited, there seemed to be some justification in making the price higher than for a regular edition, but under no circumstances is there any excuse for highway robbery, so I made the retail price of the book $5.00.
  I have kept a very few copies, and I am glad to be able to comply with your request for two, which I now send you by registered post.

Yours

glad you are going back to America. What's the good of Europe, anyhow. – It is still highly probable that we shall appear in the spring. Brewster sailed a week ago for Ceylon. But I don't much want to go east. Probably we shall come to the States.

You must send me also a cheque book from New York. I shall have to draw some money unless somebody pays me something in England. I have only forty-odd pounds in the bank: don't want suddenly to find myself penniless. – Did you sell any of your Liras this summer – ? you really should have done.

Yesterday came from Seltzer the October *Dial*, with a piece of *Sea and Sardinia*, very much cut up.[1] Damn them for that. Last week Ruth Wheelock – of the Amer. Consulate in Palermo – arrived back from New York.[2] She had seen Seltzer. He is bringing out *Sea and Sardinia* at the end of this month, at $5. a copy.[3] Why don't *you* tell me this news? And why doesn't Seltzer send me *proofs* even if he doesn't wait to have them back corrected. I like to see them. Why are people so annoying. I hear also he has *Tortoises* ready.[4] Why the hell didn't he send me a copy by Miss Wheelock? – I have no word from him for six weeks or more. – I expect Miss Wheelock over from Palermo this weekend, shall hear the latest news from her.

I am doing the stories rather desultorily. Have just got 'The Horse-Dealer's Daughter' back from the typist in Florence:[5] it's a new story, or an old one rewritten 7000 words.[6] Will send it you to New York. – Also am just at the end of quite a different story – 'The Captains Doll' – about 16 or 20,000 words I should think – long.[7] Will send you that also when it's typed. I sent Seltzer direct the *Fantasia of the Unconscious* (provisional title) with introduction answering critics. I don't know whether I shall finish *Mr Noon*. I get so annoyed with everybody that I don't want to tackle any really serious work. To hell with them all. Miserable world of canaille.

– Now I was interrupted in this letter, so it won't get you in London, and I shall send it to N. York. – Please send me a detailed account of everything doing in America. I want to know exactly what is being published and what

---

[1] Excerpts from the essays 'As Far as Palermo' and 'The Sea' appeared in *Dial*, lxxi (October 1921), 441–51 and from 'Cagliari', 'Mandas', 'To Sorgono' and 'To Nuoro' in lxxi (November 1921), 583–92.

[2] Ruth Wheelock (1891–1958), a secretary in the American Consulate, was DHL's typist for *Sea and Sardinia*, *Mr Noon*, etc; she had also participated in his fruitless search for a boat (see *Letters*, iii. 698–9).

[3] The book was actually published on 12 December 1921.

[4] Seltzer published *Tortoises* on 9 December 1921.   [5] Florence] Palermo

[6] The story was originally entitled 'The Miracle' and was first mentioned in a letter of 12 January 1917 (see *Letters*, iii. 74 and n. 2; see also Tedlock, *Lawrence MSS* 93). DHL's typist for this and several later MSS (including 'The Captain's Doll') was Mrs Carmichael.

[7] The story was included in the volume entitled *The Ladybird*, published by Secker, March 1923, and *The Captain's Doll* when published by Seltzer, 21 April 1923.

isn't. Pinker and Huebsch always kept me in the dark, and I wont have it.

Heseltine is altogether a shady bird: too shady, I should say, to risk himself and his precious wife in court.

Is Curtis Brown doing anything with *Sea and Sardinia* in England? What is Secker's attitude to it?[1] Shall we let him have it without pictures, if he won't have it with? – or shall we not?

And what about Thayer and the *Gentleman from S[an] Francisco* story? Have you heard anything more?

We have just been trying the new Fontana Vecchia wine: though it shouldn't be tried till Novem 11th. – I dont like it very much – it's going to be *rough*. I'm glad I had a barrel of last years from the Vigna Spagnuola.

Greet America from me.

D. H. Lawrence

2362. To Earl Brewster, 2 November 1921
Text: MS UT; Brewster 33–7.

Fontana Vecchia, *Taormina*, Sicilia
2 Novem 1921.

Dear Brewster

Yours and Achsah's from beyond Crete received today: and by coincidence, one from Alpha.[2] So the family voice was uplifted in one strain on this feast-day of All-Souls. Anyhow you've got as far as Port Said.

No, I don't understand a bit what you mean about rightness and about relationships and about the world. Damn the world, anyhow. And I hate 'understanding' people, and I hate more still to be understood. Damn understanding more than anything. I refuse to understand you. Therefore you can say what you like, without a qualm, and never bother to alter it. I shan't understand.

I do wonder what Ceylon is like. The ship sounds rather fun, if rather awful. Of course I should have to make those Australian two-legged organs tune up a bit if I was there. I believe they think they're most awfully IT.

I've been in a hell of a temper for three weeks: blank refused to see anybody after the Fisher's last visit: and only the Baron Stempel came and gave me a headache. I begrudged him his tea: and detested him. I've been so disagreeable to old Grace, rooking me, that now she creeps about as if a dagger was at her neck. I've written such very spiteful letters to everybody that now the postman never comes. And I believe even the old Capra[3] doesn't have her belated kid for fear I pounce on her. – But it is a world of *canaille*: absolutely.

[1] He published an edition of the book with illustrations in April 1923.
[2] Alpha Barlow.   [3] 'Goat'.

Canaille, canaglia, Schweinhunderei,[1] stink-pots. Pfui! – pish, pshaw, prrr! They all stink in my nostrils.

That's how I feel in Taormina, let the Ionian sea have fits of blueness if it likes, and Calabria twinkle like seven jewels, and the white trumpet-tree under the balcony perfume six heavens with sweetness. That's how I feel. A curse, a murrain, a pox on this crawling, sniffling, spunkless brood of humanity.

So, what's it like in Ceylon? I'd much rather go to Mars or the Moon. But Ceylon if there's nothing better. Is everybody there as beshitten as here? I'll bet they are.

There isn't any news, so don't ask for any. I believe Seltzer is bringing out my *Sea and Sardinia* book just now: and poems called *Tortoises*. I finished the *Unconscious* book and sent it to America with a foreword answering some of my darling critics. Called it provisionally *Fantasia of the Unconscious*. – Call it *Fantasia* to prevent anybody tying themselves into knots trying to 'understand' it. Since when I did up a short story, and suddenly wrote a very funny long story called 'The Captains Doll' – which I haven't finished yet. But I have just got it high up in the mountains of the Tyrol, and don't quite know how to get it down without breaking its neck. – If I hadn't my own stories to amuse myself with I should die, chiefly of spleen.

This afternoon I have got to go into paese for the first time for ten days, to buy some things. If I die before I get back, you'll hear by the next post, maybe.

Today is Tutti i Morti.[2] Last night the cemetery was lit up with bunches of light like yellow crocuses. Carmelo of course, vestal that he is, was trimming the two lamps before his father's pidgeon-hole, and waiting on guard lest anyone stole the said lamps, which, according to Grazia,[3] are finissime, ma belle, di cristallo intagliato – sa – non ci sono altre cosi in tutto il cimitero, no signore, ne in Taormina tutta.[4] She leans on the parapet of our balcony – spaventata[5] – terrified of the ghost of her poor dead Beppe. She has never been in the cemetery since he died: and only twice has prevailed on herself even to pass the cemetery wall. What had she done to him, that she fears his avenging spirit so deeply? The bitch – She comes sheltering under my wing because, I suppose, she thinks I'm such another tyrant and nuisance, such as he was.

I have been reading Giovanni Verga's Sicilian novels and stories. Do you

---

[1] 'Rabble, swineherd's dog', i.e. dirty wretches.

[2] '[Day of] All the Dead', i.e. All Souls' Day. On the eve of this holiday, candles are lit in cemeteries to commemorate the dead

[3] Grazia Cacópardo was the mother of Carmelo (d. 1957), Francesco ('Ciccio'), DHL's landlord at Fontana Vecchia, and Francesca ('Ciccia').

[4] 'the finest, but beautiful, of carved crystal – you know – there are no other such things in the whole cemetery, no Signore, not in all of Taormina.'   [5] 'frightened'.

know them? When once one gets into his really rather difficult style (to me), he is very interesting. The only Italian who does interest me. I'll send you some if you like – But probably you'll be reading Sanscrit and speaking Cinghalese by now.

I don't know anything about the future. My stock of English money is almost gone. England will provide me no more. I await Mountsier's arrival in America, and then he will tell me how many dollars are to my name. I hope about 2500 or 3000. I feel at the moment I don't care where I live, that people are bloody swine – or bloodless swine everywhere – and here at least I have a fair space of land and sea to myself. But if you tempt me one little bit I'll splash my way to Ceylon. Be sure though and tell me how much a house costs, and a pound of bacon and a dozen eggs. Don't be on a damned high Bhuddistic plane. I'm in no mood to stand it. – And if you do come back to Europe, come to Sicily, not to Capri.

Tell Achsah B[rewster] that I am grateful for the news of the Vail veil – or loin-cloth. Does she then think that my own fig-leaf is too diminutive? and does her modesty alone prevent her telling me so. Oh fie!

We saw Earl photographs, and Achsah photographs, and Schaler photo-graphs,[1] and a whole wall-paper-pattern of Harwood photographs at the Fisher's. – Tempi passati vostri! ma son' tristi, questa tempi passati: o troppo passati, o non abbastanza.[2]

I will write again when a gentle spirit moves me.

> – What though the spring breezes blow soft on Ceylon's isle.
> Though every prospect pleases, and only man is vile.[3]

                                        riverderci   D. H. Lawrence

2363. To Mabel Dodge Sterne, 5 November 1921
Text: Luhan 5–7.

                              Fontana Vecchia, Taormina, Sicily
                              5th November, 1921

Dear Mabel Dodge Sterne[4]

I had your letter this afternoon and read it going down Corso: and smelt the

---

[1] Fred Shaler, an American artist, friend of the Brewsters. He and Earl Brewster had been students together in New York.

[2] 'Your time is past! ah but I am sad, this time is past: either too much past, or not enough.'

[3] 'From Greenland's Icy Mountains', the famous hymn by Bishop Reginald Heber (1783–1826) ['. . . spicy breezes . . . o'er Ceylon's . . .'].

[4] Mabel Dodge Sterne, née Ganson (1879–1962), wealthy American patron of the arts, who (with her third husband) had gone to join the art colony at Taos, New Mexico, and urged DHL to do likewise. m. (1) Carl Evans, 1900 (2) Edwin Dodge, 1903 (3) Maurice Sterne, 1916 (4) Tony Luhan, 1923. Author of *Lorenzo in Taos* (New York, 1932).

Indian scent, and nibbled the medicine: the last being like licorice root, the scent being a wistful dried herb.

Truly, the q-b and I would like to come to Taos[1] – there are no little bees. I think it is quite feasible. I think I have enough dollars in America to get us there. Are you practical enough to tell me how much it would cost, per month, for the q-b and myself to keep house in Taos? We are *very* practical, do all our own work, even the washing, cooking, floor-cleaning and everything here in Taormina: because I loathe servants creeping around. They poison the atmosphere. So I prefer to wash my own shirt, etc. And I *like* doing things. – Secondly, is there a colony of rather dreadful sub-arty people? – But even if there is, it couldn't be worse than Florence. – Thirdly, are your Indians dying out, and is it rather sad? – Fourthly, what do the sound, *prosperous* Americans do in your region? – Fifthly, how does one get there? What is the nearest port? I might get a cargo boat to bring us, from Palermo.

I believe I've heard of Taos, and even seen pictures of it, photographs – at Leo Stein's house in Settignano.[2] Have I? And are you a relative of the Maurice Sterne, artist, who was at Anticoli this summer?[3] I've only heard of him.

I believe what you say – one must somehow bring together the two ends of humanity, our own thin end, and the last dark strand from the previous, pre-white era. I verily believe that. Is Taos the place?

I have already written the second book to *Psychoanalysis and the Unconscious*, and posted the MS. to Seltzer, – called, provisionally, *Fantasia of the Unconscious*. I am satisfied with it for what it is. But it is the third book, which I have still to write, and which I can't write yet, not till I have crossed another border, it is this that will really matter. To me, I mean. I feel hopeless about the public. Not that I care about them. I want to live my life, and say my say, and the public can die its own death in its own way, just as it likes.

I think we may leave here in January or February. I think we will come to Taos. Write me what advice or instructions you think necessary, by return. I should have your letter by the new year.

I want to leave Europe. I want to take the next step. Shall it be Taos? – I like the *word*. It's a bit like Taormina.

D. H. Lawrence

[1] DHL refers to Frieda as 'the queen bee' or 'the q-b' in *Sea and Sardinia* which Mabel Sterne had recently read (Luhan 4).
[2] Leo Stein (1872–1947), brother of Gertrude Stein (1874–1946), American expatriate and collector of contemporary art, author of *Appreciations* (1947). DHL had met him in Settignano in late 1919 (see *Letters*, iii. 463).
[3] Her husband, Maurice Sterne (1878–1957), painter and sculptor.

We could sail from any Italian port, or even from Malta.

Do you know anything about ships from New Orleans or Galveston or anywhere near? I should really like to miss New York, for the first shot. If you should find it worth while to cable I'll pay when I arrive – or send cheque. – I would prefer to sail in January – don't know why. – Are there any trees? Is there any water? – stream, river, lake? – How far are you from El Paso or from Santa Fe. I don't see Taos on the map.

DHL

If possible I would not go to New York: perhaps Galveston, Texas, or Los Angeles. Please say.

DHL

Please don't tell anybody that we think of coming to Taos. Shall we bring any household things? – sheets, towels, etc.? How warm must the clothing be? How cold, and how hot is Taos?

The man who does most things for me is

Robert Mountsier, 417 West 118 Street, New York.

He might write you.

2364. To Robert Mountsier, [6 November 1921]
Text: MS Smith; Postmark, Taormina 7 11 21; Unpublished.

Fontana Vecchia, Taormina, Sicily
Sunday. 6 Novem.

Dear M[ountsier]

I had a letter yesterday from Mabel Dodge Sterne – do you know who she is? – from *Taos, New Mexico*: do you know anything about that? – She says she can give us a *house* there, and everything we need. And I think it is there I should like to go.

Write me at once what you think.

I should like to sail if possible in January or early February. Do you know anything about a cargo boat that might take us from Palermo, Naples, or any Italian port or even – Malta or Marseilles – to New Orleans or Galveston Texas or somewhere there?

Be sure and send me cheques so that I can have some money: and perhaps, if it were safe, even 1000 dollars in *notes*. I am getting very low in English. Have had to buy clothes.

I have finished 'The Captain's Doll': good, but I don't know if it will sell. You would come to Taos to see us. – Be sure and answer at once.

D. H. Lawrence

If you like to write to M D Sterne, her address is just Taos, New Mexico.

2365. To Martin Secker, [8 November 1921]
Text: MS UInd; Postmark, Taormina 8 NOV 21; Secker 44.

Fontana Vecchia, *Taormina*. Sicilia
9 Nov 1921

Dear Secker

I return the solicitor's letter.[1] I should think the most likely thing is that Heseltine is trying to blackmail you. It is quite in character. And then he would like to draw some limelight on to himself. He is an impossible person. But money is at the bottom of it. And I'd see him in several hells first.

But I'm sorry you have the annoyance. It must be so, however, while the world is full of Canaille.

Best wishes   D. H. Lawrence[2]

2366. To S. S. Koteliansky, [10 November 1921]
Text: MS BL; Moore 672-3.

Fontana Vecchia, *Taormina*, Sicilia
10 Novem.

My dear Kot

I have meant day after day to write. But this summer my whole will-to-correspond has collapsed.

I had yours about Thayer. Did he ever properly acknowledge yours? And he ought to have paid you by now. I wonder if you are hard up. If you are, you won't hesitate to tell me, will you. My English money is at the last crumbs, but thank goodness I've got some dollars in America – when Mountsier will put me into touch with them. So just let me know if you are in need.

Mountsier I suppose has gone back to New York. He is one of those irritating people who have generalised detestations: his particular ones being Jews, Germans, and Bolshevists. So unoriginal. He got on my nerves badly in Germany.

[1] See p. 94 n. 1.
[2] Secker replied on 15 November 1921 (Secker Letter-Book, UIll):

Dear Lawrence,
    Many thanks for yours of the 9th. Since I wrote last I have had protracted negotiations and correspondence with the solicitors. It was necessary to come to some decision without delay, and the matter has now been settled by the payment of £50 damages and £10.10 costs, Heseltine agreeing to accept your modifications in the text. These were the best terms I could manage. It was quite clear that Heseltine would have gone into court, and even if a jury had assessed the damages at *nil*, the defence and costs could not have been less than three or four hundred pounds. I have now gone to press with a new edition, so that it will once more be on sale after a lapse of three months I hope there will be no further bother.
    How is the new book going, and when can I hope to publish?

Yours sincerely,

What are you doing about the rest of the Bunin book? Who is working over your translation? Perhaps Woolf.[1] If it isn't very long, I'll do it if you wish me to.

I am getting my short stories into order, and settling up my MSS. I want to get all straight. I want to feel free to go away from Europe at any minute. I am so tired of it. It is a dead dog which begins to stink intolerably. Again I entertain the idea of going to America. A woman offered us a house, an adobe cottage in Taos, New Mexico, on a mountain with Indians near. Really, I want to go. I will go to the States. Really, I think the hour has struck, to go. Basta la mossa![2] I hope we can go in January. I hope we can get a merchant ship from Palermo or Naples to New Orleans or to Galveston in Texas. You will say it is just my winter influenza which makes me think of America. But finally I shall go. But don't tell anybody.

I feel very sick with England. It is a dead dog that died of a love disease like syphilis.

Here nothing happens. It has been very warm and scirocco, and one's head feeling as if it were going to float away. Now suddenly it is very cold, and snow on Calabria. The devil's in the world. We see a few people here. But nobody who means anything at all to me.

Secker wrote in a great funk because Heseltine is threatening a law-suit against *Women in Love*, for libel. He says Halliday is himself and the Pussum is his wife. Well, they are both such abject shits it is a pity they cant be flushed down a sewer. But they may try to extort money from Secker.

I ought to have written to Barbara, but I simply hadn't it in me. Why should I? I see Murry and the long-dying blossom Katherine have put forth new literary buds.[3] Let 'em. I did a second volume to *Psychoanalysis and the Unconscious*, and sent it to America. Nowadays I depend almost entirely on America for my living. I think Seltzer has just published at five dollars the slight travel book *Sea and Sardinia*. If he sends me copies I will send you one.

Tell me if there is any news. I know there isn't, except the old startler that All is Bloody.

Greet Sonia, Grisha, and the long-plaited Ghita.

And be greeted.

D. H. Lawrence

[1] See p. 23 n. 2.   [2] 'Enough of moving!'
[3] Murry's *Poems, 1916–20* had been published in September 1921, Katherine Mansfield's *Bliss and Other Stories* in December 1920 (New York, 1921).

2367. To Edward Garnett, 10 November 1921
Text: MS NYPL; Postmark, Taormina 12 NOV 21; Huxley 528–9.

Fontana Vecchia, *Taormina*, Sicilia
10 Novem.˙ 1921

Dear Garnett

Thank you for the MS of the story, which came today.[1] I hope it was not a nuisance to you to send it.

No, I wont read Homer, my atom of Greek is too infinitesimal. But if you want to read Homer, I'll send him you. Somebody made me a gift of him. And then, if you want to read Homer, why, you needn't make the mistake of reading me.

No my dear Garnett, you are an old critic and I shall always like you, but you are also a tiresome old pontiff and I shant listen to a word you say, but shall go my own way to the dogs and bitches, just as heretofore. So there.

I ordered *Women in Love* for you from Secker. If he doesn't send it you, go to 5 John Street and kill him at once. When you get it, if you get it, and when you read it, if you read it, don't for a moment imagine you are wrestling with the *Iliad*. Just remember that it is your young friend so–and–so, wipe away all your homeric illusions, and bear nobly on.

It is lovely here, and the morning landscape is just like Homer. But only the landscape. Not man. I hope you *will* come one day.

If it is quite easy for you to find out, tell me what translations of the Sicilian Giovanni Verga have appeared in English. His two chief novels are *I Malavoglia* and *Mastro-don Gesualdo*. Then the short sketches, the volumes, are *Cavalleria Rusticana* and *Novelle Rusticane* and *Vagabondaggio* and another.[2] He is *extraordinarily* good – peasant – quite modern – Homeric – and it would need somebody who could absolutely handle English in the dialect, to translate him. He would be most awfully difficult to translate. That is what tempts me: though it is rather a waste of time, and probably I shall never do it. Though if I dont, I doubt if anyone else will – adequately, at least.

I am glad Bunny is set up all right with a wife. Of course you'd *say* she was Irish even if she was a nigger as black as soot and with lips like life-belts. But I'm sure she's nice, Irish or not. I haven't heard from him, so I cant send him two antimacassars or a set of toilet-tidies until I do. Of course he may have turned over a new leaf and started, like *John Bull*, to disapprove of me. I hope not, it is so unoriginal.

---

[1] See p. 100 n. 2.
[2] *Vagabondaggio* (Florence, 1887). *Vita dei Campi* (Milan, 1880) later reissued as *Cavalleria Rusticana*.

I will send back the *Grenzen der Seele*.

Tell me if you come across any more MS.

Secker is due to have all my next three books, but he may prefer to have novels.

Greet Mrs Garnett – and I hope everything is lovely at the Cearne.[1] Here the roses are just rushing into bloom, in masses, now the rain has come. But today is suddenly cold, and it has snowed on Etna and on Calabria.

Saluti.   D. H. Lawrence

2368. To Martin Secker, 10 November 1921
Text: MS UInd; Postmark, Taormina 12 NOV 21; Secker 44–5.

Fontana Vecchia, Taormina, Sicily
10 Nov. 1921

Dear Secker

Of course *all* the Halliday-Pussum scenes in *W[omen] in Love* are *purely* fictitious. No shadow of a resemblance to them ever happened, as far as I know.

I am going to send *Aaron's Rod* to Curtis Brown. He and Mountsier hate it. Probably you will too. But I want you to publish it none the less. That is to say, I don't in the least want you to if you don't wish to. But I will have the book published. It is my last word in one certain direction.

I am getting together my short stories for a book. They are quite innocuous, I suppose. Do you want to do them? And if so, when? Let me know.

I started a novel in the Venice lagoons. If I didn't get so disgusted with everybody and everything I'd finish it.

Heseltine ought to be flushed down a sewer, for he is a simple shit.

Oh, please do send a copy of *Women in Love* to Edward Garnett, 19 Pond Place. Fulham Road. *S.W.3*. Don't fail, will you?

Send me all the news.

D. H. Lawrence

What is happening in London about *Sea and Sardinia*? I believe Seltzer has it out already.

2369. To Michael Sadleir, 11 November 1921
Text: MS UNCCH; Unpublished.

Fontana Vecchia, Taormina, Sicilia
11 Nov. 1921

Dear Sadler

I am putting together a book of short stories: and asking Secker, who has

---

[1] The Garnetts' home near Edenbridge, Kent; for DHL's description of it see *Letters*, i. 314.

first right to it, if he wants it. If he wants to bring it out in 1922, I suppose I must not include 'Wintry Peacock' at all. Or until when do you give me? And then in America? Does your reservation hold good there also?[1] Please let me know, so that I can fix the MS.

When is Blackwell going to publish this *New Decameron* volume?[2] I had a note from him, but he didn't say anything. Do you think you might send me two copies when it is out?

In the New Year I should so like to make a voyage and see a bit more of the world. If I can manage it – perhaps I cant, but I want to try – then I shall have to collect all my sous. Then if I ask you for the money for 'Wintry Peacock', do you think I could have it? Only if I can find my ship.

Yours   D. H. Lawrence

2370. To Dr Anton Kippenberg, 12 November 1921
Text: MS SVerlag; Unpublished.

Fontana Vecchia, Taormina, Sicilia.
12 Novem. 1921.

Dear Dr Kippenberg

I was so pleased with the proofs of the *Rainbow*. The translation seems to me good and solid: perhaps a bit heavy: but then it is very hard for me to get used to myself in another language. – But now the proofs have ceased coming. I do hope you have not suspended the printing. I do hope it is still going ahead.

The fantastic behaviour of the Mark is rather appalling. But I have an absolute belief in Germany's power to save herself: just as I am very much afraid that England is going to ruin herself. Europe is really a hopeless place. Nowadays it's just a *sauve qui peut*:[3] and the devil take the hindmost: which in the end will be England.

I am thinking about the payment for *The Rainbow*. Under the circumstances, I am sure you will not want to pay in English money, as you agreed. Don't you think it would be best if we agreed over a certain number of German Marks, and you pay them to my mother-in-law, Baronin von Richthofen? It seems to me, the longer we leave it the more hopeless the situation becomes. If you would tell me what sum, in Marks, you think just, then we can agree, and you can send a cheque to my mother-in-law, and the matter can be settled.

Of course I only suggest this, as it seems a simple way under the circumstances. If you do not approve, let matters remain as they are.

I must thank you for the final volumes of the *Pandora* and *Biblioteca*

---

[1] Sadleir obviously agreed to the inclusion of the story in *England, My England* when Seltzer published the volume in New York, October 1922. Cf. Letter 2422.
[2] See p. 31 n. 1.   [3] 'every man for himself'.

Mundi.[1] I am sending one or two specimen copies to a bookseller in London.
They are such charming books to look at. – I wish things were different.

Yours very Sincerely   D. H. Lawrence

2371. To Baroness Anna von Richthofen, 15 November 1921
Text: MS UCB; Unpublished.

Fontana Vecchia, *Taormina*, Sicilia
15 Novem. 1921

Meine liebe Schwiegermutter
    Wo ist mein Deutsch? – ich muss dir schreiben. Du hättest die Feigen.
Waren sie wirklich gut, oder verdorben? Du hast den Hinke ein Platz
gefunden. Das ist gut. Die ganze familie hängt noch aus dir.
    Wir haben wenig neues. Nur eine Sache. Eine Frau die heisst Mabel Dodge
Sterne – bekannt in America, aber nicht sehr – hat mir geschrieben von Taos,
Neu Mexico, V. S., das wir da gehen sollen. Taos ist eine indiane Städtlein,
auf einem Berg, 2000 Meter über Meer, und 35 Kilometer von dem
Eisenbahn. Es gibt ein triber von Indianer, frei, die sind da gewesen seit der
Sündflut. Sie wohnen in grossen pyramidischen Häusen, und beten an der
Sonne. Sie sagen das Taos ist der Sonnemittel von unserm Welt. Ich glaube es
wär interessant. Die Frau wird uns haus und Möbel geben, wenn wir nur
gehen wollen. Vielleicht gehen wir dann. Man braucht in diesen Tagen eine
neue Welt. Vielleicht nächtes Jahr gehen wir, und kucken es an. Was sagst du?
Es wär gut für mich, nach Amerika zu gehen. Wenn ich nur Amerikanische
Erzählungen oder Romanen schreiben könnte, ich meine, sie sollen auf
Amerikanische Erde spielen, dann würde ich Geld kriegen. Und es kommt
mir vor dass man für die Zukunft etwas neues finden muss, hier in Europa ist
alles beinah fertig, aus, ge-endet. Und so muss man auch fertig sein. Wir
müssen an Friedel und Marianne und Hardu auch denken. Wir werden Taos
überlegen, nicht wahr? – Der Seltzer, mein Verleger in Neu York hat mir
telegrafiert dass er findet *Aaron's Rod* wonderful, overwhelming. Das freut
mir mehr, weil der Mountsiger hatte das Buch sehr ungern. Es ist der Roman
der ich in Ebersteinburg geschrieben habe, unter die Bäume dort in der
Wälder.
    Der Mountsier ist von London nach New York am 5n November weg-
gefahren. Er soll mir sofort schreiben, als er da kommt, wie viele Dollars ich

---

[1] The final volumes of the *Pandora* series (launched in 1920) were *The Summoning of Everyman*,
Fioretti di San Francesco and *Great Political Documents of the United States of America*.
Volumes in the *Bibliotheca Mundi* (begun in 1920) continued to appear beyond 1921 (cf. *Letters*,
iii. 679).

habe dort in der Bank. Ich hoffe viele. Dann kann ich dir mehr geben. Die Mark ist ganz verrückt geworden. Du muss mir schnell sagen wenn dein Gelt schwindet.

Wir erwarten auch die *Sea und Sardinia* bücher von New York. Sie sollen für fünf Dollar verkauft werden. Das ist viel: 25 shillings. Aber sie haben die Bilder von Juta, die wir in Ebersteinburg hatten. Sie waren in Amerika gedruckt, wegen Sankzionen. Ich habe die Druckbogen noch nicht gesehen, habe ein wenig Angst dass die Farben schlecht ausgekommen seien. Wann das Buch kommt, schick ich dir gleich ein Exemplär.

Hier sind wir fleissig gewesen. Die Frieda hat plötzlich drei neue Röcke – oder Anzüge – dresses, meine ich. In Capri hat sie schone hell-graue Flannell gekauft, und der Schneider hat ein ganz hübsches coat-and-skirt gemacht. Aber das war schon vor drei Wochen. Jetzt hat sie drei Stück von Sizilianischer Stoff gekriegt. Es ist ein Art Leinen mit ein wenig Seide gemischt: alles in der Bergen hier oben gemacht, in der Dörfe ist Leinen und Seide gewachsen, da gesponnen und gefärbt und gewoben. Sie machen, wie alle Bauern, nur Karrierte Formen: wie *plaid*. Der Eine ist karriert hell-grün und magenta und gelb, und[1] ein wenig dunkel blau, der andere ist rose-veilchen und braun mit weissen Linien, und der letzte grosse karrierte Veilchen-farbe und Lindenblumegrün. Der eine ist schon fertig – die Schneiderin hat es gestern gebracht. Schön, sehr schön – und altmodish wie die Ewigkeit. Sie hat auch feine neue weisse Schuhe, von gutem weissen Leder machen lassen. Diese sind heute gekommen. Ich habe zwei Bilder gemalt – der einer rund, wie ein Teller, in einem goldenen Rahmen – alles rund wie ein Rundspiegel. Es ist vier dicke[2] nette blonde Weibschen die sich in einem grünen Teich badeten, und haben plötzlich angst, und fliehen. Der anderer ist ein Masaccio Copie, sehr bunt, drei Könige und Marie, Esel und Kuh, Ritter und Pagen und edlen Pferden: schön. Wir haben einen alten Rahmen, altgold, hand-geschnitten, für diesen. Schade das ich dir keinen schicken kann, hübsch und fertig eingerahmt. Dann habe ich zwei Novellen geschrieben. 'The Captain's Doll', das spielt in Deutschland und Zell: der anderer, 'The Fox', in England. Ich will alle meine Manuskripten fertig haben. So bringe ich ein Buch von Novellen und Erzahlungen zusammen. Aber ich habe doch zu viele für einem Buch.

Wir haben so schönes Wetter gehabt. Dann kamen fünf Tage mit kaltem Wind, ein wenig schnee auf Calabria – ich kuck es an mit deinem Opernkucker – und viel, viel Schnee auf Etna, ganz tief gekommen, unten nach die Bäume, die Röcke von Etna. Dann ist Etna riesig schön. Sie raucht ziemlich viel. Der

---

[1] und] der   [2] dicke] fette

Rauch kommt unseren Weg. Die Sonne scheint durch gold und orangenfarbig, bös, wie ein Löwe. Dann war ich erkältet für vier Tage: hatte angst dass meine Nase wie Schnee in Sommer ganz wegschmelzen sollte. Aber es ist besser. Jetzt ist es scirocco, von Afrika: warm, nass, nebelig, ein heisser, nasser, furchtbarer Wind, mit grossen Paketen von weissen Nebel nieder auf dem Meer. Die Rosen haben es doch gern. Sie sind hunderte: rose Rosen, und gelb, und rot, viele viele. Wir haben auch sechs Schalevoll im Haus. Dann blüthet die ganze Luft von Orangenduft. Die Orangenbäume und Mandarinen sind voller Blumen. Auch die grosse, grosse weisse Trompetblumen hangen hunderte so still und tot weiss unter die[1] Blätter, und duften suss und fremd wie India. Die erste Narcissus sind schon hier: kleine kleine Bisschen, und daisies und crocus und cyclamen, alle wild im Garten.

Die Frieda will etwas an Frl. Bader schenken. Ich schick dir nur ein Pfund – oder zwei. Gieb der armen Bader ein Pfund – oder 1000 Mark, wenn die Valuta immer noch so hoch und wahnsinnig ist. Was überbleibt, behalte. – Heute kommen drei alte Jungfrauen zum Thee. Oh jeh, oh jeh!

– Brauchst du etwas Thee aus England. Ich lass es schicken.

D. H. Lawrence

Frieda schreibt an der Bader. Vielleicht wenn die Valuta hoch ist und du kriegst viel für dien Pfund, kannst du an der drei Kinder etwas schenken.

Frieda hat kleine Sachen aus deinem Kochbuch gemacht – wunderbar gut ausgekommen – die Fassnachtsüsse für heut sind kleine Engeln.

– Sie lässt dir sagen das die Karrierte stoffen sind nicht sehr Karriert, und sie sieht *nicht* fett aus darin.

Du lässt immer grüssen Else und die Kinder alle, nicht wahr?

[My dear Schwiegermutter

Where is my German? – I must write to you. You had the figs. Were they really good, or spoiled? You have found Hinke a place. That's good. The whole family still depends on you.

We've got little news. Only one thing. A woman called Mabel Dodge Sterne – known in America, but not very – has written to me from Taos, New Mexico, U. S., that we should go there. Taos is a little Indian town, on a mountain, 2000 metres above the sea, and 35 Kilometres from the railway. There's a tribe of Indians, free, who have been there since the Flood. They live in great pyramidal houses, and worship the sun. They say Taos is the solar centre of our universe. I think it would be interesting. The woman will give us house and furniture, if we'll only go. Perhaps we shall go, then. One needs in

---

[1] unter die] unter von

these days a new world. Perhaps next year we'll go, and look at it. What do you say? It would be good for me, to go to America. If only I could write American stories or novels, I mean, they should take place on American soil, then I should get money. And it seems to me that for the future one must find something new, here in Europe everything is nearly done, over, ended. And so must one also be done. We must also think of Friedel and Marianne and Hadu. We shall consider Taos, shan't we? – Seltzer, my publisher in New York, cabled to me that he finds *Aaron's Rod* wonderful, overwhelming. That makes me happier, because Mountsier disliked the book very much. It is the novel I wrote in Ebersteinburg, under the trees there in the woods.

Mountsier left London for New York the 5th November. He is supposed to write to me immediately he gets there, how many dollars I have there in the bank. I hope many. Then I can give you more. The Mark has gone quite crazy. You must tell me quickly if your money runs out.

We are expecting too the *Sea and Sardinia* books from New York. They are supposed to be sold for five dollars. That's a lot: 25 shillings. But they have got the pictures by Juta, that we had in Ebersteinburg. They were printed in America, because of Sanctions. I've not yet seen the proofs, am a bit afraid the colours may have come out badly. When the book comes, I'll send you a copy directly.

Here we've been busy. Frieda has suddenly got three new skirts – or suits – dresses, I mean. In Capri she bought lovely light-grey flannel, and the tailor made a quite pretty coat-and-skirt. But that was already three weeks ago. Now she has got three pieces of Sicilian cloth. It is a sort of linen mixed with a little silk: all made up here in the mountains, in the village is grown linen and silk, spun there and dyed and woven. They make, like all peasants, only chequered designs: like *plaid*. One is chequered light-green and magenta and yellow, and a little dark blue, the other is rose-violet and brown with white stripes, and the last one large chequered violet and linden-blossom green. The one is already finished – the seamstress brought it yesterday. Lovely, very lovely – and old-fashioned as eternity. She also had fine new white shoes made from good white leather. These came today. I have painted two pictures – the one round, like a plate, in a golden frame – all round like a round mirror. It is four plump nice blonde females who have been bathing in a green pool, and are suddenly frightened, and flee. The other is a Masaccio copy, very colourful, three kings and Mary, ass and cow, knights and pages and noble horses: beautiful. We have an old frame, old-gold, hand-carved, for this one. Pity I can't send you one, nice and ready framed. Then I have written two novelettes. 'The Captain's Doll', which takes place in Germany and Zell: the other, 'The Fox', in England. I want to get all my manuscripts settled up. That way I shall collect a book of novelettes and short stories. But I've got rather too many for one book.

We had such beautiful weather. Then came five days with cold wind, a little snow on Calabria – I look at it with your opera glasses – and much, much snow on Etna, come quite low, down towards the trees, the skirts of Etna. Then Etna is immensely beautiful. She smokes rather a lot. The smoke comes our way. The sun shines through, gold and orange, angry, like a lion. Then I had a cold for four days: was afraid my nose should melt clean away like snow in summer. But it's better. Now it is scirocco, from Africa: warm, wet, misty, a hot, wet, dreadful wind, with great patches of white mist low on the sea. The roses really like it. They are hundreds: pink roses, and yellow, and red, many many. We've also got six bowlfuls in the house. Then the entire air blooms with orange fragrance. The orange-trees and mandarins are full of blossoms. Also the great, great white trumpet-flowers hang in hundreds so still and dead-white beneath the leaves, and smell sweet and foreign as India. The first narcissi are already here: tiny tiny bits, and daisies and crocuses and cyclamens, all wild in the garden.

Frieda wants to give something to Frl. Bader. I send you only one pound – or two. Give the poor Bader a pound – or 1000 marks, if the exchange is still so high and insane. What's left over, keep. – Today come three old maids to tea. Oh God, oh God!

– Do you need some tea from England. I'll have it sent.

D. H. Lawrence

Frieda is writing to the Bader. Perhaps if the exchange is high and you get a lot for your pound, you can give the three children some.

Frieda has made little things from your cookery book – turned out wonderfully well – the Shrovetide sweets for today are little angels.

– She says to tell you the chequered materials are not very chequered, and she does *not* look fat in them.

You always give greetings to Else and all the children, don't you?]

2372. To Donald Carswell, 15 November 1921
Text: MS YU; Postmark, Taormina 18 NOV 21; cited in Carswell 157–9.

Fontana Vecchia, *Taormina*. Sicilia
15 Novem. 1921

Dear Don

Many thanks for your letter: also to Catherine for hers. About the trews, that is all I want to know.[1] Very good. I've done the story and can just correct it where it needs.

---

[1] See Letter 2359.

Am glad you're going to earn money. What has Speyer done to forfeit his nationality? – or to make them say so.[1]

For that Halliday business I made some slight alterations: I gave Halliday lank black hair and Pussum lank yellow hair. But Secker writes that Heseltine refuses in any way to accept these modifications, and says – or his lawyer says – he is now going to bring an action against the book for libel. Heseltine is a thoroughly rotten sort, so is the woman. He is only doing it for blackmail and to advertise himself: chiefly the last. I think it's disgusting that such a person is allowed to air himself and preen himself in court. He's a foul sort. – But I hope Secker will be up to him.

I hear the weather is cold and awful in England. Here it has had a sharp cold touch, but now scirocco in hot billows of wet and clinging mist – and rain. Damn scirocco.

We've got no news except that a woman called Mabel Dodge Sterne writes from Taos, New Mexico, saying we can have a furnished adobe house there, for ourselves, and all we want, if we'll only go. It seems Taos is on a mountain – 7000 feet up – and 25 miles from a railway – and has a tribe of 600 free Indians who she says are interesting, sun-worshippers, rain-makers, and unspoiled. It sounds rather fun. I believe there's a little bunch of American artists there, though.[2] But that might make it easier just to live. Fun it would be if one could get a merchant ship to New Orleans or Galveston, Texas, and miss that awful New York altogether. Dont you think? Tell me if you know anything about such a place as Taos. – Of course I haven't settled anything – and we have talked so often of a move, and never made it. – But don't tell anybody else, will you?

I am expecting every day *Sea and Sardinia* – the slight Sardinia travel book, from New York. It has got Juta's coloured illustrations. As soon as I get copies I'll send you and Cath. one. Also Seltzer is bringing out *Tortoises*, poems as a chap-book, this month. I'll send that too when I get it. I wanted to send Cath. the 'Adolf': the Rabbit Sketch: but have lost MS and printed copy and everything.[3] How the devil I've managed it I don't know. Shall have to write to New York for a copy of the *Dial*, where it appeared. Ask Catherine another thing. Seltzer wanted to bring out the poems 'Apostolic Beasts' as a chap-book too. (I know it should be Evangelic or Apocalyptic.)[4] And he wanted, if

---

[1] Sir Edgar Speyer (1862–1932), banker associated with the firm of Speyer Brothers, London, had been convicted of treachery during the war; on 14 December 1921 his naturalisation was revoked.

[2] Taos had been attracting American artists in increasing numbers since the turn of the century. The Taos Society of Artists held its first meeting in 1915.

[3] 'Adolf', the story of the Lawrence children's pet rabbit, appeared in *Dial*, lxix (September 1920), 269–76.

[4] 'The Evangelistic Beasts' section of *Birds, Beasts and Flowers* was never published separately by Seltzer.

so, to have a cover design representing the four beasts of the Evangelists –
from the Apocalypse – Man, Lion, Bull, and Eagle.[1] – In mediaeval Missals
and Books of Hours and such, sometimes one comes across fascinating
diagrams of the four beasts. If ever you see one, tell me where and if it would
reproduce for a cover design.

Everybody hated *Aaron's Rod* – even Frieda. But I just had a cable from
Seltzer that he thinks it wonderful. Maybe it is just a publisher's pat. Anyhow
it's better than a smack in the eye, such as one gets from England for
everything – as Cath for her *Camomile*. If only she'd called it Rose-hearted
Camellia they'd have supped it up. Pah-canaille. Canaille, canaglia,
Schweinhunderei!

You'll be just enjoying yourself in this Speyer case. I'm so glad. As for him,
if he has to fob out some of his money, good for him.

The post is very bad here. One train fell in a river in Calabria, and all post
and all luggage lost irretrievably: stolen, of course. Now the fascisti and
communisti are at it in Rome. The Catholic church is a deep one. It is trying to
form a Catholic world league, *political*, and taking more the Communistic line.
It is working hard in Germany and Austria and here – and in France – and also
America. It may turn out a big thing. I shouldn't wonder if before very long
they effected a mild sort of revolution here, and turned out the king. It would
be a clergy-industrial[2]-socialist move – industrialists and clergy to rule in the
name of the people. Smart dodge, I think. If the exchange falls again they'll
effect it. Then they'll ally with Germany and Austria and probably France,
and make a European ring excluding England. That seems to be the idea.

Hope your ship is sailing nicely, and J. P.[3] and all flourishing.

D. H. Lawrence

There are clouds of all sorts of new birds in the garden, suddenly come
south. And the storks are passing in the night, whewwing softly and
murmuring as they go overhead.

2373. To Earl Brewster, 16 November 1921
Text: MS UT; Brewster 37–9.

Fontana Vecchia, *Taormina*, Sicily
16 Nov. 1921

Dear Brewster

How then is Ceylon? I have been thinking of your arrival. It has blown, the
wind, and snowed on Calabria, and sciroccoed till we are all of us in fragments.
But now it's fair again. How has it been beyond the Gulf of Aden?

---

[1] See Revelation iv. 7.   [2] industrial] capitalist
[3] The Carswells' son, John Patrick (1918–   ).

I am tired of here, I can't *belong* any more. And now you have gone so far, Ceylon seems like a coloured illustration in a book to me: not real. And all the east seems like the stage.

I had a letter from Mabel Dodge Sterne from Taos, New Mexico – and she says won't we go there. She offers us a house: an adobe cottage – and all we want. Taos has a tribe of Indians, there since the Flood. It is a centre of Sun worship. They say the sun was born there. It is 6000 feet up on a mountain – and 25 miles from the railway. But of course there are some American artists there. – Yet I want to go. The Indian, the Aztec, old Mexico – all that fascinates me and has fascinated me for years. *There* is glamour and magic for me. Not Buddha. Buddha is so finished and perfected and fulfilled and vollendet,[1] and without new possibilities – to me I mean. So it seems to me. The glamour for me is in the west, not in the fulfilled east. It is a shame to write you like this. But my spirit stubbornly says it to me. Of course I have not decided. I shan't make a move till the new year. But I think truly I would rather go to Taos than to Ceylon. And sail to New Orleans or Galveston or even Los Angeles. You will be angry. But it seems to me my fate.

Still I want to hear about Ceylon, if you think it is *your* fate. And of course Achsah is to write, and she is to say what she *really* thinks of it.

I have had a bit of flu so haven't been out much. Kitson was here[2] – and Rosalie. They talk of you and of Schaler. And Miss Fisher and Miss Bunch from Palermo:[3] the latter wondering why you never answered her letters. I tell her about Buddha and she says, so hot and injured:

'But I thought he was a *christian*!'

'Oh probably,' say I. And I always laugh. It always affects me as being funny, when people say 'he is a *christian*!' It is like being on the stage in a costume play. I told you they are going to erect an English church here for £30,000 sterling. But the chief mover, il Signor Duca, is detained in Rome where he has been meeting Mrs Evans,[4] because the fascisti and communisti are hitting one another again and making a railway strike.[5]

Of news there is none particular. I had a cable from Seltzer that he thought *Aaron* wonderful, overwhelming. Glad to hear it, I'm sure. *John Bull* is in such

---

[1] 'consummated'.

[2] Robert Hawthorn Kitson (1873–1947), English expatriate in Taormina, was an amateur water-colourist and expert photographer. See *Letters*, iii. 552 n. 2.

[3] Miss Bunch is unidentified.

[4] The 'Duca's' – Alexander Nelson Hood's – sister; she shared his villa in Taormina. (See Nehls, ii. 86–7.)

[5] The Fascists, under the leadership of Benito Mussolini (1883–1945), were engaged in attacks on communists (and alleged communists) which included beatings, murder and arson. There were railway strikes in major Italian cities throughout November.

a dirty mess himself, having swindled half England in his Victory Club, or something like that, and being on trial for weeks, that he is not going to be allowed to suppress *Women in Love*.[1] The other dirty mongrel continues to persist in suing for libel, but I am hoping he too will get a good kick on the rump. So perish my enemies. I haven't got *Sea and Sardinia* yet, but the *Dial* published mutilated bits in Oct and Nov. I have been busy getting my MSS into order – as far as possible – so that I can clear out and be free. So I have brought the short stories up to the scratch, ready for a volume: and written a long short story 'The Captains Doll', which I think is interesting, and put a long tail to 'The Fox', which was a bobbed short story.[2] Now he careers with a strange and fiery brush. I hope you will read him some time, because then you will see that I am not really drawn Buddhawards, but west.

Nevertheless I hope you are having a good time and holding the hands of Cinghalese Saints with proper gusto. I'll bet one can have a lovely villegiatura[3] in Ceylon, saints or no saints, Buddha or not. I can't help rather hating Buddha, the cross-legged pigeon. I can't even help putting my spite and irreverence against him into this letter. So it's high time I stopped.

Send the news nevertheless. Be greeted, all of you.

D. H. Lawrence

2374. To Robert Mountsier, 18 November 1921
Text: MS Smith; Postmark, Taormina 19 NOV 21; Unpublished.

Fontana Vecchia, Taormina, Sicily
18 Novem 1921

Dear M[ountsier]

I am still persisting in my intention to come to Taos. I would like *very* much, best of all, to be able to go through the Panama Canal to Los Angeles or San Francisco. I have a terrible desire to land on the Pacific shore, even if it costs considerably more. I want you[4] at your end to see if you can find me a ship to do this. I asked Mabel Dodge Sterne too if she knew of ships. I know that Maurice Sterne – who I think is her brother[5] – a painter – he has had

---

[1] Horatio William Bottomley (1860–1933), founder and editor of *John Bull* which, on 17 September 1921, had called on the police to prosecute *Women in Love* (see p. 88 n. 2). Bottomley had begun a libel action against a former associate who had published a pamphlet entitled 'The Downfall of Horatio Bottomley, M.P. – His latest and greatest swindle – How he gulled poor subscribers to invest one-pound notes in his Great Victory Bond Club.' Revelations made during his unsuccessful libel action resulted in his being charged (March 1922) with fraudulent conversion; in May he was sentenced to 7 years penal servitude.

[2] DHL had cut 'The Fox' in 1919 for publication in *Hutchinson's Story Magazine* where it appeared in November 1920. The final version of the story is about three times its original length.   [3] 'country-house'.   [4] you] to   [5] See p. 111 n. 3.

something in the *Dial* – he was in Anticoli when we were in Austria – I know a ship-owner gave him a cargo-boat passage out here, and he said it was lovely. I don't know if he is in America now. I suppose Mabel D. would know.

Taormina is looking very lovely – and the people are all very nice: but it's no good. I want to come away. I want to leave in January if possible. Messina, Catania, Siracuse, Palermo, Trapani are the Sicilian ports: failing these, any Italian port, or Malta.

I put a long new tail on the 'Fox'. It will be a good book of stories. I am doing a Magnus MS. about the Foreign Legion in Algiers which I will send.[1] I am going to send the *Aarons Rod* to Curtis. Your letter and his about *Aaron* annoyed me. – Seltzer however has cabled that he liked the book.

I heard of quite a large yacht sold in Nice a few weeks back for about £250 sterling. But I am sure, if I come to America, and if we want to cruise the South Seas, in two years time we can get our little vessel. But first I must come to America.

Do do what you can about getting a boat to bring us over. If there is nothing, we shall have to come Fabre line to New York.

D. H. Lawrence

2375. To Mabel Dodge Sterne, 21 November 1921
Text: MS Brill; Luhan 9.

Fontana Vecchia, *Taormina*, Sicilia
21 Novem. 1921.

Dear Mabel Dodge Sterne

This is a line to say I am persisting in my intention to come to Taos in January. I haven't yet heard anything about a ship: have a very great desire to find a cargo-boat that will land me in Los Angeles or San Francisco. I have a very great desire to land on the Pacific coast. I hope to be in Taos in February.

Look at Leo Stein bursting into a new Jewish psalmody![2]

I asked Robert Mountsier to chase ships for me at that end: am doing my best at this end.

Till we meet, then.

D. H. Lawrence

---

[1] Maurice Magnus (1876–1920), American, joined the French Foreign Legion during the 1914–18 War and deserted after it. DHL met him through Norman Douglas in Florence, November 1919; Magnus followed DHL to Sicily in early 1920 and went on the same ship to Malta in May 1920. He committed suicide in Malta, November 1920. DHL was now engaged on what would be his Introduction to Magnus's *Memoirs of the Foreign Legion* (Secker, 1924), which caused his quarrel with Douglas (see also Letter 2432).

[2] DHL enclosed the following 'disagreeable, malicious' letter from Leo Stein (Luhan 9–11):

Settignano–Firenze,
Nov. 9, 1921

My Dear Lawrence

> Rich and Red
> Bury the dead,
> And a soul prepare
> For the rich and the rare;
> Rise from the grave
> On a bellying wave;
> Ganglionic back
> Hew snicker-snack;
> Fly free O my heart
> Light-quivering dart;
> There, sheer, you behold her
> Cling, amplectinous shoulder.

I have but lately read your book on consciousness, and recall how once you would have sent to the New Republic the things that you were about to write on that subject. I am afraid that they would never have gotten by. The N.R.'s are a rather conservative lot and would have been inclined to judge rather harshly your flight on the wings of scientific imagination. I doubt whether they have gotten much beyond Tyndall in that direction.

Your work is of course in several respects in a familiar tradition. The title recalls Schopenhauer, and might well have been, The Fourfold Root of Sufficient Being. On the other hand it continues the work of the Natur-Philosophen. It makes me think of Oken and of science like the following: "Die Mathematik ist auf das Nichts begründet, und entspringt mithin aus dem Nichts." "Der Sehnerv ist ein organisirter Lichtstrahl, das Hirn eine organisirte Sonne, das Auge eine organisirte farbensonne, Regenbogen."

I am a little discouraged, however, by your materialism. Here we are started off from the belly. Disguise it as you will, the belly is made for food, and food is made for the belly. The back is, as everyone knows, made for resistance, for do we not in resistance get our backs up? Then we pass to a more lyrical note to "The Angel Israfel, whose heart-string is a lute," and so by ultimate progression, to the embracing arms which, of course, come from behind, else would we be left out from our own embraces if we embraced only from front. That would make an embrace a sorry isolation, and so once more is the world justified in the wisdom of its poets.

The hour of war spiritualism is running to its end, and I should not be surprised if the moment were come for the founding, in the sunny glens of Southern California, of the new Laurentian Brotherhood of the Fourfold Root of Sufficient Being. It might carry as its Oriflamme the Blazing Beard of which the Sun in the High Heavens is the sufficing symbol, and the brethren might intone, in their triumphal progress, something like the following:

> In Plexus and Ganglion
> We rise, we rise,
> Freud and Einstein we leave
> To conceptual sties,
> In the Prophet's wisdom
> Alone we are wise
> As sensationally upward
> The spirit flies
> And warms to its home
> In the star-tented skies.

Of course I do not insist on the intrinsic importance of this chant. It is, perhaps, a little too much in the romantic temper and might not float easily in the amniotic juice of a modern womb. Pray accept the goodwill which prompts it rather than the evil deed which is the outcome, and believe me ever yours

Leo Stein.

Kindest regards to your wife.

2376. To Martin Secker, 23 November 1921
Text: MS UInd; Postmark, Taormina 24 Nov 21; Secker 45.

Fontana Vecchia, *Taormina*, Sicilia
23 Novem 1921

Dear Secker

It makes me sick with rage to think that Heseltine got that money out of you.[1] *Really*, one should never give in to such filth.

I am sending Curtis Brown the MS. of *Aarons Rod*. I want it to be published simultaneously with Seltzer's. Mountsier and CB. both prophesy that you'll dislike *Aarons Rod*, and refuse to publish it. Please yourself. Seltzer cabled two days ago that he thought it 'wonderful, overwhelming.' Dont know if that is just an Americanism.

Do you think Douglas will identify himself with Argyle and be offended?[2] I should think not. – I have practically got ready the book of short stories: having it typed in Florence – When do you think to do *The Rainbow*?

Yrs D. H. Lawrence

2377. To Curtis Brown, 23 November 1921
Text: MS UT; Unpublished.

Fontana Vecchia, *Taormina*, Sicilia
23 Nov. 1921

Dear Curtis Brown

I am sending you today the MS. of *Aaron's Rod*, for Secker. I don't want him by *any means* to publish it before Seltzer is ready at the American end: if Secker wants to publish it.

I am going to send you shortly a batch of short stories for a volume: some unpublished ones.

Is anything happening in England about *Sea and Sardinia*? I suppose Seltzer has got his out by now, though I've seen no signs of it yet.

Hope all goes well.

Yrs D. H. Lawrence

P. S. I have just received the enclosed from Secker. I don't quite see his point about the short stories not being counted one of the five *books*.[3] Jonathan Cape asked me if I had any book of short things to offe[r.][4] Anyway February would be too soon for the short stories. I want to try the magazines, particularly in America. – If Secker is going to be cautious, so am I.

Please let me know about *Sea and Sardinia*.

D. H. Lawrence

---

[1] See p. 113 n. 2.   [2] See p. 54 n. 3.
[3] DHL was under contract to Secker for five books which Secker insisted were to be full-length novels unless he agreed to the contrary. Two had so far been published: *Women in Love* and *The Lost Girl*.   [4] MS torn.

2378. To Robert Mountsier, 26 November 1921
Text: MS Smith; Postmark, Taormina 28 NOV 21; Unpublished.

Fontana Vecchia, *Taormina*, Sicily
26 Novem. 1921

Dear Mountsier

I was very much annoyed to receive this morning your letter announcing your sailing on the 16th. Of course I fully concluded you had gone on the 5th., according to your previous letter. Otherwise I would have asked you for more blank cheques, which I need. Can't you then even keep me informed of your movements? – I have had no direct information from New York since I was in Zell. This is quite preposterous. I have seen no sign of proofs of *Sea and Sardinia* and its pictures, or of *Tortoises*: indeed no sign of anything. I will write to Seltzer about this.

I wish to know also if he received the MS of *Fantasia of the Unconscious*.

I hope you have by now sent me a statement of our accounts, also some means of getting at some money. I want Blank Cheques, because I believe I can get dollars even here in the village.

I intend to come to America in the New Year. Am trying to find a cargo boat here, to sail to Los Angeles or San Francisco. I am afraid it will be difficult. If I fail we shall come by the Fabre line to New York. I shall post no MS. to you until I hear from you. I don't think I want *The Dial* to mess about with *Aarons Rod*. I hated their snipping up such bits of *Sardinia*.[1] – Why haven't they paid Koteliansky?

D. H. Lawrence

I would prefer that *The Dial* published 'The Captain's Doll': which has 34000 words.[2] I will send the MS.

Seltzer cabled that he found *Aaron* 'wonderful, overwhelming'. – I have sent the English MS. to Curtis Brown. – dont want Thayer to see it.

I heard from Secker that he paid £50 hush-money to Heseltine, and 10 guineas costs. I loathe his giving in to such dirt.

Make Seltzer publish the introduction to the *Fantasia*, make him.

I just had Seltzer's letter – met the postman in the Corso – I cant make the alterations because I have now no MSS – but will look through the handwritten MS, and see if I can do it.

He can leave out what he likes.

---

[1] See pp. 74 n. 2 and 107 n. 1.
[2] 'The Captain's Doll' was not published in any magazine.

2379. To Thomas Seltzer, 26 November 1921
Text: MS UT; Postmark, Taormina 29 NOV 21; Lacy, *Seltzer* 28–9.

Fontana Vecchia, *Taormina*, Sicilia
26 Novembre 1921
Dear Seltzer
The postman gave me your letter in the Corso this evening: your letter of Nov 11th. That is a marvellous quickness.

About *Aaron*: I haven't got any type-written corrected MS. so don't quite know how it stands. I have only my hand-written MS – which luckily I haven't yet burned. If you really must modify Argyle – I think he is so funny, though Mountsier calls him a foul-mouthed Englishman – you can do so at your discretion, by just lifting a word or two. I'll go through the Marchesa MS. tonight.[1]

Do print the introduction to the *Fantasia*. The motto today is fight, fight, and always fight. Let them have it: they well deserve it, and they can't really do one much harm.

Of course I am dying to see *Sea and Sardinia*. Yes, I want you one day to publish the *European History*. I feel here too near to Greece and Rome to want to write a history about them. – Curse the Austrians for not sending that Cable. – If *Tortoises* is not much go as a chap-book, no more chap-books.

I have got two long stories: 'The Captain's Doll', 34,000 words and 'The Fox' about the same. I will send them to Mountsier the minute I get the typescript from Florence. I think they are very interesting.

I am persisting in my idea of coming to America, as I told you. January or February I hope to sail. *Ought* I to come to New York? I see red when I think of Kennerley and *Sons and Lovers*.[2] Would it be better if I personally were on the scene to have a shot at him? – Or can I continue to chase my ship to take me to Los Angeles or San Francisco. May be a wild-goose chase, but I'll just try. People in London urge me to go there – they say I could do things in England now. But no, England has made me too angry. I will come to the States to try it: but to fight, to fight. All the better to put their rabbity backs up.

---

[1] Though Argyle was certainly modelled on Douglas, a precise original for the Marchesa del Torre is not known. The character may have derived in some degree from the American wife of the Marchese Carlo Torrigiani whose Sunday at-homes were famous in Florence. (For textual changes made in Seltzer's and Secker's editions, see *Aaron's Rod*, ed. Mara Kalnins, Cambridge University Press.)

[2] Mitchell Kennerley (1878–1950), New York publisher, had published *Sons and Lovers* in 1913 and continued to issue reprints. DHL continued to complain that 'America has had [*Sons and Lovers*] for nothing' (E. D. McDonald, *A Bibliography of the Writings of D. H. Lawrence*, Philadelphia, 1925, p. 12). But see *Letters*, ii. 165.

'The Fox' and 'The Captain's Doll' are so modern, so new: a new manner. Then I will send seven or so other stories, shorter. — I don't want to start anything serious now before I leave.

I have been angry at not having any definite news from New York since August. Perhaps there has not been much to say. But I always want to know exactly what is happening, so please tell me always, direct. And always send me proofs of whatever is appearing, even if you don't wait to have them returned.

To me *Fantasia* is important. But they'll try to push it aside as if it didn't matter. That's why it's better to go out against them tooth and nail and make them uneasy about what *they're* going to say. Print the introduction, and to hell with them. For this book one must put up a fight.

Yours   D. H. Lawrence

I have looked through the original MS. It is no good, I can't alter it. But if you like to follow the type-script, which I have often written over, in the scenes you mention, and if you like to leave out what is written over, I don't think you need fear the public much. And if you like to leave out a sentence or two, or alter a phrase or two, do so. But I can't write anything different. Follow the original typescript.

2380. To Dr Anton Kippenberg, 28 November 1921
Text: MS SVerlag; Unpublished.

Fontana Vecchia, Taormina, Sicilia
28 Novembre 1921

Dear Dr Kippenberg

Thank you for your letter of the 22nd. I shall be quite content if you pay eighteen thousand Mark for *The Rainbow*. Please do send it to my mother-in-law

Frau von Richthofen, Ludwig-Wilhelmstift, BadenBaden.

If she could have it for Christmas it would make her very happy.

Do not be downhearted about the fate of Germany. He laughs longest who laughs last. I agree with you entirely about the folly of giving in to French megalomania. But there is nothing final about that. England is drifting to a real German alliance, at last beginning to realise that this is her only way to save herself. You would not believe how England is *hated* in France and Italy — and in America. Her only chance of saving herself is by a close commercial agreement with Germany. Now she sees it. Only they are still afraid of public opinion: I mean the government and the middle classes. You would be surprised if you knew the *volte face* in middle-class opinion. For instance an Englishwoman here the other day said: — 'Yes, I got the book in the Tauchnitz

edition.[1] I know it is German, but then it would be awful for all of us if
Germany really were bankrupt, so I want to do my bit to prevent it.' – And this
is the ordinary stupid, middle-class Englishwoman. Wait – wait – only wait. If
Europe survives, Germany will survive as a great and leading nation. If
Europe is determined on suicide, then there's no help. Basta la mossa. – There
is a *very real* hatred of France here in Italy, and Briand's words in Washington
have sent them all, the Italians, into fits.[2] – They are trying to throw the
government once more. If they succeed, I believe the *church* will come into
power, backed by the communists, and there will be an immediate alliance
with Germany and Austria. Wait – wait – only wait. Germany has seen worse
days, in spite of all that the German professors flung in my face when I was in
Germany. – I am an Englishman – but good God, I am a *man* first. And as a
man I loathe the mob – and a nation can easily degenerate into a mob. Siamo
uomini.[3]

I send you a criticism of *Sons and Lovers* by Robert Saudek. It appeared in
the Prazer Presse. – I expect also a light travel book of mine, with coloured
illustrations. It is just appearing in New York, at five dollars a copy – title *Sea
and Sardinia*. I will send you a copy.

Best of wishes.

D. H. Lawrence

2381. To Curtis Brown, 1 December 1921
Text: MS UT; Unpublished.

Fontana Vecchia, *Taormina*, Sicily
1 December 1921

Dear Curtis Brown

I enclose a letter from Arnold Lunn about a collection of *Georgian Stories*.[4]

---

[1] Charles Bernhard von Tauchnitz (1816–95), German publisher, founded the 'Tauchnitz
Edition' of British and American authors in 1841 and of German authors in English translation
in 1868.

[2] Aristide Briand (1862–1932), prime minister of France (1921–2) and French representative at
the Washington Conference (1921–2). On 21 November, Briand gave a speech defending
France's refusal to disarm because of the continuing threat of Germany. He stressed Germany's
ability to mobilise 7,000,000 men through maintenance of a reserve army under various guises,
and of German industry's readiness to manufacture munitions. Briand's speech was reported
unsympathetically by H. G. Wells (1866–1946) in European newspapers, where DHL may
have read the account. The *Times* carried a report which included ample quotation (22
November 1921, p. 10).   [3] 'We are men.'

[4] (Sir) Arnold Henry Moore Lunn (1888–1974) had written to DHL on 2 November 1921
requesting a story from *The Prussian Officer* (published by Duckworth in 1914 and by Huebsch
in 1916) for a collection of *Georgian Stories* to be published by Chapman & Hall in June 1922.
Lunn's stated aim was to give the same stimulus to the art of the short story as had been given to
poetry by the *Georgian Poetry* volumes. Royalties were to be equally divided among the
contributors (who included Sheila Kaye Smith, Katherine Mansfield and Alec Waugh).
DHL's 'The Shadow in the Rose Garden' was included in the volume.

I have answered that I am willing that they should print one of the stories from *The Prussian Officer*. Will you please ask Duckworth if he consents[1] – and also Huebsch in New York? – and then settle the matter for me?

> Yours Sincerely   D. H. Lawrence

2382. To Robert Mountsier, 1 December 1921

Text: MS Smith; Postmark, Taormina 1 DIC 21; Unpublished.

> Fontana Vecchia, *Taormina*, Sicilia
> 1st Decem. 1921

Dear Mountsier

I send you various MSS. by registered post today.

1. 'The Fox', about 33,000 words. (first part was published in *The Strand Magazine*, London)[2]
2. 'The Captains Doll' – about 34 000 words. *New*.
3. 'Samson and Delilah' (pub. in *English Review* two years ago)
4. 'Fanny and Annie'. (pub. in *Hutchinsons Magazine* in London)
5. 'The Blind Man' (pub. in *English Review* a year ago)
6. 'Hadrian' – originally 'You Touched Me' (published in *Land and Water* in 1920)
7. 'Monkey Nuts' – unpublished.
8. 'The Horse-Dealers Daughter' – unpublished.

I hope you have kept a copy of 'Wintry Peacock', from the *Metropolitan*.[3]

I shall send duplicates to Curtis Brown when I hear from you. I am doing a third long story – 'The Thimble' – to go with 'Fox' and 'Captain's Doll' in one volume. – Then I have three stories still to send you, enough to make up a volume of Short Stories. I want 'The Fox', 'The Thimble', and 'The Captains Doll' to be one volume by themselves – about 80,000 words.[4]

It is evidently going to be difficult to find a ship to New Orleans or Los Angeles: so, as New York will be so cold, we may have to wait till March to come. But we will see. – Seltzer must make himself any small modifications of *Aarons Rod*. Make him publish the introduction to *Fantasia*.

> Yrs   D. H. Lawrence

---

1 Gerald de l'Etang Duckworth (1871–1937), stepson of Leslie Stephen and thus half-brother to Virginia Woolf, had founded his publishing firm in 1898. His list included Stephen, Virginia Woolf, Charles Doughty, Belloc and Galsworthy, as well as DHL whose *Trespasser*, *Love Poems* and *Sons and Lovers* he had published before *The Prussian Officer*. (See the *Times* obituary, 30 September 1937.)

2 DHL was in error here: the first periodical publication of the story was in *Hutchinson's Story Magazine* (see p. 126 n. 2).

3 Stories nos. 3 – 8 , and 'Wintry Peacock', were all collected in *England, My England*. For details about their earlier publication see Roberts A23.

4 'The Thimble' (first published in *Seven Arts*, i, March 1917, 435–48) was re-written as 'The Ladybird'. Then, together with the other two novelettes, it was collected in *The Ladybird, The Fox, The Captain's Doll*.

2383. To Baroness Anna von Richthofen, 2 December 1921
Text: MS UCB; Unpublished.

Fontana Vecchia, *Taormina*, Sicilia
2 Decem. 1921

Meine liebe Schwiegermutter.

Ich hatte deine Postkarte über die Bader und ihre Tausand. Armes Bäderle, sie kriegt es doch nicht! Nein, die Frieda hat ihr *nicht* geschrieben. Wir hatten schon angst von dir und deiner Familienwut: wüssten schon dass du eine lange Zahl von Annie und Marianne, Hardu und Friedel und Hans und dir selber zu rechnen hättest. So, sie kriegt ein Paar Schuhe. Die Frieda sagt dass sie werden nur Hausschuhe aus Stoff, und nicht aus Leder sein. Ach, die Weiber! Aber es ist schon recht, Charity begins at home. Ich weiss nicht wie man es übersetzt.

Heute kam der Else ihr Brief. Wenn nur der Hinke nicht ein 'fanullone' sei: ich meine, ein unglücklich der nimmer sein Leben gut treiben weisst. Ist er nur unglücklich oder fehlt sein Seelenkraft? Nur soll die Annie ihm *nimmer* Geld schenken. Das wär ein hoffnungsloser Anfang.

Aber, Gotteswillen, lass niemand dies lesen, sonst ist das Fett im Feuer.

Hier siehst du den Kippenbergerbrief. Alles scheint schön zu sein. Baue aber deine Hoffnungen nicht zu hoch. Ich habe ihm geschrieben, ich bin ganz zufrieden mit den 18 tausend Mark: und habe ihm gesagt, es wäre schön, wenn er das Geld zu dir für Weinacht schickte. Hoffentlich thut er so. Die Frieda aber will ihren Stock in dem Rad stecken. Sie giebt es so aus, dass du nur 12 Tausend behältest, und schenkst sechs tausend weg: jedes Kind 500. oder was, und weiter weiss ich nicht. Sie soll dir selber schreiben. Aber erst fange die Ganz, dann lass' sie kochen. Du hast das Geld noch nicht.

Von Amerika nichts weiter. Die Reisekostet furchtbar – 250 Dollar Neapel bis New York: 150 Dollar New York bis New Orleans: 50 Dollar New Orleans bis Taos. Aber vielleicht können wir ein Schiff direkt nach New Orleans finden – nachher.

Die Friedeleanzüge sind fertig: der eine hat alte silberne Spitze auf Ärmeln und Hals, der anderer goldene Spitze: nicht hell. Du sollst an Else sagen, ich habe den Morgenanzug in einen schönen Hausanzug machen lassen. Es sieht sehr schön aus, ich kann es den ganzen Tag tragen. – Meine Schwester schreibt mir, ihr Bub war sehr krank. Jetzt ist sie, mit ihm am Meer, in Bournemouth, bleibt noch ein Paar Wochen.

Das Wetter ist wieder schön gewesen. Unser *Podere* wird gepflügt. Kommt ein schwarzer, Sarazenischer Mann, eine kleine junge Frau in gelbem Kopftuch, ein barfuss Bub, zwei Kühe, ein junger silberner Stier mit schwarzen Augenbogen, eine feines Merinoschaf, ein schwarz-und-braun Ziege, und ein gelber Hund: und ein Esel, du lieber gott, der singt für zwanzig.

Der Mann mit den zwei Kuhen pflügt, die Frau schneit die lange Gräser, und laüft nach dem Bub mit hoch erhobenen Stock, will ihn schlagen: der Stier geht einsam herum, und kost mit uns, das Merinoschaf bleibt in der nähe von Mann und Hund. Sie sitzen alle zusammen und essen unter dem Sorbapfelbaum, und die Kühe kriegen Heu, der Hund kriegt brot, die Leute essen brot und zwiebel, trinken wein mit wasser. So bis Sonnenuntergang. Sie sind sehr nett. Sie arbeiten schon zwei Wochen hier im Garten. – Der Etna raucht viel schwarzer Rauch. Die Fremden kommen nicht viele: immer schlechter Streiken auf dem Eisenbahn. Gestern war das Meer hart und blau wie ein blauer Steinboden. Heute plötzlich Wind, Wellen, und Schaum. Sei gegrüsst. Sei geduldig. Grüss alle.

DHL

Unsere Ziege hat zwei junge – ein schwarzer Bubziege, und eine schwarz-und-braune Mädelziege. Leider essen wir nächste Woche den Bubbok. Er ist aber so lustig. Es thut mir weh.

Ich schriebe an meiner Schwester, sie soll Thee schicken. Die Else soll den Halb haben.

[My dear Schwiegermutter

I had your postcard about the Bader and her thousand.[1] Poor Bäderle, she doesn't get it after all! No, Frieda did *not* write to her. For we were afraid of you and your familial fury: we knew you had a long list of Annie and Marianne, Hadu and Friedel and Hans and you yourself to consider. So, she gets a pair of shoes. Frieda says they will only be house shoes of cloth, and not of leather. Oh, females! But it's quite all right, Charity begins at home. I don't know how one translates it.

Today came Else's letter. If only Hinke were not a 'fanullone':[2] I mean, an unfortunate who never knows how to lead his life well.[3] Is he just unfortunate or does he lack spiritual strength? Only Annie ought *never* to give him money. That would be a hopeless beginning.

But, for God's sake, let nobody read this, else the fat's in the fire.

Here you see the Kippenberg letter. All seems to be fine. But don't build your hopes too high. I wrote him I am quite satisfied with the 18 thousand marks: and said, it would be fine if he sent the money to you for Christmas. Hopefully he will do so. But Frieda wants to poke her stick in the wheel. She declares that you are only to keep 12 thousand, and give six thousand away: each child 500 or whatever, and further I don't know. She should write to you herself. But first catch the goose, and then let it be cooked. You've not got the money yet.

[1] See p. 72 n. 2 and Letter 2371.   [2] 'an idler, a lazy person'.   [3] See p. 76 n. 2.

From America nothing further. The journey costs frightfully – 250 dollars Naples to New York: 150 dollars New York to New Orleans: 50 dollars New Orleans to Taos. But perhaps we can find a ship direct to New Orleans – later on.

The Friedel suits are finished: the one has old silver lace on sleeves and neck, the other gold lace: not bright. You should tell Else, I have had the morning suit made into a lovely house suit. It looks very lovely, I can wear it the whole day. – My sister writes me, her boy was very ill.[1] Now she is with him at the seaside, in Bournemouth, stays another couple of weeks.

The weather has been beautiful again. Our *podere* is being ploughed. Comes a black, Saracen man, a little young woman in yellow kerchief, a barefoot boy, two cows, a young silver bull with black eyebrows, a fine merino sheep, a black-and-brown goat, and a yellow dog: and an ass, oh dear Lord, that sings for twenty. The man with the two cows ploughs, the woman cuts the long grasses, and runs after the boy with high-upraised stick, wants to hit him: the bull goes lonesomely about, and flirts with us, the merino sheep keeps near to man and dog. They all sit together and eat under the sorb-apple tree, and the cows get hay, the dog gets bread, the people eat bread and onion, drink wine with water. So till sundown. They are very nice. They've been working two weeks already here in the garden. – Etna smokes a lot of black smoke. Not many tourists come: always worse strikes on the railway. Yesterday the sea was hard and blue like a blue tile floor. Today suddenly wind, waves, and foam. Be greeted. Be patient. Greet all.

                                                                        DHL

Our goat has two young – a black boy-goat, and a black-and-brown girl-goat. Unfortunately next week we're eating the boy-ram. But he is so jolly. It hurts me.

I'm writing to my sister to send tea. Else should have half.]

2384. To Jan Juta, 3 December 1921
Text: MS UT; Unpublished.

Fontana Vecchia, *Taormina*, Sicilia
3 Decem. 1921

Dear Johnnie

Your letter this minute. Like you I've waited and waited for *Sardinia*. It was due out, *finally*, on Novem. 15th. I hear from New York that the pictures are *beautiful*, but to my rage haven't seen a thing (I mean the reproductions of course). It is to be sold at five dollars: dear. I have written and cursed Seltzer, and told him to send you books and proofs *at once*! But no result. That beastly

[1] Ada Clarke and her son John.

Mountsier put off going to New York till Nov 22nd., so I haven't heard from him either. I have written and damned them all.

The Burr is due here[1] – con la mamma – either today, tomorrow, or Monday. Strikes are popping like crackers all the time – molta incertezza[2] everywhere. I have arranged for Burr to stay in Beau Séjour, just below Bristol, and to have use of Studio garden. Hope she'll be happy. 40 Lire a day: Diodoro now *60* – also Mrs Dashwood.[3]

The Wheelock is back in Palermo – hated America apparently – hopes very much to go to Dresden with Dreyfus, the Consul, who is moving there this week.[4] If she can't go to Dresden she will be in despair, as she hates the Vices.[5]

I had a letter from Alan's sister from Java – she seemed a bit fed with A. – Glad to hear he is flourishing, and that the door-mouse didn't come unhinged.

Philip Heseltine, that filthy rat, threatened Secker with a libel lawsuit because he said he was Halliday in *Women-in-Love*, and Secker paid £50. hush-money. He'll get it back out of me, I know. Curse them all. – Seltzer cables that he finds *Aaron's Rod* – 'Wonderful, overwhelming' – but he wants a bit of modification for the darling 'general public.' May the general public die of colic. Mountsier and Curtis Brown disliked *Aaron* very much.

Of course you will not have to *pay* anything for *Sea and Sardinia*. If Seltzer hasn't sent you six presentation copies I will threaten to abandon him. I hope it may make us both some money.

Now for plans. – A woman called Mabel Dodge Sterne, wife of Maurice Sterne – wasn't he at Anticoli? – wrote me a long letter pressing me to come to *Taos, New Mexico*, U. S. A. New Mexico is the U. S. state adjoining Mexico proper. Taos is 6000 ft high, is 25 miles from a railway, has a tribe of aboriginal Indians, said to be very interesting, who live in huge pyramid houses made of dry-brick. This woman offers us a house and everything if we will go. So I have written to say I will go. If it were possible I would go in January or February. But it seems impossible to find a ship to anywhere except New York. And New York in midwinter would probably lay us out. So it may be March. But we are going. *Let us meet in Taos.* It is only about one day's journey from real Mexico. *Fun to do an amalgamate book out there* – But we must learn *Spanish*. – The Americans of course would love a book on their own States. We might see.

Do greet the Brett Youngs for me.[6] Tell them I called at Fraita last April,

[1] Elizabeth Humes.   [2] 'great uncertainty'.   [3] An expatriate Englishwoman.
[4] Louis Goethe Dreyfus, Jr. (1899–   ), American consul at Palermo (1920-1); he became consul at Dresden 15 November 1921.   [5] I.e. the Vice-Consuls.
[6] Francis Brett Young (1884–1954), doctor and novelist, lived with his wife Jessica in Anacapri (in their Villa Fraita), though at this time they were visiting South Africa, Juta's native country. The Brett Youngs knew the Lawrences on Capri (1919–20) and helped them to find the Fontana Vecchia in March 1920. See *Letters*, iii. 438 n. 2.

with Brewster, and thought it *charming*. I wished they'd been there. I am getting so sick of these piffling pleasant people here, and their silly jibber-jabber. Feel I shall die if I have to hear much more. Very few forestieri[1] because of strikes etc. Taormina Corso just one long arcade of junk shops now. Things dearer than ever, more faked, food tiresome as it always was. If only Etna would send down 60,000,000,000 tons of boiling lava over the place and cauterise it away. I'll bet Naxos was a foul hole, before Etna kindly crozzled[2] it to a cinder. – But she – Etna – has been looking very lovely, deep, deep snow, and heavy smoke blowing this way, sun sultry through the smoke. Italy has a kind of waste, barren, écoeuré[3] feeling, it seems to me. I want to be off. If only I could get a ship to New Orleans or to Los Angeles.

Frieda is very well and has got three new frocks. She is also quite ready to be off, she says.

I have done three long stories: 'The Fox', 'The LadyBird', and 'The Captain's Doll'. They just make a volume. Please me, so be damned to everybody else.

Yes my boy, I know you'll soon be sick on Cape Candy and 'fondness.' You need somebody wholesomely to detest you.

Greet Alan for me. Tell him to open a junk shop in Cape Town, and sell *all* his presents at a good profit. Otherwise he made a mistake going east.

I will write the moment any of the various swine who owe me precise information make their grunts audible: and I will let you know exactly what we are doing. I have had my old brown suit turned ready to set off: al rovescio, carino: inside out.

The duca has gone off to Maniace with Mrs Evans, who is considerably the worse for wear. Taormina – British – is seething over the building of an English church, to cost £30,000 sterling. Mabel Hill says if they won't build it on *her* bit of land she won't give a penny, or even lend her countenance to the work.[4] It needs her brutto musaccio,[5] that it does.

a rivederci, buona sera, stia bene.

D. H. Lawrence

2385. To Marie Hubrecht, 3 December 1921
Text: MS Hubrecht; Unpublished.

Fontana Vecchia, *Taormina*, Sicilia

3 Decem. 1921

Dear Miss Hubrecht

Carmelo tells me you think you will not come this winter to Taormina. I am

---

[1] 'strangers'. [2] 'shrivelled' (dialect). [3] 'nauseous'.
[4] Mabel Hill, an expatriate Englishwoman, had lived in Taormina for about 20 years and was locally renowned for her piety and philanthropy. See *Letters*, iii. 491 n. 1.
[5] 'ugly mug'.

sorry we shan't see you. Everything here is very much the same. I went to the studio this afternoon, and Carmelo and I straightened many of the books. The furniture is all packed together in one half of the room – I don't think it will come to any harm. My wife and I go down, sometimes, and one day I want to make tea there, on the primus stove. May we use your cups? – or would you rather not? – The books are a great mess. There are so many old magazines and old reviews that seem to me utterly useless. When you do come you will have to get rid of them, they only cumber up the place. As for building, everything is *so* expensive, and the workpeople are so difficult, I'm sure it would only be a great expense of money and patience to you. Bowdwin has still got a dozen workpeople down at Rocca Bella. The place will not be ready for months. And the workpeople swarm around, of course. It is no longer very nice down there.

Bowdwin himself is much better: though he is still lame, and cannot close his eye. Didn't you hear the details of the affair? It was a young scoundrel who had twice asked Bowdwin to lend him money, because he wanted to marry. Then one evening in the darkness after dinner as Bowdwin was coming up from the Beau Séjour where he is staying, to go to the village, just as he was coming up the curved path from the lower gate of Rocca Bella, he heard a voice above him say 'Fermate'[1] – He stopped. And the voice from above him, you know the garden is above the path, rather high, down towards that low gate – the voice from above said 'Le mani su!'[2] – Bowdwin threw up his arms. He could just see an indistinct figure of a man in the dark on the garden above him. 'Siete armato?' said the voice. 'No.' – ' Datemi il portafoglio – '[3] Bowdwin gave the portfolio from his pocket – and there was nothing in it but a few letters – not a Lira. Then suddenly, before he knew, the man struck at him from above with an axe. It caught him on the brow, and missed the left eye by a hairsbreadth. It is an awful gash even now. Bowdwin fell back, with one idea, to get over on to the highroad. He got to the wall and fell down on to the road. In doing so he injured his foot frightfully – he will be lame for life. He crept on all fours to Beau Séjour, crying *Aiuto!*[4] – It was a marvel he wasn't killed – The fellow went straight into the village to chat with the Carabiniere and establish an alibi. But Bowdwin denounced him because he recognised his voice. The fellow denied it for two days, and there was no proof. Then after two days he confessed. – Now he has threatened to murder Bowdwin when he comes out of prison and to cut the faces of Bowdwin's workpeople. – Altogether it is a very nasty affair, and I can never go to Rocca Bella without feeling it in the air. The fellow is a regular criminal.

The weather is not good: sometimes very cold, then suddenly scirocco and

[1] 'Stop'.   [2] 'Hands up!'
[3] 'Are you armed?' . . . 'Give me your pocketbook'.   [4] *'Help!'*

volumes of mist and rain. Nobody seems very content. There are very few forestieri in this village because of the continual railway strikes and railway disasters. People are afraid to come. The Corso is one long string of antique shops, all moaning because nobody comes to buy. The hotels are very expensive. Timeo, Diodoro and Mrs Dashwood are charging L[ire] 60 a day after Christmas – and everything one has to buy is correspondingly dear. It costs me nearly twice as much to keep house here, as it did in the spring of 1920.

Grazia is very well. You knew Carmelo had a new baby – a third: a tiny little thing, a girl, born in September. I am afraid they are not very happy. Giovanna complains of him and says he is a bad husband to her – unkind. Ciccia also has a new baby: also a girl.[1] It was born about a month ago. Ciccia has been rather ill, and had a bad cough. She seems better now. She is craving all the time to go to America and join her husband Vincenzo. Carmelo also wants to go to America. They are all discontented.

It is possible we may go also to America in the spring. A friend wrote and offered us a house in New Mexico. I too am tired of Europe. There seems no hope in it. Of course I have not decided anything yet.

I had a letter from Juta this morning. He is in South Africa with his mother, and Insole has joined him, after having *done* China and Japan and Sumatra. Juta wants us to go to Mexico in the summer, and he paint and I write a travel book. Then afterwards he thinks of going to Paris.

I think I have told you all the news. We are continually borrowing your books from the studio, but I always scrupulously take them back. It is so nice that you let us use the studio. But we have not been down much since that awful Bowdwin affair: and since all that furniture is packed in. – Carmelo asked me to tell you that he settled his L[ire] 125 with me. He is anxious to know what to do about the Galifi money. But I do not quite understand that business. Anything I can do for you here I shall be glad to do.

My wife sends her best greetings, with mine.

Yours Sincerely   D. H. Lawrence

2386. To Mabel Dodge Sterne, 4 December 1921
Text: MS Brill; Luhan 13–14.

Villa Fontana Vecchia, Taormina, Sicilia
4 December 1921

Dear Mrs Sterne

I had your cable this morning. We are persisting in the Taos intention. I

---

[1] Francesca ('Ciccia') Cacópardo.

have written many letters: all I find so far is that I can get a steamer to New Orleans from England. That will do if nothing else. I wait still for answers from Genoa. I still hope to sail in January, or February at latest.

I must thank you for Bjerre's book, which I have read, and which I found interesting: pretty sound, it seemed to me.[1] But I rather hate therapy altogether – doctors, healers, and all the rest. I believe that a real neurotic is a half devil, but a cured neurotic is a perfect devil. They assume perfect conscious and automatic control when they're cured: and it is just this conscious-automatic control that I find loathsome.

However – till we meet.

D. H. Lawrence

I would prefer that the neurotics died.

2387. To Mary Cannan, [5 December 1921]
Text: MS Lazarus; Moore 678–9.

Villa Fontana Vecchia, *Taormina*, Sicilia
Monday 5 Decem.

My dear Mary

Wonderful to be going to Honolulu! Sounds a thrilling trip across Canada. I believe you can sail from Vancouver.

We of course have got a plan too. A woman wrote and said we could have a house and all we want in Taos, New Mexico, one of the Southern states of U.S.A. – Taos is a little town with a tribe of aboriginal indians. It is 6000 ft. high, 25 miles from a railway station, and near the desert of Arizona. There is a little colony of American artists there, and that may be horrible. But we are going. I am waiting to hear from Mountsier how many dollars I have in America – but I'm sure there are enough. I have written to various places for a steamer to New Orleans or to Los Angeles. I wrote to Cooks in Marseilles, about a boat to New Orleans. I *do* hope they'll answer, because I think there's a steamer goes from Marseilles. If the money comes all right from America, and I get the boat, we shall sail in January: and if not in January, then in February. If we go from Marseilles we shall come and see you. I too want to be off. And then if we're in Taos when you come back from Honolulu, you can come and see us there. It is not so *very* far from San Francisco. – But don't tell anybody yet that we are planning this. One plans so many things – If I don't like Taos or New Mexico we shall go south to real Mexico. But I must avoid New York. And New Orleans is, I hear, a lovely place.

---

[1] Probably *The History and Practice of Psychoanalysis* by Poul Carl Bjerre (1876–   ), trans. Elizabeth N. Barrow (Boston, 1916; 1920).

Before you go, seize a good moment and sell your Italian Liras, then they'll be off your mind. This country is sickening, and such a muddle ever increasing. I am tired of it. There are not many forestieri here, all afraid of strikes and railway smashes. And the village moaning: thousands of antique shops with doors wide open and nobody to go in. Food dearer and more impudent than ever. I shall be glad to go.

We see the usual crowd: and have even given in to going to Woods now. Am so bored really by all the triviality – oh God! Then Juta's 'Bettina'[1] and her mother are come here, to stay two months – in Beau Séjour. And I don't want them: Juta is in S. Africa, and Insole has joined him there from Java. He – Juta – wants to come to Mexico in March and do a book with me. Of course he is pining to see the *Sardinia* book – but no signs of it yet. I think it came out about the 20th Novem: – price five dollars. I *heard* that Juta's illustrations had come out beautifully.

The weather chops and changes – very cold, then very Scirocco and muggy. The old stagers are all here – and we seem to get all mixed up with them. I want to go. I know them too well now, there's no getting away from them.

I will let you know when I get a steamer. Meanwhile send me your news. I also feel as if I were leaving for good. So tired of Europe. Is Miss Muir with you yet?[2]

F[rieda] sends love.

D. H. Lawrence

2388. To Curtis Brown, [7–12 December 1921]
Text: MS UT; Huxley 532–3.

Fontana Vecchia, *Taormina*, Sicily
7 Decem. 1921[3]

Dear Curtis Brown,

I sent you what MSS are ready of the stories. The first part of 'The Fox' was published in *Nash's Magazine*.[4] 'The Captains Doll' is quite new. I am writing a third: 'The Lady Bird' – about the same length – 30,000 words or so. These three I want to go in one volume by themselves. I will send 'The LadyBird' as soon as it is done. These I call the three novelettes.

The true short stories I send are

1. 'Samson and Delilah' (pub. *English Review*)
2. 'Fanny and Annie' (pub. *Hutchinsons*)

---

[1] Elizabeth Humes.
[2] Molly Muir had been a friend of Mary (and Gilbert) Cannan since c. 1908.
[3] Though written on 7 December, the letter was not posted until 12th. See p. 144 n. 4.
[4] See p. 134 n. 2.

3. 'The Blind Man' (*English Review*)
4. 'Hadrian' – originally 'You Touched Me'(pub. in *Land and Water*)
5. 'Monkey Nuts' – unpublished.
6. 'The Horse-Dealers Daughter' – unpublished.
7. 'Tickets Please' – *Strand Magazine.*[1]
8. 'The Primrose Path' – unpublished.

Besides these I have two more short stories with the typist in Florence: hope to send them you in a few days. And then a last one, 'England my England', I am working on.[2] I think these will be quite enough short stories. If not there are two animal sketches, 'Rex' and 'Adolf', which I can send.[3] Both have appeared in *The Dial* in America.

Secker wants a book of short stories quick, for the spring. I think better let him have these little stories – not the three novelettes. Tell me what you think. – I believe *Land and Water* cut 'You Touched Me' ('Hadrian'). I will ask Mountsier to send a true copy from America. – Wonder if you are back from America.

Yrs.   D. H. Lawrence

PS   I waited for the MSS. of the two other short stories, which I now enclose with the rest.[4]

1. 'Tickets Please': pub. in *Strand Magazine*
2. 'Primrose Path': unpublished

There remains now only 'England my England' which was pub. in *English Review*, but which I am re-writing. Also the 'novelette' – 'The Ladybird'. – which is nearly ready.

I have sent Mountsier *duplicates of all these*.

2389. To Robert Mountsier, 7 December 1921
Text: MS Smith; Postmark, Taormina 8 DIC 21; Unpublished.

Fontana Vecchia, *Taormina*, Sicily
7 Decem 1921

Dear M[ountsier]

I have sent Curtis B[rown][5] the same batch of short stories as I sent you. I hope soon to have the others ready.

Secker wants to publish a vol. of short stories in *early* spring, *before* he does *Aarons Rod*: to do *Aarons Rod* in May or June.[6] If he does this, I think he had

[1] 'Tickets, Please' was published in *Strand* (April 1919).
[2] 'England, My England' appeared in *English Review*, xxi (October 1915), 238–52.
[3] 'Rex' appeared in *Dial*, lxx (February 1921), 169–76. See also p. 123 n. 3.
[4] By 'MSS' here DHL meant typescripts; he received them on 12 December from the typist, Mrs Carmichael (Tedlock, *Lawrence MSS* 94).   [5] Curtis B.] Secker
[6] Secker published *Aaron's Rod* in June 1922, and *England, My England* not until January 1924.

better do the little stories, *not* the three novelettes ('Fox etc – '). He will not be simultaneous with Seltzer in that case. Write quickly what you think, also to Curtis Brown. 'Wintry Peacock' would be excluded from the English vol., but not, I think, from the American. I may let him include 'Rex' and 'Adolf' if he is short: but I think he won't be.[1]

I think you have now two typed copies of 'You touched Me' – re-christened 'Hadrian'. If so, would you please make any tiny alteration from the new MS. I sent, on to your original, and then post one of them to Curtis Brown, asking him to use this for the complete vol. I find that *Land and Water* cut the story: and I sent Curtis B. the *Land and Water* pages. If you haven't got a duplicate, don't bother.

I am expecting to get a passenger ship to New Orleans: perhaps from Marseilles. – Haven't heard from you yet. Shall want dollars for the passage – or English pounds. Am dying to see *Sea and Sardinia* – is it sent to England yet? – Why such a *long* time?

DHL

2390. To Martin Secker, [7–12 December 1921]
Text: MS UInd; Secker 45.

Villa Fontana Vecchia, *Taormina*, Sicily
7 Dec. 1921

Dear Secker

I have sent Curtis Brown the MS. of six stories. Two more are at the typist's. One I am working on. I think these are enough – though there are two little animal stories you might have, besides.

I am finishing the third of three little novelettes – each about 33,000 words. I want these to be a book by themselves, later.

If we agree about the book of short stories, when do you think you could have it out? I cannot have the MS. ready before 1st January, I am afraid – not complete.

Yrs   D. H. Lawrence

P. S. I waited for the two extra stories, so send Curtis B. now the MSS of *eight* short stories and the two *long* stories besides –

---

[1] The same stories appeared in both the English and American editions of *England, My England*; 'Rex' and 'Adolf' were excluded, 'Wintry Peacock' included.

2391. To Robert Welsh, 9 December 1921
Text: TMSC Garnett, R.; Unpublished.

Sicily,
9th December, 1921
Robert Welsh Esq., Solicitor, Ayr.[1]

Dear Sir,

I have just received your letter of 2nd December, telling me of the James Tate Black Memorial prize for my Novel *The Lost Girl*.[2] I have received no previous letter. Daniel cannot have forwarded the one containing the cheque; he has this address.[3] Of course I am very pleased especially pleased at having at last some spark of friendly recognition out of Britain. It has been mostly abuse.

Would it be simpler to pay the hundred pounds direct into my account with the L[ondon] C[ounty] W[estminster] and Parr's Bank, 263 Strand, London W. C. 2?[4] The Italian post is somewhat uncertain. But just as you wish.

And will you tell me the name of the Professor of English Literature at Edinburgh University?

Thanking you for your kindness.

Yours faithfully,   D. H. Lawrence

2392. To Baroness Anna von Richthofen, [10 December 1921]
Text: MS UCB; Frieda Lawrence 120.

Fontana Vecchia, *Taormina*, Sizilien
Sonntag. 10 Decem.

Liebe Schwiegermutter

Ich bin froh, dass du den Chek hast. Aber störe du dich eben nicht, dankbar zu sein. Das Geld ist da: gut, und genug gesagt.

Die Frieda behaltet nichts. Wir haben noch ein Glück. Der Professor of English Literature in Edinburgh Univertäts hat mir einen Preis besagt: 100

---

[1] Robert Welsh (1874–1960) studied law at the University of Glasgow, was admitted solicitor in 1897 and set up practice on his own account c. 1910. Later he was one of the Honorary Sheriffs in Ayr. His firm administered the James Tait Black Prize on behalf of his clients, the Black family.

[2] The prize was for £100; it had been established in memory of James Tait Black, the Edinburgh publisher; and it was awarded on the recommendation of the Regius Professor of Rhetoric and English Literature in the University of Edinburgh, at this time (Sir) Herbert Grierson (1866–1960). In 1921 two prizes were awarded: for the best novel, DHL's *The Lost Girl*; for the best biography, G. M. Trevelyan's *Lord Grey of the Reform Bill*.

[3] Welsh had presumably addressed DHL c/o C. W. Daniel, the publisher of his play *Touch and Go* (1920).

[4] DHL recorded in his diary, 29 December 1921, that Welsh had paid £100 into his bank (Tedlock, *Lawrence MSS* 95).

Pfund für den *Lost Girl*. Das ist ein Glücksfall. Ich hoffe das ich nächste
Woche das Geld kriege. Hundert Pfund Englisch ist ja nettes Geld.
Bitte Schwiegermutter, schick dem Hadu nein nein – besser dass alle
dasselbe haben – 500.[1] Der Bub braucht es vielleicht mehr wie die andern.
Der Hinke schreibt tüchtig. Es klingt mir aber ein Bisschen übertüchtig,
übermoralisch, und engnäsig, und blassblütig. Aber du weisst besser wie ich.
Gut wenn du ihn hilfen könnst.
Wir schicken keine Weihnachtspaketen – die Post ist so eine Schwierigkeit,
hier in Italien. Aber wenn das Buch kommt, schick ich das. – Ich bin so
zufrieden, das du dich so gesund findst. Aber *vorsicht* vor Weihnacht. Geh du
auf kleinen stillen Füssen, mach kein übermütiges Rausch.

DHL

Ein furchtbarer Wind. Tausende weisse Lämmchen auf dem hart-blauen
Meer, und die Segelschiffe die laufen angstvoll mit einem halben Flügel.
Die Frieda hat hunderte gute Leckerle gebacken – sehr[2] gut – heut Morgen
gemacht.

[Dear Schwiegermutter
I am glad you have the cheque.[3] But just don't you bother to be grateful.
The money is there: good, and enough said.
Frieda is keeping nothing. We have another bit of luck. The Professor of
English Literature at Edinburgh University has awarded me a prize: 100
pounds for the *Lost Girl*. That's a windfall. I hope I get the money next week.
A hundred pounds English is quite nice money.
Please Schwiegermutter, send Hadu – no no – better that all have the same
– 500. The boy needs it perhaps more than the others.
Hinke writes diligently. It sounds to me however a bit too diligent, too
moral, and narrow-nosed, and pale-blooded. But you know better than I.
Good if you could help him.
We are sending no Christmas parcels – the post is such a difficulty, here in
Italy. But when the book comes, I'll send it. – I am so pleased that you find
yourself so healthy. But *beware* of Christmas. Just you go on little still feet,
don't get cockily tipsy.

DHL

An awful wind. Thousands of little white lambs on the hard-blue sea, and
the sailing ships that run anxiously with half a wing.
Frieda has baked hundreds of good dainties – very good – made them this
morning.]

[1] nein nein – besser dass alle dasselbe haben – 500.] geheimnisvoll tausend Mark, stets funf
Hundert   [2] sehr] she   [3] From Kippenberg: see Letter 2383.

2393. To Robert Mountsier, 12 December 1921
Text: MS Smith; PC v. Carl Spitzweg, 'Ein Einsiedler, Geige spielend'; Postmark,
Taormina 12 DIC 21; Unpublished.

[Fontana Vecchia, *Taormina*, (Messina) Sicily]
12 December. 1921

I sent you today MSS. of two stories – 'Tickets Please' – pub. in *Strand Mag.*
in 1918 – England only – and 'The Primrose Path', quite unpublished. – Still
seeking ship to New Orleans.

D. H. Lawrence

2394. To Martin Secker, 17 December 1921
Text: MS UInd; Postmark, Taormina 17 DIC 21; Secker 46.

Fontana Vecchia, *Taormina*, Sicily
17 Decem. 1921

Dear Secker

I am getting a ship from Palermo to go to New Mexico. And am tight for
money. Would it inconvenience you to pay me in any money owing on the *Lost
Girl*? – L[ondon] C[ounty] W[estminster] and Parrs Bank – 263 Strand –
W.C.2. Please do it if you can. If not, just let me know.

I have sent *all* the short stories but one, to C[urtis] B[rown], told him to let
you see them. The last I must still work on. Of the three novelettes, all are
finished, but one is at the typist still. – I will send the last short story in about
ten days time.

Let me know by return about the money, so that I know what I can do.
Greetings for Christmas.

D. H. Lawrence

2395. To Dr Anton Kippenberg, 19 December 1921
Text: MS SVerlag; Unpublished.

Fontana Vecchia, *Taormina*, Sicilia
19 December 1921

Dear Dr Kippenberg

I hear from my mother-in-law that she has the cheque for eighteen
thousand Mark, from you. How pleased she is! She can have a real Christmas.
– Many thanks for sending the money so promptly and kindly to her. I hope in
time the translation of *The Rainbow* will pay you back.

My wife and I think of going to America in the early New Year – to New

Mexico, where we have friends. I would like to try the New World. This old
Europe does take the heart out of one. – But I will let you know what we do,
exactly.

Many good wishes for the season.

D. H. Lawrence

2396. To S. S. Koteliansky, [20 December 1921]
Text: MS BL; PC v. Buste de Femme, Titien; Postmark, [. . .] 21 DIC 21; Zytaruk 230.

[Fontana Vecchia, *Taormina*, (Messina) Sicily]
Dec 20

I sent you and Sonia a book for Christmas – though I feel very unChristmas-
like. We really do think of going to *New* Mexico – which is still USA. A
compromise. No, I cant come back to England – can't. Don't believe in your
good simple people. – All Murrys etc.

Has that miserable *Dial* paid you?[1]

I wish we could sail in Jan.

DHL

2397. To Violet Monk, [20 December 1921]
Text: MS SIU; PC v. Dosso Dossi, Portrait d'homme avec beret; Postmark, Taormina 21
DIC 21; Unpublished.

[Fontana Vecchia, *Taormina*, (Messina) Sicily]
20 Dec.

I had those MSS.[2] Very many thanks – hope you are better of your pains. We
are preparing for Christmas – but dont feel a bit like it. We think of sailing
away to New Mexico in the New Year – hope it will come off. How is Miss
Lambert? So sunny and beautiful here just now – warm as summer.

Best wishes from us both.

D. H. Lawrence

2398. To Robert Mountsier, 21 December 1921
Text: MS Smith; Postmark, Taormina 21 DIC 21; Unpublished.

Fontana Vecchia, *Taormina*, Sicilia
21 Decem. 1921

Dear M[ountsier]

I had your letters and chequebook today. Many thanks. Dont bother any
more about the money, I can cash these cheques here.

[1] See p. 23 n. 2.   [2] See p. 28 n. 4.

I am so glad to know you are back in New York. I feel I can trust you. And is there a publisher on earth that one can *really* trust? I hope Seltzer isn't going to go bankrupt again.[1] – I will not write him *any* business letter at all, now I know you are back.

I wrote to Mitchell Kennerley telling him I am coming to the States and that I *intend* to have my own out of him.

I have finished the third of the *novelettes* – 'Ladybird' – and will send it you when it comes from the typewriter.[2] With 'The Fox', 'The Ladybird', and the 'Captains Doll', I think you have a rather nice volume. – Then I am finishing today or tomorrow, D.V. – the last of the short stories – 'England, My England'. The vol of short stories to begin with 'Tickets Please' and perhaps to bear that title.

If I am to finish *Mr Noon* it shall be in the States.

You are discouraging about Taos. Yet I will go there. I dread the New York region, and feel I shall like New Mexico, even if I dont care for Taos and Mabel Dodge. There is a possibility of a cargo boat from Palermo to New Orleans in January, so Tagliavia[3] writes me. I shall know definitely in a few days. Otherwise I shall sail from France. I shall cable Seltzer when I leave – he has a cable address. Will you then let Mrs Sterne know at once.

Dont be so sure you won't come to see us in Taos. – If we don't like it we can move on a bit. Juta wants me to meet him in Mexico City in March, to do another joint travel book. What do you think?

Koteliansky still is not paid for *The Gent[leman] from San Francisco*. Why?

I heard that I was to have the James Tait Black prize for *The Lost Girl* – £100 – from Edinburgh University: But haven't got the money yet.

Shall write immediately there is news.

DHL

Don't put me off Taos: If ever I am coming to America, let me come now.

I can do a foreword[4] for the 'Beasts' if it comes as a chapbook. But see first how *Tortoises* goes.

Huebsch sent me two copies of his new *Rainbow*, and said he thought the 1000 he printed were sold.

---

[1] A letter from Seltzer's wife, Adele, to her sister on 8 November 1921 makes his financial plight clear: 'People think marvels of Thomas that he has held his own during these fearful times. Old established businesses have gone crash, and he has kept up. But it has been a miserable struggle' (Lacy, *Seltzer* 178).   [2] typewriter] publisher   [3] Unidentified.   [4] foreword] chapbook

2399. To Catherine Carswell, [21 December 1921]
*Text:*MS YU; PC v. [Fresco depicting Pius II being crowned by Frederick III, from the Piccolomini library, Duomo, Siena]; Postmark, Taormina 21 DIC 21; cited in Carswell 138, 159.

[Fontana Vecchia, *Taormina*, (Messina) Sicily]
21 Decem.

I sent you an American novel I thought amusing.[1] Hope you'll have a good Christmas. We really want to sail away to New Mexico in Jan. or Feb. – feel so unbearably tired of Europe. Tell me how you are.

DHL

2400. To S. S. Koteliansky, 26 December 1921
Text: MS BL; cited in Gransden 28.

Fontana Vecchia, *Taormina*, Sicilia
26 Dec 1921

Dear Kot

I got the cheque for £12 – odd. I *wish* you would let it be $\frac{1}{4}$ for mc – I am not justified in taking half. – *The Dial* should have paid you *more*, also.

I had a return touch of influenza – and Christmas in bed. But I don't care. It saved me going out to a horrible Xmas dinner.

We really think of going to New Mexico. I am toiling to find a ship. A woman offers us a house in Taos, near Santa Fe: mountains – 6000 ft. high – aboriginal indians – sun worship – fine bright climate. I want to find a ship to New Orleans or Galveston or Los Angeles. Will sail in Jan. or Feb. if possible. It is U.S.A., so not off the map. I am afraid there is a colony of New York artists in Taos. Evil everywhere. But I want to go – to try.

We only saw the Carswells in Florence in September – voilà tout.[2]

Be kind enough to send me a packet of primus stove *needles*, will you – they only cost a few pence – as *sample*, registered is the best way to post. Don't do it except when it is absolutely no trouble. – I sent[3] you *Contes Drolatiques*[4] – hope you got it.

Cold here.

saluti   DHL

[1] Probably John Dos Passos, *Three Soldiers* (1921). See also Letter 2432 and n. 3.
[2] 'that's all'.   [3] sent] send   [4] See p. 40 n. 2.

2401. To Mabel Dodge Sterne, 28 December 1921
Text: MS Brill; Luhan 12–13.

Taormina
28 December 1921

Dear Mabel Dodge Sterne

Your letter and the little MSS[1] came this morning.

Good, we are coming. I haven't found a cargo boat yet, but from Bordeaux to New Orleans a boat on 15th. January. It is just possible we may get that. But I have to wait for letters and money arrangements. If we miss this boat, we shall sail a month later – by the next. This is the Transatlantique passenger service. So at any rate we should be in Taos in March. I want very much to come, and wish I could start tomorrow.

Thank you for all the information. It seems to me we shall live as cheaply there as here – almost. If the rooms of the little house are not too small, we'll have that. And I'll pay you the usual rent. I hope I needn't all my life be so scrubby poor as we have been: those damned books may sell better. But money never worries me. I've got apparently about 2000 dollars to come with: enough.

I too believe in Taos, without having seen it. I also believe in Indians. But they must do *half* the believing: in me as well as in the sun. Vediamo.[2]

I must learn Spanish. I don't know any.

allora, fra poco[3]   D. H. Lawrence

2402. To Martin Secker, 29 December 1921
Text: MS UInd; Postmark, Taormina 29 DIC 21; Secker 46.

Fontana Vecchia, *Taormina*, Sicilia
29 Decem. 1921.

Dear Secker

Thank you for your statement of account and for paying the £17,,19 ,,0 into my bank.

You will by now have read the MSS of the stories. I have finished everything, only wait for the typist. I should like the title 'Fanny and Annie' changed to 'The Last Straw'.[4] Please note it.

I am just deciding on a ship to New Orleans – hope to sail in January – February at latest.

I am making some modifications in *Aaron's Rod*, for Seltzer. You can see them when they're done.

Best wishes for the New Year.

D. H. Lawrence

---

[1] Unidentified.   [2] 'Let us see.'   [3] Lit. 'then, in short time'.
[4] This change was not made by Secker or in any subsequent publication of the story.

P. S. Will you please henceforth make out all accounts to Curtis Brown for the *Lost Girl* and for everything.

DHL

2403. To Angela Easterbrook, 29 December 1921
Text: MS UT; Unpublished.

Fontana Vecchia, *Taormina*, Sicily
29 Decem. 1921

Dear Miss Easterbrook[1]

Thank you for your letters of 12th and 21st December. Yes, it is quite all right to order *The Prussian Officer* on my account – About *Tortoises* I have done absolutely nothing in England. Let Curtis Brown act entirely according to his own discretion in the matter – I don't mind if Secker has it or not.[2]

I have finished 'Ladybird' and 'England my England' – and only wait for the typist. Will you please make all arrangements with Mountsier for the American end.

I enclose note from *Chatto and Windus*. I should like Brown to ask them if they are going to leave *Look We have Come thr[ough]* out of print.[3] In that case I should like him – Brown – to take the responsibility for the book.

I also enclose Secker's statement. Would you mind glancing at the agreement and seeing if I get 1/6 per copy over 2000 or over 3,000. I wish also you would take charge of all Secker's accounts with me, have them made out to you – to Curtis Brown, that is. – I will write Secker to this effect.

I am thinking of sailing with my wife for New Mexico, in January or February. So I would like to have everything straight.

Best wishes for the New Year.

D. H. Lawrence

2404. To Catherine Carswell, [30 December 1921]
Text: MS YU; PC v. La Catastrofe di Messina – Corso Vittorio Emanuele; Postmark, Taormina 30 DIC 21; cited in Carswell 159.

[Fontana Vecchia, *Taormina*, (Messina), Sicily]
30 Dec.

Send you today a copy of *Tortoises*. Wonder if you'll like the appearance.[4] If

---

[1] Angela Easterbrook was Albert Curtis Brown's secretary for several years until she left in the 1920s to be married.
[2] The book was never published in England.
[3] Chatto & Windus did not re-issue the volume (see p. 176 n. 2).
[4] The book's outward appearance is described in Roberts (A19): 'Greenish-brown decorative paper boards, upper cover decorated with a colour print of Fujiyama by Hiroshige for the background; a huge tortoise is suspended from a scaffolding by a rope secured around his middle; at the bottom of the scaffolding in pseudo-oriental lettering: TORTOISES.'

ever you see a reproduction of the four Evangelical Beasts – Matthew, Mark, Luke, John as Man, Bull, Lion, Eagle – from some old illumination – such as would do for the cover design of my Apostolic Beasts – do send it me. – We are seriously thinking of sailing to New Orleans and going to Taos in New Mexico, to try that – hope to get off in Jan. or Feb. – I had your p.c. – perhaps Christmas was jolly none the less. I had a cold and was in bed. I hate Christmas anyhow. Best of wishes for the New Year.

DHL

2405. To Earl Brewster, 2 January 1922
Text: MS UT; Brewster 43–4.

Fontana Vecchia, Taormina, Sicilia
2 Jan. 1922

Dear Brewster

I had your letter about Kandy. It sounds lovely, the coloured, naked people and the big elephant coming round the corner and the temple throng. I guess you'll love it after a while. I feel I can't come – that the east is not my destiny. More and more I feel that meditation and the inner life are not my aim, but some sort of action and strenuousness and pain and frustration and struggling through. All the things you don't believe in I do. And the goal is not that men[1] should become serene as Buddh[a][2] or as gods, but that the unfleshed gods should become men in battle. God made man is the goal. The gods are uneasy until they can become men. And men have to fight a way for the new incarnation. And the fight and the sorrow and the loss of blood, and even the influenzas and the headache are part of the fight and the fulfilment. Let nobody try to filch from me even my influenza. – I've got influenza at the moment, but it only makes me more unbuddhing.

I have decided to go to Taos in New Mexico. There are Indians there, and an old sun magic – And I believe that the clamorous future is in the States. I do not want peace nor beauty nor even freedom from pain. I want to fight and to feel new gods in the flesh.

We are looking for a ship. At present I can only find one from Bordeaux to New Orleans – and Bordeaux is so far. So probably we shall sail from Palermo to New York on February 6th. The address in Taos will be

c/o Mrs Maurice Sterne, Taos, New Mexico.

But always safe is my publisher:

c/o Thomas Seltzer, 5 West 50th Street, New York City.

I sent you two days ago a copy of *Tortoises* – poems – to Kandy – I hope they will come.

---

[1] men] the Gods and   [2] MS reads 'Buddh'.

Write and tell me what you are doing. Old Major Fraser died on Saturday and is being buried today down at Mazzaro by the sea.[1] It was time for him to die.

For myself, I am weary of Taormina, and have no desire to stay in Sicily or in Europe at all.

Greet Achsah and the child, and be greeted.

D. H. Lawrence[2]

2406. To Angela Easterbrook, 3 January 1922
Text: MS UT; Unpublished.

Fontana Vecchia, *Taormina*, Sicily
3 Jan 1922

Dear Miss Easterbrook

Do please let the short stories, the unpublished ones, be published in the magazines, if possible – though even for that I wish it could be in conjunction with Mountsier at the American end. Secker can wait a while.

I expect to send 'Ladybird' and 'England my England' at the end of the week. – I will let you know when I fix my ship to sail. It will probably be February 6th.

Yours   D. H. Lawrence

Secker would never be ready till May, anyhow. It always takes him a long three months to get a book out. So you could take until May for the serials.[3]

DHL

I have no duplicat[e][4] except 'The Primrose [Path']'[5] – you could get them ma[de] from Secker's MS. – I can send you 'The Primrose Path' only: will do so tomorrow. That only leaves 'The Horse De[aler's] Daughter' and 'Monkey Nuts'.

2407. To Robert Mountsier, [9 January 1922]
Text: MS Smith; Unpublished.

Fontana Vecchia, *Taormina*, Sicily
9th. Jan. 1921

Dear Mountsier

I send you here the MSS of 'The Ladybird' – 30,000 words: also of

---

[1] A Scotsman retired from the Indian army, who collected Greek carvings and paintings; his home was at Mazzarò, n. of Taormina.

[2] An unidentified person added, after DHL's signature: 'My love to you all three. Bebie'.

[3] 'The Fox' was the only one of the three short novels included in *The Ladybird* to appear first in serial form (in the *Dial*, May–August 1922).

[4] MS torn.   [5] 'The Primrose [Path']] Horsedealers Da[ughter]

'England my England', 13 000 words. 'The Ladybird' is *quite* new: 'England my England' is all re-written, absolutely: but it appeared in a poorer form in the *English Review* in 1915. – I enclose handwritten MSS of 'Fox' and of 'Captains Doll', so that I needn't cart them about.

I have not yet heard if you have received the MSS. of *all* the other stories – or any of the other stories. Have you got them by now? I do hope so.

I have your letter giving me an account of the moneys – 1,400 dollars, that is: also your note of Dec. 7th. saying the other 400 are paid in. Nothing further.

I have the *Tortoises* books: very handsome, but I am surprised to see them so expensively got up. This is not a chap-book. There is *still* no sign of *Sea and Sardinia*: nor of the *Aaron* MS. which Seltzer is sending for me to make alterations. Italian post bad again.

I told you I received the book of cheques. I think I shall be able to manage with these, though since the Banca di Sconto has gone smash – or stopped paying – it is impossible to cash anything here in the village.[1]

I had flue for a fortnight: otherwise we should really have sailed from Bordeaux to New Orleans by the Cie Gle. Transatlantique on Jan. 15th. Now we must wait – perhaps we shall come on Feb. 5th sail from Palermo by the Fabre line, to New York, ship *Providence*. I shall cable Seltzer and he must tell you. Perhaps the Consul in Leghorn will get me a cargo boat fit to sail on. – In case I come to New York, look how much it costs to take a ship down to Galveston, instead of going overland to Taos.

I hear from Juta he has had a rather serious accident to his foot, on the mountain there.

Has Huebsch sent you a statement for the *Rainbows* sold and for the other books? I *must* tackle Kennerley if I come.

I have posted MSS of all these stories to Curtis Brown – or his representative.

Have got a headache and don't feel well. Hope you're all right.

Yrs   D.H. Lawrence

2408. To Thomas Seltzer, 9 January 1922
Text: MS UT; Postmark, Taormina 11 GEN 22; Lacy, *Seltzer* 29–32.

–   Fontana Vecchia, *Taormina*, Sicilia
9 Jan. 1922

Dear Seltzer
   Today has come *Sea and Sardinia*, and a few days ago *Tortoises*. They are

---

[1] The Banca Di Sconto, one of the three principal Italian commercial banks, had lacked business confidence for some time; then other banks refused to honour its cheques and it was forced to suspend dealings on 29 December 1921.

handsome books, and must have cost a good deal. But you can't call *Tortoises* a chap-book. Did you intend it for one? I think the pictures have come out well – only the reds a bit weary. I do hope Juta will be pleased. Poor Jannie, he has hurt his leg so badly out there on that beastly Table Mountain, and is struggling on crutches. I do hope he'll soon be on his proper feet. He is just the man for the American public – so handsome and pictorial.

Today I sent off the last of the story MSS to Mountsier. I do hope by now he has all. The three stories, 'The Fox', 'The Ladybird', and 'The Captains Doll', will, I think, make a really interesting book – perhaps even a real seller. Then there is the book of short stories proper. When the MS. section of *Aaron* arrives from you, and I have done that, then I have finished with writing for a bit, thank god. I am sick of the sight and thought of manuscripts. But to amuse myself on shipboard and so on I shall probably go on with a translation of the Sicilian novel *Mastro-don Gesualdo*, by Giovanni Verga. It is some thirty years old already, and perhaps is already translated in America. Will you find out? – It interests me very much, as being one of the genuine emotional extremes of European literature: just as Selma Lagerlöf or Knut Hamsun may be the other extreme, northwards.[1] But Verga seems to me more real than these.

I've got this flu which keeps coming – so feel unhappy for the moment. But for this we'd probably have sailed from Bordeaux to New Orleans by the *La Salles* – Transatlantique SS – on January 15th. Now maybe we shall take the *Providence*, Fabre line, from Palermo to New York, leaving Palermo February 5th. I shall cable you when it is decided, and you will please tell Mountsier.

They are in a stew here over the failure of the Banca di Sconto. Let us hope it will end all right. But Italy is rocky. I am tired of Europe – really tired in my bones. There seems to be no getting any forrarder. What I want in America is a sense of the future, and be damned to the exploited past. I believe in America one can catch up some kind of emotional impetus from the aboriginal Indian and from the aboriginal air and land, that will carry one over this crisis of the world's soul depression, into a new epoch.

Did they tell you that they gave me £100 sterling for the James Tait Black Memorial prize for the best English novel of 1920. It was judged by the Professor of English literature in Edinburgh University.

It is cold here, the snow almost coming down to us, on the hills – Etna all white and black – many many little birds fluttering everywhere. Thank goodness powder has become so dear.

I look forward to seeing you. What fun it will be to be in Taos. I look forward to it immensely, and wish I could start tomorrow. Juta and Insole

---

[1] Selma Ottilia Lovisa Lagerlöf (1858–1940), Swedish novelist and short story writer, Nobel laureate in 1909, first woman member of Swedish Academy (1914). Knut Hamsun (1859–1952), Norwegian novelist, Nobel laureate in 1920.

press me to go to Nyasaland,[1] and trek across to Lake Tanganyika. But no, I have said I will come to America.

Be greeted   D. H. Lawrence

2409. To Jan Juta, 9 January 1922
Text: Moore, *Intelligent Heart* 286–7.

Fontana Vecchia, Taormina, Sicily
Jan. 9, 1922

I heard from Burr from Rome – who had it from Mrs Wroe,[2] from Suia – that your hurt leg is more serious than you made me think. I *do* hope it isn't really bad. Of course with all those Tanganyika trekking plans, I thought it was just a temporary sprain. I *do* hope it's not anything serious, and that it is quite better by the time you get this letter.

Today has come *Sea and Sardinia*, so we are thinking hard of you. I expect you have your copies. What do you think? The *reds* are disappointing – and there is a certain juiciness about the colours that I don't like – but otherwise they are not bad, I think. Do tell me your impression. I'm sure the text will be a bit of a blow to you – so wintry and unidyllic. And see yourself and M. Alain![3] Bet you'll think you aren't *half* nice enough, both of you. Never mind, you have now made your bow before the world. The wrapper makes me scream with agony – but you can't prevent the Americans.[4]

I am sorry we can't do the Tanganyika trip. But I am not sufficiently moneyed. – I got £100 for that prize fo[r] the *Lost Girl*, though. Did I tell you?

It is awfully cold here, the snow right down Monte Venere and on Forza all sprinkled white – Etna a shrouded horror. I hate it when it's cold. Yet the first bits of almond blossom are sparking out, and the first of those magenta anemones that Alan calls Venus tears.

I keep on with the Taos trip. If I'd been well enough we'd have sailed from Bordeaux to New Orleans on the 15th of this month. Now perhaps on the 5th Feb. we'll go Fabre line from Palermo to New York, and then overland from there. Unless some casual steamer turns up. But I expect to be in Taos by March *and then you can come when you like!* After all, the Americans would *love* a book on their own country and what with Rockies and Indians and deserts – big deserts lie below Taos, which is on a plateau 6000 ft high – and Mexicans and Cowboys – *you ought to find something to paint and I to write.*

[1] Now Malawi.   [2] Unidentified.
[3] The description of Juta and Insole in *Sea and Sardinia*, chap. VIII.
[4] The book had 'a white paper dust-jacket printed in black with a colour illustration of "Fonni" by Jan Juta reproduced on the upper cover' (Roberts A21).

Today thank heaven I have sent off the last of my MSS – three long-short stories, will make a really interesting book those three – 'The Fox', 'The Ladybird', and 'The Captain's Doll': then a collected book of short stories, most of them re-written. Oh I fairly loathe the sight of manuscripts, and the *thought* of publishing. Oh I get so sick of everything: and so double-sick of Taorminity.

But we've got good dry olive wood and the salotta is warm and thank God the wind is still. Only tomorrow five awful people to tea. – By the way have you heard of Gilbert Cannan out in S Africa – with young Mond and Gwen, the polyandrous wife?¹ Mary Cannan of course going off like a wick-wack about them. But I am callous.

We were so distressed for fear the leg might be worse than we thought. Send word that it is better.

I had a letter from Mrs Wroe about Mexico – thought her rather a twaddler.

2410. To Curtis Brown, 9 January 1922
Text: MS UT; Unpublished.

Fontana Vecchia, *Taormina*, Sicily
9 Jan 1922

Dear Curtis Brown

I post you today the MSS of 'The Ladybird', 30,000 words: quite new – and 'England my England' 13,000 words: re-written, but appeared in an old form in the *English Review* in 1915. I enclose also spare copy of 'The Primrose Path'.²

I hope you will be able to dispose of some of the stories serially – in conjunction with Mountsier in America.

Basil Blackwell of Oxford asks me for a book of short stories. Do you think he might have one – failing Secker?

If Secker doesn't want to do *Aaron's Rod*, I don't mind a bit.

Wonder if you are back from America – or if you are Miss Easterbrook.

Yours   D. H. Lawrence

---

¹ Henry Ludwig Mond (1898–1949), later 2nd Baron Melchett, m. Amy Gwen Wilson in January 1920. She was formerly mistress to Gilbert Cannan; he had deserted his wife, Mary, on her account. For over a year from October 1920 Cannan had been touring South Africa; he met the Monds while there (Gwen was South African by birth) and briefly re-established their curious three-cornered relationship.   ² 'The Primrose Path'] England My.

2411. To Baroness Anna von Richthofen, [10? January 1922]
Text: MS UCB; Frieda Lawrence 121–2.

[Fontana Vecchia, *Taormina* (Messina) Sicily]
[10? January 1922][1]

[Wir mussen][2] nur ein sehr gutes Schiff auswählen. Es *kann* so sein, das wir nächsten Monat abfahren. Aber nichts sicher. Und wenn wir da sind, in Amerika, und ich kann Geld verdienen, dann können wir schön wieder nach Deutschland kommen, dich zu besuchen. Wenn man nur die Dollars hat, ist Amerika nicht weiter von Baden wie Taormina: und vielleicht nicht so weit. Das weisst du gut.

Ich habe ein bisschen Influenza gehabt: es war sehr kalt, der Schnee kam näherer und näherer, die Bergen hinunter, Monte Venere war weiss, und unserer eigene Monte Diretto. Bis zu uns könnte der Schnee aber doch nicht kommen, das Meer sagt nein. Und jetzt, Gott sei dank, wieder warm wie sommer, Schnee geflogen, Meer blau, die Mandeln eifrig zu blüthen. So tausende viele Vögeln sind herunten gekommen, mit der Kälte, Goldfinke, Schwarzköpfe, Blauköpfe, Rotschwänze, Rotbrüste, alle so bunt und lustig. Und Gott sei dank, Pulver ist jetzt so teuer, die grossmutigen Italiener können keine Patronen mehr kaufen.

In dieser Zeit arbeite ich nicht. Ich habe, seit wir wieder hier sind, drei lange Novellen geschrieben, die ein ganz nettes Buch machen sollen. Auch habe ich meine kleine Novellen gesammelt, fertig für ein Buch. So, für den Moment bin ich frei, und will nichts weiter anfangen, sonst vielleicht will ich einen grauen Sizilianischen Roman übersetzen – *Mastro-don Gesualdo*, von Giovanni Verga. Es ist echt Sizilianisch, und man kann darin sehen, wie schwarz und schwer und hoffnungslos sind diese Sizilianer, *innerlich*. Äusserlich solche schönheit: innerlich Dreck und Grauen: und *Geld*. Nein, schwiegermutter, hier in Europa kann nichts neues ankommen. Nur können sie die alte Bindfaden immer kauen. – Die Banca di Sconto, vielleicht die Grosseste Bank in Italien, ist verkracht – zahlt nicht – und *so* eine schwarze Wolke über alle Leute hier. Das Geld ist das Blut eines Italiener's. Er sagt es

[1] DHL was ill with a bout of flu for a fortnight in December 1921 – January 1922. He speaks of having the flu in a letter to Thomas Seltzer dated 9 January 1922 and mentions 'snow almost coming down to us' and flocks of birds. On 11 January he wrote to Mary Cannan that he had been ill for a fortnight. Thus from internal evidence 10 January seems an appropriate date for this letter.
[2] The manuscript for this letter is incomplete: the first page is missing. Frieda published the incomplete manuscript in "*Not I, But the Wind . . .*" (1934) as two separate letters. The German edition of her book, *Nur Der Wind* (1936), included the incomplete manuscript as a single letter and the translator or editor supplied the words, 'wir mussen' at the beginning to complete the first sentence as the editors have done here.

immer – vuole il sangue mio – er will mein Blut haben – wenn er muss etwas zahlen. – Aber es ist doch grausam. Wahrscheinlich aber wird die Regierung hereinkommen, und gut machen.

Heute hatten wir deinen Brief an Frieda. Wie nett für die Annie, wenn sie an Oster heiraten kann. Dann hat sie kaum Vater oder Mutter mehr, und alles kann freier und freundlicher werden. Ich bin so froh dass es geht dem Hinke so gut mit seinem Geschäft.

Frieda will auch ein Wort schreiben. Wir sitzen in unserer Salotta, warm und still, mit der Lampe auf dem Tisch. Draussen, durch die Thüre sieh ich wie eine Dämmerung das Mondbeleuchtete Meer, und den Mond durch die Bignonia Blätter von unserm Terrasse: und alles ganz still, nur von Zeit zu Zeit kracht der Ofen.[1] Wenn ich denke, dass wir weg gehen, bin ich auch ein wenig melancholisch. Aber innerlich bin ich sicher das ich gehen muss. Dies ist ein schones Ende, aber besser ein schwerer Anfang wie ein Ende nur.

Grüsse alle. Sage an Else dass ich hatte alle Briefe: und Friedel schreibt so gut English. Sicher haltet er mein Deutsch für wenig. Es freut mich sehr dass du die Annie dabei hast, und bist nicht allein, diese lange Winterabende.

Bleib immer wohl. Ich schreibe schnell wieder. Du sollst eine Verbeugung vor aller Stiftsdamen machen, in meinem Namen.

dein Schwiegersohn   D. H. Lawrence

Das armes Bäderle war so krank: es thut mir leid. Wie geht die Else? Ich will ihr Bücher schicken nachher.

[We must choose only a very good ship. It *can* be so, that we shall sail next month. But nothing certain. And when we're there, in America, and I can earn money, then we can easily come to Germany again, to visit you. If only one has the dollars, America is no farther from Baden than Taormina: and perhaps not so far. That you know well.

I've had a bit of flu: it was very cold, the snow came nearer and nearer, down the mountains, Monte Venere was white, and our own Monte Diretto. But to us the snow just couldn't come, the sea says no. And now, thank God, again warm as summer, snow flown, sea blue, the almonds eagerly blossoming. So many thousands of birds have come down, with the cold, goldfinches, blackheads, blueheads, redtails, redbreasts, all so colourful and gay. And thank God, powder is now so dear, the generous Italians can't buy any more cartridges.

At this time I am not working. I have, since we have been back here, written three long novelettes, which should make quite a nice book. Also I have

---

[1] Ofen.] Herd.

collected my little novelettes, ready for a book. So, for the moment I'm free, and don't want to begin anything else, except perhaps I want to translate a grey Sicilian novel – *Mastro-don Gesualdo*, by Giovanni Verga. It is truly Sicilian, and one can see in it how black and heavy and hopeless are these Sicilians, *inwardly*. Outwardly such beauty: inwardly dirt and horror: and *money*. No, schwiegermutter, here in Europe can come nothing new. They only can keep chewing the old strings. – The Banca di Sconto, perhaps the largest bank in Italy, has gone broke – doesn't pay – and *such* a black cloud over all the people here. Money is the blood of an Italian. He always says it – vuole il sangue mio – he wants my blood – when he has to pay anything. – But it is really horrible. Probably, however, the government will come in, and make good.

Today we had your letter to Frieda. How nice for Annie, if she can marry at Easter. Then she will hardly have father or mother anymore, and all can become freer and friendlier. I am so glad Hinke is doing so well with his business.

Frieda wants also to write a word. We sit in our salotta, warm and still, with the lamp on the table. Outside, through the door I see like twilight the moonlit sea, and the moon through the begonia leaves of our terrace: and all quite still, only from time to time the stove crackles. When I think of our going away, I'm also a bit melancholy. But inwardly I am certain that I must go. This is a lovely end, but better a difficult beginning than an end only.

Greet all. Tell Else I had all letters: and Friedel writes English so well. Surely he thinks little of my German. I am very glad you have Annie with you, and are not alone, these long winter evenings.

Keep well always. I'll write again soon. You should make a bow before all the Stift ladies, in my name.

your son-in-law   D. H. Lawrence

Poor Bäderle was so sick: I'm sorry. How is Else? I want to send her some books later on.]

2412. To Mary Cannan, 11 January 1922
Text: MS Lazarus; Unpublished.

Fontana Vecchia, Taormina, Sicily
11 Jan 1922

My dear Mary

Well I am sending you *Sea and Sardinia* today, and hope you'll like it. Secker is bargaining with Seltzer for 1000 sheets, for an English edition. The pictures have come out pretty well – not too well, alas – the reds are poor. – We heard that Juta had hurt his leg on the mountain there in S. Africa – now from his sister, that it may be very serious, and make him always lame. I truly hope not.

There was a boat from Bordeaux to New Orleans on Jan 15th. If I'd been ready enough I'd have caught it. There may be another in a month. If not I shall sail from Palermo to New York on Feb 5th, though I don't want to go to New York.

I have had flu for a fortnight and such bad headaches, but now thank heaven feel better.

A lovely warm springlike day – the days when I love Taormina still. Pity you cant be here for a month.

Send news.

DHL

2413. To Martin Secker, 11 January 1922
Text: MS UInd; Postmark, Taormina 12 GEN 22; Secker 46–7.

Fontana Vecchia, *Taormina*, Sicily
11 Jan 1922

Dear Secker

I am writing Curtis Brown that I agree to a 15% on *Sea and Sardinia*, but that I don't want any more that 13-as-12 clause.

Send me those 50 sheets of *Women in Love* quickly, because we may leave at any time. But please tell me *what I get* for these 50 signatures.[1] What do I make on those fifty copies? I want to be paid for the signatures.

I hope to leave at latest Feb. 5th. But will let you know.

Yrs   D. H. Lawrence

2414. To Curtis Brown, 11 January 1922
Text: MS UT; Unpublished.

Fontana Vecchia, *Taormina*, Sicilia
11th Jan. 1922

Dear Curtis Brown

Your letters of 4th. and 5th. inst. today. I agree to a royalty of 15% on the published price of the Secker edition of *Sea and Sardinia*. But please eliminate from the contracts that thirteen-copies-count-as-twelve clause. I consider it unjust. I have mentioned it to Secker.

I have sent duplicates of *all* the Stories to Mountsier, though I haven't

---

[1] The first edition, English issue, consisted of fifty copies made up from sheets of the Seltzer first edition (November 1920). Published June 1922 at 63s (compared with Secker's trade edition at 9s.). For the royalty payment on the autographed edition see p. 199 n. 2.

heard if he has got any of them yet. I hope you have 'Ladybird' and 'England my England' now.

My wife and I will be sailing very shortly to America – I hope on Feb. 5th at the latest. Of course I shall let you know.

Yours   D. H. Lawrence

2415. To J. B. Pinker, 12 January 1922
Text: MS UNYB; Unpublished.

Fontana Vecchia, *Taormina*, Sicily
12 Jan 1922

Dear Pinker

I hear that *Look We Have Come Through* has been for some time out of print. Will you please ascertain at once from Chatto and Windus whether they intend to re-print the book. If so, *when*. And if not, whether they are willing to terminate the agreement. – I suppose there is a six-months-out-of-print clause, anyhow.

Will you be so good, also, as to tell me the number they printed – that is the number sold.

Yours Sincerely   D. H. Lawrence[1]

2416. To Jack Clarke, 12 January 1922
Text: Lawrence–Gelder 120–1.

Sicily.
12 Jan. 1922

I am sending you an hourglass to remind you that you are piling up your years. Here the peasants hardly ever have clocks, and they still measure an hour by the sandglass. . . . I hope it will arrive unbroken – trust to luck. I hope you'll have digested your Christmas pudding before you tackle your birthday cake. Your festivities tread on each other's heels. Love from Auntie Frieda and me.

2417. To Angela Easterbrook, 12 January 1922
Text: MS UT; Unpublished.

Fontana Vecchia, *Taormina*, Sicily
12 Jan 1922

Dear Miss Easterbrook

I wrote Chatto and Windus and told them what I thought of them, for a discourteous paltry behaviour. Will let you know about *Look We Have Come Through* when I hear.

Yrs   D. H. Lawrence

[1] See p. 176 n. 2.

2418. To S. S. Koteliansky, 14 January 1922
Text: MS BL; Postmark, Taormina 15 GEN 22; Moore 684–5.

Fontana Vecchia, *Taormina*, Sicily
.14 Jan 1922

My dear Kot

I had the *Dial* by the same post as your letter. They are impudent people, I had told them not to put my name. Of course they did it themselves. But I don't really care. Why bother.

I had the empty envelope of the primus needles: just ripped a bit at the side, and the packet extracted. Inevitably. But that also doesn't matter, because Smythe[1] brought me three packets from England, two days ago.

I keep chasing ships to get to New Orleans, so as to avoid New York. But every ship seems either to go somewhere else, or to decide not to go at all at the last minute. I may get a Cie Transatlantique boat from Bordeaux next month – or I may go White Star, Naples to New York, next month. We will see. I feel like you, that I am messing about on the edge of everything. But I feel also I *can't* come back into Europe. – Taos I hear has a colony of New York artists there. Oh God! Yet I feel it is my destiny at least to *try* the States, if only to know I hate them. Dunque – ![2] – And here, everybody is pleasant and has tea-parties and at least £500 a year. And it feels so empty. What isn't empty – as far as the world of man goes.

I too think of the Bucks cottage fairly often and still sometimes lull myself with: 'Ranane Sadihkim Sadihkim Badanoi.'[3] If only there were some of the dark old spirit of that left in the world! Meanwhile one is eight years older, and a thousand years more disconnected with everything, and more frustrated. Quoi faire! Che fare?[4]

I am glad you liked the 'Gent' when he was done. Of course you do exactly as you like about the Wolff book:[5] that has nothing to do with me. Only send me a copy when it comes. – Apparently Secker is going to buy sheets of *Sea and Sardinia* from Seltzer. I will send you a copy of that when it appears: which, if I know Secker, will be in about ten months' time.

Well, at least it is sunny and there is a bit of spring in the air, the sun is warm and the almonds are in bud. Why should one get depressed. But I have had flu – not badly – for three weeks.

If we go to Taos, and if we get on there, perhaps you will come too: if there

---

[1] Unidentified.   [2] 'So – !'
[3] The Triangle, Bellingdon Lane, Chesham, Bucks, where the Lawrences lived August 1914–January 1915 and where, at Christmas, Kot sang the Hebrew musical version of Psalm xxxiii. 1 ('Rejoice in the Lord, O ye righteous') quoted here. (See *Letters*, ii. 252 n. 1 and 2.)
[4] 'What to do! What to do?'   [5] See p. 23 n. 2.

could be something doing: and if you would like to back me up. Vediamo!
a rivederci, e sta bene, e molti saluti a Sonia anche a Ghita e Grisha.[1]

DHL

2419. To Cecily Lambert and Miss Furlong, 14 January 1922
Text: MS SIU; Unpublished.

Fontana Vecchia, *Taormina*, Sicily
14 Jan 1922

Dear Lambert and Miss Furlong
    I have your letter of 31st December only this morning, and reply at once.
Alas, we are booked to leave next month for America for New Mexico. But we
may be delayed, and the sailing may be deferred. Yet I am afraid in any case we
shall be gone by mid-March.
    For cheapness, I should come overland. If you can bear the weariness of
long journeys, you can travel second class – there's very little difference. Get
Cooks to book you a room in Paris and wherever else you wish to stay. Paris to
Turin is 24 hours – quite bearable. You can stay overnight in Turin, if you
have booked a room. It ought to cost you only about 5/- a night each. Cooks
can book you at hotels and *everything*, and you have everything paid – no need
to bother. That is the best way. An ordinary hotel costs *en pension*, in Italy,
about 40 Liras a day: which is about nine shillings. You can in the cheaper
towns like Florence find hotels for 30 Lire. All the hotels speak English and are
quite decent. At all big stations there is a Cooks man, who will tell you what
you want. Hotel tips are now charged you in the bill: an additional[2] 10% or
12½% or 15% on your bill: so you have no tipping to do unless somebody does
something out of the way for you. A porter at the station gets about a Lira for
every piece of handluggage he carries for you. You won't have any trunks.
Carriages – horse carriages, the same – all have taximeters, and you pay by the
clock – luggage in front extra. It is all much easier nowadays. But it's an
infernal journey down to Sicily. If you come second, sleep in Paris, Turin, and
Rome. From Rome to Taormina is about 21 hours.
    Don't think of going Cooks *conducted*.[3] See what they'll book you hotel
rooms for, leaving you free. Be sure *never* to arrive in a place like Rome without
having your hotel room ready booked. Otherwise you'll be in the hand of
thieves, touts and God knows what. The hotels are *very* full in the spring.
    If it happens we are gone from here, and still you want to do your trip, go to

---

[1] 'Until we meet again, and keep well, and many greetings to Sonia also to Ghita and Grisha.'
[2] MS reads 'addional'.
[3] A journey on which Thomas Cook and Son, tourist agents, provided a 'conductor', or guide,
i.e. a specially organised journey.

Milan, Como, and Venice: that is lovely, and not *nearly* so far. You can go Paris to Milan without changing, and Milan to Como in only 1½ hours, Milan to Venice about 7 hours. And North Italy is much cheaper, much simpler and honester than the south. I think myself the journey from Genoa southwards is terribly fatiguing – a horror of 40 hours. In Venice you can get quite nice pension for 35 Lire a day. Venice is lovely.

I should love to see the bungalow. Who knows, we may be in England before very long, even if we go to New Mexico. I will let you know at once the moment our plans are *fixed*. I don't know why your letter took so long. About six days is usual.

Many good wishes to you both from my wife and me.

Yours D. H. Lawrence

2420. To Thomas Seltzer, 14 January 1922
Text: MS UT; Postmark, Taormina 17 GEN 22; Lacy, *Seltzer* 32.

Fontana Vecchia, *Taormina*, Sicilia
14 Jan. 1922.

Dear Seltzer

The typed MS. of *Aaron's Rod* came today. I again tried altering it. I can modify the bits of Argyle's speech. But the essential scenes of Aaron and the Marchesa it is impossible to me to alter.[1] With all the good-will towards you and the general public that I am capable of, I can no more alter those chapters than if they were cast-iron. You can lift out whole chunks if you like. You can smash them if you like. But you can no more alter them than you can alter cast iron.

There you are. It's your dilemma. You can now do what you like with the book. Print only a limited edition – leave out anything you like for a popular edition – even if you like substitute something of your own for the offensive passages. But it is useless asking me to do any more. I shall return you the MS. on Monday. Then say no more to me. I am tired of this miserable, paltry, haffling and caffling world – dead sick of it.

D. H. Lawrence

2421. To Curtis Brown, 16 January 1922
Text: MS UT; Unpublished.

Fontana Vecchia, *Taormina*, Sicilia
16 Gennaio 1922

Caro Curtis Brown

Thank you for recovering the extra ten guineas from Secker – I must say I

[1] See Letter 2379 and n. 1.

admire his mistakes. I suppose you paid it into the Law Courts Branch of the L[ondon] C[ounty] W[estminster] and Parr's Bank.

Mountsier writes in a frenzy, saying that Secker must not forestall Seltzer in publishing any of the books – Short Stories or otherwise. Do for heavens sake try and settle with him – Mountsier.

Hope all goes well otherwise.

Yrs   D. H. Lawrence

Please keep the animal sketches 'Adolf' and 'Rex' apart. I want later to do a small book of them.

Of course *Sea and Sardinia* will count as one of the five books in the Secker agreement.[1]

DHL

2422. To Robert Mountsier, 18 January 1922
Text: MS Smith; Unpublished.

Fontana Vecchia, *Taormina*, Sicily.
18 Jany. 1922.

Dear Mountsier

I enclose a little paper of answers to questions – hope they are all there.

I had Seltzers ten copies of *Sardinia*: a nice book, I think. The pictures are good too, only the reds a bit dull and some of the blue-greens juicy. Did I say this before?

Suddenly that I am on the point of coming to America I feel I *can't* come. Not yet. It is something almost stronger than I am. I would rather go to Ceylon, and come to America later, from the east.

Perhaps Juta will come to Ceylon and we'd do a book there. Did I tell you he'd hurt his foot on Table Mountain and seems rather badly lame for the moment. I hope it will get better. – I shall have just enough English money to get me to Ceylon – or America: then I must use dollars.

I got the *Dial* with the Bunin story – thanks for it. I didn't want my name on the translation really, but too late to bother.

I sent back the type MS. of *Aaron* to Seltzer because it was just physically impossible to me to alter it. He may do as he likes now. I just won't alter it: can't, the alterations won't come: and the general public can go to hell in any way it likes.

I shall let you know immediately I decide *fina* my voyage.

Yrs   DHL

.

---

[1] See p. 129 n.3.

Fontana Vecchia. 17 Jan. 1922
Answers to Questions

1. I promised to give Juta one-third of my profits on *Sea and Sardinia*. Have not heard from him if he accepts.

2. Secker has not mentioned to me anything about my paying for the Heseltine blackmail money: so I have said nothing. If Secker pays blackmail that is not my affair.[1]

3. Have written to Curtis Brown that they shall keep 'Adolf' and 'Rex' apart, for a possible animal sketch-book later.

4. 'Wintry Peacock' is committed to Basil Blackwell until Jan 1st. 1924: for *England*.[2] The agreement, I believe, does not touch America. He gave me £21. for the story – which was very good. You might write and tell him that you conclude that the American rights are still free:

    49 Broad Street, Oxford.

   There is no agreement save by letter: and no mention of America. When I specially said to Blackwell – 'Does this include America?' he did not answer – so I conclude it doesnt.

5. I wrote to Curtis Brown to arrange for publication dates with *you*. Meanwhile I sign no agreement with Secker save for *Sardinia* (if he wants it).

6. I don't know what you mean by a missing chapter of *Studies in C[lassic] A[merican] Lit[erature]*.

7. I enclose Huebsch letter.[3] Have you had his statement?

8. I got sheets of *Women in Love* from Secker for me to sign: but reply to him I won't sign them till I know what it will profit me.

9. Secker sent me a statement and cheque of £17"10"0 for sales of *Lost Girl* (over and above the advance[4] paid) up to June last. It seemed to me he ought to have raised the royalty to 1/6 after 2000, whereas he was still paying 1/- per copy. I sent the statement to Curtis B. to enquire into. Secker replied to them: 'I was under the impression that the royalty did not rise until 2,500. However I have now corrected this and enclose cheque for ten guineas, for the excess royalties.' – How's that for cool cheek?

10. Have the enclosed 'copy' from Huebsch – so good that you now have control of all the Doran agreements.[5] We may as well keep on friendly

---

[1] See p. 113 n. 2.   [2] See Letter 2251 and n. 2.   [3] Missing.   [4] advance] royalty
[5] George H. Doran (1869–1956), American publisher (see *Letters*, ii. 417 n. 5). As early as March 1914 he had shown himself ready to publish three of DHL's books (see *Letters*, ii. 223) but in the event published none; the rights to publish *The Prussian Officer* (1914), *Twilight in Italy* (1916) and *Amores* (1916) were transferred by Doran to Huebsch (see *Letters*, ii. 610 n. 4). DHL's specific reference was probably to a letter from Doran to Huebsch, 6 April 1921 (quoted in

terms with Huebsch. He says he sent you statements up to 31 Oct – sold
1116 *Rainbows*. I want to know if he is going to re-print it.
11. Can't we get at that beast Kennerley. Do talk it over with Seltzer.

2423. To Earl Brewster, 18 January 1922
Text: MS UT; Brewster 44–6.

Fontana Vecchia, *Taormina*, Sicilia
18 January 1922

Dear Brewster

Your letter of 16 December just come. And suddenly, for the first time, I
suddenly feel you may be right and I wrong: that I am kicking against the
pricks. I have misinterpreted 'Life is sorrow'.[1] That is a first truth, not a last
truth. And one must accept it as one's first truth, and develop from that. I
verily believe it.

The groundwork of life is sorrow. But that once established, one can start to
build. And until that is established one can build nothing: no life of any sort. I
begin to agree. I took it one must *finish* with the fact that *Life is sorrow*. Now
again I realise that one must get there, and having arrived, then begin to live.

Good then: as a basis, *Life is sorrow*. But beyond that one can smile and go
on.

Only – only – I somehow have an imperative need to fight. I suppose it
depends *how* one fights.

No, I believe you are right. Probably there, east, is the *source*: and America
is the extreme periphery. Oh God, must one go to the extreme limit, then to
come back?

I only know it seems so much *easier*, more peaceful to come east. But then
peace, peace! I am *so* mistrustful of it: so much afraid that it means a sort of
weakness and giving in. Yet I believe you're right. The very word you say, that
Ceylon is *heavy*, makes me think you are right.

And the fact that I have felt so *spiteful* against Bhudda makes me feel I was
unsure all the time, and kicking against the pricks.

We have made all arrangements to go to Taos, New Mexico. But we have

Huebsch's letter to Mountsier, 31 December 1921, MS UT) in which Doran wrote: 'If Mr
Mountsier will accept the suggestion which I made to him yesterday, namely, that upon his
giving me a definite release I will hand over to him all contracts dealing with the affairs of Mr.
Lawrence, provided he will relieve us from further responsibility and consideration. We will
also offer to Mr. Mountsier any necessary assurance which he might need in facilitating the
complete and satisfactory transfer of all arrangements into a direct connection between you
[Huebsch] and him.'
[1] A principle of Buddhism: human existence is painful because man desires that which is
transitory and can be freed from these desires only by taking the 'path' taught by the Buddha.

booked no passage. Shall I come to Ceylon? Dio mio, I am so ridiculous, wavering between east and west.

I believe I shall not go to America. What is the good after all of going to where everything is just *unlearnt* and confused to the utmost. Perhaps it is true, Buddhism is true realism, *things as they are*. And America is utterly *things as they are not*. – But the future – where is that? Must one go through the utter unreality of America: or keep a continuity? I'd better begin to make sure.

Later: Well now, I'm writing at once about ships to Colombo. I shall cable to you if we are actually coming, when we book passages. I hope to sail next month.

So – a rivederci.

D. H. Lawrence

2424. To S. S. Koteliansky, 20 January 1922
Text: MS BL; Postmark, Taormina 21 GEN 22; cited in Gransden 28.

Fontana Vecchia, *Taormina*, Sicily
20 Jan. 1922.

My dear Kot

Will you post me a copy of the *Occult Review*: and if possible a catalogue of books on occult science: there is a publisher whose name I forget.[1] Any time when you are near Charing Cross Road will do. You said you wanted to send me something. – *The Occult Review* – or *The Occultist Review*: that also I forget. I should just like to see this months issue.

Well, I said I was going to America. But the moment I feel the ship is there to take me, I fight shy. I *can't* go to America. Not yet. It is too raw for me, and I too tender for it. We must wait a bit. I have got a friend in Kandy, Ceylon, who asks me to go there and stay with him. I think I shall do that: quite soon. I feel I can fortify myself in the east, against the west. You will say I am foolish: but it is my destiny. I do intend later to go to America. But I must first have something else inside me.

I believe Secker is going to bring out *Sea and Sardinia*. It is just a light sketch book: but personal: so it would amuse you. I will send you a copy when it is ready.

You will be glad to have Sonia back. I shudder to think of that[2] cave, the flood of newspapers rising silently in a fog of cigarette smoke, and you swimming slowly and hopelessly, in the heavy ocean of printed slush, gasping to sink.

[1] The publisher was William Rider; DHL had shown an interest in his *Occult Review* in 1918 (see *Letters*, iii. 299).   [2] that] all

Greet Sonia, and I hope she is happy to be back in the cavern,[1] and I hope
she'll order the cart for the newspapers at once.

DHL

P.S. The brilliant idea strikes me that you might ring up Thomas Cooks,
Ludgate Circus, and ask them what boats there are from *Malta* or *Naples* to
Colombo, Ceylon, and what is the price of a cabin for two, first class: or berths
for two, first class. I have written to Malta and to Naples, but you never know
those people, plus the Italian post. – Any ship from S. Italy or Malta to
Colombo.

DHL

2425. To Robert Mountsier, [20 January 1922]
Text: MS Smith; Postmark, Taormina 21 GEN 22; Unpublished.

Taormina
20 Jan.

Dear Mountsier
    This is a note about a *Finn*, J.W. Nylander, who was a sailor. He writes in
Swedish: is translated into German.[2] I have sent a vol. of his stories, in
German, to Seltzer, to see what he thinks of them. I think you could get some
of them into the *more popular* magazines: am almost sure you could. But it
would need finding a Swedish translator. Nylander is very poor: but you could
make it worth your while, even if you charged him a *high* per centage at first, to
get him going a bit: because a hundred dollars will [mean] a[3] great deal to him.
He is not translated into English[4] *at all*. Do try and do what you can.

D.H. Lawrence[5]

    address,
            J W Nylander, Sleependen, nr. *Kristiania*, Norway

2426. To Thomas Seltzer, 20 January 1922
Text: MS UT; Postmark, Taormina 21 GEN 22; Lacy, *Seltzer* 33.

Fontana Vecchia, *Taormina*, Sicily
20 Jan. 1922

Dear Seltzer
    This is a note simply about J W. Nylander, who is a Finn who is here, was
once a sailor, has written sea-stories, in *Swedish*, is translated into German,

---

[1] Kot's residence at 5 Acacia Road, St John's Wood, was familiarly known as 'the cave' or
'cavern'.
[2] John Wilhelm Nylander (1869–1949), Swedish author. DHL read the German translation
Seevolk (Leipzig, 1910) (see next letter). DHL's efforts on his behalf were apparently of no
avail.   [3] MS reads 'will a a'.   [4] English] German
[5] DHL recorded in his diary that, also on 20 January, he wrote to Mountsier sending 'statements
of $836' (Tedlock, *Lawrence MSS* 95).

but not into English: and who is poor. I am sending you by this post *Seevolk*, a volume[1] of stories: he says not the best. They are a bit *soft*: yet I think 'Jim Lawson' – and 'Die Frau auf dem Southern Cross' good; and even 'Idyll'. Would the magazines do them if they were translated; do you think? And if so do you think you could find a translator who would share royalties – *Swedish*, remember? And would you speak to Mountsier about it, if you think it any good? Nylander will send you three[2] other volumes in German translation. The man is poor, and so modest and shrinking: please do find time to give the matter a bit of attention. I shall trust you to do this.

Yrs   D. H. Lawrence

address,

J. W. Nylander, Sleependen, nr. Kristiania, Norway.

No matter *what* your decision, be so kind as to write him a word and tell him.

2427. To Martin Secker, 21 January 1922

Text: MS UInd; Postmark, Taormina 22 GEN 22; Secker 47.

Fontana Vecchia, Taormina, Sicily
21 Jan. 1922

Dear Secker:

I have got the fifty sheets of *Women in Love*. I think you ought to give me twenty per-cent on signed copies. I get fifteen on unsigned, so why throw in the signature?

And I think I will turn over the whole business to Curtis Brown. So I will send him the signed sheets, and you can have them if you'll give me the 20%.

Would you like 'Tickets Please!' for the title of the short-story book?[3] I had thought of that. It fits pretty well.

I am not working on anything at the moment, because I am waiting to go away. At the last moment I believe I shall funk America and go to a friend in Ceylon. I want to sail next month.

I hear from Huebsch that he sold out his five-dollar edition of *The Rainbow* at once.[4] Why don't you take your courage in your hands and do the book this year? You would certainly sell it.

Is *Women in Love* selling again? – your ordinary edition.[5]

---

[1] volume] bunch   [2] three] four

[3] At least as early as 12 June 1922 Secker referred to the 'short-story book' as *The Blind Man and Other Stories* (Secker Letter-Book, UIll).

[4] See p. 106 n. 2.

[5] On 15 November 1921, Secker had written: 'I have now gone to press with a new edition, so that it will once more be on sale after a lapse of three months' (see p. 113 n. 2). This new edition incorporated the changes DHL agreed to make to pacify Heseltine, and others which Secker seems to have made himself.

I want to turn over all the business and financial things to Curtis Brown: so will you henceforward make all statements and payments for *Lost Girl* and *Women in Love* to him.

                                                              Yrs   D. H. Lawrence
Did you not want *Tortoises?*[1]

2428. To Curtis Brown, 21 January 1922
Text: MS UT; Unpublished.

                                              Fontana Vecchia, *Taormina*, Sicily
                                                                   21 Jan 1922.
Dear Curtis Brown

I am sending you by this post fifty signed sheets for Seckers *edition de luxe Women in Love*. He offers me 15% on these fifty. I ask for 20%, to pay me for this signature. He hasn't fixed price yet. I have told him I'm arranging the matter through you. Let him have the sheets when he agrees to the 20%.[2]

I have told him I want him to make all statements and all payments through you – for *Lost Girl* and *Women in Love*. So will you take these under your wing, please.

Did Secker refuse *Tortoises?*

                                                              Yrs   D. H. Lawrence

2429. To Catherine Carswell, 24 January 1922
Text: MS YU; cited in Carswell 160–1.

                                              Fontana Vecchia, *Taormina*, Sicilia
                                                                   24 Jany. 1922
My dear Catherine

I had your letter: am sorry about the flu. I had it too, and it lasts such a long time. Thank goodness it did not keep me long in bed, but I've had it since Christmas and have hardly shaken it off yet. I believe it is partly an organic change in one's whole constitution – through the blood and psyche. We are at the end of our particular tether, and the breaking loose is an uncomfortable process.

My sister said you sent the plates so nicely and safely packed.[3] She was so delighted with them. I do hope you didn't hate all the trouble.

I sent you the chap-book of *Tortoises*. Hope you have it. My sisters irritate me by rather loftily disapproving. I really am through with them: shall send them no more of my books. Basta? – I had one or two copies of the American *Sea and Sardinia*: but Secker is doing it in London, and I will have him send

---

[1] Secker did not publish *Tortoises* separately, although the poems appeared in his edition of *Birds, Beasts and Flowers* (1923).   [2] See p. 199 n. 2.   [3] See Letter 2343.

you a copy. He is buying sheets and pictures from Seltzer. It is quite amusing,
I think. – He doesn't like my *Aaron's Rod*. That rod, I'm afraid it is gentian's
root or wormwood stem. But they've got to swallow it, sooner or later –
miserable tonicless lot. – I am waiting to read the *Camomile*. Send me proofs if
you have a double set, and I'll return them. I hope it's bitter too.

I have once more gone back on my plan. I shrink as yet from the States.
Ultimately I shall go there, no doubt. But I want to go east before I go west: go
west via the east. I have a friend called Brewster, who went with wife and child
from here last autumn to Kandy, Ceylon. He has got a big old ramshackle
bungalow there, and is studying Pali and Buddhism at the Buddhist
monastery, and asks me to come. So I shall go there. We had almost booked
our passage to America, when suddenly it came over me I must go to Ceylon. I
think one must for the moment withdraw from the world, away towards the
inner realities that *are* real: and return, maybe, to the world later, when one is
quiet and sure. I am tired of the world, and want the peace like a river: not this
whiskey and soda, bad whiskey too, of life so-called. I don't believe in
Buddhistic inaction and meditation. But I believe the Buddhistic peace is the
point to start from – not our strident fretting and squabbling.

There is also a little Finn here called Nylander: J. W. Nylander. He was a
sailor, then Captain of a tramp steamer. Then he wrote sea-stories, in
Swedish. I read one volume, *See-volk*, in German translation. He is about 50 –
has wife and child – and pension from the Finnish[1] government. But Finnish
money is down like Italian. So they are very poor. They are returning to
Norway at the end of March. He would very much like his stories translated to
English: has written to an Englishwoman in Finland to do them. But then they
would have to be put into proper literary shape. I said you might do that for
him. The stories are all sea-stories: a bit soft, a bit weak, but not bad really.
Since Norwegian-Scandinavian stuff is rather the boom, I thought if you
wouldn't mind the bother of going over the stories you might get some of the
magazines to publish them. But if you think it is not worth your while, just say
so. J. W. Nylander, Porta Catania, Taormina, until end of March: then
Sleependen, near Kristiania, Norway. If you get on pleasantly by letter you
might perhaps one day have a trip to Norway. – I have written to Mountsier
and Seltzer about the stories in America. – You would have to try and arrange
simultaneous publication with Mountsier:

> *Robert Mountsier, 417 West 118th Street, New York.*

– If you *do* do the stories, don't forget to write Mountsier to see what he is

---

[1] Finnish] Swedish

doing, will you. – Of course you would take a just per-centage of any profits: and if America did *your* translation too, then a percentage of that also. It might amuse you, and isn't hard work.[1]

The weather is vile here: really wicked. But one must possess one's soul in patience. Now I hope you are well again, and J[ohn] P[atrick] and Don happy.

D. H. Lawrence

2430. To Curtis Brown, 25 January 1922
Text: MS UT; Unpublished.

Fontana Vecchia, *Taormina*, Sicily
25 Jany. 1922.

Dear Curtis Brown

I enclose Chatto's letter about *Look We Have Come Through!*[2] Will you please preserve this, and henceforth take charge of the book.

Yours   D. H. Lawrence

I haven't heard if you have received the last of the stories – 'England my England'!

2431. To Curtis Brown, 26 January 1922
Text: MS UT; Huxley 535–6.

Fontana Vecchia, *Taormina*, Sicilia
26 Jany. 1922

Dear Curtis Brown

Glad you are back; hope well and successfully back. But Miss Easterbrook and I got a lot done in the meantime.

---

[1] Catherine Carswell was not amused: though sympathetic towards Nylander she found his stories uninteresting and returned them to him 'with regrets' (Carswell 161–2).

[2] The letter (TMS Chatto & Windus) reads as follows:

January Nineteenth
Nineteen Twentytwo

Dear Sir,

In reply to your favour of the 12th inst., we wrote to you on December 14th in response to yours of the *7th of that month* as follows:

'In reply to your letter of the 7th inst., we regret that we are unable to send you a copy of "Look! We have Come Through" as the book is out of print with us. Our last statement accounted for all the copies printed.'

We subsequently received a letter from Messrs. Curtis Brown, but as your Agreement was made through your agent, Mr. Pinker, we thought it only right to inform Messrs. Curtis Brown of this fact.

The last statement showed that the edition of 1000 copies has been accounted for; and as we have no plant, we do not propose to reprint the volume; and the rights we acquired under our Agreement with you now revert to you.

We are, yours very faithfully
Chatto & Windus

This is answer to her letter of 20th. inst.

1. I enclose both agreements, signed by me. You will look after them.
2. I enclose proof of 'Almond Blossom' poem for the *English Review*.[1]
3. Glad you have all the stories. For heaven's sake – the *English Review* published 'England my England' in 1915, under that title: although the story is entirely re-written. But best not send it out again serially, unless with a note to that effect. Anyhow no magazine will want it. For the rest of the stories, all right.
4. You *don't* enclose the letter from Mountsier which you mention, but I guess he has written me the same direct.
5. I can't alter 'Hadrian',[2] because I have nothing to alter it by. I will tell Mountsier to send a duplicate.
6. I didn't alter the original MS. at all, of *Aarons Rod*. Or only a few words. I couldn't. Seltzer sent me a clean typed copy of the book, begging for the alterations for the sake of the 'general public' (he didn't say *jeune fille*). I sat in front of the MS and tried: but it was like Balaams Ass, and wouldn't budge.[3] I couldn't do it: So I sent it back to Seltzer to let him do as he pleases. I would rather Secker followed the true MS, if he will – and vogue la galère.[4]
7. I have made *no* arrangement for the publication of *Studies in Classic American Literature*, but Seltzer is booked to publish them in New York, so for heaven's sake consult him, or I shall have more fat in the fire. I should rather like Cape to publish them. – *Is your MS. of these complete?*
8. I can't go to America: another Balaam's Ass. But when I try to turn my travelling nose westwards, – *grazie!* – he won't budge. So, after vainly shoving and prodding the ass of my unwilling spirit, to get him on board and across the Atlantic, I have given up, and am writing to Cooks at Naples to book berths on the *Osterley*, sailing from Naples Feb. 26th. for Colombo. I have a friend in Kandy learning Buddha in a monastery there – so I shall go with my wife there, for a bit. Wish me god-speed. (not into the monastery)
10. Before I go I am asking Pinker to release to me what books of mine he still keeps the collecting rights over, and if he'll do it, then I'll put everything, all my English publications, under your wing: if you'll take them.

Meanwhile Benedicite!

D. H. Lawrence

I suppose you had Chatto's letter which I forwarded! One for us, Miss Easterbrook, and be damned to them!

---

[1] 'Almond Blossom' appeared in *English Review*, xxxiv (February 1922), 101–4.
[2] It had been and continued to be published as 'You Touched Me'. See Letter 2388.
[3] See Numbers xxii. 21–35.   [4] 'come what may'.

2432. To Robert Mountsier, 26 January 1922
Text: MS Smith; Postmark, Taormina 29 GEN 22; Unpublished.

Fontana Vecchia, *Taormina*, Sicilia
26 Jany 1922

Dear Mountsier

First and foremost, do please send a duplicate of 'Hadrian' to Curtis Brown.

Then today I am sending you the MS. of Maurice Magnus' 'Dregs: Experiences of an American in the Foreign Legion':[1] together with an introductory memoir by myself. The memoir is just literal truth, so when you've read it you will know all there is to know. When you read the 'Dregs' you'll probably be as disgusted and horrified as Magnus was at the actual reality. But be patient, and don't give up.

This is the rest. Magnus' MSS. were delivered over to Michael Borg, whom I call Mazzaiba in the 'Memoir': Magnus owes about £100 in Malta.[2] I wish you could get a publisher to give some $400 for the Magnus MS: sale outright: for the American rights, that is. If any publisher would take it, in spite of its 'awfulness' – preferably a biggish man like Doran, to follow Dos Passos book[3] – if *possible* – then he might give $400 to buy the book outright, Magnus' book, not my memoir. You might make some *separate* agreement for my 'Memoir', so that we too earned something. But for 'Dregs' itself you would draw up an agreement with *Michael Borg, 34 Fuori la Mina, Valletta, Malta* – Tell him the highest offer you can get – if you can get one – and ask him if he agrees. Then settle with him. For my introduction, arrange something separately, as you think best.

That is for American Rights. Grant Richards did offer to buy the English rights.[4] But I *don't want* my introduction sold to England. The American publisher might arrange an English sale for 'Dregs' alone. And *Norman*

---

[1] It was Secker (later the publisher of the book) who proposed that the title should be *Memoirs of the Foreign Legion* (*Letters from a Publisher*, p. 19).

[2] Magnus was notoriously improvident and importunate. After his death his principal creditors in Malta (including Michael Borg) refused to part with the MS of *Memoirs* to Norman Douglas (named by Magnus as his literary executor); they sent it to DHL in the hope that he might ensure its publication and that they might thereby recover their debts. Despite allegations subsequently made about DHL's motives, it becomes clear here that he wanted the main agreement to benefit Borg.

[3] Doran had published *Three Soldiers* (1921), the first major work by John Dos Passos (1896–1970). MS reads 'Los Passos'.

[4] Grant Richards was a general publisher specialising in religious and literary works (he published the 'World's Classics' series before it was transferred to O.U.P.). DHL knew of him as the publisher of Anna Wickham's poems (*Letters*, ii. 400, 417); no other connection is known.

Douglas, – c/o *Thomas Cook and Son, Via Tornabuoni, Florence* – would do an introductory memoir for the English edition. – *But*, in case Douglas *didn't* do the introduction, and anybody really wanted mine, in England – they can have it if they pay for it, I don't care. But I'm not keen on its going to England. Now probably you will refuse to handle this MS at all: think it too impossible. If you do feel like that, please hand it over to Seltzer and I'll have his advice on it.

A publisher can cut anything he thinks absolutely must be cut.

Perhaps you will hate my associating myself with such a book. But I don't care.

I have written to book berths on the *Osterley*, sailing from Naples for Colombo on Feby 26th. We should then be in Ceylon by March 14th – by heaven's grace. The address in Ceylon would be c/o *E. H. Brewster,* '*Ardnaree*', *Kandy, Ceylon.* I shall cable Seltzer when we leave, and he'll tell you.

I have transferred $200 to my English bank – the L[ondon] C[ounty] W[estminster] and Parrs Bank, 263 Strand W.C.2. – and $50 to Haskard, Palazzo Antinori, Florence – my bank in Italy. I hope your Liras werent in the Banca di Sconti.

No more news for the moment. I have been dragging on with this flue, and feel limp. Be patient about these extraneous MSS.

Yrs   D.H. Lawrence

P.S. If I cable to Seltzer that we are sailing, will you be so good as to send Mable Dodge a line at once, so that she knows. I have written to her – but not finally: and she might not understand a 'Ceylon' cable unless she had the letter.

DHL

I enclose in the MSS photographs of Magnus and one of the portrait of his mother.

2433. To Mary Cannan, 27 January 1922
Text: MS Lazarus; Unpublished.

Fontana Vecchia, Taormina, Sicily
27 Jany 1922

My dear Mary

I am glad you were amused by *Sardinia*. I hear Secker is buying sheets complete from Seltzer to bring it out in April or May.

We have suddenly changed our plan. As I do every time, I have balked at

America. When it comes to going, I can't go. A Balaam's Ass inside me. And so
– we are going to Ceylon. I have written to Cooks at Naples to book me berths
on the *Osterley* – Orient Line – sailing from Naples on Feby 26th. – to
Colombo. It takes about 14 days. I don't know yet whether there will be berths
for us. But if there are we shall go. It costs £74 each, which of course turns my
bones to water. But I don't care. I must go out of Europe now. We shall join
the Brewsters. He has got a big bungalow in the hills near Kandy, and is
studying with the Buddhist monks in the Buddhist monastery there. He loves
it – and says at last he feels as if he were come into his own. I want to go now. I
feel it will give one rest, peace, inside one: this Ceylon. I dont know why I feel
that, but I do. Whereas New Mexico would only be more exciting and
afterwards wearing, I'll bet.

The address in Ceylon is,

    c/o E. H. Brewster, 'Ardnaree', *Kandy*, Ceylon.

If we get there and like it, then you must come. Later on I want to go forward
to China: and then at last across to America, to New Mexico. I shall have to go
to America at length. But not yet. Postpone the evil day. – Ceylon seems nearer
to you, doesn't it? And more congenial? I bet we shall be meeting you in the
harbour at Colombo.

Do you want really to send me something? Then send me a fountain pen,
mine *flows* so badly and I discard it. A fairly broad nib: and a pen that really
flows without flooding. I like an Onoto, self-filling, if they are just the normal
half guinea price there in that beastly France. If they are dearer, send me any
one: but not an expensive one: you know I hate expensive things. – Then when
I write with a pen that *will* write, I shall bless you. I still have a stump of pencil
in a little silver pencil case you gave me at Cholesbury,[1] – and it is the pencil I
depend on: a wee stump now, and a battered little case: but there it is, always
on the go.

Yes, go to Spain, you'll like it. I'd go if we weren't going further. Shall tell
you when we are fixed up.

                        D. H. Lawrence

2434. To J. B. Pinker, 27 January 1922
Text: MS UNYB; Unpublished.

                    Fontana Vecchia, *Taormina*, Sicily
                            27 Jany. 1922.

Dear Pinker

    I haven't had your answer to my letter about *Look We Have Come*

---

[1] When the Lawrences lived at Chesham, Bucks., in 1914, Gilbert and Mary Cannan were nearby
at Cholesbury (see *Letters*, ii. 212). DHL appeared to remember the period with pleasure (see
ibid., iii. 251–2).

Through!: but Chattos themselves wrote that they did not intend to re-print the book, and so the agreement terminates.

I wonder if you would mind releasing to me the rights over the other books which were placed by you, and on account of which monies must be paid to you by the publishers. There is only *The Prussian Officer* with Duckworth, and the *New Poems* with Secker.[1] Is that not so? And they bring in no money. It would be so much simpler if you could let Secker and Duckworth know that you no longer wish to be responsible for the books, so that the accounts can be[2] sent direct to me, along with the accounts[3] of the previously published books.

Anyhow please let me know how you feel about this. I am thinking of sailing away next month – to Ceylon.

Yours Sincerely   D. H. Lawrence

2435. To Mabel Dodge Sterne, 27 January 1922
Text: MS Brill; Luhan 16–17.

Fontana Vecchia, *Taormina*, Sicily
27 Jan. 1922

Dear Mabel Dodge Sterne

Is it vile of us to put off Taos for the moment.[4] But I have a Balaam's Ass in my belly which won't budge, when I turn my face west. I can't help it. It just stubbornly swerves away in me. I *will* come. But a detour. I am writing to book berths on the *Osterley* from Naples, Feby. 26th. for Colombo, Ceylon. The address will be

c/o E. H. Brewster, 'Ardnaree', Lake View Estate, *Kandy*, Ceylon.
But the telegraphic address just Brewster, Ardnaree, Kandy. I feel it is my destiny to go east before coming west. Only to stay a short time: perhaps a year. But to get quite calm and sure and still and strong. I feel America is so *unreligious*: it's a bad word: and that it is on the brink of a change, but the change isn't quite ready yet, so I daren't come. And I feel you yourself are *harried* out there. Come and join us in Ceylon – as soon as you can – and then after, let us go together to Taos.

I had your letter of New Years Day. I sent you *Tortoises*. I will come to the Indians, yes. But only via the East. There is something will not let me sail west for America.

[1] *The Prussian Officer and Other Stories* published by Duckworth, 26 November 1914; *New Poems* published by Secker, October 1918.   [2] can be] are   [3] accounts] previous
[4] DHL's remark presupposes that Mabel Sterne has received Frieda's letter of the previous day announcing the change of plan: 'We were coming *straight* to you at Taos, but now we are not. Lawrence says he can't face America *yet* – he doesn't feel strong enough! So we are first going to the East to Ceylon . . .' (Luhan 15–16).

You want to send Brill to hell and all the analytic therapeutic lot.[1] And I don't like Stein, a nasty, nosy, corrupt Jew. Voilà! Time we got clear of all that stuff.

No, *never* adapt yourself. Kick Brill in the guts if he tries to come it over you. Kick all America in the guts: they need it. Foul enough, with their over-riding of life. But when the hand has fallen on them a bit heavier, they will change. Only wait. But meanwhile, withdraw for a little peace: a breathing space.

No, spit on every neurotic, and wipe your feet on his face if he tries to drag you down to him. And Stein is a shitten Jew. And all that 'arty' and 'literairy' crew, I know them, they are smoking, steaming shits. My blood turns to gall: I want to go and have it sweetened a bit: away from them all, in the old, old east. Later we'll tackle 'em.

Come to Ceylon. Come at once – via San Francisco and China – and we'll prepare ourselves for the later Onslaught on to that Land of Promise of yours.

Benedicite   D. H. Lawrence

2436. To Benjamin Huebsch, 28 January 1922
Text: MS UT; Unpublished.

Fontana Vecchia, *Taormina* Sicily.
28 Jan. 1922.

Dear Huebsch

Thank you for your letter telling me about *The Rainbow*. I hope by now Mountsier has taken over everything from Doran. –[2] What do you intend to do about *The Rainbow*? – Will you print it again, or not.

I ought to be coming to America. Heaven knows why I always balk it at the last minute but I do. Now I am arranging to sail next month from Naples to Ceylon: to stay in Ceylon a few months at least; and then perhaps come on to the United States. Europe is a weary place, and I want to leave it.

I enclose a *Notruf* about the niggers in Germany.[3] I think it's rather

---

[1] Dr Abraham Arden Brill (1874–1948), Mabel Sterne's psychiatrist in New York. Lecturer on psychoanalysis and psycho-sexual sciences at Columbia University, lecturer and clinical professor of psychiatry at New York University. Author of many books on psychoanalysis and translator of Jung.

[2] The agreement that Huebsch should publish *The Rainbow* was negotiated through George Doran & Co. when Pinker was DHL's agent (see *Letters*, ii. 420 n. 2). Thus Doran later became involved in the legal dispute when Mountsier employed the firm of Stern and Ruben to retrieve all the rights from Huebsch.

[3] After the war France stationed some black troops in the Rhineland and Ruhr; their behaviour caused a public outcry and a call for swift action. A *Notruf* ('a cry for help') was printed at least twice – the second post 15 November 1921 – appealing, in highly emotive terms, for action by the white races to prevent further assaults by 'black and brown savages' on 'defenceless German women and children'. See R. Pommerin, *Der Rheinland Bastarde: Das Schicksal einer Farbigen Deutschen Minderheit, 1918–1937* (Berlin, 1979).

sickening of the French: they are altogether rather sickening just now. Can't you say something in the *Freeman*[1] about it? – or get somebody somewhere else to do it? It should be stopp[ed.][2]

Yours sincerely   D. H. Lawrence

2437. To Curtis Brown, 1 February 1922
Text: MS UT; Unpublished.

Fontana Vecchia, *Taormina* Sicily
1 Feby 1922

Dear Curtis Brown

I return Arnold Lunn's agreement[3] and the Secker agreement for the book of short stories.[4] The Lunn business seems a great fuss for a trifle.

About Secker. I agree that if *Sardinia* counts as one of the five books, the short stories need not count.[5] I agree to the £35 advance on royalties. But dont you think the 15% royalty should rise to 20% after the first 2000 are sold: or at *least* after the first 3000? I think so myself, decidedly.

Did I tell you I have written for berths on the *Osterley* sailing from Naples to Colombo on Feb. 26th? I haven't got the answer yet.

Yrs   D. H. Lawrence

---

[1] Huebsch's New York weekly magazine.   [2] MS torn.   [3] See p. 133 n. 4.
[4] *England, My England.*
[5] Curtis Brown wrote at once to Secker and received the following letter dated 7 February 1922 (Secker Letter-Book, UIll):

Dear Mr Curtis Brown,
I am afraid I cannot see my way to agree to D.H.Lawrence's wish that "Sea and Sardinia" should form one of the books of my "Women in Love" contract. This contract, I have already pointed out, was intended to apply to full length novels, and unless it is made clear beforehand (as in the case of these three novelettes) it is obvious that I can only interpret the clause in this way.
I will read the three novelettes, and bearing in mind that it is to form one of the books under my contract should I accept it, will let you know my decision in a few days.
I do not care to make any proposal for reprinting the Chatto & Windus volume of poems unless I can acquire also the poems published by Duckworth & Co.
Yours sincerely

Secker reiterated his standpoint about *Sea and Sardinia* in a further letter on 14 February; he took the opportunity to counter an argument presumably made by Curtis Brown about the volume of short stories: 'As for the short stories, you speak as if Mr Lawrence had done me a favour by letting me have them. So far from that being the case, I only accepted the collection out of my general interest in the author's more serious work.'

2438. To S. S. Koteliansky, 2 February 1922
Text: MS BL; Postmark, Taormina 3 2 22; cited in Gransden 28.

Fontana Vecchia, Taormina, Sicily.

2 Feby 1922.

My dear Kot

Thank you for your letter, for the *Occult Review*, and for the Cooks letter: all safely come.

The fares are awful! But I want to go. Probably we'll go second class from Malta, and bust my dollars. I want to go to the east: I believe one will find a bit of peace there. After all I am not so clever but that my life consists in a relation between me myself, that I am, and the world around me, that I am in contact with, and which may or may not be illusory. But anyhow I need now another illusion: palm-trees and elephants and old old religions and yellow-dark people. Vado pùre! – anche questo mese. Ci ho li un amico Americano, Brewster: lui vuol studiare il buddismo. Ha una casa grande e vecchia vicina a Kandy – non è mica ricco – sposato, con una bambina. Andiamo aggiungerci a lui. Sai che sono stanco qui, a sbraitare con tutta questa gente. Sai che bisogna andarmene, via, via: sì, sì, non posso più qui. Sai che ci sono sempre gli angeli e gli arcangeli, troni, poteri, cherubini, serafini – tutto il coro costà. Ma qui sempre queste bestie battisate chi fanno udirsi, questi e nient' altro. Io me ne vo. Camminando si arriva: neppure nel sepolcro: ma un po' fuori di questo mondo troppo troppo umano. Tante cosé che ci sono nascoste: devo attaccarmi vi, a quellì.

Perchè scrivo italiano, sbagliato anche? Perchè son'sciocco, ma stanco a modo, e vorrei cambiarmi la pelle, come la biscia. Ogni modo me ne vo. C'era una volta il paradiso laggiù, in Ceilan. Tu non credi? Io sì. Cerco anche un po queste paradiso. Abitava proprio lí, Adamo, quell' antenato.

Cosa vuoi, dunque? Cosa me ne vuoi? Ch'io mi chiudo in una grotta Numero 5, come tu? Dio liberi! – in una tana pieno zeppo di giornali? Mai, amico mio, mai. Foglie di cannella, non di giornali.

Un poco triste anche, come quella biscia quando deve cambiarsi la pelle. Ma senza guai non ci sono guadagni. Ti! – tu mi dispiaci: rannichiarsi lá in fondo di una tana No. 5, senza arrischiarti nemmeno un pelo della barba: – cosa devo pensare di te? – anche il rospo va alla caccia: ma tu, accoccolato in un cantuccio della tana, non fai niente che gracchiare. No no! La vita è da spendere, non da conservarvi.

Benedicite   DHL

Comando a Seltzer di mandarti questi *Tartaruge*. Non ti piaceranno pure.

[Anyhow I'm going – this very month. I have an American friend there, Brewster. He wants to study Buddhism. He has a large old house near Kandy –

he is not at all rich – married, with a little girl. We are going to join him. You know I'm tired here, of yelling with all of these people. You know that I need to go away, away, away: yes, yes, I can't go on here anymore. You know there are always the angels and the archangels, thrones, powers, cherubims, seraphims – the whole choir there. But here these baptised beasts always make themselves heard, these and nothing else. I'm going away from here. Walking one arrives: if not to the grave, at least a little bit outside this human, too human world. There are so many things hidden to us: I have to attach myself to them.

Why do I write in Italian, and what's more incorrect? Because I'm a fool, but tired in a way, and would like to change my skin, like the serpent. Anyway, I'm going away from here. There was once paradise down there, in Ceylon. Don't you believe it? I do. I'm also looking for a bit of this paradise. Adam, that ancestor, was living right there.

What do you want then? What do you want from me? That I close myself into a grotto number 5, as you do? God deliver me! – in a cave crammed full with newspapers? Never, my friend, never. Leaves of cinnamon, not of newspapers.

I feel a little bit sad too, like that serpent when he must change his skin. But without difficulties there are no rewards. There! – I'm not pleased with you: crouching there are the bottom of cave No. 5, without risking even one hair of your beard: – what must I think of you? – even the toad goes hunting: but you, huddled in a small corner of your cave, all you do is caw. No, no! Life is to be spent, not saved.

Bless you   DHL

I'm asking Seltzer to send you *Tortoises*. You won't like it either.]

2439. To Jean Starr Untermeyer, [2 February 1922]
Text: MSC UT; Nehls, iii. 669.

Fontana Vecchia, *Taormina*, Sicilia
2 July 1922[1]

Dear Mrs. Untermeyer[2]

I received your two books of poems, also your letter. The poems I have read – most of them aloud to my wife. I think the greatest achievement is when pure

---

[1] The text is a copy in an unknown hand written on paper initialled 'PHC'; the date is clearly an error.

[2] Jeanette ('Jean') Starr (1886–1970), American poet, m. 1907, Louis Untermeyer (1885–1977), American poet. She had published her poems, *Growing Pains* (New York, 1918) and *Dreams Out of Darkness* (New York, 1921); presumably they were the volumes sent to DHL. The Untermeyers had been admirers of DHL for some time and had, in December 1919, sent him the equivalent of $100 (see *Letters*, iii. 445 and n.).

speech goes straight into poetry, without having to put on Sunday clothes. One is so weary weary of affectations and showing off. But as for the 'struggle' – heavens where is it going to land us? Where is it going to land you? We shall see the next step in your next book of poems.

My best wishes to Louis Untermeyer. We *were* coming to America, my wife and I. Now we are going to Ceylon – This month I hope. They say Paradise was once in Ceylon. Was it ever in America. Or will it be? Or is America where Paradise is perfectly lost? Even that's an achievement. Hope I may meet you and your husband one day.

Yours very sincerely   D. H. Lawrence

2440. To Robert Mountsier, 7 February 1922
Text: MS Smith; Postmark, Taormina 8 2 22; Unpublished.

Fontana Vecchia, *Taormina*, Sicily
7 Feby 1922

Dear Mountsier

The James Tait Black prize is a sum of money bequeathed by the widow of James Tait Black Publisher, for the best English novel of each year, judged by the Professor of English Language and Literature in Edinburgh University. Is that enough?

Will you please add these definite facts to the 'Memoir of Magnus' – modify my last paragraph. The mother was the daughter of the *Emperor Frederick* and therefore half-sister of the present ex William:[1] Magnus therefore Wilhelm's nephew. Her portrait by *Paul* is in the *Doria* gallery in Rome. When the book appears – if ever it does – be sure to send a copy to
Don Mauro Inquanez, Montecassino, Prov. di Caserta.
Montecassino is the monastery itself.

I have engaged berths on the *Osterley*, sailing from Naples on the 26th of this month for Colombo – address
c/o EHBrewster, 'Ardnaree', Lake View Estate, *Kandy*, Ceylon.
– Juta telegraphs from the Cape that he will join me in Ceylon in April.

A lad called Whitney Warren, son of an architect in New York has taken Fontana Vecchia from me – seems a nice boy.[2] I have done about one-third of Vergas novel *Mastro-don Gesualdo* – translated it I mean. I have written to the publishers in Milan about copyrights. – Poor old Verga went and died exactly as I was going to see him in Catania. But he was 82 years old.

---

[1] Magnus's mother, Hedwigis Rosamunda Liebetrau Magnus (1845–1912). Cf. 'Introduction to *Memoirs of the Foreign Legion*', in W. Roberts and H. T. Moore, eds, *Phoenix II*, 1968, p. 360.
[2] Whitney Warren, a New York architect, had studied in Paris at L'Ecole des Beaux Arts; he died in 1943. His son (who bore the same name) has not been traced.

I believe you were right about Taos. Now we'll see what Ceylon does for us.
I signed the agreement with Secker for the short stories not to appear before
next autumn. Do arrange the simultaneous publication with Curtis Brown.

I'm sorry the *Dial* takes that scrap of *Aaron* – What good are 35 dollars
anyway?[1] – one cheapens oneself. I rather wonder too that you send the
Metropolitan two stories at the same time.[2] The more they think they can
reject the less theyll take.

A man H J Forman is here – an American writer – dull but nice. Seems to
want to do an article on me, and I of course rather hate it. Shall not submit to
any actual interview.[3] – The place is full of Americans – this will soon be an
American colony pure and simple. Bonner is back – a little less perky and a
little more pushing, but not going down very well.[4] They all snub him, but
he's not so bad. Why should he bother to *push*, especially among this silly
crowd. The most *trivial* people in the world, but all really very nice and
amiable.

Well Ceylon next.

DHL

I wrote the letter to Doran, to hand over any money to you.

2441. To Curtis Brown, 8 February 1922
Text: MS UT; Huxley 536–7.

Fontana Vecchia, *Taormina* Sicily
8 Feby. 1922

Dear Curtis Brown,

I enclose a letter from Pinker. I want you to take over *all* my books: all the
Duckworth books and the Secker books, and have all accounts made out to
you, and all payments. Then you'll have all my English work in your hands.
I'll write to Duckworth tomorrow. Will you take everything under your wing?

Se vuole Dio – we are sailing from Naples on the *Osterley*, Orient Line, on
26th Feby, for Ceylon. The address in Ceylon is

c/o E. H. Brewster, 'Ardnaree', Lake View Estate, Kandy, Ceylon.

---

[1] Mountsier's statement of account, submitted to DHL in July 1922 (TMSC Smith), confirms
that he received $35 from the *Dial* for the right to print a selection from chap. XIV of *Aaron's Rod*
(in February 1922).

[2] Whatever stories were offered to *Metropolitan* none was accepted.

[3] Henry James Forman (1879–1966), American journalist, editor and author. His 'With D. H.
Lawrence in Sicily' appeared in the *New York Times Book Review and Magazine*, 27 August
1922.

[4] Bonner was an expatriate American whom DHL knew in Taormina in 1920; he wrote an opera
and hoped that the Metropolitan Opera House would stage it for him (*Letters*, iii. 634). In
January 1921 he took a letter from DHL to Mountsier (ibid., iii. 644–5).

I am nearly half-way through the translation of a Sicilian novel, *Mastro-don Gesualdo*, by Giovanni Verga. He just died – aged 82 – in Catania. I think he is so very good. I have written to the publishers, Fratelli Treves, of Milano, about copyright: but I hear there is no strict law between England and Italy. Ask *Secker*, I see he just published *Tre Croci*.[1] I believe there was a translation of *Mastro-don Gesualdo*, done by a Mary A. Craig, in 1893, I believe. But it will have disappeared. Will you find out about it? – I will send you the MS. – all that is finished – before I leave. Afraid I shan't have it done. Such a good novel. Verga is the man who wrote *Cavalleria Rusticana*.

I expect I shall have time for a reply from you. We leave this house on the 22nd for Naples. Any *late* letter you could post on the *Osterley*, or address to the

S. S. *Osterley*, Orient Line, Naples, in partenza febbraio 26.

The story 'Witch à la mode' hasnt come from Pinker.[2]

Think this is all this time.

D. H. Lawrence

2442. To Michael Borg, 10 February 1922
Text: MS UT; Unpublished.

Fontana Vecchia, *Taormina*
10 Feb. 1922.

Dear Michael Borg

This is to introduce you to Mr H. J. Forman, an American writer, who is coming to Malta for a few days to look at the island and gather impressions. If there is anything you could tell him or do for him, to help him to find the interesting points of Malta, I should be so glad.

Poor Magnus, I heard of another nasty bit of swindling which he did a few days before he left for Malta. – The manuscript by the way has gone to Mr. Mountsier, and he will write direct to you. Mr Forman did not know Magnus – I told him only a few facts.

I have written for berths on the *Osterley*, leaving Naples on the 26th: I expect I shall get them. If not I shall fly to Malta and go P. and O.

Best wishes from us both.

D. H. Lawrence

---

[1] Secker published *Three Crosses* (November 1921), a translation (by Rina Capellero) of *Tre Croci* (Milan, 1920) by Federigo Tozzi (1883–1920).

[2] DHL had been trying to recover this MS from Pinker since February 1920 (see *Letters*, iii. 473); see Letter 2446 below. The story was published posthumously, in *Lovat Dickson's Magazine*, June 1934.

2443. To Rosalind Baynes, [10? February 1922]
Text: MS UN; Huxley 537–8.

Fontana Vecchia, *Taormina*, Sicily
Friday

My dear Rosalind

Your letter yesterday. Our great news is that we are going to Ceylon – to friends who have gone and taken a bungalow near Kandy. He is studying Buddhism at the monastery. The address will be

c/o E. H. Brewster, 'Ardnaree', Lake View Estate, *Kandy*, Ceylon.

I don't know how long we shall stay or what we shall do but I want to go – Am tired of tea partying here. We are supposed to be sailing on the 26th. of this month from Naples, by the *Osterley*, Orient Line, to Colombo. Isn't it thrilling.

As for Godwin, he is just a lump. Quite right for him to marry into the Church.[1]

I don't think I'd go to Austria with the babies if I were you.[2] It is beautiful, but I was awfully depressed there, and not well. It is the life-exhaustion feeling. But you might like it. It is not *wildly* cheap – but fairly so. Innsbruck itself is no good: you'd have to go to a village round about: Mayrhofen, in the Zillertal – You might ask Perceval. Our place Zell-am-See is dear. But Douglas would know of a place. – Then Windeam said he had a *lovely* inn near Bozen – Bolzano – in the mountains: and Meran is lovely. Then the people here go to Asolo, north of Padua, and love it and say it's cheap. But go to the Garda, because a lake is so lovely, plus the mountains. The steamers that will carry you here and there, quite cheap, are such fun. I loved the Garda. We were at Gargnano, half way up. We were at a farm-place called San Gaudenzio – and loved it.[3] I've forgotten the peoples' names – Maria and Paolo. Maria a strong peasant does everything for you. A lovely place for children. But you ought to run up and look at it first – Stay at the *Cervo* – inn. Gargnano – take steamer from Desenzano. Riva at the top of the lake is a *jolly* place, but might be hot. If I were you I'd go to the Garda. The mountains are lovely and wild behind. If you had a friend to explore. At the *Cervo* – a little hotel – was a German wife of the Italian proprietor – we liked her.[4] We had a flat in the Villa Igeia – She'd remember us: in 1912–13.

I have been busy translating Giovanni Verga's *Mastro-don Gesualdo* into

[1] See p. 67 n. 2. Baynes' second wife was the niece of the Archbishop of Canterbury.
[2] Her 'babies' were Bridget (b. 1914), Chloë (b. 1916) and Jennifer Nan (b. 1918).
[3] The Lawrences lived in Gargnano, at the 'Villa Igéa', from 18 September 1912 till 30 March 1913; they then moved to a farmhouse, San Gaudenzio, owned by the Capelli family, until 11 April.
[4] The Lawrences held Signora Samuelli in high regard: see *Letters*, i. 520 and n. 3.

English. Do you know Verga? Sicilian, so good: especially *Gesualdo* and *I Malavoglia* and some of the *Novelle*.

I am asking Seltzer to send you to Villa Ada a copy of the Canovaia *Tortoise* poems:[1] also *Sea and Sardinia*. But it will take a while for them to come from New York.

I get awfully irritated with theoretic socialism like Berties.[2]

You will be taking Bridget to Switzerland: you can look at the Garda then. On Como I stayed two years ago in *Argegno*, and liked it extremely.[3] Such fun having excursions into the hills and then on the lake as well. There is a café-pastry cook shop just opposite the quay in Argegno – with an English wife: and very friendly. They'd tell you about a pension. And Como is on your way.

I don't a bit know how long we shall be in Ceylon – or what after. We were *almost* on board ship for America when I suddenly backed out – didn't want to go.

It's horrid weather here, and almond blossom full out.

I expect we'll leave about the 20th from here. If you write at once we'll get it. F[rieda] sends love. We'll meet again somewhere, that's certain.

DHL

2444. To Mary Cannan, [12? February 1922]
Text: MS Lazarus; Moore 691–3.

Fontana Vecchia, *Taormina*, Sicilia
Sunday.

My dear Mary

The pen and seal have come: with the pen I write this letter, and it seems to be running famously. The lapis seal is perfectly lovely: I don't think the setting a bit too elaborate. Beautiful, I think it. I love feeling the stone. But whatever made you suddenly send me this wildly expensive gift! – I love the way that the blue of lapis lazuli seems to live inside a film of crystal, as it were. Now I hope it will stay with me all my life, and seal all my affairs of state and solemnity. Of course the two people who have seen it think that *I* ought not to be having anything so grand. 'That's the sort of thing to be lying on Plum's table', said the Fisher. Damn Plum.[4] I suppose she thinks I ought to be stamping my wax with a thimble top or a wet thumb-end.

[1] See p. 67 n. 1. DHL wrote the *Tortoise* poems at Villa Canovaia in September 1920.

[2] Bertrand Arthur William Russell, 3rd Earl Russell (1872–1970), distinguished mathematician and philosopher. Fellow of Trinity College in 1895; because of his campaigning as a pacifist during World War I, he was temporarily deprived of his Fellowship, fined and imprisoned. DHL met Russell through Lady Ottoline Morrell in 1915; they became increasingly hostile to one another during this year-long association. By 'theoretic socialism', DHL may allude to Russell's *The Practice and Theory of Bolshevism* (1920). (See *Letters*, ii. 273 n. 2.)

[3] DHL was on a walking-tour with Percy and Irene Whittley in August 1920.

[4] Unidentified.

It is so cold. The almond blossom is out, and looks and *feels* like snow. I don't even like the look of it: it gives me that sick feeling of snow.

I am filling in my time translating a Sicilian novel, *Mastro-don Gesualdo*, by Giovanni Verga: he died last month. It is so good. – But I am on thorns, can't settle.

I have sent the deposit money for the berths on the *Osterley*, sailing from Naples on the 26th.: two weeks today. The thought of going gives me a sinking feeling: the wrench of breaking off. But I want to go. I suppose I shall be sitting draped in a sheet, cross-legged and smiling at my own pancia,[1] like Buddha, in about a fortnight after I get to Ceylon. See me. The address by the way is

c/o E. H. Brewster, 'Ardnaree', Lake View Estate, *Kandy*, Ceylon.

Don't talk about goodbyes. Think what fun for you to be stepping off at Colombo under your parasol, and me and Frieda there two sights to behold in pith helmets and black goggles. The very thought of it makes you know it is inevitable.

> What though the spicy breezes
> Blow soft o'er Ceylon's isle[2]

Don't have any doubts about it.

I shall write you again of course before we go. We shall leave this house on the 22nd – for Naples. A young American called Whitney Warren has taken the house.

I have got your London bank address: but keep me informed of everything.

I think myself that the Austrian Tyrol, though lovely, is depressing. I'm sure Spain is more fun. But people are a *bit* disagreeable everywhere.

Albert Stopford is here – the man who made some sort of scandal, I don't know what.[3] He's really very nice: but getting oldish.

I did such a 'Memoir' of Maurice Magnus, to go in front of his horrid *Legion* book. If it's published – in America – they shall send it you. You'll have to read it. Our Malta trip!

Well Mary, thank you so much for the pen and my blue seal. Don't think of goodbyes, only of parasols and P. and O. liners and pith helmets and palm trees and us shouting 'There she is!' from behind our goggles, as you wave from the upper deck.

DHL

---

[1] 'belly'.   [2] See p. 110 n. 3.
[3] On 20 November 1918, Albert Stopford (b. 1860) was charged with 'improper behaviour towards a soldier in the Scots Guards' (*Times*, 21 November 1918); the next day he was convicted and sentenced to 12 months imprisonment with hard labour. Stopford, an art dealer, was related to the family of the Earl of Courtown, hence Frieda's description of him as 'an aristocrat' (Tedlock, *Lawrence MSS* 318).

2445. Marie Hubrecht, 15 February 1922
Text: MS Hubrecht; Unpublished.

Fontana Vecchia, *Taormina* Sicilia
15 Feby. 1922

Dear Miss Hubrecht.

We are leaving on the 26th. of this month by the *SS. Osterley* from Naples for Ceylon. We are going to join the Brewsters. I don't know how long we shall stay there – but six months at the least. Juta wants to come in April and paint there. The address will be

'Ardnaree', Lake View Estate, *Kandy*, Ceylon.

Do write to us there.

By the way the book with the Juta pictures – *Sea and Sardinia* – is out in America, and is due in England in March. I have ordered you a copy to be sent to you, along with *Women in Love* as soon as the book is out: to be sent to the Witte Huis. If it doesn't come, write to

Martin Secker, 5 John Street, Adelphi, London W.C. 2

and ask him why. He should send both books together. And he charges me for them, and then they never arrive.

A young American called Whitney Warren has taken this house for a year. I am sorry to give it up: but I have no idea when we may be back, if ever.

It has been the most horrible weather – wind and rain all the time, and cold – utterly unlike Taormina. I shall really be glad to get away.

You will find everything quite safe in the studio[1] – we had two teaparties there, but no damage done to anything. I'm sure you'll find everything exactly as it was put away. The only thing that might have got left here is a copy or two of the loose *Harpers Magazine* or the *Studio Magazine*: things of no value. All the books are safely returned.

I do hope you are now quite well. I myself have had influenza lingering on me all winter, and do not feel quite myself even now. It is a misery.

You will write to me to Ceylon, won't you, and tell me all the news.

Best of wishes from us both, and so many thanks for letting us use the studio. Alas, it has been such bad weather we have only been once since Christmas.

Yours Sincerely   D. H. Lawrence

Carmelo asks me to enclose a note from him, and hopes you will reply.

---

[1] See the picture of Rocca Forte in *Letters*, iii.

2446. To J. B. Pinker, 15 February 1922
Text: MS UNYB; Unpublished.

Fontana Vecchia, *Taormina*, Sicily
15 Feb. 1922.

Dear Pinker

Many thanks for your letter and for the story 'Witch à la Mode', safely arrived.

I am leaving with my wife, going to Ceylon – sailing from Naples on the 26th of this month. The address will be:

'Ardnaree', Lake View Estate, *Kandy*, Ceylon

in case you ever need it.

Yours Sincerely   D. H. Lawrence

2447. To Martin Secker, 15 February 1922
Text: MS UInd; Postmark, Taormina 15 2 22; Secker 47–8.

Fontana Vecchia, *Taormina*, Sicily.
15 Feb. 1922

Dear Secker

We are sailing on Feb. 26th. from Naples on *S.S. Osterley*, Orient Line, for Colombo. Address in Ceylon:

'Ardnaree', Lake View Estate, *Kandy*, Ceylon.

Don't know how long we shall be there, or anything: but want to go.

I enclose a list of the six presentation copies of *Sea and Sardinia*.[1] Will you please post them for me.

Hope I'll do a Ceylon novel. We leave this house on the 21st. A letter to the ship *S.S. Osterley*, Orient Line, Napoli in partenza Feb. 26th would get me.

Best wishes   D. H. Lawrence

The copy to Kippenberg, Insel Verlag, you ought to throw in, for trade. He has just printed *The Rainbow*.

I heard from Pinker[2] relinquishing his rights over *New Poems*. Will you

---

[1] The list is (MS UInd) as follows:
  Copies of Sea and Sardinia
  1. Miss Marie Hubrecht, Witte Huis, *Doorn* bei Utrecht, Holland. please enclose also a copy of *Women in Love* also.
  1. S. Koteliansky, 5 Acacia Rd., St. Johns Wood. N. W. 8.
  1. The Lady Cynthia Asquith, Stanway, Winchcombe, Glos.
  1. Mrs Catherine Carswell, Holly Bush House, Holly Mount, Hampstead N. W. 3.
  1. Miss Elsa Weekley, Great Maplestead Vicarage, near Halstead. Essex.
  1. Mrs Rosalind Baynes, Villino Ada, Fiesole, Florence
  1. Dr Anton Kippenberg, Insel Verlag, Kurzestrasse 7, *Leipzig*. Germany
[2] Pinker] Secker

therefore make all statements and payments for these to Curtis Brown. Will you also kindly send one copy of *New Poems* to Don Mauro Inguanez, *Montecassino*, Prov. di Caserta, Italy.

2448. To S. S. Koteliansky, [17 February 1922]
Text: MS BL; PC; Postmark, Taormina 18 2 22; Zytaruk 238.

[Fontana Vecchia, *Taormina*, (Messina) Sicily]
Friday.

We leave Taormina on Monday for Palermo – throes of packing – We sail from Naples on the 26th by *SS. Osterley*, Orient Line for Colombo – about 14 days. Address:
'Ardnaree', Lake View Estate, *Kandy*, Ceylon.
Write me a line at once. I ordered you *Sea and Sardinia* from Secker – tell me if he sends it. Feel so queer, actually to be going. But am glad – so glad – Palm trees and elephants and dark people: incantevole![1]

DHL

2449. To Enid Hilton, 17 February 1922
Text: MS UCLA; Unpublished.

Fontana Vecchia, *Taormina*, Sicily
17 Feby 1922
Dear Enid[2]
Your letter just come: finds us in the throes of packing up. We leave on Monday morning for Palermo – sail from Naples on the 26th for Colombo. The address will be:
'Ardnaree', Lake View Estate, *Kandy*, Ceylon.
Heaven knows how long we shall stay, or how we shall like it.
Your news quite thrilling. I agree, best for you to keep your job. Why sit idle in some tiresome little flat? Yes, save up for a holiday. Take a second-class ticket to *Milan*. Stay one night at Hotel Como or Hotel du Nord: then go on to *Como*. Stay in the *Barchetta* restaurant, near the lake: it has rooms: about 25 Liras for a double-bedded room. Take trips up the lake to various places – then move eastwards – you can walk from Lecco to Lake Iseo – and again from

---

[1] 'enchanting!'
[2] Enid Hopkin (1896–   ) had recently married Laurence Hilton. She was the daughter of DHL's old and, for him, influential friends, William ('Willie') Edward Hopkin (1862–1951) and his wife Sarah Annie ('Sallie') (1867–1922), both of them prominent in Eastwood's political and intellectual life. See *Letters*, i. 176 nn. 2, 5.

Iseo to Lake Garda – wild and mountainous. On Garda stay at Gargnano, at the Hotel del Cervo. It is lovely country: should cost you about 10/- a day each if you're careful. Always ask prices before you take rooms. – From Desenzano, if you feel like a dash to Venice, it is only three hours. Stay there in the Casa Petrarca, Grand Canal: they speak English. I think you'd feel more comfortable in the Italian lakes than in Austria, though the latter is much cheaper. But not happy. Better write for a room at Venice if you want to stay. I expect you will pay about 40 Liras a day each, *en pension*, without wine. The exchange is now about 90 Lire to £1.

On Como I stayed at Argegno – liked it very much. I liked the steamers on the lakes so much. And May is a perfect month. Plan it out in Baedeker. In the big towns the hotels are apt to be *very* full: but not in Como and[1] such places. At all big stations is a Cook's man: he'll tell you everything. And so many English people are travelling, you need never be afraid. The towns like Milan are rather dear – but ask for a cheap bedroom: about 25 francs for the two of you. One says francs or Liras irrespective. Learn just a bit of Italian.

I send you a Baedeker and a couple of other books. Many good wishes from us both for your future. I am so sorry about your mother. This in a rush of one thing and another.

Yrs   D. H. Lawrence

No, your mother did not send me a wedding-card – I knew nothing.

2450. To Catherine Carswell, [17 February 1922]
Text: MS YU; PC; Postmark, Taormina 18 2 22; cited in Carswell 162.

Taormina.

Friday

My dear Cath.

We leave Taormina on Monday for Palermo, en route for Naples. We sail from Naples on the 26th. by *SS Osterley*, Orient Line – for Colombo. Takes about 14 days. Feel so thrilled – Address:

'Ardnaree', Lake View Estate, *Kandy*, Ceylon.

Write me there. Had your letter – so glad such good news of *Camomile*.[2] Ordered you *Sea and Sardinia* from Secker – tell me if he sends it. Nylander so pleased that you wrote him. – Throes of packing! – but am glad. I want to go. One day you and Don will come – I dreamed of elephants.

DHL

---

[1] and] At   [2] See p. 52 n. 3.

2451. To Thomas Seltzer, 17 February 1922
Text: MS UT; Postmark, Taormina 17 2 22; Lacy, *Seltzer* 33.

Fontana Vecchia, *Taormina*, Sicily
17 Feb. 1922

Dear Seltzer

We are sailing from Naples on the 26th. inst by the *Osterley*, for Colombo.
The address:

'Ardnaree', Lake View Estate, Kandy, Ceylon.

Will you be so kind as to send a copy of *The Lost Girl* and of *Sea and Sardinia* to Mrs Leader-Williams, Palazzo Atenasio, *Taormina* – Sicily.[1]

Hope I'll do a Ceylon novel. – Am so glad to be moving out of Europe.

D. H. Lawrence

2452. To Robert Mountsier, 17 February 1922
Text: MS Smith; Postmark, Taormina 17 2 22; Unpublished.

Fontana Vecchia, *Taormina*, Sicily
17 Feb. 1922

Dear Mountsier

We are definitely sailing on the *Osterley* from Naples on the 26th. inst. for Colombo. Address

'Ardnaree', Lake View Estate, Kandy, Ceylon.

The typist – Miss Carmichael, 7 Via Faentina, Florence – will send you the first half of the translation of *Mastro-don Gesualdo*. As Harpers did the other Verga novel in 1891, they might like to do this.[2] Apparently there is *no* definite copyright law between England and America – and Italy. And Verga is dead. – I will send you the rest as soon as it's done, with a small foreword on Verga. – Treves are no longer the publishers in Italy – and the only claimants on the novels are the heirs.

Will you please send at once to Curtis Brown a copy of 'Melville – *Moby Dick*' essay from the *Studies in C[lassic] A[merican] Literature*. It is missing from my MS. Curtis wants to offer it to Jonathan Cape.[3]

Will send another line before leaving.

D.H. Lawrence

---

[1] Basil and Lilian Leader-Williams were acquaintances of DHL's in Taormina; they were antique dealers.
[2] Harper and Brothers published *The House by the Medlar-Tree*, trans. Mary A. Craig, intro. by William Dean Howells (New York, 1890; 1891).
[3] Cape did not accept the book; it was first published in England by Secker (1924).

2453. To Curtis Brown, 18 February 1922
Text: MS UT; Unpublished.

Fontana Vecchia, *Taormina*, Sicily
Sat. 18 Feby 1922

Dear Curtis Brown

Had your letters: am sending you today MSS of *Studies in Classic American Literature*. The *English Review* published the first eight, the *Nation* published 'Whitman', and some other little paper published 'Blithedale Romance'.[1] Leaves only 'Dana' and 'Melville' for periodical publication: both unlikely. *One Essay is missing*: 'Herman Melville's *Moby Dick*'. I have written to Mountsier to send it you at once. – If Seltzer is delaying the publication of these *Studies* I don't see why Cape shouldn't go ahead, I shall tell Mountsier so. That is if Cape will publish them. – Be sure you follow the sequence of chapters as I have written it out. Be sure to have the *Moby Dick* chapter from Mountsier. Be sure to mention the *English Review*: I liked Harrison for doing these. – Write also to Mountsier asking him to send the *Moby Dick* essay.

I enclose the letter from Treves about Verga.[2] My typist in Florence will send you the first half of the MS. translation all I have done: (Mrs Carmichael, 7 Via Faentina, Florence). It appears there is not any strict copyright law between England and America, and now that Verga is dead, a publisher can go ahead.[3] So I am told. But I enclose Treves' letter.

Wildly busy packing. We leave this house on Monday: sail on the 26th on the *Osterley*. You have the Ceylon address.

Tanti saluti   D. H. Lawrence
Address till 26th. Hotel Santa Lucia, Naples.

2454. To Robert Mountsier, [18 February 1922]
Text: MS Smith; Postmark, Taormina 19 2 22; Unpublished.

Fontana Vecchia
Sat. 19 Feb. 1922

Dear M[ountsier]

I enclose the last three sheets of the 'Whitman' essay. Please substitute

---

[1] The essay on Hawthorne's *Blithedale Romance* was first published in Seltzer's edition of *Studies in Classic American Literature* (1923). However the essay had reached proof stage for the *English Review* (Roberts E382f), but was not published. For details of the publication of the other essays referred to, see Roberts A25.

[2] The Milan publishers Fratelli Treves informed DHL (TMS UT, 9 February 1922) that the translation rights were reserved by the author; that they might have been acquired by another firm; but that they would normally pass to Verga's heir.

[3] The information about the publication in England of Verga's novels which DHL gives in Letter 2457 is also written on this letter in a hand that cannot be confidently identified.

them in the MS., and let these be printed. Then there will be nothing censurable also. And *this* is what I mean. You will see where it goes on.

Please send Curtis Brown the *Moby Dick* essay at once. And if Jonathan Cape wants to print *Studies in C[lassic] A[merican] Lit[erature]* before Seltzer is ready, I believe a little previous English puffing would help Seltzer's sale. I would like these essays to come out as soon as possible.

We leave on Monday for Palermo – am just finishing packing. A wrench! But I want to go. – Round the world will bring us to America.

Au revoir   D. H. Lawrence

2455. To Baroness Anna von Richthofen, [19 February 1922]
Text: MS UCB; PC; Postmark, Taormina 20 2 22; Frieda Lawrence 124.

Fontana Vecchia
Sunday.

Meine liebe Schwiegermutter

Wir sitzen reise-fertig: 4 Koffer, ein Hauskoffer, ein Buchkoffer, F[rieda]'s und mein. – und dann zwei Valisen, Hut-koffer, und die zwei ganz kleine stücke: grade wie Abraham fortfahrend nach einem neuen Land. Mein Herz zittert jetzt, meiste vor Schmerz – das weg-gehen von unserm Heim und die Leute und Sizilien. Aber ich will 's vergessen, und nur an Palmen und Elefanten und Affen und Pfauen denken. Morgen 10:34 reisen wir fort: essen in Messina, wo wir müssen umsteigen: kommen ½ 9 an Palermo – und so an den Hotel Panormus, wo wohnt die Freundin. Donnerstag nacht nach Neapel, mit schiff: und da in Hotel Santa Lucia. Dann Sonntag morgen auf dem *S.S. Osterley*, Orient Line, nach Ceylon. Das Schiff geht weiter, nach Australien. Du hast die Addresse:

'Ardnaree', Lake View Estate, *Kandy*. Ceylon.

– Denke, es ist nur 14 Tage von Neapel. Wir können immer schnell wieder kommen, wann wir genug haben. Vielleicht hat die Else auch recht, vielleicht kehren wir wieder[1] nach unserm Fontana. Ich sage nicht nein. Ich mache nichts fest. Heute geh ich, morgen kehre ich wieder. So ist es. Ich schreibe dir wieder von Palermo wann ich Zeit habe. Ich denke an dich.

DHL

[My dear Schwiegermutter

We sit ready to travel: 4 trunks, one household trunk, one book trunk, F[rieda]'s and mine. – and then two valises, hat-box, and the two quite small pieces: just like Abraham faring forth to a new land.[2] My heart quivers now,

---

[1] wieder] uns   [2] Cf. Genesis xiii. 1ff.

mostly with pain – the going away from our home and the people and Sicily. But I want to forget it, and only think of palms and elephants and apes and peacocks. Tomorrow 10:34 we leave: eat in Messina, where we must change: arrive 8.30 in Palermo – and so to the Hotel Panormus, where our woman friend lives. Thursday night to Naples, by ship: and there at Hotel Santa Lucia. Then Sunday morning on the *S.S. Osterley*, Orient Line, to Ceylon. The ship goes on, to Australia. You have the address:

'Ardnaree', Lake View Estate, *Kandy*. Ceylon.

– Imagine, it is only 14 days from Naples. We can always come back quickly when we have had enough. Perhaps Else is quite right, perhaps we shall return to our Fontana. I don't say no. I'm settling nothing. Today I go, tomorrow I return. So it is. I'll write you again from Palermo if I have time. I think of you.

DHL]

2456. To Curtis Brown, 19 February 1922
Text: MS UT; Unpublished.

Fontana Vecchia, *Taormina*, Sicily
19 Feb. 1922

Dear Curtis Brown

Let Secker go ahead with *Sea and Sardinia*. Did I ever insist that it *should* be one of the five books? – I dont think I did. Because of course I realise it is a limited selling book. And I want him to do it. I think you have mistaken me about it. Anyhow I don't feel it need count as one of the five.

Leaving here tomorrow.

D. H. Lawrence

2457. To Curtis Brown, 24 February 1922
Text: MS UT; Postmark, Napoli 24 II 1922; Huxley 539–40.

[Grande Albergo Santa Lucia, Napoli][1]
Friday 24 Feby 1922

Dear Curtis Brown

I sent you a letter saying please agree to Secker about *Sardinia*.[2]

[1] Here and in the two letters following, DHL used the hotel's headed notepaper.
[2] Curtis Brown had probably told DHL about Secker's letter to him, 16 February 1922 (Secker Letter-Book, UIll):

Dear Mr. Curtis-Brown,

I am much obliged for your letter of the 14th, from which I note that it is settled that "Sea and Sardinia" shall be published as a separate book outside my contract. Naturally our previous arrangements now stand.

I agree to Mr. Lawrence's suggestion that I should pay a 20% royalty on the signed copies of

I asked him please to make all accounts with you: and wrote the same to Duckworth. I hope too that you will soon make your first penny.

Treves wrote to me – I ought to have sent the letter. They said that all copyright was kept for himself by 'il povero Giovanni Verga' – and that they would now revert to his heirs: that is his nephews – since Verga died in January. Treves are no longer the publishers of Verga. The publisher in London was J. R. Osgood, published the novels

The House by the Medlar Tree (*I Malavoglia*) 1891
Mastro-Don Gesualdo 1893 trans Mary A. Craig.
first of these pub. America by Harpers.

I wrote to Catania to Prof Zanboni, but he didn't answer.[1]

Treves told me very little – I don't even know who publishes Verga now – they certainly did in 1920 still – but anyhow the publisher has no control over the copyright, apparently. – Mrs Carmichael will send you half the Verga MS. – We sail on Sunday – I am so sleepy just come off the Palermo boat.

Sincerely   D. H. Lawrence

I presume you got the signed sheets for Secker's *Women in Love* special Seltzer[2] copies. I consider he *ought* to pay me for those signatures, but if the gnat sticks in his throat and he doesn't want to, let him go ahead without bothering – I don't care.

DHL

Yes, of course Mountsier must keep the American control.

Of course I want you to take control also of Secker's little *de luxe* edition of *Women in Love*.

2458. To Robert Mountsier, 24 February 1922
Text: MS Smith; Postmark, Napoli 24. II 1922; Unpublished.

[Grande Albergo Santa Lucia, Napoli]
Friday 24 Feb 1922

Dear M[ountsier]

We sail on Sunday – two days hence – for Ceylon.

All right, I won't write to Seltzer about such a thing as corrections. I thought that didn't interest you particularly.

I have told Secker I want Curtis to do *all* my business – have even got a

"Women in Love" and I will let you know as soon as I have decided what price the book is to be. Will you meanwhile be good enough to send me the signed pages?

I have now read the three novelettes and agree to accept them as the fourth book under my contract, the other three being "The Lost Girl", "Women in Love" and "Aaron's Rod" receipt of the proof of which I am anxiously awaiting from America.

Yours sincerely

---

[1] Unidentified.   [2] Seltzer] edition

release from Pinker and have turned over all *Duckworth* books into his hands.[1]
– Secker wanted to give me 15% on the *deluxe W[omen] in Love*s with my
signature and I said he should give 20%. I sent the signed sheets to Curtis
B[rown].

I'll look for the 'Ass' poem.[2] If it is lost it is lost, and addio.

I wrote you all about the *Studies in C[lassic] A[merican] Lit[erature]*.

Dont be depressed about books – they'll sell one day.

I have transferred so far $490 – that is 400 to the English bank and 90 to
Haskard in Florence. But of the latter, the first cheque No. 1. disappeared
letter and all in this sweet post. But it was crossed to Haskard, so can't be
cashed. – I can cash cheques in Ceylon.

Haven't heard from Juta save cables saying he can join us in Ceylon in
April.

I hope you have had all my letters – I seem to write so many. – I think Curtis
is a little piqued at having so much work from me, and as he says, *not a penny*. I
can't help it. – Do you feel the same? Pazienza!

I am glad I am going east and not west – read *Main Street* and it gave me
horrors.[3] Italy is getting also impossible – sort of going to pieces,
demosutised.[4]

Dont be depressed.

Benedicite DHL
'Ardnaree', Lake View Estate, *Kandy*, Ceylon.

2459. To Thomas Seltzer, 24 February 1922
Text: MS UT; Postmark, Napoli 24. II 1922; Lacy, *Seltzer* 34.

[Grande Albergo Santa Lucia, Napoli]
24 Feb. 1922

Dear Seltzer

So we have left Sicily and on Sunday – two days hence – the boat sails for
Ceylon. Feel upset at going – but glad to leave Europe – will come west
eastwards.

The book business is not good, Mountsier says, and everybody seems
depressed. Never mind – pazienza chi va piano va lontano.[5]

Greetings to you.

D. H. Lawrence

---

[1] I.e. *The Trespasser* (1912), *Love Poems and Others* (1913), *Sons and Lovers* (1913), *The Prussian
Officer and Other Stories* (1914), *Twilight in Italy* (1916), *Amores* (1916),
[2] Written in March 1921, first published in *Birds, Beasts and Flowers*.
[3] *Main Street* (New York 1920), the novel that first established the reputation of Sinclair Lewis
(1885–1951). It is a devastating picture of American small town provincialism.
[4] A coinage from 'demos' (the people, proletariat).
[5] 'patience, he who goes slowly goes far'.

2460. To S. S. Koteliansky, [25 February 1922]
Text: MS BL; PC v. Roma Arco di Tito Bassorilièvo delle Quadriga; Postmark, Napoli 25.
II 1922; Zytaruk 238.

Naples
Sat.

We sail tomorrow on the *Osterley* – write to Ceylon.

DHL

2461. To Catherine Carswell, [25 February 1922]
Text: MS YU; PC v. [Painting of three girls in field]; Postmark, Napoli 25. II 1922; Moore,
Poste Restante 65.

Naples
Sat

We leave tomorrow on the *Osterley*. Write to Ceylon.

DHL

2462. To Rosalind Baynes, [25 February 1922]
Text: MS UT; PC v. Gargnano [waterfront]; Postmark, Napoli 25. II 22; Unpublished.

Naples.
Sat

We leave tomorrow by the *Osterley* – send us a line to Ceylon.

DHL

2463. To Mabel Dodge Sterne, [25 February 1922]
Text: MS Brill; PC; Postmark, Napoli 25. II 1922; Luhan 17.

Naples
Sat

We are sailing tomorrow for Ceylon – you have the address – I wonder if you
will feel like a dash to the east – I feel rather bad about suddenly backing out of
all I had decided, Taos and America – and you were so kind – But it is my
destiny.

D. H. Lawrence

2464. To Ada Clarke, [25 February 1922]
Text: MS Clarke; PC v. Cagliari – Nuovo Palazzo Comunale. Filippo Figari: Portatero di Doni (dettaglio); Postmark, Napoli 25. II 1922; Unpublished.

Naples.
Saturday

We leave tomorrow by the *Osterley* – I havent heard from you. I couldn't send the flower picture. Write to Ceylon.

Love   DHL

2465. To Mary Cannan, [28 February 1922]
Text: MS Lazarus; Moore 693–4.

[R.M.S. 'OSTERLEY.']¹
Tuesday. 28 Feb.

My dear Mary
    Here we are full at sea – should come in sight of Crete today. It is lovely lovely weather – blue Mediterranean – the ship *so* comfortable. We are second class and it is quite perfect, because the people are so quiet and simple and nobody shows off at all. The boat is nothing but comfort – like a luxurious hotel this second class. First is no different, except one deck more – but *more showing off* – dances etc. It cost £140 for the two of us, Naples to Colombo. First class only ten pounds more.
    We come to Port Said on Thursday, then through the Suez Canal.
    I love it really – it is so roomy and comfortable, and at sea. We are due to arrive at Colombo on the 13th.
    I am glad to leave Italy – it has become a hateful country. Did you get your 5000 out of the Banca di Sconto? If so transfer it at once, the country is more shaky than ever and the exchange is good for you.
    I bet you'll be coming to Ceylon. This boat left London on the 18th. and called at Toulon for mail – quite near you.

a rivederci   DHL

2466. To Baroness Anna von Richthofen, [28 February–1 March 1922]
Text: MS UCB; Frieda Lawrence and Desmond Hawkins, trans., 'Two Letters of D. H. Lawrence, Written on the Way to Ceylon, Addressed to Frau Baronin von Richthofen', *Twentieth Century*, iv (January 1933), 1–2.

[R.M.S. 'OSTERLEY.']
Dienstag 28 Feb.

Meine Liebe Schwiegermutter
    Wir sind zwei Tage fort: kamen aus Neapel Sonntag abend, 8 uhr. Montag

¹ In this and subsequent letters DHL uses the ship's headed notepaper.

Morgen, 8 Uhr kamen wir durch die Enge von Messina: und dann
Stundenlang sahen wir unsere Etna, wie eine weisse Königin, oder eine weisse
Hexe da im Himmel stehend: so zauberschön, aber ich meine schlimm. Sie
sagte mir 'Komm du wieder her' – ich sagte nur nein, aber weinte innerlich
vor Schmerz – Trennungschmerz.

Das Wetter ist wunderschön – blaue Himmel, blaues Meer – still. Heute
sehen wir kein Land, nur die lange weisse dünne Wolken wo liegt
Griechenland. Später sollen wir Crete (Candia) sehen. Wir kommen
Donnerstag an Port Said, da geht dieser Brief an Land: wir auch, für ein Paar
Stunden. Dann gehen wir durch die *Suez Canal*, und so in das Rote Meer.

Das Schiff ist prachtvoll – so bequem, so viel platz, und nicht viele
Reisende. Die Plätze sind nicht die Hälfte besetzt. Es ist grade wie ein ganz
'Luxus' Hotel. Morgens, 7 Uhr, kommt der Steward mit einer Tasse The und
fragt ob man sein Bad nehmen will, und warm oder heiss oder wie. Um 8 uhr.
klingt Frühstück: und so ein *Menu*: gekochte Birnen, Porridge, Fish, Speck,
Eier, Bratwurste, Beefsteak, Nieren, Marmalade – alles da. Dann nachher
geht man oben, sitzt herum, kosen oder croquet-spielen – elf uhr kommt der
Steward mit einer Tasse Bovril – 1 uhr. Mittagsessen – Suppe, Fish, Huhn
oder Truthahn, Fleisch entrées – immer viel zu viel – 4. uhr Thee – 7 uhr.
Diner – ach nein, man isst immer. Aber man hat auch Appetit am Meer: wann
es so still ist und himmelschön wie jetzt.

Ich finde es merkwurdig, dass es so still ist, so ruhig, so zivilisiert: die Leute
alle so still und selbstverständlich, und *so* eine Reinheit, alles so sehr bequem.
Ja, es ist doch besser wie Italien, die Italiener sind jetzt nicht gut: niederich
geworden. Die Frieda hat sich in Neapel erkältet, und du solltest doch sehen,
wie gut mit ihr sind der Steward und die Stewardess, als sie im Bett liegt –
kommen so schnell mit Thee und Sodawasser oder was sie will, und immer so
zärtliche Manieren. Nach Italien ist es merkwurdig. Nein, die Zivilisation ist
eine schöne und feine Sache, wann es nur lebendig bleibt, und wird nicht
ennuyée.

Ich kann dir wieder von Aden schreiben – und dann nicht mehr, bis
Ceylon. Jetzt geh' ich unten, und seh ob die Frieda aufgestanden ist. – Heute
geht ihre Erkältung schon besser.

Schade dass du nicht da warst, in Neapel, uns an Bord kommen zu sehen:
mit Köffer kind-und-kegelerie: Körben von Orangen und Äpfeln (geschenkt)
und einem längen Brett, das ein Stück ist von einem Sizilianischen Wagen,
sehr bunt gemalt mit zwei Szenen vom Leben von Marco Visconte – die Else
weisst wie schön sind diese Sizilianischen Wagen: und die facchini die ruften
immer: Ecco la Sicilià – Ecco la Sicilia in viaggio per l'India.

Für den Moment a riveverci – die Frieda soll ein Wort auch schreiben –

DHL

[Frieda Lawrence begins]
Liebe mère,
    Also hier sind wir so selbstverständlich als ob man auf diesem Schiff geboren wäre – Lawr hat ja alles beschrieben – Es ist so still und friedlich, mich ärgert meine Erkältung den ganzen Winter hatte ich gar keine – ich kann gar nicht verstehen warum nicht alle Leute die genug Geld haben nicht um die Welt reisen es ist so *einfach* – 1000 Grüsse

F. –

[Lawrence continues]
    Den ganzen Nachtmittage haben wir Crete gesehen, mit Schnee auf den Bergen – so gross, die Insel: auch eine andere kleinere Insel, ganz gelb und wust, mit riesigen Abgrunden. Jetzt ist die Sonne unten, das Himmelrand rot, das Meer Tinteblau, und der kleinst, dünnste, schärfste Mond der ich je gesehen habe. Es ist schon ganz warm.

Mitwoch

    Heute nur warm und still – kein Land gesehen, Möwen und zwei Schiffe – kommen Morgen vormittag an Port Said – Briefe einwerfen heut Abend vor 10. uhr.

DHL

[My dear Schwiegermutter
    We've been gone two days: sailed from Naples Sunday evening, 8 o'clock. Monday morning, 8 o'clock we came through the Straits of Messina: and then for hours we saw our Etna, like a white queen, or a white witch standing there in the sky: so magically beautiful, but I think wicked. She said to me 'Come back here' – I only said no, but wept inside with pain – pain of parting.
    The weather is marvellous – blue sky, blue sea – still. Today we see no land, only the long white thin clouds where Greece lies. Later on we should see Crete (Candia). We come Thursday to Port Said, there this letter goes ashore: we too, for a couple of hours. Then we go through the *Suez Canal*, and so into the Red Sea.
    The ship is splendid – so comfortable, so much room, and not many travellers. The spaces are not half occupied. It's just like a really luxurious hotel. Mornings, 7 o'clock, the steward comes with a cup of tea and inquires whether one wants to take his bath, and warm or hot or how. At 8 o'clock breakfast is sounded: and such a *menu*: stewed pears, porridge, fish, bacon, eggs, fried sausages, beefsteak, kidneys, marmalade – all there. Then afterwards one goes above, sits about, flirting or playing croquet – eleven o'clock the steward comes with a cup of Bovril – 1 o'clock lunch – soup, fish, chicken or turkey, meat entrées – always much too much – 4 o'clock tea – 7

o'clock dinner – oh no, one is always eating. But one also has an appetite at sea: when it is so still and heavenly beautiful as now.

I find it remarkable that it is so still, so peaceful, so civilised: the people all so quiet and natural, and *such* cleanliness, all so very comfortable. Yes, it really is better than Italy, the Italians are now no good: become base. Frieda caught a cold in Naples, and you just ought to see how good with her are the steward and the stewardess, as she lies in bed – come so quickly with tea and soda water or whatever she wants, and always such gentle manners. After Italy it is remarkable. No, civilisation is a beautiful and fine thing, if only it remains alive, and doesn't become ennuyée.

I can write to you again from Aden – and then no more, till Ceylon. Now I'm going below, and see if Frieda has got up. – Today her cold is a bit better.

Too bad you were not there, in Naples, to see us come on board; with trunks bag-and-baggage: baskets of oranges and apples (given us) and a long board, which is a piece of a Sicilian cart, very colourfully painted with two scenes from the life of Marco Visconte[1] – Else knows how lovely are these Sicilian carts: and the facchini kept calling: Ecco la Sicilia – Ecco la Sicilia in viaggio per l'India.[2]

For the moment a rivederci – Frieda should also write a word –

DHL

[Frieda Lawrence begins]

Liebe mère,

Well, here we are as naturally as if one had been born on this ship – Lawr has already described everything – It is so still and peaceful, my cold annoys me, the entire winter I didn't have one – I just can't understand why all people who have enough money don't travel round the world it is so *simple* – 1000 greetings.

F.–

[Lawrence continues]

The entire afternoon we've seen Crete, with snow on the mountains – so big, the island: also another smaller island, all yellow and barren, with great ravines. Now the sun is down, the rim of the sky red, the sea ink-blue, and the smallest, thinnest, sharpest moon I've ever seen. It is already quite warm.

Wednesday

Today only warm and still – seen no land, gulls and two ships – come tomorrow forenoon to Port Said – post letters this evening before 10 o'clock.

DHL]

---

[1] Milanese general, d. 1329.
[2] 'porters kept calling: Here is Sicily – Here is Sicily on the way to India.'

2467. To Lady Cynthia Asquith, 28 February 1922
Text: MS UT; Unpublished.

[R.M.S. 'OSTERLEY.']
28 Feb. 1922

I ought to have told you before of our great plunge! – we are going to Ceylon to refind the Paradise it once was. What do you bet that we find it. I've got a friend in Kandy who is taking Buddhism terribly seriously (not theosophy) – studying in the monastery of the Tooth.[1] Perhaps I too shall study in that same molar monastery, but no matter how wise I ultimately become, I shan't be a Buddhist.

It is lovely on the Mediterranean – so blue and pure. Yesterday for hours our own Etna hovered in the air behind us, like a white witch. I nearly wept, of course, but hardened my heart and said no my lady!

The address will be:
'Ardnaree', Lake View Estate, *Kandy*, Ceylon.
Do write me a line.

I ordered Secker to send you a copy of *Sea and Sardinia*, to Stanway, when it is ready. *See you get it.*

I so nearly went to America this time – then at the 11th hour couldn't. There is such a gulf between us and west – greater than between us and east. After all, one is nearer to the *innerliche* East than to the äusserliche[2] West.

Send me a line –

Benedicite D. H. Lawrence

2468. To Norman Douglas, 4 March 1922
Text: MS YU; Unpublished.

[R.M.S. 'OSTERLEY.']
4 March 1922

Dear Douglas

I ought to have written from Naples to tell you we were leaving Italy – thank the Lord I am away from Taormina, that place would have been the death of me after a little while longer. Here we are going to Ceylon. At the eleventh hour I couldnt simply face America – the magnetism shoved me away. So we are going to Ceylon. A friend who had the Villa Quattro Venti at Capri has taken a bungalow near Kandy and is studying Pali in the Buddhist monastery – so we shall go and stay with them for the first to see how we like it. The address is 'Ardnaree', Lake View Estate, *Kandy*, Ceylon. Send me a line sometimes.

[1] Actually the Temple of the Tooth, the home of a Buddhist monastery.
[2] '*inward* . . . outward'.

I sent the Magnus MS to America but so far hear nothing of it.

The voyage is rather lovely really, though you would hate being shut up with all the people. Hope you are flourishing. F[rieda] joins in many greetings.

D. H. Lawrence

2469. To S. S. Koteliansky, [7 March 1922]

Text: MS BL; Postmark, Colombo 13 MR 22; cited in Gransden 28

[R.M.S. 'OSTERLEY.']

Tuesday 7 March

My dear Kot

I got your cable to the ship – so nice of you to think of us. Here we are ten days at sea. I like it so much: everybody pleasant and no showing off, and plenty of room. The ship isn't half full, except the third class. We have come second, and it is perfectly comfortable and is good as anyone could wish. I enjoy it very much.

We are now in the Arabian Sea steering straight for Colombo, where we arrive on Sunday night or Monday morning. The sea is lovely, with white 'lambs' everywhere, but the boat is as steady as a street.

We had a few hours in Port Said, and it is still just like *Arabian Nights*, with water-sellers and scribes in the street, and Koran readers and a yelling crowd. And I loved coming through the Suez Canal. It takes 18 hours – and you see the Arabs and their camels and the rosy-yellow desert with its low palm-trees and its hills of sharp sand. Almost one seems to walk through it. It gave me rather a nostalgia for the desert. Then Mount Sinai like a vengeful dagger that was dipped in blood many ages ago, so sharp and defined and old pink-red in colour. – I spend the day talking small-talk with Australians on board – rather nice people – and translating *Mastro-don Gesualdo* and having meals – and time passes like a sleep – the curious sense that nothing is real except just this ship – nothing exists except just this ship. I do wonder how we shall feel when we get off and are in Ceylon. At the moment it seems as if we should just go on for ever on this boat. But it is so nice too. – You have the address:

'Ardnaree', Lake View Estate, *Kandy*, Ceylon.

Greet Sonia   DHL

2470. To Baroness Anna von Richthofen, [7 March 1922]

Text: MS UCB; Frieda Lawrence and Hawkins, *Twentieth Century*, iv (January 1933), 2–3.

[R.M.S. 'OSTERLEY.']

Arabian Sea.

Dienstag 7. März

Meine liebe Schwiegermutter

Vielleicht kann ich diesen Brief für Aden einwerfen, heut' Abend, aber wir machen keinen Halt. Wir sind so weit gekommen – und so schön. Wir waren

drei Stunden im Port Said, und es war ganz wie die Tausend und Eine Nächte
– Es war Morgen, 9 uhr, unde die Damen [Frieda Lawrence interjects] von
Port Said [Lawrence continues] waren alle[1] fort, einzukaufen: kleine
wackelnde Haufen von schwarzen Crêpe, und zwei Houri-augen zwischen
Schleir und mantel. Komish ist die kleine Röhre die über der Nase [Frieda
Lawrence interjects] steht [Lawrence continues] und haltet Schleier und
Kopftuch zusammen. Kam ein char-a-banc, mit zwanzig schwarzen Frau-
paketen. Dann hat eine von der Frauen ihre Schleier zürüch-gezogen und
nach uns gespuckt, weil wir hässliche Christianer waren. – Aber alles sieht
man noch: Bettler, Wasser-träger, der 'scribe' der sitzt mit seinem kleinen
Tisch und schreibt Briefe, der Alter der liesst den Koran, die Männer die
rauchen ihren 'chibouks' im offnen café und auf dem Trottoir. – Und was für
Leute: schöne Türken, Nigger, Griecher, Levantine, Fellaheen, drei
Bedouinen aus der Wüste, wie Tiere, Araber – wunderbar. – Wir haben Kohle
an bord genommen, und dann Mittag wieder fort, im Suez Canal. Das ist *sehr*
interessant. Der Kanal ist 88 Meilen lang, und man kann nur 5 meilen in
[Frieda Lawrence interjects] der [Lawrence continues] Stunde fahren. Da
sitzt man auf diesem grossen Schiff und fühlt sich wirklich am land, langsam
fahrend auf einem stillen Landschiff. Die Ufer sind ganz nahe man kann leicht
eine Orange an den Araben werfen, die an dem Ufer arbeiten. Dann sieht man
schön, wunderbar, die Sahara Wüste – oder Desert, wie sagt man. Der
Wasserweg geht eng und allein durch rot-gelben Sand. Von Zeit zu Zeit
Araber mit Kamelen an den Ufer arbeiten, und schreien immer Hallo! Hallo!
als das grosse Schiff so langsam vorbei färht. In der weite kleine schärfe
Sandhügeln, so rosa-gold und scharf, und der Horizont scharf wie ein Messer-
rand, so klar – dann ein Paar einsame Palmen, einsam und verloren in dem
starken Licht, klcin, wie Leute die nicht hoch gewachsen sind – dann wieder
nur Sand, gold-rosa, und scharfe Sandhügeln, so scharf und deutlich und klar,
nicht wie die Wirklichkeit, wie ein Traum. Langsam kam der Abend, und wir
so still, man dächte wir gingen nicht mehr. Tausend Möwen fliegen herum,
wie ein Schneesturm, und ein grosser schwarzer Raubvogel, allein und
grausam, so gross, zwischen tausenden weissen schreienden schnell gehenden
Seevögeln. Dann kamen wir an den Bitter-See – flache Seen die ganz weit
gehen – und langsam Sank die Sonne hinter den Wüsten, mit wunderbaren
Farben, und als die Sonne heruntergeganen war, dann *so* ein Himmel, wie ein
Schwert brennend grün und rosa. Schön war es, ich habe nichts so
übermenschlich gesehen. Man fühlte sich nahe an den Toren vom alten
Paradies, ich weiss nicht wie, aber etwas nur *halb* menschlich, etwas von einem
Himmel mit grossen stolzen hochmütigen, auch grausamen Engeln. Die

[1] On more than 70 occasions during this letter, Frieda corrected DHL's German (as here, 'allen'
was changed to 'alle').

Palmbaüme siehen so klein aus. Die Engeln sollen viel höher sein, und jeder
mit einem Schwert. Ja, es ist ein Grenz-land. – Nächsten Morgen waren wir
grad im Roten Meer – Stand der Mount Sinai da, rot wie altes, getrocknes
Blut, nakt wie ein messer, und so scharf, so unnatürlich scharf, deutlich, wie
ein 'poinard' [Frieda Lawrence interjects] Dolch [Lawrence continues] der
ist in Blut gestocken [Frieda Lawrence interjects] getaucht [Lawrence
continues] gewesen, und seit lang wieder getrocknet, und ein bisschen
'rusted', [Frieda Lawrence interjects] verrostet ist [Lawrence continues] und
immer da, wie etwas schreckliches, zwischen Mann [Frieda Lawrence
interjects] dem Menschen [Lawrence continues] und seinem verlorenen
Paradies. Alles ist Semitisch und grausam – nakt, scharf, kein Baum, kein
Blatt, kein Leben: der mörderliche Wille und Eisen von Idee und Ideal –
Eisen, Wille, und Ideal – so stehen diese furchtbare Ufer von diesem Roten
Meer, das heiss ist wie ein Ofen, ohne Luft. Es ist ein merkwürdiger Ausgang,
durch dieses Rote Meer – Bitter. Hinten lieglt endlich Jerusalem,
Griechenland, Rom und Europa – vollendet und vorbei, ein grosser
furchtbarer Traum. Mit Juden ist es angefangen, mit Juden kommt es zu
Ende. Du solltest Sinai sehen, dann könntest du es wissen. Das Ideal ist
schlimm gegen den Mensch gewesen: und Jahveh ist Vater von dem Ideal,
und Zeus und Jupiter und Christus sind nur Söhne. Und Gott sei dank Sinai
und Rotes Meer sind vorbei und vollendet.

Gestern vormittag kamen wir durch die Enge von Bab-el-Mandeb, wieder
in die Freie. Ich bin so froh dass wir diesen Weg gekommen sind. Gestern
sahen wir immer Land – Arabien – nakt und wüst, aber nicht so rot und scharf
und wie getrocknetes Blut. Heute sehen wir kein Land – aber sollen [Frieda
Lawrence interjects] später an [Lawrence continues] Cap Socotra vorbei
gehen. – Das Schiff hat 15 Stunden gewonnen – wir sind 15 Stunden vor
unserer Zeit. Vielleicht kommen wir Sonntag nachtmittag in Colombo an statt
Montag. Es ist sehr warm, aber immer Luft: das Meer ist mit weissen
Lämmchen bedekt, aber das Schiff still und sicher. Wir haben nicht einen
einzigen schlechten Moment gehabt – alles hier am Bord so freundlich, so gut
und bequem. Ich arbeite an der übersetzung von *Mastro-don Gesualdo*, und
habe meinen Tintenfass auf Deck fallen lassen. Die *Osterley* soll mein
schwarzes Zeichen immer tragen. – Um elf Uhr morgens kriegen wir nicht
mehr Bovril, aber Eis. Die Frauen tragen alle bunte Sommerkleider. Abends
tanzt man. Wir sehen jetzt die kleinen fliegendenfische, die sind ganz silber
und fliegen gerade wie Schmetterlinge so lustig. Dann auch schwarze
Porpoises [Frieda Lawrence interjects] Delphine [Lawrence continues] die
laufen wie frohliche kleine schwarze Schweine herum.

Benedicite DHL

Nein, man kann nur in Colombo einpostieren.

[My dear Schwiegermutter

Perhaps I can post this letter at Aden, this evening, but we make no stop. We've come so far – and so beautifully. We were three hours in Port Said, and it was just like the Thousand and One Nights – It was morning, 9 o'clock, and the ladies of Port Said were all abroad, to shop: little waddling heaps of black crêpe, and two houri-eyes between veil and mantle. Comical is the little tube that stands over the nose and holds veil and headshawl together. Came a charabanc, with twenty black woman-parcels. Then one of the women drew back her veils and spat at us, because we were hateful Christians. – But one sees everything still: beggars, water-carriers, the 'scribe' who sits with his little table and writes letters, the old man who reads the Koran, the men who smoke their 'chibouks' in the open café and on the pavement. – And what people: handsome Turks, Niggers, Greeks, Levantines, fellaheen, three bedouins from the desert, like animals, Arabs – wonderful. – We took on coal, and then at midday off again, in the Suez Canal. That is *very* interesting. The canal is 88 miles long, and one can only travel 5 miles an hour. There one sits on this great ship and feels oneself really on land, slowly travelling on a still land-ship. The banks are quite near, one can easily throw an orange at the Arabs who work on the bank. Then one sees beautiful, wonderful, the Sahara Wüste – or Desert, how does one say it. The waterway goes narrow and alone through red-yellow sand. From time to time Arabs with camels are working on the bank, and always shout Hallo! Hallo! as the great ship passes by so slowly. In the distance little sharp sandhills, so rosy gold and sharp, and the horizon sharp as a knife edge, so clear – then a couple of lonely palms, lonely and forlorn in the strong light, small, like people who have not grown tall – then again only sand, gold-pink, and sharp sandhills, so sharp and defined and clear, not like reality, like a dream. Slowly came the evening, and we so still, one would have thought we no longer moved. A thousand gulls flew about, like a snowstorm, and a great black bird of prey, alone and cruel, so large, among thousands of white, screaming fast-moving seabirds. Then we came to the Bitter Lake – shallow lakes that extend quite far – and slowly the sun sank behind the desert, with wonderful colours, and when the sun had gone down, then *such* a sky, like a sword burning green and pink. Beautiful it was, I've seen nothing so superhuman. One felt oneself near the gates of the old Paradise, I don't know how, but something only *half* human, something of a heaven with great proud haughty, also cruel angels. The palm-trees look so small. The angels should be much taller, and each with a sword. Yes, it is a borderland. – Next morning we were just in the Red Sea – There stood Mount Sinai, red as old, dried blood, naked as a knife, and so sharp, so unnaturally sharp, defined, like a 'poinard' (dagger) that was stuck (dipped) in blood, and has long since dried again, and is a bit 'rusted', and always there, like something dreadful, between man and his lost Paradise. All is Semitic and cruel – naked, sharp, no tree, no leaf, no life: the murderous will and iron of idea and ideal – iron, will, and ideal – so stand these terrible shores of this Red Sea, that is hot as an oven, without air. It is a strange exit, through this Red Sea – Bitter. Behind lies at last Jerusalem, Greece, Rome and Europe – fulfilled and past, a great terrible dream. With Jews it began, with Jews it ends. You ought to see Sinai, then you could know it. The ideal has been wicked to man: and Jahveh is father of the ideal, and Zeus and Jupiter and Christ are only sons. And thank God Sinai and Red Sea are past and fulfilled.

Yesterday forenoon we came through the Straits of Bab-el-Mandeb, again into the open. I'm so glad that we came this way. Yesterday we always saw land – Arabia – naked and barren, but not so red and sharp and like dried blood. Today we see no land – but later on are supposed to pass Cape Socotra. – The ship has gained 15 hours – we are 15 hours ahead of our schedule. Perhaps we'll arrive Sunday afternoon at Colombo instead of Monday. It is very warm, but always air: the sea is covered with little white lambs, but the ship still and steady. We've had not a single bad moment – everybody here on board so friendly, so good and comfortable. I am working on the translation of *Mastro-don Gesualdo*, and dropped my ink bottle on deck. The *Osterley* shall always wear my black mark. – Mornings at eleven o'clock we no longer get Bovril, but ice-cream. The women all wear colourful summer frocks. Evenings one dances. We see now the little flying fishes, they are all silver and fly just like butterflies so gaily. Then also black porpoises (dolphins) that run about like frolicsome little black pigs.

Benedicite   DHL

No, one can post only in Colombo.]

2471. To Reginald Turner, [7? March 1922]

Text: Stanley Weintraub, *Reggie: A Portrait of Reginald Turner* (New York, 1965), p. 199.

[R.M.S. 'OSTERLEY.']
[7? March 1922]

['In a letter written as the *Osterley* sailed through the Red Sea, and filled with vivid images of mountains, sea and desert, he asked the friend he had made fun of as "Algy"[1] to go to a certain shop in Florence and buy coloured ribbons for Frieda, to be sent on to them at their destination.']

---

[1] Reginald ('Reggie') Turner (1869–1938), journalist and novelist, whom DHL had met in Florence (where Turner was a permanent resident) in September 1920. DHL probably used him as the model for Algy Constable in *Aaron's Rod*. See *Letters*, iii. 594 n. 4.

2472. To Rosalind Baynes, [8 March 1922]
Text: MS BucU; Huxley 540–1.

[R.M.S. 'OSTERLEY.']
Wednesday 8 March

My dear Rosalind

Here we are on the ship – ten days at sea. It is rather lovely – perfect weather all the time, ship steady as can be, enough wind now to keep it cool. We went on shore at Port Said – and it's still like Arabian nights, spite of all. Then I loved coming through the Suez Canal – 5 miles an hour – takes 18 hours – you see the desert, the sand-hills, the low palm trees, arabs with camels working at the side. I like it so much. Now we are in the Arabian Sea, and expect to come to Colombo on Monday morning: 15 days voyage.

The ship is *so* pleasant – only about half full – or less – so plenty of room. We have come second class, and it is perfectly comfortable and nice, couldn't want anything better. Alas, it cost £140 for the two of us. But I had to get out of Europe. In Ceylon we stay with friends. There are children on board having the time of their lives. – I am translating Vergas *Mastro-don Gesualdo*, to pass the time. – By the way I should be so glad if you would some times send me an old Italian novel or book that you have done with – if it is interesting. I should like to go on reading Italian. – The people on board are mostly simple Australians. I believe Australia is a good country, full of life and energy. I believe that is the country for you if you had anything specific in mind. If we don't want to go on living in Ceylon I shall go to Australia if we can manage it.

I ordered you *Sea and Sardinia* and *Tortoises*, I hope you will get them – the former from England, Secker, the latter from America, which takes a long time.

Being at sea is so queer – it sort of dissolves for the time being all the connections with the land, and one feels a bit like a sea-bird must feel. – It is my opinion that once beyond the Red Sea one does not feel any more that tension and pressure one suffers from in England – in Europe altogether – even in America I believe – perhaps worse there. I feel so glad I have come out, but don't know how the money is going to behave: Can't help it.

Write and tell me all that happens –

'Ardnaree', Lake View Estate, *Kandy*, Ceylon.

It seems difficult in this world to get a new *start* – so much easier to make more ends. F[rieda] sends many greetings – she is a bit dazed by the sea.

DHL

2473. To Margaret King, [14 March 1922]
Text: MS Forster; PC v. Dam Street, Colombo; Postmark, [. . .]; Unpublished.

Colombo
Tuesday 14 Mar

We arrived yesterday morning after an excellent voyage – leave this afternoon for Kandy – very hot here, hope it will be cooler among the hills.

Brewster met us at the wharf, so everything has been easy and nice.

love   DHL

2474. To Robert Mountsier, [14 March 1922]
Text: MS Smith; PC v. Clock Tower, Colombo; Postmark, [. . .]; Unpublished.

[Colombo]
14 March

We got here yesterday – Colombo very hot. Going up to Kandy this afternoon with Brewster – think I shall love these tropics.

DHL

2475. To Robert Mountsier, 23 March 1922
Text: MS Smith; Unpublished.

Ardnaree, Lake View Estate, Kandy – Ceylon.
23 March 1922

Dear M[ountsier]

Here we are, settled in with the Brewsters and four black servants amid bread-fruit and palm-trees. It is very hot. – lovely to look at – but I doubt if I shall stay very long in Ceylon. Probably in a few months move to Australia – and then finally from Sydney to San Francisco.

I want to have a letter of credit for $1000, good for here and for Australia. Here the bank is National Bank of India, Kandy. In Australia I don't know – but I should call at Perth, in West Australia, and go on to Kandy. I have so far had out only $450. But it cost an awful lot getting here.

I shall finish *Mastro-don Gesualdo* this week. I shall send it to Mrs Carmichael to type and forward to you. Make one alteration, please. Where I say the ' parish ' lands – in the auction of the parish lands – please change *parish* to *communal* – the auction of the communal lands.[1] I don't believe I shall write a line in Ceylon – at least not here in the hot part. And I think in about three months we shall move on.

No more news then. I'll write to Mr Hastings in Charleroi.

D. H. Lawrence

---

[1] See *Mastro-don Gesualdo* (Seltzer, 1923), p. 40, l. 28.

Today the Prince of Wales[1] comes to Kandy and we go to see the Perahara with 120 elephants.

If you want any help from Italy about the Verga book I'm sure Mrs Carmichael, 7 Via Faentina, Florence – will help you.

2476. To Emily King, 24 March 1922

Text: MS Lazarus; Vivian de Sola Pinto, 'D. H. Lawrence: Letter Writer and Craftsman in Verse', *Renaissance and Modern Studies*, i (1957), 7–8.

Ardnaree. Lake View Estate. Kandy. Ceylon

24 March 1922

My dear Sister

Your birthday has gone by and I haven't sent you anything. But it has been such an eventful time, with not a quiet moment. I enclose a bit of Ceylon lace, that the native women make by hand: and a little purse or cigarette case that they weave. These easily go into a letter.

We have been in the bungalow a week. It is about a mile or mile and a half from Kandy, looking down on the lake: very lovely. It stands uphill among a sort of half wild estate – cocoa-nut palms and cocoa – and jungle trees – almost like the jungle. We sit on the verandahs and watch the chipmunks and chameleons and lizards and tropical birds among the trees and bamboos – there's only a clear space of about three yards round the house. We've got four servants – two men, one ayah, one boy of fifteen – but nothing is ever done: except meals got ready. It is very hot in the sun – we have sun helmets and white suits – but quite pleasant sitting still. If one moves one sweats. There's a good deal of room in the bungalow, and practically no furniture except chairs and a table or two. It is rather fascinating, but I don't know how long we shall stay.

Yesterday the Prince of Wales was here – great doings. We were down at the Perahera at night – were just opposite the Prince. Poor devil, he is so thin and nervy: all twitchy: and seems worn out and disheartened. No wonder, badgered about like a doll among a mob of children. A woman threw a bouquet, and he nearly jumped out of his skin.

But the Perahera was wonderful: it was night, and flaming torches of cocoanut blazing, and the great elephants in their trappings, about a hundred, and the dancers with tomtoms and bagpipes, and half naked and jewelled, then

---

[1] Later Edward VIII (1894–1972); he abdicated in 1936 and was given the title of Duke of Windsor. He reviewed the *pera-hera* – a religious procession of elephants in front of which white cloth is spread so that the sacred animals do not tread on the ground – from the Temple of the Tooth. Devil dancers, drummers and pipers take part in the festival, which includes fireworks as well.

the Kandyan chiefs in their costumes, and more dancers, and more elephants, and more chiefs, and more dancers, so wild and strange and perfectly fascinating, heaving along by the flames of torches in the hot, still, starry night. Afterwards fireworks over the lake, and thousands and thousands of natives, so that it looked like some queer dream when the fire flared up and showed their thousands of dark faces and white wraps packed on the banks.

One doesn't do much here, I tell you – though Brewster goes every day to the Temple to learn the sacred language of the Buddhists – Pali. I wish you could see it all – it is most strange and fascinating. But even at night you sweat if you walk a few yards.

I expect the post will soon be bringing English mail.

Love to you all.

D. H. Lawrence

Frieda bought this lace. The purse will do for card-case or anything.

2477. To Irene Whittley, 25 March 1922
Text: MS UT; Unpublished.

'Ardnaree', Lake View Estate, *Kandy*, Ceylon.
25 March 1922

Dear Irene Whittley

We had your letter today. My sister had told me you had changed your flat, and I waited for the address. But what a shame you've had this bad luck. I'm so awfully sorry. And the brown shoes, I know I shall never see them. I shall write at once to Taormina that they be returned to you. You go to the post office and claim them back. They will at least fit Billie.[1]

And here we are in Ceylon. We sailed on Feb. 26th from Naples, and have been here just a fortnight tomorrow. It is all very wonderful, but we are almost too dazed yet to know what we feel. We are staying with the Brewsters in a Bungalow on a half wild estate of Palm and cocoa on a hill above Kandy lake, about a mile out of Kandy: with four black servants and no furniture in the house, and a terrific heat from 10.0 till 4.0, the rest lovely, not too hot. I wonder how long we shall stay – I haven't an idea. But if I intend being here above a month or two I shall look for a house for ourselves. You wouldn't be able to trip over for your holiday, though.

The Prince of Wales was here on Thursday, and great doings. But poor little devil, he looked worn out, and thoroughly depressed, and so nervy and twitchy. The Perahera at night with all the torches, elephants, and devil dances was quite wonderful. I loved it. But I still am not quite sure where I am: sort of look round for myself among all this different world.

---

[1] Unidentified.

I'm sorry about your father.[1] I expect now you'll have one worry after another with the pair of them, so make up your mind and stiffen your neck, and then if they will only keep hale and hearty for another dozen years it will be like a gift to you.

Frieda is like me a bit dazed with this world of palm trees and dark swarming people. But she loves it. She bids me say we never had your Christmas letter – we didn't – and sat and wondered. If you can't get the shoes back, I will send you a cheque for them.

Many greetings to you both: I do hope that now you are going to have a run of good luck and peace.

D. H. Lawrence

2478. To Catherine Carswell, [25 March 1922]
Text: MS YU; PC v. Fishing Boat; Postmark, [. . .]; Carswell 165.

Ardnaree, Lake View Estate, Kandy
25 March.

We are here and settling down – very hot at first – but one soon takes naturally to it – soon feels in a way at home – sort of root race home. We're in a nice spacious bungalow on the hill above Kandy in a sort of half jungle of a cocoa-nut palm estate – and cocoa – beautiful, and such sweet scents – The Prince of Wales was here on Thursday – looks worn out and nervy, poor thing – the Perahera in the evening with a hundred elephants was lovely – But I don't believe I shall ever work here.

DHL

2479. To Anna Jenkins, 28 March 1922
Text: MS WAPL; Huxley 541-2.

'Ardnaree', Lake View Estate, Kandy. Ceylon.
28 March 1922

Dear Mrs Jenkins[2]

Well, here we've been for a fortnight – rather lovely to look at, the place – but very hot – and I don't feel at all myself. Don't think I care for the east. Shall try going up to Nuwara Eliya next week.[3] But this address always good.

---

[1] Capt. Short.

[2] Anna Louise ('Pussy') Jenkins, née Burt (1873–1945), m. 1895, Arthur George Jenkins (1868–1917), solicitor, who became Mayor of Coolgardie and Member of the Legislative Council. Anna Jenkins, daughter of Hon. Septimus Burt (1847–1919), Q.C., Attorney General for Western Australia, could perhaps be described as a somewhat eccentric socialite. Nevertheless she was a keen musician – she spent several years in London studying music with Percy Grainger – and patron of the arts. It appears that when she met the Lawrences on the *Osterley* between Naples and Ceylon, Anna Jenkins encouraged them to visit Australia and offered them accommodation in her father's family home, Strawberry Hill, Adelaide Terrace, Perth, where she continued to have a studio.   [3] See Letter 2495.

I doubt if we shall stop long – two or three months: then come on. My mind turns towards Australia. Shall we really come and try West? I have a fancy for the apple-growing regions, south from Perth: have a great fancy to see apple trees in blossom: and to be really 'white'. I feel absolutely dead off Buddhism, either Nibbana or Nirvana, Kania or Karma.[1] They can have Buddha.

But we saw the Perahera and the Prince of Wales – the former a wonderful sight, the latter a pathetic one.

Tell me if you think we *should* like W. Australia – if not we'll go straight to Sydney.

Greetings from my wife and me.

                                                                    D. H. Lawrence

2480. To Robert Pratt Barlow, 30 March 1922
Text: TMSC NWU; Huxley 542–3.

                                    Ardnaree. Lake View Estate. Kandy. Ceylon.
                                                                    30 March 1922

Dear Pratt Barlow,[2]

We have been here these last 18 days: the heat in the middle of the day rather overwhelming, but morning and evening delicious: the place beautiful, in its way very, the jungle round the house, palms and noisy, scraping and squeaking tropical creatures: good-looking, more-or-less naked, dark bluey-brown natives. But all a bit extraneous. I feel I don't belong, and never should. I think next week we shall go up higher to Nuwara Eliya.

I wonder what you are doing. This will probably follow you to England. We were at the Perahera here for the Prince of Wales. It was wonderful, gorgeous and barbaric with all the elephants and flames and devil dances in the night. One realizes how very barbaric the substratum of Buddhism is. I shrewdly suspect that high-flownness of Buddhism altogether exists mostly on paper: and that its denial of the soul makes it always rather barren, even if philosophically etc more perfect. In short, after a slight contact, I draw back and don't like it.

The Prince of Wales seemed sad and forlorn. He seemed to be almost the *butt* of everybody, white and black alike. They all secretly hate him for being a Prince, and make a Princely butt of him – and he knows it. My sympathy was with him.

I wonder what you and Cunard[3] thought of the last tirade at your house.

---

[1] 'Nibbana' and 'Kania' are the Pali eqivalents of 'Nirvana'.
[2] Robert Pratt Barlow, an Englishman, had resided in Sicily since before 1914; a man of some wealth and an intimate friend of the Duca di Bronte, he lived in a large house on the hill above Spisone beach.   [3] Unidentified.

Probably nothing. But I do think, still more now I am out here, that we make a mistake forsaking England and moving out into the periphery of life. After all, Taormina, Ceylon, Africa, America – as far as *we* go, they are only the negation of what we ourselves stand for and are: and we're rather like Jonahs running away from the place we belong.[1] That is the conclusion that is forced on me. So I am making up my mind to return to England during the course of the summer. I really think that the most living clue of life is in us Englishmen in England, and the great mistake we make is in not uniting together in the strength of this real living clue – religious in the most vital sense – uniting together in England and so carrying the vital spark through. Because as far as we are concerned it is in danger of being quenched. I know now it is a shirking of the issue to look to Buddha or the Hindu or to our own working men, for the impulse to carry through. It is in ourselves, or nowhere, and this looking to the outer masses is only a betrayal. – I think too the Roman Catholic Church, as an institution, granted of course some new adjustments to life, might once more be invaluable for saving Europe: but not as a mere political power.

But this I know: the responsibility for England, the living England, rests on men like you and me and Cunard – probably even the Prince of Wales – and to leave it all to Bottomleys[2] etc is a worse sin than any sin of commission.

Best wishes from my wife and me.

D. H. Lawrence.

2481. To Robert Mountsier, 3 April 1922
Text: MS Smith; Postmark, Kandy 3 AP 22; Unpublished.

Ardnaree, Lake View Estate, Kandy. Ceylon.

3 April 1922

Dear M[ountsier]

I posted you yesterday by registered MS. post the remainder of *Mastro-don Gesualdo*: you will get it typed in New York. Do please look through it carefully, and remember to change 'parish' lands into 'communal.' – Today from Seltzer came the other Verga book, *The House by the Medlar Tree* pubd. by Harpers. Mary A. Craig's translation. I should think you might easily persuade Harpers to do *Gesualdo*. Mary Craig's translation, though good, lacks the real snap and flavour: too soft and pleasant, you know.

I had your letter here, saying the *Met[ropolitan]* sent back the two stories.[3] I heard from Curtis B[rown] that *Hutchinsons* were publishing 'Monkey

---

[1] See Jonah i–iv. Jonah, told by God to preach to the wicked city of Nineveh, intentionally took a ship in a different direction.
[2] See p. 126 n. 1.   [3] See p. 187 and n. 2.

Nuts'.[1] But I have no word from him about anything else. Wonder what you think of the Magnus MS. I keep hearing more things about him: to the bad: Here it is monstrous hot, like being in a hot bell-glass. I don't like it a bit. I don't like the east. It makes me feel sick in my stomach: seems sort of unmanly. I shall cable you for money, and go away: probably go on to Australia, as it is in the direct route, and look at that. Then if I don't like it, to San Francisco from Sydney. So there we are. If I cable you (or Seltzer): *Perth*: that means Perth, West Australia – address.

c/o Mrs Jenkins, Strawberry Hill, Perth. W. Australia.

If I cable you Sydney, write c/o Thomas Cook and Sons. Heaven knows what will become of this bit of money by the time we come to a stop. But I can't help it. Travelling itself is hellish costly, but while we sit here we spend little. I'm not working and feel I never should work in the east. But then I want also to lie fallow for a bit. I might translate one or two Verga Sketches from *Novelle Rusticane*.[2] I believe they are not copyrighted at all. Tell me what you think of *Mastro-don*.

I expect soon to hear from you about various things – also from Curtis B.

Yes, we'll have to pay the 8% tax. I feel I don't care about anything.

Of course if I cable for money I don't want the letter of credit I asked for.

Yrs   D. H. Lawrence

I wrote Doran what you asked. As for Pinker, requiescat.[3] – Ones enemies fall slowly but surely into oblivion. The sons are said to be semi-idiot.

Typing *Lost Girl* cost £16.

Aarons Rod about the same but Mrs Carmichael only 3 Lire a thousand words, and 1.50 for carbon copy: cheaper.

2482. To S. S. Koteliansky, [3 April 1922]
Text: MS BL; PC v. Temple elephants at Katugasto; Postmark, [. . .]; Gransden 28.

Kandy.

3rd April

So hot here – and I don't like Ceylon – shall probably go on in about three weeks time to Australia – one may as well move on, once one has started. I feel I dont care what becomes of me.

DHL

---

[1] 'Monkey Nuts' appeared in the *Sovereign* (22 August 1922), not in *Hutchinson's Magazine*.
[2] Sketches collected in *Little Novels of Sicily* (New York, 1925). The Brewsters described him doing these translations in the mornings on the verandah (Brewster 250).
[3] Pinker died suddenly in New York on 8 February 1922.

2483. To Robert Mountsier, 3 April 1922
Text: MS WAPL; Priday, *Southerly*, xv (1954), 4–5.

Kandy
Apr 3rd 1922

Mounthier, 417 West 118 St, NY City.
Cable thousand dollars national bank of India Kandy not letter credit.
Lawrence

2484. To Mary Cannan, 3 April 1922
Text: MS Lazarus; cited in Vivian de Sola Pinto, ed. *D. H. Lawrence after Thirty Years, Catalogue of an Exhibition Held in the Art Gallery of the University of Nottingham, 17 June–30 July, 1960* (Nottingham: University of Nottingham, 1960), p. 33.

Ardnaree, Lake View Estate. Kandy. Ceylon.
3 April 1922

My dear Mary

Well here we are three weeks. This is the hottest month in Ceylon – and the heavens are white hot from 10.0 till 6.0. The bungalow is outside Kandy on a hill among trees – a sort of jungle of palm (cocoanut) and bread-fruit trees etc – pretty view. Sharp wooded hills, Kandy lake below – birds shriek and pop and cackle out of the jungle, creatures jerk and bounce about. We have about half a dozen black servants, barefoot and silent moving and silly. The native life is picturesque – but to tell the truth, rather silly. The east, the bit I've seen, seems silly. I don't like it one bit. I don't like the silly dark people or their swarming billions or their hideous little Buddha temples, like decked up pigsties – nor anything. I just don't like it. It's better to see it on the cinema: you get there the whole effect, without the effort and the sense of nausea. It just makes me feel sick at the pit of my stomach. Dear Mary, *never* travel round the world to look at it – it will only make you sick. Take a nice little house somewhere quiet, and we'll come and stay with you. One only goes further and fares worse.

We saw the Prince of Wales and the Perahera. Poor little devil, he sat perfectly still, expressionless and ghastly, looking down on this heaving procession of elephants and princes and devil-dancers and torch flames – it was 11.0 at night – and tom-toms and weird singing.[1] It was wonderful – so barbaric – as a spectacle wonderful: elephants, princes, dancers, dancers princes and elephants – endless – and great flames from Cocoa-nut torches. But the poor Prince is simply at his last straw of endurance – so nervous and irritable – would hardly open his mouth to anybody.

[1] singing] dancing

It is a roomy bungalow with verandahs all round – Brewsters nice. But I'm not going to stop here. In a months time I hope to be gone – I don't know where – perhaps to Australia. I'll let you know. Anyhow take my advice and dont take far flights to exotic countries. Europe is, I fancy, the most satisfactory place in the end. Have a house and invite us to stay with you when we've spent every *sou* escaping from the places we've rushed into.

Hope all is well with you – send news.

DHL

2485. To Catherine Carswell, [3 April 1922]
Text: MS YU; PC v. Native Bullock Cart; Postmark, [. . .]; Unpublished.

[Kandy]
3 April

Had Don's letter – glad you're flourishing – here very hot – I think we shall go on to West Australia quite soon – tropics not really my line – not active enough.

DHL

2486. To Anna Jenkins, [3 April 1922]
Text: MS WAPL; PC v. Tom Tom Beaters; Postmark, [. . .]; H. E. L. Priday, 'D. H. Lawrence in Australia – Some Unpublished Correspondence', *Southerly*, xv (1954), 3–4.

Kandy.
Monday 3 April

I have just cabled to New York for money – can't stand Ceylon – too hot and sticky – shall come right on – probably by the boat from Colombo April 24th – arrive Freemantle May 4th. What do you say to that? hope you won't just hate it, the quickness – but I think we'll just stay a day or two in Perth, then go on, either south in W[est] A[ustralia] or to Sydney. Hope you're well.

D. H. Lawrence

Excuse card – this place makes me irritable.
–

2487. To Else Jaffe, [3 April 1922]
Text: MS UT; PC v. Mount Lavinia Hotel and Katamaran, Colombo; Postmark, [. . .]; Unpublished.

Kandy.
3 April

Here we are sweating our heads off – palm trees and black people and heat –

and a tropic taste in everything and a tropic smell – too much for me – I think we shall move on quite quickly to West Australia – go down to the apple growing regions.

    – I am no bird to swelter in the tropics. I will let you know.

DHL

2488. To Hilda Brown, [3 April 1922]
Text: MS Cotterell; PC v. Ceylon Elephant; Postmark, Kandy 3 AP 22; Nehls, ii. 122.

Kandy. Ceylon.

[3 April 1922]

Here we are in the heat among the black people – but I think we shall go on to Australia.

    How are you all.[1] Many greetings from us both.

D. H. Lawrence

2489. To Mabel Dodge Sterne, [3 April 1922]
Text: MS Brill; PC v. Fishing Boat; Postmark, [. . .] 3 AP 22; Luhan 21.

Kandy –

3 April

I had your note, but neither book nor necklace so far – however, they will come. Ceylon is an *experience* – but heavens, not a permanence. I think we shall go right on, in about 3 weeks time and look at Australia – then from Sydney to San Francisco, if I've got any money. Write a line to me c/o Mrs Jenkins, Strawberry Hill, Perth. West Australia. If we move on so quick, we'll soon see Taos.

DHL

2490. To Rosalind Baynes, [3 April 1922]
Text: MS BucU; PC v. Bulls on the Road; Postmark, [. . .]; Unpublished.

[Kandy]

3 April

So hot here – sticky – don't like the east so far – think we shall move on in about three weeks time to West Australia – look at that – feel I don't care where I go and what I do.

DHL

---

[1] Hilda Brown and her parents were DHL's neighbours in Hermitage, Berks., December 1917–May 1918.

2491. To Mary Cannan, [5 April 1922]
Text: MS Lazarus; Unpublished.

Ardnaree. Kandy
5 April

My dear Mary

Your letter from Monte Carlo today. Now you will be in London – in the snow! – Here the heat is terrific – and I hate the tropics. It is beautiful, in a lush, tangled, towsled, lousy sort of way. The natives too are quite good looking, dark-skinned and erect. But something about it all just makes me sick – there is something smooth and boneless, and a smell of cocoanut oil and sickly fruits – that I can't bear. I loathe the tropical fruits, except pineapples, and those I can't digest: because my inside has never hurt me so much in all my 36 years as in these three weeks. – I'm going away. I plan to go on the 24th inst. to West Australia – that is, if my money is cabled me from New York in time. – And then goodbye to the east, for me. Sickly. *Don't you travel.* Get a nice little house in Sussex or Hants. If I dont like W. Australia, shall go on to Sydney.

If I don't like that, then California. If I don't like America, then England. I'm making no bones about it – intend to satisfy myself as to what I *do* want – feel perfectly reckless. If I cable you from some corner of the earth to lend me money, don't leave me in the lurch.

Of course I shan't be working a stroke – but that isn't the point. I need this bitterness, apparently, to cure me of the illusion of other places. I shall cable Curtis Brown – 6 Henrietta St – when I leave for Australia. If I say *Perth* the address will be

c/o Mrs Jenkins, Strawberry Hill, Perth. W. Australia.

You can ring him up if you're in London.

Don't weep over distances – they probably send me home to England sooner and surer than anything ever would.

DHL

2492. To Anna Jenkins, [8 April 1922]
Text: MS Cockburn; Unpublished.

Kandy.
8 April

Dear Mrs Jenkins

This to tell you that if my money comes quick from New York, and if there is room on the *Orsova*, we shall sail on that boat for Fremantle on the 24th of this month: arrive about 4th May. We shall come up to some hotel in Perth and then call on you.

Ceylon just makes me feel ill all the time – Our friends also can't stand it and are going back to Europe.

Greetings from us both.

D. H. Lawrence

I am giving your address for one or two letters: do you mind my taking this liberty?

2493. To Mabel Dodge Sterne, 10 April 1922
Text: MS Brill; Luhan 18–19.

Ardnaree. Kandy. Ceylon.

10 April 1922

Dear Mabel Dodge Sterne

I have your two letters, but still no sign of book or necklace. Speriamo.

No, the East doesn't get me at all. Its boneless suavity, and the thick, choky feel of tropical forest, and the metallic sense of palms and the horrid noises of the birds and creatures, who hammer and clang and rattle and cackle and explode all the livelong day, and run little machines all the livelong night; and the scents that make me feel sick, the perpetual nauseous overtone of cocoanut and cocoanut fibre and oil, the sort of tropical sweetness which to me suggests an undertang of blood, hot blood, and thin sweat: the undertaste of blood and sweat in the nauseous tropical fruits; the nasty faces and yellow robes of the Buddhist monks, the little vulgar dens of the temples: all this makes up Ceylon to me, and all this I cannot bear. Je m'en vais. Me ne vo'. I am going away. Moving on.

I have cabled for money from New York, and anxiously await the return cable so that I can book berths on the *Orsova*, on the 24th. of this month, for West Australia: about 10 days from Colombo to Fremantle. The address there will be

c/o Mrs Jenkins, Strawberry Hill, *Perth*. W. Australia.

I don't know how long we shall stay there: but I shall take my steamer-ticket right to Sydney. I want to look at Australia, and try what it's like. If I don't care for it, then I can very easily come on. There are steamers every fortnight from Sydney to San Francisco: and San Francisco is not far from Taos. And I shall be fulfilling my real desire to approach America from the west, over the Pacific. I hope I shall arrive in Taos with ten cents left in my pocket – ten cents left to me in the world, even. Knees of the Gods.

I still of course mistrust Taos very much, chiefly on account of the artists. I feel I never want to see an artist again while I live. The Indians, yes: if one is sure that they are not jeering at one. I find all dark people have a fixed desire to jeer at us: these people here. They jeer behind your back. But heavens, I don't see much in them to admire, either. They seem to be built round a gap, a hollow pit. In the middle of their eyes, instead of a man, a sort of bottomless pit. That's Buddhism too. Buddhism seems to me a very conceited, selfish show, a vulgar temple of serenity built over an empty hole in space. No no, these little darkie people don't impress me, upon actual contact. The place, Ceylon, is a real prison to me, oppressive, and I want to get out. Two weeks today, pray God.

I wish I could come to America without meeting the awful 'cultured' Americans with their limited self-righteous ideals and their mechanical love-motion and their bullying, detestable negative creed of liberty and democracy. I don't believe either in liberty or democracy. I believe in actual, sacred, inspired authority: divine right of natural kings: I believe in the divine right of natural aristocracy, the right, the sacred duty to wield undisputed authority. Naturally I find myself in diametric opposition to every American – and everybody else, besides Americans – whom I come across. Nevertheless, there it stands.

Well, so far so good.

Yrs   D. H. Lawrence

2494. To Austin Harrison, 11 April 1922
Text: MS Harrison; Huxley 543–4.

Ardnaree. Kandy. Ceylon.
11 April 1922

Dear Harrison

I got the proofs of 'The Horsedealer's Daughter' here this morning. No good sending them back – you'll have printed the thing doubtless by the time you get this.[1]

I've been in Ceylon a month and nearly sweated myself into a shadow. Still it's a wonderful place to see and experience. There seems to be a flaw in the atmosphere, and one sees a darkness, and through the darkness the days before the Flood, marshy, with elephants mud grey and buffaloes rising from the mud, and soft-boned voluptuous sort of people, like plants under-water, stirring in myriads.

I think I shall go on to Australia at the end of the month. Ask Curtis Brown for my address if you want it, will you?

Yrs   D. H. Lawrence

[1] 'The Horse-Dealer's Daughter' appeared in *English Review*, xxxiv (April 1922), 308–25.

2495. To Robert Mountsier, [16 April 1922]
Text: MS Smith; Postmark, Kandy 17 AP 22; Unpublished.

Ardnaree. Kandy. Ceylon.

Easter Sunday.

My dear M[ountsier]

The bank got the cheque from the bank of Hongkong in Colombo: I got Rupees 3,481.[1] I have booked berths on the *Orsova* for the 24th to West Australia – but taken tickets to Sydney. Shall try Australia, and if I don't like it come on to San Francisco. We travel second class, which is quite good, but even so, it is expensive: from Naples to Colombo £70. each, from Colombo to Sydney Rupees 1,650 the two tickets: about £112 or so. Alas, there goes the money. But it can't be helped, I insist on finding some place I *may* like.

Ceylon is very interesting to look at, but would be deadly to live in. It *was* very hot, and I nearly sweated myself into the grave. But the rains have come, and it is cooler. – I am glad I came. I am glad I looked at this corner of the east. Then one has no more illusions about it. From a cinematograph point of view it can be fascinating: the dark, tangled jungle, the terrific sun that makes like a bell-jar of heat, like a prison over you: the palm-trees and the noise and the *sullenness* of the forest: and then the natives, naked, dark, in all shades of darkness from yellow to mauve black, suave, smooth, in their way beautiful. But curiously enough, the magnetism is all negative, everything seems magnetically to be repelling one. You never for a second feel at one with anything: always this curious black tropical hostileness, this underneath gloom. And sometimes my God it's the most melancholy thing I've ever struck: the sense of apathy, black, dark, empty apathy, as if nothing ever *could* matter, not really, not in our sense of the word: and the feeling that there is a lid down over everything. All Ceylon has a lid down over it. Yesterday we went to Nuwara Eliya, the hill station, 6000 ft. up. I thought we should get through the lid: but no, it presses tighter there. And all the white people on the island were flocking there, to be cool, grimly determined at least to seem to enjoy themselves. Queer it is, so different from what I expected. I am glad to have experienced it: but would die if I had to stay. I am glad to have seen something at least of these Oriental millions, and of this vaunted Buddhism. The last is to me a barren, dead affair: and the teeming millions don't seem to me as if they would ever do much, unless it were something wicked.

In despair I went on translating Vergas *Novelle Rusticane*: short sketches: very good. It seems this little volume was never copyrighted. I'll send you all I have done before I leave. – I enclose you here a little grass purse for cigarettes.

---

[1] See Letter 2483.

. Hope you are well and all is going well.

Yrs   DHL

Perhaps I'd better put the purse separate as sample.

2496. To S. S. Koteliansky, 17 April 1922
Text: MS BL; Postmark, Kandy 18 [. . .]; [Stephen Spender], ed., 'Letters to S. S. Koteliansky',
Encounter, i (December 1953), 31–2.

Ardnaree. Kandy. Ceylon.
17 April. 1922

My dear Kot
    I had your letter. You are right, Ceylon is too hot. One sweats and sweats,
and gets thinner and thinner. I am not staying. We are sailing next Monday,
24th, for West Australia – the address
        c/o Mrs Jenkins, Strawberry Hill, *Perth*, West Australia.
It has been lovely to *see* Ceylon. But I feel the East is not for me. It seems to me
the life drains away from one here. The old people here say just the same: they
say it is the natives that drain the life out of one, and that's how it seems to me.
One could quite easily sink into a kind of apathy, like a lotus on a muddy pond,
indifferent to anything. And that apparently is the lure of the east: this
peculiar stagnant apathy where one doesn't bother about a thing, but drifts on
from minute to minute. I am not at all sure that we shall like Australia either.
But it seems to me en route. We shall stay with Mrs Jenkins for a time: if we
don't care for that, go on to Sydney. I am taking a ticket to Sydney, as it only
costs £6. more. And then after trying Sydney and New South Wales, if I don't
like that we shall go across the Pacific to San Francisco, and then I shall have to
sit down and earn some money to take the next stride, for I shall be blued. But
I don't care. Now I have started, I will go on and on till I am more or less sure.
And if I like none of the places I shall come back to Europe with my mind
made up, and settle down permanently in England or Italy. So there's the
programme.
    Of course one doesn't work here at all – never would.
    I send you a little Kandy brass tray *via* my sister. I hope it won't take long
for you to get it: if the post doesn't swallow it. The lion is supposed to be a
Buddha symbol, but it might just as well be the lion of Judah.[1] – By the way I
detest Buddha, upon slight contact: affects me like a mud pool that has no
bottom to it. – One learns to value what one actually knows and possesses, and
to have a wholesome indifference to strange gods. Anyhow these little rat-hole
Buddhist temples turn my stomach.
    Well, next from Australia.

Yrs   D. H. Lawrence

[1] The 'Lion of Fo' or 'Lion of Buddha', a stylised image of a snarling lion, representing the
guardian of a Buddhist temple. A lion was also the emblem of the tribe of Judah.

2497. To Amy Lowell, [17 April 1922]
Text: MS HU; PC v. Milch Cow and Baby, Ceylon; Postmark, Kandy 18 AP 22; Moore, *Intelligent Heart* 288.

Kandy. Ceylon.
17 April.

We have been here the last six weeks – wonderful place to look at, but too hot to live in. Now we are going on to Australia – and if we don't like that, then San Francisco. – By the way I never got your last book that you said you sent me.[1] – How are you? Write me a line c/o Robert Mountsier, 417 West 118 St.
Frieda sends many greetings.

D. H. Lawrence

2498. To Benjamin Huebsch, 17 April 1922
Text: MS UT; Unpublished.

Ardnaree. Kandy. Ceylon.
17 April 1922

Dear Huebsch
Your letter and the *Freeman* found me here[2] – I didn't come straight to America after all: may come roundabout. We are sailing on to Australia at the

[1] See p. 97 n. 6.
[2] Huebsch had written on 3 March (TMSC LC) as follows:

Dear Lawrence,
Yours of January 28th arrived recently and with it the German call for help in the matter of France's negro troops in Germany. As the opportunity presents itself we will probably comment on this sickening horror in the *Freeman* though it is very difficult to make a dint in American public opinion when everybody is selfishly concerned in his personal and parish interests. However, Americans are not worse than other people in this respect. You know that in the past we have devoted space to articles by Morel and others on the subject of the French army of occupation.
Do you see the *Freeman* with any regularity? I am mailing you the last three numbers, in one of which (No. 103) there happens to be a review of your "Sea and Sardinia". I suppose that I ought not to address newspapers to you because of the traveling plans that you mentioned, but doubtless you have arranged with someone to forward your mail.
As to "The Rainbow", it is not my intention to let it remain out of print, but to replenish the supply in response to the demands of the market. I think, and so do your friends here, that in view of the original notoriety my handling of the book has been effective in that there has been no threat of suppression. This leaves the way open to the production of new editions without interference. Just now it would seem as if the latest edition served to meet immediate requirements. By the way, I am sending a check for $250 on account to Mountsier via Doran.
You will, of course, be interested in America when you come, but if you are leaving Europe because it is a weary place, you are due for a sad disappointment because in those matters which in Europe weary you, you will find young America senile and decrepit. I am afraid that the German, "Dort wo Du nicht bizt, dort ist das Gluck", is ringing in your ears.
Yours sincerely

end of the month. If you have to write me, best write c/o Robert Mountsier, as we are an uncertain quantity.

Yours   D. H. Lawrence

2499. To Percy Whittley, [17 April 1922]
Text: MS UT; PC v. Native Boutique or Shop; Postmark, Kandy 18 AP 22; Unpublished.

Kandy.

17 April

Dear W[hittley]

I have heard nothing further of the parcel – have you? We are finding Ceylon too hot – sailing on at the end of the month to Australia, to look at that – if we don't like it, then on to San Francisco: and so home, when I can find the money for the fares. Anyhow I'll satisfy my mind as to what I do and what I don't want. – Wonder how you two are.

Yrs   D. H. Lawrence

2500. To Catherine Carswell, [17 April 1922]
Text: MS YU; PC v. Kandy, The Mountain Capital of Ceylon; Postmark, [. . .]; Unpublished.

Kandy,

17 April –

We are sailing on at the end of the month to Australia – find Ceylon too hot and enervating, though it was lovely to look at it. The east is queer – how it seems to bleed ones energy and make one indifferent to everything. – If I don't like Australia I shall go on to San Francisco – now one is started, nothing like keeping going.

Yrs.   DHL

2501. To Rosalind Baynes, [17 April 1922]
Text: MS BucU; PC v. Animal Bathing, Ceylon; Postmark, Kandy 18 AP 22; Unpublished.

Kandy.

17 April

We've sweated here for six weeks – wonderful to look at it all, but no good to live in. So we are going on to Australia at the end of the month, to try that. I shall write and tell you what I find there. And if we don't like it we shall go on to San Francisco, if there's the money left. Once started, best keep going till one is sure.

DHL

2502. To Bessie Fisher, [21 April 1922]
Text: MS Lazarus; PC v. Village Scene, Ceylon; Postmark, Kandy 21 AP 22; Unpublished.

Kandy
21 April.

– Had your letter yesterday – so glad to have all your news, so sorry that it is mostly bad. Poor everybody with flu – and poor Mrs Evans! – and poor Williams![1] I am feeling more myself now, as it has rained in torrents and so it is cooler. It was hot like a prison in a dream. But we are going on. We sail on Monday for West Australia, and the Brewsters hope to sail at the end of the month for Marseilles – destination uncertain. We have had good times here – but I like Buddha *much less* than ever on closer acquaintance. The east is not for me – that I am sure of. What *is* for me, I dont know. – I'll write again.

DHL

2503. To Sallie Hopkin, 21 April 1922
Text: MS NCL; PC v. Sinhalese Village, Ceylon; Postmark, Kandy 21 AP 22; cited in Paulina S. Pollak, *Journal of Modern Literature,* iii (February 1973), 31.

Kandy.
21. April.

My dear Sallie –
I was dreaming of you and Willie – and it seems far away, to Eastwood. We have been here six weeks: wonderful to look at, but my, it has been hot; too hot: so we are going on to Australia, to look at that: sailing from Colombo on Monday. – Did Enid ever get the books and letter I posted just before we left Taormina?[2] I didn't hear from her. – The east is really wonderful pictorially, but judging from this bit, I don't really like it: too boneless and negative. No, I'd never be a Buddhist. I hope you are both well. I'll write from Australia. F[rieda] sends love.

DHL

2504. To Robert Mountsier, 22 April 1922
Text: MS Smith; Postmark, Kandy 22 AP 22; Unpublished.

Ardnaree. Kandy.
22. April 1922

Dear M[ountsier]
I am sending you today by registered MS. post the first 88 pages of Verga's *Novelle Rusticane*: 70 pages remain to follow. You might possibly sell these to a

---

[1] Unidentified.   [2] See Letter 2449 and n. 2

magazine – *Harpers* might be interested, or the *Yale Review*. You might get Carlo Linati (address c/o *Dial*) to do an article on Verga.[1]

We are going down to Colombo this afternoon to stay with Judge Ennis till Monday,[2] when we sail for Fremantle – W. Australia – address as you know, c/o Mrs Jenkins. Strawberry Hill. Perth. W.A.

I have not heard from you for some time: alas, the *Orsova* will bring the mail, but we shan't get it. It must follow by the next ship, 22 days later!

I've got about £90. left of my $1000. Oh dear! – It was good of you to cable that money so promptly.

I wish I had heard from you before we left. Trust all goes well, and you are doing well for yourself. Shall write from the ship.

DHL

What *are* you doing for yourself by the way? what sort of work. I cabled Seltzer yesterday: Sailing Fremantle. Hope he got it and told you.

But I am not really sorry to be leaving Ceylon – though it has a certain melancholy sort of magic. What does one wander looking for? – I guess I know.

You will of course supply Curtis Brown with a typed-copy of the *Novelle*.

2505. To Curtis Brown, 22 April 1922
Text: MS UT; Huxley 544–5.

Ardnaree. Kandy. Ceylon.
22 April 1922

Dear Curtis Brown

I cabled you today – *Sailing Fremantle*. Hope you got the cable. We sail for West Australia on Monday. Address me as I said –
c/o Mrs Jenkins, Strawberry Hill, Perth, West Australia.

The *Orsova* will bring the mail, but alas, we shan't get it, as we sail by her. That means another months delay, don't wonder therefore if you get no answers to your letters.

Yrs   D. H. Lawrence

I expect Mountsier will send you shortly the first half of another Verga translation, of the *Novelle Rusticane*: – short stories of Sicily: I suggest as title the title of one of the stories 'Black Bread' – Sicilian short stories, by Giovanni

---

[1] Carlo Linati (1878–1949), Italian critic whose work had been published in the *Dial*; later he translated 'The Fox' and 'The Ladybird' into Italian (Roberts D112).

[2] Hon. George Francis Macdaniel Ennis (1868–1934), Puisne Justice in the Supreme Court, Ceylon, 1912–25. He had previously served as a judge in several African countries. m. Ethel Kirkland, 1904. In *Kangaroo*, chap. x, DHL made use of his surname for one of the leaders of the Digger movement.

Verga. – I am given to understand that this *vol.* was never copyrighted by Verga. You might possibly sell some of the sketches to the magazines.

DHL

2506. To Martin Secker, 24 April 1922
Text: MS UInd; Postmark, Slave[. . .] 24 AP 22; Secker 48.

'Braemore', Bullers Rd., Colombo, Ceylon
24 April 1922

Dear Secker

Will you please send a copy of *Women in Love* to Mrs Ennis at the above address. Been staying a few days here – leave this afternoon for Australia: address

c/o Mrs Jenkins, Strawberry Hill, Perth, West Australia.
Heaven knows when I shall get my mail now.
Hope everything goes well. Let me know.

Yrs   D. H. Lawrence
name *Mrs Ennis*, wife of Judge Ennis.

2507. To Ada Clarke, [24 April 1922]
Text: MS Clarke; PC v. Double Bullock Cart with full load, Colombo; Postmark, [. . .] 24 [. . .] 22; Unpublished.

Colombo
24 April.

We sail this afternoon to Fremantle. The brass trays were posted to you. Write me to Perth.

DHL

2508. To Lady Cynthia Asquith, 30 April 1922
Text: MS UT; Postmark, Fremantle 4 MAY 22; Huxley 545–6.

[R.M.S. 'Orsova'.]¹
Sunday. 30 April 1922

Here we are on a ship again – somewhere in a very big blue choppy sea with flying fishes sprinting out of the waves like winged drops, and a catholic Spanish Priest playing Chopin at the piano – very well – and the boat gently rolling. – I didn't like Ceylon – at least I liked looking at it – but not to live in. The east is not for me – the sensuous spiritual voluptuousness, the curious sensitiveness of the naked people, their black, bottomless, hopeless eyes – and the heads of elephants and buffaloes poking out of primeval mud – the queer

¹ DHL used the ship's headed notepaper.

noise of tall metallic palm-trees: ach! – altogether the tropics have something of the world before the flood – hot dark mud and the life inherent in it: makes me feel rather sick. But wonderful to have known. – We saw the Prince of Wales at the Kandy Perahera – a lonely little glum white fish he was sitting up there at the Temple of the Tooth with his chin on his hands gazing blankly down on all the swirl of the east like a sort of Narcissus waiting to commit black suicide. The Perahera wonderful – midnight – huge elephants, great flares of cocoanut torches, princes like peg-tops swathed round and round with muslin – and then tom-toms and savage music and devil dancers – phase after phase – and that lonely little white fish of a Prince up aloft – and the black eyes and black bright sweating bodies of the naked dancers under the torches – and the clanging of great mud-born elephants rearing past – made an enormous impression on me – a glimpse into the world before the Flood. I can't get back into history – The soft, moist, elephantine pre-historic has sort of swamped in over my known world – and on one drifts.

But you said not about India but about us. No, I am not angry – no more of my tirades – the sea seems so big – and the world of elephants and buffaloes seems such a vast twilight – and by sheer, or mere proximity with the dark Singhalese one feels the vastness of the blood streams, so dark and hot and from so far off – what does life in particular matter? – why should one care? – one doesn't. – Yet I don't believe in Buddha – hate him in fact – his rat-hole temples and his rat-hole religion. Better Jesus.

We're going to Australia – heaven knows why: because it will be cooler, and the sea is wide. Ceylon steams heat – and it isn't so much the heat as the chemical decomposition of ones blood by the ultra-violet rays of the sun. I don't know what we'll do in Australia – don't care. The world of idea may be all alike, but the world of physical feeling is very different – one suffers getting adjusted, but that is part of the adventure. I think Frieda feels like me, a bit dazed and indifferent – reckless. – I break my heart over England when I am out here. Those natives are *back* of us – in the living sense *lower* than we are. But they're going to swarm over us and suffocate us. We are, have been for five centuries, the growing tip. Now we're going to fall. But you don't catch me going back on my whiteness and Englishness and myself. English in the teeth of all the world, even in the teeth of England. – How England deliberately undermines England. You should see India. Between Lloyd George and Rufus Isaacs etc we are done.[1] – You asked me a year ago who had won the war

---

[1] David Lloyd George (1863–1945), Prime Minister 1916–22 and one of DHL's *bêtes noires* (see *Letters*, iii. 48). Rufus Daniel Isaacs, 1st Marquess of Reading (1860–1935), formerly British Ambassador in Washington, had become Viceroy of India in 1921. He was facing serious political agitation led by Gandhi, rebellion in Madras and in the Punjab.

– we've all lost it. But why should we bother, since it's their own souls folks have lost. It is strange and fascinating to wander like Virgil in the Shades –[1]

Don't buy *Sea and Sardinia* because I shall have to pay Martin Secker for it. He must send it you. It will amuse you.

I'm glad the boys are well, and that Herbert Asquith likes reading other people's books. That's better than having to read one's own: and it's much better to be doing something than nothing. I merely translate Giovanni Verga – Sicilian – *Mastro-don Gesualdo* – and *Novelle Rusticane* – very good – to keep myself occupied. If your husband would like to read them – the translations – tell him to ask Curtis Brown.

F[rieda] greets you.

D. H. Lawrence

we get there on Thursday – to Fremantle.

The address will be, as far as I know:

c/o Mrs Jenkins, Strawberry Hill, Perth, West Australia.

a quite safe address anyhow.

2509. To Robert Mountsier, [4–7 May 1922]
Text: MS Smith; Postmark, Darl[ington] 8 MY 22; Unpublished.

[Savoy Hotel, Perth][2]
4 April 1922

Dear M[ountsier]

Well here we are – landed today on same boat as Annie Besant.[3] Seems a queer godforsaken place: not so much new as non-existent, in the real sense: though they call themselves very 'alive.' Air beautiful and pure and sky fresh, high – that part really good. Dont know how long I shall stay – probably go on to Sydney in about a fortnight. My ticket carries me so far. I'm doubting if I shall be long in Australia. Shall most probably be in America by July or August – try Taos *en passant*. Don't be surprised if I cable you for more dollars from Sydney, to pay my ship to San Francisco – and if I cable be sure to answer. If I use up every sou, you must ask Seltzer to advance me a bit. I'll see this damned world, if only to know I don't want to see any more of it. – Au revoir.

DHL

This is the most expensive hotel I've ever stayed in – leave it tomorrow.

---

[1] I e. Virgil as Dante's guide through Hell and Purgatory in the *Divine Comedy*.
[2] For this letter and the next DHL used the hotel's headed notepaper.
[3] Annie Besant (1847–1933), prolific author on religious, philosophical and political affairs; President of the Theosophical Society; and a champion of nationalism and education in India.

Sunday:

came up to a boarding house on the edge of the bush –[1] wierd country, as if the people were not *really* here: only accidentally here. Sky and air really wonderful, – I think we shall go on to Sydney. You might write me there c/o Thomas Cook and Son. That is quite safe. Heaven knows when I shall get letters.

DHL

2510. To Mabel Dodge Sterne, [4–7 May 1922]
Text: MS Brill; Luhan 21.

[Savoy Hotel, Perth]
4 April 1922

Dear Mabel Dodge Sterne

Well here we are – a raw hole it seems. Got here this morning. Shall have to wait a fortnight or so for a boat on to Sydney. Doubt if Australia will see much of me. At the rate I'm going, I ought to be in Taos easily by August. Will you still have a little house for me?

I never got the book and necklace you sent to Ceylon.

Grüsse   D. H. Lawrence

Sunday

Came out into the bush: wonderful sky and air and freshness. But don't think I shall stay long. Send me a line to Sydney – c/o Thomas Cook and Son, Sydney. That is quite safe.

DHL

2511. To Robert Mountsier, [6 May 1922]
Text: MS Smith; Unpublished.

[Savoy Hotel, Perth]
6 April[2]

Dear M[ountsier]

Here we are in W[est] A[ustralia]. Rum Show – but lovely air and sun – going into the hills – will write.

DHL

---

[1] At the suggestion of Anna Jenkins, who had met the Lawrences on their arrival in Fremantle, they moved on 6 May to a guesthouse, 'Leithdale', at Darlington about 40 miles e. of Perth. The guesthouse was run by two nurses, Mary Louisa ('Mollie') Skinner (1878–1955) – later to be co-author of *The Boy in the Bush* (1924) – and her Quaker friend, Ellen ('Nellie') Beakbane.
[2] This note, apparently written after DHL began Letter 2509, was probably posted with it.

2512. To Anna Jenkins, [13 May 1922]
Text: MS WAPL; PC v. Crystal Terrace, Mammoth Cave, W.A.; Postmark, [. . .] 13 MAY 22;
Priday, *Southerly*, xv (1954), 4.

Sat. morning
Booklovers.[1]

Came into town for an hour – leaving by 12.20. Have decided to go on to
Sydney by the *Malwa* on Thursday – no house at Darlington. When shall we
see you – What of your black hut?

D. H. Lawrence

2513. To Baroness Anna von Richthofen, 15 May 1922
Text: MS UCB; Frieda Lawrence 140.

Darlington. West Australia.

15 Mai 1922

Meine liebe Schwiegermutter
    So, die neuen Juden sollen weiter wandern. Die Frieda ist so entäuscht. Sie
hatte gehoffnet, dass hier fündete sie ein neues England oder Deutschland,
mit viel, viel grossem Raum und lustigeren Leuten. Das Land ist hier:
Himmel hoch und blau und neu, sowie man kein Atmen daraus genommen
hätte: und die Luft ist neu, stark, frisch wie silber: und das Land ist furchtbar
gross und leer, immernoch unbewohnt. Die 'Bush' ist grau und endlos, kein
Lärm, still, und die weissen Stämme von den Gum-trees alle etwas gebrannt:
ein Wald, ein Vor-wald: nicht ein Uhrwald: etwas wie ein Traum, ein
Dämmerungwald das noch nicht einen Tag gesehen hat. Es ist *zu* neu, siehst
du: zu weit. Es braucht noch hunderte Jahren vor es leben kann. Dies ist das
Land wo die ungeborenen Seelen, fremde und nicht zu kennen, die in 500
Jahren geboren sein sollen, wohnen. Ein grauer, fremder Geist. Und die
Leute die hier sind, sind nicht wirklich hier: nur wie Enten die auf der Fläche
des Teiches schwimmen: aber das Land hat ein 'viertes Dimension,' und die
weisse Leute schwimmen wie schatten über die Fläche davon. Und sie sind
keine neue Leute: sehr nervös, neurotique, sowie sie schlecht schlafen, immer
mit einem Gespenst in der Nähe. Ich sage, ein neues Land ist wie schärfe
Wein in welchem schwebt wie eine Perle der Seele eines einkommendes Volk,
bis es dieser Seele untergebrochen ist – oder geschmolzen – oder vergangen.
    Aber das ist dumm. Donnerstag fahren wir weiter, mit dem P and O Boot
Malwa – nach Adelaide, Melbourne und Sydney In Adelaide bliebeu wir
einen Tag: schlafen eine Nacht an Land in Melbourne: und kommen am 27n.
an Sydney: 9 Tage von Fremantle. Das wird interessant sein. Wir haben
unsere Fahrkarten von Colombo bis Sydney. Ich geh so gern immer weiter.

[1] 'The Booklovers' was the famous bookshop founded in Perth by Mrs Frances Zabel in 1900; it
    became a popular meeting place for literary people.

Ich denke, von Sydney gehen wir nach San Francisco, und bleiben ein paar Wochen in Tahiti. Und so, die Welt herum.

Ach Schwiegermutter, es muss so sein: es ist mein Schicksal, das Wandern. Aber die Welt ist rund, bringt uns wieder Zurück nach Baden.

Be well.

DHL

[My dear Schwiegermutter

So, the new Jews shall wander on. Frieda is so disappointed. She had hoped that here she would find a new England or Germany, with much, much great space and jollier people. The land is here: sky high and blue and new, as if no one had ever taken a breath from it; and the air is new, strong, fresh as silver; and the land is terribly big and empty, still uninhabited. The 'bush' is hoary and unending, no noise, still, and the white trunks of the gum trees all a bit burnt: a forest, a preforest: not a primeval forest: somewhat like a dream, a twilight-forest that has not yet seen a day. It is *too* new, you see: too vast. It needs hundreds of years yet before it can live. This is the land where the unborn souls, strange and not to be known, which shall be born in 500 years, live. A grey, foreign spirit. And the people who are here, are not really here: only like ducks that swim on the surface of the pond: but the land has a 'fourth dimension,' and the white people swim like shadows over the surface of it. And they are no new people: very nervous, neurotic, as if they don't sleep well, always with a ghost nearby. I say, a new land is like sharp wine in which floats like a pearl the soul of an incoming people, till it, this soul, has broken down – or melted – or passed away.

But that's foolish. Thursday we are going on, by the P. and O. boat *Malwa* – to Adelaide, Melbourne and Sydney. In Adelaide we stay one day: sleep one night on land in Melbourne: and arrive on the 27th. in Sydney: 9 days from Fremantle. That will be interesting. We have our tickets from Colombo to Sydney. I like so much to keep moving on. I think, from Sydney we shall go to San Francisco, and stay a couple of weeks in Tahiti. And so, round the world.

Oh Schwiegermutter, it must be so: it is my destiny, to wander. But the world is round, brings us again back to Baden.

Be well.

DHL]

2514. To Earl Brewster, 15 May 1922
Text: MS UT; Brewster 51.

Darlington. West Australia
15 May 1922

Dear Brewster

Well! – it is even as you say: six weeks will see us through Australia, I verily believe. At least we are going on next Thursday by the P. and O. boat from Fremantle to Sydney.

We are here about 16 miles out of Perth – bush all round – marvellous air, marvellous sun and sky – strange, vast empty country – hoary unending 'bush' with a pre-primeval ghost in it – apples ripe and good, also pears. And we could have a nice little bungalow – but – But – BUT – Well, it's always an anticlimax of buts. – I just don't want to stay, that's all. It is *so* democratic, it feels to me infra dig. In *so* free a land, it is humiliating to keep house and cook still another mutton-chop. We go east, to Sydney. And there, no doubt, I shall cable at once for more money, to cross the Pacific. – But I find we can take a boat stopping at Fiji, Pego, Honolulu – or another one stopping at Tahiti and somewhere else. I'm determined to *try* the South Sea Isles. Don't expect to catch on there either. But I love trying things and discovering how I hate them.

How I *hated* a great deal of my time in Ceylon: never felt so sick in my life. Yet it is now a very precious memory, invaluable. Not wild horses would drag me back. But neither time nor eternity will take away what I have of it: Ceylon and the east. – One day I shall go round the world again, and go from Africa to North India and Himalayas and if possible Thibet: then China and Japan. One day. Then basta. 'We have no abiding city here –'[1]

I wonder where you are, you three. I haven't a notion. And where I shall be myself, a month hence, I haven't a notion. Toiling on, toiling on –

I wonder how James is, and Cook, and ayah, and Banda. Dio benedetto, che giorni![2]

I wonder where you are, and how long your face is.

DHL

2515. To Curtis Brown, 15 May 1922
Text: Huxley 547.

Darlington, West Australia.
15th May, 1922

Dear Curtis Brown, –

We've been here in W[est] A[ustralia] for a fortnight, and are taking the P. and O. boat *Malwa* on to Sydney on Thursday. I've had no mail for five weeks, but hope to get my letters from the *Malwa* in Perth before we sail. Don't write to me before I send you an address. We shall probably go on from Sydney across the Pacific, and I want to stop in the South Sea Islands a bit, if I can: and ultimately land in Taos, New Mexico – where I was going first.

[1] Hebrews xiii.14 ['For we have not here an abiding city, but we seek after the city which is to come' (R. V.)]   [2] 'Good God, what days!'

It's queer here: wonderful sky and sun and air – new and clean and untouched – and endless hoary 'bush' with no people – all feels strange and empty and *unready*. I suppose it will have its day, this place. But its day won't be our day. One feels like the errant dead, or the as-yet-unborn: a queer feeling. It is not. And the people are not. And there is a queer, pre-primeval ghost over everything. Flinders Petrie says that a colony is no younger than its mother-country.[1] In many ways it is older: more nerve-worn. Queer world altogether. Will send an address soon.

D. H. Lawrence

2516. To William Siebenhaar, [16 May 1922]
Text: TMSC NWU; Unpublished.

Leithdale, Darlington.
Tuesday.

Dear Mr. Siebenhaar,[2]

Thank you for your letter and post-card. We are actually leaving on Thursday by the *Malwa*. It seems ungrateful to be running away so soon from W[est] A[ustralia], when it has been so kindly and quite lovely. But one has a devil of restlessness.

We think of coming to Perth on Thursday morning, and I will call on you at your office. Then we can arrange a luncheon: either you come to us, or we to you. Many thanks for the invitation.

Good luck to get a copy of the *Rainbow*.

Till Thursday then.

D. H. Lawrence

2517. To Anna Jenkins, [17 May 1922]
Text: MS WAPL; Priday, *Southerly*, xv (1954), 4–5.

Darlington.
Wednesday.

Dear Mrs Jenkins

No cure for depression except to feel downright devil-may-care.

---

[1] Sir William Matthews Flinders Petrie (1853–1942), Egyptologist; author of many books on archaeology and anthropology. DHL read Petrie's *History of Egypt* (1894) in 1916 (see *Letters*, ii. 538 and n. 1; 556).

[2] William Siebenhaar (1863–1937), b. Holland and emigrated to Western Australia in 1891 after some years teaching in England. He was a government official from 1895 until 1916 when he was suspended for alleged seditious activities, his anarchist politics having brought him under suspicion. He was later reinstated. Siebenhaar published *Dorothea, A Lyrical Romance in Verse* (c. 1910); with Alfred Chandler, *Sentinel Sonnets* (Melbourne, 1919); a translation of *Max Havelaar* (1860) by Multatuli (pseudonym for Eduard Douwes Dekker, 1820–87), with an introduction by DHL (Knopf, 1927); as well as some writing for newspapers and literary magazines. m., 1899, Lydia Bruce Everard.

We'll be in tomorrow morning – Mr Siebenhaar wrote urging us to lunch. I said we would either lunch with him or ask him to lunch with us. Now it occurs to me that you might hate him lunching with us at the Savoy. I'm sure I am only being polite to him. So ring up the Booklovers tomorrow at 9.30 and tell me if I'm to put him off. I can easily invent a story. Then we can have our lunch at the Savoy in *moderate* peace.

I believe we need not be on board until 3.0 or 3.30: boat leaving at 4.0, according to time-table. I'll call at P. and O. at 9.0 in the morning and make sure. But as I have to get all my luggage down from Perth, and as I suppose I'd better do it myself, please don't think of motoring us. We'll go by train to Fremantle. – bags and all.

à demain.

D. H. Lawrence

2518. To S. S. Koteliansky, 20 May 1922
Text: MS BL; Postmark, [. . .] 22 May [. . .]; cited in Gransden 28.

[P & O.S.N.Co. S.S.][1]
20 May 1922

Dear Kot

Here we are in the Gt. Australian Bight, rolling on again. We stayed two weeks in Western Australia: weird land, marvellous blue sky, clear air, pure and untouched. Then the endless hoary grey 'bush' – which is gum trees, rather thinly scattered, like a thin wood, with a healthy sort of undergrowth: like a moor with trees. People very friendly, but slow and as if unwilling to take the next step: as if everything was a bit too much for them. We are going now to Sydney – calling at Adelaide and Melbourne. We get to Sydney on May 28. I don't know how we shall like it – but Frieda wants to have a little house and stay a few months anyhow. She is tired of moving on. But I like it. I like the feeling of rolling on. I shall have to cable to Seltzer to give me money and he'll have to give it me. I don't care. – I think from Sydney we shall visit the South Sea Islands – think of our 'Rananim' – on the way across to San Francisco. If you were here you would understand Katherine so much better.[2] She is *very* Australian – or New Zealand. Wonder how she is. – I got a mail in Perth just as I left – nothing from you. – Things follow after me in time. I haven't got an address – perhaps

c/o Thomas Seltzer, 5 West 50th. St., N. York

---

[1] For this and the next five letters DHL used the shipping line's headed notepaper. He did not consistently supply the name of the ship.
[2] Katherine Mansfield was born in New Zealand and spent her childhood there.

or else wait till I can tell you. It's a long time now to England – boat takes six weeks – fortnightly mail. – I'm not working – don't want to. How are you all?

DHL

2519. Cyril Beaumont, 20 May 1922
Text: MS Lazarus; Unpublished.

[P & O.S.N.Co. S.S.]
20 May 1922

Dear Beaumont[1]

I got your letter two days ago in Perth – West Australia. We are wandering round – stayed two months in Ceylon – now going to Sydney – then I don't know where.

I would have liked to do a foreword to Richard Aldington's Goldoni play – but now it will be too late and complicated.[2] For Richard's sake I would have liked to do it. Where is he now?

About poems I don't know. Curtis Brown is my agent now. Ask him. Have you seen *Tortoises*, that Seltzer brought out in America? You might like to do that.

Write me c/o Curtis Brown, 6. Henrietta St. W. C. 2.

Yrs   D. H. Lawrence

2520. To Amy Lowell, 20 May 1922
Text: MS HU; Damon 606.

[P & O.S.N.Co. S.S.]
20 May 1922

My dear Amy

Here we are rolling gently in the Great Australian Bight, on a sea swelling from the Antarctic. It is very nice. Once having started wandering I feel I shall never stop. We stayed two months in Ceylon and two weeks in West Australia. I got your letter two days ago in Perth, an hour before we sailed. Glad everything goes on. – This makes two books you have sent me to Germany, and neither of them have I got.[3] – As for Keats, while there's a human being

---

[1] Cyril William Beaumont (1891–1976), bookseller and publisher; he had published DHL's *Bay* (1919). 1917–31 he ran the Beaumont Press specialising in the work of contemporary writers; he was himself an authority on the theatre and classical ballet. See *Letters*, ii. 212n.

[2] Richard Aldington (1892–1962), poet, novelist and, later, biographer of DHL. Beaumont published his translation of the play by Carlo Goldoni (1707–93), *Le Donne di Buon' Umore*, as *The Good-Humoured Ladies* (January 1923). Arthur Symons supplied the introduction after DHL declined.

[3] In fact, Amy Lowell had sent only one book to Germany, *Fir-Flower Tablets* (see p. 97 n. 6). The other book referred to was *Legends*, which DHL received.

left on earth the last word will never be said about anything.[1]

I am enjoying the face of the earth and letting my Muse, dear hussy, repent her ways. 'Get thee to a nunnery' I said to her.[2] Heaven knows if we shall ever see her face again, unveiled, uncoiffed.

The earth – and man is a strange mystery: always *rather* what you expected, and yet oh, so different. So different. One wonders if all books are just so many parish magazines. – The talk is just on top.

Alas for me and my erotic reputation! Tell them I have sent my Muse into a nunnery while I took a look at the world.

I expect we shall come via the South Seas to America.

Greet Mrs Russell. Not having a secretary to sign my letter I sign it myself.

D. H. Lawrence

please address me c/o Robert Mountsier or of Thomas Seltzer.

2521. To Achsah Brewster, [20 May 1922]
Text: MS UT; Brewster 53.

[P & O.S.N. Company's S.S.] Malwa
[20 May 1922]

Dear Achsah

We got your letter and Earls in Perth two days ago – you will be in the Mediterranean by now. – Amused to hear how Ardnaree blew the lid off after we'd gone. I can see the overseer doing his prayers at Earls feet, and Earl not kicking him. – We get to Adelaide on Monday, and to Sydney on tomorrow week. Feel a bit in dread of it: the towns are awful – yet the land is new and strange and remote and gives one something. I find all the South Sea Isles lie at[3] hand at Sydney – must visit them. F[rieda] says she must stay at least three months in or near Sydney – we'll see. I am not thinking of any work. This boat very pleasant. P. and O. Imagine the *Osterley* taking you back again! – Of course Earl was quite right to read the gland book[4] – I call that perfectly legitimate. A book is public, not like a letter. – I got a letter from Seltzer urging me to go to India and write a book on it. Too late this time. But one day I'll go again. All Indian servants on board here: I wouldn't have missed Kandy for anything. – Ardnaree.

DHL

[1] Amy Lowell had apologised for writing about an author who had already received so much critical attention as Keats. She was engaged on a biography of him.
[2] *Hamlet* III. i. 124.   [3] at] to
[4] Louis Berman, *The Glands Regulating Personality; A Study of the Glands of Internal Secretion in Relation to The Types of Human Nature* (New York, 1921). Mabel Sterne sent the book to Ceylon for DHL.

2522. To Jan Juta, 20 May 1922
Text: Moore, *Intelligent Heart* 290–1.

[P & O.S.N.Co. S.S.] Malwa
May 20, 1922

I got your letter two days ago in Perth, W[est] Australia. Now we are rolling in the Gt.Australian Bight, en route for Sydney. Ceylon was lovely to look at but not to live in. Seltzer wanted me to go to India and do a book on that with you – I didn't feel like it. Perhaps later we will. – We stayed two weeks in West Australia – weird place. Don't know how long we shall stay in Sydney – perhaps a month or two – then on into the South Seas, and so to America, to Taos. I've no idea where I shall get the money for the steamer fares, but I don't care. I find on these boats one can travel perfectly second class – nicer than first, simpler – now that there is hardly anybody coming out this way. We are less than thirty passengers second class – nice simple people. – I feel that once I have rolled out of Europe I'll go on rolling. I like it so much. But F[rieda] still hankers after 'a little 'ome of 'er own.' I, no. – But I love straying my own way. – Australia has a marvellous sky and air and blue clarity and a hoary sort of land beneath it, like a Sleeping Princess on whom the dust of ages has settled. Wonder if she'll ever get up. – I'm not working – don't want to – and it takes me now about two months to get a letter. I don't know where Bettina is, or I'd write to her. – America seems to have loved your pictures.[1] Write me
　　　c/o Robert Mountsier, 417 West 118 Street, New York.
– How is Alan? – And E. Africa. – As for me, I have started rolling and can't stop yet. Downhill.
　　　Would you have liked to do India? It's fascinating, if one can bear it, and if one avoids most of the English.
[Frieda Lawrence begins]
　　　Amy Lowell in raptures over your pictures – why dont you say what your family said? Where's Alan? Love to Renée if you see her –[2]

Frieda

2523. To Robert Mountsier, [26–30 May 1922]
Text: MS Smith; Postmark, Thirroul 30 MY 22; Unpublished.

[P & O.S.N.Co. S.S.] Malwa
25 May 1922[3]

Dear M[ountsier]
　　　I had your letter just as we left Perth: collected it at the post office. It had no

---

[1] In *Sea and Sardinia* (so far published only in America).
[2] Réné Hansard, Juta's sister.
[3] In the course of the letter DHL says that they arrive in Sydney 'tomorrow' (i.e. 27 May 1922); the letter was therefore started on 26 May.

news except that you suggested I should go to India and do a book of that. Too late. And one couldn't do a book of India just now: everything too tender and inflamed.[1] And America wouldn't care for the things I had to say, either. But later on – another year – I will go to India again, in the cool season, and when things are different.

I had a letter from Amy still angry about *Tortoises*. She says Seltzer is getting a name as a merely erotic publisher and that is bad for me. Dear respectable Amy with her eccentric cigar.[2]

I sent you the final *Novelle Rusticane* MS. from Perth. Hope you have it, and that it's some good. If it is no trouble to you I wish you'd look out a little alteration. I have just discovered that 'tirare su una presa' is a colloquialism for 'take a pinch of snuff.' I was puzzled by it. In *Mastro-don Gesualdo*, in the auction scene of the sale of the communal lands, before Gesualdo makes the *second* bid – 'tirava su una presa' – You'll find I had 'made another bid' – and crossed it out – and put 'went one higher' – or something like that – and crossed it out again. If you can find the place, put 'took a pinch of snuff.' – The same in the story 'His Reverence' – where he and the Baron sit and bargain – Also, when I say they played *Loo*, in 'His Reverence' (also I think in *Gesualdo*, but I can't remember) – we'd better make it Piquet or something like that. Loo is too gambly and for too many people. The game is tre-sette: three-seven: played by two people.

They are trifles, but you will correct them if they are not a trouble.

So Seltzer is publishing *Fantasia*.[3] Well, I like his courage. I wonder if he'll do anything with it. I begin to feel one had better leave the public to stew in its own juice, and not struggle with them. But I suppose the only thing to do is to keep on.

I doubt if I shall ever like Australia. The country is rather wonderful, with its clear sky and air and sense of emptiness. If I were chucking up the literary sponge, and turning my back on the world, and going to live just for my own sake and pleasantness, I'd stop in Australia. One could live in the bush for next to nothing, and a great free land. But I suppose I must hang on at least till I've tried America. The sense of futility grows – and it's nice to know there is this country – the North West particularly – where one could lose oneself away from the world.

We are on the P. and O. boat *Malwa* – mostly people from India – some fleeing to a surer land. But I doubt, myself, whether India will ever bust up. It seems to me what will happen will be that all the civil jobs will gradually[4] go in

---

[1] See p. 234 n. 1.
[2] Amy Lowell's cigar-smoking had been public knowledge since 1913 when U.S. newspapers carried headlines that the sister of President Abbott Lawrence Lowell of Harvard smoked cigars.
[3] He published *Fantasia of the Unconscious* on 23 October 1922. [4] gradually] gradually all

to the hands of natives, and that corruption and semi anarchy will follow – and then either the slow driving out of the British, or the appeal to Britain to return and keep order. One thing seems to me evident. It is the Brahmins bidding for the *absolute* caste power – caste seems to me worse than slavery. But India will fall into chaos once the British let go. The religions are so antagonistic – Hindu and Mahommedan – and then Buddha. They may keep Britain in power, out of fear of each other. Then again, they may not. But all this 'nationalism' and 'self-government' and 'liberty' are all tripe. They've no more notion of liberty than a jackal has. It's an absolute farce. The whole thing is, like Bolshevism, anarchistic in its inspiration – only anarchistic: just a downthrow of rule, and a chaos. And anyhow, the dark races *don't have* any sense of liberty, in our meaning of the word. They live and move and have their being[1] according to the inspiration of *power* – always *power*, whether private or public, just or unjust. They can't understand the stuff we mean by love or liberty. We can't understand it ourselves anymore, it seems to me.

And Australia, Australia is liberty gone senile – gone almost imbecile. The human life seems to me very barren: one could never make a novel out of these people, they haven't got any insides to them, to write about. And everybody says the government is bankrupt: but then people like to talk in scares. But in Melbourne harbour lie rows and rows of steamers, laid up, can't find cargoes at all. The Union line have half their steamers idle. Nothing doing. Meanwhile immigrants rolling in, and a laborer demanding his pound a day or 25/-.

I wonder if the American consul will want to kick at giving me a visa.

We arrive in Sydney tomorrow morning. I've got nearly £50. in my pocket, no more. I shall have to be cabling for dollars. I shall try New South Wales, to see if I want to stop there and write a novel. If I don't, I shall set off across the Pacific, calling at some of those precious Isles, to see what *they* are like. And then, to San Francisco. Since it's on the way, and cheap, we'll go to Taos just to try it. Further than that I don't know. Did you read Somerset Maugham's *Trembling of a Leaf* –? –Pacific Isles tales?[2] I'll send them you. Make it *not* attractive *at all*. Bisogna vederi coi sui occhi.[3] You'll be looking down your nose at the way I blue the dollars. But it can't be helped. I hope there is another safe thousand by now. Heavens! If not you must get Seltzer to advance it me. Don't leave me beached out here.

I like being at sea. If I don't like even America, then I'll sit down and earn a ship, and we'll have a ship for a few years. We'll see.

I'll add a line in Sydney. Don't know when the mail goes.

au revoir   DHL

[1] Acts xvii. 28 ['we live . . . our being'].
[2] W. Somerset Maugham (1874–1965), *The Trembling of a Leaf: Little Stories of the South Sea Islands* (October 1921).   [3] 'One must see with one's own eyes.'

Thirroul
Tuesday. 28 May.[1]

We've taken a little house on the edge of the Pacific here: the weirdest place you ever saw. It costs 30/. a week: but living is fairly cheap. But it's *awfully* expensive getting about. Sydney is a great fine town, and a wonderful harbour. But I like Australia less and less. The hateful newness, the democratic conceit, every man a little pope of perfection – I shall cable you next for money. Then I intend to sail by the *Marama* – July 6 or the *Sonoma* – July 12th – for San Francisco. If I dare spend the money I shall stop and look at the Isles. – I am going to try to write a romance – or begin one – while I'm here and we are alone. But I long for Europe, and especially for Sicily. – Is America awful like this?

DHL

Chapman and Halls have published in London a vol of stories *Georgian Stories* with one of the stories out of *Prussian Officer* in it: 'Shadow in a Rose Garden,' Duckworth agreed.[2] Now *Putnams* are to publish the book in America, and Chapman and Hall write and ask me if I'd ask Hucbsch to let Putnam use the story. I said I would. So I enclose my letter to Huebsch – Send it or not as you like – but just see what he's doing and get him to let Putnam have the story.

DHL

2524. To Chapman and Hall Ltd, 28 May 1922
Text: MS Lawlor; Unpublished.

Sydney. Australia.
28 May 1922

Dear Sir

I got your letter about Putnam and the short stories here in Sydney yesterday. Am sorry for the delay. I will write at once to B. W. Huebsch – I told Arnold Lunn about him.

I shall be leaving in July for the South Seas and San Francisco. If you should have anything to write me, please address it

c/o Robert Mountsier, 417 West 118 Street, New York City.
Yours Sincerely   D. H. Lawrence

Messrs Chapman and Hall
11 Henrietta St. W. C. 2.

---

[1] The postscript and Letters 2527 and 2528 are misdated. The *Malwa* arrived in Sydney on Saturday, 27 May. The Lawrences stayed a day or two in the city before moving 40 miles southwards on the coast to the house they were to occupy, 'Wyewurk', in Thirroul. The correct date for this postscript and the other two letters is Tuesday, 30 May.

[2] See p. 133 n. 4.

2525. To Benjamin Huebsch, 28 May 1922
Text: MS Smith; Unpublished.

Sydney. Australia
28 May 1922

Dear Huebsch

I got a letter from Chapman and Halls here (much belated) asking if I'd write you for permission for Putnams to publish the story 'Shadow in a Rose Garden' in the volume *Georgian Stories* which has apparently appeared already in London – The story is one contained in *The Prussian Officer*.[1]

You might let Putnams know what you feel about it, if you haven't already done so. It may be a good advertisement. Though why *that* story? – Of course *I* am willing they should have the story, if you are.

Yours sincerely   D.H. Lawrence

P.S. Am sailing from Sydney in July: best address me
c/o Robert Mountsier, 417 West 118 St.
– Would you be so good as to send a copy of *Look We Have Come Through* and of (or[2] else *New Poems*) to
Mrs A. L. Jenkins, Strawberry Hill, Perth. West Australia.

DHL

2526. To Hugo Throssell, [28 May 1922]
Text: Katharine Prichard, 'Lawrence in Australia', *Meanjin*, ix (Summer 1950), 252–3.

[Sydney]
[28 May 1922]

[3]['Lawrence wrote from Sydney to say that he had already fled from the West, in something like a panic, finding Australia a remote and terrifying place. He mentioned a nostalgia for Sicily'.]

2527. To Baroness Anna von Richthofen, [30 May 1922]
Text: MS Jeffrey; Frieda Lawrence 142.

'Wyewurk'. *Thirroul*. New South Wales. Australia
28 May 1922

Meine liebe Schwiegermutter

Diesmal schreib ich dir auf Englisch, ich muss schnell sein.[4] We got to Sydney on Saturday, after a fine journey. I like the P. and O. boats, with the

---

[1] Huebsch published the first American edition of *The Prussian Officer* in 1916 (and of *Look! We Have Come Through!*, 1918; *Amores*, 1916; and *New Poems*, 1920).
[2] of (or] of "*Amores*" (or   [3] See p. 251 n. 2.
[4] 'This time I'll write to you in English, I must be quick.'

dark servants. But that was a frightful wreck of the *Egypt* in the Bay of Biscay.[1]
We heard of it in Adelaide. Our Captain of the *Malwa* changed from the *Egypt*
only this very voyage. He was very much upset – so was everybody. They say
the Lascar servants are so bad in a wreck – rushing for the boats. But I don't
believe *all* of it.

Anyway, here we are safe and sound. Sydney is a great fine town, half like
London, half like America. The harbour is wonderful – a narrow gateway
between two cliffs – then one sails through, and is in another little sea, with
many bays and gulfs. The big ferry steamers go all the time threading across
the blue water, and hundreds of people always travelling.

But Sydney town costs too much, so we came down into the country. We are
about 50 km. south of Sydney, on the coast. We have got a lovely little house on
the edge of the low cliff just above the Pacific Ocean – 'Der grosse oder stille
Ozean,'[2] says Frieda. But it is by no means still. The heavy waves break with a
great roar all the time: and it is so near. We have only our little grassy garden –
then the low cliff – and then the great white rollers breaking, and the surf
seeming to rush in right under our feet as we sit at table. Here it is winter, but
not cold. But today the sky is dark, and it makes me think of Cornwall. We
have a coal fire going, and are very comfortable. Things go so quickly in
Australia. It will not cost much to live here, food is quite cheap – good meat is
only fivepence or sixpence a pound – 50 Pfg. ein Pfund –

But it is a queer, grey, sad country – empty, and as if it would never be filled.
Miles and miles of bush – forlorn and lost. It all feels like that. Yet Sydney is a
huge great modern city.

I don't really like it, it is so raw – so crude. The people are so crude in their
feelings – and they only want to be up to date in their 'conveniences' – electric
light and tramways and things like that. The aristocracy are the people who
own big shops[3] – and there is no respect for anything else. The working people
very discontented – always threaten more strikes – always more socialism.

I shall cable to America for money, and sail in July across the Pacific to San
Francisco – via Wellington, New Zealand, Raratonga, Tahiti, Honolulu –
Then to our Taos. And that is the way home – coming back. Next spring we
will come to Germany. I've got a Heimweh[4] for Europe: Sicily, England,
Germany.

auf Wiedersehen   DHL

---

[1] On 20 May 1922 the P. & O. liner *Egypt* was struck and sunk by the French freighter *Seine* in
thick fog off the coast of Finistère. Nearly 100 people were drowned. Some of the Lascars were
accused of taking to the lifeboats immediately, thus preventing women passengers from getting
into them.   [2] 'The great or still ocean'.
[3] shops] stores   [4] 'Homesickness'.

I must hurry to catch the mail which leaves here tonight – leaves Sydney tomorrow, for Europe. Write to me

    c/o Robert Mountsier, 417 West 118 Street, *New York City*.

I shall get your letter in America.

Frieda ist so glücklich mit ihrem neuen Haus – macht alles so schön.[1]

                                      DHL

2528. To Anna Jenkins, [30 May 1922]
Text: MS WAPL; Huxley 547–8.

                          'Wyewurk'. Thirroul. N. S. W. Australia

                                        28 May 1922

Dear Mrs Jenkins

Well here we are – in a little house to ourselves on the edge of the cliff some 40 miles south of Sydney. It's a weird place – with coal-mines near. I believe I wish I'd stayed in Darlington. In fact I'm sure I do. Australia goes from bad to worse in my eyes. Sydney and the harbour are quite one of the sights of the world. But the quality of the life is absolutely too much, or too little for me. Talk about crude, raw, and self-satisfied. If every American is a King or Queen, I'm sure every Australian is a little Pope all on his own, God's Vicar. 'There is nothing better than me on earth', he seems silently to proclaim, not with tongues of angels or tones of silver either:[2] and not always silently. I've got a bitter burning nostalgia for Europe, for Sicily, for old civilisation and for real human understanding – not for this popery of sacred 'conveniente' – Everything is 'so convenient', they keep telling you. They can keep their convenience. –

And I shan't be able to leave till July – the *Marama*, July 6th at the earliest – and a poky little steamer. God how I hate new countries: They are *older* than the old, more sophisticated, much more conceited, only young in a certain puerile vanity more like senility than anything. I do wish I had stayed in Western Australia. Trop tard![3]

You were so awfully nice to us too – and here we don't know a soul: nor want to. I found your letter to Mr Toy[4] – but don't know if I shall present it. So much for gratitude from me. But I feel I simply can't face *knowing* anybody: it's enough to look at 'em.

We shall go on to San Francisco: have taken this house 'Wyewurk' (why not wireworks) for a month. Meanwhile my Psalm is 'Lord remember David'.[5] Of course F[rieda] is happy for the moment tidying the house.

---

[1] 'Frieda is so happy with her new house – makes all so lovely.'
[2] Cf. 1 Corinthians xiii. 1.   [3] 'Too late!'
[4] Anna Jenkins had provided DHL with a letter of introduction to Mr Toy of the *Sydney Bulletin*. See Nehls, ii. 151.   [5] Psalm cxxxii. 1.

Remember me nicely to Mrs Gawler.[1] Tell her I agree with her, I am a fool.

The Pacific is just under a little cliff – almost under the doorstep: and heavens, such a noisy ocean.

I am ordering you poems.

It would seem like sarcasm to ask you to come to Sydney. But if you feel like it, do come – plenty of room here.

Many greetings from us both.

D. H. Lawrence

Had a letter from Mr Throssell, husb. of Katharine Pritchard. Too late again.[2]

DHL

Threw *Dorothea* and Sonnets into the Ocean from the ship.[3] – *Malwa* empty, and quite pleasant.

2529. To Mabel Dodge Sterne, 3 June 1922
Text: MS Brill; Luhan 23.

c/o Thomas Cook and Son. Sydney. N.S.W.

3 June 1922

Dear Mabel Dodge

Here we are in a little house on the edge of the Pacific, which ocean rolls loudly nearly into the house. We've come about 40 miles south of Sydney. Australia is not a bad country qua country. But I am so weary of these utterly à terre democratic peoples. Probably America will be as bad.

I have started a novel and if I can go on with it I shall stay till I've finished it[4] – till about end of august. But if I can't work I shall come on to America. I'll send you a cable merely saying the boat. I suppose Sterne, Taos, New Mexico will find you. The steamers are

Union Line	Marama–July 6th.	arrive San Francisco July 31.
	Tahiti. Aug 10th.	,, ,, ,, Sept. 4th.
	Marama Sept 7th	Oct 2nd

---

[1] May Eva Gawler (b. 1873), m. Douglas George Gawler, son of the second governor of South Australia; a close friend of Anna Jenkins in whose company she had met the Lawrences shortly after their arrival in West Australia. She is recorded as having said to DHL 'you are a fool' (Nehls, ii. 134).

[2] Captain Hugo Vivian Hope Throssell (1884–1933), V.C., son of the Australian Prime Minister George Throssell. He had invited the Lawrences to visit him and his wife near Darlington, not knowing that they were already in New South Wales. Throssell's wife wrote under the name of Katharine Susannah Prichard (1884–1969); she had published three novels: *The Pioneers* (1915), *Windlestraws* (1916) and *The Black Opal* (1921).

[3] Cf. p. 240 n. 2.   [4] *Kangaroo* (1923). The title first appears in Letter 2539.

	Sonoma July 12th	,,	,,	,,	July 31st
Oceanic Line	*Ventura* Aug 16th	,,	,,	,,	Sept 4th.
	Sonoma Sept 13th	,,	,,	,,	Oct 2nd.

These sailings may be altered a bit, but not much.

It seems to me it is a good thing I came round the world to Taos. I shall be much more likely to stick it when I get there.

I hear the glands book arrived in Ceylon and was sent on, so I shall get it.

I do hope I shall get from your Indians something that this wearily external white world cant give, and which the east is just betraying all the time. Meanwhile have patience with our vagaries.

If I was really going to give up struggling with life I'd come to Australia. It is a big empty country, with room to be alone.

I want this to catch the *Tahiti*, which sails June 8th. and is due in Frisco on July 3rd.

tanti saluti   D. H. Lawrence

2530. To Robert Mountsier, [3 June 1922]

Text: MS Smith; PC v. The Bulli Lookout, South Coast, N.S.W.; Postmark, Thirroul 6 JE 22; Unpublished.

['Wyewurk', Thirroul, New South Wales, Australia]
June 3rd.

– We have come to Thirroul, about 40 miles south from Sydney, and are established in a house on the edge of the Pacific. Rather nice. I want to do a novel, and if it goes I shall stay a month or two – if not, come on to San Francisco. The boats are

	Marama. July 6.	arr. S. Frisco	Jly 31
Union	*Tahiti* Aug 10	,, ,,	Sept 4
Line	*Marama* Sept 7	,, ,,	Oct 2

Sonoma July 12	,, ,,	July 31
Ventura Aug 16	,, ,,	Sept 4
Sonoma Sept 13	,, ,,	Oct 2

I shall cable for money, and name ship. We shall call at Taos to look at it. Hope all goes well.

DHL

am having my mail addressed to you.[1]

---

[1] The postscript is written on the verso of the postcard.

2531. To S. S. Koteliansky, [5 June 1922]
Text: MS BL; PC v. The Beach, Thirroul, South Coast, N.S.W.; Postmark, Thirroul 6 JE 22; Zytaruk 243.

Thirroul, N.S.W.

5 June.

We have come down here about 40 miles south of Sydney – taken such a nice little bungalow on the very edge of the Pacific – can bathe all to ourselves. It is queer – a big, free land, rather fascinating. But I feel awfully foreign with[1] the people, although they are all English by origin. It is rather like the Midlands of England, the life, very familiar and rough – and I just shrink away from it. If I can write we shall stay a few months. Then I really think we shall cross to San Francisco.

Write me a line

  c/o Robert Mountsier, 417 West 118 Street, New York.

So long since I had any mail.

DHL

 Pardon the p.c. – I can't bring myself to write letters here.

2532. To Earl Brewster, [5 June 1922]
Text: MS UT; PC v. The Beach, Thirroul, South Coast, N.S.W.; Postmark, Thirroul 6 [. . .] 22; Brewster 54.

Thirroul.

5 June.

– We have come down here about 40 miles south of Sydney – have a very nice bungalow with the Pacific in the garden – really – but it is so noisy. I am trying to write – and if I can get on we shall stay a month or two. But I think anyhow by autumn we shall be in America – Australia is a wonderful country in itself – but as usual – l'uomo non mi piace.[2]

 Frieda is very happy with her house – and we can bathe all to ourselves. Send me a line

  c/o Robert Mountsier, 417 West 118 St. New York.

DHL

---

[1] with] from   [2] 'man doesn't please me' (cf. *Hamlet* II. ii. 322).

2533. To Ada Clarke, [5 June 1922]
Text: MS Clarke; PC v. The Bulli Lookout, South Coast, N.S.W.; Postmark, Thirroul 6 JE
22; Lawrence–Gelder 121-2.

Thirroul.

5 June.

– We have taken such a nice little furnished bungalow, right on the sea – we
can bathe all to ourselves – like it so much. Australia is awfully nice, as a
country – the bit I have seen of it. But of course one does not feel one belongs to
the people. Sicily especially spoils one for the new, raw countries and their
rough sort of friendly and unfriendly manners. I hope you got the ring I sent
from Perth. Had your letter three days ago saying Jackie and Gertie gone to
Florence. You'll be thinking of summer holidays when you get this. Send me a
line

c/o Robert Mountsier, 417 West 118 St. New York.

DHL

2534. To Baroness Anna von Richthofen, 9 June 1922
Text: MS UCB; Frieda Lawrence 144.

Thirroul N. S. W.

9 June 1922

Meine liebe Schwiegermutter

Wir hatten zwei Briefe heute: Anita's Hochzeit Brief auch: und die
Nachrichten von Johanna, das sie Max verlassen will. Ach Gott – Revoluzion
und Erdbebung! Aus[1] deinen zwei Briefen kommst du mir ein bisschen bös
vor. Bist du bös dass wir weiter gekommen sind, wie wandernde Juden? Ich
sag dir wieder, die Welt ist rund, und bringt den rollenden Stein wieder
zuhaus. Und ich muss gehen, bis ich etwas finde, das mich beruhigt. Letztes
Jahr habe ich es in Eberstcinburg gefunden. Da habe ich *Aaron's Staub* fertig
gebracht, und mein *Fantasia von dem Unbewustsen*. Und jetzt ist *Aaron*
erscheint, und diesen Monat kommt die *Fantasia* auch in New York. Und ich,
ich bin in Australien, und plötzlich schreibe wieder – ein wahnsinniger[2]
Roman von Australien. So geht's. Ich hoffe, ich kan es fertig haben, in August.
Dann, Schwiegermutter, wieder am Meer. Wir wollen das Schiff *Tahiti*
nehmen, das von Sydney fährt am 10n August fort: kommt am 16n. an
Wellington in New Zealand: dann nach Raratonga und dann Papeete, Kapital
von den Insel Tahiti, im Mittel des Pazific Ozean – und dann, Sept 4, an San
Francisco, California. Von San Francisco nach *Taos*, in New Mexico. Und ich

---

[1] On at least eleven occasions – as here where she substituted 'Aus' for DHL's 'Von' – Frieda
corrected DHL's German in this letter.   [2] wahnsinniger] wahnsiginer

glaube, in dem Frühling, du wirst uns wieder in Baden Baden sehen. Ich habe grade Geld genug, uns nach Taos zu bringen. Und dann nichts. Aber es kommt immer.

Wir sind sehr nett hier. Du würdest dieses Haus sehr gern haben: das grosse Zimmer mit offnem Feuer und schöne Fenster mit kleinen roten Vorhänge, und die breite *Verandahs*, und das Gras und das Meer immer gross und lärmig unter die Füsse. Wir baden Mittag, wenn die Sonne sehr warm ist, und die Ufer ganz, ganz einsam: nur die Wellen. – Das Dorf ist neu und roh – die strassen sind nicht gebaut, alles Sand und Lehm – interessant ist es. Die Leute sind alle sehr freundlich, und doch für mich fremd. Briefträger und Zeitungbub kommen auf Pferden reitend, und pfeifen mit Polizeipfeife wenn[1] sie die Briefe eingeworfen haben – oder die Zeitung. Fleisch ist so billig – zwei gute Schafszungen, 60 Pf. – und ein grosses Stück *Beef*, genug fur zwolf Leute, zwei Mark. Schöne Obst haben wir auch – Apfeln, Birne, Passion Fruit, Persimmons: und wunderschöne Butter und Milch. Und Himmel und Erde so neu, sowie Man kein Atmen noch davon genommen hätte, kein Fuss darauf getreten. Die grosse Geistladung die so schwer wiegt, in Europa, existiert gar nicht hier. Man fühlt sich etwas wie ein Kind, das keine wirkliche Sorgen hat. Interessant ist es – eine neue Erfahrung.

Est ist dein Geburtstag in einem Weilchen. Ich schick dir ein paar Pfennige, du kannst immer noch ein Thee mit Altweibern haben. Grüsse alle.

Die arme Else. Ich schreibe an ihr.

Leb wohl   DHL

[My dear Schwiegermutter

We had two letters today: Anita's wedding letter too: and the news from Johanna, that she wants to leave Max.[2] Oh God – revolution and earthquake! From your two letters you seem to me a bit angry. Are you cross that we have come farther, like wandering Jews? I tell you again, the world is round, and brings the rolling stone home again. And I must go till I find something that brings me peace. Last year I found it at Ebersteinburg. There I finished *Aaron's Rod*, and my *Fantasia of the Unconscious*. And now *Aaron* is out, and this month comes *Fantasia* too in New York. And I, I am in Australia, and suddenly writing again – a weird novel of Australia. So it goes. I hope to have it done by August. Then, Schwiegermutter, again to sea. We want to take the ship *Tahiti*, that sails from Sydney on 10th August: gets in on the 16th. to Wellington in New Zealand: then to Raratonga and then to Papeete, capital of

---

[1] wenn] als
[2] They were divorced in 1923; Johanna then married Emil von Krug (1870–1944), a Berlin banker.

the island Tahiti, in the middle of the Pacific Ocean – and then, Sept 4, at San Francisco, California. From San Francisco to *Taos*, in New Mexico. And I believe, in the spring, you will see us again in Baden Baden. I've just enough money to get us to Taos. And then nothing. But it always comes.

We're very nice here. You would like this house very much: the big room with open fire and lovely windows with little red curtains, and the broad *verandahs*, and the grass and the sea always big and noisy under our feet. We bathe at midday, when the sun is very warm, and the beach quite, quite lonely: only the waves. – The township is new and raw – the streets aren't paved, all sand and clay – it's interesting. The people are all very friendly, and yet foreign to me. Postman and newspaper boy come riding on horses, and whistle with a police whistle when they have dropped the letters in – or the newspaper. Meat is so cheap – two good sheep's tongues, 60 Pf. – and a great piece of *beef*, enough for twelve people, two marks. Lovely fruit we have too – apples, pears, passion fruit, persimmons: and marvellous butter and milk. And sky and earth so new, as if nobody had yet taken one breath from it, set one foot on it. The great spiritual freight that weighs so heavily in Europe doesn't even exist here. One feels somewhat like a child that has no real cares. It's interesting – a new experience.

It's your birthday in a little while. I send you a few pfennigs, you can still have a tea with old wives. Greet all.

Poor Else. I'll write to her.

Farewell   DHL]

2535. To Robert Mountsier, 9 June 1922
Text: MS Smith; Postmark, Thirroul 9 JE 22; Unpublished.

'Wyewurk', Thirroul, New South Wales.
9 June 1922

Dear M[ountsier]

I had your letter of May 10th yesterday – direct to Sydney – and the one of April 20 today, from Kandy, scolding me for wanting money cabled. I am sorry it is a nuisance. How about the next lot? I've got just £31. here now: and it costs me about £3. a week to live, lowest estimate, here in this house. I've paid the rent (30/- week) till June 26th. If I stay till August, and sail on the *Tahiti*[1] on August 10, I should have six more weeks rent to pay – £9. Would leave me about £22. for the eight weeks and the getting back to Sydney and on board. *Just* might be done. The fare to San Francisco is £60 first, and £40 second. We have come second[2] so far, but they say these boats are so small

---

[1] *Tahiti*] Somona   [2] second] first

there is practically no deck accommodation second. I think we shall have to go first. That means £120 clear: then some money for landing at the other end, and to get to Taos with. I'm afraid I shall need at least £160. But I don't want to change money back and forth from dollars to pounds: and I know Cooks wont give me dollars if they can possibly help it. I tell you what. Unless you hear from me by cable, get Thomas Cooks in New York to cable their Sydney people seven hundred dollars as soon as possible after you get this letter, and I'll book August sailings. If you have anything to advise me, cable here deferred rate. I won't cable you at all unless an emergency arises. But I must have money enough when I land in Frisco to get us to Taos. I'll tell Cooks in Sydney what I'm doing. I'm sorry to be a bother – and to swallow *all* the money.

If the novel I have begun (pitched in Australia) keeps on at the rate it is going at, it should be ready by August. But it is a rum sort of novel, that'll probably bore you. So don't count on it.

I am writing to Seltzer today to ask him to return to you *Mr Noon* and *Birds Beasts*.

What is your book?[1] I am most interested – want to see it.

I *hope* Seltzer hasn't posted copies of *Aaron* to me to Ceylon or anywhere.

Don't tell anybody I am coming to America. Don't let Seltzer either. I don't want people to know.

Could you post at once a copy of 'Adolf' and a copy of 'Rex' or do you think 'Tickets Please' would be better? It must be short – to

Herrn Dr Anton Kippenberg, Insel Verlag, Kurzestrasse 7. *Leipsig* for him to translate into German for his *Insel Almanach*: and tell him he is to choose which he uses. Or if you like send only 'Adolf'.[2]

Michael Borg is a timid fool. I hope he's answered by now. My letters to him will take another 6 weeks.

Put this fragment of a cheque for those old Imagiste Poems to the account.[3]

Did you get my three pages of new ending to 'Whitman'?[4]

I'm glad you manage Seltzer. One day we'll prosper. I haven't written to him – Seltzer – for a long time, till now. Feel he's a bit fishy but we must be careful and make the best of him. No doubt he means well.

I feel rather keen to write an American novel, after Australia.

D.H. Lawrence

It's quite lovely here.

[1] Mountsier's book was entitled *Our Eleven Billion Dollars: Europe's Debt to the United States* (Seltzer, 1922). What Mountsier regarded as Seltzer's failure adequately to promote his book helped to sour his (and thus perhaps DHL's) relations with the publisher.
[2] Kippenberg's firm published annually, *Insel-Almanach auf das Jahr.* 'Adolf' never appeared in it.   [3] Cf. p. 96 n. 1.   [4] See Letter 2454.

Perhaps the best would be to cable the money in pounds – £160 – from America – then I'd not have much to change back into dollars. But do as you think best.

Anita v. Schreïbershofen is married to Ernst v. Hinke – and Johanna is going to get divorced from Max and is going to marry Emil Krug! – Revolution in the family. – My mother in law wails at this long distance, and wants us to come nearer.

After all it's better to travel and spend the money and feel one moves in life, than to sit still in nothingness.

I hope the Consul won't make a fuss about visas – make us have through tickets to Europe, or something vile.

I've had no news for ages from Curtis Brown or Secker[1] – don't know what's happening, do you? – Keep all letters till I get to America.

DHL

2536. To Thomas Seltzer, 9 June 1922
Text: MS UT; Postmark, Thirroul 9 JE 22; Lacy, *Seltzer* 34–5.

Thirroul. New South Wales.

9 June 1922

Dear Seltzer

Well we've got so far – about fifty miles south of Sydney, in a little house to ourselves quite on the sea: very nice; a weird country, though. I have begun a novel, and it seems to be going well – pitched in Australia. Heaven knows if anybody will like it – no love interest at all so far – don't intend any – no sex either. Amy Lowell says you are getting a reputation as an erotic publisher: she warns me. I shall have thought my reputation as an erotic writer (poor dears) was secure. So now I'll go back on it.

Will you please hand back to Mountsier the MSS. of *Mr Noon* – till I see what I'll do further with it – and of *Birds Beasts and Flowers*. Please let him have them at once. – Did you like the Three Stories?[2]

I do hope you didn't post copies of *Aaron's Rod* to me here or to Ceylon.

---

[1] The two men had, however, been corresponding in DHL's absence (Secker Letter-Book, UIll). Secker's letter to Curtis Brown, 28 February 1922, informing him that the typescript of *Aaron's Rod* was with the printer, included the following remarks about the novel: 'There are certain paragraphs and passages which are quite unpublishable and as Mr. Lawrence has given Seltzer a free hand to make certain amendments, I gather that this permission applies to me also.' For the consequences see Roberts A21 n. 2. With the same letter he returned 'The Ladybird', 'The Fox' and 'The Captain's Doll' which were to form the fourth book under his contract with DHL. This book, Secker told Curtis Brown on 21 March, would be published in November 1922 (it was actually published in March 1923).

[2] 'The Captain's Doll', 'The Fox' and 'The Ladybird', published by Seltzer as *The Captain's Doll* (see p. 107 n. 7).

Hear it is going well. Please send a copy to Amy, and to Mabel Dodge Sterne, *Taos*, and to

Mrs A. L. Jenkins, Strawberry Hill, *Perth*. West Australia: also to Juta if you have his address, also to

Frau Dr Else Jaffe-Richthofen – Konradstrasse 16. *München* also to

EH Brewster, c/o Thomas Cook 90 rue du Rhône, *Geneva*, Switzerland.

We think of staying here till August, then crossing to San Francisco and so to Taos. But I'll let you know definitely.

When we get to America we'll see you. Hope the Consul won't want to refuse us visas. – I should like very much to write an American novel, after this Australian[1] one: on something the same lines. But we'll see. One has to do what one can do. Only Germany helped me to the finish of *Aaron*.

I want so much to know how *Fantasia* goes – and to see it in print. Send it to Mabel Dodge also – and to Brewster – and to my sister in law Else Jaffe.

I should expect to land in San Francisco either on Sept 4th[2] by the boat *Tahiti* (via Wellington, Raratonga, Papeete) – or else on the same day by the *Ventura* – via Pago Pago and Honolulu. But *don't* tell anybody we are coming. We shall go to Taos. And I don't want anybody to know we are there.

Feel we shall be seeing you soon. Till then, prosper.

Yrs   D. H. Lawrence

2537. To Mabel Dodge Sterne, 9 June 1922
Text: MS Brill; Luhan 24.

'Wyewurk', *Thirroul*. New South Wales.

9 June 1922

Dear Mabel Dodge

I have as good as decided to stay here till August – because I think I can finish my Australian novel, or near enough, by then. We shall probably take the boat *Tahiti*, arriving in San Francisco Sept 4th. I'll write again when I book berths. The *Tahiti* sails August 10th.

I want you please *not* to tell anybody we are coming. I want to be really apart from most people – same as here. Here I have not let anybody know I am come – I don't present any letters of introduction – there isn't a soul on this side of Australia knows I am here, or knows who I am. And that is how I prefer it. It's a queer novel I'm writing, but it interests me. – I have ordered Seltzer to send you a copy of *Aarons Rod* and of *Fantasia of the Unconscious*, which follows *Psychoanalysis and the Unconscious*.

---

[1] Australian] *English*   [2] 4th] 10th

I build quite a lot on Taos – and the pueblo. I shall be so glad if I can write an American novel from that centre. It's what I want to do. And I have learned a lot coming here.

We shall have blued all our money on steamships, so shall want to be very obscure and economical till a little more grows up. Of course I shall have enough to get along with.

I wonder if we shall find the winter very cold! But I look forward to it very much. I wonder if we shall go to that farther off pueblo you wrote about.

I feel now it actually won't be long before we are in New Mexico.

D.H. Lawrence

2538. To Dr Anton Kippenberg, 9 June 1922
Text: MS GSArchiv; Unpublished.

Thirroul. N. S. W. Australia
9 June 1922

Dear Doctor Kippenberg

I had your letter of 24 April today – it has followed me so far. I have written to my agent Robert Mountsier, in New York, to send you two sketches to choose from, for your *Insel Almanach*. I know the *Almanach* very well – have known it for years. I hope the manuscripts will reach you in time, if not, you can lay them by.

We shall be leaving Australia in August, I think, for San Francisco. This is a very pleasant country to be in – so new, and without that weight of anxiety and weariness in the air which weighs on us in Europe. But they are all the time talking about the Commonwealth being bankrupt, the paper money having no value, and the threatening revolution of Labour. The world is all alike – weary with its old forms. But here the earth and air are new, and the spirit of place untouched.

If you have to write me, please address me
c/o Robert Mountsier, 417 West 118 Street. *New York City*.

Yours Sincerely   D. H. Lawrence

2539. To Thomas Seltzer, 11 June 1922
Text: MS UT; Lacy, *Seltzer* 36.

'Wyewurk', Thirroul. South Coast. N. S. W.
11 June 1922

Dear Seltzer

Wrote you yesterday – today come the copies of *Aaron* – Many thanks – book looks so nice – haven't plucked up courage to look out the cut parts yet.

Baroness Anna von Richthofen c. 1924

Else Jaffe c. 1919

Achsah, Harwood and Earl Brewster, Capri c. 1923

Jan Juta c. 1921

Mollie Skinner 1922

William Siebenhaar

Amy Lowell

Mabel Dodge Luhan 1923

Tony Luhan

D. H. Lawrence, 1923, from a portrait by Kai Götzsche

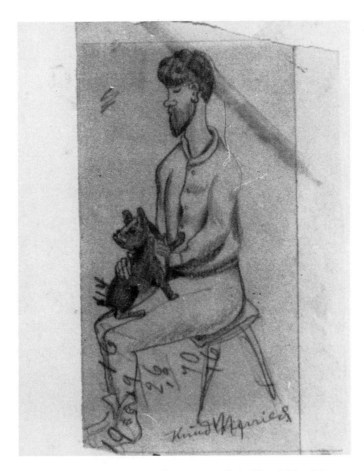

D. H. Lawrence, 1923, from a portrait by Knud Merrild

Willard Johnson, Witter Bynner and D. H. Lawrence, Santa Fe 1923

Idella Purnell, Lawrence, Frieda, Willard Johnson, Dr George Purnell, Mexico 1923

Idella Purnell c. 1925

Thomas and Adele Seltzer c. 1920

Dorothy Brett, 1922, from a self-portrait

Don't bother therefore to send the copies I asked you to post. But don't post me *Fantasia* here, if you haven't done so. Send out for me instead the five or six copies I asked you to send – and keep the rest till I come.

I think I'm calling my new novel *Kangaroo*. It goes so far – queer show – pray the gods to be with me, that I finish by August.

Yrs   D. H. Lawrence

2540. To Martin Secker, 11 June 1922
Text: MS UInd; Secker 49.

Thirroul. S. Coast. New South Wales
11 June 1922

Dear Secker

Am here in a house on the Pacific writing a novel – queer sort of quite different novel, pitched in Australia. We think of staying till August, then to California. Please write to me c/o Robert Mountsier, 417 West 118 St. New York City – and tell me all you're doing, and what books you're publishing and what not. I've just received copies of *Aaron* from Seltzer – haven't yet looked what he cut – he says its selling. What of the English *Sea and Sardinia?*[1]

Of my six presentation copies of any book you publish, please post one only to me, c/o Mountsier. Of the rest, if it is the *stories*, please send a copy to

1. Mrs L A Clarke, Grosvenor Rd. Ripley nr Derby.
2. Mrs S. King. 480 Main St. Carlton nr Nottingham
3. S. Koteliansky – 5. Acacia Rd. N. W. 8.
4. The Lady Cynthia Asquith – *Stanway* – Winchcombe – Glos
5. Mrs Mary Cannan, 6 Inverness Place, Bayswater W. 2

But don't send *Aaron's Rod* to the first two. Send those two copies:

1. Miss Barbara Low – 13 Guilford St. W. C. 1.
2. Miss Elizabeth Humes, American Embassy, Piazza San Bernardo. Rome

Dont fail me about this, will you?

The new novel goes well, and I hope to call it *Kangaroo* and finish it by August. Unberufen![2]

Australia a weird country – fascinating – but humanly non-existent. Yet so much space and sun and unwornout air.

Yrs   D. H. Lawrence

Wonder if any of my mail went down on the *Egypt.*

---

[1] See p. 108 n. 1..
[2] 'Touch wood!' (lit. 'unbidden').

When you bring out the short stories 'Tickets Please'[1] – please send a copy to my mother in law

Frau Baronin von Richthofen, Ludwig Wilhelmstift, Baden Baden.

2541. To Else Jaffe, 13 June 1922
Text: MS Jeffrey; Frieda Lawrence 146–9.

'Wyewurk', *Thirroul*. South Coast. N. S. W. Australia
13 June 1922

Dear Else

I have been wanting to write to you. The Schwiegermutter says that Friedel is ill with jaundice. I am so sorry, and do hope it is better by now.

I often think of you here, and wonder what you would think of this. We're in a very nice place: have got a delightful bungalow here about 40 miles south of Sydney, right on the shore. We live mostly with the sea – not much with the land – and not at all with the people. I don't present any letters of introduction, we don't know a soul on this side of the continent: which is almost a triumph in itself. For the first time in my life I feel how lovely it is to know nobody in the whole country: and nobody can come to the door, except the tradesmen who bring the bread and meat and so on, and who are very unobtrusive. One nice

---

[1] I.e. the volume eventually entitled *England, My England* published by Seltzer in October 1922 but not by Secker until January 1924. When replying to this letter from DHL, on 25 July 1922 (TMS Smith), Secker indicated his preference for 'The Blind Man' over 'Tickets Please' as the lead story in the volume:

Dear Lawrence,
    I am very glad to have your letter of June 11th to which I hasten to reply.
    All goes well here and the sales of "Aaron's Rod" up to the end of last month amount to 1716 copies. The book is in circulation at The Times Book Club and Mudies but Smith and Boots will not circulate it though I went to a great deal of trouble to try and overcome their objections. Mudie as a matter of fact, only gave in after the first reviews had appeared. I am posting you a copy care of Mountsier.
    The collection of short stories I would like, with your permission, to call "The Blind Man" which I think is a better title than "Tickets Please". The trouble however with the book is that it is too short, making only 250 pages. It would be all right if I could include the Blackwell story "Wintry Peacock", and I should like to know the exact terms on which Blackwell purchased this story, with a view to adding it.
    But, in any case, I want to defer the book of short stories until after I have published the three novelettes which volume I want to call "The Lady Bird". I think it would be inadvisable to follow up the book of short stories with the three novelettes; the sequence "The Lady Bird", "The Blind Man" and your new novel would be preferable.

Secker concluded by lamenting Seltzer's failure to supply him with sheets of *Sea and Sardinia*, thus preventing him from publishing the book in England; he also welcomed the prospect of receiving *Kangaroo* as soon as possible.

thing about these countries is that nobody asks questions. I suppose there have been too many questionable people here in the past. But it's nice not to have to start explaining oneself, as one does in Italy.

The people here are awfully nice, *casually*: thank heaven I need go no further. The township is just a scatter of bungalows, mostly of wood with corrugated iron roofs, and with some quite good shops: 'stores.' It lies back from the sea. Nobody wants to be too near the sea here: only we are on the brink. About two miles inland there is a great long hill like a wall, facing the sea and running all down the coast. This is dark greyish with gum trees, and it has little coal-mines worked into it. The men are mostly coal-miners, so I feel quite at home. The township itself – they never say *village* here – is all haphazard and new, the streets unpaved, the church built of wood. That part is pleasant – the newness. It feels so free. And though it is midwinter, and the shortest day next week, still every day is as sunny as our summer, and the sun is almost as hot as our June. But the nights are cold.

Australia is a weird, big country. It feels so empty and untrodden. The minute the night begins to go down, even the towns, even Sydney, which is huge, begins to feel unreal, as if it were only a daytime imagination, and in the night it did not exist. That is a queer sensation: as if the life here really had never *entered in*: as if it were just sprinkled over, and the land lay untouched. – They are terribly afraid of the Japanese. Practically all Australians, and especially Sydney, feel that once there was any fall in England, so that the Powers could not interfere, Japan would at once walk in and occupy the place. They seriously believe this: say it is even the most obvious thing for Japan to do, as a business proposition. Of course Australia would never be able to defend herself. – It is queer to find these bogeys wherever one goes. But I suppose they *may* materialise. – Labour is very strong, and very stupid. Everything except meat is exorbitantly expensive, many things twice as much as in England. And Australian apples are just as cheap in London as in Australia, and sometimes cheaper. It is all very irritating.

This is the most democratic place I have *ever* been in. And the more I see of democracy the more I dislike it. It just brings everything down to the mere vulgar level of wages and prices, electric light and water closets, and nothing else. You *never* knew anything so nothing, Nichts, Nullus, niente, as the life here. They have good wages, they wear smart boots and the girls all have silk stockings; they fly round on ponies and in buggies – sort of low one-horse traps – and in motor-cars. They are always vaguely and meaninglessly on the go. And it all seems so empty, so *nothing*, it almost makes you sick. They are healthy, and to my thinking almost imbecile. That's what the life in a new country does to you: it makes you so material, so *outward*, that your real inner life and your inner self dies out, and you clatter round like so many mechanical animals. It is very like a Wells story – the fantastic stories. I feel if I lived in Australia for ever I should never open my mouth once to say one word that meant anything. Yet they are very trustful and kind and quite competent in their jobs. There's no need to lock your doors, nobody will come and steal. All the outside life is so *easy*. But there it ends. There's nothing else. The best society in the country are the shop-keepers – nobody is any better than anybody else, and it really *is* democratic. But it all feels so slovenly, slip-shod, rootless, and empty, it is like a kind of dream. – Yet the weird, unawakened country is wonderful – and if one could have had a dozen people, perhaps, and a big piece of land of ones own – But there, one can't. There is this for it, that here one doesn't feel the depression and the tension of Europe. Everything is happy-go-lucky, and one couldn't *fret* about anything if one tried. One just doesn't care. And they are all like that. *Au fond* they don't care a straw about anything: except just their little egos. Nothing *really* matters. But they let the *little* things matter sufficiently to keep the whole show going. In a way it's a relief – a relief from the moral and mental and nervous tension of Europe. But to say the least, it's surprising. I never felt such a foreigner to any people in all my life as I do to these. An absolute foreigner, and I haven't one single word to say to them.

But I am busy doing a novel: with Australia for the setting: a queer show. It goes fairly quickly, so I hope to have it done by August. Then we shall sail via New Zealand and Tahiti for San Francisco, and probably spend the winter in Taos, New Mexico. That is what I think I want to do. Then next spring come to Europe again. – I feel I shall wander for the rest of my days. But I don't care.

I must say this new country has been a surprise to me. Flinders Petrie says new countries are no younger than their parent country. But they are older, more empty, and more devoid of religion or anything that makes for 'quality' in life.

I have got a copy of *Aaron's Rod* for you, but am not sure whether I may post it from here or not. Trade relations with Germany don't start till August.

Write to me c/o Robert Mountsier, 417 West 118 Street. New York. – I wish I had good news of you. Frieda sleeps after her bathe.

D. H. Lawrence

If a girl called Ruth Wheelock sends you a little note I gave her to introduce her to you, I think you'd like her. American, was in the consulate in Palermo – we knew her there and in Rome – both like her.

DHL

She's not got any money, unless she earns some or her father gives her some.

2542. To Earl Brewster, 13 June 1922
Text: MS UT; Brewster 54-7.

'Wyewurk', Thirroul. N. S. W.

13 June 1922

Dear Brewster

I suppose this will eventually reach you. Here we are in a very nice bungalow – 30/- a week – on the very edge of the sea, with a weird new 'township' between us and the dark wall of hills which stands up two miles inland. It is weird, weird country. Of course the people are all you think they are: and less than that. But within 1000 miles there isn't a soul that knows us. I don't present any letter of introduction, and don't intend to. I never knew before how wonderful it was to know absolutely nobody, for a vast distance around one. The tradesmen leave goods in the morning, that is all. Material existence is very easy indeed, the life of the people being *absolutely* external. What else have they to do but make it so. We do everything for ourselves, and not a soul can come to our door.

In a way I am sorry you haven't seen this country. It is extraordinarily subtle, *unknown* country. The gum trees are greyish, with pale trunks – and so often the pale, pure silver dead trees with vivid limbs: then the extraordinary *delicacy* of the air and the blue sky, the weird bits of creek and marsh, dead trees, sand, and very blue hills – it reminds me of Puvis de Chavannes more than any country I have seen:[1] so apparently monotonous, yet when you look into it, such subtly different distances, in layers, and such exquisite forms – trees, flat hills – strange, standing as it were at the *back* of the vision. It needs Japanese treatment – or Puvis. By the way his *Winter* is in Melbourne art gallery. I still hated his self-conscious sentiment and rather snivelling outlook. But love that detaily patterny subtle layering of distances. Only not the foolish human figures – classic remains.

The Glands book came today: also I've got the *Aaron's Rods* from Seltzer – will send you a copy to Cook Geneva if I don't hear from you next mail. I am writing another novel – pitched here in Australia – a weird thing of a novel. I am hoping to get it done by August, as it goes well so far. If I do we shall sail to San Francisco via Tahiti – and go to Taos. You might write c/o Mabel Dodge Sterne, *Taos*, New Mexico. We should arrive in San Francisco on Sept 4th. all being well. Don't write here.

---

[1] Pierre Puvis de Chavannes (1824–98), French painter principally known for his murals which are notable for their absence of depth and their flat areas of colour. Among the murals Puvis executed for public buildings in Paris were *Summer* and *Winter* (1891–2) for the Hôtel de Ville. A replica of *Winter* (painted in 1896) is in the National Gallery of Victoria in Melbourne.

It is winter here – but lovely sunny days. The sun is a lovely creature here. Only the nights are cold. And the sea is marvellous, so big, so many colours, with huge unfolding breakers and an everlastingly folded secret. That's the charm here: the folded secret. This would be a lovely country if one wanted to *withdraw* from the world: really. It has a sustaining magic of its own. – Humanly speaking, of course, it just *is not*.

Well I hope you and Achsah and the child are settled happily somewhere. Frieda is sleeping after bathing. Where shall we meet next?

DHL

Achsah, the *clock* is our only time-piece, the green parrot with red beak stands like the Holy Ghost beside him, along with the red (Nuwara Eliya) candlestick and the brass is quite dazzling. We use your shell butter plate every day: and I find lovely shells here, and if only there was a jeweller he should make you hatpins and buttons out of them. Frieda doesn't finish her Buddha embroidery because she housewifes.

Your little black embroidered *Greek* bag, given in Capri, also hangs on a nail for ornaments – It's a pretty room – and big, big as Ardnaree's big room. Pity you cant come to tea. We bake good cakes and tarts and eat them *all* ourselves. Perhaps that's the most lonely feeling – eating all the cakes oneself.

The living is quite cheap once one is settled in, though things aren't cheap: except, of course, meat, of which you get huge joints thrown at you. The apples *are* good: but the orchards a disappointment as they don't let the trees grow taller than man-high so they can pick them easily. – There are also oranges and lemons, but not like Sicily.

I have had moments of Heimweh for Europe – and for the *glamour* of Ceylon. But in truth I sit easier in my skin here than anywhere. The sea is extraordinary good company, especially when you have firm sands to walk on.

Frieda is making herself a house dress of blue and black stripe flannelette – so blue! Poor Achsah.

I should think we'll be in Europe next spring.

Have you found the tobacco shop yet? I shall be a queer old cove taking snuff by the time I get back to Europe.

2543. To Mabel Dodge Sterne, [19 June 1922]
Text: MS Brill; PC; Postmark, Thirroul 19 JE 22; Luhan 25.

['Wyewurk', Thirroul, New South Wales, Australia]
20 June 1922

I had your letter of May 12th today – and two days ago the *Glands* book. But no sign of the necklace. I suggest you write to the Postmaster, Kandy, and ask where it is, and ask to have it returned. I will write to him also. – Am stuck in my novel – wish we could get away from here in July, but fear I shall have to wait till August for money. – I am sending you a copy of *Aarons Rod* by this post. I asked Seltzer to send you a copy of *Fantasia*. Hope you get it.

D. H. Lawrence

2544. To Thomas Seltzer, 21 June 1922
Text: MS UT; Postmark, Thirroul 21 JE 22; Lacy, *Seltzer* 36–9.

'Wyewurk', *Thirroul*. New South Wales.

21 June 1922

Dear Seltzer

We are planning to sail from Sydney on August 10th by *S.S. Tahiti*, Union Line, arrive in San Francisco on the morning of Sept 4th., all being well. You said you would come and see me as soon as I landed in America. It would be great fun if you could come to San Francisco and meet us: especially if both Mrs Seltzer[1] and you were there. We'd go to some quiet and inexpensive hotel – I see one can easily have a room for $1.25 or $1.50 a day – and we wouldn't tell anybody we were there. Except Mabel Dodge Sterne, and she might posssibly come too. Which we *might* all like: or hate. Anyhow we are pledged to go from San Francisco to Taos. But I don't want *any* strangers to know, or any foolish reporters. Here in N. S. W. not a soul knows about me, I don't present any letters of introduction: and I like that much the best. Before we leave I shall cable you the name of the boat – *Tahiti*, via Wellington and Tahiti, arrives Sept 4th, and *Sonoma*, Oceanic Line, sails Aug 16 and arrives Sept 4th, the same – but not such a nice route. I hope Mountsier will have sent me the dollars to come with. Do ask him if he has.

I have done more than half of the novel: the Lord alone knows what anybody will think of it: no love at all, and attempt at revolution. I do hope I shall be able to finish it: not like *Aaron*, who stuck for two years, and *Mr Noon*, who has been now nearly two years at a full stop. But I think I see my way. Seven weeks today till we sail.

No, I wouldn't like to live always in Australia – unless I'd had enough of the world altogether, and wanted to lose myself. It would be a good place for that. Weird country. Has its fascination.

What fun if we saw you in Frisco.

D. H. Lawrence

I want this to catch the *Niagara*: then you should have it by July 20th.

If I cable the boat to you, be sure and tell Mountsier. Did you ever get the cable from Kandy, 'Sailing Fremantle'? I don't believe you did.

DHL

[1] Adele Seltzer, née Szold (1876–1940).

2545. To Robert Mountsier, [21 June 1922]
Text: MS Smith; Postmark, Thirroul 21 JE 22; Unpublished.

'Wyewurk', Thirroul. New Sth. Wales.

21 June

Dear M[ountsier]

I hope by the time you get this you will have cabled me the money to Sydney: *without* cursing me for the bother.

We still stick to plan of sailing by the *SS Tahiti* on Aug 10. Arrive San Francisco Sept 4th. Seltzer said before he'd come and see me as soon as I landed, so I ask him can't he meet us in San Francisco. For some reason the U.S.A. is the only country in the world that I shrink from and feel shy of: Lord knows why. I'd rather you could have come and met us: always imagined you meeting us in New York. But alas, it costs so much, and I shall have no money left in the Charleroi. Sangue di dio, we never have a sou! Else I'd say take the money from that.

Wonder what we shall think of Mabel Dodge and Taos. If we don't like it, shan't stay more than a fortnight or so.

Done a bit more than half of *Kangaroo* – now slightly stuck. You'll never like it – though there isn't so much as the letter S of sex.

Feel this would be such a good country to disappear into, when one had had enough of the world. It tempts one to disappear.

Frieda just a bit seedy. Change for her. – Wish we wouldn't get two winters.

a riverderci   DHL

2546. To Mabel Dodge Sterne, [21 June 1922]
Text: MS Brill; Luhan 25–6.

[Frieda Lawrence begins]

'Wyewurk', Thirroul, New South Wales

[21 June 1922]

Dear Mabel Dodge,

We are sitting here perched on the Pacific, lovely for that and the air and space but the tin cans and newspapers *flying* all over the *ugly* little town behind are not to be thought of – And quite a nice statue of an 'Anzac'[1] stands at the corner, just like a forgotten milk can, no grass round it or *anything*, only filthy paper flying and a tin cinema show near – I *can not* bear it – except this place alone on the cliff of the sea with a nice big beautiful room and big terraces all round. We are reading the Gland book in turns – I find it interesting, but it always is funny when a man sees salvation in 'glands', they know in 'part' – L[awrence] has written a novel, gone it full tilt at page 305 – but has come to a

---

[1] A soldier in the Australian and New Zealand Army Corps (1914–18).

stop and kicks – I am *glad* to sit still for a little before we start the 24 days to San Francisco, but it will be I hope the jolliest part of the journey – and we are *both* looking forward to Taos, keep us dark at *first* anyhow, but *terribly* dark – We dont know a soul here, rather fun – nobody has 'discovered' L – The necklace must wait till I come to you, I shall be so cross if it is lost – but I am sorry that you had so much bother with it, the post can be so irritating – I looked inside the gland book for the necklace and had a genuine ten minutes disappointment, till I remembered that it *was'nt* with the gland book – with relief. – August the 10th we start: By the way *dont give* us too little a place to live in, we are much too quarrelsome – it's quite fatal – We can afford it nowadays, I mean we are'nt as poor as we used to be – but we must'nt be too much on top of each other or we get on each other's nerves – I cannot really imagine Taos – In spite of pictures – So I shall see it in the 'flesh' soon –

> Every good wish   Frieda Lawrence
the name of this bungalow, it's an 'Australian' joke! we believe, on why work? –

[Lawrence begins]

> June 21.

– We'll get this off by the *Niagara* via Vancouver. I posted you *Aarons Rod* yesterday. Asked Seltzer to send you *Fantasia of the Unconscious* – which should be out. I wrote to Ceylon with very careful instructions to have the necklace returned to you. It *may* turn up here meanwhile: also the notes.

Unless something untoward happens – unless the Consul refuses a visa or my money doesn't come from Mountsier or anything tiresome like that, we should be in Frisco on the morning of Sept 4th. Why don't you come for a trip and meet us? I'll cable you the boat just before we sail. I expect we shall have to go first class on these small boats. Damn steamer fares. – Of course I must pay *rent* for whatever house you let us have. No, not too small, if it can be avoided – the house. We both like to keep sufficiently clear of one another.

> DHL

The address 'Wyewurk', *Thirroul*, New South Wales, is good till August – And *New South Wales* is one word.

2547. To William Siebenhaar, 21 June 1922
Text: TMSC NWU; Unpublished.

> 'Wyewurk', *Thirroul*, Sth. Coast, N.S.W.
> 21 June 1922

Dear Mr. Siebenhaar,

I should have thanked you sooner for all your kindnesses in West Australia, and for the poems and the *Western Mail*,[1] which interested me very much. When it comes to writing poetry, we are at opposite ends of the rope. For me you are too classical – and for you I am afraid I should be just outside the pale. Nevertheless when I get to America I shall send you a copy of one of my vols.

We are here in a cottage on the edge of the Pacific: rather lovely. Australia itself has a weird fascination: but the social side doesn't attract me a bit. I am trying to do a novel: may heaven help me. We think to sail on August 10th. by the boat *Tahiti* to San Francisco. Until then, stay here in this house, which we like, and make excursions around.

I read *Max Havelaar* essay, and found it interesting.[2] But of course it *is* too long for a periodical. But no doubt if there were a revival of interest in the book or its author you would get an editor to publish it – or at least part of it. – easily. If you would care to take the trouble of translating say the first fifty pages of *Max Havelaar*, and would send me the MS., I would submit it to the best publishers in New York, and they could arrange then with you for the book. What New York publishes, London will publish. But you should also find out about the *copyright*, and the previous translations. Probably the copyright has run out by now.

I suppose you are at Darlington a good deal now. Remember us both very kindly to your wife, I hope she enjoys her country cottage.

If you see Miss Skinner, of Leithdale, tell her to send me a line if she has any news of her own work.

With best wishes from us both,

D. H. Lawrence

2548. To Catherine Carswell, 22 June 1922
Text: MS YU; Carswell 167, 168, 169.

Thirroul. Sth Coast. N. S. W.
22 June 1922

My dear Catherine

Camomile came last week – reached me here – the very day I sent you a copy of the American *Aaron's Rod*. I have read *Camomile*, and find it good: slighter than *Open the Door*, but better made. Myself I like that letter-diary form.[3] And I like it because of its drift: that one simply must stand out against the social world, even if one misses 'life'. Much life they have to offer! Those Indian Civil servants are the limit: you should have seen them even in Ceylon: conceit

---

[1] The Christmas number (1897) of *Western Mail* contained his translation of excerpts from *Ongeluckige Voyagie* [*The Voyage and Shipwreck of The 'Batavia' on the Australian Coast*] (Amsterdam, 1648) by E. François Pelsaert (d. 1630). Siebenhaar might have sent a copy to demonstrate his ability as a translator.   [2] See p. 240 n. 2.
[3] The narrator, Ellen Carstairs, tells her autobiographical story through a diary for the benefit of her friend, Ruby Marcus. (The *Times* reviewer, 20 April 1922, found the novel 'disappointing' after Catherine Carswell's first novel, *Open the Door!*)

and imbecility. No, she was well rid of her empty hero, and all he stands for: tin cans. It was sometimes very amusing, and really wonderfully well written. I can see touches of Don (not John, Juan, nor Giovanni, thank goodness) here and there. I hope it will be a success and that it will flourish without being trodden on.

If you want to know what it is to feel the 'correct' social world fizzle to nothing, you should come to Australia. It *is* a weird place. In the *established* sense, it is socially nil. Happy-go-lucky dont-you-bother we're-in-Austrylia. But also there seems to be no inside life of any sort: just a long lapse and drift. A rather fascinating indifference, a *physical* indifference to what we call soul or spirit. It's really a weird show. The country has an extraordinary hoary, weird attraction. As you get used to it, it seems so *old*, as if it has missed all this Semite-Egyptian-Indo-European vast era of history, and was coal age, the age of great ferns and mosses. It hasn't got a consciousness – just none – too far back. A strange effect it has on one. Often I hate it like poison, then again it fascinates me, and the spell of its indifference gets me. I can't quite explain it: as if one resolved back almost to the plant kingdom, before souls, spirits and minds were grown at all: only quite a live, energetic body with a weird face.

The house is an awfully nice bungalow with one *big* room and 3 small bedrooms, then kitchen and washhouse – and a plot of grass – and a low bushy cliff, hardly more than a bank – and the sand and the sea. The Pacific is a lovely ocean, but my, how boomingly crashingly noisy as a rule. Today for the first time it only splashes and rushes, instead of exploding and roaring. We bathe by ourselves – and run in and stand under the shower-bath to wash the *very* seaey water off. The house costs 30/- week, and living about as much as England: only meat cheap.

We think of sailing on Aug 10th. via Wellington and Tahiti to San Francisco – land on Sept 4th. Then go to Taos. Write to me:

c/o Mrs Mabel Dodge Sterne, *Taos*, New Mexico. U.S.A.

– I am doing a novel here – half done it – funny sort of novel where nothing happens and such a lot of things *should* happen. Scene Australia. – Frieda loves it here. But Australia would be a lovely country to lose the world in altogether. I'll go round it once more – the world – and if ever I get back here I'll stay. – I hope the boy is well, and Don flourishing, and you as happy as possible.

DHL

2549. To Anna Jenkins, 30 June 1922
Text: MS WAPL; Priday, *Southerly*, xv (1954), 5–6.

'Wyewurk', Thirroul. Sth Coast. NSW
30 June 1922

Dear Mrs Jenkins

Why not come with us on the *Tahiti* on Aug 10th? Would it be too dear? It costs about £110 I think. It is £60. first and £50 second class to Frisco from Sydney – vice versa – on the *Tahiti* – £60 and £40 on the *Sonoma* (American Line). You can easily go second from New York to England. We thought of going 1st to Frisco because it is a long trip. But you see the Pacific Isles – Raratonga and Tahiti – what fun! Doesn't it tempt you? And even to see Thirroul. Much more fun.

Madame Septcheveux is priceless: Signora Settecapelli: Settecappelli.[1] Those pink legs bowled me over. The corpse of Dorothea wouldn't be so bad, but supposing those pink legs washed up on one's doorstep, years after? And Lady Bareham. Weren't there even seven hairs on the ham?

Frau Drossel – Mrs Throssel V. C. was also rather priceless – an infant son in a newspaper cutting V. C.[2]

Been to Wollongong today: fierce cold wind: blew my hat in the sea, me after it, wave rose, all but washed me away for ever.

How also is the unmarried Mr Bachelor?

D. H. Lawrence

The address when we *do* get to America is:
    c/o Mrs Mabel Dodge Sterne, *Taos*, New Mexico. U. S. A.
Have those letters been an infernal nuisance to you. I am so sorry. I wrote to the postmaster at Perth to send them direct *here*. They are fools to bother you.

2550. To Katharine Throssell, 3 July 1922
Text: MS Throssell; Prichard, *Meanjin*, ix (Summer 1950), 253–4.

'Wyewurk', *Thirroul*. South Coast. N. S. W.
3 July 1922

Dear Mrs Throssell

Your letter, I suppose, means you are up and about and wearing your little V. C. like a medal at your breast. May he be a rosy cross. – I understand you are prouder of that little newspaper clipping than of all the yards you've had before, for books.

I am sorry, really, that we didn't get your husband's letter before we left W[est] A[ustralia]. Don't imagine either that I am bolting as fast as all that from Australia. We're not going till August 10th – and three months in one place isn't so bad. For some things too I love Australia: its weird, far-away natural beauty and its remote, almost coal-age pristine quality. Only it's too far for me. I can't reach so awfully far. Further than Egypt. I feel I slither on

---

[1] Settecapelli (literally 'seven hairs') was identified by Anna Jenkins as William Siebenhaar, author of *Dorothea* (Nehls, ii. 151). And see the final postscript of Letter 2528.
[2] Katharine Throssell had sent DHL a newspaper cutting about her son, Ric's, birth (Nehls, ii. 153) See p. 251 n. 2. and Letter 2550.

the edge of a gulf, reaching to grasp its atmosphere and spirit. It eludes me, and always would. It is too far back. It seems to me that generation after generation must people it with ghosts, and catastrophes water it with blood, before it will come alive with a new day of its own. Too far for me: strains my heart, reaching. But I am very glad to have glimpsed it. And I would dearly have liked to see all the things you told me of. – We went into the Art Galleries at Adelaide and Melbourne. But nobody has *seen* Australia yet: can't be done. It isn't visible. Most nearly Puvis de Chavannes *Winter* at Melbourne – if he weren't so sickeningly affected with his people. But landscape – very Australian – detailed, yet frail and atmospheric. Oh there is a great magic here. But frightens me. (I know Puvis has nothing to do with Australia.)

As for America, I go to it rather with dread, and fully expect to hold my ears and cover my eyes and bolt, as you did. But perhaps not.

Australia seems to me a most marvellous country to disappear into. When one has had enough of the world – when one doesn't want to wrestle with another single thing, humanly – then to come to Australia and wrestle with its Sleeping Beauty terrors. No, just to drift away, and live and forget and expire in Australia. To go away. It is a land where one can go out of life, I feel, the life one gets so sick of.

Do you like *Sons and Lovers* so much? – I am sorry, I don't know your books. But *Sons and Lovers* seems a long way back, to me. They've got a copy of *The Rainbow* in the Perth Literary Institute: or had when I was there.

I hope, when I wander disconsolately back to Australia, you will let me see your son, your books, your husband and your farm. Where is Greenmount? exactly? What do you grow on your land? – My wife wants a little farm more than anything else, she says. But how should I sit still so long?

Yours Sincerely   D. H. Lawrence

2551. To Robert Mountsier, [7 July 1922]
Text: MS Smith; Unpublished.

'Wyewurk', *Thirroul*, N.S.W.
July 7.

Dear M[ountsier]

This man[1] writes to say that he would like to know if I will commit to 'them'

---

[1] DHL wrote to Mountsier on the letter he had received from Giuseppe Prezzolini, Italian agent for the (American) Foreign Press Service. Prezzolini wrote from Rome on 26 May 1922:

Egregio Signore,
   Pochi giorni prima della morte di Giovanni Verga per preghiera del comune amico Edgard Ansel Mowrer, io Le spedii un biglietto di presentazione per il nostro grande de scrittore, del qualo si accingeva a tradurre i *Malavoglia*.

the business of procuring a publisher for the Verga books, or if I was in communication with other publishers. If you want any help, you might write him – G. Prezzolini. Perhaps anyhow just send him a line.

I have only two chapters to add to my novel. I think you'll dislike it and disapprove of it even more than you did of *Aaron*. Can't be helped. – I think I shall post you the MS by the *Makura* on July 20th – sailing to Vancouver. Then you can let us have the typed MS as soon as I get to America.

I shall post this by the *Sonoma* – July 12th – that is if she's still carrying mail. I'll write you again by the *Makura* on the 20th – and that is the last boat before the *Tahiti*. I am now expecting your cable with the money. I saw the Consul in Sydney and the visas will be all right. So the *Tahiti* will be the boat, if your money-cable arrives.

I shall cable Seltzer the one word *Tahiti*, before we sail: also Mabel Dodge the same.

I should like, if I could, to write a New Mexico novel with Indians in it. Wonder if it would be possible.

I don't mind if Verga brings me little money – but get a royalty rather than a sum down.

I *do* want to hear news of everything. No letters from you.

DHL

2552. To S. S. Koteliansky, 9 July 1922
Text: MS BL; Spender, *Encounter*, i (December 1953), 32–3.

'Wyewurk', Thirroul. N.S.W.
9 July 1922

My dear Kot.

I had your letter, and the Bunin book next day. But not the Mrs Tolstoi reminiscences.[1]

> Desidererei ora sapere se Ella ha compiuto la traduzione e se intende affidare a noi la cura di farla pubblicare in America?
> Mi dica pure se Ella fosse in trattative con altri editori e mi creda Suo devato.

[Dear Sir,
   A few days before the death of Giovanni Verga, at the request of our mutual friend Edgar Ansel Mowrer, I sent you a letter of introduction for our great writer, whose *I Malavoglia* you had taken in hand to translate.
   I should now like to know if you have completed the translation and if you intend to entrust to us the task of having it published in America?
   Tell me also if you have entered into negotiations with other publishers, And believe me,
Yours faithfully]

[1] *The Gentleman from San Francisco and Other Stories* (May 1922); *The Autobiography of Countess Sophie Tolstoi*, trans. S. S. Koteliansky and Leonard Woolf (Hogarth Press, June 1922).

What a pretty cover Bunin has! But the tales are not very good: 'Gentleman' is much the best. Some of Wolf's sentences take a bit of reading. Look at the last sentence on p. 71.[1]

You should have had *Sea and Sardinia* and *Aaron's Rod* by now: unless Martin Secker is playing me dodges and not sending out the presentation copies as I asked. – I shall be able to read this famous *Ulysses* when I get to America.[2] I doubt he's a trickster.

We still propose sailing on August 10th. by the *Tahiti*, to San Fancisco: arrive Sept 4th. Send me a line and tell me all the happenings. I heard from a friend in Paris that the Bunin book was noticed in the *Times*.[3] What was the notice like? – I had Cath. Carswell's *Camomile* here: slight, but good, I thought. What are the notices of that? – By the way, don't you think Secker ought to try that *Shestov* again now?[4] You press him about it, and I'll write him too. It would certainly sell some now.

I have nearly finished my novel here – but such a novel! Even the Ulysseans will spit at it.

There is a great fascination in Australia. But for the remains of a fighting conscience, I would stay. One can be so absolutely indifferent to the world one has been previously[5] condemned to. It is rather like falling out of a picture and finding oneself on the floor, with all the gods and men left behind in the picture. If I stayed here six months I should have to stay for ever – there is something so remote and far off and utterly indifferent to our European world, in the very air. I should go a bit further away from Sydney, and go 'bush.' – We don't know one single soul – not a soul comes to the house. And I can't tell you how I like it. I could live like that forever: and drop writing even a letter: sort of come undone from everything. But my conscience tells me not yet. So we go to the States – to stay as long as we feel like it. But to England I do not want to return. – Though no, I don't think you flatter me. I do think I've got more in me than all those fluttering people, good and bad, in London. But they are antipatico. They are distasteful to me.

Write me a line, c/o Mountsier – or else just to *Taos*, New Mexico. U.S.A .

---

[1] 'Perhaps, too, there was in her soul a drop of purely feminine pleasure that here was a man to whom she could give her small commands, with whom she could talk, half seriously and half jokingly as a mentor, with that freedom which their difference in age so naturally allowed – a man who was so devoted to her whole household, in which, however, the first person – this, of course, very soon became clear – was for him, nevertheless, she herself.'

[2] James Joyce's *Ulysses* was published in Paris in February 1922 by Sylvia Beach (Shakespeare and Company).

[3] The reviewer focused almost entirely upon the title story about which he remarked: 'A better translation is hardly possible' (*Times*, 17 May 1922).

[4] Secker published Leon Shestov, *All Things are Possible*, trans. S.S. Koteliansky with a foreword by DHL, in 1920. See *Letters*, iii. 380 n. 3.   [5] previously] henceforth

Greet Grisha and Sonya and the tall Ghita, and starve Fox[1] for one day, for my sake.

Yrs   DHL

2553. To Mabel Dodge Sterne, 9 July 1922
Text: MS Brill; Luhan 27.

'*Wyewurk*', Thirroul. N.S.W.
9 July 1922

Dear Mabel Dodge

Just a word to catch the *Sonoma*, sailing on Wednesday.

I had your cablegram: 'Expecting You.' I am only waiting for Mountsier's cable with my money to engage berths on *The Tahiti*. I was in Sydney, and the Consul will give the visas all right. I'll cable you the word *Tahiti* the day before we sail, if nothing goes wrong: and nothing will go wrong. That will mean we are in San Francisco on September 4th. It would be great fun if you came to meet us, but of course not unless it would amuse you too. Seltzer *might* come.

I have nearly done my novel: *such* a novel. I hope you have *Aaron's Rod*, and *Fantasia*.

I wish we could settle down at – or near – Taos – and have a little place of our own, and a horse to ride. I do wish it might be like that.

I had a note from the Customs – some sort of parcel from the U.S.A. It may be the necklace. There is one more boat sails – to Vancouver – after the *Tahiti*, so I can send you one more note.

Till then.

Yrs   D. H. Lawrence

2554. To Robert Mountsier, 17 July 1922
Text: MS Smith; Postmark, Thirroul 18 JL 22; Unpublished.

'Wyewurk'. Thirroul. New South Wales.
17 July 1922

My dear M[ountsier]

Your second letter from Elizabeth today[2] – dated May 25th. Rather depressing accounts of sales: *Sea and Sardinia* only 685, and *Aaron*, which from your previous letter I had hoped was going well, now not so well. All we can do is to grin and bear it, for the present. I shall still have my day. Don't be too impatient with Seltzer. He may be dodgy, but believe me you'd hate Houghton or Mifflin[3] or Doran worse. I'm sorry they don't think *Mastro-Don*

---

[1] The Farbmans' dog.   [2] I.e. Elizabeth, Pennsylvania.
[3] The two men – Henry Oscar Houghton (1823–95) and George Harrison Mifflin (1845–1921) – had merged their publishing interests as long ago as 1880 to form the Boston publishers, Houghton Mifflin Co.

Gesualdo a profitable spec. But oh damn them and their profitable ventures to everlasting Hell. Basta.

I have packed up the MS. of *Kangaroo* to send it to you by the *Makura*, via Vancouver. She sails on Thursday 20th. I have no doubt you will dislike it very much, and think it worse even than *Aaron*. But again, be patient. I want you to have the MS. typed ready to send to me when I get to America, so that I can go through it again. Also send me all suggestions that occur to you, I want you to do so: only be *patient* even with the things you don't like. Don't post any copy to England. But you are letting Curtis B[rown][1] have copies of the Verga books, aren't you?

I am waiting for the cable for the money. It should be here by now, approximately, if you had my letter by the *Ventura*. I have booked berths on the *Tahiti*. But suddenly I see her advertised date for sailing is changed[2] to August 16th. That means she would not reach San Francisco till Sept 10th. I suppose. When I cable Seltzer I will just say date of arrival – 4th or 10th. But anyhow you could find out from a New York shipping office – the *Tahiti*, Union Line.

Do you hate having to cable more money? Never mind. In America we will really sit still and spend nothing. I wonder if Seltzer will come to San Francisco – Probably not. He too will be getting a bit tired of me if the sales are so small. I believe he does his best. Mabel Dodge may come – with her Indian Tony.[3] A redskin welcome! I want to go to Taos and try it there. If possible, I should like to write an American novel with Indians in it. Vediamo. But of course I tie myself to nothing. We may hate Taos and leave it in a fortnight. As God wills.

I see there is a Railway strike in U.S.A.[4] I believe you will have bad Labour troubles in the next few years, amounting almost to revolution. There must come a break somewhere. – And when there has come a break, then I shall come into my own. As things are, never. Because the 'public' that now is would never like me any more than I like it. And I hate it – the public – the monster with a million worm-like heads. No, gradually I shall call together a choice minority, more fierce and aristocratic in spirit. One cannot hurry these things. Sempre pazienza![5]

There is a great charm in Australia. If it weren't for fighting the world to the last gasp, I would stay here and lapse away from the world into the bush, into Australia. – Frieda says she is determined to have a little farm in America. I am willing, if it comes off.

[1] Curtis B.] Seltzer   [2] changed] suddenly
[3] Antonio ('Tony') Luhan (d. 1963), a Taos Pueblo Indian; he married Mabel Sterne in 1923.
[4] A massive strike by railway shopmen began on 2 July 1922 and lasted until 14 September.
[5] 'Always patience!'

I wonder where we shall see you. You said you would never come to Taos. But I feel we shall see you soon. So auf Wiedersehn.

DHL

I have written to Michael Borg.

It is a wildly windy day, and the Pacific looks like a snow-storm. Australia is in many ways a very attractive country. The people are all simple and easy going and nice – though we don't know anybody – don't want to – prefer it alone.

DHL

2555. To Thomas Seltzer, 18 July 1922
Text: MS UT; Postmark, Thirroul 18 JL 22; Lacy, *Seltzer* 39–40.

'Wyewurk'. Thirroul. New South Wales.
18 July 1922

Dear Seltzer

Just a line to say that the advertised date for the sailing of the *Tahiti* is suddenly changed from August 10th to August 16th. So that if you *were* coming to San Francisco – I don't suppose you are – then I should think our boat would arrive September 10th instead of September 4th. Of course you can always make sure by enquiring at a shipping office – S. S. *Tahiti*, Union Line. New Zealand.

But I am not sure it will be the *Tahiti*, because I haven't got any cable of money yet from Mountsier. I hope it will come soon. They are holding me a cabin on the boat.

I finished *Kangaroo* on Saturday – I don't suppose you'll like it a bit. I heard from Mountsier and he said *Sea and Sardinia* had only sold 685, *Aaron* about 3000. That's few of *S and S*. – I hope *Aaron* will go on selling. Depressing to have such petty sales always. – I must come to America and try and do a novel there, that's all.

tanti Saluti   D. H. Lawrence

This will catch the *Makura* – via Vancouver – last mail before the *Tahiti*.

2556. To Mabel Dodge Sterne, 18 July 1922
Text: MS Brill; Luhan 27–8.

'Wyewurk', Thirroul. New South Wales.
18 July 1922

Dear Mabel Dodge

The notes of Taos and the photographs – very interesting – but not the necklace. F[rieda] laments this. But I wrote urgently about it to Kandy.

I still haven't got the money from Mountsier, so can't finally engage berths. But they are holding cabin no. 4. for me on the *Tahiti*. I see the advertisement

of her sailing has suddenly changed the date from the 10th. to the 16th.
August. If she sails on the 16th then I don't suppose she arrives in San
Francisco till September 10th instead of 4th. I very much want to catch the
Tahiti – have done my novel, and have nothing further to do here. – I wish the
money would come. I'll cable you the date of arrival when we are leaving.

a bientôt   D. H. Lawrence

This will catch the *Makura* via Vancouver: and that is the last boat before
the *Tahiti* – the last mail. We shall stay a couple of days or so in San Francisco
any way: just to look at it.

2557. To Achsah Brewster, 24 July 1922
Text: MS UT; Brewster 57–60.

'Wyewurk'. Thirroul. N. S. W.

24 July 1922

My dear Achsah

Your letter of June 8th from Chexbres today:[1] we had wondered and
wondered where you were – So glad to hear of you rejoicing among the
meadows, instead of shuddering under the zinc roof of Ardnaree. Don't take
either psychoanalysis or glands too seriously: glands are only little wheels in
the working, and complexes are a myth, they don't exist. The gland man
amused me by his crossness more than by his theories. Of course the idea that
you can supply pituitrin and adrenalin and so forth to make a race of supermen
is just as absurd as any other panacea. But he comes a *bit* nearer to the origins of
consciousness. – I hope Seltzer has published and posted to you the *Fantasia
of the Unconscious*, as I asked him to. I will post you *Aaron* today, to Geneva. I
kept you a copy. – Does Earl still moan his Orient? No, I don't. Superficially,
sometimes, I am drawn to its glamour. But when I remember and realise, I feel
sick at the thought of it. No no, the east is not for me. Still I should like one day
to go to the Himalayas, and by Java and Sumatra and China and Japan to San
Francisco. Later.

We are still in our Wyewurk (I told you it was an Australian humorism Why
work?) Australia has a weird and wonderful fascination. I cannot but think
that Earl would have found it a *very* attractive landscape to paint – though no
strong colour: and you would love practising the new notes of gum-trees and
cabbage palms and tree-ferns. The atmosphere is very beautiful, very clear,
yet very frail. – Though it is winter, it has been perfect weather, (hot sun) save
for some cold winds from the mountains – until yesterday, when there came a
gale of wind and rain from the sea, and it is still blowing and splashing, the sea

---

[1] The Brewsters had left Ceylon for Switzerland; they were living e. of Lausanne, near the n.
shore of Lake Geneva.

loud and *hoarse*, like a northern sea. Usually it *booms* – like drums and a rattle of kettle-drums. We are waiting to go to Sydney to engage finally our berths on the *Tahiti*, sailing August 10th. Then September 4th San Francisco, and so to Taos, New Mexico. – I wrote a sort of novel here – short – you won't care for it at all. But this bit of landscape and atmosphere pretty clear. – We haven't known a single soul here – which is really a relief. I feel if I lived all my life in Australia I should never know anybody – though they are all very friendly. But one feels one doesn't want to talk to any of them. – Though there is a great fascination in the country itself: a sort of lure in the bush. One could pass quite out of the world, over the edge of the beyond. But it is just a bit too soon. That's why I go on to America – If I stayed in Australia I should really go bush.[1] But there is still some fight to fight, I suppose. – Frieda finished the Buddha embroidery, and it looks *very* nice: shimmery and silky and pale yellow and pink and pale green. She is now doing the vase of flowers, the background bright blue with wash-blue. Having done my novel I am out of work until we sail – but we have only a fortnight longer here. – I shall be penniless utterly when I get to Taos: but then I shall only be as usual. Why on earth did you send the 8/6 – quite absurd. I even owed Earl Rs. 3. The little 'Big Ben' clock ticks gaily: but alas, we knocked the green parrot off the mantel and he broke.

DHL

I am now going to start learning Spanish, ready for the Mexicans. – Have no news of publishing or anything – till I get to America. – We shine our brass as blatantly as possible – where is yours? No doubt we'll see you in America.

DHL

2558. To Baroness Anna von Richthofen, 31 July 1922

Text: MS Moore; PC v. Bulli Pass, South Coast, N. S. W.; Postmark, [Thirr]oul 31 JL 22; *D. H. Lawrence; An Exhibition of First Editions, Manuscripts, Paintings, Letters, and Miscellany*, ed. Earl Tannenbaum (Carbondale: South Illinois University Library, 1958), pp. 53–4.

['Wyewurk', Thirroul, New South Wales, Australia]
31 Juli 1922

Wir hatten deinen Brief vom 28 Mai Heute. Gestern waren mit Freunden in Auto auf diesem 'Pass', und im Bush: wunderwoll. Die Blumen kommen – Fruhlingsanfang. Wir haben vier verschiedene 'Mimosa' gefunden – alles ist so fremd, so anders. Siehst du im Bild den 'Tree-fern' – Baumfarrenkraut: es gibt sehr viele, und sie sind so hubsch. Wir haben nur zehn Tage mehr – machen die Koffer wieder fertig.

[1] I.e. 'go into the country, leaving the city behind' (with the possible ambiguity of 'going berserk').

Wir haben alle deine Briefe gut erhalten: warum hast du die unsere nicht? Bleib wohl.

DHL

[We had your letter of 28 May today. Yesterday were with friends by motor-car on this 'pass', and in the bush: wonderful. The flowers are coming out – beginning of spring. We found four kinds of 'mimosas' – all is so strange, so different. You see in the picture the 'tree-fern' – Baumfarrenkraut: there are very many, and they are so lovely. We have only ten more days – getting the trunks ready again.

We have received safely all of your letters: why don't you have ours? Keep well.

DHL]

2559. To William Siebenhaar, 2 August 1922
Text: TMSC NWU; Unpublished.

'Wyewurk', *Thirroul*, N.S.W.

2 August 1922.

Dear Mr. Siebenhaar,

I should have answered your letter before, but we have been away. And now next week we leave for good: we sail on the 10th. on the *Tahiti*. I wonder how you got on with Multatuli.[1] My address in America will be

c/o Mrs. Mabel Dodge Sterne, *Taos*, New Mexico, U.S.A.

I suppose we shall stay there a month or two.

We have had such a big storm here, nearly blew the sea out of its hollow. Now it has gone quiet, but the whole foreshore is changed and spoilt.

My wife wishes to be remembered to Mrs. Siebenhaar: I hope things will go pleasantly for you.

Yours Sincerely   D. H. Lawrence

2560. To Katharine Throssell, 6 August 1922
Text: MS Throssell; Prichard, *Meanjin*, ix (Summer 1950), 254.

'Wyewurk.' *Thirroul*. N. S. W.

6 August 1922

Dear Katherine Prichard

Thank you for the books that came two days ago.[2] I am returning the two that have your name in them, and keeping *Black Opal* and *Eyes of Vigilance*,

---

[1] See p. 240 n. 2.

[2] Katharine Prichard recalled sending her own novel, *The Black Opal*; *Eyes of Vigilance* (Melbourne, 1920), a volume of poems by Furnley Maurice (pseudonym of Frank Leslie Thomson Wilmot (1881–1942), Australian poet and manager of the Melbourne University Press); the poems and plays of Louis Esson (1879–1943); and *Songs of Reverie* with music by Henry Tate (1873–1926), Australian composer and musicologist. See Nehls, ii. 154. (DHL makes use of the surname 'Wilmot' in *Kangaroo*, chap. VI.)

though I don't know whether you intend me to have them for good. I have read
the plays and nearly all the poems. The plays seem to me like life, and the
poems are real. But they all make me feel desperately miserable. My, how
hopelessly miserable one *can* feel in Australia: *au fond*. It's a dark country, a
sad country, underneath – like an abyss. Then, when the sky turns frail and
blue again, and the trees against the far-off sky stand out, the glamour, the
unget-at-able glamour! A great fascination, but also a dismal grey terror,
underneath.

We sail on Thursday – 10th.: we are keeping *Black Opal* to read on the ship.
If ever I come back it will be for good.

I am sending you my last novel, though you won't care for it. If ever you
want to send a line: c/o Robert Mountsier, 417 West 118 Street, New York
City is always good. – How is the tiny V. C. of your bosom?

D. H. Lawrence

The immediate address is just *Taos. New Mexico. U.S.A.*

2561. To S. S. Koteliansky, [8 August 1922]

Text: MS BL; PC v. The Main Road, Thirroul, South Coast, N.S.W.; Postmark, Thirroul
8 AU 22; Zytaruk 246.

['Wyewurk', Thirroul, New South Wales, Australia]
8 August. – Tuesday.

Countess Tolstoi came two days ago – have read her – rather sad, and a bit
ridiculous: very interesting. Had your letter too. Hope Secker sent you *Aaron*
as bidden. We are packed up, and go to Sydney tomorrow – sail on Friday.
The sea is lovely and calm – I look forward to the voyage – hope it will be
pleasant. – America will seem much nearer to England – probably we shall be
in London next spring. How do you like the look of Thirroul? The houses are
all wood and tin – but it is nice here, so easy, and sunny. Greet the cave-
dwellers.

DHL

2562. To Else Jaffe, [15 August 1922]

Text: MS Jeffrey; PC v. Guides Pipy and Eileene . . . Whakare-warewa; Postmark,
Wellington 15 AUG 1922; Unpublished.

[Wellington]
15 August.

At the Antipodes – for a day only – on to Raratonga and Tahiti – shall hear
from you in America.

DHL

2563. To Catherine Carswell, [15 August 1922]

Text: MS YU; PC v. Guide Emma, Whakare-warewa; Postmark, Wellington 15 AUG 1922; cited in Moore, *Poste Restante* 67.

Wellington
15 Aug.

Here for a day – on to Raratonga and Tahiti – San Francisco Sept 4. Shall hear from you in America.

DHL

2564. To Ada Clarke, 15 August 1922

Text: MS Clarke; PC v. Mitre Peak, Milford Sound; Postmark, [Welling]ton [. . .]; Lawrence–Gelder 122.

Wellington
15 Aug

Here we are at your antipodes – don't want to stop here though – Sail this afternoon. – are on a nice boat.

DHL

2565. To Katherine Mansfield, [15 August 1922]

Text: MS NZNL; Harry T. Moore, *The Priest of Love* (1974), p. 352.

[Wellington]
[15 August 1922]

[In an undated letter Katherine Mansfield told Middleton Murry: 'I had a card from Lawrence today – just the one word] Ricordi [– how like him. I was glad to get it though.'][1]

2566. To Robert Mountsier, [20 August 1922]

Text: MS Smith; PC v. Aaorangi, Rarotonga; Postmark, Rarotonga 20 AO 22; Unpublished.

[Rarotonga, Cook Islands]
20 August

I hope I shall see you before you get this – here for the day only – Having a good trip, quiet, empty sea: and two Wednesdays in this week, which makes it seem like a year. Next call Tahiti – then Frisco – still feel quaky about America – if I shall like it. F[rieda] very proud because she won the whist drive last night.

DHL

---

[1] The postcard with its one-word message (meaning 'remembrances') was sent to Katherine Mansfield, from her birthplace Wellington, via Lady Ottoline Morrell: see Letter 2703.

2567. To Lady Cynthia Asquith, 20 August 1922
Text: MS UT; PC v. Takuvaine, Rarotonga; Postmark, Rarotonga 20 AO 22; Unpublished.

[Rarotonga, Cook Islands]
20 August 1922

Calling here on the way to Frisco – pleasant wide lonely sea, calm – but of course clash of deck games and entertainments aboard here – gentleman gently practising the Saxophone in the music room – F[rieda] very proud having won the whist drive – wonder where you are for the summer. We call at Tahiti next – then San Francisco – still shy at the idea of America – Travel would be so nice if fewer people travelled – you'd probably hate it – a ship like a big boarding-house staggering over the sea. – Write me a line to America – to *Taos*, New Mexico, U. S. A. – I have no news from England for a long time.
D. H. Lawrence

2568. To Earl Brewster, [20 August 1922]
Text: MS UT; PC v. Avatio Rarotonga; Postmark, [. . .]; Brewster 60.

[Rarotonga, Cook Islands]
20 Aug.

Here for a day – such a lovely island – temple – flowers, great red hibiscus – tropical *almost* but not at all sweltering. Wish you'd come this way.
DHL

2569. To Compton Mackenzie, [20 August 1922]
Text: MS UT; PC v. Rarotonga [Tropical scene]; Postmark, Rarotonga 20 AO 22; Compton Mackenzie, *My Life and Times: Octave Five* (1966), p. 235.

[Rarotonga, Cook Islands]
20 Aug

Calling here for the day – very lovely – Tahiti next – then Frisco. Wonder how you are.
D. H. Lawrence

2570. To Ada Clarke, [20 August 1922]
Text: MS Clarke; PC v. Aaorangi, Rarotonga; Postmark, [. . .]; Lawrence–Gelder 122.

Rarotonga
20 Aug. –

Such a lovely island – calling next at Tahiti – it's really almost as lovely as one expects these South Sea Islands to be.
Love,   DHL

2571. To Bessie Fisher, [22 August 1922]
Text: MS Lazarus; PC v. Tahiti [Tahitian family scene]; Postmark, Papeete 23–8 22; Unpublished.

Tahiti
22 August

Lovely voyage across the Pacific – hot here – staying till tomorrow afternoon – so beautiful to look at, but Papeete spoilt – let us have a word at *Taos*, New Mexico, USA. Hope you had a good summer.
Both greet you.

D. H. Lawrence[1]

2572. To Catherine Carswell, [22 August 1922]
Text: MS YU; PC v. Tahiti, Climbing for and Husking Coconuts; Postmark, Papeete 23–8 22; Carswell 169.

Tahiti –
22 Aug

Here till tomorrow afternoon – beautiful – but Papeete a poor, dull, modernish place.

DHL

2573. To Emily King, [22 August 1922]
Text: MS Needham; PC v. Tahiti, Vaitapika River; Postmark, Papeete 23–8 22; Unpublished.

Tahiti.
22 Aug

Staying here till tomorrow afternoon – such a lovely sea and land – but the town all spoilt – hot enough too.

Love   DHL

2574. To Ada Clarke, [22 August 1922]
Text: MS Moore; PC v. Tahiti, A Tahitian; Postmark, Papeete 23–8 22; Lawrence–Gelder 123.

Tahiti.
22 Aug

Sail on tomorrow afternoon – hot – lovely island – but town spoilt – don't really want to stay. But having a very good trip.

love   DHL

[1] A postscript in an unknown hand reads: 'Saluti tanti al Postino Salvatore' ('Many greetings to Postman Salvatore').

2575. To Compton Mackenzie, [22? August 1922]
Text: Mackenzie, *My Life and Times: Octave Five*, p. 235.

[Tahiti]
[22? August 1922]

If you are thinking of coming here don't. The people are brown and soft.
DHL

2576. To Robert Mountsier, [22 August 1922]
Text: MS Smith; PC v. Tahiti, The Fisherman's Home; Postmark, Papeete 23–8 22;
Unpublished.

Tahiti
22 Aug

Stay till tomorrow afternoon – lovely – but Papeete disappointing – dead, dull, modern, French and Chinese.

DHL

2577. To Mary Cannan, 31 August 1922
Text: MS Lazarus; Moore 713–4.

[R.M.S. Tahiti][1]
31 August 1922

My dear Mary
Well here we are after 21 days on board this ship – everybody getting very nervy and on edge. We were a day at Rarotonga and two days at Tahiti: very pretty to look at, but I didn't want to stay, not one bit. Papeete is a poor sort of place, mostly Chinese, natives in European clothes, and fat. We motored out – again beautiful to look at, but I never want to *stay* in the tropics. There is a sort of sickliness about them, smell of cocoa-nut oil and sort of palm-tree, reptile nausea. But lovely flowers, especially Rarotonga. These are supposed to be the earthly paradises: these South Sea Isles. You can have 'em.
We get to San Francisco on Monday morning, and I shall be glad. We're about 60 passengers in the first saloon – mostly quite nice, but one simply aches to be alone, away from them all. Imagine 25 days confined with 60 Australians, New Zealanders, Americans, and French – never able to get away from them. You'd simply hate it. To be alone, and to be still, is always one of the greatest blessings. The more one sees of people, the more one feels it isn't worth while. Better sit quite still in one's own room, and possess one's own soul. Travel seems to me a splendid lesson in disillusion – chiefly that. We've had always beautiful weather, smooth seas, have neither of us ever felt ill –

[1] DHL used the ship's headed notepaper.

only ship-weary, one gets. At Tahiti we took on a Crowd of cinema people who have been making a film 'Captain Blackbird.'[1] They are rather like successful shop-girls, and the men like any sort of men at the sea-side. Utterly undistinguished. That's how it all is – so undistinguished, so common.

I wonder how long we shall stay in America. Thank heaven Mountsier sold me a story for $1000.[2] So I can come on if I want. Thank heaven it won't be New York. I expect we shall stay a few days in San Francisco, and perhaps look at the Yosemite Valley. But you can believe that sights don't mean much to me. Thank heaven Taos is a tiny village.

I feel almost sure we shall come on to England in the spring. Then we shall see you. So far, I like Taormina as well as anything I have seen: we may go back there. But after shifting so much one just longs to sit still in some remote place of one's own. Nothing so uninspiring as one of these ships. F[rieda] sends love – shall look for a letter from you.

DHL

2578. To Robert Mountsier, 4 September 1922
Text: MS Smith; Telegram; Unpublished.

San Francisco
4 September 1922

Robert Mountsier
Arrived penniless telegraph draft care Palace Hotel San Francisco.

Lawrence[3]

2579. To Mabel Dodge Sterne, [4 September 1922]
Text: MS Brill; Luhan 28.

[Palace Hotel, San Francisco][4]
Monday

Dear Mabel Dodge
I had your letter and telegram on board – sounds perfectly lovely – very many thanks. The General Post Office is shut today so I can't get the other

[1] 'Captain Blackbird' was a working title for the melodrama *Lost and Found On A South Sea Island* by Goldwyn Pictures (February 1923), directed by R. A. Walsh. The cast included House Peters (Captain Blackbird), Pauline Stark, Antonio Moreno, Mary Jane Irving, Rosemary Theby, George Siegmann, William V. Mong, Carl Harbaugh, David Wing. In the film, Captain Blackbird goes to Pago Pago where, after a series of complications, he and his men rescue his daughter from warring natives.
[2] 'The Captain's Doll' was sold to *Hearst's International* (see Letter 2600) although the magazine later released it (see Letter 2723). DHL credits Mountsier with the initiative; Seltzer, writing to Mountsier, 22 June 1922, claimed that he had effected the sale (Lacy, *Seltzer* 225, 226, 228).
[3] An undated draft in Mountsier's hand of what appears to be the text of a telegram in response to DHL's urgent plea reads as follows (MS Smith): D H. Lawrence, Palace Hotel, San Francisco.
   Call at Western Union office nearest your hotel for hundred dollars telegraphed you this morning. If you need more before letter containing four hundred reaches you telegraph me care Walker, Elizabeth, Pennsylvania.
[4] Here, and for the next letter, DHL used the hotel's headed notepaper.

letter till tomorrow. And I can't telegraph you our day for arrival in Lamy because once more, like an ass I spent all my money and arrive here with less than $20, so must wait till Mountsier wires me some. I have telegraphed to him already. There is money in the bank.

I think we shall leave *Thursday* – perhaps even Wednesday. I thought of stopping off at Yosemite Valley but feel – oh damn scenery. So intend to come straight to Lamy.

Shall telegraph you immediately I am fixed up – tomorrow, I fondly hope. And we ought to be with you by Saturday. It sounds all so delightful.

Tante belle cose di noi due.[1]

D. H. Lawrence

2580. To Baroness Anna von Richthofen, 5 September 1922
Text: MS UCB; Frieda Lawrence 169.

[Palace Hotel, San Francisco]
5 September 1922

Liebe Schwiegermutter

Wir sind gestern angekommen – die Reise war immer gut. Jetzt sitzen wir hier im Palace Hotel: das erste Hotel von San Francisco, war erst nur eine Eisenhütte wo die Ochsenwagen einmal abspannten: jetzt ein grosses Gebäude mit Post und Laden drinnen, wie eine kleine Stadt in sich selber: kostet sehr viel, aber für ein paar Tage es macht nicht. Wir waren 25 Tage auf dem Meer und sind immer noch Landkrank – der Boden sollen auf und hin gehen, das Zimmer soll von den Maschinen zittern, das Wasser soll herumrauschen – und tut es nicht. So ist man Landkrank, der feste Boden tut beinah weh. – Wir haben viele Schiffsfreunde hier, sind noch eine freundliche Kompagnie.

Ich meine, wir fahren Dienstag oder Freitag nach Taos: zwei Tage im Zug, und 100 Km. im Auto. Wier haben so nette Briefe und Telegrammen von Mabel Dodge Sterne und von Mountsier: die Mabel Dodge sagt: 'Als Sie aus San Francisco fahren sind Sie meine Gäste: so schick ich Ihnen die Eisenbahn Fahrkarten.' So Americanisch! – Alle sind sehr nett, alles sehr *bequem*: bequem, bequem. Ich hasse wirklich diesen Mechanischen *Comfort*.

Ich schicke dir thirty[2] dollars: ich habe keine Englische 'cheques' bis ich nach Taos komme. Nachher schick ich Englisches Geld: aber besser ein bisschen zu einemal, wenn die Valuta immer steigt. – Braucht die Else auch vielleicht etwas Geld? – Ich weiss noch nicht was ich habe – aber in Taos wird unser Leben beinah nichts kosten: Hausfrei, holzfrei – –

Bleibe wohl, schwiegermutter – ich warte auf deine Nachrichten.

DHL

[1] 'Very best regards from both of us.'   [2] thirty] zwanzig

[Dear Schwiegermutter

We arrived yesterday – that journey was good all the way. Now we sit here in the Palace Hotel: the first hotel of San Francisco, was first only a corrugated iron hut where the ox-wagons once unhitched: now a great building with post and shops in it, like a little town in itself: costs very much, but for a couple of days it doesn't matter. We were 25 days at sea and are still landsick – the floor should go up and down, the room should tremble from the engines, the water should swish round about – and doesn't. So one is landsick, the solid ground almost hurts. – We have many shipboard friends here, are still a friendly company.

I think we'll go Tuesday or Friday to Taos: two days by train, and 100 km. by motorcar. We have such nice letters and telegrams from Mabel Dodge Sterne and from Mountsier: Mabel Dodge says: 'When you leave San Francisco you are my guests: so I am sending you the railway tickets.' So American! – Everybody is very nice, everything very *comfortable*: comfortable, comfortable. I really hate this mechanical *comfort*.

I send you thirty dollars: I have no English 'cheques' till I get to Taos. Afterwards I'll send you English money: but better a little at a time, if the exchange keeps rising. – Does Else perhaps need some money too? – I don't know yet what I've got – but in Taos our life will cost next to nothing: house free, wood free – –

Keep well, schwiegermutter – I wait for your news.

DHL]

2581. To Robert Mountsier, 5 September 1922
Text: MS Smith; Telegram; Unpublished.

San Francisco
Sept 5, 1922

Received money many thanks leave here Saturday.

Lawrence

2582. To Margaret King, [5 September 1922]
Text: MS Ascherman; PC v. Seals on the Rocks, near Cliff House, San Francisco; Postmark, [. . .] 1922; Unpublished.

[Palace Hotel, San Francisco]
5 Sept.

Arrived yesterday – motored round the town and saw these seals this afternoon – it's a fine town but a bit dazing – we leave Friday for Taos – expect letters there.

DHL

2583. To Robert Mountsier, 6 September 1922
Text: MS Smith; Postmark, San Francisco SEP 6 1922; Unpublished.

[Palace Hotel, San Francisco][1]

6 Sept 1922

Dear M[ountsier]

Well, here I am in America – San Francisco very pleasant, and not at all overwhelming, except rather expensive: in fact, *very*, according to my mere European idea. We have a room here for $7. a day, but eat out quite moderately. But I don't like dollars and bits and dimes and nickels: one starts too big. – It is sunny and nice, and we've gone an automobile trip round the city. There is still a *bit* of Bret Harte – R.L. Stevenson unfinished 'West' about it: not much.[2] Terrible the noise of *iron* all the while, breaks my head: and the black, glossy streets with steel rails in ribbons like the path of death itself.[3] Terrifying, that is. But night, with great masses and bunches of light, and lights splashing and starring and running up and down and round about, bewildering, beautiful too, a sort of never-stop Hades. I went to a cinema and with jazz orchestra and a huge and voluminous organ. Either it is all crazy or I am going.

We leave Friday night for Taos. I simply daren't stop off at Yosemite or Grand Cañon: feel I might drop dead if any more stupendousness assails me. I may gain courage later. Mabel Dodge meets us at Lamy and motors us thence. She has the house all ready, sounds very nice, really. You must take back your word and come there: to Taos. Though I believe we stop a day or so with her at Alice Corbin Henderson's house in Santa Fe.[4] She sent a cutting about *Women in Love* suppressed[5] – *so*! – I haven't heard a word from Seltzer – not a sign. What's got him? Tomorrow I want to go up Mt. Tamalpais and be a Moses on Pisgah.[6] hope to find your mail at post office tomorrow: I got Mabel Dodge's. F[rieda] quite happy here: we have boat friends in all the hotels.

a rivederci   DHL

---

[1] Here, and in Letters 2587–9, DHL used the hotel's headed notepaper.
[2] Francis Brett Harte (1836–1902) worked as a journalist in San Francisco as well as writing stories remembered for their humorous portrayal of the West, its thieves and outcasts more than its conventional inhabitants. Robert Louis Stevenson (1850–94), Scottish novelist, poet and essayist, who published his recollections of California, *The Silverado Squatters* (1883).
[3] Reference to the trolleys and cable cars in San Francisco.
[4] Alice Corbin Henderson (1881–1949), American poet and editor who founded *Poetry* magazine with Harriet Monroe and was its associate editor from 1912–16. Author of *The Spinning Woman of the Sky* (1912), *Red Earth* (1920), and co-editor with Harriet Monroe of *The New Poetry: An Anthology* (New York, 1917) in which DHL's poem 'Grief' appeared. m. 1905, William Penhallen Henderson (1877–1943), American painter and architect.
[5] See Letters 2587 n. 1, 2597 and 2608.   [6] See Deuteronomy xxxiv. 1.

2584. To Robert Mountsier, 7 September 1922
Text: MS Smith; Telegram; Unpublished.

San Francisco
Sept 7 1922

Leave tomorrow night mail not arrived telegraph hundred dollars.

Lawrence

2585. To S. S. Koteliansky, [8 September 1922]
Text: MS BL; PC v. Old Chinatown, San Francisco; Postmark, San Francisco SEP 8 1922; Zytaruk 247.

[Palace Hotel, San Francisco]
8 Sept.

Been here a day or two – sunny, hot, noisy, but not unpleasant. Leave tonight for Santa Fe – will write properly from Taos, where I expect my mail.
Greet everybody.

DHL

2586. To Catherine Carswell, 8 September 1922
Text: MS YU; PC v. Street Flower Venders, San Francisco; Postmark, San Francisco SEP 8 1922; cited in Carswell 169.

[Palace Hotel, San Francisco]
8 Sept.

Been here a few days – quite pleasant, but very noisy and iron-clanking and expensive – we leave tonight for Santa Fe: I will write you from Taos, where I expect my mail.

DHL

2587. To Amy Lowell, 8 September 1922
Text: MS HU; Damon 621.

[Palace Hotel, San Francisco]
8 Sept. 1922

Dear Amy
    Well here I am under the Star-spangled Banner – though perhaps the Stripes of persecution are more appropriate.
    San Francisco is sunny and pleasant, though noisy and full of the sound of iron. We leave tonight for Santa Fe. Send me a line,
        c/o Mrs Mabel Sterne, *Taos*, New Mexico

– to tell me how you are: unless of course the new prosecution of *Women in Love* makes you feel that least said soonest mended.¹

We still feel a bit dazed after the long trip across the Pacific. Will take me some time in a little quiet place to myself to gather together the me that is me. Pour tous les autres, je m'en fiche.²

Greet Mrs Russell. Frieda sends her Wiedersehen.

D. H. Lawrence

2588. To Thomas Seltzer, 8 September 1922
Text: MS UT; Postmark, San Francisco SEP 8 1922; Lacy, *Seltzer* 40.

[Palace Hotel, San Francisco]
8 Sept 1922

Dear Seltzer

Here we are in the land of the free; sunny and warm out here, and less strenuous than I imagined, though very iron-noisy.

I thought I should have had a word from you – but there is nothing. Mountsier said he telegraphed to you. The mail is late, so we are going on without it; we leave tonight for Santa Fe, meet Mabel Dodge there. She sent me a cutting about suppression of *Women in Love*. Pfui! – But I haven't had any real news for ages. – I shall be glad to hear from you and to know what is happening. Apparently I have arrived in the land of the free at a crucial moment.

Yrs   D. H. Lawrence

2589. To Robert Mountsier, 8 September 1922
Text: MS Smith; Postmark, San Francisco SEP 8 1922; Unpublished.

[Palace Hotel, San Francisco]
Friday evening. 8 Sept. 1922

Dear M[ountsier]

I got the second $100 this morning – good job I did, for the mail hasn't

---

¹ Amy Lowell replied on 16 September (Damon 621–2) and commented on this remark: 'Are you really such a silly fellow as to suppose that the suppression of "Women in Love" can make a difference to me? I think "Women in Love" one of your very finest books, and this suppression business makes me sick. Everybody knows that I am one of your chief champions in this country . . .' The incident relating to the novel was the seizure from Seltzer's office in July of *Women in Love*, together with Arthur Schnitzler's *Casanova's Homecoming* (1922) and the anonymous *A Young Girl's Diary* with a foreword by Freud (1921), by John S. Sumner, Secretary of the New York Society for the Suppression of Vice. Sumner proceeded to take out a prosecution against Seltzer but a New York magistrate decided against him in September. (See G. T. Tanselle, 'The Thomas Seltzer Imprint', *Papers of the Bibliographical Society of America*, lviii, 1964, 394–6.)

² 'For all the others, I don't care.'

arrived and won't come today. I left the address for it to follow me to Taos. Apparently there is a delay.

I am glad to be going into a bit of quiet. One feels quite dazed, dragged over all this space of distance.

Not a word from Seltzer. Is he having prosecution troubles? – is that it? Very welcoming telegrams from Mabel Dodge. – We leave tonight on the 8.0 o'clock train direct, and arrive Sunday afternoon. Mabel Dodge motors us from Lamy.

I'm sorry I get no letters, no news – but I expect there is nothing cheering to hear.

a riverderci   DHL

2590. To Johanna von Schreibershofen, [12 September 1922]
Text: MS UCB; PC v. The Church, Pueblo of Laguna; Postmark [. . .]; Unpublished.

Taos.
12 Sept

Unsere Freundin hat uns gestern hier gebracht, 100 Km im Auto über die hohe Wüste. Wir haben ein sehr schönes *Adobe* Haus – in der Nähe ein Berg, die Wüste herum. Aber wir sind noch nicht da – es ist zu weit.

DHL

[Our woman friend brought us here yesterday, 100 km by motorcar over the high desert. We have a very pretty *adobe* house – nearby a mountain, the desert around about. But we are still not here – it's too far.

DHL]

2591. To Baroness Anna von Richthofen, [12 September 1922]
Text: UTul; PC v. Pueblo of San Juan North of Santa Fe N. M.; Postmark, Taos SEP 14 1922; Unpublished.

Taos.
12 Sept.

Wir kamen gestern mit Mabel Dodge Sterne 100 Km. über die wüste – sehr schön – und sind jetzt in dem feinsten neuen *Adobe* Haus – nein, so fein waren wir nimmer. Wir hatten heut Morgan deine zwei Briefe, auch einen Brief von Else. Traurig ist Deutschland – Taus ist über 2000 Meter hoch – die Sonne noch heiss – Tausende Grüsse.

DHL

[We came yesterday with Mabel Dodge Sterne 100 km. over the desert – very beautiful – and are now in the finest new *adobe* house – no, so fine we've never been. We had this morning your two letters, also a letter from Else. Sad is Germany – Taos is over 2000 metres high – the sun still hot – Thousands of greetings.

DHL]

2592. To Margaret King, [12 September 1922]
Text: MS Ascherman; PC v. A Mirage on the Arizona Desert; Postmark, Taos SEP 14 1922; Unpublished.

Taos.

12 Sept

We arrived here yesterday – motored 75 miles over the desert from Santa Fe. This place is 7000 ft. up – wonderful. Expect letters from you.

DHL

2593. To Earl Brewster, [12 September 1922]
Text: MS UT; PC v. An Indian Mother; Postmark, Taos SEP 14 1922; Brewster 60.

Taos.

12 Sept.

We got here yesterday – found your letter and Achsah's – glad you liked *Aaron* – You seem to be still pining for the east. It is wonderful here – we drove 75 miles across the desert from Santa Fe – but you couldn't paint it.

I'm still dazed and vague – will write soon.

DHL

2594. To Thomas Seltzer, [12 September 1922]
Text: MS UT; Postmark, [. . .] SEP [. . .] 1922; Lacy, *Seltzer* 41.

[Taos, New Mexico][1]

12 Sept

Dear Seltzer

I found here your letters to Australia, sent after me, but no other sign of you. I do hope you weren't intending to go to San Francisco.

Mabel Dodge met us at Lamy and brought us here – 75 miles across a really wonderful desert. She has built us this summer this lovely adobe house, and

---

[1] Here and on several occasions later (e.g. Letters 2595, 2607, 2622, 2639), DHL used printed notepaper headed 'Las Cruzes, Taos, New Mexico'; its significance is unknown.

made it so beautiful. Really we are quite overwhelmed. But you must come here. You can get a stage automobile from Santa Fe.

It is high up, 7000 feet, so I am just feeling a bit dizzy and sleepy, and feel as if my own self were trailing after me like a trail of smoke, some of it still in Australia. How much of me is here I don't know – just the clockwork.

Well I shall be glad to know at least where you are, and how.

D. H. Lawrence

Received telegram – hurray!

DHL[1]

2595. To Robert Mountsier, [12 September 1922]
Text: MS Smith; Postmark, Ta[os] SEP 14 1922; Unpublished.

[Taos, New Mexico]
Tuesday. 12 Sept

Dear M[ountsier]

We got here last night – 75 miles very bumpy drive across the desert – but very impressive. Mabel Dodge is very nice – we are in a bran new 'dobe house, *very* delightful, just on the Indian Reservation. She has done it all most beautifully for us – really beautiful – 4 good big rooms and a kitchen – you must come and see. She built the house for us, but in Tony's name[2] – Tony is the Indian 'husband' – nice too, but silent. Of course as yet we are chiefly bewildered: and dazed: you know it is 7,000 ft. up, and I'm not yet at the altitude.

I have your letter with the German letters enclosed:[3] but nothing yet from San Francisco forwarded: and no sign from Seltzer.

Did you ever get *Kangaroo*? – No mention of it from you.

More anon, when I know where I am.

DHL

Of course M. D. lives 200 yards away – she's a sort of queen with various houses scattered round; and dependants.

Shall I just ask them at the bank to cash Charleroi cheques.

About how much credit have I at the Charleroi bank – roughly? – I must send something to Germany.

[1] DHL wrote his postscript on the verso of the envelope.
[2] The house where DHL stayed was always known as 'Tony's house'. See Letter 2661.
[3] The enclosures cannot be identified.

2596. To Robert Mountsier, [c. 12 September 1922]
Text: MS Smith; Unpublished.

[Taos, New Mexico]
[c. 12 September 1922][1]

Wrote these people that *I* was willing but they must settle with you and Curtis [Brown].

DHL

2597. To S. S. Koteliansky, 18 September 1922
Text: MS BL; Postmark, Taos SEP 20 [. . .]; cited in Gransden 29.

Taos. New Mexico. U.S.A.
18 Sept 1922

My dear Kot.

I have your letter. We arrived in Taos from San Francisco on the 11th. – but Mabel Sterne immediately sent me motoring off to an Apache gathering 120 miles away across desert and through cañons. Weird to see these Red Indians – the Apaches are not very *sympatisch*, but their camp, tents, horses, lake – very picturesque. This is high tableland desert country, 6000 ft. up: and then mountains near. Mabel Sterne, who is a rich American woman, lends us this new and very charming *adobe* house which she built for us: because she wants me to *write* this country up. God knows if I shall. America is more or less as I expected: shove or be shoved. But still it has a bigness, a sense of space, and a certain sense of rough freedom, which I like. I dread the pettyfogging narrowness of England. Still, I think to come on in the spring. It is still hot, sunny here, like summer.

I am so sorry you are ill and forlorn in the cave. I wish you could come out.

If Secker hasn't sent you a copy of *Aaron*, it is because he is a nasty little fellow. – I think the book sells pretty well here. Seltzer had a 'suppression' trial – *Women in Love*, and Schnitzler and *Young Girl's Diary* – and he won with triumph. So he telegraphs. I believe I have got £500. in the bank, so if you

---

[1] Edward O'Brien and John Cournos wrote to DHL from England on 23 June 1922 asking for permission to include 'The Horse-Dealer's Daughter' in *The Best British Short Stories* for 1923. The letter was sent care of J. B. Pinker and must have been forwarded to Australia where DHL then was. It is improbable that he received the letter in Australia, and the first mail forwarded from Australia was received by DHL on 12 September 1922 in Taos. Hence his letter to O'Brien and Cournos (which is missing), and this letter, must have been written from Taos, probably in September 1922.

Edward Joseph Harrington O'Brien (1890–1941) was an American author and editor; John Cournos (1881–1966) was a Russian-born author, editor and autobiographer who had lived in Philadelphia but now lived in London. The two men included DHL's story in *The Best British Short Stories of 1923* which they edited (and published in January 1924).

want any, I hope you'll say. Say if you are hard up. I have taken money from you and not felt in any way constrained, so surely you can do the same with me. – I am paying back at last the little bit that Eddie Marsh and Ottoline once gave me: so long ago.[1] – If you are short of money, just say 'Yes, I am hard up.'

I will write again very soon. Letters should not take more than a fortnight now. This is not so far away: but 30 miles from the railway, over the desert. Hang on, and don't let them get you under.

DHL

2598. To Edward Marsh, 18 September 1922
Text: MS NYPL; Unpublished.

Taos. New Mexico. U. S. A.
18 Sept. 1922

Dear Eddie

Thank you for the *G[eorgian] P[oetry]* cheque.[2] We at last have come to rest for a moment here high in the desert middle of nowhere. I think to stay here the winter.

I have meant and meant to send you that £20. which you so nobly lent me long ago.[3] But you know me and my finances. But I enclose the cheque, and very many thanks.

I just got back from motoring many miles through desert and cañons to the Apache dance. There they were, the Redskins, in their tents, with barking dogs and a lake near by. The world is a weird place.

Many greetings to you from us both.

Yrs   D. H. Lawrence

P. S. Of course do include 'Snake' in *G. P.*[4] – I got both your letters *today* only.

2599. To Thomas Seltzer, 19 September 1922
Text: MS UT; Postmark, Taos SEP 20 1922; Lacy, *Seltzer* 41–2.

Taos. New Mexico.
19 Sept. 1922

Dear Seltzer

At last I have your letter. I am glad you won that case:[5] now you ought to be able to go freely ahead.

---

[1] See the Letter following and Letter 2609.
[2] For royalties from *Georgian Poetry 1911–1912* (1912) and *Georgian Poetry 1913–1915* (1915).
[3] Marsh sent £20 to DHL in November 1915 (*Letters*, ii. 432).
[4] 'Snake' appeared in the *Dial*, xxi (July 1921), 19–21, before being included in *Georgian Poetry 1920–1922* (December 1922).   [5] See p. 292 n. 1.

Amy is just a cupboard that loves itself. I'm glad that by sheer intuition I gave her a few slaps last time I wrote her. She goes off my list now.

I am very anxious to see *Fantasia*.

I am sorry Mountsier and you have come to daggers drawn. Or perhaps it is just as well to fight a bit. Anyhow I'll leave it to you to fight it out, because truly I know nothing about it. Mountsier doesn't tell me. And you see I've got to be friends with both of you. For my part, I think you have stuck up for me well, as a publisher, and I want us to be on good terms. We must meet and have a talk and pour a little oil of laughter on the troubled waters. Won't you run over here? Mabel Sterne will lend you a studio. She is very nice and has a good opinion of you.

I have a letter from Secker very angry, apparently, about not getting sheets of *Sea and Sardinia*. What about that? Also informing me he is doing the three novelettes under title *Ladybird first*, soon, before he does the book of short stories.[1] That must be seen to. I have written him and Curtis Brown. I wonder if I'll get a novel out of here? It would be interesting if I could.

I wait a letter with more news of the 'case' from you.

                                          Yrs   D. H. Lawrence

I was away five days motoring into the Apache country to see a dance – Indian:[2] so I am still strange here, not orienté. The place is 6000 ft. high, and takes a bit of getting used to: makes me feel dazed. I expect Mountsier will be coming over to see me – you won't have to be here both at the same time, or blood might flow. – You take the stage motor-car from Santa Fe.

2600. To Martin Secker, 19 September 1922
Text: MS UInd; Postmark, Taos SEP 20 1922; Huxley 550–1.

                                          Taos. New Mexico
                                          19 Sept. 1922

Dear Secker

We got here last week – and since then I have been away motoring for five days into the Apache country to see an Apache dance. It is a weird country, and I feel a great stranger still.

I have your letter of July 25. Mountsier says *he* is trying to publish *Ladybird* here, and that the book must by no means appear in England before it is settled. I got $1000 from *Hearsts* for 'Captains Doll' – for the *International*.

---

[1] See pp. 107 n. 7 and 144 n. 6.
[2] The dance took place at the Jicarilla Apache Reservation. See DHL's essay 'Indians and an Englishman', *Dial* lxxiv (February 1923), 144–52 and *Adelphi* (November 1923), reprinted in *Phoenix* 92–9.

And it is this kind of money I have to live on. England makes me about £120 a year; if I got no more than that I should have to whistle my way across the globe. Therefore America must have the first consideration. On the English crust I could but starve, now as ever.

I finished *Kangaroo* and wait for Mountsier to send me the typescript. Then I'll revise it and let Curtis Brown have it.

Since last Christmas Curtis has paid less than £100. into my bank for me. Well, if that is all England cares about my books, I don't care if England never sees them.

Of course I know it's not your fault – and that it is thin rations for you as well as for me. But I can't help it. If America will accept me and England wont, I belong to America.

I might do you another short story to fill up your 'Blind Man' book.[1] Seltzer is calling it *England my England*. Let me know about this.

Do send me all the news. How is Compton Mackenzie? Send me news of him.

Yrs   D. H. Lawrence

Seltzer is just bringing out *Fantasia of the Unconscious* – and the short stories next month.

I am angry about *Sea and Sardinia* and Seltzer.[2]

Tell me, do you ever intend to print *The Rainbow* again, or don't you? – You heard of Seltzers 'suppression' victory over here. He is coming out at once with a three dollar edition of *Women in Love*. I heard from London that the book was out of print there. *Is that so?*

Will you please send a copy of *Women in Love* to

Mrs Dorothy Larking,[3] Villa Primerose, *Juan les Pins*, Alpes Maritimes, France.

Did you send copies of *Aaron* to my sisters:

Mrs L. A. Clarke, Grosvenor Rd, Ripley near Derby.

Mrs S. King, 480 Main St., Carlton nr Nottingham.

If not please do – though I didn't intend them to have it. And did you send Koteliansky a copy – please do that – 5 Acacia Rd. N. W. 8.

---

[1] See p. 262 n. 1

[2] Secker's own irritation at his failure to persuade Seltzer to come to terms over an English edition of *Sea and Sardinia* is evident in several letters in the Secker Letter-Book from February 1922 onwards.

[3] Wife of Capt. Dennis A. H. Larking (1876–1970), R.N. retd, who was Naval Attaché in Rome in 1919. The connection with DHL is not known.

2601. To Robert Mountsier, 19 September 1922
Text: MS Smith; Postmark, Taos SEP 23 1922; Unpublished.

Taos. New Mexico.
Tuesday. 19 Sept. 1922

Dear M[ountsier]

I was away five days motoring to the Apache country to see an Indian dance. Very interesting – Mabel Dodge very generous.

All the letters have come on from San Francisco. The drafts I shall deposit in bank here, to be going on with.

I had a telegram and a short letter from Seltzer about his 'Victory'. He complains that you sent him an ultimatum, and that you insist that copyrights shall be made in *my* name.[1] What about this? – I will be quite wary with him. But do you be patient, don't gall him too much.

Send me *Kangaroo* to revise. It won't serialise. – You see Secker is doing the *Ladybird* book first. What about it? Did you have *Novelle Rusticane* typed? If so will you send a copy to Curtis Brown, because Basil Blackwell, Oxford, wants to see the Verga books.[2]

I won't write more for the moment.

DHL

It is very pleasant here. I don't know how long we'll stay – am dazed and not yet really here – I will tell you after a fortnight or three weeks. – But you had better come and see me here, and pay the railway expenses from my account. Once you are here it will cost nothing. I guess Seltzer will be appearing. No, I have told Seltzer nothing about Verga or *Kangaroo*. I don't mind if he defers *Studies* till Spring.

This place is over 6000 ft.up, and apparently takes a bit of getting used to, especially after a sea voyage.

You must tackle Curtis Brown about Secker. I will do the same.

If you come, I will ask Mabel Dodge to lend you the Studio, about 100 yards away, and you can eat with us. But we mustn't have Seltzer here at the same time. Let me know. – If it doesn't *suit* me here, I shan't stay more than a month.

DHL

Let me have *Kangaroo* MS. as soon as possible – I suppose you've received it. Send me the typed MS. to revise.

---

[1] See p. 314 n. 6.
[2] The first English edition of these stories, under the title *Little Novels of Sicily*, was published by Basil Blackwell in March 1925.

2602. To E. M. Forster, 20 September 1922
Text: MS KCC; Huxley 552.

Taos. New Mexico. U.S.A.
20 Sept. 1922

Dear E. M.[1]

We got here last week from San Francisco – from Sydney – Found your letter. Yes I think of you – of your saying to me, on top of the downs in Sussex – 'How do you know I'm not dead?' – Well, you can't be dead, since here's your script. But I think you *did* make a nearly deadly mistake glorifying those *business* people in *Howards End*. Business is no good.

Do send me anything you publish, and I'll order Seltzer to send you two of my books which are only published here – one appearing just now.

Taos is a tiny place 30 miles from the railway high up – 6000 ft – in the desert. I feel a great stranger, but have got used to that feeling, and prefer it to feeling 'homely'. After all, one is a stranger, nowhere so hopelessly as at home.

I think we shall stay here the winter, so when you feel moved to it, write again. Frieda sitting on an iron-grey pony jogging through the sage-brush still, out of her qualms, spoke of you and Brahma. I didn't care *at all* for Buddha. Sono morti della vera morte, quelle persone.[2]

Saluti buoni   D. H. Lawrence

I've just come back from motoring five days into the Apache Country, to an Apache feast. These are Red Indians – so different – yet a bit chinesey. I haven't got the hang of them yet. Here is a pueblo of the grain-growing Indians.

Tell Leonard Woolf he might like to publish my translation of Giovanni Verga's *Novelle Rusticane*, if he asks Curtis Brown for it.

DHL

2603. To Curtis Brown, 20 September 1922
Text: MS Lazarus; Moore, *Intelligent Heart* 300.

Taos. New Mexico. U. S. A.
20 Sept. 1922

Dear Curtis Brown

I was away five days motoring to the Apache country to an Indian feast there, so only got your letter last night. This is now my address – and I think I'll be here all the winter.

---

[1] DHL had known Edward Morgan Forster (1879–1970), the novelist and critic, since January 1915 (see *Letters*, ii. 262 n. 2). Initially he found *Howards End* (1910) – to which he refers below – 'exceedingly good and very discussable' (ibid, i. 278).
[2] 'They are the dead of the true death, those people.'

Thank you for the account rendered. I'll write Duckworth this mail, and tell him once more to send in accounts to you.

I finished *Kangaroo*, and when I receive typescript from Mountsier, will revise it and let you have it.

Secker *ought not* to publish the three novelettes before they are through here. You know Hearsts are printing 'The Captain's Doll' in the *International* and giving me $1000. Mountsier is trying to place 'Ladybird' also. And *this* is the money I live on. To let Secker publish just as he pleases would simply take the bread out of my mouth. You know how much I get from England. Not enough to pay my steamer fare or even my house rent. If England doesn't want to read me, I don't care. I don't care if my books are never published over there. You complain that it doesn't pay you to handle my books. Well, that's not my fault. If you don't want to handle them, then leave them. Non mi fa niente.[1]

I had a letter from Basil Blackwell saying he would like to see the Verga translations, *Mastro-don Gesualdo* and *Novelle Rusticane* – with a view to publishing. You might let him see the MSS.

If Secker wants another story for the short story book, I will[2] do it. But of course 'Wintry Peacock' is pledged till 1923.

Send me all news. I hope letters will now take only 10 days or a fortnight.

                                          Yours Sincerely   D. H. Lawrence

2604. To Emily King, [20 September 1922]
Text: MS Needham; PC v. Interior of House, Isleta Pueblo; Postmark, [. . .] SEP 20 1922; Unpublished.

                                          Taos. – New Mexico
                                          20 Sept.

Found your letter here – glad you are all well. – We arrived on my birthday but I have been away five days motoring to the Apache country to visit the Indians there. It is very fine here – but queer, 6000 ft up. I will write a letter very soon.
                                          Love.   DHL

2605. To Anna Jenkins, 20 September 1922
Text: MS WAPL; Huxley 551–2.
                                          c/o Mrs Mabel Sterne. *Taos*. New Mexico. U.S.A.
                                          20 Sept. 1922

Dear Mrs Jenkins

Just a line to you to say we have arrived at last and have got our feet on earth again. I found your letter here – glad you seem settled:

---
[1] 'It doesn't matter to me.'   [2] will] must

We motored here 75 miles from Santa Fe across the desert – nearly shaken to bits. The house Mrs Sterne built for us – a long adobe house, one room deep and one story high, here on the Indian Reservation. It is quite smart inside, and sort of brown mud outside. The place is 6000 ft. up, so one's heart pit-a-pats a bit. I haven't got used to it yet. It is sunny, and *hot* in the sun, but the rain is beginning.

But still I haven't extricated all of me out of Australia. In one part of myself I came to love it – really to love it, Australia. But the restless 'questing beast' part of me kicked me out, and here I am.

We got pretty tired of the *Tahiti*, though she was comfortable. But the people uninspiring. We picked up a cinema crowd at Papeete, all of them hating one another like poison, several of them drunk all the trip.

Frieda is boiling wild plums that the Indians brought us – I must rush to supervise, of course. Write again and tell us news. We'll meet somewhere. Many greetings from both.

D. H. Lawrence

2606. To Ada Clarke, [20 September 1922]
Text: MS Clarke; PC v. The Church, Pueblo of Laguna; Postmark, [. . .] 1922; Lawrence–Gelder 123.

Taos. N. Mexico, U S A
20 Sept.

We arrived here on 11th. – my birthday – found your letter – many thanks, but too extravagant: F[rieda]'s brooch very pretty. I have been away five days motoring to the Apache Reservation to an Apache feast – it is very fine and wild out here – but we are settling in, already making jam of peaches, and of wild plums that the Indians bring. Your tennis place sounds fine – glad you make nice things for yourself. I ordered you *Aarons Rod* in spite of the fact that you wont like it. I will write a letter in a day or two.

Love. DHL

2607. To Rachel Annand Taylor, 21 September 1922
Text: MS UCLA; Postmark, Taos SEP 2 [. . .] 19 [. . .]; Majl Ewing, ed., *Eight Letters by D. H. Lawrence to Rachel Annand Taylor*, (Pasadena, California, 1956), p. [13].

[Taos, New Mexico U.S.A.]
21 September 1922

Dear Rachel Annand Taylor[1]
Of course I remember you – and 'Where are the knights that rode away' –

---

[1] Rachel Annand Taylor (1876–1960), Scottish poet and biographer whose poems DHL had known since November 1909 and whom he had first met early in 1910 at the home of Ernest and Grace Rhys. (See *Letters*, i. 141 n. 2.)

and a frail little dinner-party where the china seemed to crack if one spoke aloud. Of course I remember also *Fiammetta* –

'We know their roses and their rods –'[1]

Thank you anyhow for the Edinburgh prize: though I realise you awarded it with misgiving.[2] You have died so many times, and each time *Fiammetta* appears a frailer, subtler flame. As for me, deaths leave me only more aggressive. So there you are – an ignis fatuus – and there am I bellowing in the mud of the marsh. It gets us differently. Why yes, I think I see the frail flame of your laughter at *Tortoises*. In the light of that flame it is to me too a good comic.

But I won't mention the life-urge any more. And I wish you safe anchorage still in the world, tenuous though the threads may be.

D. H. Lawrence

2608. To Earl Brewster, 22 September 1922
Text: MS UT; Brewster 61–3.

Taos. New Mexico. U. S. A.
22 Sept. 1922

Dear Earl

I found your letter, and Achsah's, here. Glad you liked *Aaron*.

Well, we are in the home of the brave and the Land of the Free. It's free enough out here, if freedom means that there isn't anything in life except moving *ad lib* on foot, horse, or motor-car, across deserts and through canyons. It is just the life outside, and the outside of life. Not *really* life, in my opinion.

But you should see me, in your white riding breeches, a blue shirt, a cowboy hat, and your white tie, trotting on a bay pony with an Indian, across to the Pueblo. Frieda too. It is very sunny indeed. The Indian Pueblo is still, earthbrown, and in a soft, sun-soaked way aboriginal. I like it. But it is like looking from the top of a hill way back down to a village one has left and forgotten: a bit écoeurant.[3] I am of course a great stranger here. And I feel there is a curious grudge, or resentment against everything: almost in the very soil itself.

The house is a very smart adobe cottage Mabel Sterne built for our coming: built in native style.

[sketch][4]

---

[1] The first quotation in the paragraph was indelibly associated with their first meeting at the Rhys home: see *Letters*, i. 180. It is unidentified. The second is from Rachel Annand Taylor's own poem, 'The Prologue of the Dreaming Women', *The Hours of Fiammetta* (1910), p. 11.
[2] She appears to have been involved in some way with the award to DHL of the James Tait Black Memorial Prize (see Letter 2391 and n. 2).   [3] 'sickening, disgusting'.
[4] DHL's sketch shows the position of the cottage in relation to Mabel Sterne's house as well as to natural features – stream, desert and mountains.

It is just one story high, has four rooms and a kitchen, and is furnished with a good deal of 'taste' in simple Indian or home-made furniture and Mexican or Navajo rugs: nice. The drawback is, of course, living under the wing of the 'padrona'. She is generous and nice – but still, I don't feel free. I can't breathe my own air and go my own little way. What you dislike in America seems to me really dislikeable: everybody seems to be trying to enforce his, or her, *will*, and trying to see how much the other person or persons will let themselves be overcome. Of course the *will* is benevolent, kind, and all that, but none the less it is other people's will being put on me like a pressure. I dislike that: and I despise it. People must be very insufficient and weak, wanting, inside themselves, if they find it necessary to stress themselves on every occasion. Mancano troppo.[1] They are, it seems to me, short of something vital in their own souls.

I don't know how long I shall stick it: probably, as a sort of lesson to myself, until the spring. Then I shall come away. But if I dislike it *too* much, I shall leave as soon as I decide that it is too much. The sun, the free desert, the absence of Europe's stiflingness – that is good. But this absurd will-pressure and the sense of a host of people, who must all have an inferiority complex somewhere, striving to make good over everybody else, this is only ignominious, it seems to me.

Seltzer had a case: the 'Vice' people tried to suppress *Women in Love* and other books: Seltzer won completely, and is now claiming $10,000 damages.

I expect to receive copies of *Fantasia of the Unconscious* before the end of the month. Of course I shall send you one.

Tell me where you are now. Many greetings to Achsah and the child – she will soon be a Mademoiselle.

D. H. Lawrence

2609. To Lady Ottoline Morrell, 22 September 1922
Text: MS UT; Postmark, Taos SEP 2[. . .] 192[. . .]; Unpublished.

Taos. New Mexico. U. S. A.
22 September 1922

Dear Ottoline

Will you please let me pay back the £15 which you so kindly lent me during the hard days.[2]

Yours Sincerely   D. H. Lawrence

---

[1] 'They lack too much.'
[2] Lady Ottoline, like Edward Marsh (see Letter 2598), had sent money to DHL in November 1915 when he was hoping to go to Florida (*Letters*, ii. 447 and n. 1).

2610. To Thomas Seltzer, 22 September 1922
Text: MS UT; Lacy, *Seltzer* 42–3.

Taos. New Mexico.
22 Sept. 1922

Dear Seltzer

Will you please do a little thing for me. Send me a Spanish-English dictionary, and a book to begin to learn Spanish from. Those shilling paper folders published by Kühl or Kunze – yes, Kunze[1] – are quite good. One needs Spanish here. I must find a teacher too.

Can you send me also a copy of James Joyce's *Ulysses*. I read it is the last thing in novels: I'd best look at it.

Mabel Sterne says when you come to Taos she will be glad to put you up in her house. She has plenty of room, and servants. We shall be glad to see you any time. You take the motor stage which leaves Santa Fe at midday, 75 miles over the desert, or you take the other stage from Taos Junction, only about 30 miles.

I hope you will get your $25000 damages from the Vice man.

Yrs   D. H. Lawrence

Could you send me too that Herman Melville book – *Herman Melville, Poet and Mystic*:[2] – I will go over the *Studies in C[lassic] A[merican] Literature* again:

Any news of *Fantasia* yet?

Have you got the MS. copy of *Studies in Classic American Literature*? I should like to go through them again.

DHL

2611. To Robert Mountsier, [22 September 1922]
Text: MS Smith; Postmark, Santa Fe SEP 2[. . .] 1922; Unpublished.

Taos. New Mexico.
Friday. 22 Sept.

Dear M[ountsier]

Thank you for forwarding all the letters. I had only the telegram from Seltzer, and a letter from him forwarded from San Francisco: nothing new. I understand about the 'case' now.[3]

Mabel Sterne says if you come here, you can have the Studio, which is 50 yards from both houses, or you can stay in her house, as she has lots of room, and servants to do the work. It is very nice here: we learn to ride horseback, F[rieda] and I. – But I don't altogether like living under anybody's wing. Too smothering. And I don't want anybody to be *kind* to me.

---

[1] Unidentified.
[2] Raymond M. Weaver, *Herman Melville, Mariner and Mystic* (New York, 1921).
[3] See p. 292 n. 1.

Seltzer of course never started for San Francisco – and never intended to. But of course he was busy with the 'case'. I will let you know immediately I hear anything definite from him: and I won't commit myself with him, not to anything. I am getting to be a wise and disillusioned bird.

Will you please post me the *Studies in C[lassic] A[merican] Literature* – a Manuscript copy – I should like to go over them again. I have asked Seltzer for the book on Melville.

more anon

DHL

Be sure and send the MS. of *Kangaroo* when it is ready.

2612. To Harriet Monroe, 23 September 1922
Text: TMSC NWU; Huxley 553.

Taos, New Mexico
23 Sept., 1922

Dear Harriet Monroe:

Well here we are in the fair middle of the New World: feeling a bit strange so far, but getting used to it. The desert is yellowish, and Taos mountain soft and unwilling, as I sit here and look at it. Like an unwilling woman. I should say, wouldn't you, the most unwilling woman in the world is Thais: far more unwilling than Cassandra.[1] The one woman who *never* gives herself is your free woman, who is always giving herself. America affects me like that.

Alice Corbin came here along with us. I like her very much. But her mouth talks of freedom and her eyes ask only to have freedom taken away; *such* freedom. The Land of the Free. Thank God I am not free, any more than a rooted tree is free.

I am glad you publish 'Turkey-Cock' and 'Evening Land'.[2] 'Turkey-Cock' is one of my favorites.

When we come eastwards, I hope we shall see you. Meanwhile – Ave!

D. H. Lawrence

2613. To Alice Corbin Henderson, 23 September 1922
Text: MS UT; Postmark, Santa Fe SEP 23 1922; Unpublished.

Taos. New Mexico.
23 Sept 1922

Dear Alice Corbin,

Thank you so much for sending the Spanish Grammar. I hope to swallow it bit by bit. I haven't found a teacher yet.

---

[1] Thais, a famous Athenian courtesan who, according to legend, encouraged Alexander the Great to set fire to the palace of the Persian kings at Persepolis. Cassandra, daughter of King Priam of Troy, was a prophetess whose predictions were never believed.

[2] 'Turkey-Cock' and 'The Evening Land' appeared in *Poetry*, xxi (November 1922), 59–67.

We read the 'Jim' poem.[1] It comes out very straight and real, as I like it to come. But, cara, cara mia, what then is freedom? What is freedom for a woman? to be free to come and go, and change and change back again? After all, I never saw a primrose wiggling itself up a spire like a tuberose.

> 'The primrose by a river's brim
> A yellow primrose was to him
> And nothing more —'[2]

To her, alas, it was a whole galaxy of flowers, a whole parterre: from sweet-william to salpiglossis.

What is the primrose *to itself*? Why, it is the quintessence of yellow primrosiness, e nient' altro.[3] It stays deep, deep at home in itself and blossoms its own still core. Neither ranging outwards nor *scope*. Only its very self. And you can only be your very self by abiding by yourself, primrose unadulterated, forfeiting all the rest, columbine and passion-flower. And fidelity to yourself means fidelity single and unchanging, to one other one. The first change is a tearing at the quick of your own integrity and being, primrosiness. Woman can be truly true to one man only: and man the same to one woman. The rest is lapses. Perhaps we must lapse to know we have lapsed. But it is lapses. And the only real experience is the experience that goes deep into the singleness of the self, not this roving business.

Of course it's absurd of me to write to you like this. But it's just my 'Jim to Julia.'

I hear Harriett Monroe is publishing two of my poems in November's *Poetry*: 'Turkey-Cock', one of my favourites.

We don't see much of the young Alice.[4] La jeunesse goes its own divided way. But she is coming in to a meal today.

I want to remind you that you are to ask me for a present. I'm waiting for you to tell me what it is to be, so don't fail. Even if you ask for my new cow-boy hat, or worse, my old bast shoes.

a riverderci   D. H. Lawrence

P.S. Will you tell me, supposing we should ever want to move a little way off from Taos, if you think we could find a little furnished house in the Santa Fe neighbourhood, and what, approximately the rent would be?

P.P.S. Thank you for the letter about *Sons and Lovers*.

---

[1] Unidentified.
[2] William Wordsworth, 'Peter Bell', i. 248–50 ['A primrose by . . . And it was nothing more'].
[3] 'and nothing more'.
[4] Alice ('Corbinetta') Oliver Henderson (1907–   ), Alice Corbin Henderson's daughter and, in December 1922, to become the wife of Mabel Sterne's son, John Ganson Evans (1902–78).

2614. To William Siebenhaar, 25 September 1922
Text: TMSC NWU; Huxley 553–4.

Taos, New Mexico, U.S.A.
25 Sept. 1922

Dear Mr. Siebenhaar

Yesterday came your letters – two – and the first part of *Max Havelaar*.[1] I read these chapters and liked them very much. I think your translation is perfectly splendid: you seem to me to have caught so well the true spirit of the thing. Really it seems to me a first rate translation. Only the poem, alas, comes out rather tedious. That particular kind of poem is very difficult to keep alive: even if it is very living in the original, which I rather doubt.

I shall wait till I get a few more chapters before forwarding the MS. to my agent, to put before the publishers. If only they won't say it is too 'old-fashioned'. That is the cry they raise against the Sicilian, Giovanni Verga, one of whose novels I translated, because I think him so good. They want things modern and thrilling; ah, they weary me.

We stayed a week in San Francisco, then came on here: motored about 100 miles across the desert from Lamy, via Santa Fe. It is a weird country, this high desert plateau covered with pale, yellow-flowering sage-brush, broken by the deep cañons where the rivers flow, and again interrupted by the Rocky Mountains which in this part seem to sit ponderously on the plain. Taos is about 7,000 ft. above the sea.

We have got a very charming house on the edge of the desert, one mile from the Mexican Plaza – the village – and three miles from the old Indian pueblo. There are about 600 Indians in the pueblo – very nice they are. We go riding on horseback with them across the space, and enjoy it immensely. Then on Saturday is their great 'dance', to which Indians come from a hundred miles round, Apaches, Navajos. We are all the time on the go: not still like in Australia.

Well, I hope we shall have good luck with the publishing of *Max Havelaar*. Vediamo! I shall look out for the rest of the MS.

My wife sends many greetings, with mine, to Mrs Siebenhaar and to you. Remember me to Miss Curtis.[2] I had a letter from Mrs Jenkins, from London. She seems more contented now.

Best of wishes.

Yours Sincerely   D. H. Lawrence

---

[1] See p. 240 n. 2.
[2] Probably Phyllis Curtis who worked at 'The Booklovers' bookshop of which she subsequently became proprietress (Nehls, ii. 475).

2615. To Else Jaffe, 27 September 1922
Text: MS Jeffrey; Frieda Lawrence 170–2.

Taos. New Mexico. U. S. A.
27 Sept. 1922

My dear Else.

Well here we are in the Land of the Free and the Home of the Brave. But both freedom and bravery need defining. The Eros book came, and I shall read it as soon as we get breathing space. Even though we are in the desert, in the sleepy land of the Mexican, we gasp on the breath of hurry – We have got a very charming adobe house on the edge of the Indian Reservation – very smartly furnished with Indian village-made furniture and Mexican and Navajo rugs, and old European pottery. Behind runs a brook – in front the desert, a level little plain all grey, white-grey sage-bush, in yellow flower – and from this plain rise the first Rocky Mountains, heavy and solid. We are 7000 ft. above the sea – in a light, clear air. The sun by day is hot, night is chilly. At the foot of the sacred Taos mountain, 3 miles off – the Indians have their pueblo, like a pile of earth-coloured cube-boxes in a heap: two piles rather, one on one side the stream, one on the other. The stream waters the little valley, and they grow corn and maize, by irrigation. This pueblo owns 4 square miles of land. They are nearer to the Aztec type of Indian – not like the Apaches, whom I motored last week to see – far over these high, sage-bush deserts and through cañons. – These Indians are soft spoken, pleasant enough – the young ones come to dance to the drum – very funny and strange. They are catholics, but still keep the old religion – making the weather and shaping the year: all very secret and important to them. They are naturally secretive, and have their backs set against our form of civilisation. Yet it rises against them. In the pueblo they have mowing machines and threshing machines, and American schools, and the young men no longer care so much for the sacred dances. – And after all, if we have to go ahead, we must ourselves go ahead. We can go back and pick up some threads – but these Indians are up against a dead wall, even more than we are: but a different wall. – Mabel Sterne is very nice to us – though I hate living on somebody else's property and accepting their kindnesses. She very much wants me to write about here. I don't know if I ever shall. Because though it is so open, so big, free, empty, and even aboriginal – still it has a sort of shutting-out quality, obstinate. Everything in America goes by *will.* A great negative *will* seems to be turned against all spontaneous life – there seems to be no *feeling* at all – no genuine bowels of compassion and sympathy; all this gripped, iron, *benevolent* will, which in the end is diabolic. How can one write about it, save analytically. Frieda, like you, always secretly hankered after America and its freedom: it's very freedom *not* to feel. But now she is just beginning to taste the iron ugliness of what it means, to live by this will *against* the spontaneous inner life, superimposing the individual, egoistic will over the real genuine sacred life. Of course I know that you will jeer when I say there is any such thing as sacred spontaneous life, with its pride and its sacred power. I know you too believe in the screwed-up human will *dominating* life. But I don't. And that's why I think America is neither free nor brave, but a land of tight, iron-clanking little *wills*, everybody trying to put it over everybody else, and a land of men absolutely devoid of the real courage of trust, trust in life's sacred spontaneity. They can't *trust* life until they can *control* it. So much for them – cowards! You can have the Land of the Free – as much as I know of it. – In the spring I want to come back to Europe.

I send you £10. to spend for the children – since you suffer from the exchange, I hope in this little trifle you can profit by it. F. sends her love.

D. H. Lawrence

P. S. If you want winter clothing, or underclothing, for the children or yourself or Alfred, write to my sister Mrs L. A. Clarke, Grosvenor Rd. Ripley near Derby – tell her just what you want, and she will send it. I shall pay her – I have told her you will write – so dont hesitate.

2616. To Mary Cannan, 27 September 1922
Text: MS Lazarus; Moore 719–20.

Taos. New Mexico. U.S.A.

27 Sept. 1922

My dear Mary

Your letter of Aug. 2nd. came on today – why the devil Seltzer was so long forwarding it, I don't know.

We got here on the 11th. San Francisco was not unpleasant – in fact quite pleasant – but it made no great impression on me. Here we have a very pretty 'adobe' house, just on the edge of the Indian Reservation: Mabel Sterne built it for us this summer. It is furnished very prettily, with Mexican rugs and blankets and mostly village-made furniture. It looks very nice. The big house is about 200 yards away – an adobe pile. I don't much like being on the grounds of a *padrona*: but Mabel Sterne is quite generous and we do just as we please. – Just behind the house is a brook with trees – in front, the *desert*, covered with grey, yellow-flowering sage bushes – and about four miles away, the mountains, standing heavy on the plain. It is beautiful enough: and we are 7000 ft. above the sea. But the sun is still very hot during the day, the nights coldish. Three miles off is the pueblo, the Indian village: a queer place. Mabel Sterne has with her one of the Indians – Toni – a big fellow – nice – they have been together several years. We are kept busy – being driven out in the car over the desert to wild places – on Monday we went right into the Rocky Mountains, which are beautiful, the aspens gold as daffodils. And then we are learning to ride horseback. Almost every day one of the Indians comes with the horses, and we ride over to the pueblo, and round the desert. It is great fun, if a bit tiring. – This week-end the Taos Indians have their festa, and the Indians come from many miles around. I drove in the motor two days to the Apache country, to the Apache festa. – So you see us really in America: on the go.

Whether I *really* like it is another matter. It is all an experience. But one's heart is never touched at all – neither by landscape, Indians, or Americans. Perhaps that is better so. Time, I suppose, that one left off feeling, and merely began to register. Here, I register.

I have written you various letters, which I hope you got. Barrie and C[ynthia] A[squith] – well, I suppose they must both have substitutes, and money is a fine cement. Thank you so much for saying I could borrow from you. Now, thank goodness, I believe I have even got £500 in hand, so am even in a position to lend, instead of borrowing.

We shall probably stay in America all winter – here or elsewhere – but in the spring I want to come to England. I even begin to get a bit homesick for England, though I still feel angry against it. I plan to come in the month of April.

I hope you enjoy your trip to Venice and Lucca. Tell me what Italy is like now. My heart still turns most readily to Italy. – That beastly Banca di Sconto![1] What a mercy you were out of it as much as you were. – As for Gilbert, he has lapsed into the land of ghosts, in my soul.

Remember me to everybody. And believe me, travel is a great weariness, as well as an excitement.

F[rieda] sends love.

DHL

2617. To Catherine Carswell, 29 September 1922
Text: MS YU; Carswell 170–2.

Taos. New Mexico. U. S. A.
29 Sept. 1922

My dear Catherine

Your letter from the Tinners Arms[2] came last night. I always think

---

[1] See p. 156 n. 1.
[2] Where the Lawrences stayed in Zennor, Cornwall, February – March 1916, before moving into Higher Tregerthen.

Cornwall has a lot to give one. But Zennor sounds too much changed.
Taos, in its way, *is* rather thrilling. We have got a *very* pretty adobe house, with furniture made in the village, and Mexican and Navajo rugs, and some lovely pots. It stands just on the edge of the Indian reservation: a brook behind, with trees: in front, the so-called desert, rather like a moor but covered with whitish-grey sage brush, flowering yellow now: some 5 miles away the mountains rise. On the North – we face East – Taos mountain, the sacred mt. of the Indians, sits massive on the plain – some 8 miles away. The pueblo is towards the foot of the mt., 3 miles off: a big, adobe pueblo on each side the brook, like two great heaps of earthen boxes, cubes. There the Indians all live together. They are pueblos – these houses were here before the conquest – very old: and they grow grain and have cattle, on the lands bordering the brook, which they can irrigate. Mabel Sterne has an Indian lover lives with her. She has had two white husbands and one Jew: now this. She is pretty rich, has a big house 200 yards away, and another house and a studio besides this. We drive across these 'deserts' – white sage scrub and dark green piñon scrub on the slopes – On Monday we went up a cañon into the Rockies to a deserted gold mine. The aspens are yellow and lovely. We have a pretty busy time, too. I have already learnt to ride one of these Indian ponies, with a Mexican saddle. Like it so much. We gallop off to the pueblo or up to one of the cañons. Frieda is learning too. Last night the young Indians came down to dance in the studio, with two drums: and we all joined in. It is fun: and queer. The Indians are much more remote than negroes. – This week-end is the great dance at the pueblo, and the Apaches and Navajos come in wagons and on horseback, and the Mexicans troop to Taos village. Taos village is a Mexican sort of plaza – piazza – with trees and shops and horses tied up. It lies 1 mile to the south of us: so four miles from the pueblo. We see little of Taos itself. There are some American artists, sort of colony: but not much in contact. The days are hot sunshine: noon very hot, especially riding home across the open. Night is cold. In winter it snows, because we are 7000 feet above sea level. But as yet one thinks of midsummer. We are about 30 miles from the tiny railway station: but we motored 100 miles from the main line.

Well, I'm afraid it will all sound very fascinating if you are just feeling cooped up in London. I don't want you to feel envious. Perhaps it is necessary for me to try these places, perhaps it is my destiny to know the world. It only excites the outside of me. The inside it leaves more isolated and stoic than ever. That's how it is. It is all a form of running away from oneself and the great problems: all this wild west and the strange Australia. But I try to keep quite clear. One forms not the faintest inward attachment, especially here in America. America lives by a sort of egoistic *will*, shove and be shoved. Well, one can stand up to that too: but one is quite, quite cold inside. No illusion. I will not shove, and I will *not* be shoved. Sono io!¹

In the spring I think I want to come to England. But I feel England has insulted me, and I stomach that feeling badly. Però, son' sempre inglese² – Remember if you were here you'd only be hardening your heart and stiffening your neck³ – it is either that or be walked over, in America.

DHL

In my opinion a 'gentle' life with John Patrick,⁴ Don, and a gentle faith in life itself, is far better than these women in breeches and riding-boots and sombreros, and money and motor-cars and wild west. It is all *inwardly* a hard stone and nothingness. – Only the desert has a fascination – to ride alone – in the sun in the forever unpossessed country – away from man. That is a great temptation, because one rather hates mankind nowadays. But pazienza, sempre pazienza! – I am learning Spanish slowly, too.

DHL

2618. To Robert Mountsier, 29 September 1922
Text: MS Smith; Postmark, Espanola SEP 30 22; Unpublished.

[Taos, New Mexico]
Friday. Sept. 29. 1922

Dear M[ountsier]

I got 'Democracy' MS.⁵ – This is the only letter I've had from Seltzer since I am here – it was forwarded from Palace Hotel.⁶ But before receiving this I got a forwarded telegram 'Complete success, Judge praises your book,

---

¹ 'I am myself!'   ² 'But, I am always English'.   ³ Cf. Letter 2620 and nn. 1 and 2.
⁴ See p. 124 n. 3.
⁵ DHL had sent off to the editors of the periodical, *The Word*, at The Hague, four essays on 'Democracy' on 6 October 1919; three were published between 18 October and 6 December, but the first publication of the fourth has not been traced (see *Letters*, iii. 404 n. 1). The 'MS' cannot be precisely identified; it may have been one of the four extant typescripts. See *Reflections on the Death of a Porcupine and Other Essays*, ed. Michael Herbert (Cambridge).
⁶ Seltzer's letter (on the verso of which DHL wrote to Mountsier) was dated 6 September 1922 (TMS Smith); it reads as follows:

Dear Lawrence:
    It has upset me dreadfully that I couldn't be in San Francisco to meet you as I had fully planned to do. If I had known the exact date at least a week in advance I might have arranged to do it. But it was difficult to get information. The steamship company has no office here. I wired to the San Francisco office and received no reply.
    I expect a decision soon on the case about which Mabel Dodge has probably told you. It is important for me to be here when the decision is announced. We hope it will be favorable, in which case I suppose there will be a great demand for WOMEN IN LOVE. I have had the book set up for a popular $3.00 edition, so as to have it ready when the need arises.

Seltzer'[1] – then a repetition of this telegram direct to Taos, with words 'where are you' added. That is absolutely all. – I have written him that he has an invitation from Mabel Dodge to stay with her. But no answer. – I wrote exactly as you suggest – pleasantly, good-humouredly, but waiving all matters of business. I will continue to do so. I think he knows my attitude and that's why he doesn't write. Very well, that is his affair. It doesnt trouble me. – I asked him to send me also the Herman Melville book, and a Spanish dictionary. We'll see if he does it.

I wonder why you want to publish this 'Democracy' as a separate little book? Do you think it is worth while publishing little books? Does Seltzer? As for the 'Lion and Unicorn' article,[2] I don't even remember anything about it, and am afraid I have burnt all traces of it. But if you like I can easily write another 5,000 or 10,000 words on to this. But do you really want a little 'Democracy' book? Let me know.

When does 'Fantasia' appear? – We can decide *Kangaroo*'s date between ourselves, when you've read it. I should have thought early spring.

I am settling down a bit better here, and Mabel Sterne is learning to leave us alone, and *not* to be a padrona. I pay for everything I have, so don't feel indebted – though I must say she is naturally generous. One thing, I am learning to ride horseback, on one of her indian ponies – F[rieda] as well. I can

Our friends have come to our aid in great shape and the whole press of the country has fought vigorously on our side. I was not wrong about Amy Lowell. I did not even want to ask her. But a friend of mine insisted that she ought to be and offered to get her help. She refused. This is all the more surprising as nearly all authors, even the most conservative, were highly indignant at the suppression of these books and showed a great readiness to assist, some of them offering their help voluntarily.

Another reason for my staying is that I have to see the fall publications through, among them your FANTASIA OF THE UNCONSCIOUS which is due in about two weeks and ENGLAND MY ENGLAND to be published in about a month.

Mountsier has suddenly, without any preliminaries, sent me an ultimatum from his country retreat to have the copyrights for all your future books taken out in your name. I am not used to receiving ultimatums. I see no reason for the change. You are thoroughly safeguarded by the present arrangement; and in general your affairs are safer in my hands than elsewhere. A change now would look rather bad for me and what's bad for me cannot be good for either of us. It seems Mountsier wants to pick a quarrel with me. Let him. I will fight.

AARON'S ROD is now in the third edition and is selling fairly.

I am sending enclosed a copy of my letter to you in Australia which you have probably not received.

Yesterday I sent Mountsier a check for you for $200 and expect to send him another check for $200 soon.

Will see you soon. I am glad you have come at last. I hope you and Mrs. Lawrence like it here.

Yours

[1] See p. 292 n. 1.
[2] Probably Part I of 'The Crown', subtitled 'The Lion and the Unicorn Were Fighting for the Crown', which appeared in *Signature*, 4 October 1915. See *Reflections*, ed. Herbert.

go now, and gallop across these spaces. I like that so much. And the big open place has a fascination. So I may stay on some months. If so you will come, and I will hire the Studio for you – it is only 100 yds. from us – and you will eat with us. Let us see. – This week end is the Indian fiesta¹ – fun. But I'd never make a stunt of these Indians. They're quite nice, and all that –

au revoir   DHL

F. very pleased with the photographs of her mother.

I never thanked your sister for so kindly inviting us. Please do say *thank you* to her.

One could have a good time in this country, and as cheaply as Europe, if one were so minded.

DHL

I had two welcoming letters from Amy – she feeling a little bit uneasy, as I had twitted her without knowing.

He said in a letter to Australia that *Aaron* had already sold 6000 copies.

(You mustn't think too badly of Seltzer. You see I never could send *your* letters to him. Let us go gently.)²

2619. To Witter Bynner, [c. October 1922]
Text: Bynner 8–9.

[Taos, New Mexico]
[c. October 1922]³

⁴If we don't like Taos, or find neighbors here oppressive, we can go to Mexico. Perhaps you and the Spoodle⁵ could come with us.

---

¹ The San Geronimo fiesta, a celebration of the harvest, took place at the Taos Pueblo on 29 September.
² The final three paragraphs were written on the recto of Seltzer's letter, DHL's final, parenthetical remark being placed immediately following Seltzer's statement, 'I will fight'.
³ By the end of September DHL's letters had begun to hint at the deterioration of his relationship with Mabel Sterne, but it was not until late October or early November that the open break occurred and the Lawrences moved to Del Monte Ranch on 1 December. The tone of this letter suggests that it was probably written some time in October, before the serious quarrel took place.
⁴ DHL's correspondent was Harold ('Hal') Witter Bynner (1881–1968), an American poet at whose house in Santa Fe the Lawrences had spent their first night in New Mexico. A Harvard graduate (1902), Bynner spent some years in publishing, taught briefly (1918–19) at the University of California, travelled extensively in the east especially China, and then settled in Santa Fe. The poetry of China and of the American Indians exerted powerful influences on his own. He published his account of his relationship with DHL in *Journey with Genius* (1951).
⁵ DHL's nickname for Willard ('Spud' or 'Spoodle') Johnson (1897–1968), American journalist and editor. He was editor and co-founder of the 'little magazine', *Laughing Horse*, 1922–39, to which DHL contributed. Johnson was a close friend of and, for a time, secretary to Bynner.

2620. To Harriet Monroe, 4 October 1922
Text: TMSC NWU; Harriet Monroe, 'D. H. Lawrence', *Poetry*, xxxvi (May 1930), 92.

Taos, New Mexico
Wednesday, 4 October 1922

Dear Harriet Monroe

If there is time make the tiny alterations at the end of 'Turkey Cock'. What do I find? God knows. Not, not freedom – but freedom is an illusion anyhow, as you suggest. A tension like a stretched bow, which might snap, but probably won't. Something a bit hard to bear. 'Stiff-necked and uncircumcised generation'[1] – That inhuman *resistance* to the divinity – would be perhaps superhuman and 4th dimensional. But always resistance. Reminds me of the great cries of the Old Testament: 'How long will ye harden your hearts against me.'[2] But who is Jehovah in this case, I don't know. An Almighty however, not a Dove! A Thunderbolt, not a Logos.

Probably we'll stay here all winter. I'd like to do a novel here.

Yes, I shall be glad to see you and Chicago: spite of terrors.

D. H. Lawrence

2621. To Mabel Dodge Sterne, [c. 6 October 1922]
Text: MS Brill; Luhan 65–6.

[Taos, New Mexico]
[c. 6 October 1922][3]

So you are *mise en scéne*. Now I want:

1. The meeting with Maurice[4]
2. John,[5] M. and you in Santa Fe
3. How you felt as you drove to Taos
4. What you *wanted* here before you came.
5. First days at Taos.
6. First sight of Pueblo
7. First words with Tony
8. Steps in developing intimacy with Tony
9. Expulsion of M.

---

[1] Acts. vii. 51 ['Ye stiffnecked and uncircumcised in heart in heart and ears, ye do always resist the Holy Ghost'].
[2] A biblical-sounding cry, but not an accurate quotation (Cf. 1 Samuel vi. 6; Psalms xcv. 8).
[3] In Letter 2622 DHL tells Mountsier that he is doing a novel on Mabel Sterne and her Indian set in Taos and refers to notes she prepares for him. It is likely that this letter was written about the same time.
[4] Maurice Sterne, Mabel's second husband; they moved together to New Mexico.
[5] John Ganson Evans, Mabel Sterne's son by her first husband.

10.   Fight with Tony's wife.[1]
11.   Moving in to your house

While away, if away long, *post* me the notes.
Sempre pazienza.

DHL

You've got to remember also things you don't want to remember.

Please write me a note about how it was when you met Maurice at Lamy, just how it felt. You see this is the jumping off ground.

You told me you wrote some time during Maurice's 'reign', a sort of story you thought was good. I wish you could find that for me. I might incorporate it, perhaps. I might also later incorporate some poems of yours that you sent me – about Tony and being alone in a strange house at night before he came. I've got that. – Then anyhow would be your own indubitable voice heard sometimes.

I don't want you to read my stuff till the end – it will spoil your view.

I have done your 'train' episode and brought you to Lamy at 3 in the morning.[2]

2622. To Robert Mountsier, 6 October 1922
Text: MS Smith; Postmark, [. . .] 1922; Unpublished.

[Taos, New Mexico]
Friday. Oct 6th 1922.

Dear M[ountsier]
Your letter of Sept 30th

1.   When *Kangaroo* MS. comes I'll consider all you say. Meanwhile let Seltzer see the copy you hold, at once, and he can decide publication. I can't see any hurry, really, but leave it to you 'business' people. – Yes, I meant to put a last chapter, as you suggest. – Might we not discuss the 'war episode' with Seltzer? I don't like little, scrappy books of bits.
2.   I'm sure I answer everything on the nail.
3.   I think we at least ought to get some money out of Kennerley, and has he the right to sell the book as he wishes?[3] I'd rather have had some say. But we won't offend Boni's till we have a definite course of action.[4] I feel I must recover hold over that book.

[1] Tony Luhan's first wife was Candaleria Romero (d. 1950), a Taos Pueblo Indian. (Mabel Dodge Luhan followed the outline of events provided by DHL, in her autobiographical volumes, except for this item, about which she wrote nothing.)
[2] From the abortive attempt to write a novel, a seven-page fragment survives now called 'The Wilful Woman'. See *St. Mawr and Other Stories*, ed. Brian Finney (Cambridge, 1983).
[3] See p. 131 n. 2.
[4] Boni and Liveright of New York (they published the Modern Library edition of *Sons and Lovers*, introd. John Macy, in 1922).

4. I suppose we'll stay on here now. By fighting M[abel] S[terne] and paying every cent on the nail one gets more clear. You must come here, as we agreed.

5. I still don't hear a word from Seltzer, though he sent me Spanish Dictionary and Melville book as I asked. I asked him to get me James Joyce's *Ulysses*, to see what it's like. Perhaps he couldn't.

6. I found a rough draft of ' Ass.'[1] Will send it. I told Seltzer to give you MS of *Birds Beasts* – from Australia. Now I'll ask for it for myself.

7. I doubt if I want to finish *Mr Noon*. One day I might.

8. Am doing a M. Sterne novel of *here*: with her Indian: she makes me notes. Wonder how we shall get on with it. I don't let her see my stuff.

9. I owe Secker the *Kangaroo* book as the 5th. – (3 novelettes being the fourth, he doesn't count the short stories).[2] So how can I get out of his Australian rights.[3]

10. Wont Seltzer owe me quite a bit on *Women in Love*?

11. Let Seltzer see *Kangaroo* at once.

12. Where *is Fantasia*?

Adios   DHL

[Frieda Lawrence begins]

Friday

Dear Montague,

Excuse pencil. Lawrence has the only ink – you ought to come here – I *love* the land and like Mabel D – L. was just on the defensive. Cant you warn Boni and Liveright that they have no *right* to *Sons and Lovers*? *Clever* dodge of Kennerley – you ought to come here – I *also* feel that *perhaps* the war part does not come in that *Kangaroo* book – Lawr has actually begun a novel about here and Mabel D – It's *very* clever the beginning, it will be rather sardonic! Dear faithful Mountsier, I am so amused at your fight with Seltzer – I am sure Seltzer will be quite beyond himself with his triumph. You and I will have to have a talk! I am *wild* about Kennerley, now is the moment to fight him – Would it not be best to write to Boni and L – direct? What did you say that Seltzer had sold 6000 *Aaron*'s? Do come and *dont* have scruples – you *do* deserve that trip!

Lawrence took my space away!

a rivederci!   F –

---

[1] See Letter 2458.   [2] See p. 129 n. 3 and p. 199 n. 2.

[3] Mountsier had proposed that DHL reserve the Australian rights to *Kangaroo* and that the novel be issued in an Australian edition which would pay royalties to DHL. (The usual arrangement would have been for Secker to sell sheets to an Australian binder or to export copies of the English edition.) Secker agreed to the exclusion but, after DHL broke with Mountsier in February 1923, Secker issued his edition of the novel (1923).

Thank you for My mother's photos – She always sends you greetings!
Please send a *Sea and Sardinia* to
Miss *Elsa Weekley, c/o Mrs Bruce Weekley, Great Maplestead Vicarage,*
                          Halstead, Essex.
We ride!

[Lawrence continues]
When we do!!

2623. To Thomas Seltzer, [7 October 1922]
Text: MS UT; Postmark, [. . .] O[CT] 7 1922; Lacy, *Seltzer* 43–4.

                                      Taos. New Mexico.
                                      Friday. 7 October
Dear Seltzer
    I received the Spanish Dictionary and Grammar and Melville book, for
which many thanks. Couldnt you find *Ulysses*? If you could just *lend* it me, to
read. I suppose I ought to read it.
    Why have you not written me one line to here? Are you so very busy, or just
holding off?
    Mountsier says he's posted me the typescript of the Australian novel
Kangaroo. I'll revise it when it comes. He wants it published this fall. I am
neutral. He wants me to cut out my own long 'war' experience, condense it to a
couple of pages for *Kangaroo*, and publish the 'experience' apart, perhaps
with 'Democracy'.[1] What do you say to this? I am doubtful. I asked
Mountsier to send you the other typed MS of *Kangaroo at once*. I want you
also, quickly, to send me on all you have to say. I am willing to make revisions
of all sorts. Do you think the Australian Govt. or the Diggers[2] might resent
anything? Let me know this as soon as possible.
    Send me please the MS. of *Birds Beasts and Flowers*, so I can go through it
again.
    Where is *Fantasia*?
    I *wish* you had got *Sons and Lovers*. *Can't* we do anything?
    Be sure and write about *Kangaroo* immediately.
                                       Yrs   D. H. Lawrence

---

[1] The 'war' experience is contained in the 'Nightmare' chapter in *Kangaroo*. See also Letter
    2618.
[2] In *Kangaroo* the 'Diggers' are a para-military group who plan to seize political power in
    Australia; by this reference DHL may be glancing at the 'King and Empire Alliance' which
    perhaps served as a model for his fictional Diggers. (For further information see Robert
    Darroch, *D. H. Lawrence in Australia*, Melbourne, 1981.)

2624. To Robert Mountsier, [11? October 1922]
Text: MS Smith; Unpublished.

[Taos, New Mexico]
Wednesday,[1]

Dear M[ountsier]

I was mailing you the poems when your letter came.

All right, you come here and try this for a bit. Mabel Dodge says she does not rent her places, because then[2] everybody would say 'you rented it to him, so why not to me.' But the Studio is there and you're quite welcome to it. – If you can't take it then we must get a room in town. As for paying for your food, nay, we're no longer so poor. You can make your own breakfast and eat with us.

You had better come by Santa Fe, I think. At Santa Fe take the stage motor car which leaves at midday, and gets here at 6.0 or 6.30: a very bumpy bad road over desert. Ask him to drive you to Mrs Sterne's – it's about $\frac{3}{4}$ mile from the plaza. Any heavyish luggage send express from Santa Fe to Taos – c/o Mrs Sterne – by Taos Junction. The express man goes to and from Taos Junction – about 30 miles. Santa Fe is 75 miles.

DHL

Bring for me, if its handy, a lid for my kettle, five inches diameter – any sort of lid, though the kettle is enamel. My lid fell down the well, and I cant get another.

Don't bother if it's not handy. – And bring two egg-cups, there are none here.

Bring *rough* clothes for here. Its hot in the day, cold in the night.

Mabel Sterne's motor is away with Tony going round the pueblos about Indian land laws, or I'd come in it to Santa Fe, to meet you.

2625. To Willard Johnson, [12 October 1922]
Text: MS YU; Unpublished.

Taos.
12 Oct.

Dear Johnson

Publish the enclosed or not, as you like.[3]

Greet Bynner from me, and be greeted.

D. H. Lawrence

---

[1] Dated with reference to Letter 2628.   [2] then] they

[3] DHL enclosed the text of a letter (actually a review of Ben Hecht's satiric *Fantazius Mallare; A Mysterious Oath*, Chicago, 1922) which Johnson published in *Laughing Horse*, iv (December 1922). Since, as DHL remarks about a later offering for the same periodical, it is 'an article in shape of letter' (Letter 3000), it is not included here. (For an account of the furore which followed Johnson's publication of the article, see Bynner 10–12.)

2626. To Mabel Dodge Sterne, [c. 15 October 1922]
Text: MS Brill; Luhan 101.

[Taos]
[c. 15 October 1922][1]

Dear M[abel] S[terne]

Frieda says she doesn't want to walk this afternoon. Would you like to ride a bit with me? Would you feel safe.

I did an 'Eagle' poem.[2] I'll type it on your Corona if I may.

DHL

2627. To Thomas Seltzer, 16 October 1922
Text: MS UT; Postmark, Taos OCT 17 1922; Lacy, *Seltzer* 44.

Taos. New Mexico.
16 October 1922

Dear Seltzer

Thank you for your letter – All right then, January.[3]

I think we shall stay the winter here – but it will be cold – sunny too.

Have gone through *Kangaroo* – many changes – it is now as I wish it. I want to *keep in* the war-experience piece: and I have made a new last chapter. Now it is as I want it, and it is good. I'm glad it's done. You'll like it much better.

I'm still waiting for *Fantasia*.

Yrs   D. H. Lawrence

2628. To Robert Mountsier, 16 October 1922
Text: MS Smith; Postmark, [. . .] OCT 17 1922; Unpublished.

Taos.
Monday October 16. 1922

Dear M[ountsier]

Have finished *Kangaroo*. Have kept in the *War* piece. Have added last chapter. Have made many alterations. Am waiting to hear from you before I post.

Am telegraphing you today. It is much better to come to *Raton*, New Mex. and either take the stage from there to Taos, 120 miles, a days trip: stage on Mondays, Weds., and Fridays, I think: or you go on in the train, a side line, Raton to Ute Park, and take the *same* stage at Ute Park, only about 30[4] miles to Taos, I think.

---

[1] Mabel Sterne records that DHL's later letter dated 15 January 1923 (Letter 2692) about the 'Eagle' poem was written three months after DHL wrote the poem as a result of a trip into the desert with her.

[2] 'Eagle in New Mexico', first published in *Birds, Beasts and Flowers*.

[3] Most likely a reference to Seltzer's intention to publish *The Gentleman from San Francisco and Other Stories* in January 1923. (It was first published by the Hogarth Press in May 1922.)

[4] 30] 40

This is 300 miles nearer, and a day quicker, than the Santa Fe line.
The three trains from La Junta arrive Raton:

Fast Mail express:	3.05. P.M.	*Train* Leave Raton:	5.20. P.M.
California Ltd.:	1.10 P.M.	Arr Ute Park:	1.45 P.M.
Daily Pullman (No 9):	4.25 P.M.		

If Tony is back with motor car we'd meet you at Ute Park: or fetch you in the
morning. Otherwise stage.

No more just now.

DHL

2629. To Robert Mountsier, 16 October 1922
Text: MS Smith; Telegram; Unpublished.

Taos, N Mex
Oct 16 1922

Book to Raton   sleep there take stage to Taos   Mondays Wednesdays
Fridays

Lawrence

2630. To Robert Mountsier, 18 October 1922
Text: MS Smith; Postmark, Taos 20 OCT 1922; Unpublished.

[Taos, New Mexico]
18 Oct 1922

Dear M[ountsier]
    In answer to your letter of 11th.
    We'll have to wait about *Sons and Lovers*, I suppose. Pity we can't punish
Kennerley.
    Kangaroo is ready to send to you. I am keeping in the war episode: it must be
so. The book is now as I want it. Ought one to put a tiny foreword note,
apologising to Australia?
    But anyhow Secker won't want to accept *Studies*[1] as a fifth: and he'll cut up
very rough if I don't give him *Kangaroo*. I don't like him either – I might give
him the option of *Studies*, and then offer him *Kangaroo* reserving Australian
rights for myself. But in that case how shall I proceed with Australia?
    There must be somewhere *four* of those 'Crown' essays, published in that
pamphlet *The Signature*.[2] I wrote six, but have burned the lot. I could no
doubt get the four *Signatures* from Koteliansky. I must then write an addition
if you *want* it. But let us see first how *Fantasia* goes. It isn't here yet.

---

[1] 'Studies'] Kangaroo
[2] Only three issues of the *Signature* appeared (4 and 18 October, and 4 November 1915); each
    contained a chapter of DHL's 'The Crown'. See *Letters*, ii. 17–18.

I told Seltzer I was asking you to give him carbon copy of *Kangaroo*. But all right, let him wait. He hasn't sent *Birds Beasts*. I suppose you got 'Ass' and 'Goat'.[1] I have now got 'Eagle in New Mexico'.

I send this to Elizabeth. Let me know your movements.

I don't hear from England what Secker is doing. I *bet* he'll be doing the three Novelettes. Curtis doesn't answer me. I don't like him either. He hates having to play second fiddle to American publication. What better does he deserve. – But I'll *bet* Secker is going ahead with the 3 novelettes because he *likes* them. He's calling them *Ladybird*.[2] You'll see, he'll bring them out pretending to have had no word to the contrary.

If this is so, then Seltzer must do them also in early spring: and we must make the order of publication:

1. *Fantasia*
2. *Ladybird* etc.
3. *Studies in C[lassic] A[merican] [Literature]* (shall we call this Studies of the American Daimon, Demon?)
4. *Birds Beasts*

That still leaves *England my England*, 'Democracy' and *Kangaroo* on our hands. It is a good bit. But we must *make* Seltzer get these other books out – or go to somebody else. If you go to New York – and do go – then call on these Boni Liveright people.

I asked Seltzer to get me the loan of *Ulysses*.

About your coming here. – I still suffer being on M[abel] S[terne]'s 'estate' and under her protection: I don't breathe free. But probably I'll stay through the winter. The rest of Taos we see *very* little of: have met one or two middle-aged sort of artists, quite nice, but I feel I've nothing to do with them. – If you come, you'd best have the little house, it's warmer, cosier, easier to heat. Days are sunny, like summer, nights *cold*. It will be the same, more or less all winter – sun always warm, but nights freezing, and snow later. We[3] burn cedar-wood. It isn't very expensive – about two dollars a week. M.S. won't accept rent for reasons I gave before. But my house is supposed to belong to Tony, I shall pay him. About meals – we are rather erratic. Best if you walked the half mile to the hotel for midday dinner – quite good, cost 75 cents – and had evening meal with me or with MS., just as it happens. No paying for this, it is a trifle of trifles, don't talk of it. Those would be all your expenses. – There are

[1] The poems 'He-Goat' and 'She-Goat', first published in *Birds, Beasts and Flowers*.
[2] Secker had written to Curtis Brown on 6 October (Secker Letter-Book, UIll): '. . . I would prefer to make "The Ladybird" the next publication in this country. I am willing to defer it for a reasonable period, not exceeding June next, to suit American publication . . .'
[3] We] These

five or six horses in the corrall: all nice and friendly, and the desert perfect to ride over. – We really see very little of Taos.

If you come, could you bring me a couple of gold ten-dollar pieces and three or four five dollars, from the bank: for the servants at Christmas. If it's a trouble, don't bother. If you come, do all you can in New York and come with a free mind. I suppose you'd live easily on $10. a week all told, once you are here. Come to Raton – Seltzer says he'll come here first week in January. – Let me know if I shall send *Kangaroo*. – Come here if you feel like it: you'd enjoy the country, at least. Come to Raton. Let me know.

DHL

Could you send me, or have sent me, two copies of *Look We Have Come Through* and a copy each of *Amores* and *New Poems*.

All right, go ahead against Kennerley as you think best. Alice Corbin Henderson said she'll write somebody about approaching him privately.

When does *The Captains Doll* appear?[1]

2631. To Amy Lowell, 19 October 1922
Text: MS HU; Damon 622–3.

Taos. New Mexico.
19 Oct. 1922

My dear Amy

Well, we have been here for five weeks, and are more or less getting used to it. We have a gay little adobe house on the edge of the desert, with the mountains sitting round under the sun. The Indian pueblo is about two miles off, and Taos Plaza one mile. We don't see much of the 'world' – save Mabel Sterne and her visitors.

The land I like exceedingly. You'd laugh to see Frieda and me trotting on these Indian ponies across the desert, and scrambling wildly up the slopes among the piñon bushes accompanied either by an Indian, John Concha, or a Mexican, José.[2] It is great fun. Also we go to hot springs and sit up to our necks in the clear, jumping-up water.

Of course, humanly, America does to me what I knew it would do: it just *bumps* me. I say the people charge at you like trucks coming down on you – no awareness. But one tries to dodge aside in time. Bump! bump! go the trucks. And that is human contact. One gets a sore soul, and at times yearns for the understanding mildness of Europe. Only I like this country so much.

I wasn't aware of being in a nest of your enemies: but I must have been,

---

[1] See p. 107 n. 7.
[2] Concha (1877–1969) was a Taos Pueblo Indian who often accompanied DHL when he went riding; José worked for Mabel Sterne.

according to you.[1] We slept the very first night in New Mexico at Witter Bynners house in Santa Fe, and Alice Corbin was there. They talked of you too, but everything quite nice and I should never have suspected enemies. A bit critical of your work, of course, but that goes without saying. When poets talk of my poetry I don't expect them to leave one line hanging on to another – Shreds!

Seltzer won his 'case' all right, and seems mighty pleased. He sold out his *de luxe Women in Love*s and now has a two dollar edition, I hear.[2] He is supposed to bring out *Fantasia of the Unconscious* this week. I'll send you a copy when he sends some to me: though I don't suppose it is in your line. He urges me to come east, and has a house for me in Connecticut. But I like this land so much, and shrink from the witches cauldron of New York. So he must come to Mahomet[3] – can't spell it – for Mahomet isn't budging yet awhile.

I have done two poems here: my first in America. Wonder whom I shall send them to. Harriett Monroe has two from *Birds Beasts* in November's *Poetry*.[4]

No, the books you sent me never came on. Probably Germany wouldn't let them out without a licence. That's how it is – I shall look forward to the new one.

You don't say how your health is: I hope it's quite mended. And I really look forward to meeting you again. So does Frieda. We both send many greetings – also to Mrs Russell.

Yrs   D. H. Lawrence

2632. To William Siebenhaar, [19 October 1922]
Text: TMSC NWU; PC; Unpublished.

Taos.
19 Oct.

Received Chapter Five[5] but rather loose. Put a string through the next. Think it very good.

D. H. Lawrence

[1] In a letter to DHL, 16 September 1922, Amy Lowell referred to Santa Fe as 'the nest of my enemies'; she particularly named Alice Corbin Henderson and Witter Bynner as hating her (Damon 621–2).
[2] Seltzer exploited the publicity surrounding the attempt to suppress *Women in Love* by bringing out a trade edition of the novel on 18 October 1922. The edition of 3,000 copies was sold out three days before publication and Seltzer had to order a second printing (Lacy, *Seltzer* 244).
[3] Mahomet] Ma Mahota (For the proverbial story to which DHL alludes, see M. P. Tilley, *A Dictionary of Proverbs in England*, Ann Arbor, 1950, M1213.)
[4] See p. 307 n. 2.   [5] Of *Max Havelaar*.

2633. To William Hopkin, 25 October 1922
Text: MS NCL; Pollak, *Journal of Modern Literature*, iii, 31.

Taos. New Mexico. U. S. A.
25 Oct. 1922

Dear Willie

I heard this minute from Ada about Sallie.[1] – But I knew Sallie was turning away to go. And what can one do. Only it hurts, the inevitable hurt. Our life coming to an end.

But Sallie had a fine adventurous life of the spirit, a fine adventurous life. And it's the adventure counts, not the success. If she was tired now, at least it was after a vivid travel with you. You travelled a fine adventurous way together, and if the arriving is in a waste place, what does it matter! What does it matter, you made a long trek, like pioneers. And you two led me over some frontiers, as well. And if Sallie had to go to sleep, being really tired, having gone a long way for a woman; and if you or I have to go on over queer places, further: well, the rest of the journey she goes with us like a passenger now, instead of a straining traveller.

Nevertheless, one uses words to cover up a crying inside one.

But one has got to live. – Here, on this high desert, it seems so remote, and so near – even to Devonshire Drive.[2] The aspens on the mountains are yellow, gangs of donkeys and horses wander over the pale, sage-bush desert. The night freezes, the day is hot. Frieda and I ride every afternoon, till sundown, when the sun sinks clear behind a far-off mesa. – It seems so far – and yet so near in thought. Frieda sends her love. – There will be another grave in that cemetery now, down Church Street.[3] 1 makes me feel I am growing old.

Never mind, one must strike camp, and pack up the things, and go on. With love, that belongs to the old life.

D. H. Lawrence

England seems full of graves to me.[4]

2634. To William Siebenhaar, 25 October 1922
Text: TMSC NWU; Huxley 559.

Taos, New Mexico.
25 Oct. 1922.

Dear Mr. Siebenhaar

I have Chapter 7. of *Max Havelaar*. I wish you'd done the whole book. One

---

[1] Sallie Hopkin (see p. 194 n. 2) died on 5 October 1922.
[2] The Hopkins lived in Devonshire Drive, Eastwood.
[3] The Eastwood cemetery where the Lawrence family were buried.
[4] Cf. DHL's poem 'Spirits Summoned West' (published in *Adelphi*, October 1923) for which this sentence provides the opening line.

needs to have the whole, to get an impression. What there is, I like *very* much. I send it to my agent today, for him to place before the publishers. He will write you. He is: Robert Mountsier, 417 West 118th. St. New York City.

It is wonderful here, with the aspens yellow on the Rocky Mts., the nights freezing, the days hot, the horses and asses roaming on the whitish, sage-brush desert. My wife and I ride all the afternoon, and love it. But it isn't *sympatisch* like Australia: more of the will.

Greet Mrs. Siebenhaar and be greeted.

Yours   D. H. Lawrence.

2635. To Robert Mountsier, 25 October 1922
Text: MS Smith; Unpublished.

[Taos, New Mexico]
Wednesday 25 October 1922

Dear M[ountsier]

Your letters returned. Don't irritate Seltzer if you needn't.[1] I'll keep silent.

1.   I had no proofs of *England my England*.

2.   There's no complication here. You can have the little house for

---

[1] DHL is alluding to a letter from Mountsier to Seltzer, 18 October 1922; Mountsier had sent DHL a carbon copy on which DHL wrote this reply. Mountsier's letter read as follows:

Dear Mr. Seltzer.

I have your check for $500 for royalties due D. H. Lawrence.

Regarding the royalty percentage for "Sea and Sardinia", I said I was willing to take the matter up with Lawrence after he had arrived in this country. Lawrence has written me that he wishes me to handle all the business of his books and that I may make whatever decisions I think best for his interests. From the time you first mentioned it, I have been against any reduction from 15 per cent, as you know. So the royalty stands at the 15 per cent you agreed to pay. Ignoring altogether the fact that Juta has to be paid from Lawrence's percentage, I consider any request for reduction because "Sea and Sardinia" hasn't sold as rapidly as we wish for no more justifiable than would be an author's request to a publisher for an increase over the agreed percentage because the publisher sold more than the author expected him to.

As to your writing that it is too late to change the copyright line, you know that you were notified by me about the change in the copyright line of "Fantasia of the Unconscious" and "England, My England" even before the copyright lines were set. Note the copyright line that I wrote on the printer's proof of "Fantasia," and my letters.

What I had to say about payments was not "totally unwarranted," as you choose to say. Thank you for the information given me in this last letter of yours.

Please let me know just how the "Sea and Sardinia" English edition matter stands. Secker is again making his usual complaints. What are your two offers for selling him bound copies or an edition run off especially for him? I think the matter should be definitely put up to Secker through Curtis Brown in this way. I have a letter for Lawrence in which it is pointed out that there are over one hundred typographical errors and inconsistencies in "Sea and Sardinia." Such mistakes have been none too few in most of the Lawrence books that you have published, so can't you make a special effort to eliminate them?

Sincerely Yours

yourself. – But John Evans, M[abel] S[terne]'s son, has a ranch, very nice, about 16 miles from here.[1] We might possibly fix up that, and live there. It has a 2-room block-house, and two other little one-room houses. – You'd love this country. So I suppose you'll come, after a few more hesitations.

3. I shall post you *Kangaroo* today to New York. – I enclose also a part of the MS. of a translation of a Dutch classic, *Max Havelaar*, by a writer 'Multatuli', about Java – done by a man in West Australia, and I promised him I'd have you show it to publishers. It's a queer work – real genius. Do something with it if you can, will you?

4. F[rieda] thinks the last chapter of *Kangaroo* too shallow. Do you.

5. I am doing an article about Indians and the Bursum Bill.[2] I may send it direct to the *Dial*, for quickness and because you may be leaving New York. But I'll tell them its your affair.

It's very lovely here now: ice in the morning, hot days, aspens yellow. F. and I ride alone now, all the afternoon. I work all morning. – But we don't get much time to ourselves. – Wish really we could go to that ranch, more alone. But it is rather inaccessible.

Grüsse   DHL

P.S. Tell me how much I owe to Juta.

Taos is enough for address. No post-delivery – MS's Mexican fetches all letters.

2636. To Mabel Dodge Sterne, [c. 25 October 1922]
Text: MS Brill; Luhan 103.

[Taos, New Mexico]
[c. 25 October 1922][3]

Yes, we won't ride – neither do I want to go in the buggy today – am gathering the last apples and will finish them later.

DHL

[1] Mabel Sterne had given this ranch to her son, John Ganson Evans, but he sold it back to her in 1922 shortly before his marriage. It is best known as Kiowa Ranch where DHL and Frieda lived 1924–5.

[2] In this article, 'Certain Americans and an Englishman' (eventually published in the *New York Times Magazine*, 24 December 1922) DHL wrote against the Bursum Land Bill which threatened to deprive the Indians of their land.

[3] The tone of this note suggests that it was written when the relationship between DHL and Mabel Sterne began to deteriorate; hence the conjectural date *c.* 25 October.

DHL's note was written on the back of the invitation to which he was responding:
Dear Lawrences,
Don't you think its too windy and dusty to ride the horses? Tony will take us out with the buggy about 3 o'clock if you like.

Mabel.

2637. To Robert Mountsier, [27 October 1922]
Text: MS Smith; Unpublished.

Taos
Friday 26 Oct.

Dear M[ountsier]

Just a word. I sent *Kangaroo* to 417 W., by insured parcel post.

The eggcups came. But *why* did you trouble your people. Many thanks.

Enclosed post card. Would you order a copy of *Look We Have Come Through* and *New Poems*[1] for this man.

If you see Seltzer, ask him if he really sent *Ulysses* – said he did. It hasn't come. Neither *Fantasia*.

Am busy doing an article on the Indians.

Still lovely autumn – very cold nights. Woman telegraphed me would I lecture at the club – Colonial Club, I think, New York[2] – M[abel] S[terne] says a rich club. I said I wasn't coming East till spring.

Little house ready for you whenever you like to come. Don't fuss about it.

DHL

2638. To Robert Mountsier, [28 October 1922]
Text: MS Smith; Unpublished.

Taos. New Mexico.
Saturday.

Dear M[ountsier]

This additional to yesterday: I don't think I can bear to be here very long: too much on Mabel Sterne's ground, she arranges one too much as if one were a retainer or protégé of hers: and thank you, I don't choose to be anybody's protégé. I'll stick it a month: and then what? Isn't Long Island terribly cold in winter? Hadn't we better stay somewhere south till spring? I can easily find myself a place somewhere else. I don't feel I want to be frost-bound all winter.

But I won't be bullied, even by kindness. I won't have people exerting their wills over me. Whoever does will get a jar. – I'll stick this a month longer, till I have arranged something else.

In the end it costs one more, also, paying them back for the things they have arranged for one, and which one didn't really want than it would if one had been left to make one's way all alone.

I wrote Harriett Monroe.

I cashed the drafts easily here.

Yrs. DHL

[1] *New Poems*] *Amores* (The man in question has not been indentified.)
[2] See Letter 2650.

2639. To Willard Johnson, 30 October 1922
Text: MS YU; Unpublished.

[Taos, New Mexico]
30 October 1922

Dear Mr Johnson

I had your letter this evening. Alice Corbin comes to Santa Fe in the morning so will bring this. Don't bother about apologies: one writes when the spirit moves. As for the 'Jeunesse' letter, much best burn it now, it has done all its work – Or best still, give it to Alice Corbin and let her burn it. Her feminine curiosity couldn't bear it otherwise. I'm sorry I couldn't see the mordant irony etc of Mr Hechts book. But heaven, they might put me in prison as they have done him. Martyred in such a cause.

Tell Bynner I'll answer him when I've quite made out the apple boughs and arching willows and streams under, like a dinner plate.

Belli saluti   D. H. Lawrence

2640. To Roy Chanslor and Willard Johnson, [c. 30 October 1922]
Text: Bynner 11.

Taos, New Mexico
[c. 30 October 1922][1]

[D. H. sent Chanslor and Johnson a frantic wire not to publish the review of Hecht's satire, *Fantazius Mallare*; it ended with] Heavens what a cause to be martyred for![2]

2641. To Bessie Freeman, 30 October 1922
Text: MS UNYB; Postmark, Taos OCT 31 19[. . .]; Moore, *Intelligent Heart* 302–3.

Taos. New Mexico.
30 Oct. 1922

Dear Bessie Freeman[3]

This is just a line to say how do you do, and where are you, and what are you up to. We are here as usual thick in things: even too thick. It has been the

---

[1] Dated with reference to the previous letter.
[2] Roy Chanslor, who co-edited *Laughing Horse* with Willard Johnson, told Bynner that they had initially decided not to publish DHL's startling review of Hecht's book. Hecht had been arrested in Chicago; Chanslor and Johnson feared the same fate. However DHL sent a telegram (ending with the words printed) urging them not to publish his review; this annoyed Chanslor and Johnson and made them determine to proceed. The review appeared in *Laughing Horse* with all four-letter words omitted and blanks left. See Bynner 11.
[3] Elizabeth ('Bessie') Wilkeson Freeman (1876–1951), whom DHL met through Mabel Sterne, her friend since their girlhood in Buffalo. m. (1) John Knox Freeman (2) 1934, C. J. Hamlin.

Bursum Bill till we're sick of it. I've done an article, Alice Corbin's done one, John Collier's done one.[1] The last named is still trotting on his reforming mission somewhere Zuni way.[2] We are supposed to go and meet him at San Domingo on Nov. 5th., Sunday, where all the elders from all the pueblos are to meet and have a Bursum Bill pow-wow. M[abel] S[terne] is very keen on going. Your old friend of the Apache trip is *not* keen. He doesn't love a motor-car. Besides, it has snowed these two days, and been so cold I have almost cried. I shall *not* be trailed to Santo Domingo if it's like this.

Tony is home: had to abandon John Colly – as John Concha invariably says, in Santa Fe, because he, Tony, had such a toothache. Fortunately it was better when he got home. – Put 2 + 2 together.

John Evans got back from Wyoming[3] last night, having motored 1,000,000 miles since Wednesday – in his new car. He now wants to marry young Alice in 4 weeks time, and take her to the Buffalo grandmother's for January 4th, when my young gentleman comes of age. Whether this speed will be allowed him, remains to be seen. – Alice Corbin is here, and leaves tomorrow, full of admiration etc for Mabel, but a little worried in her maternal self, the young Alice being not yet 16. – Lee Witt didn't go home to Nina for a fortnight:[4] went instead to his Mexican woman and had influenza with her. Nina infuriated, pondered a divorce. He growing tenderer, said if Mrs Berry went he'd come home.[5] Mrs Berry went, he came home, cried, Nina's heart melted in her, the divorce is postponed.

No no, no more gossip. We still ride: on Sunday through the snow up glorietta: very lovely too. My little pony quite likes me: and gran'fer is wedded to Frieda, and nearly hangs himself up on the barbed wire when she won't ride, and we trot off alone. I always think of you as my first riding companion; and my first Indian mate – You'll see yourself in my 'Pueblos and an Englishman' article if ever anybody publishes it.[6]

We never thanked you for the newspapers: but we do.

When shall we see you again?

[1] John Collier (1884–1968), American social worker and author who later became Commissioner of Indian Affairs (1933–45). He had organised the American Indian Defense Association. With his wife and three sons, Collier lived next door to the Lawrences in Taos.
[2] I.e. in the territory of the Zuni Indians, w. of Taos.
[3] Wyoming] Colorado
[4] Lee Witt (1871–1929), 'a one-armed former sheriff' (Moore, *Priest of Love*, p. 360). Cornelia ('Nina') Rumsey Wilcox (1880–1968), b. in Buffalo, m. (1) Henry Adsit Bull, 1901; divorced 1916; (2) Lee Witt, 1921; divorced 1923.
[5] Meta Berry. When Nina Witt left Taos for New York after divorcing Lee Witt, she took Meta Berry with her as housekeeper and cook.
[6] The essay (with the portrait of DHL by Jan Juta) was published as 'Indians and an Englishman' in *Dial*, lxxiv (February 1923), 144–52. Bessie Freeman is not recognisable in the published version.

Ugh, I don't like this cold weather.
How is your Paul.[1]
Many greetings from us both.

D. H. Lawrence

2642. To Mabel Dodge Sterne, [30? October 1922]
Text: MS Brill; Unpublished.

[Taos, New Mexico]
[30? October 1922][2]

Could you send me the MS. of my Bursum article – I think the girl must have missed a page out.

I would rather it went in a monthly, whole, than snipped up in a daily. It will have no effect there. We'll see what Lippman says.[3]

Beastly cold and horrid day.

DHL

2643. To Bessie Freeman, [31 October 1922]
Text: MS UNYB; Moore, *Intelligent Heart* 305.

Taos. New Mexico.
Tuesday.

Dear Bessie Freeman
I wrote you yesterday, not knowing Mabel had telegraphed to you. Today we have been up to John's ranch – about 20 miles from here. It was so lovely: and really free, far more so than here. Frieda wants us to go and live there. We'll try it first for a week, because it will be colder. But I think we shall do it – and try to make a *real* life there. It is much more splendid, more *real*, there, than here. You must come too and see how you like it.

Mabel says you want to sell your Los Angeles house. Sell it. Sell it before you come here, if you can: or put it in an agent's hands. Then come, and let us plan a new life. I was thinking you might like to take up the next 'homestead' lot to us, and have your house: and Mabel would take up another lot adjoining. And the rule would be, no *servants*: we'd all work our own work. No

---

[1] Probably her brother (cf. DHL's letter to Mabel Luhan, 15 July 1927).
[2] This letter was written after the completion of DHL's article on the Bursum Bill and before 31 October (see Letter 2644).
[3] Walter Lippmann (1889–1974), renowned American political journalist, on the editorial staff of the *New York World* (editor 1923–31). Mabel Sterne had already wired him about DHL's article.

highbrows and weariness of stunts. We might make a central farm. Make it all
real. This is too unreal for me.

There's the idea, anyhow – if it attracts you, we can talk more about it.
So no more till I see you.

Yrs   D. H. Lawrence

2644. To Robert Mountsier, 31 October 1922
Text: MS Smith; Postmark, Taos NOV 2 1922; Unpublished.

[Taos, New Mexico]
31 October 1922

Dear M[ountsier]

I send you by this post, registered MS., an article I did on the Indians and
the Bursum Bill. I send duplicate to Scofield Thayer, *The Dial* – 156 W. 13th.
Street, asking him if he can possibly put it in December's *Dial* because the
Bursum Bill is supposed to come before Congress in December, having
already passed Senate.[1] So unless it appears in December, all the Bursum part
will be useless – but the rest holds good. I said he could cut the article as he
chose. You might ring up and ask him what he's doing, and make any
arrangements. Mabel Sterne also telegraphed to Walter Lippmann c/o *New
York World*, to ask *him* if he could get the article in sections in a daily. But I
don't want it cut up into a daily if I can possibly help it. Better the *Dial* or
anybody monthly. See what you can do about it.

The second thing is a new plan. It isn't quite a success living here – not quite
real, somehow. M.S. has got a ranch, 180 acres, on Rockies foothills, about 20
miles away, wild. We went there today. It is *very* lovely. There are two rather
poor little houses – most of the lot is timber – all rather abandoned. But we
think of going there either this week or next, to try it. If we find it possible,
move in there. The ranch is utterly abandoned now, so it will be a good thing
for it to have somebody there. If we go, come there with us, and we'll make a
life. It's a wonderful place, but difficult to get at. If we like it in the long run,
MS. says she will let us have it. It's a wonderful place, with the world at your
feet and the mountains at your back, and pine-trees. And one could take up
other 'homestead' lots if one liked. I tell you in preparation. You'd have one of
the houses: they almost adjoin. We'd have to get a few repairs done: But I'll say
definitely when we've been again. Meanwhile what are your plans?

DHL

---

[1] The Bursum Bill was debated in the House of Representatives, 14 December 1922.

2645. To Mabel Dodge Sterne, [31? October 1922]
Text: MS Brill; Luhan 103.

[Taos, New Mexico]
[31? October 1922]

Best walk. – Or else ride. Frieda wont ride, though I prefer it. Perhaps best walk.[1]

We'll mail a copy to Thayer this evening. I'll get it done now. But it will take me about an hour.

DHL

2646. To Thomas Seltzer, 6 November 1922
Text: MS UT; Postmark, [. . .] NOV[. . .] 1922; Lacy, *Seltzer* 44.

Taos. New Mexico.
6 Nov. 1922.

Dear Seltzer

The books all came today – *Fantasia, England my England, Women in Love* and *Ulysses*: all very nice, but a terrible wrapper on *Women in Love*.[2] – I hope they will do well for us. – I take it *Ulysses* is just *lent*, and I will return it to the sender – who is he? – in about a week's time.

We must begin to arrange your visit. We plan to go to Santo Domingo pueblo – about two hours from Santa Fe – on the 23rd. or 24th. December. How would it be if you met us in Santa Fe and we all went to the dance? Mabel Sterne's car would hold us. Let me know: letters seem to take long.

We have just come back from a camping on a little abandoned ranch Mrs S. has about 16 miles from here – on the Rockies foothills. – Lobo. I think my wife and I will go and live there: but come here for your visit: or part of it at least: part we might all spend at Lobo. Is Mrs Seltzer coming? we shall all be glad to see her. Now let us fix up this visit, or we shall be getting criss-cross.

Tell me about your proposals for spring publication. I sent Mountsier the corrected MS of *Kangaroo* to New York.

Yrs   D. H. Lawrence

2647. To Robert Mountsier, 6 November 1922
Text: MS Smith; Postmark, [. . .] NOV 7 1922; Unpublished.

Taos. N. M.
6 Nov. 1922

Dear M[ountsier]

We've just got back from the ranch at Lobo. It's much colder there, but

---

[1] walk.] ride.
[2] 'The Seltzer dust-jacket is cream paper printed in black and red; the upper cover is illustrated with the head of a woman with streaming hair' (Roberts A15).

fine. We're going to live there. There are two cabins, one 2-room, the other 3-room. We want workmen to go this week and fix them up. You can have the little one. Much snow, but beautiful – forest – We'll have horses. There is a corrall and stabling. I shall pay M[abel] S[terne] a rent for the ranch, not much. You can share that, and food, and have no qualms. But we shall have to buy feed for horses. – It will be rough – wild – but very fine. You don't mind it rough. – I don't know how much leggings cost: but not much. Or we order from stores in Pueblo, Colorado, or in Kansas City: quite cheap. I actually wildly bought a pair Justins Cowboy boots – 20 dollars – but *very* nice. You should see me – cowboy hat, good one, $5: sheepskin coat – $12.50 – corduroy riding-breeches, very nice, $5. (You know Justins Cowboy boots are 'world famous'? – I didnt. There are others much cheaper.)

I got your letter with a statement of account – haven't looked at it yet. Enclose p.c. from *Poetry*.

Fantasia, *England my England*, *Women in Love*, and *Ulysses*, all came today: the last lent.

I hope your hand will be better – We shall have to chop much wood. – F[rieda] and I went up to Lobo with a Mexican – Sabino. We hauled a good deal of wood into the yard with Sabino's wagon. – The nearest neighbour is two miles – but very nice people, called Hawkes:[1] got 1000 acres.

Don't have any more accidents. I shall hate you if you have them down here.

I sent *Kangaroo* and 'Indians and an Englishman' article to New York. Did I tell you Seltzer said he had no MS. of *Birds Beasts*? – that you took it away from him.

I still feel a bit too close to MS. here: the Wing.

DHL

You must let us know which way you are coming: No doubt Tony would come with[2] the car to Ute Park to fetch you – I'd come with him. I believe you *can* sleep at Ute Park now. The stage from Santa Fe runs 3 days a week now – rather irregularly – I think there still is no place at Ute Park to sleep.

Oh, the well had to be dug deeper, so the kettle lid was dug out. – We use the egg cups daily.

I'll put this cheque in my Taos bank, to save bother – you reckon it.[3]

DHL

---

[1] Alfred Decker Hawk (1862–1950) and his wife Lucy Moore Walton Hawk (1864–1942) owned
    Del Monte Ranch; they were the Lawrences' landlords (1922–3) during their winter there with
    Knud Merrild and Kai Götzsche.   [2] with] to
[3] This final paragraph was written on the postcard from the *Poetry* editors (cf. Letter 2648) which
    DHL enclosed for Mountsier.

2648. To The Editor, *Poetry, A Magazine of Verse*, 6 November 1922
Text: MS UChi; Unpublished.

Taos. New Mexico.
6 Novem. 1922

Dear Sir

Thank you for the cheque for eighty dollars, for poems, which I have received today.[1]

Yours truly   D. H. Lawrence

2649. To Mabel Dodge Sterne, 7 November 1922
Text: MS Brill; Unpublished.

[Taos, New Mexico]
Nov 7. 1922

Dear Mabel.

I too will put it in black and white.

1. I don't believe in the 'Knowing' woman you are.

2. I don't believe in the 'good' woman you are: that 'good' woman is bullying and Sadish.[2] i.e. I utterly disbelieve in your 'heart'.

3. I don't believe in the lie of your 'submission' to Tony. As well say you 'submit' to Lorraine.[3]

4. I believe that, at its best, the central relation between Frieda and me is the best thing in my life, and, as far as I go, the best thing in life. –

5. You are *antagonistic* to the *living* relation of a man and his wife: because you only understand a sort of bullying: viz Tony, John Evans and the rest. – So, I count you antagonistic to the living relation between Frieda and me.

6. I have to pay for 'stamps and cigarettes' because you would find some way of insulting me on their score if I didn't.

7. It strikes me I have paid you pretty fully for all the 'emotion' you have expended, and more than paid for all the 'goodness'. I have still to pay for some of the bullying and mischief.

8. It disgusts me when you say it is chic for Lorraine to have one red eye.

9. I don't care a straw for your money and the things you 'give' – because after all it is on these you finally take your stand. It is on these you base your generosity. Bah, generosity!

---

[1] See p. 307 n. 2. The payment also covered 'St Matthew' in advance of publication in *Poetry*, xxii (April 1923), 27–31. (This information is contained on the postcard from the *Poetry* editors sent by DHL to Mountsier with the preceding letter.)

[2] I.e. sadistic.   [3] Mabel Sterne's dog, a French bull terrier.

10.   I will *never* help you to think, and 'flow' as you want: neither do I want to
      prevent you from so doing. Bubble as the hell you like.
Which is my Bursum Bill, and Basta.
Basta!

D. H. Lawrence

Nina Witt having arrived a propos – you believe in 'conjunctions' – has
read your letter and this.

DHL

2650. To Robert Mountsier, [11? November 1922]
Text: MS Smith; Postmark, Ta[os] NOV [. . .]; Unpublished.

[Taos, New Mexico]
Saturday

Dear M[ountsier]
   Your letter. You'll be in New York now.
   We've had to give up the ranch. House can't be mended: and too much
snow. We could have it in spring. We'll go and look at it.
   I believe *New Republic* is a bit stuffed with Bursum Bill.
   I told you the kettle lid was fished up.
   Snow has begun to fall. It may any time stop up the road to Raton Road, so
that's not safe. We were up there yesterday. *Very* cold. Snow falling today.
Best come to *Denver*, Colorado, and there change and take the train on the
Denver and Rio Grande Railway and come to *Taos Junction* station. That is
only 25 miles, and Long John[1] meets the train every day with the stage motor.
He'll bring you to Mrs Sterne's. So come *Denver*, Colo., then on D and R.G.
Ry. – change I think at Alamosa. This is shorter than Santa Fe, quicker, and
quite safe.
   I had a telegram from the Colony Club – Mrs Elizabeth Sage Hare – wants
me to lecture. You might see her and say it is 'possible' in spring. But not
probable.
   Bring a pound of Ridgways Tea only – and some Kolynos tooth paste. –
Yes, bring a bit of writing paper.
   Tell Seltzer I'm doing *Studies* again – Americanising them: much shorter.
Hope to do them soon. He wants this MS. and 'Captains Doll'. Give these to
him, he wants to send them to the printer.
   Have read *Peter Whiffle*.[2]
   Know nothing about Radio.

---

[1]   John Harris Dunn (1857–1954), stage driver from Taos to Taos Junction.
[2]   Carl Van Vechten, *Peter Whiffle: His Life and Works* (New York, 1922).

Bring the gold pieces: for Christmas presents – please.

Seldes wrote[1] – very nice – *Dial* December full. Get somebody to use the article, even if they cut all Bursum out of it.[2]

Yrs   DHL

2651. To Bessie Freeman, [14 November 1922]
Text: MS UNYB; cited in Moore, *Intelligent Heart* 305.

Taos. N. Mexico.
Tuesday 14 Nov.

Dear Bessie Freeman

Careless woman, you sent me somebody else's letter.

Very many thanks for the little Spanish dictionary. I have learnt quite a lot.

We can't go to the ranch this winter. The house is broken in, and too late to repair it. So we stay on in this house. All expecting you here.

The John and Alice wedding due about Dec. 16. in Santa Fe. Then they stay on here for a bit.

People here called Shevskys – he a Turk, San Francisco wife:[3] nice.

Very cold. Snow on the mountains, but the desert clear again.

Am just going to the Rio Grande hot springs. Dont you want to come too? Frieda sends many greetings, with mine.

a riverderci   D. H. Lawrence

2652. To Alice Oliver Henderson, 14 November 1922
Text: MS UT; Unpublished.

Taos.
14 Nov. 1922

Dear Corbinetta[4]

I hope you are having a good time stitching the gladdest of rags. Meanwhile *au revoir*, till after the greatest of occasions.

D. H. Lawrence

[Frieda Lawrence begins]
Dear young Alice,

Here is a small wedding-present[5] – Get something you like – I hope you are all well and cheerful – We shall go to San Domingo for the dance and hope to see you then –

My best wishes for you – Love to you and your mother.

Frieda Lawrence

---

[1] Gilbert (Vivian) Seldes (1893–1970), journalist and drama critic; managing editor of the *Dial*, 1922–3.
[2] DHL had included the text of the bill itself in his article 'Certain Americans and an Englishman'.   [3] Unidentified.   [4] See p. 308 n. 4.   [5] The present was a cheque.

2653. To Robert Mountsier, [14 November 1922]
Text: MS Smith; Postmark, Taos NOV 15 1922; Unpublished.

Taos. N. M.
Tuesday.

Dear M[ountsier]

Answer this man[1] about lectures, will you – I don't want to appear personally.

A nice letter from Seldes. I think it good if the *Dial* will do the Indian article in their Jan. issue – cutting out the politics. I tell Seldes so. But leave it to you.

Am busy re-writing *Studies*.

Very cold here. Do you think you can stand an altitude of 7000 ft? – But you'll have nice warm rooms: very nice.

If Seltzer likes to do *Kangaroo* for the spring, I am willing.

No more this minute.

DHL

2654. To F. Wubbenhorst, 14 November 1922
Text: TMSC Smith; Postmark, [. . .]; Unpublished.

Taos, New Mexico.
14 Nov. 1922

Dear Mr. Wubberhorst,[2]

I am returning to-day, by insured parcel post, the copy of *Ulysses* which you so kindly lent me. That is, I take it you lent me your copy, since your name was on the outside of the wrapper. Seltzer did not say.

I am sorry, but I am one of the people who can't read *Ulysses*. Only bits. But I am glad I have seen the book, since in Europe they usually mention us together – James Joyce and D.H. Lawrence – and I feel I ought to know in what company I creep to immortality. I guess Joyce would look as much askance on me as I on him. We make a choice of Paola and Francesca floating down the winds of hell.[3]

With many thanks for the loan of the book.

Yours sincerely,   D.H. Lawrence

---

[1] Unidentified.
[2] Nothing is known of DHL's correspondent other than that he lived in New York and was an acquaintance of Seltzer's (cf. Letter 2660). (The spelling of his name in the heading is DHL's, taken from the parcel wrapping.)
[3] In Dante's *Inferno*, Paolo and Francesca inhabit the second circle (reserved for carnal sinners), where they are blown by stormy winds, the analogue to their passions when they were living.

2655. To Robert Mountsier, 18 November 1922
Text: MS Smith; Postmark, Taos NOV 20 1922; Unpublished.

Taos.
18 Nov. 1922

Dear M[ountsier]

Another 'lecture' letter. Please answer it.

Have you let Seltzer have MS. of 'Captain's Doll' and *Kangaroo*. I think I should like him to do *Kangaroo* this spring, but I certainly want him to bring out *Studies*. Of these I have re-written the first five. They won't take me long. – Then I think I'll try a Taos novel. I'll see.

Shall I send you the MS of *Studies* as I finish them? You see I am uncertain of your movements.

Did I tell you the lid came: after the other had been dug out of the well. But it will do so nicely for the little Italian saucepan, which never had a lid.

The snow, thank heaven, has nearly melted. I don't like it.

Wonder how *Fantasia* and *England my England* are going.

Yrs   DHL

If Seltzer does *Kangaroo* in spring, what shall I do exactly about Secker?[1]

---

[1] Mountsier replied on 23 November (MS Smith);

Dear Lawrence,

Your letter of the 18th received a little while ago. The lecture letter has been answered. . .

As for the MS. of "The Captain's Doll": I'll get "The Fox" from "The Dial", and "The C's Doll" story itself from Hearst's. "The Dial" is still flirting with "The Ladybird", but I see Seldes Monday and get a definite reply.

I have to go over the rewritten parts of "Kangaroo" to see if they have been typed without mistakes. I did not read any of the changes in MS. . . .

"Fantasia" and "England my England" are going quietly, but well enough, I think, taking into consideration the crowded book market, and the unpopularity of volumes of these kinds. "Sea and Sardinia" has picked up a bit, for the christmas trade.

Let us agree on this – to have Seltzer get "Studies" out first of all. I now have nightmares of you spending the rest of your life rewriting it!

. . . All right this gives the following line-up for your 5-*book* contract with Secker:

1. "Lost Girl"
2. "Aaron's Rod"
3. "Sea and Sardinia"
4. "Psychoanalysis and the Unconscious" and "Fantasia" (counted as one)
5. "England my England"
6. "Studies in Classic American Lit."
7. "The Captain's Doll"

Remember that one of Secker's inducements was his promise to publish "The Rainbow", and he admitted to me last year that he didn't know if the court decision would allow him to do so.

Certainly nobody can insist that the "Kangaroo" is included in any 5-book contract.

This leaves "Democracy" and "Birds, Beasts and Flowers", perhaps till next fall, along with your next book. I thought you had really decided to do the Taos novel with Mabel Dodge and her Indian in it. Please enlighten me further on this . . .

2656. To Thomas Seltzer, 19 November 1922
Text: MS UT; Postmark, Taos NOV 20 1922; Lacy, *Seltzer* 45–7.

Taos. New Mexico.
19 Novem. 1922

Dear Seltzer

Will you do a little thing for me. Please have your clerk send a parcel of books to my sister – including *Aaron's Rod, England my England, Fantasia, Psychoanalysis and the Unconscious,* and your *Bee* book, and perhaps *Batouala,*[1] and any other you think she would like. Make her a nice parcel, and charge it all to me. The address:

Mrs L. A. Clarke, Grosvenor Rd., *Ripley near Derby*, England.

If you send them book post, it saves customs fuss.

Mountsier is at last in New York, so you will settle everything with him. – I hope the books go well enough.

Please also send a copy of *Aaron's Rod* and a copy of *England my England* to

Mrs. S. King, 480 Main St., *Carlton near Nottingham*, England.

Don't fail to send these, will you. I want them to have the books for Christmas.

Let me know about your coming here for Christmas. It has snowed deep, but thank goodness melted again in the hot sun.

I hope Mountsier has given you *Kangaroo*.

Greetings   D. H. Lawrence

I am busy with *Studies in Classic A[merican] Lit[erature]* – you'll like them much better, I think; much sharper, quicker.

DHL

2657. To Robert Mountsier, [19? November 1922]
Text: MS Smith; PC v. [Lawrence's Adobe house in Taos]; Postmark, Taos NOV [. . .]; Unpublished.

[Taos, New Mexico]
Sunday:

Your letter of 13th. – told you we've given up ranch. If you don't want M[abel] S[terne] little house you can have another just near for $10. a month. But best take MS. I got the riding breeches at the store here – they have good things for out west. – If we *press* the ranch, when you get here, we can still have it. Come and see. – Is Seltzer coming for Xmas? – This is a picture of our house – the festoon is red chilis.[2] I asked Seltzer to send some books to my sister. – – What about those poetry books you were sending?

DHL

---

[1] Seltzer published *The Adventures of Maya, The Bee*, by Waldemar Bonsels (1881–1952), and *Batouala*, by René Maran, both in 1922 and both trans. Adele Seltzer.
[2] Red chillies were commonly hung in a bunch like bananas to dry, serving also as decoration.

2658. To Mabel Dodge Sterne, [20? November 1922]
Text: MS Brill; Unpublished.

[Taos, New Mexico]
[20? November 1922][1]

The type girl rang up and said she fixed the charges with you, and that you said 'all right' – and that you even asked her what a 'folio' was, (100 words). I said I'd speak to you about that – and that the charge was too high. Of course if you *did* agree to a price, that's that.

We'd better not come tonight to supper – give ourselves time to cool down.

DHL

Mrs Hawke offered us their cabin for the winter. Perhaps we'd better accept that and simplify everything.

2659. To Robert Mountsier, [28 November 1922]
Text: MS Smith; Postmark, Taos [. . .] 2[. . .] 19[. . .]; Unpublished.

Taos.
Tuesday

Dear M[ountsier]

I return your letter received this morning.[2] Tomorrow I will send you the first eight – out of twelve – of the *Studies*. You may think them too violent now, to print. Anyhow they are the first reaction on me of America itself. And they are much shorter.

I leave you to decide dates. Only try and choose the best possible moment for *Kangaroo*. It is my feeling it should come out *soon*: but you and Seltzer decide.

Yes, you do the arranging with Curtis Brown, if you can: so I needn't write him. You write him about 'Captains Doll' and *Kangaroo*.

The news of the moment is that we are leaving Mabel Sterne's territory: it is unbearable. We go to Lobo: but not to the ranch I spoke of. To the next ranch: a beautiful place. We get a very good log cabin with all we want for $100., till end of March: milk and meat on the ranch.

It is a big ranch, but not much worked. Hawk is a gentleman – at present the old people have gone to California, leaving only Bill Hawk (about 25), his newly-married wife, and the daughter Elizabeth – about 21.[3] They live in the

---

[1] DHL's first mention of moving to the Hawk ranch occurs in the next letter to Mountsier. In the previous letter to Mountsier DHL made no mention of the Hawk ranch and apparently assumed they would spend the winter elsewhere; hence 20 November seems an appropriate date for this letter. [2] See p. 341 n. 1.

[3] William Hawk (1891–1975), Rachel Woodman Hawk (1898–), Elizabeth Moore Hawk (1902–71).

biggest house. They have about 100 cattle – but the ranch is half desert and half mountain. It's a lovely place. We shall have three or four horses at our disposal.

With us are going two Danes – painters – Knut Merrull (28) and Kai Götzsche (32) – very nice fellows.[1] They will have a little cabin of three rooms. They have no money, hardly. I want Seltzer to let Merrull do my book-jacket designs – he is a very clever decorator – and some designs for *Birds Beasts*.

When you come, you will have a room with us – or in the big house – or else we will fix up a third cabin for you. We'll be warm. The Danes pay $50 dollars for their cabin – till April. They have a Ford car – 4-seater. – The address is

c/o Mr Hawk, Del Monte Ranch, *Valdez*, New Mex.

It is about 17 miles from here. You will still come to Taos – then we meet you.

But don't write to the Ranch till you hear from me there.

Letters are delivered there every day: from Taos through Valdez – and another delivery from the north, through Questa.

Seltzer still says he'll come last week in Decem., with Mrs Seltzer.

We were so sorry about the tonsils. But you are a terror. What do you imagine you will have next?

You'd better come and be fixed up. It's lovely and sunny at Lobo – warm – big. And we'll go to the hot springs: hot and lovely.

I think if I wrote the M[abel] S[terne] novel, and the Indian, it would be just *too* impossible. Might make me also *too* sick. – But I think I'll do a novel out here.

Do hope you're feeling stronger.

DHL

I sent back *Ulysses* – thought it was only a loan – Seltzer said it was *given* me. Ask him to let you read it. It wearied me.

DHL

2660. To Thomas Seltzer, [28 November 1922]
Text: MS UT; Lacy, *Seltzer* 47–8.

Taos.
Tuesday.

Dear Seltzer

Just a word to tell you our news. We are going a little way from Taos, to the

[1] Knud Merrild (1894–1954) and Kai Guldbransen Götzsche (1886–), Danish painters who came to USA in 1921 and whom DHL had met at the home of Walter Ufer (1876–1936), Chicago painter and member of the Taos Society of Artists, and his wife Mary Monrad Frederiksen Ufer. Merrild recorded their experiences with the Lawrences, and DHL's letters to the two friends, in *A Poet and Two Painters* (1938).

Del Monte ranch, about 17 miles away. We shall have a good 5-roomed log cabin there – and a lovely wild place. This is a bit too much Mabel Dodge. You must come there. We are due to go on Friday next – day after Thanksgiving. But I'll write you the exact address when we get there. It's only 1½ hrs. in a car: three hours on horseback.

Two young Danes – artists – go with us, and they will have a 3-room cabin on the ranch, so we shall have company. In the big house are the young Hawks – Bill and his wife – and Elizabeth. They are nice: the father a 'gentleman' – but not rich. It's a lonely, lovely place – under the mountains, over the desert: very open.

The Danes – Knud Merrull and Kai Götzsche – don't have much money. Merrull is a *very* clever designer, head of the Artists Decorators Society in Copenhagen.[1] I want you to let him design my book-jackets; and do some wood-cuts for *Birds Beasts* – pay the ordinary price. Will you do that? I will have him send a design for *Kangaroo* jacket.[2] And then if you can give him a bit more work, please do. Because he has a great sense of beauty, and is modern. You'll see when you come.

We shall be so pleased to see Mrs Seltzer too.

Of course there is no breach with Mabel Sterne – no doubt she will want us all to come and stay here a bit, when you come.

I've nearly done *Studies*. It is the American Demon indeed. Lord knows what you'll think of them. But they'll make a nice little book: much shorter. I'll write again directly.

I sent back *Ulysses* to Mr Wubbenhorst – thought it was only a loan. Thank you so much for getting it me. But I do *not* want you to pay for books for me. Please charge them to me, or I feel uneasy.

And when you come, if you can *lend* me Herman Melville's *Pierre* and *Mardi*, I should like it. They belong only to a set, I believe.[3]

Ulysses wearied me: so like a schoolmaster with dirt and stuff in his head: sometimes good, though: but too mental. I thought the Ben Hecht book silly: not a bit good.

Yrs   D. H. Lawrence

[1] Merrild was president of Anvendt Kunst, an organisation of Danish artists which he founded in 1917.
[2] Merrild subsequently produced designs for *Kangaroo*, *Studies in Classic American Literature* and *The Captain's Doll*; Seltzer bought them but used only the last (Roberts B47).
[3] *Pierre; or, The Ambiguities* (New York, 1852) and *Mardi; and a Voyage Thither* (1849) were readily available only in the Constable Standard Edition, *Mardi* in 1922, *Pierre* not until 1923.

2661. To Tony Luhan, [30 November 1922]
Text: MS Brill; Luhan 106.

[Taos, New Mexico]
30 December. 1922[1]

Dear Tony

Thank you so much for letting us live in your house. I hope you won't find it much the worse for wear.

Let me give you a few dollars for its christening.

Come over soon with Mabel to see us at Lobo.

Yrs   D. H. Lawrence

2662. To Mabel Dodge Sterne, [1 December 1922]
Text: MS Brill; Luhan 105–6.

[Taos, New Mexico]
Friday.

Dear Mabel

Just leaving. No word yet about horses: will send a note by Sabino.

I think you will find everything in the house, except a dish and a plate, smashed, and two blankets, the red stripe and the blue stripe, which we borrow to wrap up in. I'll see these come back safely. Then I feel a bit guilty about the big water-tin, accepting the loan of it.

Hope everything was nice in Santa Fe.

So very many thanks for lending us this new house.

Let us hear what is happening. We shall see you soon.

DHL

2663. To Mabel Dodge Sterne, [1? December 1922]
Text: MS Brill; Unpublished.

Del Monte Ranch. *Valdez*
Friday[2]

Dear Mabel

Thank you for the MS. you sent.

Yrs   D. H. Lawrence

---

[1] The Lawrences moved to Del Monte Ranch on 1 December; hence this letter was probably written on 30 November.
[2] It seems reasonable to assume that the MS referred to here is the Bursum Bill article which DHL asked for in late October. In the confusion of leaving the Taos house he forgot to thank Mabel Sterne for the manuscript in the note he left, and this was his first opportunity to do so after arriving at the Hawk ranch.

2664. To Knud Merrild, [2 December 1922]
Text: MS UT; Merrild 67.

Del Monte Ranch. Valdez.
Saturday

Dear Merrild

Lizzie was awful[1] – Sabino had to pull us in with horses. But we are here. It is very nice.

Buy indiarubber boots from McCarthy's store,[2] the white ones $4.50 a pair. Buy a pair also for Götzsche[3] – (I don't mean overshoes, but indiarubber boots).

Buy also some fumigating stuff from the drug store, to fumigate your cabin. And two pieces of glass, one $17\frac{1}{2}$ inches x $7\frac{1}{2}$ ins and the other 8 inches x 12 inches.

Bring a pound of cheese.

Did Higgins change the mail address?[4]

I'll pay the things.

Great fun up here – have been out all morning getting wood. Do hope your face-swelling is better.

Greet Ufer and Mrs Ufer, and be greeted.

D. H. Lawrence

2665. To Mabel Dodge Sterne, [2 December 1922]
Text: MS Brill; Luhan 106.

Del Monte Ranch.
Saturday

Dear Mabel

Got here after a struggle yesterday. Spent a hard morning getting wood.

We shan't want the horses – better not have them, anyhow, as Hawk lets his stay out all winter. But Tony's were in stable last night – and well fed and watered.

Frieda says among the washing is one of her pillow-slips. We'll have it some time, as we've only four.

Jerry Mirabar brought good wood[5] – hope nobody steals it. And his wife is tanning five skunk skins for Frieda – hope she'll do them nicely.

Jolly up here – come and see us.

DHL

---

[1] An old Ford touring car belonging to Götzsche and Merrild.
[2] The Bond-McCarthy Store, owned by Frank Bond and John H. McCarthy (1873–1944).
[3] Götzsche] Merrild   [4] Possibly Victor Higgins (1884–1949), Taos painter.
[5] Jerry Mirabal (1886–1980) was the Taos Pueblo Indian who now appears on a postcard with the caption 'Famous Taos Indian'. An older postcard bears the caption: 'Jerry – well-known model of Taos . . . has done his share towards making Taos artists famous'.

Say if you want me to send back your two blankets at once – I can give them to John.

DHL

2666. To Robert Mountsier, [3 December 1922]
Text: MS Smith; Postmark, Valdez DEC 4 1922; Unpublished.

Del Monte Ranch. *Questa*, New Mexico
Sunday 2nd Dec 1922

Dear M[ountsier]

Well we are here – settled in – in a log cabin, an old one – four rooms and kitchen – rough but warm. One of the Danes is here, and we have cut down a big dead balsam tree, and sawn it into 5 lengths: some work. It is snowing, but not cold. The house is very warm.

When you come, come to Taos as agreed, from Denver. We'll probably all stay at Mabel Sterne's for a day or two. Thank God we are off her territory – but the parting was friendly.

We can arrange you here – you can't decide when you come. At the big house there is only Bill Hawk and his new wife – 3-months married – and Elizabeth Hawk – aged 21. The others are gone for the winter. The best, perhaps, is if you have a room and breakfast there, and then eat with us. It's only about 4 minutes. There are other cabins – but you'd be too lonely – and the house is very warm. They're nice people. – The Danes are near the Hawk house, in a 3-room cabin. If you *really* want, we'll fit you a cabin too – but it would be lonesome at nights.

I sent *Studies* up to 'Dana'. Will finish them soon. Note address – but letters will come on from Taos.

F[rieda] is happier here: though it is primitive. It is very beautiful.

DHL

2667. To Thomas Seltzer, [3 December 1922]
Text: MS UT; Postmark, Valdez DEC 4 1922; Lacy, *Seltzer* 51.

Del Monte Ranch. *Questa*. New Mexico
Sunday 2 Decem 1922

Dear Seltzer

Well we have moved – are cosy in a 5-room old log cabin among the pines above the desert. It is here you'll have to come. But come to Taos all the same, and probably we'll all stay at Mabel Sterne's for a day or two. I am glad to be on free territory once more – but we remain quite friendly. She was always nice – only somewhat *blind* to anything except her own way. I'll meet you at Taos.

It is rough here – really – and snow. But the house warm, even if there's no furniture. Will Mrs Seltzer mind? Will you?

We spent the morning sawing a pretty big tree into lengths – one of the Danes and I. We get our own fuel. This afternoon we rode through sleet and slush to San Cristobal – through the trees, downhill. They are littlish piñon trees, nothing tall. Me on a 'pacing' horse with swivel legs. A pacer, they call it!

Don't come if you mind roughness. Otherwise it's great fun, and very beautiful wild country.

I'll try and get *Studies* finished.

Yrs   D. H. Lawrence

I am not sure if we'll go to the Santo Domingo dance – but probably *not*.

2668. To S. S. Koteliansky, 4 December 1922
Text: MS BL; Postmark, [. . .] DEC 7 1922; cited in Gransden 29.

Del Monte Ranch. Questa. New Mexico.
4 Decem. 1922

My dear Kot

I have been waiting for an answer from you to my last letter. I asked you too to send to Mountsier a copy of each of the *Signatures* if you still had any. Why this non-answering. I hope you're not downright ill at last. That cave! You ought to be out of it.

You see we've moved. Too much Mabel Sterne at Taos. This is only 17 miles away – but another world. The last foothills of the Rocky Mts. – forest and snow mountains behind – and below, the desert, with other mountains very far off, west. It is fine. We have an old 5-room log cabin – and chop down our trees and have big fires. It is rough, but very agreeable. Then we ride horseback when we have time. I feel very different.

America makes one feel hard – would make one feel bitter, if one were not too old for bitterness.

I asked Seltzer to send you a copy of *England my England*, short stories. I won't send you *Fantasia of the Unconscious*, that would bore you. And you must be sick of books, anyhow.

I'll send a word to Katharine, via you. Perhaps. Anyway greet her from me.

I intend to stay here till March or April: if I don't move before. Seltzer is coming at Christmas to see me. Oh God! – I am repeatedly invited to go East and lecture. I might be a rich man. But shoulder to shoulder with Gilly and Hughie Walpole, no.[1] I won't go.

---

[1] Gilbert Cannan and the novelist (Sir) Hugh Walpole (1884–1941) had both undertaken lecture tours in USA (see Letter 2670).

I still think to come to England in the spring. What is happening in the world? We never see a newspaper – save the *Denver Post*, which is all Headlines and Murder. I know nothing. What is going to happen? Anything? I dreamed that Albert Stopford came to see me and told me that something big, very big, was imminent: like another war. Dreams! I don't care anyhow.

Do you remember the Christmas in Bucks?[1] – a cycle seems to have revolved since then, and come back somewhat to the same place. I feel a *bit* like I felt in Bucks. Rananim!

Well, be well. God knows what a state you're in. Are you fat, fox-like? Many greetings to Sonia and Ghita and Grisha.

DHL

2669. To Baroness Anna von Richthofen, 5 December 1922
Text: MS UCB; Frieda Lawrence 173–4.

Del Monte Ranch. *Questa*. New Mexico.

5 Decem. 1922

Meine liebe Schwiegermutter

Siehst du, wir haben wieder geflogen – oder wir *sind* wieder geflogen. Aber nicht weit – nur 25 Km. Und hier sitzen wir in einem alten Holzhaus – 5 Zimmer – sehr primitiv – auf diesem grossen Ranch. Hinten die Rocky Mountains – Tannenbäume – Schneeköpfe – herum, die Hügeln, Tannenbäume und Zedar und auch Greasewood, das ist eines graues Büschlein von der Wüste. Unten, die Wüste, gross und flach und wie ein Schattenteich, sehr weit. Und in der Ferne, mehr Bergen, schnee-klein, und Sonnenuntergang. – Jetzt bist du im Bild. Die *Hawk* Familie wohnen 5 Minuten unten – und dann kein Haus für 4 Kilom. Hinten, kein Haus für 300 Km. oder mehr. Sehr wenig Leute. Ein leeres Land – Sehr schön auch. Wir haben ein grossen Balsam-tanne untergeschlagen – oder geschnitten – und in Stücken gehackt – wie ein Steinbruch, das goldenes Holz. Wir haben für Kameraden zwei junge Dänen, Maler: sie gehen in dem kleinen 3-Zimmer Cabin in der nähe. Der Hawk – ein junger Mann, 30 Jahr – hat 150 halb-wilde Viehe – und eine junge Frau – ist nett – nicht reich.

Du hast über Mabel Dodge gefragt: Amerikanerin – reich – einziges Kind – von Buffalo, am Lake Erie – Bankleute – 42 Jahr alt – kurz, dick – sieht jung aus – hat drei Ehemänner gehabt – ein Evans (tod), ein Dodge (geschieden), und ein Maurice Sterne (Jude, Russisch, Maler, Jung) (auch geschieden). Hat jetzt ein Indianer, Tony, ein fetter Kerl. Hat viel in Europa gelebt – Paris, Nice, Florenz – ist etwas berühmt in New York, und wenig geliebt – sehr

[1] See p. 165 n. 3.

gescheit als Frauenzimmer – noch eine Kulturträger – spielt gern die
'patroness' – hässt die weisse Welt, und liebt die Indianer aus Hasse – ist sehr
'nobel', will sehr 'gut' sein, und ist sehr schlimm – hat eine furchtbare Wille
zur Macht – Frauenmacht, weisst du – wollte eine Hexe werden, und, in
derselbe Zeit, eine Maria von Bethany an Jesus' Füssen – eine dicke weisse
Krähe, ein girrende Unglücksraben, eine kleine Buffalo.

Die Leute in Amerika wollen alle *Macht*; aber eine persönliche, kleine,
niedrige Macht: bullying. Sie sind alle *bullies*.

Höre nur, Deutschland, Amerika ist der grosseste *Bully* die Welt hat noch
gesehen. Macht ist stolz. Aber bullying ist demokratisch und niedrig.

Genug. Wir sind immer noch 'freunde' mit der Mabel. Nehmen aber diese
Schlange nicht in der Busen.

Weisst du, diese Leute haben *nur* Geld. Nichts weiter wie Geld. Und dass
die Welt *will* das Geld, wollte alle das Geld haben – so ist Amerika stark, stolz,
übermächtig. Wenn man nur sagen könnte: 'Amerika, ihr Geld ist Scheiss;
geh und scheiss mehr' – dann wäre Amerika ein Nichtle.

[My dear Schwiegermutter

You see, we have flown again – or we *are* flown again. But not far – only 25
km. And here we sit in an old log cabin – 5 rooms – very primitive – on this big
ranch. Behind, the Rocky Mountains – pine-trees – snow-peaks – round
about, the hills, pine-trees and cedars and also greasewood, that's a grey little
bush of the desert. Below, the desert, big and level and like a shadow-pond,
very wide. And in the distance, more mountains, snow-small, and sunset. –
Now you've got the picture. The *Hawk* family live 5 minutes below – and then
no house for 4 kilom. Behind, no house for 300 km. or more. Very few people.
An empty land. – Very beautiful too. We hacked down a big balsam-pine tree
– or cut – and chopped it in pieces – like a stone quarry, the golden wood. We
have for comrades two young Danes, painters: they go in the little 3-room
cabin nearby. Hawk – a young man, 30 years – has 150 half-wild cattle – and a
young wife – is nice – not rich.

You asked about Mabel Dodge: American – rich – only child – from
Buffalo, on Lake Erie – bankers – 42 years old – short, stout – looks young –
has had three husbands – an Evans (dead), a Dodge (divorced), and a Maurice
Sterne (Jew, Russian, painter, young) (also divorced). Has now an Indian,
Tony, a fat fellow. Has lived much in Europe – Paris, Nice, Florence – is
rather famous in New York, and little loved – very clever for a female –
another culture-bearer – likes to play the 'patroness' – hates the white world,
and loves the Indians out of hate – is very 'noble', wants to be very 'good', and
is very wicked – has a terrible will to power – woman power, you know –

wanted to become a witch, and, at the same time, a Mary of Bethany at Jesus's feet[1] – a stout white crow, a cooing raven of misfortune, a little buffalo.

The people in America all want *power*; but a personal, petty, mean power: bullying. They are all *bullies*.

Just listen, Germany, America is the biggest *bully* the world has yet seen. Power is proud. But bullying is democratic and mean.

Enough. We are still 'friends' with Mabel. But don't take this serpent to our bosom.

You know, these people have *only* money. Nothing further than money. And as the world *wants* the money, wanted to have all the money – so America is strong, proud, overpowerful. If one could only say: 'America, your money is shit; go and shit more' – then America would be a little nothing.[2]]

2670. To Mary Cannan, 5 December 1922
Text: MS Lazarus; cited in Vivian de Sola Pinto, ed. *D. H. Lawrence After Thirty Years*, p. 34.

Del Monte Ranch. Questa. New Mexico.
5 Dec. 1922

My dear Mary

We lead such a strenuous life I get no letters written. We have come 17 miles from Taos: are now settled in an old log cabin, 5 rooms, on this ranch on the foothills: mountain forest and white snow behind – desert, like a great dim pool below – and other mountains, west, far away: We've been busy tidying round – now are comfortable. Two young Danes, painters, are having another 3-room cabin. We cut down a great balsam pine, and tomorrow are going to haul it in. We all go riding – the country is quite wild – hills and low pines, dropping to desert. It is very beautiful and all that.

But still, I say, America is not a sympathetic country. One doesn't like the people. They are just *never* simple and human: but never. I like the Mexicans better.

We think to stay here till March or April – then go east. For the summer, cross the sea again: most likely to England.

I get many invitations to go to New York and lecture. But with Gilbert and Hughie Walpole there, should be surely *de trop*: Anyhow I shan't go.

I am sending you by this post a copy of *England my England*, short stories. I hope you get it for Christmas.

The letters from Taos will still come on. Taos is the nearest post-office, south. But from the east, Questa, 35 miles, is the nearest post office.

---

[1] See Luke x. 39.   [2] The MS is incomplete.

Frieda loves it here as a place. Anything, so long as one can avoid the American people. The country is gorgeous, in its hard, resistant way.

Didn't I tell you about *Kangaroo*? It's an Australian novel with no women in it: more political, you might say – more a thought adventure if you like. I think a great deal of it, but don't expect it to be popular. – I seem to have a pretty good sale over here – *Women in Love* has sold about 10,000 in the cheap edition, 3000 in the other.

I still get rather feeble letters from the Taorminese – they say no forestieri in Italy. Too much fascisti, I suppose.[1]

What is England like? I even had a letter from Ottoline. She says people tend too much to *withdraw*. Can you wonder? I see Murry boosts me a bit – patronisingly.[2] But I have no use for him. Gilbert, over here, says I am very nice when I pick daisies, but useless when I do *people*. If I did him and Gwen and the Mondanity![3]

It is snow here – coyotes howl at night – sun very hot during the day. America makes one feel one has swallowed a rather big pebble.

I hope you'll have a good Christmas. Love from F[rieda] and me.

DHL

2671. To Lady Cynthia Asquith, 5 December 1922
Text: MS UT; Unpublished.

Del Monte Ranch. *Questa*. New Mexico.
5 Decem. 1922

This is to greet you for Christmas. I hear you are a popular authoress.[4] What next? Anyhow you'll never write a sex novel. *Peccato*! Write one then about J. M. [Barrie].[5]

I order you my book of short stories.

We have come about 17 miles from Taos – have an old 5-room log cabin on a wild ranch – Rocky Mts – desert below – fell trees and cut 'em up to burn – ride horseback in cowboy hat and cowboy boots – Frieda on a tall white stalk of a mare. Basta.

Do you see it all?

We think to stay till April. Then probably England. What about England,

---

[1] In October 1922 Mussolini had seized control of the government; armed Fascist violence was common.

[2] DHL may have seen Murry's review of *Aaron's Rod* in *Nation and Athenaeum*, xxxi (12 August 1922), 655–6. Though the review is highly commendatory – '*Aaron's Rod* is the most important thing that has happened to English literature since the war, more important than *Ulysses*' – Murry's manner is occasionally offensive. See Draper 177–80.   [3] See p. 159 n. 1.

[4] Lady Cynthia was writing a series of articles under the heading 'The Woman's View' for the *Times*.   [5] See p. 32 n. 6.

anyhow? I dreamed Albert Stopford came to see me and said something big
was imminent – like another war.

We never get a paper.

Had a letter from Ottoline.

Is your husband still 'Hutchinson'?[1] Very good to me.

Now don't *really* go and deteriorate, JMming and Lady's Worlding.

D. H. Lawrence

2672. To Knud Merrild, [5 December 1922]
Text: MS UT; Merrild 68.

Del Monte Ranch. Valdez
Tuesday

Dear Merrild

Pity you couldn't come out yesterday. William Hawk is coming in on
Thursday with his Ford – he will bring you out if you don't come before.

Götzsche says bring a tin of varnish remover, and look at *canvas*, at
Gersons.[2]

Did you get the other goods, or not?

Greet the Ufers.

D. H. Lawrence

2673. To Thomas Seltzer, 5 December 1922
Text: MS UT; Postmark, Taos DEC 7 1922; Lacy, *Seltzer* 52.

Del Monte Ranch. *Questa*. New Mexico
5 Dec. 1922

Dear Seltzer

I have your letter of Nov. 28, and clippings.

I will meet you then in *Taos* on the 25th – if you come straight through. If
you don't care about going to Santa Fe, then everybody says it is best to come
to Denver, Colorado, change there on to the Denver and Rio Grande railway,
and come down to *Taos Junction Station* changing, I think, at Alamosa again.
This is only 25 miles from Taos, and the stage runs every day. Sometimes the
Santa Fe stage doesn't run for two or three days. We'll probably stay a day or
two in Taos, then come here. So glad Mrs Seltzer can come. – I told you, we
are only 17 miles from Taos.

You know the Insel Verlag has published a translation of *The Rainbow*.[3]

---

[1] See p. 32 n. 5.
[2] Gerson Gusdorf (1869–1951), b. Germany, came to New Mexico in 1885, started 'Bond-
McCarthy-Gusdorf' in 1905 with Frank Bond and John H. McCarthy, and then opened his
own general store, known locally as 'Gerson Gusdorf'.
[3] *Der Regenbogen*; see p. 40 n. 1.

I know Murry too well to care what he says, one way or another. 'When I open my mouth let no dog bark.'¹

Have done all *Studies* except the last two – sent the first VIII to Mountsier. Will finish in a week (Deo volente).

Do you really want to publish my James Joyce remarks? No, I don't think it's quite fair to him.

It is fine here – but rough. Will you mind that?

Do please send books to these people, for Christmas.

DHL

2674. To Thomas Seltzer, [post 5 December 1922]
Text: MS UT; Lacy, *Seltzer* 51–2.

[Del Monte Ranch, New Mexico]
[post 5 December 1922]²

Dear Thomas

Bring me if you can the figures for the income tax – I must get that done. The Kingfisher fishing in the ink is for you – twist the top and it's an inkwell. *Il Penseroso* is for Adele.

DHL

Bring me that brown copy of *The Rainbow* if it's handy, and I'll expurgate it.

2675. To Robert Mountsier, 8 December 1922
Text: MS Smith; Unpublished.

Del Monte Ranch. *Questa*, New Mex.
8 Dec. 1922

Dear M[ountsier]

I think Seldes must have sent this to me by mistake.³ It came this minute. I return to you.

What are you doing?

DHL

I'll have a shot at the Sherman book when it comes.⁴

---

¹ *The Merchant of Venice*, I.i. 94 ['when I ope my lips . . .'].
² It seems reasonable to suppose that this unfranked note was included with the Christmas gifts for the Seltzers and written in December after plans for the Seltzers' visit were firm.
³ The enclosure is missing.
⁴ *Americans* (New York, 1922) by the literary critic Stuart Pratt Sherman (1881–1926). DHL's review, 'Model Americans', appeared in the *Dial*, lxxiv (May 1923), 503–10. (Sherman's review of *Studies in Classic American Literature*, entitled 'America Is Discovered', appeared in *New York Evening Post Literary Review*, 20 October 1923.)

2676. To Baroness Anna von Richthofen, [8 December 1922]
Text: MS UT; Unpublished.

[Frieda Lawrence begins]

Del Monte Ranch, Questa, New Mexico
[8 December 1922][1]

Liebe mère

Hier sitzen wir hoch oben, so schön in unserm Holzhaus, wir haben sehr geschafft und es nett gemacht – Lawrence und 2 junge dänische Maler haben einen meterdicken Baum gehackt – Alles ist so gut und unverfälscht, dicken Rahm auf der Milch und vom Kalb und vom Schwein so viel Du willst – Über Weihnachten ist ein grosser Rehtanz der Indianer – Lawrence's Verleger kommt mit seiner Frau von New York, die Nächte sind kalt aber am Tag die herrlichste Aussicht bis Colorado hin – weit, weit über ein unbewohntes Land – Heute kam ein Indianer um hinter uns in den Bergen auf Bärenjagd zu gehen – Wir haben riesige Holzfeuer einen Keller voll Äpfel – nachmittags reiten wir – L. hat Dir für Weihnachten Dollars geschickt – Gieb der Camilla und der Hadu etwas, die gute Kramerin muffelt ja nicht mehr – den Rest mach Weihnachtsgeschenke und den Rehbraten für's Haus – Ich habe nette Sachen für Euch – aber ich bring sie mit – Je, dies ist mein Weihnachtsbrief – Du hast ja Döchtere und Anita um Dich – Hat Hadu sein Geld ? ? Und Else schreibt Du seist so frisch – Also wenn wir kommen können Frau Geheimrat Sprünge machen – Bald ist der kürzeste Tag, ich habe Narzissen in Vasen und jede Knospe wird ängstlich beaügt – Es ist ein Glück dass man so viel aushält – Manchmal wundert's mich doch, Tropenhitze und hier sind wir 9000 Fuss hoch alles in einem Jahr – Eben hab ich einen schönen noblen Artikel von Kayserlingk gelesen – Schrieb ich Else je, dass in Kandy eines der wenigen Bücher die ich fand eines von Alfred Weber war –

Ein gutes Fest wünsch ich Euch allen von Herzen, wir schmücken einen lebendigen Christbaum im Freien und machen ein grosses Feuer –

Eure F.

Dein Stoff kam von Griffin an Spalding!

[Lawrence begins]

Adresse:

Del Monte Ranch *Questa*, New Mexico. U.S.A.

Ich schrieb dir vor drei Tagen – hast du es?

DHL

[Dear mère

Here we sit high up, so splendid in our wooden house, we have worked hard and made it nice – Lawrence and two young Danish painters chopped down a

---

[1] The conjectural date assumes that DHL was referring , in his brief message, to Letter 2669.

metre-thick tree – Everything is so good and unadulterated, thick cream on the milk and from calf and from pig as much as you want – During Christmas there will be a big deer-dance by the Indians – Lawrence's publisher is coming with his wife from New York, the nights are cold but in the day the most magnificent view all the way to Colorado – far, far across an uninhabited land – Today an Indian came to go bear-hunting in the mountains behind us – We have huge wood fires a cellar full of apples – afternoons we ride – L. has sent you dollars for Christmas – Give Camilla[1] and Hadu some, the good Kramerin is after all no longer sulking – with the rest make Christmas gifts and the venison roast for the House – I have nice things for all of you – but I'm bringing them with me – Lord, this is my Christmas letter – You have after all daughters and Anita around you – Does Hadu have his money? ? And Else writes you are so lively – So if we come Frau Geheimrat can live it up – Soon it will be the shortest day, I have narcissi in vases and anxiously eye each bud – It's lucky that one can endure so much – Sometimes it really amazes me, tropical heat and here we are 9000 feet high all in one year – I've just read a beautiful noble article by Kayserlingk[2] – Did I ever write Else that in Kandy one of the few books I found was one by Alfred Weber –

I wish you all a good Christmas from my heart, we are decorating a living Christmas tree outdoors and are having a big fire –

Your F.

Your cloth came from Griffin and Spalding![3]
[Lawrence begins]
I wrote to you three days ago – do you have it?

DHL]

2677. To Mabel Dodge Sterne, [10? December 1922]
Text: MS Brill; Luhan 108–9.

Del Monte Ranch. *Valdez*, New Mex.
Sunday
Dear Mabel
Thank you for the honey, which came from you or via you, I don't know. Also Frieda's shoes from Santa Fe: fit.

I don't know now if you are home or not.

We are settled in – very nice – Danes in their cabin. Today we rode all four

---

[1] Unidentified.
[2] Presumably a publication by Count Hermann Keyserling (1880–1946), the popular German social philosopher from whom DHL quoted in 'Aristocracy' which was included in *Reflections on the Death of a Porcupine* (Philadelphia, 1925).
[3] The principal and most expensive department store in Nottingham.

to the hot springs – Manby's – did me good to soak. I rode Elizabeth's horse – nice horse to ride.

Seltzer says he and his wife leave New York[1] on the 22nd. Dec. and come straight to Taos. His wife has a fortnight's leave: from what, I don't know.[2] I said I would meet them in Taos: and see the Christmas dance at the pueblo.[3] I want you to let me know at once if you wish us to come to you for a day or two, or not. Of course you may be full up – or you may be going away. Then I would just stay a night with the Seltzers' in Taos and come on here. Tell me, so I can arrange.

Why don't you come over here and see us? Or if you don't want to come here – don't you? – then we'll meet you at John's Ranch and picnic there.

Life has been just a business of chopping wood, fixing doors, putting up shelves, eating and sleeping, since we are here. There is still much more to do, but it can wait.

No news from the outer world.

Let me have bill for the honey and shoes.

If we come to you for Christmas, I'll bring mince pies. I made some mincemeat. And I want to make Christmas puddings. But now I have to bake! Great success, Graham's bread.[4]

Pup growing huger.[5]

Saluti buoni   DHL

2678. To Robert Mountsier, 12 December 1922
Text: MS Smith; Unpublished.

Del Monte Ranch. *Questa*. New Mexico
12 Dec. 1922

Dear M[ountsier]

Your note of Nov. 28th received only today. Well, Seldes has made a fool of us over that Indian article, and over 'Ladybird'.[6] We'll cut him out. Those 'mistakes' are always subconscious-intentional, if not deliberate. You should go ahead, without minding my letters, except my letters to you.

I hope you got the first of the *Studies*. The rest are finished – tied up – when I can get them to the post office they'll come on: probably Thursday. They'll

---

[1] New York] Santa Fe
[2] Adele Seltzer was employed as social secretary to Therese Loeb Schiff, widow of banker Jacob Henry Schiff (1847–1920).
[3] On Christmas Day at the Taos Pueblo either the buffalo dance or the deer dance is performed, the other being held on 6 January. On both occasions, visitors are permitted. See Blanche Grant, *The Taos Indians* (Taos, 1925) for descriptions of the dances.
[4] I.e. made with Graham flour.
[5] A French bull terrier, offspring of Mabel Sterne's 'Lorraine': 'Bibbles' in the poem of that title, also called 'Pips' and 'Pipsey'.   [6] See p. 329 n. 2 and p. 341 n. 1.

no doubt horrify you. But then you'll see their form is now final. Bed-rock.
You don't say anything definite about your movements. I've discovered two nice rooms adjoining the Danes cabin: used as store rooms. I'll have to get William Hawk to let me have them: and somebody in Taos to lend a stove and bit of furniture. I guess William will charge about $10. a month. Quite enough too. But you'd be all right there.

I expect to be at Taos over Christmas – meet[1] the Seltzers there, if they come. What about you? – It's much nicer here than on M[abel] S[terne] territory.

Seltzer sent me *Maya the Bee* and *Batouala*. Don't think much of either.

DHL

You don't say how your *health* is.

I told you Seldes asked me to review a book about America – book hasn't come yet – but I wont do it now.

2679. To Mabel Dodge Sterne, [14 December 1922]
Text: MS Brill; Unpublished.

Del Monte Ranch. Valdez.
Thursday

Dear Mabel

Thank you for answering at once about Christmas. You are right, it would be a bit stiff. I hadn't realised the wedding cum Noël cum Bynner mix-up that it would be. Fraid I should be the least happy. I'll bring the Seltzers on here, if they come, straight.

It has snowed deep here now – inaccessible for some days, I am afraid. Looks as if it had only rained on the desert.

All seasonable wishes for the wedding etc. – My, but it's a broth.

DHL

Yes, the story amused me. So did your other letter, with the invitation to tour the east with the Indians. You as an aesthetic Buffalo Bill! Why don't you remember my wicked [. . .]ce[2] in time?

P.S. I found the bill for the shoes – $7.50. I take it you paid this. Enclose cheque for $8.50: which covers the honey, does it?

This minute I have a letter from Mrs Harwood asking us there.[3] So shall just stay the two nights with the Seltzers' chez elle.

---

[1] meet] see   [2] MS detective.
[3] Elizabeth Case ('Lucy') Harwood (1867–1938), had come to Taos in 1914, interested in painting and drawing; she became a local patron of the arts, establishing the Harwood Foundation in December 1923.

Also a letter from Mountsier saying he arrives somewhere about the 20th or 21st. Lord, what an influx!

DHL

2680. To Bessie Freeman, 15 December 1922
Text: MS UNYB; Moore, *Intelligent Heart* 306–7.

Del Monte Ranch. *Valdez.* New Mexico.

15 December 1922

Dear Bessie Freeman

You see we have moved: Mabel was too near a neighbour. We have come to the Hawk's ranch – next to John Evans ranch – about 17 miles from Taos: have an old 5 room log cabin, and are very comfortable. We plan to stay till April, so perhaps you'll be through with your house-selling by then. Perhaps it is true, you shouldn't part with your chippendale: if it's a comfort to you to have it. Perhaps we shall see you.

We have no particular news: are going down to Taos on the 24th, and staying a day or two with Mrs Harwood – you remember, from whose house I turned back one morning. Thomas Seltzer and his wife are due to arrive in Taos on the 25th – my publisher – then we shall come on here. Mabel will be full with a wedding + Xmas lot: not my line at all. John Evans marries the young Alice Henderson on the 20th of this month. She is fifteen years old. And he will be 21 in January. But I don't care for him: a very untrustworthy youth, seems to me. I am glad to be out of it all. The young couple will live in our (Tony's) house – and proceed east to the grandmother's for his coming of age. At least, such is the programme. All the same to me. – Dear Bessie Freeman, I must tell you I don't like Mabel very much. Elle me parait fausse. La strega.[1]

We have quite a good time here: cut down a big tree and with great exertions sawed it and split it up. And oh, it burns away so fast in all the fires. I think grudgingly when I scatter red embers: all my labours gone into smoke! But it was a sweet balsam pine tree, very bright in the burning. We struggle with pack-rats and pigs and cats. We've got one of Lorraine's little black pups that is now growing up into a young termagant. We go riding: I on a high sorrell thoroughbred that nearly splits me as I split my logs with wedges. – In a 3-room cabin are two young Danes, painters, nice: good neighbours. And Mountsier is coming next week. Snow is quite deep round us: but no snow on the desert below. The coyotes howl by the gate.

You know Sarah Higgins has left Victor – pro tem. at least – and gone to

---

[1] 'She seems false to me. The witch.'

New York.[1] Suppose she thinks she can bring down bigger game. Doubt it. She's taken the baby. He is growing a beard and being a lost soul. Nina Witt says she's going to England in Jan., Lee Witt having been badly defeated in politics – nose out of joint.[2] Nina to study some sort of co-ordination healing stunt under some doctor in London. Wish her joy of it. The Gaspards have gone: he in tears, for his lost years, apparently: lost something.[3]

Did you get the copy of *England my England* I sent you? – long ago. I know quite a lot of Spanish out of the little red book.

We say we are going to *Greenland* in the summer. Are we?

This is to wish you a happy Christmas, from us both.

D. H. Lawrence

2681. To Tony Luhan, 15 December 1922
Text: MS Brill; Unpublished.

Del Monte Ranch. Valdez.

15 Dec. 1922

Dear Tony

Thank you for the long letter. That must have been fine, seeing the Shalico's dance.[4]

But why did you send back the cheque? It was not necessary. Dinero ò no, nos comprendemos, nosotros dos hombres. Como hombres, nos comprendemos.[5]

That reminds me, I left that owl in the back porch of your house. I meant to burn it. No se porqué la señora mi has mando esa fea ave de la noche. ¿Qué quisiese ella decir? No mi servo di estas cosas.[6]

Su amigo   D. H. Lawrence

---

[1] Sara Parsons (1901–), daughter of the American painter Sheldon Parsons, m. Victor Higgins, 1919.

[2] Witt probably ran for County Commissioner; as a Democrat in a Republican county, he had little chance of winning.

[3] Leon Gaspard (1882–1964), Russian painter, was not admitted into the Taos Society of Artists. He spoke English with a thick Russian accent, was not easily understood, and there may have been jealousy over his considerable ability as a painter. He left Taos for Japan and China, returning after several years, at which time he was better received. m. Evelyn Adell (d. 1956), an artist in her own right.

[4] Zuni ceremonial dance which celebrates the advent and departure of the Kachinas, deified ancestral spirits. The dancers impersonate the Shalakos, mythical beings of extraordinary height.

[5] 'Money or not, we understand, we two men. As men, we understand.'

[6] 'I don't know why the senora sent me this ugly bird of the night. What did she wish to say? These things are not for me.'

2682. To Catherine Carswell, 17 December 1922
Text: MS YU; cited Carswell 173–4.

Del Monte Ranch. *Questa*, New Mexico
17 Dec. 1922

My dear Catherine

This is late for Christmas. But I ordered you a copy of *England my England*, which I hope you get in time.

You see we have made a little move – only 17 miles. Taos too much Mabel Sterne and suppers and motor drives and people dropping in. This is, materially, very fine. We have an old 5-room log cabin on this big wild ranch on the Rocky foothills – the snow mountains behind – a vast landscape below, vast, desert, and then more mountains West, far off in Arizona, a sky-line. Very beautiful. Trees all behind and snow – The ranch people dont do much – they are educated people – more or less – only three of them now – young man and wife, and his sister – name Hawk. Very nice and kind – live in house three minutes below – have about 125 head of cattle – and ranch 1500 acres – but mostly wild. The coyotes come down howling at evening. We've got two young Danish artists in a tiny log cabin – they came along with us – and we all chop down trees for our burning, and go off riding together. Altogether it is ideal, according to one's ideas. But *innerlich*, there is nothing. It seems to me, in America, for the inside life, there is just blank nothing. All this outside life – and marvellous country – and it all means so little to one. I don't quite know what it is one wants – because the ordinary society and 'talk' in Europe are weary enough. But there is no inside life-throb here – none – all empty – people inside dead, outside bustling (sometimes). Anyhow dead and always on the move. Truly I prefer Europe. Liberty – space – deadness. – I'm expecting Thomas Seltzer and wife for Christmas – we go to Taos – also Mountsier. There will be an Indian dance at the pueblo – but the Indians are very american – no inside life. Money and moving about – nothing more. I suppose we'll stay another three months here – then come east – come to Europe – perhaps via Greenland. I know now I don't want to live anywhere very long. But I belong to Europe. Though not to England. I think I should like to go to Russia in the summer. After America, it appeals to me. No money there (they say). When you write to poor Ivy,[1] ask her how it would be for me and Frieda to spend a few months in Russia – even a year. I feel drawn that way. – Am not writing here. – *Kangaroo* is due for February. I seem to have a fair sale over

[1] Ivy Litvinov, née Low (1889–1977), novelist and friend of Catherine Carswell. m. 1916, Maxim Litvinov (1876–1951), later Soviet foreign commissar (1930–9). She met DHL in 1914 and was now living in Russia.

here – *Women in Love* going now into 15,000. Why do they read me? But anyhow, they *do* read me – which is more than England does.

Very many greetings from us both.

D. H. Lawrence

2683. To Mabel Dodge Sterne, [19 December 1922]
Text: MS Brill; Luhan 109–10.

Del Monte Ranch. *Valdez.*
Tuesday.

Dear Mabel

Your letter just come. I have decided not to come to Taos at all for Christmas. Mountsier remains indefinite, and the Seltzer's are no more definite than they were. So I'll have them brought straight out here when they do come: and I must be here to receive them.

No, I don't feel convivial.

Hope you'll have a good time with your festivities.

Yrs   D. H. Lawrence

2684. To Elizabeth Harwood, [19 December 1922]
Text: MS Brill; Luhan 110.

Del Monte Ranch. *Valdez.* New Mexico
Tuesday.[1]

My Dear Mrs Harwood

Your letter has only just arrived. It was a shame to trouble you about all those other people. I have decided not to come to Taos at Christmas, these arrivals being so indefinite. When Mountsier and the Seltzers do come I will have them brought straight out here. Your invitation was so very kind, it seems a shame not to accept it. But it will be much simpler as it is. I must look after the Seltzer's as soon as they come. Will you please accept my thanks and my regrets.

The Danes too thank you very much, but will feel too shy to come to your house alone.

With all good wishes.

D. H. Lawrence

[1] Although DHL tells Elizabeth Harwood that her letter 'has only just arrived', he actually received it the previous Thursday (Letter 2679). It was after he had received the letter from Mabel Sterne (to which he replied in Letter 2683) implying that she had arranged for Elizabeth Harwood to extend the invitation, that he decided to remain at the ranch for Christmas.

2685. To Robert Mountsier, [27 December 1922]
Text: MS Smith; Unpublished.

Del Monte Ranch. Lobo.

Wed.

Dear Mountsier

The Seltzers are here – Expect you will arrive Saturday. Go to the Columbian Hotel for the night. I think William Hawk and I will come out on Sunday morning in the Ford truck to fetch you. Hope you have a good journey.

Yrs   DHL[1]

2686. To Robert Mountsier, [29 December 1922]
Text: MS Smith; Unpublished.

Del Monte Ranch. Valdez (Lobo)

Friday night

Dear Mountsier

William Hawk says he will bring you out tomorrow night if you arrive by the stage. Seltzer leaves Tuesday morning. Hope you have had a good journey.

Yrs   D.H. Lawrence

If you dont come out with William, best hire a taxi and come in that. Oakleys have a taxi which usually comes here – Richard Oakley.[2]

DHL

2687. To John Middleton Murry, 30 December 1922
Text: MS NYPL; cited in Murry, *New Adelphi* 414.

Del Monte Ranch. *Questa*. New Mexico.

30 December 1922

Dear Jack

I had your letter yesterday. Heaven knows what we all are, and how we should feel if we met, now that we are changed. We'll have to meet and see. I think of coming to England in the late spring or early summer: perhaps go down to Mexico City and sail from Vera Cruz. The longer I am in America, the less I want to go east, to Chicago or Boston or New York. Don't mind evading them, even if it is a mere evasion. Thomas Seltzer and wife are here: he's a nice tiny man, I think I trust him really.

It is good fun on this ranch – quite wild – Rocky Mts – desert with Rio

---

[1] DHL addressed the envelope containing this letter: 'Mr Robert Mountsier due to arrive *Saturday* by favour of the stage'.

[2] Richard Bannerfield ('Uncle Dick') Oakley (1861–1936), b. England, ran a taxi service in Taos.

Grande Canyon away spreading below – great and really beautiful landscape – looking far far west. We ride off to the Rio Grande to the hot springs, and bathe – and we chop wood and wagon it in, and all that. But there's no inside to the life: all outside. I don't believe there ever will be any inside to American life – they seem so dead – till they are all destroyed.

Greet Katharine and I hope she is well in Fontainebleau where the Kings used to be. 'In *my* country we're *all* Kings and queens', said Mrs Ashley, American woman,[1] to the Duca's sister, in Taormina. And by Jove they are – of their own muck-heaps, of money if nothing else.

Mispah![2]   D. H. Lawrence

2688. To Frederick Carter, 31 December 1922
Text: MS UT; Unpublished.

Del Monte Ranch. *Questa*, New Mexico. U. S. A.

31 Decem 1922

Dear Mr Carter[3]

I had your letter two days ago. – No, I don't know your engravings. *Studies in Classic American Literature* have not appeared in book form. They are due this spring here in America, but re-written and all different – no esotericism.

What you write about the Apocalypse interests me very much. If you have two MSS. I should be glad to read one: and then if it seemed to me I could be useful, I would try to submit it to a suitable publisher here. In England I should think Rider would be the man to publish it – he does all the esoteric books. Get a copy of the *Theosophist Review*, or the *Occult Review* – monthly – and you'll see the kind of books Rider publishes, also his address, which I forget. Then if you think he is the right man, write him a letter and ask him if he would care to read the MS.

Anyhow I should be glad to hear what happens to the MS., and to read it if possible.

Yours Sincerely   D. H. Lawrence

---

[1] Unidentified.
[2] Cf. Genesis xxxi. 48–9: 'Therefore was the name of it called Galeed; and Mizpah, for he said, The Lord watch between me and thee, when we are absent one from another.'
[3] Frederick Carter (1883–1967), painter and etcher. He studied in Paris and Antwerp, returned to England and took up book illustrating. He was also interested in astrology and the occult. The MS in which he sought to interest DHL was concerned with symbolism in the Book of Revelation; it was later published by Elkin Matthews as *The Dragon of the Alchemists* (1926). For a full account of the association between Carter and DHL see *Apocalypse and the Writings on Revelation*, ed. Mara Kalnins (Cambridge, 1980), pp. 3–24.

2689. To Jan Juta, [1 January 1923]
Text: Moore, *Intelligent Heart* 308.

Del Monte Ranch, Questa, N. M.
1 Jan. 1922

I had your letter from Paris two days ago. Meant to write many times but had no address. Seltzer is here – with his wife. He is a tiny Jew, but trustworthy, seems to me. I still don't understand about English *Sea and Sardinia* – God knows what these publishers do between them.[1] Mountsier is due to arrive here this very evening. He will bring me a statement of sales. We both get *some* money for *Sea and Sardinia*: but not a great deal. Still, it will be worth having. I will send you a cheque the moment I know what the sales are – or what Seltzer has paid in. – The Americans are like that – ask you to send them things and then they won't use them. *They are no more sympathetic at home than they are in Europe.* It's a barren country, humanly. Taos was nice – but so much artistic small beer – paint purely in terms of dollars. We have come to this wild ranch – only about 17 miles from Taos – live in an old 5-room log cabin, and chop down trees and ride away on horseback to the Rio Grande. Quite a good life, physically. It is very splendid landscape – Rocky Mountains behind, and a vast space of desert in front, with other mountains far west. Very fine indeed, the great space to live in. But humanly nothing. There are two Danes came along with us, two painters, live in a little log cabin. We have quite good times riding and working. I don't want to write here. I think of going in a few weeks' time down into Mexico – to Mexico City – don't know how long to stay: then to Europe in the summer. But nothing certain. Luckily *Women in Love* sells well, so I am not so poor.

I knew Alan would go flat back to the dreary middle classes. Many greetings to Réné from us both. I heard from Burr[2] in Vienna. We will meet again this summer. Many many good wishes for the New Year.

2690. To Willard Johnson, 4 January 1923
Text: MS YU; Unpublished.

Del Monte Ranch. *Valdez*. N. Mexico
4 Jan 1923

Dear Willard Johnson
Thank you for your letter and the copy of *The Laughing Horse.*[3] It's a sad

---

[1] Secker's anger at Seltzer's procrastination was conveyed to Curtis Brown on 16 January 1923 (Secker Letter-Book, UIll): 'I should be very much obliged if you would kindly inform Mr Seltzer that as I have now waited exactly one year for the sheets of "Sea and Sardinia" I have now decided to manufacture an edition of the book in this country, so that he need not give the matter any further thought.'   [2] See p. 25 n. 6.
[3] See pp. 321 n. 3 and 331 n. 2.

laugh, a galled horse. I wish you hadn't printed the article – perhaps you wish so too – but since it is done, no matter. – No, I don't want to write a word about anything just now. – Seltzer has gone on to Los Angeles and San Francisco, and I don't know what he wants. He'll be in New York in a week's time. Perhaps next month I'll be starting on a trip to Old Mexico. If so, I'll call on you and Witter Bynner in Santa Fe, and we'll go on where we left off.

Yrs   D. H. Lawrence

2691. To Thomas Seltzer, 4 January 1923
Text: MS UT; Postmark, [. . .] JAN 6 1923; Lacy, *Seltzer* 54–5.

Del Monte Ranch. *Questa*. New Mexico
Thursday. 4 Jan. 1923

Dear Seltzer

I imagine Mountsier is going to settle down to ranch life and forget literary agency for the time being. Anyway I wont have him doing anything I don't want. – Personally he is being very nice: he'll like the life here – has gone riding today to Questa with Rachel Hawk: to the satisfaction of both. I'm glad he enjoys himself. Best that he should forget books. He talked only of some contracts he had had drawn up, starting with a 15% royalty. I don't know how that affects you. In England I start at 15%. But I want to be quite just, and you to be the same. I shall go through the *Studies in Classic American Literature* MS. and let you have it as soon as the last four type-written chapters come from New York. If you want to make any minor alterations, you are free to do so. Mountsier wants *Studies* published first, before *Kangaroo*. What do you think?

I enclose the last words of *Kangaroo*: the last page. Dont lose it.

Looking at Merrild's book-jacket designs again, I think that one for *Kangaroo* with the small figure in the middle is rather weak and abstract-looking: might lead one to expect something theoretic.

I am going through the Verga MS. – 'Black Bread'[1] – the short sketches: then I'll send it you. I want to know what you think of *Mastro-Don Gesualdo*.

Tell me how your trip west was. And what you think of the trip to Mexico.

What a rush you had for that Stage – or that train! And Oakley's car arrived at 10.45, if you please!

It is a lovely day. If Adele Szold were here we'd go riding. As it is I'll just stroll down to the post-box with this letter. – Yesterday William killed a steer – and that young Pips would not be kept away[2] – became shamefully sick – got well spanked – and so has gone to live with the Danes. There let her stay. She's

---

[1] An early title for *Little Novels of Sicily*, which contained 'Black Bread' and other short sketches by Verga.   [2] See p. 358 n. 5.

got no loyalty. To me, loyalty is far before love. Love seems usually to be just a dirty excuse for disloyalties.

Tell Adele Szold the white bowl had a pudding made in it this morning.

Yrs   D. H. Lawrence

2692. To Mabel Dodge Sterne, 15 January 1923
Text: MS Brill; Luhan 102.

Del Monte Ranch, Valdez
15 Jan 1923

Dear Mabel

I looked for that first eagle poem, but am sorry I could not find it.[1] No doubt I burned it – which is just like me.

Yrs   D. H. Lawrence

2693. To Witter Bynner, 19 January 1923
Text: MS HU; Postmark, Valdez JAN 20 1923; Huxley 562.

Del Monte Ranch. *Valdez*, New Mexico
19 Jan 1923

Dear Bynner

Thank you for the poem – I think I understand it.

Thank you also for being so nice to the Seltzers. They did appreciate it.

I think we really may be coming by Santa Fe next month or in early March. I would like to go down to Old Mexico – in spite of Wilfred Ewart. I read Stephen Graham's letter to the Santa Fe newspaper.[2] Where is Graham now? I would like to find out from him just what conditions are in Old Mexico now, and have any advice he has to give – particularly about the journey from El Paso to Mexico City.

It's awfully nice of you to offer us your hospitality once more: our first and last roof in America. One can't count hotels: they only have lids.

Greetings to you

D. H. Lawrence

Of course I wouldn't pass by Santa Fe without trying to see you. I'll write in plenty of time.

DHL

---

[1] See Letter 2626 and n. 2

[2] Wilfrid Herbert Gore Ewart (1892–1922) was accidentally killed in Mexico City on New Year's Eve by a stray bullet which struck him on his hotel balcony. Stephen Graham (1884–   ), English writer and authority on Russia, toured Mexico in 1922 with Ewart and reported the death in the Santa Fe newspaper, *New Mexican*. Graham later edited *Life and Last Words of Wilfrid Ewart* (1924).

2694. To Thomas Seltzer, 19 January 1923
Text: MS UT; Lacy, *Seltzer* 56–7.

Del Monte Ranch. *Questa*. New Mexico.
Friday 19 January 1923

Dear Seltzer

I have packed up for you *Studies in Classic American Literature*. I want you to publish them this spring. If you want anything altered or eliminated, tell me the page and line – I have a third MS. – and I will send you the revision. Don't bother to post the MS.

Also in the parcel is *Ladybird*. I had a long and friendly letter from Curtis Brown with very favorable offers for *Kangaroo*. But I don't trust Secker. And Curtis Brown says Secker is making a fine book of *Ladybird*, and will bring it out in March. I knew that was what they were up to. Hurry up your printers. If you have proofs of 'Captains Doll' and 'Fox', and there is time, let me see proofs. I will send them back at once. But be sure and be ready with the book *early* in March. That Secker shall not steal a march on us, and leave us stranded in April.

Also in the parcel the three book-jackets, which I like very much. Hope you will like them too.[1]

Also the Götzsche drawing. The *Dial* might do it with my 'Indian' article, which they are printing in instalments.[2] Or you might have some other bright idea. It would help nicely to advertise. I wrote the names on the back.

Also in the parcel thousands of contracts. As I said before, I want you to agree to all you possibly can. What is impossible write plainly to Mountsier, also to me – if anything is impossible.

Mountsier suggests *Captain's Doll*, *Studies*, and *Birds Beasts and Flowers* for this spring, leaving *Kangaroo* till early autumn. I think this wise. Do you? – And Mountsier says you really don't want *Birds Beasts* decorated or illustrated. If you really dislike it, we will just make a title-page and a rather exceptionally beautiful jacket, with animals on it. Would you like that? – I never want you to agree to anything that really goes badly against your grain. Don't hesitate to tell me.

We still think of Old Mexico in March. I read Stephen Grahams letter in the Santa Fe newspaper about the death of Wilfred Ewart in Mexico City. Is Stephen Graham back in New York? If so do ask him what the travelling is like – and the journey down from El Paso to Mexico City: and any advice he has to give.

Oh, Curtis Brown has a publisher wants to do *Mastro-don Gesualdo* in

[1] See p. 345 n. 2.
[2] See p. 332 n. 6; 'Taos' appeared in *Dial*, lxxiv (March 1923), 251–4.

August in England. Tell me quickly what you want to do about it. That lawyer Stern[1] told Mountsier that in 1888 the copyright laws weren't fixed between Italy and U. S. A. Had you better make sure. – So warm here. Many Greetings.

Yrs. D. H. Lawrence

Mrs Seltzer will recognise me on Laddie, Merrild on Brownie, the buggy-horse, and Götzsche on Pinto. Götzsche is doing a real forcible portrait of me in my leather shirt and blue overalls – if he doesn't spoil it.[2]

DHL

2695. To Mabel Dodge Sterne, [20 January 1923]
Text: MS Brill; Luhan 112.

Del Monte Ranch. *Valdez.*
Saturday[3]

Dear Mabel

No, I don't think I want to go to San Ildefonso – neither, yet, to Old Mexico. I don't feel angry. But just that I want to be alone – as much alone as I am – while I am here.

Yrs D. H. Lawrence

2696. To Mrs Bergman, [21? January 1923]
Text: MS Smith; Unpublished.

Del Monte Ranch. *Valdez*
Sunday

Dear Mrs Bergman[4]

This is to present Mr Mountsier to you – I know you will be friendly to him. He is staying with us up here, and is down in Taos for the night – or perhaps two nights – for the dentist. He would like to sleep in Mrs Witt's house. Would you be so very kind as to let him in, show him which bit of wood he may burn, and tell him where the blankets are for the cot. I know you won't mind doing him this kindness.

My wife will probably be down some time this week, for the dentist too – so we shall see you and have a chat.

Grüsse   D. H. Lawrence

---

[1] Benjamin H. Stern of the legal firm Stern and Ruben (see p. 182 n. 2).
[2] DHL gave this portrait to Adele Seltzer (Lacy, *Seltzer* 266). It is now at UT and is reproduced in this volume.
[3] Dated with reference to DHL's remark in Letter 2699 that Mabel Sterne was pressing them to take a trip to Old Mexico.   [4] Unidentified.

2697. To Curtis Brown, 23 January 1923
Text: MS BPL; Theresa Coolidge, 'D. H. Lawrence to His Agent', *More Books*, xxxiii (January 1948), 23–4.

Del Monte Ranch, *Questa*, New Mexico
23 January 1923

Dear Curtis Brown

I suddenly realise that the story 'The Captains Doll', which was bought by Hearsts for their *International Magazine*, and for which I have received $1000, has not yet appeared:[1] and till it has appeared in Hearsts magazine, it cannot possibly come out in book form: that would involve me in a great deal of trouble. I will ask Seltzer to let you know quickly when Hearsts can, or will, publish the story, and the book can then appear. But till you hear, please hold Secker back, whatever you do.

Yrs   D. H. Lawrence

2698. To Thomas Seltzer, 23 January 1923
Text: MS UT; Postmark, Questa J[. . .] 23 192[. . .]; Lacy, *Seltzer* 60–1.

Del Monte Ranch. *Questa*, New Mexico
23 January 1923

Dear Seltzer

I have suddenly realised – or Mountsier has – that Hearsts have not yet used 'The Captain's Doll'. Is that so? If so, will you find out when they *can* use it, quickly, and let Curtis Brown know – Because as I told you Secker is due to bring the thing out in March. I should like you to have it out that month too.

I enclose a letter to Curtis Brown – you read it and add a word when you have found out from Hearst.

Tell Adele Szold the underwear came for Frieda today, and I will send a cheque for the five dollars when I write to her.

Hurt my hand a bit with a log of wood.

Hope you have my letters, and MSS, and all: am waiting to hear from you.

Find I have $2,200 in the bank. Suppose that will take me to Mexico.

Am busy doing the *Birds Beasts*. They will soon be done. Will you tell me as soon as you can what format you want the book to have, exactly: the size and all: and exactly what decoration you want it to have.

It is very cold again. I don't like winter. I shall be rather glad to go south to Mexico. Tell me about it, if there is anything to tell.

Yrs   D. H. Lawrence

P. S. I will send Curtis Browns[2] letter direct – not enclose it. But do please write him as soon as you can:

[1] In fact the story was never published by Hearsts.   [2] Curtis Browns] Seltzer's

Curtis Brown, 6 Henrietta St., Covent Garden, London W. C. 2
A letter from Curtis Brown just arrived saying Secker is publishing
Ladybird 'almost immediately.' Do please find out the earliest date at which it
may be published, and send enclosed cable to Curtis Brown.

DHL

2699. To Bessie Freeman, 24 January 1923
Text: MS UNYB; cited in Moore, *Intelligent Heart* 308–9.

Del Monte Ranch. *Valdez*, New Mexico
24 January 1923

Dear Bessie Freeman

I answer your letter of New Year. So sorry about the operation and etherics.
But don't you fret, I don't believe anything serious lies after. You will be all
right. Feel a bit reckless, and you'll be well.

We are still here: but I don't know for how long. I wish Palm Springs were
not so far off, and we would come and see you. But the railway! And this
expensive America – And I'm a bit tired now of *winter*: the earth frozen for so
long. I am not used to it.

Didn't you get *England my England*? What a shame. I posted it in Taos. It is
my last book of short stories. I must get you another copy from the publisher. –
The Indian article is due to appear in the *Dial*, in pieces: our Apache trip. I
don't know exactly when.

Mabel is a liar – and false as hell. Goes round in Taos saying 'I had to get rid
of the Lawrences.' And her son John Evans 'Mother had to turn the
Lawrences out.' At the same time is writing such friendly letters, pressing us
to come down, to take a trip with them to Old Mexico etc. etc. What is that but
false? But basta! I will never see her again.

The White Peacock isn't published over here, but I believe Brentano's have
it in stock.[1] My publisher Thomas Seltzer was here for a week: such a tiny little
Jew: but nice, one of the *believing* sort. He wants to get hold of *Sons and Lovers*
and then bring out a sort of uniform edition of me.

Your warning about the hard work should have been more strictly
observed. I went and hurt my hand getting huge lumps of wood into the
wagon with the Danes. But it is about better. – Yes, I'm afraid whoever sits in
Taos and isn't a bit of a scoundrel sits in a losing game.

This Valdez is about 5 miles away – just a Mexican little hole. We are 43
miles from Taos junction station – nothing nearer. About 10 miles from the

---

[1] The American edition of *The White Peacock* was published by Duffield in 1911. DHL must
have meant that it was out of print but that the New York bookstore might supply a Duffield
edition.

Manby Hot Springs down on the Rio Grande. We go down there to stew and feel good: generally ride down.

I'm busy getting my MSS into order, so I can take flight again. I don't know which way to go – whether to go east, and via Greenland to Russia – or else south, and perhaps via Palm Springs to Old Mexico, and so to Europe. What shall I do? I wait for the gods to decide me. Am at the moment all mixed up in a volume of *Birds Beasts and Flowers*, poems which Seltzer is due to bring out in May. They amuse me. And the Danes want to decorate them. – One of the Danes is painting me in a brown leather hunting shirt and blue overall trousers: but such a funny face I get.

I won't tell you any of the Taos scandal, the latest lot, it is too unpleasing. Victor however is still alone, and Sara in New York threatening to write her marriage experience. If she writes it as she recounted it to Mabel, then Poor Victor, poor Sarah, poor public at large.[1] Tant de lingerie sâle.[2]

Frieda greets you warmly. I do hope you'll be well – feel sparky. You know, you need to be sparky and a bit adventurous – it's your real nature.

a riverderci   D. H. Lawrence

2700. To Adele Seltzer, 28 January 1923
Text: MS UT; Postmark, Questa FEB 1 [. . .]23; Lacy, *Seltzer* 61.

Del Monte Ranch. Questa, New Mexico
28 Jan. 1923

Dear Adele Szold

Der Mountsier ist heute weg – fortgegangen – etc. Gott sei dank.[3] I suppose he'll be in New York in 15 days time: staying a few days in Taos – and Denver.

But I'll write Seltzer.

Thank you for sending Frieda's parcel. I wish you would send something else. Merrild has a flute and Götzsche a fiddle and we sing songs: but they want music. Could you send us a book of English songs, and one of German: just the *simple* ordinary good songs, with simple music. I would like, if you can get it, *The Oxford Song Book*, in English – If there is a simple Italian book too, we'll have that as well. It doesn't matter if there is only mandoline accompaniment music.

I am waiting to hear from Seltzer about things.

I enclose cheque for ten dollars, five of which I owe you for that Frieda parcel.

Leb wohl[4]   D. H. Lawrence

pen arrived.[5]

---

[1] See p. 361 n. 1.   [2] 'So much dirty linen.'
[3] 'Today Mountsier left – departed – went – etc. Thank God.'   [4] 'Fare well.'
[5] The postscript appears on the verso of the envelope.

2701. To Robert Mountsier, [29 January 1923]
Text: MS Smith; Postmark, Valdez JAN 30 1923; Unpublished.

Del Monte Ranch, *Valdez*, N. M.
Monday evening

Dear M[ountsier]

You'll be pleased to hear that Seltzer has sent me a fat and imposing fountain pen. No letter however.

I'm writing the Charleroi bank about the Hadu cheque[1] – which I'll send again. I am mentioning the fact that you have asked to have the pass-book sent to me: and that I'd like to see it. Also I want to say to them that while I am in America I would like to have absolute control of my account: that they are not to pay anything out of it except to my own personal signature. Will you write and say to them that you have suggested this to me.

Hope Taos is pleasant.

Yrs   D. H. Lawrence

2702. To Thomas Seltzer, 1 February 1923
Text: MS UT; Postmark, Questa FEB 5 1923; Lacy, *Seltzer* 62.

Del Monte Ranch. *Questa*. New Mexico
1st. Feby. 1923

Dear Seltzer

I got your telegram about an article this morning. Have just finished enclosed.[2] If they don't want it, burn it.

The pen came: looks very grand. Of course I'm a bit scared of it. But when I get some proper ink from Taos I'll sit down and write to you with it, and thank you.

Mountsier left on Sunday. I wished it. Whatever friendship I felt for him before, I don't feel now. I have told him I want single control of all my money. But I haven't yet broken with him as my agent, because I feel he tried. But I think the break has got to come. Voyons!

I am finishing the *BirdsBeasts* MS. I shall send it straight to you. It makes a very interesting book.

I wait to hear from you. We still think of Mexico. I don't want Adele Szold to give a party for me, like Gilbert.[3] No. Tell her I had her letter.

Would you order for me *Terry's Guide to Mexico* – I believe that is the best.[4]

---

[1] See Letter 2676.
[2] The essay – entitled 'The Future of the Novel' by DHL – was re-titled 'Surgery for the Novel – Or a Bomb', when it appeared (much edited) in *Literary Digest International Book Review*, i (April 1923), 5–6, 23.
[3] The party was presumably to celebrate Seltzer's taking over the publication of Gilbert Cannan's books in America: he published five in 1923–4.
[4] Thomas Philip Terry, *Terry's Guide to Mexico* (New York, 1923).

– Do I bother you a great deal?
Stormy weather here.
There is a poem to Bibbles, tell Adele Szold.
Götzsche finished his portrait of me. Quite interesting, in my blue overall-trousers and leather shirt. They say it has got my get-rid-of-Mountsier face. Cela peut être.[1]
Frieda sewing glad-rags as if for a departure into the world somewhere.

Saluti   D. H. Lawrence

2703. To John Middleton Murry, 2 February 1923
Text: MS NYPL; Murry, *New Adelphi* 414.

Del Monte Ranch. *Questa*. New Mexico, U.S.A.

2 Feby 1923

Dear Jack
I got your note just now via Kot about Katharine.[2] Yes, it is something gone out of our lives. We thought of her, I can tell you, at Wellington. Did Ottoline ever send on the card to Katharine I posted from there for her? Yes, I always knew a bond in my heart. Feel a fear where the bond is broken now. Feel as if old moorings were breaking all. What is going to happen to us all? Perhaps it is good for Katharine not to have to see the next phase. We will unite up again when I come to England. It has been a savage enough pilgrimage these last four years. Perhaps K. has taken the only way for her. We keep faith – I always feel death only strengthens that, the faith between those who have it.

Still it makes me afraid: As if worse were coming. I feel like the Sicilians. They always cry for help from their dead. We shall have to, cry to ours: we do cry.

I wrote you to Adelphi Terrace the day after I got your letter, and asked Seltzer to send you *Fantasia of the Unconscious*. I wanted Katharine to read it. She'll know, though. The dead don't die. They look on and help.

But in America one feels as if *everything* would die, and that is terrible. I wish it needn't all have been as it has been: I do wish it.

DHL

2704. To Robert Mountsier, 3 February 1923
Text: MS Smith; Unpublished.

Del Monte Ranch, *Valdez*. New Mexico.

3 Feby. 1923.

Dear Mountsier
Thank you for your letter, and statement. Does the return railway fare from

---

[1] 'That may be.'
[2] Katherine Mansfield d. 9 January 1923 at the Gurdjieff 'Institute for the Harmonious Development of Man' in Le Prieuré des Basses Loges, Avon, Fontainebleau.

New York cost as much as $300? You remember you said you would let me pay the railway fare only.

I had a letter from Seltzer – still insisting he cannot do business with you. And I myself have come to the conclusion that I dont really want an agent. I will go to New York and fix up the matters that need to be fixed, myself. I wish now to break the connection between you and me. I am sure you have done all you could in my interest. But now I would rather have matters in my own hands.

With regard to yourself and me, I am sure we can arrange everything amicably. But I wish to contract all future business personally, without the intervention of an agent.

Yrs   D. H. Lawrence

I wish you would notify the persons concerned: Seltzer, Huebsch, Doran etc – that in the future they are to communicate with me direct.

DHL

2705. To Thomas Seltzer, 3 February 1923
Text: MS UTul; Postmark, Taos FEB 5 1923; Lacy, *Seltzer* 63–4.

Del Monte Ranch. *Questa*. New Mexico.
3 Feby. 1923

Dear Seltzer

I had your letter yesterday.

On the main point, of Mountsier, I do agree with you. I have this minute written to him – Mountsier – that I wish to break my agreement with him, and that in future I wish to handle all my business personally.

What about future payments to him? Is he still to have the 10% on all contracts drawn up by him? I don't want to be mean with him. Advise me at once.

You know too that he was starting a lawsuit against Kennerley, for recovery of *Sons and Lovers* royalties, through that lawyer Stern: the suit to cost me from $300 to $500 dollars. What shall we do about this? Let it go on?

Also he is serving, through Stern, the notices on Huebsch, for the taking back of the books Huebsch has in his control. The notices must be served one by one, as the books fall due.

We must be very careful about these things.

If you telegraph, send a night message to me Del Monte Ranch, *Valdez*, New Mexico. The telegraph is a bit quicker that way.

Yrs   D. H. Lawrence

If it is really necessary I will come to New York, but would prefer not to come till the end of March.

DHL

I just heard from Murry that Katharine Mansfield, his wife, died suddenly. I'm sorry. – Would you post him a copy of *Fantasia* and of *England my England* and *Psychoanalysis* to
care S. Koteliansky, 5. Acacia Rd, St. Johns Wood. London N. W. 8.
And please send a copy of *Psychoanalysis* and *Fantasia* to Koteliansky himself.

DHL

2706. To Ada Clarke, [6 February 1923]
Text: MS Clarke; PC v. Valdez, New Mexico; Postmark, [. . .] FEB 9 1923; Unpublished.

[Del Monte Ranch, New Mexico]
6 Feb.

Such a long time since I heard from you – but guess nothing is wrong, or Emily would have said. It snows here, and the nights go down to 10° fahrenheit – 20 below freezing point. I am getting tired of winter. We think of going down to Mexico City next month, and sailing from Vera Cruz to England. But am not sure. – How did you like Brighton at Christmas? You did not tell me. I have had no word from you since before Christmas. How is father? I will send something for him next time I write. And how is the winter treating Jack? – Valdez is our nearest village – but nothing there.

DHL

2707. To Thomas Seltzer, 7 February 1923
Text: MS Grover; Postmark, Taos 9 FEB 1923; Unpublished.

Del Monte Ranch. *Questa*. New Mexico
7 Feby. 1923

Dear Seltzer
I wrote you last Saturday that I had sent a letter to Mountsier telling him I wished him to be no longer my agent. He has not answered, though I hear he is yet in Taos, and has an idea of remaining there even a couple of months longer. We are going in tomorrow, and I may see him. If so I will have it out with him. I wish finally to be rid of him.
I sent you the article on the future of the novel, which you telegraphed for. I hope you have everything safely.

I enclose in this letter the two poems which were omitted from *Look We Have Come Through!*, and which I would like included in any other future edition.[1] Dont lose them.

I am sending by this mail the proofs of 'Captain's Doll' and 'Fox': with a very few corrections. Let me have proof of 'Ladybird' as soon possible. – By the way, did you cable Curtis Brown? – I hear from him Secker is doing *Sea and Sardinia* by himself in England.

I also send by this post a complete MS. of *Birds Beasts and Flowers*. When you have time to read it you will agree it is a remarkable collection. I wish you would have fair type-copies made, unless you are sending it to print at once. I want Curtis Brown to have a complete copy. If you think of sending any of the poems out to the magazines, then 'Elephant', 'Mountain Lion', 'Eagle in New Mexico', 'Autumn at Taos', 'Men in New Mexico', 'Mountain Lion', 'Bibbles', 'Kangaroo', 'Bat', 'Man and Bat' are all new and unpublished.[2] A fair number of the others have appeared. – I feel rather strongly about this book of verse: feel it is really my best. If you think there is anything needs modifying – you might in the 'Goat' poems, – let me know. – I want very much to see a perfect MS. or else complete proofs of these poems, before I leave America. And I want to leave soon. For the moment I have had enough. It has been ugly enough, M. Sterne and Mountsier. Feel I must go now. Want to go down to Mexico City via El Paso. I am in no state to come to New York yet. I want to leave here in about a month's time. Then probably come up to New York by sea, at the end of May. But I must go out of the U.S.A. now. Can't stand any more.

Am glad you like *Kangaroo*.

Write me in detail your plan of spring publication: also *format* of *BirdsBeasts*, so the Danes can do a jacket and whatever decorations you decide: perhaps just a title page: so they can earn a little money to set off with.

If you make new contracts in place of those Mountsier sent, I should like you to keep in the clause reserving the copyright to me, and the clause allowing us to annul the contract in seven years. The royalty I agree to at 10%, if you really think it best, up to 5,000. Thank you for the *Women in Love* increase. Don't be offended about the seven years. I only feel now, after a long course of bad experience, I had best keep control of my things as far as possible. I shall feel easiest so. But as long as you are faithful to me I shall remain with you. Mountsier didn't believe in me, he was against me inwardly. So I will have no

---

[1] The two poems were 'Song of a Man Who is Loved' and 'Meeting Among the Mountains' (see *Letters*, iii. 145 and n. 1). There was no other separate publication of *Look! We Have Come Through!* in DHL's lifetime.

[2] 'Bat' had already appeared in *English Review* (see p. 83 n. 2). Of the other poems listed only 'Elephant' received magazine-publication: in *English Review*, xxxvi (April 1923), 297–302.

more of him. – It has been ugly, first Mabel Sterne, then him. Now I want to go away soon, and come back feeling fresh.

Greet Adele Szold.

D. H. Lawrence

2708. To Thomas Seltzer, [9? February 1923]
Text: New York Times (11 February 1923), p. 18.

Taos, N. M.

[9? February 1923]

Thomas Seltzer, 5 West Fiftieth Street, New York, N. Y.

Let Judge John Ford confine his judgment to court of law, and not try to perch in seats that are too high for him.[1] Also let him take away the circulating library tickets from Miss Ford, lest worse befall her. She evidently needs an account at a candy shop, because of course *Women in Love* wasn't written for the Ford family any more than apples are apples for their sake. Father and mother and daughter should all leave the tree of knowledge alone. The Judge won't succeed in chopping it down, with his horrified hatchet. Many better men have tried and failed.

D. H. Lawrence

2709. To Curtis Brown, 10 February 1923
Text: MS Lazarus; Moore, Intelligent Heart 310.

Del Monte Ranch. *Questa*. New Mexico. U. S. A.

10 Feby. 1923

Dear Curtis Brown

I was glad to have your letter and to know that Secker is doing *Sea and Sardinia* on his own account.[2]

I was annoyed to hear from Seltzer that those Hearst people are holding back 'The Captain's Doll' at least till June. I will let you know immediately they definitely fix their date.

I have the *Kangaroo* contract, and if I get a satisfactory answer from you about Secker and the other books, I will sign it and send it on. Meanwhile I am annoyed to find that Mountsier, instead of sending the English copy of *Kangaroo* on to you, gave the MS. to Seldes of *The Dial*. Seldes should have

---

[1] The text is that of a telegram sent to Seltzer who released it to the *New York Times*. DHL had been angered by the news that the New York Justice John Ford (1862–1941) had conferred with John Sumner, Secretary of the Society for the Suppression of Vice, about drafting a new law to forbid the circulation of books like *Women in Love*. Ford, who considered the novel 'loathsome', had discovered his daughter reading a copy supplied by a circulating library. (A case was brought against *Women in Love* in September 1923 but was dismissed by the magistrate.) [2] See p. 366 n. 1.

posted it to you, from Berlin, I hope you have it. If not write me. Write all business direct to me or Seltzer, not to Mountsier, as he is travelling about, thinks to come to Europe, and won't be able to keep count of my things over here, so won't act as my agent any longer.

I enclose the last page of *Kangaroo*, which was missing from the MS. Seldes had. Don't lose it.

I was writing Harrison for a copy of the *English Review* containing the poem 'Almond Blossom', so enclosed a couple of poems to him, told him to let you know.[1] If you have a copy of 'Almond Blossom' handy, I wish you would mail it direct, at once, to Thomas Seltzer. He will then send you a complete MS. of *Birds, Beasts and Flowers*, which I consider my best book of poems.

Yes, I hope really we can go ahead satisfactorily with Secker. I hate futile changes. But I would have no publisher rather than one who does not stand firm by me. I am coming into my own over here; it is time England accepted me too. But if they don't want to, that is their affair. I shall not disturb myself.

I think next month I shall go down into Old Mexico – to Mexico City. But I will let you know. – And come to England some time in the summer.

I asked *The Dial* to send you a copy of their current issue. It contains the first instalment of my article 'Indians and an Englishman'. Did Mountsier ever send you a copy of this? It might have been acceptable to several English periodicals. I think the *Dial* publishes the next – and I think the final – instalment in April. It has a different thing by me for March. You could get the complete MS. from them.

Yrs   D. H. Lawrence

P.S. Those Hearst people promised to publish the 'Capt's Doll' in January – They are a nuisance.

2710. To Harriet Monroe, 10 February 1923
Text: MS UChi; Huxley 563.

Del Monte Ranch. *Questa*. New Mexico.
10 Feby. 1923

Dear Harriett Monroe

I have been thinking to see you. And now we are making up our minds, instead of coming east, to go down to Mexico City in March: when I shouldn't

---

[1] See p. 177 n. 1. Presumably one of the poems DHL had now sent to Harrison was 'Elephant' (see p. 378 n. 2). It and 'Almond Blossom' were collected in *Birds, Beasts and Flowers*. (The MS of the letter is annotated, probably in Curtis Brown's office: 'Harrison has only just received the poems – hasnt even had time to read them. He will let us know. I am sending Seltzer copy of Almond Blossom.')

see you. But then I plan to return to New York at the end of May.
Anyhow I look on you as a friend.

I have made up the complete MS. of *Birds Beasts and Flowers* and sent it to
Seltzer. He will probably publish this spring. So don't be long printing
'Matthew', which you have paid for.[1] And if you want any of the New Mexico
poems, ask Seltzer to give you 'Red Wolf', or 'Mountain Lion', or 'Eagle in
New Mexico', or 'Blue Jay' – any of the New Mexico ones. Mr Mountsier is
off on his travels again, so wont be my agent. – And in front of the *Birds Beasts*
MS. I put: 'Some of these poems have appeared in *Poetry* etc.' – *Poetry* first.
It's the *publishers* who like to leave these little notices out. So if you write to
Seltzer ever, just remind him.

Be greeted.

D. H. Lawrence

2711. To Margaret King, [10 February 1923]
Text: MS Needham; PC v. [Taos Pueblo Indian]; Postmark, Questa 13 [. . .]; Unpublished.

[Del Monte Ranch, New Mexico]
Feb. 10

This is one of the Indians – the men wear their hair so, in two long plaits – and
a blanket or an ordinary cotton sheet to wrap up in: mostly the latter, so they
look like ghosts riding. Am glad to have good news about you – sorry your
mother isn't at all well. In the summer we'll see if we can't all have a good
holiday together in France or somewhere nice.

Love   DHL

2712. To Bessie Freeman, [10 February 1923]
Text: MS UNYB; PC. v. Valdez, New Mexico; Postmark, Valdez [. . .]; Unpublished.

[Del Monte Ranch, New Mexico]
10. Feb.

– So many thanks for your letter and kind invitation. But if we go to Mexico we
must go soon, or it will be too hot. So we think of going direct via El Paso in
March. – Have you by the way seen this months *Dial*? You will find the first
part of the Indian article in it – with our trip. Hope it will please you. – So glad
you are feeling better.

D. H. Lawrence

[1] See p. 337 n. 1. 'St. Matthew' was the last of DHL's poems to be published in *Poetry*.

2713. To Robert Mountsier, 10 February 1923
Text: MS Smith; Postmark, Valdez FEB 12 1923; Unpublished.

Del Monte Ranch, Valdez. N.M.
10 Feb. 1923

Dear M[ountsier]

I find a bit of difficulty as to how much exactly I must deduct from my income, for the income tax paper (By the way, I can get one from the bank on Feb. 16th only). I should be very much obliged if you could give me the figure for my net income in U S A., so I can be sure.

Yrs   D. H. Lawrence

P. S. You will send me that letter too about what you consider fair in the way of further commissions, won't you? Send it as soon as possible. And any other item that occurs to you.

2714. To Thomas Seltzer, 10 February 1923
Text: MS PU; Moore 738–40.

Del Monte Ranch. *Questa*. New Mexico.
10 Feb. 1923

Dear Seltzer

I write this with your new pen, which is a great success.

We were in Taos two days: came back yesterday. I sent you a night letter for Judge Ford et famille. Bet you didn't print it.

I met Mountsier twice: told him simply I wished to discontinue with him: firstly, because he did not believe in me and what I was doing, but was antagonistic in spirit: secondly, because he had so annoyed you, you didn't want to deal with him. In answer to the first he said, if that was my opinion, there was no use arguing about it. To which I replied, it was my opinion. In answer to the latter he said various things. – But altogether he gave me the impression he has a *bad conscience* about something: I don't know what. He hates losing the *job*, but, *au fond*, is really relieved, I think, to be released. He gave me back some MS. and Huebsch contracts, and is to send me a letter saying what he thinks he ought to get, in the way of continuing of commissions to him. He may not stay long in Taos. Then I shall ask him back for all papers and MSS of mine. I asked him to write everybody concerned and say he had ceased to be my agent.

The two points of importance seem the Huebsch notices and the Kennerley business: both in the hands of the lawyer Stern. The Huebsch notices must be served in presence of *witness* seven years after date of *publication of book*. Notice for *Rainbow* is already served. No reply from Huebsch. And then the Kennerly case, the lawyer says, cannot come to *court for two years* – and Stern is 'pessimistic'. Mountsier advises that I continue this business *with Stern personally*. What do you say?

I have your letter of Feb. 1st. I had your telegram about Mountsier yesterday, saying you will wire again. I think it is very annoying, the *Hearst* delay. I wanted those three stories out this spring. And it will be a blow to Secker. Pity nothing can be done. Magazines should have a date limit.

I was annoyed to learn from Mountsier that Seldes had the English copy of *Kangaroo*, had carted it off to Berlin, Curtis Brown hasn't got it yet. I have asked Curtis Brown to communicate direct with me and you about it. Whatever Seldes decides, I don't really want *The Dial* to print a *bit* of the book.

We won't worry about Mountsier any more. He has a bad will, I have done with him, save for winding-up trifles. Enough.

I am anxious to hear from you about the order in which the new books are to appear. Am really sorry *The Captains Doll* is held up. I *don't want you* to get a book ready for publication without letting Curtis Brown know. He sent me a very favorable contract for *Kangaroo*, from Secker. But I said I wouldn't sign it till Secker satisfied me about *Fantasia, Psychoanalysis, Studies*, and *England my England*. Secker agrees to pay 15% up to 2000, then 20% on the next 3,000, and after that, 25%. But I won't sign till I am satisfied about those other books.

I think to go to Mexico City about middle of next month. Don't bother about the Melville books or the Bernal Diaz.[1] The former I can get in England, the latter in Mexico. But I should be glad if you could send me Terry's *Guide to Mexico*, as I asked. – We'd probably be in New York by end of May again, stay till July. Tell Adele Szold the house sounds attractive. It would be fun.

I think when you get used to it you'll like Merrilds *Kangaroo* jacket. I didn't like it at first: now think perhaps it's the best. I do want them to have a few dollars to be able to go on their way with. Otherwise I must give them, and it's so much better for their pride if they can earn them. Götzsche was so pleased when he heard Adele Szold liked the drawing.[2] We wonder what she'd think of the portrait. – Did you see this month's *Dial*?

Tell me soon about *Birds Beasts*: format and everything.

I've got to fill up income-tax papers – have asked Mountsier to let me know what I've earned exactly. Hope he will do so.

Let's settle as much business as possible before I go to Mexico. And if possible, do let me see an exact MS. of *BirdsBeasts*. I have that book at heart.

Yrs D. H. Lawrence

---

[1] Bernal Díaz del Castillo, *The True History of the Conquest of New Spain*, 5 vols. (1908–16) (see Letter 2825).
[2] Lacy suggests that it may have been 'the drawing of the riders' mentioned by Frieda in a letter to Adele Seltzer, 21 January 1923 (Lacy, *Seltzer* 57–8).

I am thinking perhaps it would be better to close my account with the Charleroi Savings and Trust Co, and you open another account for me in a New York bank. What do you think?

DHL

P.P.S. I found the 'Almond Blossom' poem. Enclose it here. So the MS. of *Birds Beasts* can be complete.

DHL

2715. To Ada Clarke, [10 February 1923]
Text: MS Clarke; PC v. [Indian with blanket]; Postmark, Questa FEB 13 1923; Lawrence–Gelder 124.

[Del Monte Ranch, New Mexico]
10 Feb.

– Had your letter at last – and you all seem out of sorts. But dont envy me too much the sun here, with temperature 25° below freezing point at night. And no sort of life is all honey. – I ordered a copy of *The Dial* for you, via Emily. Am glad Aunt Ada was done out of that legacy:[1] she deserves to be, for thinking so much about it. It's good you have a woman friend in Ripley – you evidently need a new breath. The winter seems long here. If we go down to Mexico City next month it will be almost tropical there. You'll send to Germany anything they want, wont you. I'll send the money.

Love to you all.

DHL

2716. To Adele Seltzer, 10 February 1923
Text: MS UT; Postmark, Questa FEB 16 1923; Lacy, *Seltzer* 68–9.

[Frieda Lawrence begins]

[Del Monte Ranch, New Mexico]
Saturday 10. II 23

Dear Adele S[zold],

We found each a long letter yesterday from each of you! You would have laughed over the last Mountsier days! Lawrence made him feel so small even Pips, you will admire his judgment, detested Mountsier – On the very last day after Lawr. had told him, he wanted him to go – *I* was left alone with him for lunch – Lawr took some sandwiches and went off – Mountsier very sad, he had no home, no father, no mother – in Colombo some little native beggar boys run by the side of your rickshaw and say; Lady, give penny, no daddy, no mummy,

[1] Ada Rose Krenkow.

no breakfast – Lady, give penny!! He used to talk to me and with that fatal inevitability I *knew* he was'nt our sort and we not his – I did not even feel cross I just *knew* – He is a poor hollow nut, like so many people he clings to the social shell, no wonder it's all they have got if they are hollow inside! I fear Gilbert is another one – He hates Lawrence now, he cant patronise him anymore! We were both so pleased that Thomas S[eltzer] is somebody in the world. I feel L's and his success very bound up – I thought it *mean* of M. to say anything about the *Women in Love* contract of *course* we none of us thought it would sell as it has done neither did Mr Mountsier, *beforehand*.[1] He wanted to turn Lawr and Thomas into enemies – Lawrence knows well enough what he owes to you both it's more than dollars, the dollars came *after* as a result of your belief in his genius. I think you are right to take your stand definitely and finally, it's no good messing with people that are'nt worth it, or giving into them – 'Entweder, oder'[2] – Lawr wants to go to Mexico, he thinks he might write his American novel there – You know he would like to write a novel of each continent – if possible – It's awfully nice that we have so many dollars, Lawrence will feel free and I can help my people – Then we shall come to New York, it would certainly be nice for a change to live more comfortably, then in the autumn we would go to Taormina and *keep* our Fontana Vecchia as headquarters – We love it both and you would have to come and see us – I also want to see my children in England! I am looking forward now to move on – Taos is rather awful with its spite, they all detest each other – The Danes have been a tower of strength, they are really nice and you ought to hear our 'concerts' in the evening[3] – They also heartily detested Montsiger – Wytter Bynner came with an enormous motor full of Americans, I liked the thin little Johnson, but he looked so cold and frail – What fun it will be, when you show us New York! Our poor Catherine Mansfield is buried – near Paris, it was so sad and again so inevitable that she had to die – She chose a death road and *dare* not face reality! It's been a wonderful day, you never saw this place at its best –

Now I must go to the post!

Auf Wiedersehen   Frieda

I think it's a disgrace for the Allies this Ruhrbusiness[4] – Where is their love of justice, fair play, freedom now? They need never talk again!

[Lawrence begins]
Dear Adele Szold
Did you get my letter asking you for song books and enclosing ten dollars?

[1] For sales figures see Letters 2670 and 2682.   [2] 'Either, or.'
[3] For a lively description of the 'concerts' see Merrild 131–4.
[4] French and Belgian troops occupied the Ruhr on 11 January 1923.

Mail is a bit shaky out here. – I want you to have *BirdsBeasts* under your wing, to see they are nice and shapely. – It's been so cold – now a bit warmer. And the Montsiger business made me so sick. We are keen on Mexico for a trip and the Danes pining to scrape a bit of money together to go too. They are having an exhibition in Santa Fe.[1] Witter Bynner came here one day and wants to go too: but no, no Americans if possible. I feel sore with all Americans for the moment. Where are those sweets? – Baking day, and I've made buns. Pity you aren't here to tea.

a reverderci   DHL

Did Thomas print my wire to Judge Ford intact? Tell me.

2717. To William Siebenhaar, 11 February 1923
Text: TMSC NWU; Unpublished.

Del Monte Ranch. *Questa*, New Mexico. U. S. A.
11 Feby. 1923.

Dear Mr. Siebenhaar

I have received the new chapters of Multatuli: and am keeping the MS. until I have the whole, and then I shall try and persuade my publisher to publish it. Nobody seems anxious to do old-fashioned masterpieces. But I'll see if I can't make Seltzer print it.

My wife and I think of going down to Old Mexico next month, to Mexico City. I don't know how long we shall stay. Perhaps you had better address me:

c/o Thomas Seltzer, 5, West 50th. Street, New York City.

That is always safe.

We are still in snow and hard frost here. I never thanked you for the magazine you sent at Christmas. It gave me a pang of wanting to come back to W[est] A[ustralia].

Greetings from us both to you and Mrs. Siebenhaar.

Yours Sincerely   D. H. Lawrence

2718. To S. S. Koteliansky, 12 February 1923
Text: MS BL; Postmark, Questa [. . .] 1923; Moore 740.

Del Monte Ranch. Questa. New Mexico
12 Feby 1923

My dear Kot

Your letter just come with Murry's enclosed. – Yes, I feel with you about *t*hat institution.[2] – There is no easy way out – no way of ecstasy and uplifting – it's just a bitter fight through thorns – and one must fight, or die, like

[1] See Merrild 274, 276.   [2] See p. 375 n. 2.

Katharine. – It is terrible to live and see life after life collapse, and more and more ruin pile up. – I feel bitter in America – it makes one suffer, this continent, a nasty, too-much suffering.

I did write to Murry at once. And from New Zealand I sent K. a post card care of Ottoline.

I ordered you *Fantasia.*

I hope you are well.

DHL

2719. To Benjamin Huebsch, 15 February 1923
Text: MS UT; Unpublished.

Del Monte Ranch. *Questa.* New Mexico
15 Feby. 1923

Dear Huebsch

Robert Mountsier is no longer acting as my agent, so will you please address all communications to me personally. And if there is anything to settle with Thomas Seltzer, will you deal with him direct.

I expect I shall be here another month: then either to New York or to Mexico City.

Yrs   D. H. Lawrence

2720. To Robert Mountsier, 15 February 1923
Text: MS Smith; Postmark, Valdez FEB 15 1923; Unpublished.

Del Monte Ranch. *Valdez*
Thursday

Dear Mountsier

Thank you for your note of Tuesday. I shall be glad to have the tax-blank and the information. I find I have all the Statements except the one Jan 1st. to June[1] 30th. of last year. I never remember receiving this statement: only a little yellow slip in Australia. So if you could give me this, I should be much obliged: statement for the first half of 1922.[2]

---

[1] June] July
[2] Mountsier complied with DHL's request and sent a statement of receipts and expenditure, 14 December 1921 – 30 June 1922 (TMS Smith). Receipts were as follows:

Check from "New Republic" for poem, cash placed in safety deposit box	6.00
Money order from India	4.36
Dec. 19. Check from Thomas Seltzer, being balance due on royalties for "Women in Love" and "Lost Girl," as shown by statement rendered July 1, 1921	412.10

Thanks also for the suggestions offered. It is very likely I shall want to go to Europe from Vera Cruz, and not go to New York; in which case it would be very useful to have everything settled with Stern through the post.

Yrs   D. H. Lawrence

2721. To Willard Johnson, [16? February 1923]
Text: MS YU; Unpublished.

Del Monte Ranch. *Valdez*, New Mexico
Friday

Dear Johnson

I was on the very point of writing to you or Bynner. – I wish you had eaten more, and had had on a bit of Tony's fatness.

We are due to leave here on the 15th. March, stay two days in Taos.[1] So we should be in Santa Fe Saturday 17th. or Monday 19th March or thereabouts. Stay a day or so.

Why not come down to Mexico with us? It will be getting hot and rainy season coming, if you wait. We might have a good time together. And if we didnt, we could so easily and gracefully decide that one must go to Tehuantepec and the other to Yucatan. The tickets agent in El Paso – R. N Davis, Mills Building, El Paso – says a return ticket with stop-off privileges, El Paso to Mexico City, good for 90 days, costs only 67 dollars (American). The best hotels in Mexico City charge $2.50 (American) per day for a room. Tell Bynner to splash about and get ready to come along.

The Danes are due to have a little exhibition of their pictures in Santa Fe in about 10 days time: Merrild's things mostly drawings and decorations, Götsche's paintings, including a sulky-looking portrait of me. Go and look anyhow: and if you can delude anybody that can afford it into buying a trifle, tant mieux pour tous.[2]

belli saluti   D. H. Lawrence

Jan. 9.	Check from "Dial" for chapter from "Aaron's Rod"	35.00	
Mar. 15.	Cash from Thomas Seltzer for "Sea and Sardinia" advance	200.00	
Mar. 16	Check from B.W. Huebsch via George Doran Co.	263.95	
Jun. 19.	Check from Thomas Seltzer on account of royalties due to Dec. 31, 1921, on "Women in Love," "Lost Girl," "Psychoanalysis and the Unconscious," "Tortoises," "Sea and Sardinia"	200.00	
Jun. 30.	Check from Thomas Seltzer on account of royalties (ditto Jun. 19) and on account of $500 advance on "Aaron's Rod"	1,000.00	$2,121.41

Mountsier calculated his expenses and commission at $213.86, leaving a balance of $1907.55.
[1] Taos] Santa Fe   [2] 'so much the better for everyone'.

PS. The Danes would like to come down to Santa Fe for two days when their exhibition opens. But they are very hard up, and are afraid of hotel expenses. If Bynner should know of a room where they might stay and feed themselves more or less, that would save. But this is just my impertinent suggestion, don't hesitate to ignore it.

DHL

2722. To Thomas Seltzer, [18 February 1923]
Text: MS UT; Lacy, *Seltzer* 70.

Del Monte Ranch. Questa. New Mexico
Sunday. 17 Feb. 1923

Dear Seltzer

I return proofs of *Ladybird* today.

I got the assignments for the *White Peacock* from Mountsier.[1]

There are two parcels for me, I get notices, at Jaroso. These will be from Adele Szold: and many thanks to her. But don't send things by *express* to here, please: send parcel post. Jaroso is 52 miles away, in Colorado: the nearest station on the Questa side. And I have a struggle to get the things forwarded.

And do please answer all my questions soon, and write to Merrild. I think to leave for Old Mexico about the 15th March via El Paso: have written about tickets: they don't cost much. So let us get everything settled as far as possible before we go: about the books.

Grüsse   D. H. Lawrence

2723. To Curtis Brown, 20 February 1923
Text: MS BPL; Coolidge, *More Books*, xxxiii (January 1948), 23–4.

Del Monte Ranch, *Questa*. New Mexico.
20 Feb. 1923

Dear Curtis Brown

I had a telegram from Seltzer this morning that Hearsts have released the 'Captains Doll': and I write by this mail to Secker, telling him to fix a simultaneous date with Seltzer for *The Ladybird*. I have just sent back corrected proofs to New York, so the book should be ready in March some time. Will you see to this.[2]

---

[1] I.e. assignment of copyright. (DHL was continuing his efforts to retrieve the rights to his works which had become scattered among several American publishers.)

[2] Curtis Brown wrote to Secker as soon as he received this letter. Secker replied on 1 March (Secker Letter-Book, UIll):

Dear Mr Curtis Brown,

I am very pleased to have your letter of February 27, informing me that D.H.Lawrence now agrees to March publication of "The Ladybird". I am therefore starting on the necessary subscription work in London at once, and have fixed publication for the 22nd. "Sea and Sardinia" will appear immediately after Easter.

I look forward to receiving the copy of "The Kangaroo" as soon as possible.

Yours sincerely

We leave in three weeks time. When you write, please address care of *Thomas Seltzer, New York*, until I send you an address.

Yours   D. H. Lawrence

2724. To Thomas Seltzer, 20 February 1923
Text: TMSC MSC NWU; Huxley 564–5.

Del Monte Ranch. *Questa*. New Mexico.

20 Feby. 1923

Dear Seltzer

I have your telegram this morning – Tuesday. Enclose it. Am so glad Hearst's have freed 'The Capt's Doll'. Now you can publish it next month. I sent proofs yesterday of *Ladybird*. Did you tell Curtis Brown? I am writing to Secker today so shall let him know the book is free. You write Curtis Brown.

Yes, you attend to everything for me, that Stern has on hand: the Kennerley business and the Huebsch contracts. I wrote to Huebsch telling him to act with you, and with me, not with Mountsier. I enclose a letter for Stern, the lawyer, which you can hand on. – I enclose also Mountsier's letter about further royalties.[1] Let me know what you think about this. And particularly let me know about a new banking account. I think I shall get a letter of credit from the Charleroi people, and pretty well close the old account.[2]

And in future, keep my twelve presentation copies, please, and have them sent off from your office as I ask you. I enclose a list of addresses for *The Captain's Doll*. Send to me just two copies.

I hope everything will go well.

Tanti belli saluti   D. H. Lawrence

Copies of *The Captain's Doll* to be sent out.

1.   Knud Merrild.
1.   Kai Götzsche.
1.   Mrs Elizabeth Freeman, The Desert Inn, *Palm Springs*, California
1.   Mr and Mrs Joseph Brewis, 640 Riverside Drive, *New York City*.
1.   Mrs Lee Witt, *Taos*, New Mexico.
1.   Mrs Mabel Sterne, Taos, New Mexico
1.   Frau Baronin von Richthofen, Ludwig-Wilhelmstift, Baden-Baden, Germany.
1.   Frau Professor Else Jaffé, Konradstr. 16, Munich, *Germany*.
1.   Frau Johanna von Schriebershofen, Dahlmannstr. 5, Charlottenburg bei *Berlin*, Germany.
1.   Dr. E. Tuchmann, 34 Wurtembergischerstr, *Berlin*, Germany.
1.   W. Siebenhaar, Registrar Generals Office, *Perth*, West Australia.

---

[1] The letter to Stern follows; Mountsier's letter has disappeared.
[2] On 14 February DHL wrote in his diary: 'wrote Charleroi for old bank book' (Tedlock, *Lawrence MSS* 96). He did not close his account as he envisaged.

1.   Miss Ruth Wheelock, American consulate, *Palermo*, Sicily.
1.   Mrs. Humes, c/o J. C. Humes, 315 Shawmut Bank Bldg., *Boston* Mass
D. H. Lawrence

2725. To Benjamin Stern, 20 February 1923
Text: MS UT; Unpublished.

Del Monte Ranch. *Questa*. New Mexico
20 Feby. 1923

Dear Mr Stern

Mr Robert Mountsier will have written to you that he is no longer acting as my agent. I wish you would continue the business concerning Mitchell Kennerley and the Huebsch contracts with Thomas Seltzer, who knows my wishes in these matters.

Thanking you for your attention to my affairs so far.

I am

Yours faithfully   D. H. Lawrence

Mr. B. H. Stern. Stern and Ruben. *149 Broadway. New York City.*

2726. To Martin Secker, 20 February 1923
Text: MS UInd; Secker 51.

Del Monte Ranch. *Questa*. New Mexico. U. S. A.
20 Feb. 1923

Dear Secker

I hear you will soon be bringing out *Sea and Sardinia*. Send out the six copies for me, will you.

I had a telegram this morning from Seltzer that Hearsts have released 'The Captain's Doll': So will you fix a date with Seltzer for simultaneous publication. I guess the book will be ready on this side by March. And please send out for me the copies as requested.

I have the contract for *Kangaroo*. It is all right. But I just won't sign contracts for my novels and leave the other books lying unpublished. Curtis Brown will have told you.

We are leaving here in about three week's time. So write to me care of Thomas Seltzer, 5 West 50th. Street, New York City, until you hear from me again. I think of going down to Mexico City.

Yours   D. H. Lawrence

2727. To Robert Mountsier, [20 February 1923]
Text: MS Smith; Postmark, Valdez FEB 20 1923; Unpublished.

Del Monte Ranch. Valdez, N. M.
Tuesday

Dear Mountsier

Thank you for the income tax stuff. I must add on the $80 from *Poetry* to the income. But what about the deductions? Do I deduct the $300 for your trip here? If so, then I make the deductions at least $1050, instead of the $816 which you put down. Tell me if I am wrong.

Seltzer still has not answered about the contracts – only telegrams with nothing definite. He now says 'letter following.' I'll let you know what he says and we'll settle the commissions. Apparently he has seen Stern and says the 'Kennerley' case can get a decision in two weeks: this a telegram. I'll let him go ahead.

                                                                                    DHL

2728. To Bessie Freeman, 21 February 1923
Text: MS UNYB; Postmark, Valdez FEB 22 1923; Unpublished.

                                   Del Monte Ranch, *Valdez* (Taos), New Mex.
                                                                       21 Feb. 1923
Dear Mrs Freeman

Your letter today. I think we shall leave about 15th March for Mexico City. If we like it and stay some months, you will come and see us. A there-and-back ticket from El Paso is only $67. American dollars.

Could you give me one or two letters of introduction to anybody nice? I don't know if I should use them, but I might be glad.

The Danes very much want to come, if they can rake up enough money. If they can't, they'll come on in May to Los Angeles, and try and get some work with cinema companies. In that case perhaps I might ask you if your young man might introduce them – he needn't hesitate to refuse if he didn't want to.

I'm glad you are sparky: shouldn't wonder if we all did a bit of galloping in Old Mexico. Wouldnt that be fun?

If we come back to the U.S. for next winter, I shall seriously consider your Palm Springs.

How do you like the *Dial* article? The next part probably in April – the Taos pueblo. Next month is a review of mine might Amuse you.[1]

Oh, your book *Open Spaces* came on *yesterday*;[2] Mabel had written 'Excuse delay in forwarding' on the wrapper. Frieda has already read it: liked it very much. Did you get *England my England*? If not I'll order you a copy – haven't one here. I gave an order for *The Captain's Doll* to be sent to you when it comes out – next month. Thank you so much for *Open Spaces* – 'tis late Christmas here. – Apparently I am not going to be so poor as I have been – *Women in Love* selling well.

[1] See Letter 2675 and n. 4.
[2] Possibly John Charles Van Dyke, *The Open Spaces: Incidents of Nights and Days Under the Blue Sky* (New York, 1922).

If you care to send me letters for Mexico, send fairly soon, will you? And prepare yourself to come on after us, if we like it.

Frieda sends you many greetings.

D. H. Lawrence

2729. To Robert Mountsier, [21 February 1923]
Text: MS Smith; Postmark, Valdez FEB 22 1923; Unpublished.

Del Monte Ranch. Valdez. N. M.

Wednesday

Dear Mountsier

I received the enclosed today.[1] Replied that you filled in the papers: that you were told at Income Tax office the amount was below the taxation limit, that you will give the matter your attention if necessary: that you are away from New York: and that I am paying this year's tax in this State, I didn't give them Taos address – only 417 West.

I'll fill in the papers here as soon as I get your answer about deductions, and get this settled.

Yrs   D. H. Lawrence

On second thoughts, I enclose my letter to this man, and you can mail it.

2730. To Thomas Seltzer, 22 February 1923
Text: MS UT; Postmark, Questa FEB 26 1923; Lacy, *Seltzer* 72–3.

Del Monte Ranch. *Questa*. New Mexico

Feb. 22. 1923

Dear Seltzer

Your letter this evening, also the *Guide to Mexico* and other books, and sweets. For all of which very many thanks, and *please charge them to me*: I mean all the books and expenses.

Sorry about *Sons and Lovers* cheap edition.[2] That's a waste. You can only serve notices on Huebsch six months after date of *publication* of each book: not expiration of contracts. You must find out these dates from Huebsch; or I must. How is he going to act? I wrote him about Mountsier and told him to act with you on any necessary point. If you want the Huebsch contracts, I will send them, and you can keep them for me, or deposit them for me.

Yes, you do things with Stern. (What about this Stern?) But *always* tell me. If you must act quickly, on your own responsibility sometimes, do so. But

---

[1] This enclosure and the letter mentioned in DHL's postscript are both missing.

[2] Huebsch's cheap edition has not been traced (none is mentioned in the National Union Catalog).

always tell me plainly everything. That was how Huebsch annoyed me: he just left me out. So in the end I left him out. And glad I did. Always tell me openly what you are doing and intend doing with my things, else I get angry, and then I don't care any more. – I wrote Stern to act with you.

I wrote to Secker 'Captains Doll' was released, and he was to fix date of simultaneous publication with you. – I told you I wrote Curtis Brown I would sign no contract with Secker for *Kangaroo* till Secker satisfied me about *Fantasia* and *Studies* and *England my England*.

I am glad you sent Merrild the money.[1] I think, truly, the *Kangaroo* jacket will have more effect than you imagine. Merrild will do the jacket for *Birds Beasts*, in bright, tangled colour. Size 6⅝ by 8½ inches. I take it you want *no* interior decoration. But you should tell me, since I asked you.

Mountsier made out the total of my year's income, and the total of the deductions, so I shall pay in this state, where there is no *State* tax: only the 4%.[2] But do please as far as possible keep track of my income for the current year: and expenses you pay to Stern for me, and things like that.

Did you read *Mastro-Don Gesualdo?*[3] Do when you have time, and let me know. Because Curtis Brown wants an answer for England. Blackwell wants to publish it in August or September.

Secker pledged to do advertising for £100 sterling, on *Kangaroo*. I don't know, I'm sure, what he is really about. But the figures are as I tell you. I don't trust him very far. Yes, if you go to England; do speak for me. But I'll stick to Secker if he will print all of me.

I will send you *The White Peacock* papers. Stern has served the notice for *The Rainbow*.

Let me have proofs of everything as soon as they come off the press, no matter where I am.

If you can get me an interesting letter of introduction to anybody in Mexico, do. I liked that book *The Mexican People*. Do you know anything about Pinchon or Gutierrez de Lara, the authors?[4]

We are due to leave here in 3 weeks today.

I shall look for the contracts. Yes, put in the seven year clause, and give me the copyrights. Then I shall feel freer. But I had better have a place in New

---

[1] See p. 345 n. 2.   [2] For details of DHL's tax-return see Letter 2736.
[3] Adele Seltzer read it and responded enthusiastically (see Lacy, *Seltzer* 248).
[4] L. Gutiérrez de Lara and Edgcumb Pinchon, *The Mexican People: Their Struggle for Freedom* (New York, 1914). Gutiérrez, who wrote the book, was a Mexican Socialist, revolutionary and journalist who had fought against the dictatorship of Porfirio Diaz (1876–1911) and participated in the revolutionary conflict which followed the downfall of Diaz. He was shot in the town of Sirac in August 1918. Pinchon (b. 1883), novelist and biographer, translated the book for the American market.

York to keep my papers in. Would you suggest a part of a safe in a bank? – or Stern? I must also get Mountsier to transfer all papers when he returns to New York. He is still in Taos.

Dont forget to answer me, too, about a banking account.

I seem to give you a great deal of trouble. But everything is coming straight. And we will make a success of things.

Thank you so much for all the books and music and the trouble you have taken.

Yrs   D. H. Lawrence

2731. To Baroness Anna von Richthofen, [23 February 1923]
Text: MS UT; Unpublished.

[Frieda Lawrence begins]

Del Monte Ranch
23. II 23

Liebe mère,

Gestern Dein Brief dass Du Influenza hattest, wie gut, dass Dein Herz sich so brav hält – den Schinken habe ich *mit* den [   ] gegessen, er war sehr gut – Lawrence wird wenn alles gut geht viel verdienen dieses Jahr – also Frau Geheimrat können Sprünge machen – in der Beziehung – *Hattest* Du 25 dollar für Hadu and 50 für Else und Dich? Ich denk an Nusch, ich glaube sie kann ein nettes Leben haben mit Emil, denn die Schleifere ist nichts wenn man älter wird – es wird ihr aber doch schwer werden ihren alten Max zu verlassen, so viel Vergangenheit liegt zwischen ihnen, aber keine Zukunft – Lawr hat Dir 3 lange Geschichten die *Captain's Doll* heisst bestellt – In der die the 'Captain's doll' heisst – ist eine Badescene in Zell am See – Sein Verleger liebt ihn sehr und sagt zu seiner Frau Adele hast Du saubre Hände wenn ein Brief von Lawrence kommt, dann darf sie ihn lesen – Wir gehen also wohl in 3 Wochen nach Mexiko – 3 Nächte, 2 Tage – und erst einen Tag im Auto nach Taos – und einen Tag von Taos nach Sante Fe – aber man hat Schlafwagen – meinen geliebten Pichs kann ich nicht mitnehmen, es wäre zu qualvoll für ihn, aber er ist mindestens so nett wie jener Wurstl. Lawrence ist auch erkältet, hat stundenlang Eis gehackt im zugefrorenen Bach! Mountsier war zum Glück nicht im Haus, ist wieder fort – er war nervös, ritt ein Pferd, das bockte, es fiel mit ihm, Pferd tot, Mountsier ein gebrochenes Handgelenk! Aber unsre Pferde sind sanft und mild – Mein 'Selim' ist solch ein gentleman – und läuft wie ein Has – Ich freu mich auf Mexiko, wir gehen mit 2 jungen Amerikanern – Heute geht ein Frühlingslüftchen, hoffentlich fängt's bei Dir auch an! Ich schreibe *gleich* wenn wir wissen wann's nach Mexiko geht – und wo Du hinschreiben sollst – wie *gut* die Photographie und der Adulf mit Bäuchle!

[Lawrence begins]

Ich schreibe dir sofort als wir an Mexico City kommen. Aber wenn du schreiben willst, vor du hörst, die Adresse ist

Thomas Seltzer, 5 West 50th Street, New York City.

Ich schicke dir fünf Englische Pfund – wenn du einen Braten für die Stiftsdamen schenken willst, thu's.

DHL

Hast du die andere zwei eingeschriebene Briefe?

[Frieda Lawrence resumes]

Ich schick ein Packet, wenn wir hier packen, und schreibe *genau* alles was drin ist!

Brief bitte zurück.

[Frieda Lawrence begins]

[Dear mère,

Yesterday your letter that you had influenza, how good that your heart stands up so well – the ham I ate *with* the [   ], it was very good – Lawrence, if everything goes well, will earn a lot this year – so Frau Geheimrat can live it up – in that connection – *Had* you 25 dollars for Hadu and 50 for Else and you? I think of Nusch, I believe she can have a nice life with Emil, for the grind is no good when one gets older – but it will be difficult for her to leave her old Max, so much past lies between them, but no future – Lawr has ordered you 3 long stories called *Captain's Doll* – In the one called the 'Captain's doll' – is a bathing scene in Zell am See – his publisher loves him very much and says to his wife Adele if you have clean hands when a letter from Lawrence comes, then she may read it – Well, it seems we go to Mexico in 3 weeks – 3 nights, 2 days – and first a day by motorcar to Taos – and a day from Taos to Santa Fe – but one has a sleeping-car – my beloved Pips I can't take with me, it would be too distressing for him, but he is at least as nice as that Wurstl. Lawrence also has a cold, chopped ice for hours in a frozen-over brook! Mountsier happily wasn't in the house, has gone again – he was nervous, rode a horse that bucked, it fell with him, horse dead, Mountsier a broken wrist! But our horses are gentle and mild – My 'Selim' is such a gentleman – and runs like a hare – I'm looking forward to Mexico, we're going with 2 young Americans – Today there's a touch of spring in the air, hopefully it's beginning where you are too! I'll write *immediately* we know when it's off to Mexico – and where you should write to – How *good* the photograph and Adulf with little belly.

[Lawrence begins]

I'll write you immediately we get to Mexico City. But if you want to write, before you hear, the address is

Thomas Seltzer, 5 West 50th Street, New York City.

I send you five English pounds – if you want to give a roast for the Stift ladies, do so.

DHL

Have you the other two registered letters?

[Frieda Lawrence resumes]

I'll send a package when we pack here, and write *exactly* everything that's in it!

Return letter please.]

2732. To S. S. Koteliansky, 25 February 1923

Text: MS BL; Postmark, Questa FEB 27 [. . .]; cited in Gransden 29.

Del Monte Ranch. *Questa.* New Mexico
25 Feb. 1923

My dear Kot,

I had your registered letter only last night: and then brought out from Questa by a man coming here.

I have such a deep mistrust of England. When I want to come, I can't, I feel my endless mistrust won't let me. And I have fixed up everything to go to Mexico City. We leave here in two weeks time, and I expect to be in the City of Mexico on March 20th. I will let you know the address there. And then I will tell you again how I feel about coming to England. Maybe suddenly I shall decide to come. ¿Quién Sabe?[1]

I am writing this to Murry too. – I ordered you various books from Secker and Seltzer.

DHL

I have not much faith in literary ventures, either: vieux jeu![2]

2733. To John Middleton Murry, 25 February 1923

Text: MS NYPL; cited in Murry, *New Adelphi* 415.

Del Monte Ranch. *Questa.* New Mexico
25 Feb. 1923

Dear Jack

I had your letter, with Koteliansky's, last night.

And at the moment I can't come to England. Something inside me simply doesn't let me. I mistrust my country too much to identify myself with it any more. And it still gives me a certain disgust. But this may pass. I feel something must *happen* before I can come back.

[1] 'Who Knows?'   [2] 'old fashioned!'

We leave here in a fortnight. We are going down to Mexico City. I expect to be there by March 20th. Will write as soon as I have an address.

I ordered you various of my books, care of Koteliansky.

DHL

2734. To Gilbert Seldes, 25 February 1923
Text: TMSC NWU; Huxley 564–5.

Del Monte Ranch, Questa, New Mexico
25 Feb 1923

Dear Gilbert Seldes

Your letter from Semmering last evening. We were in Austria in 1921. 'The Captain's Doll' ends in Zell-am-See. I often think of Austria.

Let Curtis Brown have *Kangaroo* as soon as you can, will you? (Not *The* K.) I don't really mind if you mention it before it is published. It is usually publishers who have feelings about these things.

No, I am not disappointed in America. I said I was coming to Europe this spring. But I don't want to. We leave in a fortnight for Old Mexico. Perhaps I shall come back here. If you write, address me c/o Thomas Seltzer, 5 West 50th. St.

But I feel, about U.S.A., as I vaguely felt a long time ago: that there is a vast, unreal, intermediary thing intervening between the real thing which was Europe and the next real thing, which will probably be in America, but which isn't yet, at all. Seems to me a vast death-happening must come first. But probably it is here, in America (I don't say just U.S.A.) that the quick will keep alive and come through.

I got proofs of the Prof. Sherman criticism along with your letter. Hope it will amuse you.

Yours   D. H. Lawrence

If you go to Vienna, look up Elizabeth Humes at the office of the American Commercial Commision. I'm sure you'd like her. My wife and I like her very much.

DHL

2735. To Curtis Brown, 25 February 1923
Text: MS Forster; Unpublished.

Del Monte Ranch. *Questa*. New Mexico.
25 Feby. 1923

Dear Curtis Brown,

Your letter of 8th Feby today. I'll answer point by point.

1. I wrote you five days ago, Seltzer telegraphed that he had got 'The Captains Doll' released, and that he proposed to publish it March 15th. (no, this bit he *wrote* me two days ago: and that he wants to consult Hearsts man again before finally fixing date for publication of book – which means he had *not* written you about the release, though I *insist* he let you know everything). But I will get in to Taos and cable you.

2. Seltzer's plan is to publish:

The Captains Doll (Ladybird)	March 15
Studies in Classic A[merican] Literature	Early in April.
Birds Beasts and Flowers	– Middle September
Kangaroo	– Middle September.

3. Yes, I agree to the *Studies in C. A. Lit.* offer from Secker: no advance; 10% on first 1000; 15 per cent on next two thousand; 20% after 3,000. – But thirteen copies shall *not* count as twelve.

4. I agree that Secker omit any purely American reference in *Psychoanalysis and the Unconscious* and *Fantasia of the Unconscious*. But I want him to fix a date of publication. And same terms as for *Studies*.

5. We'll leave *The Rainbow* in abeyance for a while. Huebsch's rights lapse in a month or two, and Seltzer takes over the book. I believe Huebsch has just done a third edition.

I don't for a moment question your good faith. But Secker must either stand by me or have no more to do with me. That's certain. He knows quite well I've never been unwilling to meet him in any difficulty.

I enclose the signed *Kangaroo* contract. There is only one point I disagree with: the thirteen count as twelve clause. *I won't sign any further contract with this thirteen-count-as-twelve clause.* Do please remember this, and fix the contracts accordingly.

I expect to be here until March 14th; and in Mexico City by March 20th. I shall write you at once. Meanwhile care of Thomas Seltzer will be quicker than anything.

I will cable tomorrow or Tuesday from Taos: it is an 18 mile drive.

Thank you for looking after these things.

Yours Sincerely   D. H. Lawrence

P. S. No, I shall not sign the *Kangaroo* contract till I have Seckers dates of publication for the other books.

DHL

2736. To Robert Mountsier, 26 February 1923
Text: MS Smith; Postmark, Taos FEB 28 1923; Unpublished.

Del Monte Ranch. *Valdez*. N. Mex.
26 Feby. 1923

Dear Mountsier

I have filled in my income tax paper and am taking it in to Taos tomorrow. I went through your statements carefully, and my figures are:

Royalties	3824.67
Periodicals	1615.00[1]
gross income	5439.67[2]
deductions:	
commission	543.96
journey	300.00
expenses	345.31
total deductions	1189.27
net income	4250.40
exemption	2500.00
taxable income	1750.40
tax due $70.00	

I included in expenses the $35 for Stern, and your typing, postage, telephone costs: but none of the *personal* items. I do hope our accounts are near enough.

I expect you received the letter I sent on respecting last year's income tax returns, forwarded from New York. If there is anything to do about this, please let me know.

With regard to further commissions, I can't give you permanent commission on the contracts we went through here, because Seltzer won't sign them, and is making new ones: which I've not seen yet. And *Women in Love* doesn't come under your commission, either. Probably the best will be if I give you full commission on the receipts from Seltzer at the end of March and end of September, this year; that settling the matter between us.

We leave here about the 15th March, and shall be a couple of days in Taos. Then to Mexico City. Before I go I want to give you an address to which you can send all papers and manuscripts of mine. Tell me what MSS you have. And if you would like to keep any of them.

Anyhow let us get settled up before I[3] leave here.

Yrs   D. H. Lawrence

[1] 1615.00] 5439.0
[2] For a detailed breakdown of DHL's income see his tax return printed in Lacy, *Seltzer* 163.
[3] I] we

2737. To Thomas Seltzer, 2 March 1923
Text: MS UT; Lacy, *Seltzer* 74.

Del Monte Ranch. *Questa*, New Mexico
2 March 1923

Dear Seltzer

Your letter of Feb. 24.

My account in the Charleroi bank will expire this month. Please open me an account in the Chase National Bank: and do as you say, keep me a constant 2000 dollars to my credit. If I leave the rest in the Seltzer Corporation, *can I get it out any time I may want it?* If so, I will leave the balance in your business.

I had a letter from Curtis Brown. Secker will publish *Studies*, *Fantasia* and *Psychoanalysis* as one book, *England my England*, all before the end of this year.[1] So I let him go ahead. I don't know if Cape is any better. I have got the *Kangaroo* contract still unsigned: it binds me to offer my next novel to Secker. I want to see what he does with these pending books, first.

Curtis Brown said Blackwell wanted to do *Mastro-don Gesualdo* in August. September would be all right. I must have proofs of this.

We leave here not later than 18th inst. – Remember to send me proofs of everything. I wish I could have had proofs of *Studies* before I go: and that MS. of *Birds Beasts*. But if you print early you can send proofs early. – *White Peacock* is quite free. I'll send you the papers for it.

Grüsse   D. H. Lawrence

Curtis Brown urges me to stay with Secker.

Hope to receive *your* contracts before I leave.

DHL

---

[1] However, Curtis Brown wrote to Secker according to DHL's instructions in Letter 2735 and received the following reply dated 13 March 1923 (Secker Letter-Book, UIll):

Dear Mr Curtis Brown,
    D. H. Lawrence
    I am much obliged for your letter of yesterday. I agree to the elimination of the 13/12 clause in the future contracts, and I will now fix provisionally the publication dates for the books as follows:
    Psychoanalysis and the Unconscious   June
    Kangaroo   September
    Fantasia of the Unconscious   October
I am of course bringing out " The Ladybird" ("The Captain's Doll") this month and "Sea and Sardinia" in April, and I think five Lawrence books will be as much as it is advisable to do in one year. I will therefore postpone "England, My England" and "Studies in Classic American Literature" until 1924 . . .
                                                        Yours sincerely

2738. To Benjamin Huebsch, 3 March 1923
Text: MS UT; Unpublished.

Del Monte Ranch, Questa. N. M.

3 March 1923

Dear Huebsch

I had your registered letter last night.[1] Mountsier gave me to understand you would not care about the terminating of the contracts.

You will see, if you refer to the contract, that the seven years clause applies specifically to each novel, separately.

I must write to the lawyer in New York to see what has been done. Meanwhile I think you can go ahead with the edition now in the press. How many copies are you printing in this edition?

I am leaving in two week's time for Old Mexico: but I intend to be in New York in May or June. You can address me *care* Thomas Seltzer: or here if there is time. I will write more definitely before I leave.

Yrs   D. H. Lawrence

P. S. Will you please answer any letter that the lawyer B. H. Stern may write you on this matter.

DHL

B.W. Huebsch. 116 West 13th St. New York City[2]

---

[1] Huebsch wrote as follows on 24 February 1923 (TMS LC) in answer to Letter 2719:

Dear Lawrence,

I am just in receipt of yours dated the 15th, advising me that Robert Mountsier is no longer your agent and that future dealings between us are to be direct.

This leads me to call to your personal attention Mountsier's notice of exercise of your alleged right to terminate our interests in The Rainbow as at June 19, 1923. I trust that you will now promptly cancel such notice and permit the contract to continue in full force, especially in view of the fact that we have the new edition now on press.

If, however, you insist on a technical application of the terms of the contract, we in turn shall feel constrained also to stand upon its letter and to enforce to the full extent of the law the breach of the provision that your two novels next succeeding The Rainbow should be publishable by us.

I trust that you will not make it necessary for us to secure our rights against your opposition, but if you should maintain the course indicated by Mr. Mountsier, no way will be open to us except to invoke the aid of the courts.

I await an early word from you and sincerely hope that it will be the requested cancellation of the notice of exercise to option above referred to.

Yours truly

[2] This letter was written on the back of the next, to Seltzer, 3 March 1923; it was intended to be a copy for the information of Seltzer and Benjamin Stern. The letter actually sent to Huebsch has not survived.

2739. To Thomas Seltzer, 3 March 1923
Text: MS UT; Lacy, *Seltzer* 75.

Del Monte Ranch. *Questa.*[1] New Mexico.

3 March 1923

Dear Seltzer

I sent you B. W. Huebsch's letter about *The Rainbow* last night. Enclosed I send you the contracts for:

Three Novels (Doran, covers *The Rainbow*) – including a letter about copyrights.

'Italian Days'.[2] *Amores* (Doran)

Prussian Officer (Doran)

Look! We Have Come Through (Huebsch)

The White Peacock (Duffield – transfer papers complete).

Please keep these for me very carefully till I come to New York and can arrange a safe-deposit for all my papers.

On the back is a copy of my letter to Huebsch. I think we ought to let him get through this edition, anyhow.[3] Best let Stern deal with him in this matter. Try and be amicable and fair.

You see Doran started at 15% on this contract.

I am writing to Stern and tell him you will show him the Huebsch letter. Telegraph to me – I must know how this is to be settled before I leave.

Yrs ever   D. H. Lawrence

P. S. Would you send a copy of *England my England* to

Mrs Elizabeth Freeman, The Desert Inn, *Palm Springs.* California.

2740. To Robert Mountsier, 3 March 1923
Text: MS Smith; Postmark, Valdez MAR 3 1923; Unpublished.

Del Monte Ranch. Valdez. New Mex.

3 March 1923

Dear Mountsier

Will you write that you are satisfied if I pay you ten per-cent of all my receipts from Seltzer for this current year? – There will probably be very little from any other source.

And will you promise to send me back all MSS and papers belonging to me, as soon as you go east.[4]

---

[1] *Questa.*] *Valdez.*
[2] I.e. *Twilight in Italy.* For the variant title see *Letters*, ii. 484.
[3] See p. 474 n. 1.   [4] Mountsier was still in Taos.

Then, if you do this, I agree to your keeping the $105 from the *Dial*, on acc. of receipts due 1st. April. There will be another instalment of the 'Indians' article in the *Dial*, and the cheque for that will also go to you. We can settle about that too.

Let me have your answer.

D. H. Lawrence

2741. To Harriet Monroe, 8 March 1923
Text: MS UChi; Unpublished.

Del Monte Ranch. *Questa*, New Mexico
8 March 1923

Dear Harriett Monroe

There was nothing in 'Matthew' to correct: except I shall be glad if you get *IXΘUS*.[1]

I wonder how you'll like Europe. I may be there in the summer. May meet you in London, Paris, Munich, Rome or Madrid.

We leave here in eight days time for Mexico City.

Poetry will miss you and you'll miss *Poetry*. It will be interesting to see what Eunice Tietjens chooses.[2] Seltzer won't be publishing *Birds Beasts and Flowers* till September. If you give me an address I'll send you an autograph copy, wherever I am – on earth. – Tell *Poetry* to address me care Thomas Seltzer. 5 West 50th Street. New York City – until I send an address. – Hope you'll have a good gay summer.

D. H. Lawrence

2742. To Witter Bynner, 8 March 1923
Text: MS HU; Postmark, Valdez MAR 8 1923; cited in Bynner 17.

Del Monte Ranch. *Valdez*. N. Mex.
8 March 1923

Dear Bynner

Did Johnson get my letter, written about twenty days ago, asking if you wouldn't like to come along to Mexico City with us.

Anyhow I am fixing definitely to leave here on the 18th. and arrive in Santa Fe either on the 20th. or 21st. of this month: Stay just a night. Don't you bother about putting us up if you have things to do.

Best wishes to you both.

D. H. Lawrence

[1] DHL's poem 'St Matthew', ll. 51–2: 'Like a fish seeking the bottom, Jesus,/ *IXΘΨΣ*.'
[2] Eunice Tietjens (1884–1944), American poet and novelist who worked with Harriet Monroe as advisory editor of *Poetry*. For DHL's acquaintance with her and her writings see *Letters*, iii. 139 and n. 1, 140–2.

2743. To Frederick Carter, 8 March 1923
Text: MS UT; Unpublished.

Del Monte Ranch. *Questa.* New Mexico
8 March 1923

Dear Mr Carter

Your letter interests me, and makes me want to read your whole MS. Myself I am more interested in the microcosm than in the macrocosm, and in the gates to the psyche rather than the astrological houses. But one gets such rare hints from astrology.

I am publishing *Studies in Classic American Literature* this spring, but I have taken out all the esoteric stuff. Best keep it exoteric.[1]

I am leaving here in eight days time for Mexico City. If you write, please address me care

Thomas Seltzer, 5 West 50th Street. New York City.

And do contrive to let me see your MS. before long. It is just possible I may be in England in the summer. I will let you know.

Yours Sincerely   D. H. Lawrence

2744. To Willard Johnson, 9 March 1923
Text: MS YU; Unpublished.

Del Monte Ranch. Valdez. (Taos). N M.
9 March 1923

Dear Johnson

I have your letter this morning – sent a note to Bynner yesterday. Great fun that you will come along. I shall try to be in Santa Fe on the 20th. There is a night train, and a day train to El Paso. We my wife and I – must do passports. I am not sure if we could get everything done in El Paso if we arrived on the Mexico Express somewhere about 10.0 a.m. It leaves El Paso at 12.40. The other train – the early morning train from Santa Fe – means that we stay at night in an El Paso hotel. Though that is no worse than a night in a Pullman. What do you and Bynner think?

We want to get to Mexico City in good time before Easter. Hotels may then be crowded.

My wife wants to have the Drawing Room – save the word from El Paso.[2]

I can't fix my day exactly till I get my Letter of Credit from New York.

---

[1] MS reads 'esoteric'.

[2] DHL noted in his diary, 14 March: 'wrote Bynner [Letter 2748] . . . enclosed letter with Taos cheque for $44.10 for Drawing Room in Mr. R. N. Davis Mills Building El Paso' (Tedlock, *Lawrence MSS* 97).

The Danes so disappointed about their exhibition. I have written to Mrs Van Stone for them just now.[1] Pity they can't make a few sous. I look forward to Old Mexico. Let us have a good time.

Yrs   D. H. Lawrence

2745. To Thomas Seltzer, 9 March 1923
Text: MS UT; Postmark, Questa MAR 12 1923; Lacy, *Seltzer* 76–7.

Del Monte Ranch. *Questa*. New Mexico
9 March 1923

Dear Seltzer

Your letter of March 3rd. – Thank you for the card from Lincoln Steffens.[2]

All right, we'll drop Stern after he has arranged this bit of Huebsch matter with you. I thought he'd better do that: you and Huebsch might bite one another's heads off. But please yourself. I'll write no more to Stern.

I sent the Huebsch contracts.

I have at last finally settled with Mountsier that he is to have 10% of this years receipts from you – your March and September payments: and then *finito*! He has already got $170 on acc. from *Dial*.

By the way, would it bother you to keep the two *Dials* with my ' Indians and an Englishman' article in them.

I think, really, you are right not to make interior decorations for *BirdsBeasts*. But poor Merrild was so set on it. He has done a design for each section-cover. I told him that you would *not* use them for the ordinary edition, but that if you liked them, and if ever you wanted to print a decorated edition, you might use them for that. I think the book-jacket has a nice free feeling: hope you'll like it. Götzsche has done a jacket for *Mastro-don Gesualdo*, which I like. But I don't want you to feel pestered about these. If you don't really want them, pay for them out of my money.

Damn Ford and the suppressionists.[3] But other events will take place; that will overwhelm this small fry.

I've still got a bit of my cold. Want very much to go south. So does Frieda. I think Witter Bynner and Willard Johnson are coming along to Mexico City. Have learnt quite a lot of Spanish. Feel the U. S. A. so terribly sterile, even *negative*. I tell you what, there is no life of the blood here. The blood can't flow

---

[1] Mary Roberta ('Berta') Hurt Van Stone (1876–1959), curator of the Art Museum in Santa Fe; the museum, which had an open-door policy, had housed the exhibition by Merrild and Götzsche. Sale shows of several artists were held in the East Gallery as well as one-man shows. (The letter to Mary Van Stone is missing.)

[2] Joseph Lincoln Steffens (1866–1936), American journalist, one of the first muckrakers, author of *The Shame of the Cities* (New York, 1904), etc. Steffens had written an article, ' Into Mexico and Out', which appeared in *Everybody's Magazine* (May 1916).   [3] See p. 379 n. 1.

properly. Only nerves, nerve-vibration, nerve-irritation. It wearies the inside of my bones. I want to go. Voglio andarmene.[1]

I enclose a letter from Paris.[2] Give 'em *England my England* and *Capt's Doll* if you feel like it, and let 'em read and digest. Canaille!

Enclose also a letter from a periodical *Tempo*.[3] I wrote the Oliver Jenkins and told him to ask you for a poem from *Birds Beasts*. Give 'em 'Elephant', or one of the Taos or Lobo poems.[4] And fix a *mild* price for the poor dears.

Am looking for MS. of *BirdsBeasts*. I hope you'll print the books *early*, and send me proofs. Have you not got proofs of *Studies* yet? I wanted to see them. Guess Secker will print *Studies* before *Fantasia*.

Be sure you send a complete *Birds Beasts* to Curtis Brown.

I shall depart to Mexico leaving myself in your hands. We go next week.

Vale! DHL

2746. To Robert Mountsier, 10 March 1923
Text: MS Smith; Postmark, Valdez MAR 10 1923; Unpublished.

Del Monte Ranch. *Valdez*
10 March 1923

Dear Mountsier

Thank you for your letter. We'll take it as settled then. – You have $170 from the *Dial*, on account, and I'll send you the balance as soon as I get the money from Seltzer.

---

[1] 'I've got to go.'   [2] Missing.
[3] Oliver Jenkins, the editor of *Tempo: A Magazine of Poetry* (published in Danvers, Massachusetts), wrote to DHL on 3 March 1923 as follows (TMS Smith):

> Dear Mr. Lawrence:
> TEMPO which has been appearing regularly for two years as a verse magazine is about to enter the field as a potential journal of prose and poetry. The next number which we are to issue in May will be a classic if we can make it so. All of which comes to this: I have the audacity to ask you for a poem or a story for TEMPO.
> The following authors have been enthusiastic enough to contribute something for the May number: Waldo Frank, Amy Lowell, Ben Hecht(?), Henry Bellamann, etc. I have reasons to expect to add Carl Sandburg, James Oppenheim, Joseph Hergesheimer, Charles Finger and Eliot to this list. Won't you help me to fulfil my desire? I want to put out a magazine that will back all the others of its kind off the boards. I think that I can do it – what do you think?
> If you will just give me the satisfaction of a reply, whether you like the idea or not, I'll certainly appreciate it. And in closing I take this opportunity to thank you for the pleasure *WOMEN in LOVE, THE LOST GIRL*, many of your poems and articles, have brought to me.
> Cordially yours.
> Please understand that TEMPO is just starting and is not wealthy, but we will use all authors fairly. If you send anything, just state your own price and we'll do our best.

> DHL's reply to Jenkins has not been found.
[4] These poems are 'Eagle in New Mexico', 'The Blue Jay', 'Bibbles', 'Mountain Lion', 'The Red Wolf', 'Men in New Mexico', 'Autumn in Taos', 'Spirits Summoned West' and 'The American Eagle'.

I expect to be in Taos end of next week, for a couple of days. How long are you staying?

Yours   D. H. Lawrence

2747. To Thomas Seltzer, 12 March 1923
Text: MS UT; Telegram; Lacy, *Seltzer* 78.

[Del Monte Ranch, New Mexico]
12 March 1923

Thos Seltzer
Proceed with Huebsch but be friendly   Lawrence

2748. To Witter Bynner, 14 March 1923
Text: MS HU; cited in Bynner 17–18.

Del Monte Ranch. *Valdez.* N. Mex.
14 March 1923

Dear Bynner
   I had your letter. Do come along with us. We leave here Friday or Saturday.
   I expect to catch the stage on Monday morning, and arrive in Santa Fe by the train, Monday. Don't know what time it arrives in Santa Fe.
   Then I think we might go on *Tuesday* night, arrive El Paso Wednesday morning. In which case we need sleepers booked for Wednesday. I enclose my letter to the agent – will you forward it. If Tuesday[1] night is too soon for you to leave, let me know. I would like us to go all together. And alter the day on my letter to El Paso, booking the pullman, if you wish a later day.
   Will you telegraph me *care Lee Witt, Taos*, and tell me what day suits you.
   And put a special delivery stamp, will you, on the El Paso letter. I'll pay up all things when I see you.
   If you wish to wait a day or two longer, I will do so too. But let me know.

Yrs   D. H. Lawrence

P. S. I would awfully like to take the little black dog with us? Could we do it, do you think? How would she have to travel?

DHL

2749. To Benjamin Huebsch, 14 March 1923
Text: MS UT; Unpublished.

Del Monte Ranch.
14 March. 1923

Dear Huebsch –
   I wish you would settle the matter of *The Rainbow* with Thomas Seltzer or

---

[1] Tuesday] Wednesday

his representative. I do hope you can come to a friendly arrangement with him.

I am leaving in two days time for Mexico City. I will send you my address as soon as I get there, or you can write me *Poste restante*, if there is anything necessary to decide.

Yrs   D. H. Lawrence[1]

2750. To Thomas Seltzer, 14 March 1923
Text: MS UT; Postmark, Questa MAR 16 1923; Lacy, *Seltzer* 78–9.

Del Monte Ranch, *Questa*. New Mexico.

14 March 1923

Dear Seltzer

I telegraphed you: 'Proceed with Huebsch, but be friendly.' If he's *really* got an edition in the press, you *can't* squash it. Don't do that. – I'll put a copy of my letter to Huebsch on the back.

I've got *Birds Beasts* MS. Will send it you before I leave. I've got my letter of Credit.

Will you please pay in a thousand dollars to my account in the *Charleroi Savings and Trust Co. Charleroi. Penna.* This can be the last we will pay in to that account. But I want some money there, so I can draw a cheque or so from the cheque-book I've got. Please pay it in as soon as you get this letter.

I send you the last poem I shall write in the US this time. 'The American Eagle'. Some one might like to print it. I think I would like it put *last* in the *BirdsBeasts* MS, among the 'Ghosts'.[2]

When will *The Captains Doll* be out?

Please send a complete MS. of BirdsBeasts to Curtis Brown at once.

We expect to be in Santa Fe on Monday – leave Wednesday. If you have a last word, you could telegraph *care Witter Bynner. Sante Fe.*

I can't bear to leave the Bimsey. Either Götzsche or Mrs Freeman, who is coming to Mexico in May, shall bring him to us: or I will come back here for him.

Mountsier says he will probably leave Taos about 1st April.

I do hope everything will go well with you. I feel the Ford fuss won't come to much. But don't overwork and make yourself ill.

I'll write a note and thank Steffens. Am sorry about Gutierrez de Lara: feel I should have liked him.[3]

---

[1] This text is taken from the 'Copy of letter to Huebsch' written on the back of the letter following.

[2] The poem was placed as DHL requested.   [3] See p. 394 n. 4.

We are in the midst of packing. The sky is trying to snow. Mabel Sterne has gone to California: got herself into too great a mess with Indians etc. Nina Witt and Lee came yesterday: been in Boston since Christmas: are a bit dreary. Expect Witter Bynner goes with us to Mexico.

I put my trust in you.

D. H. Lawrence

I shall call at the post-office Mexico City for poste restante letters.

2751. To Lincoln Steffens, [14 March 1923]
Text: MS UT; Unpublished.

Del Monte Ranch. *Questa*. New Mexico
14 March 1922

Dear Mr Steffens

Thank you for the card of introduction to Mr Haberman[1] and to the University Club of Mexico City. I guess I shall suffer from the latter gentlemen. I think there should be no bridge between commercial missionaries and Mexicans who don't want 'em: rather a dense jungle of prickly pear: which I would much rather be, if I must be something metaphorical, than a bridge, *pons asinorum*.

Yours Sincerely   D. H. Lawrence

2752. To S. S. Koteliansky, [16 March 1923]
Text: MS BL; PC v. Filippo Figari, Contadino della Trexenta; Postmark, Taos MAR 18 19[. . .]; Zytaruk 252.

[Taos, New Mexico]
March. 16.

We leave tomorrow for Mexico City – expect to get there 23rd. I will send you an address as soon as I have one. Many thanks for *Signature* MS. Did Mountsier ask for it? He is no longer my agent.

DHL

2753. To Emily King, [16 March 1923]
Text: MS Needham; PC v. Costumi Sardi, Cavalcata Gallurese; Postmark, Taos MAR 1[. . .]; Unpublished.

[Taos, New Mexico]
16 March.

– We leave tomorrow – expect to arrive in Mexico City this day week – the 23rd – about your birthday time.[2] I hope you have my letter, and that you'll

---

[1] Roberto Haberman worked in the Mexican Department of Education.
[2] DHL's sister was 41 on 21 March 1923.

have a good birthday. Deep snow here. Am glad to go from winter. I'll write as
soon as we are in Mexico.

DHL

2754. To Ada Clarke, [16 March 1923]
Text: MS Clarke; PC v. Costumi Sardi, Fonni; Taos MAR 1[. . .]; Unpublished.

[Taos, New Mexico]
16 March.

We leave here in the morning – in deep snow – expect to get to Mexico City on
the 23rd. I'll send you an address from there. Hope you will get the books I
sent from Questa. Letters take so long now.

DHL

2755. Robert Mountsier, [18 March 1923]
Text: MS Smith; Unpublished.

Taos
Sunday

Dear Mountsier
We leave in the morning for Santa Fe. I meant to come round, but people
were here. I will send you a line from Mexico: also the balance of the
commission when I get Seltzer's statement. I think it is somewhere about
$4000, his royalties.
I do hope you've had a good time in Taos.

Yrs   DHL

2756. To Thomas Seltzer, [19 March 1923]
Text: MS UT; Postmark, [. . .] MAR 20 1923; Lacy, *Seltzer* 82.

Taos Junction[1]
Monday 18 March 1923

Dear Seltzer
I just had your telegram about Huebsch as we left Taos. I haven't any
Huebsch *Women-in-Love* correspondence. But very little passed. Pinker had
the MS. two years. I thought of course he had tried everybody. Came your
letter asking for the book – I sent you my MS. Then I had a letter and cable
from Huebsch saying he *hadn't* seen the MS (who knows if he had?). I cabled
you, *please release Women-in-Love*. You had sent me £50. sterling – and you

---

[1] The letter was written on Monday 19 March on the headed notepaper of Gerson Gusdorf,
General Merchandise, Taos (cf. p. 354 n. 2).

replied you couldn't release. That was all. Ask Huebsch to show you my letters. He once said to Mountsier that I was a liar, and that he could prove it from letters. He went to look for said letters and couldn't find them. – I remember that against him, you may be sure. And I will write and remind him of it. Anyhow I acted in absolute good faith in the *Women in Love* matter. You have the correspondence.

Huebsch never answered my letters from Taos.

I do hope it will straighten out without ugliness. Go softly.

Yrs   D. H. Lawrence

2757. To Adele Seltzer, [20 March 1923]
Text: MS UT; Lacy, *Seltzer* 82–3.

[Witter Bynner, P.O. Box 1061, Santa Fe, New Mexico][1]
Tuesday

Dear Adele Szold

This is the key to the little trunk with arctics and sheepskins. You can use anything any time you may want.

We leave today at 4.0 *without* the Bynners. They follow Friday. – I wrote Thomas from Taos Junction.

adios   DHL

2758. To Witter Bynner, [21 March 1923]
Text: MS HU; PC v. International Bridge between El Paso, Texas, and Juarez, Mexico; Postmark, El Paso MAR [. . .]; Unpublished.

El Paso
Wed.

We left our umbrellas – stupid! Quite an easy journey. You check baggage here over to Juarez, across river, and buy tickets and reserve pullman there – Get Mexican gold at Bank here – two to one. Hope you're ready.

DHL

2759. To Emily King, [21 March 1923]
Text: MS Needham; PC v. International Bridge between El Paso, Texas, and Juarez, Mexico; Postmark, El Paso MAR 21 1923; Unpublished.

El Paso.
21 March

This is the frontier – we cross over this morning. – Many happy returns of the

[1] This letter was written on Bynner's personal stationery.

day to you. – I didn't get a letter before I left, except the one F[rieda] answered – Hope you had the cheque.

DHL

2760. To Bessie Freeman, [21 March 1923]

Text: MS UNYB; PC v. International Bridge between El Paso, Texas, and Juarez, Mexico; Postmark, El Paso MAR 21 1923; Unpublished.

[El Paso]
21 March.

– Have your letter from Davis – very many thanks – the letters sound splendid – I am sure you will come and see us – the Danes will be very grateful to you and also for any advice Paul[1] might give – do you mind my having bothered you? It is already hot here – There are several American women travelling alone to Mexico – so *that* is all right. F[rieda] sends an Auf wiedersehn.

D. H. Lawrence

2761. To Knud Merrild, [21 March 1923]

Text: MS UT; PC v. International Bridge between El Paso, Texas, and Juarez, Mexico; Postmark, El Paso MAR 21 [. . .]; Merrild 260.

El Paso.
Wednesday

We cross over this morning – an easy journey so far – a woman on the train is taking her *cat* to Mexico: poor pussy in the baggage van, not very happy.

Grüsse DHL

Postage to Mexico costs same as in U.S.A. – letter two cents. already it is hot.

DHL

2762. To Ada Clarke, [21 March 1923]

Text: MS Clarke; PC v. International Bridge between El Paso, Texas, and Juarez, Mexico; Postmark, El Paso MAR 21 1923; Lawrence–Gelder 125.

El Paso
21 March.

We cross the frontier into Mexico this morning – already it is hot – such a change from the snow of Del Monte.

DHL

[1] See p. 333 n. 1.

2763. To Ada Clarke, [24 March 1923]
Text: MS Clarke; PC v. Aztec sculpture, National Museum, Mexico D. F.; Postmark, [. . .]
1923; Lawrence–Gelder 125–6.

Hotel Monte Carlo. Av. Uruguay 69, *Mexico*.
24 March.

Had quite a good journey here. Mexico just warm enough, and very free and
easy, like Naples – to me much pleasanter than U.S. – we shall probably stay at
least a few months, though I am not sure – I expect some friends down from
Santa Fe on Tuesday – so good to get a little wine again.[1]

DHL

2764. To Knud Merrild, [24 March 1923]
Text: MS UT; PC v. Goddess of Symbols [National Museum], Mexico, D. F.; Postmark,
Mexico D. F. 26 MAR 1923; Merrild 264.

Hotel Monte Carlo. – Av. Uruguay 69, *Mexico City*
Saturday

Arrived wearily last night – went to a big American hotel[2] – didn't like it at all –
found this little Italian hotel, very nice[3] – Mexico very pleasant, rather like
South Italy, but I feel a bit shut in, after the ranch. But the whole atmosphere
is easy, and alive: a bit of rain, too: not at all hot, but nice and warm. I think we
are going to like it.

DHL

So good to have a flask of Chianti at one's elbow again.

DHL

2765. To Emily King, [24 March 1923]
Text: MS Needham; PC v. Natives in their canoes, Xochimilco, Mexico; Postmark, Mexico
D. F. 26 MAR 1923; Unpublished.

Hotel Monte Carlo. Av. Uruguay 69. *Mexico*
24 March.

We are here, and settled in nicely for the moment – warm but not hot –
reminds me of Naples or Palermo, much more like S. Italy than U.S.A. – so of
course, I like it much better. Wonder how long post takes.

DHL

---

[1] I.e. to have escaped from 'Prohibition' in USA.
[2] The Hotel Regis, which faced Avenida Juárez.
[3] Hotel Monte Carlo, run by an Italian family named Fortes.

2766. To Bessie Freeman, [24 March 1923]
Text: MS UNYB; PC v. Ruins at San Juan Teotihuacan, Mexico; Postmark, Mexico D. F.
26 MAR 1923; Moore, *Intelligent Heart* 311.

Hotel Monte Carlo. Av. Uruguay 69, *Mexico City.*
Saturday

Got here last night – quite a good journey – tried a big American hotel and
didn't like it: this is a nice little Italian place. It is warm – not hot – rains a little
– the city pleasant – much more like S. Italy than America – haven't done
much yet but wander round. I think we are going to like it.

DHL

2767. To Baroness Anna von Richthofen, [25 March 1923]
Text: MS UT; PC v. National Museum, Mexico; Postmark, Mexico D. F. 26 MAR 1923;
Unpublished.

Hotel Monte Carlo. Av. Uruguay 69. *Mexico*
Sonntag. 25 März

So, wir sind wieder da! – und es ist viel netter wie Ver. Staaten; mehr wie
Palermo oder Neapel, warm, aber nicht heiss, und lebendig. Das Blut fliesst
wieder frei in den Adern, nicht so wie in jenem Freiheitsland, immer in
Gefängnis. Alles ist ganz ruhig, und ein nettes, menschliches Volk: keine
Menschmaschinen. – Ich schreibe dir morgen. F[rieda] hat es gern hier.

DHL

[So, we're here again! – and it is much nicer than Uni. States; more like
Palermo or Naples, warm, but not hot, and lively. The blood flows free again
in the veins, not like in that Land of Freedom, always in prison. All is quite
peaceful, and a nice, human folk: no human machines. – I'll write to you
tomorrow. F[rieda] likes it here.

DHL]

2768. To Witter Bynner, [27 March 1923]
Text: MS HU; Bynner 19.

Hotel Monte Carlo. Av. Uruguay 69. Mexico
Tuesday

Dear Bynner
    Don't know if you are coming – I met train yesterday – but give this note to
the hotel courier on chance. It is a little Italian hotel, clean and good food, but
not elegant: costs only 4 pesos a day, food and all. You can try it. We tried the

Regis – didn't care for that. – The man speaks only Spanish – we speak Italian happily in the house.

You take a taxi with hand luggage – the hotel will fetch your trunk in the morning. – Taxis about two pesos. Perhaps best take the courier with you – he's nice really. – Everything is quite easy.

Yrs　D. H. Lawrence

2769. To John Middleton Murry, 28 March 1923

Text: MS NYPL; cited in Murry, *New Adelphi* 415.

Hotel Monte Carlo. Av. Uruguay 69. Mexico City.
28 March 1923

Dear Jack

Well, we've been in this city five days. And it makes me feel I am tired of travelling. I don't like the gruesome Aztec carvings. I don't like the spirit of this continent. It seems to me sub-cruel, a bit ghastly. I'll go round a bit, and look at Guadalajara and Orizaba and so on. Then I must go to New York. But I shan't stay. By July I ought to be in England. If you know a decent cottage or place to live, keep it in mind for me. Somewhere quiet. I don't want people. Though I doubt if I shall want to stay in England the winter. Probably Sicily. I liked that best.

DHL

2770. To Thomas Seltzer, 30 March 1923

Text: MS UT; Postmark, Mexico D. F. 31 MAR 23; Lacy, *Seltzer* 83.

Hotel Monte Carlo. Mexico City
30 March 1923

Dear Seltzer

The enclosed came today.[1] I don't know which parcel it refers to. If it is Frieda's dyed stuff, we got the parcels all right, but didn't pay any C.O.D. charges – only the excess charge for bringing the things from Jaroso station. There was no request for any payment C.O.D. – I received two parcels from Jaroso, Express: the dyed stuffs, – and sweets and books (*Young Girls Diary*[2] etc). Nothing else.

I hate to bother you about this. But would you just see to it. If you did send a C. O. D. parcel, please pay for it from my account.

D. H. Lawrence

Bynner has turned up: hating this city! I like it better than at first.

---

[1] The enclosure was a letter from the American Railway Express Co. asking for information about a parcel from Seltzer to DHL at the Del Monte Ranch.　　[2] See p. 292 n. 1.

2771. To Thomas Seltzer, 4 April 1923
Text: MS UT; Postmark, Mexico D. F. 4 ABR 1923; Lacy, *Seltzer* 83–4.

Hotel Monte Carlo. Avenue Uruguay 69. Mexico.

4 April 1923

Dear Seltzer

Your letter about *Sons and Lovers*: also Stern's, just now. Witter Bynner is here. He says he has seen an advertisement of Mitchell Kennerley, announcing a new edition of *Sons and Lovers* (not the Boni and Liveright popular edition[1]). Bynner says Kennerley probably has a stock of *Sons and Lovers* in hand, and will go on selling – and underselling – you.[2] Do you know about this? If he transfers *plates* and *copyright*, what about his already printed stock?

Do I lose the $1100 dollars from Kennerley altogether?

It seems to me there is a mistake in this Release paper: that it should say *Mitchell Kennerley* where it says *David H. Lawrence*, there in the middle. However, I send the thing signed, to you, and you can do what is necessary. I think this address is quite safe.

Grüsse   D. H. Lawrence

P. S. To save time I have the form typed out, take both to the American Consul, and send you both.

DHL

Consul says it's all right now.

DHL

2772. To Nina Witt, [4 April 1923]
Text: MS Brill; PC; Postmark, Mexico D. F. 4 ABR 1923; Unpublished.

Hotel Monte Carlo. Aven. Uruguay 69. Mexico City.

4 April.

Been here nearly a fortnight – Mexico City not bad, but very American on the one hand, and slummy on the other: rather a mongrel town. The country much more attractive – but everywhere ruins of houses and haciendas. It isn't at all too hot – a little rain each day. We were at the pyramids San Juan Teotihuacán yesterday – motored about 28 miles out from here – they are

---

[1] Boni and Liveright (Seltzer's nephews, who later took over his business when he went bankrupt) had published the Modern Library edition of *Sons and Lovers* in 1922.

[2] Bynner was probably correct in assuming that Kennerley, having relinquished the plates and his interest in the copyright for *Sons and Lovers*, had continued to sell the stock he had on hand. The interpretation seems to be supported by DHL's reference (in Letter 2773) to an injunction to prevent further sales.

impressive still – very: seem to have risen out of the earth:[1] while all the
Spanish stuff is just superimposed, extraneous – and collapsing. The natives
are interesting, more alive than the Indians, bright, quick dark eyes. And there
is the same old gulf between Spanish and them – no real fusion. And the
Spanish now collapsing. We are going tomorrow to Cuernavaca. – How is my
little dog? Greet Lee – Bynner is here.

DHL

A little Italian hotel, cheap but pleasant, very.

2773. To Thomas Seltzer, 8 April 1923
Text: MS UT; Postmark, Mexico D. F. 9 ABR 1923; Lacy, *Seltzer* 85–6.

Hotel Monte Carlo. Aven. Uruguay 69. Mexico
8 April 1923

Dear Seltzer

Your letter about Kennerley's further swindle come.

I don't like kow-towing to Kennerley and letting him off everything. I
would rather you took proceedings against him on my behalf. I *hate* letting
him blankly swindle me. It would be better to bring a claim against him for
breach of contract in not paying royalties, demand payments, and restitution
of all rights to me. If the case cannot come on for a long time, bring an
injunction to stop further sale of *Sons and Lovers* – stop Boni and Liveright as
well as Kennerley.

It is time now to fight, not to be aimiable and yielding.

But sorry you have all the trouble – But *black their eyes*.

D. H. Lawrence

You will only succeed by *fighting*: and fighting again. That brings success.

DHL

2774. To Thomas Seltzer, [9 April 1923]
Text: MS Lazarus; Postmark, Mexico D. F. 9 ABR 23; Lacy, *Seltzer* 86–7.

Hotel Monte Carlo. Av. Uruguay 69. Mexico City
Monday 8 April 1923

Dear Thomas

I wrote you yesterday, best fight Kennerley. Best fight all round. You'll see
they'll all try now to put a spoke in your wheel. Think you're going too fast. So
fight 'em. Run risks if one must. But don't conciliate any further.

As for me, when it comes near time to book tickets to England, I don't want
to go. England makes me feel sick to think of: it would try to drag me down to

---

[1] Teotihuacán, or 'The City of the Gods', was the most important city in pre-Columbian Central
Mexico (33 miles n. of Mexico City). At the s. end of the city is the Temple of Quetzalcoatl.

the old thing. So I shall look for a house here in Mexico. I really like the country, feel I might like to live here. We shall go to Guadalajara and look round. – Meanwhile this address is good.

And you are caught in the toils of family and sickness and nurses and impending funerals. I am sorry for you. Don't let it drag you down too. *Let the dead bury their dead.*[1] We've got to live forward.

I feel I would like to settle down and do a novel here.

We were in Cuernavaca – where Zapato held out so long.[2] Dead, dead, beautiful cathedrals – dead Spain – dead! – but underneath, live peons. – Soldiers everywhere – riding on roof of trains to guard them – soldiers, soldiers – And ruins! Nearly all the big haciendas and big houses are ruins, shells. A great deal of waste country.

Yet I feel I should like a little hacienda – house, and a few acres of land for fruit – perhaps get Götzsche to come and help me work it. He is very helpful where there is work – and one would need to be a tiny bit reinforced in this country.

Met one or two liberals – but am weary of this liberation. It is almost as fatal as capital: perhaps worse. Criminal to want to educate these peons with our education.

Tell me one or two things:

1. Is *The Captain's Doll* out yet.
2. What about *Studies in C[lassic] A[merican] Literature?* –[3]
3. I presume you got the completed MS. of *BirdsBeasts*, with the additional 'American Eagle' poem. Also the two cover designs from Götzsche and Merrild. Hope you liked them and sent the money for them.
4. When will you be printing these things? Can I have proofs?
5. Are you sending me the *contracts* – and statement for this half year's payment? – I had word from Charleroi Savings and Trust Co. that you deposited $500/ to my credit there. That will do for the time being. But if I find a house of course I shall want money. I'd really like to settle down.
6. Curtis Brown wrote urging me to let his American office handle my stuff. Would it be simpler if I did this?

Hope things are straightening up. – With Kennerley I think it would really be best to start an action and bring an injunction to stop the sale of *Sons and Lovers* at once. Put a spoke in *his* wheel.

– Saluti.   D. H. Lawrence

[1] Matthew viii. 22 (A.V.).
[2] Emiliano Zapata (1879?– 1919), Mexican revolutionary; led the revolution after 1910, occupying Mexico City three times (1914–15); but, in 1919, he was ambushed and killed in Morelos. Statues stand there in his honour.
[3] Seltzer published *The Captain's Doll* on 21 April 1923 and *Studies* on 27 August.

2775. To S. S. Koteliansky, 11 April 1923
Text: MS BL; cited in Gransden 29.

Hotel Monte Carlo. Av. Uruguay 69, *Mexico City*
11 April 1923

Dear Kot –

We have been here about three weeks – in this noisy, ramshackle town. But it is anyhow very free and easy. We are going tomorrow to Puebla – then Tehuacan and Orizaba: It is just possible I shall take a house here for the summer – if I don't come to England. I find it so hard, when it comes to the point, to make up my mind for England – I don't know why. – Do you remember, during the war I always wanted to come to Mexico. I like it here, too: so few pretences of any sort. – The young man is a young Californian – in the picture – and the others the two Mexican chauffeurs.[1] Has Secker sent you all the books I ordered for you?

Grüsse. DHL

2776. To E. M. Forster, [11 April 1923]
Text: MS KCC; Moore, *Intelligent Heart* 311.

Hotel Monte Carlo. Av. Uruguay 69, Mexico City.
11 April

Dear E. M. –

– *Alexandria* reached me here yesterday[2] – I've begun reading the history – But what a funny task to set yourself – though I always remember the thrill you got out of that National Gallery Catalogue[3] – We've been in Mexico three weeks – like it – may stay the summer. The photograph is on top of the Pyramid of the Sun at Teotihuacan – and the third person is Witter Bynner, Amer. poet.[4] – Would you really advise me to come to England? Shouldn't I feel I was sinking in a bog? I balk coming at the last minute. Heaven knows where we'll all end. Frieda greets you.

DHL

---

[1] The text of this letter was written on the verso of a photograph of DHL, Frieda, Willard Johnson and two Mexican chauffeurs. The same is true of Letters 2777, 2778, 2782, 2783, 2787, 2810, 2811 and 2813.

[2] Forster's *Alexandria: a History and a Guide* (Alexandria, 1922).

[3] At the beginning of World War I Forster felt obliged to find a job. His friend Sir Charles Holroyd, Director of the National Gallery, offered him a post as a cataloguer (see P. N. Furbank, *E. M. Forster: A Life*, i (1977), 259–60). Forster worked on one of the Gallery's catalogues of paintings and was paid £8. 6s. 8d. per month, September 1914 to October 1915.

[4] This letter was written on the verso of the photograph described. DHL used copies of the same photograph for Letters 2779, 2780, 2781, 2786 and 2792.

2777. To Bessie Freeman, 11 April 1923
Text: MS UNYB; Moore, *Intelligent Heart* 311–12.

Hotel Monte Carlo. Av. Uruguay 69. Mexico
11 April. 1923

Dear Bessie Freeman

We are still here – and I am liking Mexico better – think now of finding a house to live here some months – in the country for preference: so you will no doubt come and see us. – We motored out to the pyramids – very fine. This picture is on the way – ourselves, Spud Johnson (Witter Bynner's friend) and the two chauffeurs. We also stayed a few days in Cuernavaca – hot, but very attractive. And tomorrow we set off for Puebla, Tehuacan, Orizaba. – This hotel is a little Italian place – we pay only 4 pesos a day each, Amer. plan, 3 meals a day. I like it very much, so would you, if you had a companion. If you were alone, perhaps better stay at the Imperial or the Regis – the former less expensive: the latter more central. Mrs Nuttall[1] – to whom Dr Lyster[2] gave us a letter – offers us a house of hers in Coyacan, a suburb here. I'd rather be farther from town. We shall make up our minds next week. – It isn't a bit too hot – but still it takes some getting used to. – Forgive the post-cards. This address is safe. Many greetings from us both.

DHL

2778. To Achsah Brewster, 11 April 1923
Text: MS UT; Brewster 70–1.

Hotel Monte Carlo. Av. Uruguay 69, *Mexico City*
11 April 1923

Your letter arrived today – we wondered so much about you. We have been in Mexico about three weeks: are just going tomorrow to Puebla, Tehuacan, Orizaba, to look at the hotter places, and see if we'd like a house somewhere, for the summer. We got no further east, in U S A, than New Mexico. I never lectured to your countrywomen – nor intend to. It's a queer world: and I doubt Earl will never like his native land. Mexico is much better – but you'd never like this either. Best stick to Italy. I intended to come back to Europe in

---

[1] Zelia Maria Magdalena Nuttall (1858–1933), American archaeologist (b. San Francisco) specialising in ancient and colonial history of Mexico; author of many books on Mexican history and antiquities. Her *Fundamental Principles of Old and New World Civilizations* (Cambridge, Mass., 1901) was one influence on DHL's *The Plumed Serpent* (1926) in which she appears as Mrs Norris. Zelia Nuttall owned a house built during the time of Hernando Cortés (1485–1547), Spanish conqueror of Mexico.　　　 [2] Unidentified.

May – shall still possibly do so – but more probably stay here. Witter Bynner, Amer. poet, is with us – and another young Californian (no, Bynner is in the picture).[1] The two crouching are the chauffeurs. We went to a bull-fight: hated it. It's a queer world. Glad you are doing well.

DHL

2779. To Knud Merrild, 11 April 1923
Text: MS UT; Postmark, Mexico D. F. 11 ABR 1923; Merrild 265–6.

Hotel Monte Carlo, Mexico City
11 April 1923.

Dear Merrild

Your letters this morning – what a schweinerei that Taos is – how glad I am I need not smell them any more. Poor Pips! – you must do as you think best with her: anyhow I'm glad Myers got a slap in the eye.[2] But Mexico would never do for Bubastis – it's so different. She'd be dead in a month. Afraid Taos is her place. – This is a picture of Johnson and me going down the steps of the Great Pyramid at Teotihuacan. He – Johnson – is sick, and staying in the American hospital here for a week: nothing serious. We are going a tour tomorrow, to Puebla, Tehuacan, Orizaba. I want to find a house. A rich Englishwoman offers us one in Coyoacan, a suburb here. But I'd rather be further away from this noisy – but rather pleasant – city. I hope you'll be able to come down. I'll tell you more definitely our plans next week. Spit on Taos for me.

DHL

2780. To Catherine Carswell, 11 April 1923
Text: TMSC Carswell; cited in Carswell 175.

Hotel Monte Carlo, Av. Uruguay 69, Mexico City.
11th April 1923.

Dear Catherine

I had your letter here to-day. We have been in Mexico nearly three weeks: like it: are going to-morrow to Puebla and Tehuacan and Orizaba, to see if we should like a house to stay the summer. Every time I am near to coming to England, I find I don't want to come – just yet. But I am never sure what I shall do in a month's time. For the moment Russia seems very far away, and not very desirable. And my prosperity is only relative – especially with so many relatives in Germany. This photograph was taken on top of the old

[1] (no, Bynner is in the picture)] (in the picture)
[2] Ralph Meyers (1885–1948), Taos painter. According to Merrild, Meyers went to see the Danes and claimed the dog 'Pips' (or 'Bubastis') as his own. Merrild threw him out of the house. (See Merrild 265–6.)

Pyramid of the Sun, at Teotihuacan. It is very impressive there – far more than Pompei or the Forum. The peons, Indians, are attractive, but Mexico City rather ramshackle and Americanised. But there is a good *natural* feeling – a great carelessness. Do hope some of your plans come good.

DHL

The third person is Witter Bynner, American poet.

2781. To Ada Clarke, [11 April 1923]
Text: MS Clarke; Unpublished.

Hotel Monte Carlo, Mexico City
11 April.
My dear Sister

Here we stand with Witter Bynner – an Amer. poet – on top of one of the ancient pyramids in Teotihuacan. I like Mexico much better the longer I stay – perhaps we shall take a house and remain for the summer – It is just hot enough for me. I bought you a very lurid Oaxaca sarape – blanket – made by the Indians of the south. I will send it when I get an opportunity – We are going to Puebla and Orizaba – leave tomorrow. Hope all goes well at Ripley, that Jack is better.

DHL

2782. To Emily King, [11 April 1923]
Text: MS Needham; Unpublished.

Hotel Monte Carlo, Mexico City.
11 April
My dear sister

Here we are with a friend and the two chauffeurs, photographed at the roadside motoring out to San Juan. There are lots of those tall organ cactus. I like Mexico better than I did – fancy I should like to take a house and stay the summer – Europe sounds so miserable, and Frieda isn't keen on coming back, with things as they are. A rich Englishwoman offers us a house in Coyoacan – eight miles out – but I'd rather be farther from the city. So we are taking a trip round Puebla and Orizaba, to see. – The young fellow is an Amer. friend – suddenly gone sick, and we've had to put him in the Amer. hospital here. How are you now?

DHL

If we dont get to England for the summer I will send you some money for a holiday. Did you get the £5?

DHL

Did Ada get the £10. for father?

2783. To Mary Cannan, [12 April 1923]
Text: MS Lazarus; Postmark, Mexico D. F. 12 ABR 1923; Unpublished.

Hotel Monte Carlo. Av. Uruguay 69. Mexico City
[12 April 1923]

I like Mexico better the longer I stay here. We are going tomorrow to Puebla –
then to Tehuacan and Orizaba. We might possibly take a house here for some
months. It isnt at all too hot – 7500 ft. up. How are you and what are you
doing? I'm getting tired of travel – but when I try to come to England,
something in me resists always – The third young man is a young Amer. friend
– the others the two Mexican chauffeurs.

Are you sitting good and still?

DHL

2784. To Lady Cynthia Asquith, [12 April 1923]
Text: MS Ritzi, Postmark, Mexico D. F. 12 ABR 1923; Unpublished.

Hotel Monte Carlo. Mexico City.[1]
[12 April 1923]

We've been here about three weeks – like it – may take a house for the summer.
I wanted to come to England but couldn't quite decide on it. Maybe I just stick
it – I had your letter just before we left U S A. There is a careless naturalness
in Mexico – the peons, Indians, still far away from us. Myself I like it. But shall
probably see you before very long.

D. H. Lawrence

2785. To Willard Johnson, [16 April 1923]
Text: MS YU; Postmark, Puebla 16 ABR 23; Unpublished.

Hotel Jardin. Puebla[2]
Monday.

Hope you're better. I'm feeble but unconquered. You don't miss much, really,
by staying in Mexico. Tomorrow morning we set off for Orizaba – once more 7
hours train. Send a line to Hotel Francia, Orizaba. Bynner buys more bits, all
the time.[3]

DHL

---

[1] This letter was written on the verso of a photograph of Mexicans in the Plaza. So were Letters
2788 and 2793.
[2] This letter – like Letters 2789, 2790 and 2791 – was written on the verso of a photograph of a
Mexican bull fight.
[3] Possibly 'onyx trifles and Spanish jewelry' for sale in Puebla (Bynner 36).

2786. To Willard Johnson, [16 April 1923]
Text: MS YU; Postmark, Puebla 17 ABR. 23; Unpublished.

[Hotel Jardin, Puebla]
Monday

We've changed again – going in the morning to Atlixco, 2 hours from here – so don't write to Orizaba – they'll forward from here. Hope you're well.

DHL

2787. To John Middleton Murry, [21 April 1923]
Text: MS BL; Postmark, Orizaba 21 ABR 23; Unpublished.

Orizaba
21 April

I've had enough of the New World – sail next week to New York – care Seltzer, 5 West 50th St. and come to England in June. Have you thought of a house for me, in the country? I want to come back.

DHL

2788. To Catherine Carswell, [21 April 1923]
Text: MS YU; Postmark, [. . .]; cited in Carswell 175–6.

Orizaba.
21 April

Had enough of the New World – sail for New York from Vera Cruz next week – and come to England about June – feel like coming back now.

DHL

2789. To Emily King, [21 April 1923]
Text: MS Needham; Postmark, Orizaba 21 ABR 23; Unpublished.

Orizaba.
21 April

I've had about enough of Mexico – think to sail at end of this month to New York – come to England in June – am tired of the New World – Write care of Thomas Seltzer.

DHL

2790. To William Hawk, [21 April 1923]
Text: MS UT; Postmark, Orizaba 21 ABR 23; Moore, *Intelligent Heart* 313.

Orizaba.
21 April

Have had about enough of Mexico – sail for New York next week – address care Thomas Seltzer. 5 West 50th. St. This country interesting for a short time, then one is through with it. – I do hope Mrs Hawk is better, and that the weather is warm – We saw this bull fight – pretty disgusting.

D. H. Lawrence

2791. To Knud Merrild, [21 April 1923]
Text: MS UT; Postmark, Orizaba 21 ABR 23; Merrild 274.

Orizaba.
21 April.

I've had about enough of this country – and continent. Think we shall sail at the end of this month to New York, and at the end of May, sail for Europe. That's what I intend to do. I've had enough of this. – We go back to Mexico City tomorrow, and I shall find mail.

DHL

2792. To Adele Seltzer, [21 April 1923]
Text: MS UT; Postmark, Orizaba 21 ABR 23; Lacy, *Seltzer* 89.

Orizaba.
21 April

Dear Adele Szold
    I do wonder how is your house of troubles. We go back to Mexico City tomorrow and I shall find mail. I've had enough of Mexico – it's quite nice, but I've had enough. And I want to go back to England. No reason why – but I just want to. So I think we'll sail for New York in about a week's time. I'd like to see Thomas and you again before I leave this continent. We ought to be in New York by the 7th. May, easily. I'll send a telegram – and if you are still in the bigger apartment – the Lord be with you – can we go in the little one, and *not* have a servant, except perhaps a char-woman twice a week? Frieda is crazy to wash dishes again. – I should never be able to write on this continent – something in the spirit opposes one's going forth. – Do hope your troubles aren't thickening.

DHL

    Spud Johnson and me descending the pyramid.

2793. To Ada Clarke, [21 April 1923]
Text: MS Clarke; Postmark, Orizaba 21 ABR [. . .]; Lawrence–Gelder 131.

Orizaba.
21 April

I've had about enough of this – expect to sail to New York from Vera Cruz in a week's time – stay a week or two in New York, and then sail to England. I suppose we shall stay with Thomas Seltzer.

DHL

2794. To Robert Mountsier, [21 April 1923]
Text: MS Smith; PC v. Perspectiva desde las Cumbres de Maltrata; Postmark, Orizaba 21 ABR 23; Unpublished.

Orizaba
21 April

Have been in Mexico a month, and have had about enough. Think of leaving soon – probably via New York. Will let you know. Haven't had any Seltzer statements yet – but maybe mail for me in Mexico City. – It was interesting here for a month, but no more.

Yrs DHL

2795. To Curtis Brown, 21 April 1923
Text: MS BPL; Coolidge, *More Books*, xxxiii (January 1948), 23–4.

Hotel Monte Carlo. Av. Uruguay 69. Mexico. D. F.
21 April 1923

Dear Curtis Brown

I have received all at once six or seven of your letters, which I answer right away.

I am glad *The Ladybird* is being well received: hope it will sell.[1] – Am glad

---

[1] Two letters from Secker to Curtis Brown (Secker Letter-Book, UIll) provide valuable background to this letter from DHL. On 27 March Secker wrote:

Dear Mr Curtis Brown
I am pretty sure "The Ladybird" is going to do well, and I have already gone to press with another edition. I wonder whether you might make enquiries from Messrs Duckworth, to ascertain if they would part with the publishing rights in the four Lawrence novels in their list, "The White Peacock", "Sons and Lovers", "The Trespasser" and "The Prussian Officer". The latter is a collection of short stories, and I believe that "The Trespasser" is out of print. It was so, at any rate, some few months ago.
I assume, of course, that Lawrence is signing the "Kangaroo" contract and those for the psychoanalysis books. These latter are in the printers hands and one will be ready next month.
Yours sincerely

also that Harrison is printing 'Elephant'.[1]

Continental Translation rights – I am glad also if that goes ahead. Keep track only of The Insel Verlag (Dr. Anton Kippenberg) of Leipsig, which has printed a translation of *The Rainbow* and is considering a second book.[2]

Kangaroo. – I enclose the signed agreement for Secker, with the 13-as-12 clause struck out. – The separate publication in Australia was Mountsier's idea. From what I saw of Australia, and considering the nature of the book, I myself do not think there is much in this separate publication business. But I leave it to your discretion, since you have already gone so far. If you decide it is not worth while, then arrange with Secker for the Australian rights.[3] But *don't* let him off at 3d. a copy. – I have written Seltzer urging him to let me have proofs of *Kangaroo*. But like every other publisher, he won't go to print till the last minute, if he can help it. – I'll see you get a copy of the revised proofs at the earliest possible moment.

BirdsBeasts and Flowers: I too am keen on this book: Seltzer plans to get it out this autumn. I certainly think Secker might pay 15% after 3,000. In fact, what I would prefer would be, no advance, 10% up to 2000, and 15% after that.

I don't know about Duckworth: nor can I lay hands at the moment on his contracts. But when I get to a place where I can unload my trunks, I will let you have what contracts I possess. Some, I fear, have disappeared in the course of my travels (By the way, though I have three separate times asked Duckworth to make statements and payments on all books, to you, he persists in sending them to me direct.) – I tried to urge him, Duckworth, to let Secker have *Love Poems* and *Amores*; D. replied he didn't wish to. Perhaps you might find a way. – If *Birds Beasts* succeed, persuade Secker to bring out an edition

Secker wrote again, on 6 April 1923:

Dear Mr Curtis Brown

Many thanks for sending me D.H.Lawrence's new collection of poems, "Birds, Beasts and Flowers". I think I shall be able to publish the book this autumn, and it will I presume be the subject of a separate agreement. I see that I published his last book of poems on a 10% royalty basis, the first 500 copies being free, so that I assume it will be quite agreeable if we fix the royalty as before and pay royalties from the beginning, with payment on publication to cover the copies subscribed.

I am also much obliged to you for enquiring from Duckworth about the early Lawrence novels. I suppose he would be equally opposed to parting with the two books of poems which he published. One day it will be well worth while having a collected volume of Lawrence's poems.

I have duly received the typescript of "Kangaroo", though I have not yet had time to read it. According to present plan this is to be published simultaneously here and in America in September.

Yours sincerely

[1] See p. 378 n. 2.
[2] Perhaps *Sons and Lovers*, published by Insel-Verlag in 1925.   [3] See p. 319 n. 3.

of *Look! We Have Come Through*, with two extra poems that belong to this book.[1] You remember Chattos relinquished their rights. *BirdsBeasts* and *Look! We Have Come Thr.* are separate, integral books. I never want them mixed or confused with anything else. But if Secker could get hold of *Love Poems and Others* and *Amores*, then he could make a collected book with *New Poems*. There is also the little volume called *Bay*, which C.W. Beaumont published. This could go in with the collection. But the selecting and arranging must be left to me. – I think this is all the business.

I am not sure how long I shall stay in Mexico. I may come to England quite soon. But address me for the time being c/o Thomas Seltzer. I enclose a photograph taken in the cloisters of Cuernavaca cathedral here in Mexico.[2] Secker might possibly like it for an advertisement.

Yours sincerely   D. H. Lawerence

2796. To Amy Lowell, 21 April 1923
Text: MS HU; Damon 638.

Hotel Monte Carlo. Av. Uruguay 69. Mexico D. F.

21 April 1923

Dear Amy

I have your letter, and the *Ciro postale*.[3] Here we are, circling uneasily round, wondering whether we shall settle for a time, or not. I would like to sit down and write a novel on the American continent (I don't mean *about* it: I mean while I'm here). But it is hard to break through the wall of the atmosphere. – I didn't really dislike the U.S.A. as much as I expected. And I don't *mistrust* it half as much as I mistrust the present England, with its false sentimentalism. So I hesitate here.

Probably I shall come to New York, by sea, before the autumn passes. Then we should both very much like to pay you a little visit, if you feel equal to visitors. While the flowers still last in your garden.

Mexico *is* interesting – but I feel I haven't got the right hang of it yet.

Remember us to Mrs Russell – and I do hope you are feeling well and strong.

Yrs ever   D. H. Lawrence

[1] When Chatto & Windus published *Look! We Have Come Through!* (1917), they insisted that 'Song of a Man Who is Loved' and 'Meeting Among the Mountains' be omitted (see *Letters*, iii. 145 n. 1).
[2] It was taken by Bynner (the negative is in the collection of Clark Kimball, Great Southwest Books); see also p. 431 n. 2.
[3] Amy Lowell sent a cheque for $5.29 on 6 April.

2797. To Edward Marsh, 21 April 1923
Text: MS NYPL; Postmark, Mexico D. F. 23 ABR 1923; Unpublished.

Hotel Monte Carlo. Av. Uruguay 69. Mexico. D.F.

21 April 1923

Dear Eddie

Thank you for the little cheque.[1] – We are still in Mexico. I tip-toe for a leap to Europe, and then hold back – don't know quite why. I suppose I must stay a little longer over here.

Greetings from us both.

D. H. Lawrence

2798. To Kai Götzsche and Knud Merrild, [21 April 1923]
Text: MS UT; Postmark, Mexico D. F. 23 ABR 1923; Merrild 292.

Hotel Monte Carlo. Av. Uruguay 69. Mexico City

21 April

Dear Götzsche and Merrild,

I found your letter here – you may have left Taos already – Mrs Freeman wrote and said she thought you only wanted her letter in *May*, but that she was writing you at once. – If you haven't had her letter, write to her:

Mrs Elizabeth Freeman, *Palm Springs*, California.

I give you a note to a man in Los Angeles.[2] Go to him if you want help.

I'm *still* going to look for a place here. Going to see a Dane[3] who has a farm, tomorrow. Send your address to this hotel the moment you have a place. If ever you get really hard up, let me know at once: both of you. – There is a quick railway down from Los Angeles to Guadalajara, where I think we may settle. – It's not so easy here. In these states almost *every* hacienda (farm) is smashed, and you can't live even one mile outside the village or town: you will probably be robbed or murdered by roving bandits and scoundrels who still call themselves revolutionaries. – But I'll try the state of Jalisco.

Yrs   D. H. Lawrence

2799. To Frederick Carter, 23 April 1923
Text: MS UT; Unpublished.

Hotel Monte Carlo. Av. Uruguay 69. Mexico. D. F.

23 April 1923

Dear Mr Carter

I had your letter of 23 March yesterday: but so far, no drawings or MS. or

---

[1] See p. 297 n. 2.
[2] Will Levington Comfort (1878–1932), American novelist, journalist and short-story writer. He gave them a letter of introduction to a banker.   [3] Unidentified.

anything beyond the letter itself. I look forward to the coming of the drawings and MS. If I get on at all with the book, I will do my best to get Seltzer, or some other suitable publisher, to bring it out. Of course it is the book as a whole that will be of real interest. – If I find myself capable, I will gladly do a brief foreword for the drawings: when I get them: and let you have it at once. Meanwhile we can only wait.

I am not quite sure how long we shall be in Mexico, my wife and I: but probably a month or two longer. This address will hold good.

I think 'Divine Numbers and Divine Names' is a beautiful title. And I think one might rouse more interest in America than in England.

Yours Sincerely   D. H. Lawrence

I hope Elkin Matthews is paying you a proper royalty.[1] He's not a very good pusher – or used not to be. Perhaps he's better now.

Does the Aztec Calendar Stone interest you at all?

2800. To Emily King, [24 April 1923]
Text: MS King; Unpublished.

Mexico. Hotel Monte Carlo
24 April

Dear Pamela

We are back here in Mexico, where it is much cooler. – I hope you had your copy of *Ladybird*. We think of going to Guadalajara at the end of the week to see some people. – You may as well use this little cheque for anything you want – and to pay for the things for Germany. – The photograph is in the cloisters at Cuernavaca Cathedral here in Morelos State.[2]

DHL

2801. To Robert Mountsier, 25 April 1923
Text: MS Smith; Postmark, Mexico D. F. 25 ABR 1923; Unpublished.

Hotel Monte Carlo. Av. Uruguay 69. Mexico City. D. F.
25 April 1923

Dear Mountsier

I still haven't got the accounts from Seltzer – but he told me that my royalties amounted to about $4,000. I don't know what his 'about' means: but feel you may be glad of the money, so send you $230.00, and we can balance up when I do at last get Thomas' statement. You have had $170.00 on account, haven't you? So the $230 will make up $400.

Huebsch making a great fuss about relinquishing the *Rainbow*, and abusing

---

[1] See p. 365 n. 3.
[2] The letter – like Letters 2805, 2816 and 2822 – was written on the verso of a photograph of DHL in the cloisters.

me as usual: so I sent him back that charity money, and told him what I thought of him.[1]

When it comes to the point of sailing for New York and Europe I shy off. I don't know why. But I feel a bad mistrust of England particularly, at the present moment. Perhaps after all we shall stay the summer here in Mexico. I think we shall go at the week-end to Guadalajara, look at that, and perhaps take a house for a month or two.

Witter Bynner is here – very companionable and nice, much nicer than I thought in Santa Fe.

Hope things go well with you. Mexico isn't a bit too hot.

Yrs   D. H. Lawrence

This address is safe.

2802. To John Middleton Murry, [26 April 1923]
Text: MS NYPL; Huxley 566.

Hotel Monte Carlo. Av. Uruguay 69. Mexico. D. F.
Thursday. Apr 27

Dear Jack

I had your cablegram this morning: wonder when and how you are beginning. Do take a chapter from *Fantasia*.[2] Arrange with Curtis Brown, he is my agent in England. I haven't a story handy – if I sit down for a while here I want to write some. You might like that article of mine in *The Dial* – Feb. – called – 'Indians and an Englishman' – about the Apaches – Curtis Brown has it.[3]

I found your letter when I got back from Orizaba. I don't see you with another wife.[4] But it will be as it will be.

I like Mexico, and am still uncertain of my movements. But feel sure I shall be in England before autumn. Only I may stay the summer here, and write a bit. I couldn't do anything in U S A. – Lunching today with the Minister of Education here[5] – they are good idealists and sensible, the present government – but I feel myself as usual outside the scheme of such things.

Hope you will let me know about the magazine, and good luck to it.

Yrs   DHL

[1] DHL noted in his diary, 21 April 1923: 'Wrote Huebsch and sent him back 200 dollars' (Tedlock, *Lawrence MSS* 98).

[2] Murry founded and edited (till 1930) the *Adelphi*, publishing the first issue in June 1923. Since *Fantasia of the Unconscious* was a principal reason for Murry's seeking to renew his friendship with DHL, it was appropriate that chap. IV from that book should be reprinted in the first issue of *Adelphi*.

[3] The article appeared in the November number of *Adelphi*.

[4] Murry married Violet le Maistre (d. 1931), an assistant on *Adelphi*, in 1924.

[5] José Vasconcelos (1881–1959), Minister of Education, 1920–5, had invited DHL to a luncheon but at the last minute was called to an emergency meeting.

2803. To Baroness Anna von Richthofen, 27 April 1923
Text: MS UCB; Frieda Lawrence 175.

Hotel Monte Carlo. Av. Uruguay 69 Mexico. D. F.
27 April 1923.
liebe Schwiegermutter

Wir sind immer noch hier, machen immer Ausflüge. Wir können uns nicht entschliessen, weg zu fahren. Morgen geh ich zu Guadalajara und dem Chapala-see. Da hat man wieder die Pacificbrise, vom Stille[1] Ozean.

Man kommt nicht gern wieder in Europa: alles ist so dumm, und schlimm-dumm, und hat keine Ende. Du muss furchtbar müde sein, mit diesem Deutschlandstragödie. Alles ohne Meinung, ohne Richtung, ohne Idee oder Geist. Nur Geldgefräsigkeit und Frechheit. Man kann nichts machen, nichts thun, nur sich langweilen und bös werden.

Hier auch in Mexico gibt's Bolshevismus und Fascismus und Revolutionen und alles was. Es ist aber mir egal. Ich gehöre nicht. Und die Indianer sind immer draussen. Revoluzion kommt und Revoluzion geht, sie bleiben dieselbe. Unsere Bewustseinmaschinerei haben sie nicht, sind wie schwarzes Wasser, darüber gehen unsere schmutzige Motorschiffe mit Stink und Lärm, das schwarzes Wasser ist geschmutzt, aber nicht wirklich ändert.

Ich schicke dir zehn Pfund, und für Else fünf. Hoffentlich kommt es bald. Es geht ein Hamburg-Amerika schiff jeder Monat von Verz Cruz nach Hamburg. Es muss schöne Frühling in Deutschland sein. Wenn nur der Mensch nicht so dumm oder schlimm wäre, wäre ich so gern in Ebersteinburg, wann die Kastanien bluthen. – Hast du noch *The Captain's Doll*? Es soll dich amusiern.

Tausend Grüsse. DHL

[Dear Schwiegermutter
We are still here, always going excursions. We can't make up our minds to leave. Tomorrow I go to Guadalajara and Lake Chapala. There one has again the Pacific breeze, from the still ocean.

One doesn't come gladly again to Europe: all is so stupid, and wickedly stupid, and has no end. You must be frightfully weary of this German tragedy. All without meaning, without direction, without idea or spirit. Only money-greed and impudence. One can achieve nothing, do nothing, only be bored and become cross.

Here in Mexico too there's Bolshevism and Fascism and revolutions and all such. But it's all the same to me. I don't belong And the Indians are always outside. Revolution comes and revolution goes, they stay the same. Our consciousness-machinery they don't have, are like black water, over which go

[1] Stille] Pazific

our dirty motor-ships with stink and noise, the black water is dirtied, but not really changed.

I send you ten pounds, and five for Else. I hope it comes soon. A Hamburg-America ship goes every month from Vera Cruz to Hamburg. It must be lovely spring in Germany. If only man were not so stupid or wicked, I would so gladly be in Ebersteinburg, when the chestnuts bloom. – Have you *The Captain's Doll* yet? It ought to amuse you.

A thousand greetings.   DHL]

2804. To Kai Götzsche and Knud Merrild , [27 April 1923]
Text: MS UT; Postmark, Mexico D. F. 27 ABR 1923; Merrild 293.

[Frieda Lawrence begins]

Monte Carlo, Mexico

Dear friends,   Friday

To-day you leave Taos and you wont be sorry – We have'nt found anything to *live* yet here, but to night Lawrence goes to Guadalajara, there is a lake near there and a pretty place and you can swim – There would be much to paint here – only these terrible revolutions have made it so miserable all these broken places – But we *do* like it – If Lawrence cant get a house at this place and does'nt like it, we go to New York and Europe – But I am glad we came anyhow – The photographs are awfully nice. I love that one of Lawrence and Pips and me – Do keep the plate, – Bynner was sorry not to be in Santa Fe to look after you – They are both nice but Bynner is an old lady and Johnson a young one – Lawrence's *Captain's Doll* is a great success in England[1] – And Mabel really married to Tony?![2] And our Pips at Ralph Myers – he is a different Pips now – And I remember when Mabel offered him to Ralph he wouldn't have her – In a Hearst's magazine I saw Ufer's picture with Mrs Berry's name – I hope you will have a good trip and that Lizzie[3] will behave – Our Fontana Vecchia has been done up and we can have it – Perhaps we shall go back – Europe seems more miserable than ever – We saw a terrible bullfight and ran away after 10 minutes – We shall think of you on the road –

Guadalajara would be near from Los Angeles!

So all good luck.

Frieda Lawrence

[Lawrence begins]

I address to Merrild because I think his name is easier for the post people – Hope you got my letter and enclosure to W L Comfort – also the letter from Mrs Freeman. I am tired of looking round here – this week-end will be the last effort. What's the good if one can't live safely in the country?

DHL

---

[1] See reviews in Draper 191–6.   [2] They were married on 23 April 1923.
[3] The Danes' car.

2805. To Thomas Seltzer, [27 April 1923]
Text: MS YU; Lacy, *Seltzer* 89.

Hotel Monte Carlo. Mexico. D. F.
27 April

Dear Thomas

I am going this evening to Lake Chapala in Guadalajara, to see if we might like to live there a while. If that is no good, we shall come to New York – shan't bother any more with here. Isn't this a nice photograph – in the cloisters of Cuernavaca Cathedral. Nothing further from you.

DHL

2806. To William Siebenhaar, 27 April 1923
Text: TMSC NWU; PC; Unpublished.

Hotel Monte Carlo, Mexico, D.F.
27 April 1923.

Dear Mr Siebenhaar

Your letter and the new batch of *Max* came today – so glad to hear the book is finished. I have the whole MS. with me, shall go through it carefully as soon as the last part comes. Then I shall urge it on my publisher. He is due to publish a translation of mine – Giovanni Verga, the Sicilian novelist – in September. If that is at all a success, I think he will do *Max Havelaar*. We have been here five weeks, and may stay the summer. I will send you an address: but the publisher Thomas Seltzer, 5 West 50th. St., New York is always good. By the way I sent you a copy of *Amores* – did you get it? So sorry Mrs. Siebenhaar is done up. We may meet in Europe.

Au revoir ⸱ D. H. Lawrence

2807. To Frieda Lawrence, [1? May 1923]
Text: Bynner 79; Telegram.

[Lake Chapala, Mexico]
[1? May 1923]¹

Chapala paradise. Take evening train. Purnells meet you in Guadalajara.² I in Chapala. If any confusion go to Hotel Cosmopolita across from station.

---

¹ The chronology of this period involving the move from Mexico City to Chapala is difficult to reconstruct. What seems certain is that DHL left Mexico City on Friday 27 April, making his way through El Fuerte and arriving in Chapala on Sunday 29 April. The Lawrences first settled in the Chapala house by the afternoon of 2 May, hence the telegram must have been sent on 1 May.

² Dr George Edward Purnell (1863–1961?), American dentist, lived with his daughter Idella Purnell (b.1901) in Guadalajara. She was a former student of Bynner's at the University of California; 1923–30 she edited a magazine of verse, *Palms*; m. (1) 1927, John M. Weatherwax; (2) 1932, Remington Stone.

2808. To Witter Bynner, [2 May 1923]
Text: MS HU; Huxley 566-7.

Zaragoza No 4. *Chapala* (Jal.)

2 May – afternoon

Dear Bynner

Thank you for looking after F[rieda] and the mountains of luggage. – We are already in our house – pleasant – near lake but not looking on it, on our own little garden: the first corner after the Villa Carmen, house next the dark trees. It belongs to the Hotel Palmera.

The Palmera is the smartest hotel – I stayed at Arzopalo, which faces the lake – manager Winfield Scott, American.[1] It's shabby, but pleasant – both charge 4 pesos a day, cheaper for long stay. There is a new hotel, Gran. Hotel Chapala, charges 3 a day.

Chapala very pleasant – just enough of a watering place to be *easy*. We can bathe from the house.

There are camions to Guadalajara in 2 hours – several a day. I must come in soon to go to the bank.

Face the unpacking.

Greet the Spoodle.

DHL

Walk about 4 minutes East from Arzopalo, along lake front.

2809. To Thomas Seltzer, 2 May 1923
Text: MS UT; Postmark [. . .] 2 MAY 1923; Lacy, *Seltzer* 91.

Zaragoza No. 4. *Chapala* (Jalisco), Mexico.

2 May 1923

Dear Thomas

Here we are in a little house of our own on Lake Chapala, a big lake not far from Guadalajara (2 hours). Frieda joined me from Mexico this morning, and we moved in. It is hot and sunny and nice: lots of room.

F. brought your letter. I suppose all the papers will come on, contracts, etc. So far nothing. I *do* hope you haven't posted me presentation copies here: I do hope you got my list, and sent them out from New York.

About the book-jackets for *Mastro-don* and for *BirdsBeasts*,[2] they were enclosed in the final corrected MS. of *BirdsBeasts* sent just before I left Taos – by registered mail. Surely you got that packet. If you look it up you will find

---

[1] Scott, a widower (his wife was Mexican), lived in the hotel with his daughter Margaret. Mr Bell in *The Plumed Serpent* was based on Scott, according to Bynner (p. 124).

[2] Götzsche designed the first, Merrild the second (Merrild 295).

the things. I'm afraid that, what with Judge Ford and the rest you have hardly time to keep track of everything.

You will see the Judge Ford business won't hurt in the long run, but meanwhile what a curse. I can tell you are almost snowed under.

Murry cabled that he is starting a new monthly and wanted to use a chapter from *Fantasia*, wanted also a story: haven't got latter.

I shall begin a novel now,[1] as soon as I can take breath.

I won't let Curtis Brown handle my American side. But don't you get too overwhelmed with work. It is what I am afraid of.

Don't I change from day to day about staying here? However, I am fixed now for a time at least. I believe you'd like it immensely. Splendid to have you both come.

Be sure and look up that corrected MS. of *BirdsBeasts* and those two book-jackets, and let me know.

Hope you got my letter enclosing the one to Huebsch, with cheque to Huebsch, paying him back.[2] Mind you send this.

I wonder if any of the letters get lost.

How is Adele Szold?

Saluti   DHL

2810. To John Middleton Murry, [3 May 1923]
Text: MS NYPL; cited in Murry, *New Adelphi* 416.

Calle Zaragoza. No 4. *Chapala* (Jalisco), Mexico.

3 May

Dear Jack

We've taken a house here on Lake Chapala – nice and hot, not too much. You'll think I do nothing but change my plans – I can't help it. I go out to buy my ticket to New York and Europe, then don't buy it. – Wonder how your magazine goes – want to see it. Wonder when the gods will let me come east. This is already the Pacific slope – near Guadalajara.

Wonder what ails me.

DHL

Did I send this card before?

---

[1] Initially called 'Quetzalcoatl', it was to become *The Plumed Serpent* (Secker, 1926).
[2] See Letter 2801 and n. 1.

2811. To William Hawk, 3 May 1923
Text: MS UT; Unpublished.

Zaragoza No 4. *Chapala.* (Jalisco), Mex.

3 May 1923

Dear William

You see we haven't gone to New York – instead have come here to Lake Chapala, 2 hrs. from Guadalajara and have taken a nice long low house with trees and flowers, by the lake. It is hot – bananas in the garden – but not uncomfortably so. My wife very glad to have a home of her own once more, hang up her embroidery and spread the serapes on the floors. We've got a Mexican family to look after us, so are forced to speak Spanish. The lake is big with low mountains round – the country very dry. It still isn't safe to live outside the villages. – How is Mrs Hawk? The Danes said more snow in Taos! Awful. We live out of doors on the verandahs in very little clothing, and bathe at evening. I do hope Rachel is well, and that you like the cabin. Do you hear that Ralph Myers has got my Bibbles? Alas!

Greet everybody from us both.

D. H. Lawrence

2812. To Kai Götzsche and Knud Merrild, 3 May 1923
Text: MS UT; Postmark, Chapala 4 MAY 23; Merrild 294.

Zaragoza No. 4. *Chapala* (Jalisco), Mex.

3 May 1923

Dear Götzsche and Merrild

F[rieda] brought your letter from Mexico yesterday: so sorry about Merrild's gum-boil: hope he's well. That beastly Taos!

Here we are, in our own house – a long house with no upstairs

[sketch][1]

– shut in by trees on two sides – we live on a wide verandah, flowers round – it is fairly hot – I spend the day in trousers and shirt, barefoot – have a Mexican woman Isabel to look after us – very nice. Just outside the gate the big Lake of Chapala – 40 miles long, 20 miles wide. We can't see the lake, because the trees shut us in. But we walk out in a wrap to bathe. – There are camions – Ford omnibuses – to Guadalajara – 2 hours. Chapala Village is small with a market place with trees and Indians in big hats. Also three hotels, because this is a tiny holiday place for Guadalajara. I hope you'll get down, I'm sure you'd like painting here. – It may be that even yet I'll have my little hacienda and grow bananas and oranges.

[1] DHL gives a rough outline of the floor-plan.

Seltzer said he never received the two book-jackets, *Mastro-Don* and *Birds Beasts*. I say he *must* have had them. He must *look*. I'm afraid he is muddled in his office. Write to him, and if he doesn't find them, you can make another copy. Meanwhile I enclose fifty dollars for them on account. If you need the money quickly, go to Will Levington Comfort, 4993 Pasadena Avenue, Los Angeles, and get him to guarantee it at a bank. I sent you a letter to him to Taos. If you haven't got it, take him this.

Heavens, Mabel *married*. – Merrild, please write me the most interesting points of the gossip concerning the event.

I did have a right bad cold in Puebla, but was better in a few days. Only then, I wanted to go back quickly to Europe. When I feel sick I want to go back. When I feel well I want to stay.

Trust this gets you safely. The money of course is for both. – You'll see how Pips doesn't belong at all in Mexico.[1] Only in Taos. Write at once.

D. H. Lawrence

2813. To Emily King, [3 May 1923]
Text: MS King; Unpublished.

Calle Zaragoza. No. 4. *Chapala* (Jalisco), Mexico
3 May

We came into this house yesterday – a long one storey place with trees – oleanders and bananas – and a Mexican woman Isabel to look after us – have to talk Spanish – Just near is a big lake, Lake Chapala – 40 miles long. It is hot – one lives in trousers and shirt – outdoors all day on the deep verandah. – I wish you could all waft over. But Mexico is much rougher even than Sicily. I don't know how long we shall stay – We have this house by the month. I like Mexico very much, when I feel up to it [   ]²

2814. To Ada Clarke, [3 May 1923]
Text: MS Clarke; Unpublished.

Calle Zaragoza No. 4. *Chapala* (Jalisco). Mex.
3 May.

We moved into a house here yesterday – a long rambling house on one floor – with flowers and trees closing in. We are in a little village, Chapala, two hours from Guadalajara, on the big Lake Chapala, forty miles long. I have the house

---

¹ Mexico] Taos   ² MS damaged.

by the month – dont know how long we shall stay. But I really like Mexico – except when I feel tired, then I want to come back to Europe. – It's a long time since I heard from anybody. How are you all?

DHL[1]

2815. To Catherine Carswell, [3 May 1923]
Text: MS YU; Unpublished.

Zaragoza No 4. *Chapala*. (Jalisco), Mexico
3 May.

Dear Catherine

– Your letter came on – glad you liked *Capt's Doll* – we've taken a long old house here on Lake Chapala, with trees on two sides, making the patio – a Mexican woman Isabel for servant – with her two children – away at end – struggle along in Spanish now. It is fairly hot – banana country – but very nice – we live out on the verandahs – I like Mexico much better than New Mex. – Russia seems far, far off just now – but I never know what I shall do next. This is already the Pacific slope – feels remote.

DHL

2816. To Lee and Nina Witt, [3 May 1923]
Text: MS Brill; Luhan 114.

Calle Zaragoza. No 4, *Chapala*. Jalisco. Mex.
3 May

Dear Lee Witt and Nina

After all we've moved in to a house – a long low house with trees – just hidden from Lake Chapala, which is a big water, 40 miles long. – It is hot – bananas in the garden – little red birds – but not too hot. I like it so much, when I'm not tired. When tired I want to go to Europe. – I had a real bad cold in Pueblo – it passed in a few days. – I may even now have my hacienda and ten peons, and grow bananas and oranges. Then you must come and see me. Meanwhile write and tell me the news – Mabel married Tony I hear – why. Send a bit of gossip now I'm far away. – It's not safe yet to live out in the country here. Pity. – we've got such a nice servant Isabel – et famille. Be greeted.

DHL

---

[1] This letter, like Letter 2815, was written on the verso of a photograph showing Frieda with market basket and parasol.

2817. To Willard Johnson, [5? May 1923]
Text: MS YU; Unpublished.

Zaragoza No 4. *Chapala*. Jalisco
Saturday

Dear Spoodle

We are settled in our house, sarapes spread about, Mexican Eagle hung on the verandah, already old stagers, with a nearly-incomprehensible Ysabel as familiar as if she had been our wet-nurse, spite of linguistic discrepancies. When you come to Chapala you shall have frequent teas with good cakes, in the garden, and it is nearly as good as Sanborn's,[1] without the stomach ache: and alas poor Spoodle, without the Elegancia. It's quite peaceful, and green.

I hope you are enjoying Guadalajara. It is possible I shall come in by Camion on Monday – or Tuesday – for the bank: in which case I shall call at Miss Purnells. Greet her from us both.

Yrs   D. H. Lawrence

2818. To Witter Bynner, [7? May 1923]
Text: MS HU; cited in Bynner 82.

Zaragoza #4. *Chapala*. Jal.
Monday

Dear Bynner

I hope the fears, the pains, and the *disgusts*, have all passed. If Guadalajara is worse than Orizaba, then alas! Damn all shops and markets, so nothing is left.

Here too the middle of the day can be hot, but morning and evening beautiful, very cool. The heat only from 12 to 4.0. Fresh wind from the lake. Our house very cool.

We intend to come in to Guadalajara tomorrow, by the first camion, leaving here about 7.0. I will call at 150 Galeano[2] to see how you are: also do the bank and a few things: then come back. We can discuss the choice of hotels here.

Do hope you are well.

DHL

2819. To Thomas Seltzer, 9 May 1923
Text: MS UT; Lacy, *Seltzer* 93–4.

Zaragoza #4. *Chapala*. Jal. Mexico.
9 May 1923

Dear Thomas

I just sent you the first lot of *Studies* proofs: as far as end of 'Poe'. I do hope

---

[1] Restaurant in Mexico City (see Nehls, ii. 235).   [2] Dr Purnell's office address.

you get them in time. I'd like the revisions made. There are one or two serious alterations in the first essay,[1] that are important to me.

I repeat again, I *do* wish you would print *Kangaroo* and *BirdsBeasts* and *Mastro-don early*, *soon*, so that I can have proofs in plenty of time. And I would like *two sets* of proofs, please. I'll write Miss Leener too, and tell her this.[2]

You are doing *Mastro-don* for September, aren't you? I am settling this with Curtis Brown. Tell me for sure.

I send the massive list of corrections of errors from Mr Feipel, who is evidently in the Brooklyn Library.[3] Pity he can't have revised proofs, if he's such a bird. His charts leave me quite cold.

Nothing has come from you except that first batch of *Studies* proofs: and the *transfers* of copyright.

It is hot here in Chapala. I like it. I have made two false starts at a novel here. Shall make a third start tomorrow. Mexico is queer: very savage underneath. It still is unsafe to live in the country: and not very safe anywhere. Somebody tried to get in here last night. It seems to me Mexico will never be safe. I have my ups and downs of feeling about the place. It will end, I suppose, in my staying as long as it takes me to write a novel – if I *can* write a novel here – then coming to New York for a time, then going to England. But I never know what I shall finally do.

Did you hear Mabel Sterne has married Tony and is going to take a ranch to live a 'freer life', and invite *paying* guests.[4] You might see what she charges. She is now Mrs Antonio Lujan. – It gives me a sort of end-of-the-world feeling. Mexico does that too. It feels like the end of the world. *Ruat caelum!*[5]

I keep wondering how your domestic affairs are: how is Adele Szold's sister, how is New York altogether? – Also how are they taking *Captain's Doll?* They won't care for it, if England likes it.

Poor Gilbert has a dreadful face, in your Announcements List.[6]

We went to Guadalajara yesterday. It's a burnt dry town. I didn't care for it much. Pearl of the west! Mostly old shell! Mexico altogether is terribly heavy, as if it had hardly the energy to get up and live. Though it's not really a case of energy. The soul of the country sulks, and won't look up. Sulks emptily through the ages.

I can read Spanish fairly well now.

Fight on!

DHL

[1] 'The Spirit of Place'.
[2] Miss Lerner was a typist in Seltzer's office (Lacy, *Seltzer* 181).
[3] Louis N. Feipel (see Letter following).
[4] Mabel Luhan considered turning her large house, Los Gallos, into a resort ranch which she would run with her friend, Edna Ferguson.
[5] '*Though heaven falls!*' (attributed to William Murray, Lord Mansfield, 1705–93).
[6] Seltzer published Cannan's novel *Annette and Bennett* in 1923.

2820. To Louis N. Feipel, 9 May 1923
Text: Moore 741–2.

Zaragoza 4, Chapala, Mexico
9 May 1923

Dear Mr Feipel:

Thank you for your rather scaring lists of errors in *The Captain's Doll* and *Fantasia*.[1] I am afraid a great deal is my own fault – hyphen or no hyphen is one to me. However, I will try to mend my ways, especially as far as orthographic inconsistency goes, remembering your eye is on every dot. And when I get a chance I'll correct every error that appears on your list.

Meanwhile many thanks for your research.

[P.S] Oh, in excuse, I've had no proofs of the books printed in America, except the story 'Ladybird'.

2821. To Bessie Freeman, 11 May 1923
Text: MS UNYB; Moore, *Intelligent Heart* 314.

Zaragoza No. 4. *Chapala.* (Jalisco), Mexico
11 May 1923

Dear Bessie Freeman

Your letter about Mabel. No, it's worse than Gibbon.[2] The submerged Continent of Atlantis.

I suppose you'll pay next time you go.

We've got a house here – very nice – green trees – a Mexican Isabel to look after us – a big lake of Chapala outside – a little village[3] Chapala – but at same side a little lake-side resort for Guadalajara, which is about 35 miles away.

It isn't too hot. If you feel like coming down, come down. I won't offer you this house, because Isabel would by no means come up to your standards, even if *we*[4] did. But there is a pleasant hotel, 4 pesos a day for a short time, 3 pesos a day if you stay a month. And a peso is about 49 cents American. Cheap enough.

Don't know how long we shall stay – a month or two. At the moment Witter Bynner is here in the hotel, with Willard Johnson. Very nice.

So come if you feel like it – either by sea over Manzanillo, or El Paso and Irapuato.

Yrs   D. H. Lawrence

---

[1] On 1 September 1922 (TMS UT) Feipel wrote to draw DHL's attention to about 70 typographical errors or inconsistencies in *Sea and Sardinia*; he wrote later about *Kangaroo* (and coincidentally met DHL on his way by train to New York in mid-September 1925).
[2] The allusion is unidentified.
[3] village] Indian   [4] *we*] you

2822. To Earl Brewster, [15 May 1923]
Text: MS UT; Brewster 71–2.

Zaragoza #4. *Chapala*, Jalisco – Mexico.
15 May.

Dear Earl

Just got your letter from Capri – No, you never wrote *me*. I answered Achsah's letter with a card – didn't know till then where you were. We have taken a house down here for a month or two – like it – a big lake – but it's never so easy living as in Europe – especially Sicily. Yet I don't know if I shall go back – don't know what I shall do – the Lord enlighten me. When I move I'll tell you. – I'm trying to write a novel – Witter Bynner is still down here. We're rather better off for money. – When I get letters from Europe then I never want to go back. When I forget the letters, I do. – You might run down here to see me. Anyhow write from New York.

DHL

2823. To Knud Merrild, [17 May 1923]
Text: MS UT; Postmark, Chapala 17 MAY 23; Merrild 298.

Chapala.
May 17th

Had your post card – glad you arrived safely, anyhow – wait to hear about the trip. Go to Will L. Comfort for any advice – 4993 Pasadena Av.[1] I told him you were coming. Nothing new from N. York. It's getting hot here. Did you hear from Taos that John Dunn's house and garage burnt down. – And how could Tony marry again, could he get a divorce from the Indian wife?[2] – Do you hate Lizzie finally, or not yet?

DHL

2824. To Adele Seltzer, [22 May 1923]
Text: MS UT; Postmark, Chapala 25 MAY 23; Lacy, *Seltzer* 94–5.

Zaragoza #4. *Chapala*. Jalisco
22 May

Dear Adele Szold

Your letter about Thomas and his nose – bad luck. The enemy almost gets us down, sometimes. Am having a hard fight myself. The enemy of all the

---

[1] For an account of the Danes' encounter with Comfort, see Merrild 298–9.
[2] According to Alice Oliver Henderson Rossin, the divorce was granted in Raton, New Mexico, by Judge Kiker.

world. Doesn't want me to write my novel either. Pazienza! Curse Kennerley, curse Huebsch, curse Boni and curse Liveright. May their bones rot inside their bodies. Curse the enormous enemy. May it burst swollen.

A hacienda! – You don't know Mexico. We have to have a young man with a pistol sleep on the terrace outside the door. I am not allowed to walk alone outside the narrow precincts of the village: for fear of being stopped, robbed, and what not. It gets awfully boring. It's really just petty crime. But the government has no control outside the towns and villages. The country is a sort of no-man's-land as far as security goes. If I thought of a little hacienda I'd have to buy a revolver for the first furnishing – and get the Danes to come down and arm them too as a military guard: – It's safe enough inside the town or here in Chapala – unless you're supposed to have money in the house. – All rather boring. I like the lake – and though the day from 12 to 4.0 is pretty hot, the rest is pleasant. And it won't get any hotter. The rains are coming. – All the Mexicans with property seem to want the United States to take over the country – Mexico enter the U. S. federation. – But I hate the *cramped* feeling of not being allowed to go freely in the country, having to watch every man to see if he's a rascal. The people here are quite nice. And at first everything *seems* so normal. Then one begins gradually to realise the uncertainty, and the limitations.

We've never had definite news of *Sons and Lovers*. I don't get *any* parcels – though some are in Mexico – nor do I get the balance of the *Studies* proofs. Don't trust the post. – Tell us if Thomas is better, and how Kennerley settled at last.

DHL

2825. To Idella Purnell, 24 May 1923
Text: MS UT; Unpublished.

Zaragoza #4. Chapala. Jal.
24 May 1923

Dear Miss Purnell

I've got nothing at all to read: find I like reading Spanish. Would it be a trouble to you to order for me from Leopoldo Font's bookshop:

Bernal Diaz': *True History of the Conquest of New Spain* (5 vols).

It costs about 12 pesos. The man said to Bynner that he had it in stock. He might give it to the camion to bring out. – And if Leopold Font publishes a catalogue of his books, I wish he'd send me one.

Bynner says it is doubtful if you are coming out this week-end – and that you had a little nervous collapse when you got back to Guadalajara. Hope it was not that you were overcome with joy at being back. – If you come this week-end we'll really picnic somewhere – all the gods being willing. – Bynner is coming in with the Newtons[1] on Monday morning, presumably. If you are not here for Sunday, I will give him the money for Bernal Diaz. – I suppose my money hasn't come yet to the bank, as I hear nothing. But I am in no particular hurry.

Remember me to Dr Purnell.

Greetings from my wife and me.

D. H. Lawrence

2826. To Thomas Seltzer, 24 May 1923

Text: House of Books, *First Editions Association Copies Autograph Letters and Manuscripts,* [1970], p. 33, Item 251.

Chapala, Mexico
May 24, 1923

My dear Thomas

. . . Yes we have to beat that Boni brute, issue a standard size book for the same price as his cheap edition[2] and while the fight lasts I'll cut down my royalty to a minimum. [Has just received copies of *Captain's Doll* and they look very nice. Feels that printing only 3000 copies might make a flaw in the supply to the public and spoil the demand. That the new novel goes its strange course fairly steadily, it is something he has wanted to do all his life. Plans for the summer, financial arrangements etc.]

Yr affmo. amigo   DHL

2827. To John Middleton Murry, 26 May 1923

Text: MS NYPL; Huxley 568.

Zaragoza #4. *Chapala*. Jalisco. Mexico.
26 May 1923

Dear Jack

Your letters of May 6. and May 9. – I knew your wire must have cost a lot – hope you had my letter or used *Fantasia* anyhow.

Don't know why I find it so hard to come to England: but I do. And when I meet Englishmen out here they make me sick. But they're the wrong sort anyhow.

I wanted to do a novel. I sort of wanted to do a novel here. I could never begin in Mexico. But I have begun here, in Chapala. – It's a big lake 90 miles long, 20 miles across: queer. – I hope my novel will go all right. If it does, I ought to finish it – in its first rough form – by end of June. Then *seriously* I want to come to Europe: via New York: stay there perhaps two weeks: be in

---

[1] Unidentified.   [2] See Letter 2771 and n. 1.

London by early August. I really think I shall manage this. It was, I suppose, that undigested novel kept me back till now. But I won't any more say finally that I will do a thing.

I am having the first slight scene of my novel – the beginning of a bull-fight in Mexico City – typed now, and will send it in two days time. It is complete in itself. Use it or not as you like. Curtis Brown is my agent, settle with him.

About magazines, it is for you to judge. I had the one prospectus you sent. When the rest come I will post them to people in America. I like the idea of a shilling monthly. But it's no good my saying how I shall feel about it till I come.

It isn't that I am so very keen on leading a remote country life. And I loathe the 'playboy' attitude to life. Oh god, there are so many playboys, not only of the western world. And I detest 'having a good time.' But when I think of England, willy nilly my gorge rises in a sort of profound mistrust. I suppose there's nothing to do but to come to England and get over it.

Ask Curtis Brown to let you see the MS. of *Novelle Rusticane* – by Giovanni Verga. They are sketches of Sicily. I translated them and a novel *Mastro-don Gesualdo*, because I admire Verga so greatly. I'll send you the tiny story 'Cavalleria Rusticana' – or 'La Lupe'[1] if you like: also Verga. Seltzer is publishing *Mastro-don Gesualdo* in the autumn – and I think Blackwell is doing it in England.[2]

A man wanted me to have a banana hacienda with him here in Mexico. I suppose anyhow I'd better see England again first. And I feel, perhaps I've no business trying to bury myself in out of the way places.

No, I think in the long run perhaps 'The Ladybird' has more the quick of a new thing than the other two stories. 'The Fox' belongs more to the old world.

Frieda wants to come to England much more than I do. She has Devonshire on her mind.

DHL

2828. To Thomas Seltzer, [26 May 1923]
Text: MS UT; Postmark, Chapala 26 MAY 23; Lacy, *Seltzer* 95.

Zaragoza #4. *Chapala*. Jal.
Sat.

Dear Seltzer

This is to ask you if you have yet got any proofs of *Kangaroo* – also of *Birds*

---

[1] These stories were published in *Cavalleria Rusticana and Other Stories* by Jonathan Cape in February 1928. None of them appeared in *Adelphi*.
[2] Cape published the first English issue of *Mastro-don Gesualdo* from the Seltzer sheets in March 1925.

Beasts and of *Mastro don Gesualdo* – And to beg you please to send me
duplicate galleys of all, by *Printed Matter* post – not by parcel.
Hope you're well.

                                                                                    DHL

No *Studies* proofs yet.[1]

2829. To Curtis Brown, 26 May 1923
Text: MS UT; Huxley 567.

                                        Zaragoza #4. *Chapala*. Jalisco. Mexico.
                                                                    26 May 1923

Dear Curtis Brown
    Your letter of 11th. May. Note you have the £125. from Secker for
Kangaroo.[2] Seltzer says he has sent *Kangaroo*,[3] *Birds Beasts and Flowers*, and
Mastro-Don Gesualdo to the printer, so proofs should not be long. I will let you
have them at once when I get them. Have you made any final arrangement
with anybody about *Mastro-don Gesualdo*?
    John Middleton Murry is starting a new magazine – 18 York Buildings.
Adelphi. W. C. 2. If he wants any bits of MS of mine that you can let him have,
please oblige him.
    I've started a new novel here – scene in Mexico. I hope it will go. If it does I
think I should have it finished in first rough draft by early July. Then I shall go
to New York for a fortnight, and come to England in August. Then we can talk
about everything.

                                                        Yrs   D. H. Lawrence

2830. To Martin Secker, 26 May 1923
Text: MS UInd; Secker 52.

                                        Zaragoza #4. *Chapala*. Jalisco. Mexico
                                                                    26 May 1923
Dear Secker
    Curtis Brown says you would like more photographs: so I send these.

---

[1] This postscript appears on the verso of the envelope.
[2] Secker had written to Curtis Brown, 10 May 1923 (Secker Letter-Book, UIll):
Dear Mr Curtis Brown,
    Many thanks for the Lawrence contract for "Kangaroo" which is quite in order. I am
sending my cheque for the advance. Certainly I will agree to the royalty terms for "Birds Beasts
and Flowers" going to 15% after 2000.
    I am very glad to have the photograph which I can put to immediate use. We ought to have
some good photographs of him over here, and perhaps you would ask him to send copies of any
which he may have taken when he reaches New York which I imagine will be his next resting
place.

                                                                    Yours sincerely

[3] *Kangaroo*] proofs of

I've started a new novel here. Hope it will go on. If it does, I think I shall go to New York in July and come to England in August. – The novel has its scene here in Mexico.
Glad you're getting the books out, and hope they'll sell.

Yrs   D. H. Lawrence

2831. To William Siebenhaar, 27 May 1923
Text: TMSC NWU; PC; Unpublished.

Zaragoza 4, Chapala, Jalisco, Mexico.
27 May 1923.

Dear Mr. Siebenhaar,
I had your letter yesterday, and today Chs. 14–16 of Multatuli. I shall be glad when I get the whole, and can settle down to it. The worst of my writing an introd. is that I don't know Multatuli's other books. We have got a house here by Lake Chapala, not far from Guadalajara. It isn't like Aimard, but very interesting.[1] It is still very like Mme. Calderon de la Barca's *Life in Mexico*. Do you know that? It is in the Everyman Library.[2] I do hope your wife is well in England. It is hot here – but rainy season is just beginning. We met Mrs. Skinner and liked her very much.[3] Give my real sympathy to Miss Skinner. Those two bungalows will feel lost. I can see it all so well. I don't know how long we shall be here, Seltzer is the safest address. The view is in the square at Mexico.

Best wishes   D. H. Lawrence

2832. To Martin Secker, 29 May 1923
Text: MS UInd; PC v. [Photograph of bullfight]; Postmark, Chapala 29 MAY.23; Secker 52.

Chapala. Jal
29 May 1923.

Dear Secker
I got the six copies of *Ladybird* today. It looks very nice. But while I am so far away, please don't ever send me more than *one* copy: send the rest out to the addresses I give. Did you send out *Ladybird* to my sisters and the others? I enclose a list for *Fantasia*.[4] Dont send me any *Fantasia*s, as I hope to be in London by end of summer. – The novel goes along. – I expect proofs of *Kangaroo* and *Birds Beasts* from Seltzer any day.

Yrs   D. H. Lawrence

---

[1] Gustave Aimard, pseudonym of Olivier Gloux (1818–83), French author of adventure novels, including stories about Mexico.
[2] *Life in Mexico* (1843; Everyman's, 1913) was written by Frances Erskine Calderón de la Barca (1804–82).
[3] Jessie Leake Skinner (c. 1854–1923), mother of Mollie Skinner, had just died. m. 1872, James Tierney Skinner.   [4] The list is missing.

2833. To Bessie Freeman, [30 May 1923]
Text: MS UNYB; cited in Moore, *Intelligent Heart* 315.
[Frieda Lawrence begins]

Chapala
30. V. 23

Dear Bessie Freeman,

Your world must have come tumbling about your ears, your whole world, when you heard that Mabel had married Tony – In my *head* I say: why not, but somewhere else it's *so* impossible – Merrild writes: the Indians dont like the marriage, and the Taos people dont, but they have something to talk about and that they *do* like – I still like Mabel, she has failed somehow in her life, but then it is so easy to fail – It's queer here, sometimes I love it, sometimes detest it, but any how such an experience – I wish you had taken this way, because where we shall be I don't know in a month's time – Lawrence is writing a novel already 250 pages – he sits by the lake under a tree and writes – We are a funny household, a wild Isabel with 2 sons and 2 girls and already we have added a young cousin and his wife she 14½! At night a mozo sleeps outside our bedrooms with a loaded revolver! because there was a scare of banditti! It feels quite safe most of the time but just occasionally it's a little scaring – but the people are gentle and friendly – this note I will send to Buffalo. Nina Witt was trying to have her children with her this summer! I want to go to Germany sometime this year and see my mother!

A nice summer to you –

With good wishes to you.   Frieda L –

[Lawrence begins]

Heaven knows where we shall be next winter – or next month, as Frieda says. I pledge myself to nothing. But I'll let you know our moves. We may see you in N York or somewhere.

DHL

2834. To Baroness Anna von Richthofen, [31 May 1923]
Text: MS UCB; Frieda Lawrence 176–7.

Zaragoza #4. *Chapala*. (Jalisco). Mexico
Frohnleichnam. 31 May

Meine liebe Schwiegermutter

Du wirst denken, wir meinen nimmer nach Europa wieder zu kommen. Es ist aber nicht so. Nur hatte ich immer die Idee, ich möchte einen Roman hier in Amerika schreiben. In den Ver. Staaten könnte ich nichts anfangen. Hier aber es geht wahrscheinlich gut. Ich habe zehn Kapitel schon geschrieben, und wenn der Herr Gott nur mich hilft, habe ich die erste volle Skizze schon fertig bei dem Ende Juni. Und jedenfals kommen wir sofort. Ich muss über New York fahren, wegen geschäft, und weil es eben kurzer und billiger ist. Aber in Juli ist New York sehr heiss, und eine hässliche Hitze, sagt man. Doch bleiben wir dort nicht länger wie fünfzehn Tagen, und von dort nach England: und von England nach Deutschland, wahrscheinlich in September: mein Geburtstag Monat, den ich gern habe.

Heute ist Frohnleichnam, und auch hier ein Prozession. Aber es gibt keine schöne Birken wie in Ebersteinburg vor zwei Jahren. Nur trägt man kleine Palmen in die Kirche. Und Palmen sind nicht schön wie unsere Bäume, und diese ewige Sonne ist nicht die Freude, wie unsere Sonne. Hier scheint es immer noch, und ist ein wenig mechanical.

Doch ist Mexico sehr interessant, ein fremdes Volk. Die meisten sind bloss Indier, dunkel wie die Leute in Ceilan, aber viel stärker. Die Männer haben die stärksten Rückgrate in der Welt, ich gläube. Sie sind halb-civilisiert, halb wild. Wenn sie nur eine neue Glaube hätten, eine neue Hoffnung, wären sie vielleicht ein neues, junges, schönes Volk. Aber als Christianer kommen sie nicht weiter, sind innerlich melancolisch, leben ohne Hoffnung, werden plötzlich bös, und arbeiten nicht gern. Doch sind sie auch gut, können sanft und ehrlich sein, sind sehr still, und sind gar nicht Geld-gefräsig. Und das finde ich wunderbar, sie hangen so wenig auf Geld und Haben, hier in Amerika, wo die Weissen hangen nur auf Geld und Haben. Die Peónen aber nicht. Er hat wirklich nicht diesen Besitzenfieber, das ist das übrige, eigentliche Weltschmerz bei uns.

Also, du weisst wo wir sind, und wie es geht bei uns. – Ich meine, ich schicke dir eine schöne *Sarape* – blanket – für deinen Geburtstag. Auf Wiedersehn

D. H. Lawrence

[My dear Schwiegermutter

You will think we mean never to come to Europe again. But it isn't so. Only I always had the idea I should like to write a novel here in America. In the United States I couldn't begin anything. But here it will probably go well. I have already written ten chapters, and if only the Good Lord helps me, I shall have the first complete sketch done by the end of June. And in that case we'll come at once. I must go via New York, owing to business, and just because it is shorter and cheaper. But in July New York is very hot, and an ugly heat, they say. Yet we will stay there no longer than a fortnight, and from there to England: and from England to Germany, probably in September: my birthday month, that I'm fond of.

Today is Corpus Christi, and here too a procession. But there are no lovely birches as in Ebersteinburg two years ago. One only carries little palms into the church. And palms aren't beautiful like our trees, and this eternal sun is not a joy, like our sun. Here it's always shining, and is a bit mechanical.

Yet Mexico is very interesting, a strange folk. Most are pure Indians, dark like the people in Ceylon, but much stronger. The men have got the strongest backbones in the world, I believe. They are half civilised, half wild. If they only had a new faith, a new hope, they would perhaps be a new, young, beautiful people. But as Christians they don't get any further, are inwardly melancholy, live without hope, become suddenly cross, and don't like to work. Yet they are also good, can be gentle and honest, are very quiet, and are not at all greedy for money. And I find that wonderful, they are so little attached to money and possessions, here in America, where the whites are attached only to money and possessions. But not the peons. He really hasn't got this fever to possess, that is the remaining, actual world-weariness with us.

So you know where we are, and how it is with us. – I think I'll send you a lovely *sarape* – blanket – for your birthday. Auf Wiedersehn

D. H. Lawrence]

2835. To Idella Purnell, 1 June 1923
Text: MS UT; Unpublished.

Zaragoza #4. *Chapala*. Jal
1 June 1923

Dear Miss Purnell

If that malheureux of a Bernal Diaz hasn't come, do please bring me something to read; your man about the U. S.[1] is too self-important and statistical, and the poets don't keep one long. If you can snatch a moment of time, buy me a Spanish novel – Pio Baroja or somebody amusing. The one Baroja I have is *César o Nada*.[2] And you might get *Soeur Philomène* (Goncourt)[3] which is on Gallardo's[4] list for 1.25. On the hot afternoons one *must* have something to read.

That miserable money, too, hasn't come.

I think this number of *Palms* is good. The first poet the worst.[5]

Greet Dr Purnell from me.

Yours Sincerely   D. H. Lawrence
Many thanks for getting the other things for me.

---

[1] Unidentified.   [2] *César o Nada* (Madrid, 1910), by Pio Baroja y Nessi (1872–1956).
[3] Edmond Louis Antoine de Goncourt (1822–96) and Jules Alfred Huot de Goncourt (1830–70), brothers, collaborated on their novels, which included *Soeur Philomène* (Paris, 1861).
[4] Unidentified.
[5] The first poet in *Palms* (Summer 1923) was Wade Wright Oliver (1890–   ), identified in 'The Poets' section as Professor of Bacteriology in the College of Medicine, Long Island College Hospital, Brooklyn, New York. Oliver later published *Sky Rider* (Portland, Maine, 1928) and *Fantasia* (Portland, Maine, 1938), two volumes of poems.

2836. To Knud Merrild, 4 June 1923
Text: MS UT; Postmark, Chapala [. . .] JUN 23; Merrild 300–1.

Zaragoza #4. *Chapala.* Jalisco. Mexico

4 June 1923

Dear Merrild

We were much entertained by your letter, and glad to find you in such good spirits. Now today comes a letter from Götzsche, who says you have got a good job and that you are happy – So perhaps Los Angeles will be your lucky city after all.[1]

I sent you a copy of *The Captains Doll*, addressed to Götzsche. I hope you got it. The cover looks very gay and lively, I think.[2]

I am busy doing a novel: hope it will continue to go well. – Mexico is still much more fun than U.S.A. – Much wilder. We have a man to sleep on the verandah with a pistol: and we may not walk outside the village for fear of being robbed or carried off by bandits. And this little village has twenty soldiers to guard it – Which is all very stupid. We've got a whole stack of servants and semi-servants living at the end of the house: not because we want them, but because they seem to have their holes there, like rabbits – Isabel, Carmen, Maria, Daniele, Pedra and Francisco. Now they're bargaining for eggs – like the devil – at 6 centavos – and we only pay 5.

I think I shall give up this house at the end of the month – and probably go to New York, stay there not more than a fortnight, then go to England. This is what I have promised to do. But whether I shall *actually* do it, I don't know. I am not very anxious to go back to Europe.

One day you must come to Mexico. It is different from anything I have seen – life has quite a different *tempo* here. – Bynner and Johnson are still here, in the hotel. – With your revolver, gun and knife you would be just right here: though they are all mostly for show. Tell me your news.

Yrs   D. H. Lawrence

2837. To Catherine Carswell, 7 June 1923
Text: MS YU; PC v. [Photograph of Lake Chapala]; Carswell 176, 182.

Zaragoza #4. *Chapala.* Jal. Mexico

7 June 1923

Dear Catherine

Your letter about the house today[3] – That's awfully nice of you: but see, we are still here. I felt I had a novel simmering in me, so came here, to this big

---

[1] Merrild was designing the ornamental decorations for the local world exposition; Götzsche working for the film company, Metro Goldwyn Mayer; both in Los Angeles (Merrild 300).
[2] See p. 345 n. 2.
[3] Catherine Carswell had offered a floor of the 'old Hampstead house' in which she and her husband now had rooms (Carswell 176).

lake, to see if I could write it. It goes fairly well. I shall be glad if I can finish the first rough draft by the end of this month. Then we shall pack up at once, go to Mexico City and sail from Vera Cruz for New York. Hope to be in England by early August, where will you be then? – I shall be glad to be back. But wanted to get this novel off my chest.

auf wiedersehen   DHL

2838. To Curtis Brown, 7 June 1923
Text: MS UT; Unpublished.

Zaragoza #4. *Chapala*. Jal.
7 June 1923

Dear Curtis Brown

I return here the agreements for *Birds Beasts* and for the three books *Studies – Psychoanalysis –* and *Fantasia*. You will note Secker did not initial the alterations.

I intend to leave here at the end of this month and come via New York to England: arrive probably in early August. – The novel goes pretty well. Hope to have it finished, in rough, before I leave here.

Yrs   D. H. Lawrence

2839. To Thomas Seltzer, [8 June 1923]
Text: MS UT; Postmark, Chapala 8 JUN 23; Lacy, *Seltzer* 96.

Zaragoza #4. Chapala. Jal.
8 June

Dear Thomas –

This to tell you that we are definitely leaving here at the end of this month: so don't post any mail here after the 19th. We ought to be in New York by July 15th. I'd like to stay there long enough to do all those *proofs*, and perhaps go through my novel: but we'd have to be in the country for that. We'll see. – Haven't heard from you for some time. Hot here. Novel more than half done.

DHL[1]

2840. To S. S. Koteliansky, 10 June 1923
Text: MS BL; PC; Postmark, Chapala 10 JUN 23; Zytaruk 254.

Chapala. Jalisco
10 June 1923

Dear Kot

Your letter today – hope the magazine does well.[2] Don't think of the money

---

[1] The text is written on the verso of a photograph of boats on the shore of Lake Chapala.
[2] The *Adelphi* for which Kot was the business manager.

– you don't owe me anything. Truly I don't want it, at the present have enough. I intend to leave here at the end of this month if I can finish the novel on which I am working. We go to New York, and ought to be in England by August. It only depends, now, on my finishing the first draft of this novel here. So – auf wiedersehen.

DHL[1]

2841. To Adele Seltzer, [10 June 1923]
Text: MS UT; Lacy, *Seltzer* 96–7.

[Frieda Lawrence begins]

Chapala
10. VI. 23

Dear Adele,

Thank you very much for your offer of tinned things! No, we get good food, all this tropical fruit and we have bought chickens that lay eggs and then we eat the chickens – It's been so hot for a day or two but then the terrific rain came – and it's still attractive – We do things with Bynner and Spud like going across the lake or into Guadalajara! Lawr- is at page 350 of a most surprising novel – Lawr- says it will take Thomas all his time to publish it – I think it is the most splendid thing he ever did – I look forward to seeing you in *less* than three weeks – As New York is so hot we will only stay 2 or 3 days; if you had thought of having us in your house *dont* do it; it will mean so much bother for so short a time, put us in a hotel near – We will go into the country – is'nt there a nice little old new England inn any where? And you would have to come – Bynner says New Hampshire is pretty, is that too far [for][2] you? I wish you could have seen this, there is something *uncowed* in these natives that fascinates us all – It's given us a lot, the country so hard and wild and unsentimental! How is Thomas, is he really quite well? Are you suffering from the heat already? How is your sister, not well I fear – Europe lies in front of me like an unknown country, because we are changed – Dont work too hard in the heat, because it pulls the strength out of you – Have'nt we triumphed over our enemies, Revenge is the joy of the gods – We shall have a lot to tell you when we come –

So auf Wiedersehen   Frieda

[Lawrence begins]

I like my new novel best of all – much. But it perhaps too different for most folks: two-thirds done. Pray the gods for the rest.

DHL

---

[1] The letter was written on the verso of a photograph of Lake Chapala.
[2] MS reads 'far you'.

Long while since I heard from Thomas. I'll bring him a sarape. Do you want anything? Say quick.

DHL

We leave this house about 26th. – see that no mail comes after 17th or 18th.

We might have a tiny cottage somewhere for a month – not far from New York.

I think I might like to stay long enough to go all through – novel and all rest of proofs.

DHL

2842. To Frederick Carter, 15 June 1923
Text: MS UT; Unpublished.

Zaragoza #4. *Chapala*. Jalisco. Mexico
15 June 1923

Dear Frederick Carter

The letter of 22nd May with drawings has just come. Meanwhile I am struggling might and main to get that previous MS. out of the post in Mexico City.[1] They must think it is a secret anarchistic work or something, for they have had it, the devils, for several weeks, and *won't* send it on. Now I have asked a friend in government service in the city to go and shoot them if they don't hand it over.[2] Mexico makes one feel like that. I'll write the moment I have it.

These drawings are beautifully executed – that's the first thing one thinks. My wife wants at once to rush for a pencil to begin to draw. For wood-engravings these are beautifully fine and flexible, and at the same time compact. The figures themselves often remind me of other things – Blake, and the *Discus-Thrower*.[3] With that fine process you might have broken from convention a wee bit more, perhaps. But I shall be very glad to see the rest of the drawings, and most glad to have the complete MS. There are so many things in the chapters I want to read. I hope you have made the complete MS. pretty full. It occurs to me, if these chapters break up easily, and if you write an easy style, we might place some short pieces of the book with the weekly or monthly magazines in New York. I might arrange that if you wished.

[1] The MS (when revised) became *The Dragon of the Alchemists*; the drawings were astrological by Carter himself.
[2] Possibly Frederic W. Leighton (1895–), American who worked under Roberto Haberman, supervising the teaching of English in the Mexico City schools. DHL met Leighton through Witter Bynner in Mexico City, and Leighton visited them in Chapala. See Bynner 21.
[3] The *Discus-Thrower* is a bronze statue by the Greek sculptor, Myron (a marble copy is in the Museo Romano).

I have been busy doing a novel here in Mexico – and hope to finish the first rough draft by the end of this month. Then we shall go to New York – be there in July – and come to England in August. I will send you word as soon as we are definitely leaving here. Then you might post the MS. to Thomas Seltzer. There is no difficulty with MSS. and papers in the U.S.A. – only here in idiotic Mexico. I mean customs. – Meanwhile I definitely hope to have that other MS. very soon.

I asked Secker to send you a copy of *Fantasia of the Unconscious*, and I will send you a copy of *The Captain's Doll* from here.

Meanwhile all good wishes.

D. H. Lawrence

By a fluke, the MS. this minute arrived. I like these drawings really better – Apocalypse comes out well in this print. Shall begin to read at once. Have sent you a *Capts Doll*.

DHL

I like the big cat – Blind Understanding – very much.

2843. To Thomas Seltzer, 15 June 1923
Text: MS UT; Postmark, Chapala 15 JUN 23; Lacy, *Seltzer* 97–8.

Chapala, Jal.
15 June. 1923

Dear Thomas

Your letter and statement today. – I should still be poor *sans Women in Love*, shouldn't I?

All right, I'll go over the 'Whitman' essay again. Wait for it.

The novel has gone well. Shall I call it 'Quetzalcoatl'?[1] Or will people be afraid to ask for a book with that name. – I've done 415 MS. pages – expect about another 100. It interests me, means more to me than any other novel of mine. This is my real novel of America. But you may just hold up your hands with horror. No sex.

Now it comes near time to leave here, I don't much want to go. I give up this house on the 30th. – if novel isn't finished, shall stay in Hotel Arzopalo long enough to get it done. Bynner and Spud still there. By the way, if ever you want a man clerk, do you think you might have Spud Johnson? He's very reliable and does good work. I think he ought to have a proper job, not be just Bynner's amanuensis.

[1] This was always the title DHL preferred; *The Plumed Serpent* was a later suggestion by his publisher. Quetzalcoatl, the nature god of Indian tribes in Mexico before the Spanish conquest, was represented by the *quetzal* – a rattlesnake covered in green feathers. He could also assume human form, wearing a bird mask. During the Classic Period (200 B.C.–900 A.D.), Quetzalcoatl was the main deity of the ruling city of Teotihuacán.

Murry's *Adelphi* came. How feeble it is! Oh God, am I going back to Europe to that?

I don't really want to go back to Europe. But Frieda wants to see her mother. Perhaps I shall have to go, this once. But feel sure I shan't stay. – Perhaps round the world again, and try to do a novel in India or China: the East. Then to America, and perhaps back to Mexico. So far, I think I like Mexico best of all the places, to live in. As Adele Sz[old] said, the life of the blood. I'm sad to go. But I suppose it's best, for the moment.

Don't give anybody that bit of the bull-fight unless you think well. I don't feel like supporting the knock-kneed *Adelphi*. Katharine Mansfields ugly bits etc.[1]

So sorry you've been seedy. But you'll be better now.

Rainy season here – cool again.

Ships sail from Vera Cruz every Sunday. We *might* sail on July 8th. – arrive N.Y. 15th. or 16th.

Have you really sent the books to the printer?

DHL

Fantasia will sell later – like *Women in Love*. Pazienza!

2844. To Thomas Seltzer, [c. 15 June 1923]
Text: MS UT; Lacy, *Seltzer* 101–2.

[Chapala, Jalisco, Mexico]
[c. 15 June 1923][2]

This is about the Chapter from *Fantasia* in the *Adelphi*[3] – which that brat Murry never acknowledged as from *Fantasia*. This man might be useful – I

---

[1] 'The Samuel Josephs', a story by Katherine Mansfield, appeared in *Adelphi*, i (June 1923), 12–19. By 'ugly bits' DHL may have been pointing to the distasteful Joseph family and its sordid habits.

[2] The letter to which DHL refers is a short note from Francis Louis (1900–65), a medical doctor from Durham County Hospital, who wrote about the chapter of *Fantasia* published in the *Adelphi* for June 1923 (see p. 432 n. 2.). Louis wrote on 1 June; DHL received his copy of the first issue of the *Adelphi* in Chapala about 15 June, so it seems likely that Louis' letter arrived at about the same time. (For an obituary of Louis see *British Medical Journal*, 11 December 1965, p. 1438.)

[3] DHL's letter to Seltzer was written on the letter he received from Louis. The letter reads as follows:

It seems rather incongruous introducing the jargon of pseudo-scientific technique into your otherwise striking piece of imaginative writing in the "Adelphi": but will you consider it an impertinence if I venture to congratulate you on your truly wonderful physiological & p[syc]hological systems? What a powerful light you shed upon the aetiology of phthisis and "neurasthenia of the Heart"!

Yours etc.,   Francis Louis.

Louis's final sentence refers to DHL's remark in the extract from *Fantasia*:'. . . there is a tendency now towards phthisis and neurasthenia of the Heart'.

suppose he is a doctor. I wrote a note to him and asked him to reply care of you. Would you mind sending him a copy of *Psychoanalysis* and of *Fantasia?*

DHL

2845. To Kai Götzsche and Knud Merrild, [17 June 1923]
Text: MS UT; Merrild 303–4.

[Frieda Lawrence begins]

Zaragoza 4, Chapala
[June 17 – 1923][1]

Dear Danes,

There is G[ötzsche']s very cross letter about the Renaissance architect[2] – It made me laugh – I am very sorry you are not having a good time – but also I am *glad*, that means I hope that you will sometime join us again and we will make a life together – To-day is Sunday – I always think of you on Sundays and wish you were coming to dinner – Isabel, the cook, has just killed our cock – he made a noise like a hen instead of crowing like a cock – We are still not sure of our fate – but if we see a place we really like, we will have it and plant bananas – I am already very tired of not doing my own work – Lawrence does not want to go to Europe, but he is not sure of what he wants – The common people are also very nice but of course really wild – And I think we could have a good time, Merrild would love the lake and swimming, we could have natives to spin and weave and make pottery and I am sure this has never been painted –

[Lawrence begins]

We are going on Tuesday up to Ocotlan on the lake to see if we can rent a little farm there. I am still doubtful if it would be safe. But if we decide on it I hope you will both come down and help us manage it. I will write to you at once when we get back: so don't write to New York to me until you hear again. And perhaps by then you will have found some good jobs. I think probably we should go to New York for a little while to settle business, even if I decided to rent a place: and come back in September, start then, before the rains end. It's our uncertain life – and things never behave as they should.

DHL

2846. To Frederick Carter, 18 June 1923
Text: MS UT; Moore, *Intelligent Heart* 317–19.

Zaragoza #4. *Chapala*. Jal. Mexico.
18 June 1923

Dear Mr Carter

I have read the 'Dragon' – and a tough 'Dragon' he is.[3] Nearly too much

---

[1] The letter was dated by Merrild (Merrild 303).
[2] The architect of a Renaissance-type building who had invited Merrild to produce some sketches for a commission and then rejected them (Merrild 302).
[3] See p. 456 n. 1.

for my brain. Why did you make him so severely astrological and zodiacal?
The side bits are so fascinating. I'm not sure even now if the 'Apocalypse' is
primarily Zodiacal. It's a revelation of Initiation experience, and the clue is in
the microcosm, in the human body itself, I believe, and the Zodiac is only used
from the table of the Zodiacal Man, and the Man in the Zodiac has his clue in
the man of flesh and blood. I believe pretty well all you say. But you're
examining and describing the cart, and from it postulating the horse. The
subtle thing is the relation between the microcosm and the macrocosm. Get
that relation – the Zodiac Man to me – and you've got a straight clue to
Apocalypsis. – The ancients thought in images. But their own great
immediate sensations and emotional experiences, how far did they know them
as experiences within the physique, particular local movements of the physical
psyche? I believe, very exactly. I believe the image for passionate desire was as
much the liver, as, say, the Mound of the Sun.[1] I believe they were dominantly
physical – *particularly* the real ancients, Egyptians and Persians. John may
have been more like Boehme.[2] But his imagery started primarily from the
physical psyche, the organic and the nervous and cerebral psyche, and
expanded into the stars. That I believe. He was seeking to project the spinal
chord into the Galactic Way. The Seals are ganglia of nerve-consciousness,
projected into zodiacal signs and star-constellations. The Dragon is the Will
and Desire. The riders are the energetic messages, releases of consciousness
and energy, resultant on the conquest by mind and will of one after the other of
the primary affective centres. The serpent girdle below the paps is the division
of the diaphragm into upper and lower man. The revelation is a conquest, one
by one, of the lower affective centres by the mind, and the New Jerusalem is
the mind enthroned.

Of course, all the *other* things are true: what happens in the microcosm
happens in the macrocosm. But the clue is in the physical psyche of man as
understood in the time of St. John. – I believe you'd find the going simpler if
you accepted that. The movement is back and forth.[3] I don't know the values
well enough, of the zodiac symbols. Why dont you do that? Establish the
human, psychic, physiological, chemical, and astronomical values of each
zodiac sign? You see why, in my reading, he reverses the order of the signs:
because the conquest is of the lower by the upper – the upward movement.
These four winds of the spirit are the four great centres of inspiration – Leo

---

[1] The meaning of this phrase is unclear. It does not occur in *The Dragon of the Alchemists* (1926),
    the published version of the MS DHL saw in 1923.
[2] Jakob Boehme or Bohme (1575–1624), German theosophist, concerned, as St John (of the Book
    of Revelation) was, with the existence of evil as a necessary antithesis to goodness.
[3] Alongside the next 14 lines of MS, DHL drew a sketch of 'Zodiac Man' to illustrate his
    argument.

being the solar plexus – the sympathetic ganglia – sagittarius the deepest, most secret, and most potent. The scorpion of the lower psyche becomes the Eagle of the upper – The clue is that the upper centres conquer the lower – but in reality Leo conquers Virgo, Cancer-Libra, Gemini-Scorpio, and Taurus-Sagittarius. Aries (the hind brain) – Capricorn-Aquarius – that is the rough progression: but I don't know the values well enough to follow exactly. It may be seals are sympathetic ganglia and vials are the corresponding voluntary ganglia, of the spine: or vice versa, I can't tell from your book, and haven't got a bible. The balance of the seven is as far as I can see

$$\text{Leo} \atop \text{Virgo}\Big\rbrace \qquad {\text{Gemini} \atop {\text{Cancer} \atop \text{Libra}}}\Big\rbrace\Big\rbrace \qquad {\text{Taurus} \atop \text{Scorpio}}\Big\rbrace \qquad \text{ARIES.}$$

Sagittarius, which lies outside the sealed body, is the first and last.

I wonder if this means anything to you.

But if only I knew enough – or anything at all about Astrology – I know nothing – I'd try fitting the astrological meanings to the natural centres of the physical psyche, and see if the order didn't come that way.

If I come to England we'll talk about it. But I may not come. I don't know why I don't want to come. I don't. Anyhow I shall go to New York, and that is nearer.

You'd never get an ordinary publisher to publish this text. It is *absolutely* unintelligible to the ordinary reader. And yet there *is* something great and liberating behind it all: makes life seem noble again. Oh I do hope your big MS is more human. It doesn't matter much after all whether the first horseman is Leo or Sagittarius or any other Zodiacal sign. It's a question of what the sign means after that, humanly. If through the Zodiac we can get at the human meaning, good. If not, no good. Why can't you help one to the unravelling of the human-physical experience of the 'Revelation'.

Because, for my part, I should like to see the end of this Return. The end of the Little Creation of the Logos. A fresh start, in the first great direction, with the polarity downwards, as it was in the great pre-Greek Æons, all Egypt and Chaldea. Greek changed the direction, the Latins went it full tilt. The great *down* direction, away from mind, to power, that was old Egypt. The sceptre, not the logos.[1]

Do excuse this if it seems impertinent to you. Hope we shall meet. Write me care Thomas Seltzer. Expect to be in New York by July 21 at latest.

Yours   D. H. Lawrence

[1] For a commentary on this letter seen in the context of DHL's reading of Blavatsky and James Pryse's *The Apocalypse Unsealed* (1910), see *Apocalypse*, ed. Mara Kalnins, pp. 4–8.

2847. To S. S. Koteliansky, 22 June 1923
Text: MS BL; Postmark, [. . .] 22 JUN 23; Moore 747.

Zaragoza #4. Chapala. Jalisco, Mexico

22 June. 1923

My dear Kot

The Dostoevsky and Tolstoi books have come: and many thanks.[1] What a dismal time Dostoevsky brought upon himself.

The *Adelphi* also came, and oh dear, I was badly disappointed. It seemed to me so weak, apologetic, knock-kneed, with really nothing to justify its existence. A sort of beggar's whine through it all. Mr Well's parsnips floating in warm butter.[2] Mr Joiner screamingly ridiculous.[3]

No really! Is this the best possible in England?

We are going to New York in July – care Thomas Seltzer. God knows if I shall be able to bring myself across the Atlantic. Probably I shall come back to Mexico. But I will let you know.

One's got to *hit*, nowadays, not apologise.

How can I write to Murry?

What do you think yourself?

Write to New York.

DHL

2848. To Bessie Freeman, 27 June 1923
Text: MS UNYB; cited in Moore, *Intelligent Heart* 317.

Chapala.

27 June. 1923

Dear Bessie Freeman

This is to say we are leaving Mexico for the present, and expect to arrive in New York about July 15th. Write

care Thomas Seltzer, 5. West 50th St. New York City.

We may see you in the east – and Mr Chamberlain[4] too – though I have lost his address.

The novel is *nearly* finished – near enough to leave. I must come to New York – and go to England. But we may come back to Mexico.

Anyhow we'll talk when we meet.

Au revoir   D. H. Lawrence

---

[1] *Dostoevsky: Letters and Reminiscences* (1923), trans. Koteliansky and J. Middleton Murry; and *Tolstoi's Love Letters* (Hogarth Press, 1923), trans. Koteliansky and Virginia Woolf.

[2] The *Adelphi* contained a review of H. G. Wells' *Men Like Gods* (1923) by H. M. Tomlinson, which was extravagant in its praise.

[3] 'Mr Joiner and The Bible' by the 'Journeyman' tells the story of a man who reads to his daughter H. G. Wells' list of the twelve most important books, one of which is the Bible. Mr Joiner then reads from the Bible and feels very happy.   [4] Unidentified.

2849. To Knud Merrild, [27 June 1923]
Text: MS UT; Postmark, Chapala 27 JUN 1922; Huxley 569–70.

Chapala.
Wednesday

Dear Merrild

We were away two days travelling on the lake and looking at haciendas. One could easily get a little place. But now they are expecting more revolution, and it is so risky. Besides, why should one work to build a place and make it nice, only to have it destroyed.

So, for the present at least, I give it up. It's no good. Mankind is too unkind.

We shall leave next Monday for Mexico City – and probably shall be in New York by July 15th. I don't expect to care for the east: don't intend to stay more than a month. Then to England. It is no good, I know I am European. So I may as well go back and try it once more.

You had a bad time chasing round, Götzsche told me. Perhaps now you will be able to make some money. I hope so.

But I really hope that before long we may meet again, all of us, and try to make a life in common once more. If I can't stand Europe we'll come back to Mexico and spit on our hands and stick knives and revolvers in our belts – one really has to – and have a place here. But if Europe is at all possible, much better there. Because the Mexicans are rather American in that, that they would rather pull life down than let it grow up. And I am tired of that. I am tired of sensational, unmanly people. I want men with some honorable manhood in them, not this spiteful babyishness and playboy stupidity and mere greediness of most people. We will go on looking and preparing, you and Götzsche and us, till we can really make a life that is not killed off as it was in Del Monte. Even if you have to go round the world before we can start, still we can wait and prepare. The 'world' has no life to offer. Seeing things doesn't amount to much. We have to be a few men with honour and fearlessness, and make a life together. There is nothing else, believe me.

Tell Götzsche I will write to him. I will settle the book-covers when I get to New York, never fear. – I had a nice letter from Götzsche's father.

Auf Wiedersehen.   D. H. Lawrence

2850. To Robert Mountsier, 27 June 1923
Text: MS Smith; Postmark, Chapala 27 JUN 23; Unpublished.

Chapala. Jal. Mexico
27 June 1923

Dear M[ountsier]

Thank you for the letter and the Cournos letter. I've written Cournos.[1]
Seltzer's account came to $4,306, so I owe you another 30.60. which I
enclose.

I've liked Mexico and have *nearly* finished a novel here – I'll have to finish it
somewhere else. We leave on Monday en route for New York, where I hope to
arrive by July 15th or July 21st – by sea. Write me care Thomas Seltzer – and
would you mind asking Taos post-office to send any letters to me on to New
York – should any more arrive. I don't suppose we shall stay in the east longer
than a month – then to England. – If I find I can't stand Europe I think I shall
come back to Mexico.

Has Taos settled down from all its excitements? And has it done your health
good staying there?

Best wishes   D. H. Lawrence

2851. To Thomas Seltzer, [27 June 1923]
Text: MS Cushman; Postmark, Chapala 27 JUN 23; K. Cushman, *DHL Review*, xviii
(Spring 1985–6), 25–31.

[Chapala, Jalisco, Mexico]
Wednesday

Dear Thomas

Will you answer Cournos about this story, at once.[2]

---

[1] The letter is missing but its contents can be inferred from Letter 2851. (At about the same time
    – 18 and 26 June – Secker was writing to Edward O'Brien also giving permission for the
    inclusion of the story in the anthology: Secker Letter-Book, UIll. Cf. p. 296 n. 1.)
[2] DHL's letter was written on the verso of the following typed letter signed jointly by Edward
    J. O'Brien and John Cournos:

Forest Hill, Oxon,
June 2, 1923.

D. H. Lawrence, Esq.,
Taos,
New Mexico.
Dear Mr. Lawrence: –
    On behalf of our publishers, Jonathan Cape of London, and Small, Maynard & Company of
Boston, we ask your formal permission to reprint your story entitled "The Horse-dealer's
Daughter" in "The Best British Short Stories of 1923, and Year Book of the British Short
Story."
    Should you grant this permission it is understood and agreed that it is conditional on
ratification by any American editor or publisher to whom you may have disposed of your

We have been away these two days down the lake, travelled a hundred miles on the water – looking at haciendas. – There is more talk of revolution and the country still very dangerous. If there is no Recognition by the U.S. – and if the U.S. lifts the embargo on firearms into Mexico – there is supposed to be a Catholic-reactionary revolution due about September – which would mean bolshevist re-reaction in the spring.[1] It's all disheartening.

I give up. I hope to sail on July 8th. for New York, as previously agreed. This is final – we have started to pack and leave here on Monday – four days. – The novel isn't finished – I must do it when my soul gets calmer. I shall telegraph you again tomorrow – and then unless I wire once more postponing, expect us on the Ward Line Boat due to arrive in New York on July 15th. If I don't wire postponing we shall sail on July 8th. Address in Mexico, after the 3rd. is Monte Carlo hotel.

I am sending the *Rainbow* agreements to Stern by this mail.

DHL

Tell Cournos to print 'Horsedealers Daughter' from *England my England* making acknowledgements to you. Perhaps better send him a copy – as you think best.

D.H.Lawrence

American copyright; that all rights of any sort in the story shall remain yours; and that the story shall be copyrighted in America in your name. We shall see that a copy of the book is sent you promptly on publication.

As the book is to be manufactured and published in America first it will not be practicable to send you a proof, but we shall take care that any alterations which you may desire are embodied if you send them to us now.

Sincerely yours,

Cournos added a note in his own hand:
Dear Lawrence
Had looked forward to a meeting with you in U.S.A., but New Mexico was too far away for my purse. Better luck another time.
Hope things are prospering with you.

Yrs. J.C.

Sorry to trouble you with this again!

DHL added for Seltzer: See over – DHL

[1] The source of DHL's anxiety, in the very unstable political situation in Mexico, was the increasing challenge to the administration of Álvaro Obregón (1880–1928) – President 1920–4 – led by Adolfo de la Huerta (1882–1955). In 1923–4 de la Huerta instigated an unsuccessful revolt against Obregón's candidate for his successor as President, Elías Calles. There never was a serious possibility of a conservative Catholic revolution, though, during the Calles administration (1924–8), the Catholic militants were in open but futile revolt. During Obregón's presidency there was considerable talk among government officials about the threat to expropriate United States oil interests. This delayed recognition of the Obregón régime by the U.S. government until 31 August 1923.

2852. To Earl Brewster, 29 June 1923
Text: MS UT; Brewster 72.

Chapala. Jal.
29[1] June 1923

Dear Brewster

Pardon this rag of a note – we are leaving Chapala – expect to arrive New York July 15th – had your letter – hope see you and Achsah and child in east (small e) – perhaps that Franconia.[2] Write care Thomas Seltzer.

Be greeted.   DHL

Your picture-book came.[3] Swank!

2853. To Thomas Seltzer, [29 June 1923]
Text: MS UT; Postmark, Chapala 29 [. . .]; Lacy, *Seltzer* 99–101.

[Chapala, Jalisco, Mexico]
29 June

Dear Thomas

Now comes word we must be vaccinated – which may possibly delay us a week. I'll let you know at once.

I've sent some books by post – trunks so full.

Saluti   DHL

2854. To Thomas Seltzer, [30 June 1923]
Text: MS UT; Postmark, [. . .] 30 JUN 1923; Lacy, *Seltzer* 101.

Chapala.
30 June

Dear Thomas

They have altered the sailings of the Ward Line ships from Sunday to Thursday – so expect to sail Thursday 12th July and arrive Thursday 19th.

DHL

passport photographs

2855. To Mollie Skinner, 2 July 1923
Text: MS WAPL; Postmark, [. . .] 2[. . .]; Huxley 570.

Chapala. Jalisco. Mexico.
2 July 1923

Dear Miss Skinner

I have often wondered if you were doing that novel.[4] – Your letter came this morning.

---

[1] 29] 27   [2] Franconia, New Hampshire.
[3] *L'oeuvre de E. H. Brewster et Achsah Barlow Brewster; 32 réproductions en phototypie précedées d'essais autobiographiques* (Rome, 1923).
[4] It was to become *The Boy in the Bush* (Secker, 1924); the novel by Mollie Skinner (see p. 236 n. 1), originally entitled 'The House of Ellis', was published as a collaboration after DHL rewrote the MS.

We are going up to New York next week: and maybe to England. I expect to find your MS. in New York. Then I shall read it carefully, and see what publisher it had best be submitted to. If there are a few suggestions to make, you won't mind, will you. I shall write as soon as I can get through.

Perhaps the best address is:

care Thomas Seltzer. 5. West 50th Street. New York City.

I often think of Darlington – can see it in my mind's eye as plain as I see the Lake of Chapala in front of me here. Perhaps we shall come back one day. – The path down the hollow under the gum trees, to your mother's cottage: and those big ducks. – Your mother didn't belong to our broken, fragmentary generation: with her oriental rugs in that little wooden bungalow, and her big, easy gesture of life. It was too small for her, really.

My wife sends many greetings.

Yours very sincerely   D. H. Lawrence

2856. To Witter Bynner, [4? July 1923]
Text: MS HU; Unpublished.

[Chapala, Jalisco, Mexico]
[4? July 1923][1]

[Witter Bynner begins]

Dear Pilgrims:

Julian wishes for some reason to start a bit earlier – I've told him we'll be ready at 9.15. Does that suit you? I've made no terms but shall pay either 75 an hour or 4 the day – as may turn out the cheaper. You might arrange with him for another boat so that everything will be ready.

Yours   WB

Jot down a word on the back of this.

[Lawrence begins]

Yes, we'll come at nine fifteen. Ask Julian about another boat.

Will it rain?

We're taking a bit of lunch.

DHL

2857. To Thomas Seltzer, 9 July 1923
Text: MS UT; Postmark, [. . .] JUL[. . .]; Lacy, *Seltzer* 102.

Hotel Arzapalo. Chapala. Jal.
9 July 1923

Dear Thomas

We leave Chapala today – it is doubtful if we can get out of Vera Cruz – very

---

[1] According to Bynner the journey on Lake Chapala was due to begin on 5 July: hence the conjectural date of this letter. See Bynner 167.

Bolshevist there, and strike imminent if not already on – won't let ships leave –
so we think to leave by rail, via *Laredo*, probably stop off a day or two in New
Orleans – arrive in New York somewhere about the 20th. I'll let you know.

DHL

2858. To Willard Johnson, [13 July 1923]
Text: MS YU; PC v. Hidalgo Street, Laredo, Tex.; Postmark, Laredo JUL 14 1923;
Unpublished.

Laredo
Friday

Had to spend a day in this hot place – they didn't put the baggage across at the
connection at Quaretaro – You watch yours at Irapuato. We've got it now,
leave in two hours for N[ew] Orleans. They will vaccinate you at the frontier
free of charge. Why pay 3 pesos? Greet everybody – hope Bynner is well.

DHL

2859. To Witter Bynner, [13 July 1923]
Text: MS HU; PC v. Sunset Route, Pecos River, as seen from high bridge; Postmark,
[. . .]; Bynner 187.

[Laredo, Texas]
Friday

– it rained all the way in Mexico – but Texas is fierce hot – queer show – don't
feel much elation being here in U.S. Do hope you're better.

DHL

2860. To Emily King, [13 July 1923]
Text: MS Needham; PC v. Hidalgo Street, Laredo, Tex.; Postmark, [. . .] 1923;
Unpublished.

Laredo.
13 July

Just crossed the frontier – going on to New Orleans today.

DHL

2861. To S. S. Koteliansky, [13 July 1923]
Text: MS BL; PC v. Under six flags, showing the Alamo, Built 1718, San Antonio, Texas;
Postmark, [. . .]; Zytaruk 256.

[San Antonio, Texas]
Friday

– Here in U.S. again – going to New Orleans – then New York – shall find
letters there. This already feels much nearer England.

DHL

2862. To Baroness Anna von Richthofen, [13 July 1923]
Text: MS UCB; PC v. The Alamo, Built 1718, San Antonio, Texas; Postmark, [. . .];·
Unpublished.

San Antonio
13 July –
Wieder in Ver. Staaten – in Texas – reisen nach New Orleans – ich habe
Mexico viel lieber wie hier. Bleib wohl.

DHL

[Frieda Lawrence begins]
   auf der Reis.

Frieda

[Again in Uni. States – in Texas – travelling to New Orleans – I like Mexico
much better than here. Keep well.

DHL

[Frieda Lawrence begins]
   on the journey.

Frieda]

2863. To Margaret King, [15 July 1923]
Text: MS Needham; PC v. Picking Cotton; Postmark, New Orleans JUL 16 1923;
Unpublished.

New Orleans.
15 July
Staying a few days in this steaming, heavy, rather dead town, then going to
New York by sea. – I hope Joan is better and that you are all able to go away for
a holiday – it has been a sad summer for you.

Love   DHL

2864. To Knud Merrild, [15 July 1923]
Text: MS UT; Postmark, New Orleans JUL 15 [. . .]923; Huxley 571–2.

[Hotel De Soto, New Orleans, La][1]
Sunday
Dear Merrild
   Here we are – got so far on the journey to New York. The moment I am back
in these States comes my old feeling of detestation over me again. But I no
longer let it trouble me. I just resist them all the time, and shall continue to do
so. Only one has to watch that in resisting them one doesn't become hard and

[1] DHL used the hotel's headed notepaper here and for Letter 2867.

empty as they are. I want to keep myself alive inside, for the few people who are still living.

I expect we shall arrive in New York on Wednesday. I shall stay long enough to correct all proofs and get my MS. typed[1] – then I suppose we shall go on to Europe. I am not very keen even on going to England. – I think what I would like best would be to go back to Mexico. If we were a few people we could make a life in Mexico. Certainly with this world I am at war.

I dreamed last night of Pips. But I feel that she too was a false little dog, a bit of Mabel Sterne.

New Orleans seems America – but more easy-going – same impudence, however.

Tell Götzsche I will write him as soon as we are in New York.

DHL

2865. To Dr George Purnell, [15 July 1923]
Text: MS UT; PC v. New Orleans, La., Weighing Cotton; Postmark, New Orleans JUL 16 1923; Unpublished.

New Orleans
Sunday

Don't care for this steamy decayed town, feel sticky all the time – much prefer even Guad[alajara] – At this rate I shall soon be back: so look out, if you hear of a little ranch for me, let me know. Thank you for all your kindness and hospitality – and excuse post cards – I can't find a sheet of note paper. My address care Thomas Seltzer, 5. West 50th St. New York.

Greet Idella.

DHL

2866. To Catherine Carswell, [15 July 1923]
Text: MS YU; PC v. Crap at Coonville, 'Now Seben Come Eleben'; Postmark, New Orleans JUL 16 1923; cited in Carswell 176.

New Orleans
Sunday

– Back in U. S. A. – regret Mexico – staying here a few days – a dead, steamy sort of place, a bit like Martin Chuzzlewit[2] – dreary – going up to New York by boat. The Mississippi is a vast and weary river that looks as if it had never wanted to start flowing. – Expect to be in England before September.

DHL

---

[1] About the proofs see Letter 2876; the MS – of *The Plumed Serpent* – was typed but not completed until early 1925.
[2] Dickens' eponymous hero visited America where he bought a piece of land which turned out to be a swamp.

2867. To John Middleton Murry, [17 July 1923]
Text: MS NYPL; Murry, *Reminiscences of D.H.Lawrence* (1933), p. 183.

[Hotel De Soto, New Orleans, La]
Tuesday

Dear Jack

Being in the U. S. makes me want to come to Europe. I really don't care for it here. We go today to Washington, for New York – and as soon as I've done all my proof-correcting etc. I shall come to England. Meanwhile I hope things are going well.

DHL

2868. To Earl and Achsah Brewster, [19 July 1923]
Text: MS UT; PC v. El Pico de Orizaba; Brewster 70.

New York
Thursday

Dear Earl and Achsah

Got here today – going to stay in a cottage in New Jersey[1] – write and let us meet as soon as you come this way – don't know how long we'll stay in this America – pray god not long. Don't like it. I *will* write a letter from the country. – Got all your letters. – Write to 5 West 50th St – care Seltzer.

DHL

2869. To Bessie Freeman, [20 July 1923]
Text: MS UNYB; Moore, *Intelligent Heart* 319.

care Thomas Seltzer. 5 West 50th St, New York City
Friday

Dear Bessie Freeman

We got in yesterday – Today are going out to New Jersey to stay in a cottage, where I can get proofs corrected. Not quite sure of the address. But its only 50 minutes out, so either you will come and see us, or we you, as soon as you are here. I find town *wearing*.

We'll talk Mexico and the future.

au revoir from us both

D. H. Lawrence

Seltzer can give you the exact address – it's his cottage.

DHL

---

[1] The cottage, belonging to a Mr Hammerslaugh, was in a remote part of the New Jersey hill country; the Seltzers renamed it 'Birkindele' allegedly after Birkin in *Women in Love* and Adele (Lacy, *Seltzer* 165).

2870. To Amy Lowell, 23 July 1923
Text: MS HU; Unpublished.

care Thomas Seltzer. 5. West 50th St. *New York City*

23 July 1923

Dear Amy

Here we are – in the Seltzer's cottage in New Jersey at the moment. Probably you are a thousand miles away. But let me know: and tell me if there is to be a meeting. I think we sail for England about 20th August.

Greetings to you.

D. H. Lawrence

2871. To Bessie Freeman, [24? July 1923]
Text: MS UNYB; Unpublished.

[care Thomas Seltzer, 5 West 50th St. New York City]

Tuesday

Dear Bessie Freeman

Only got both your letters today – post said they didn't know where to deliver. Write to 5 W. 50th St.

I am going in to New York on Thursday or Friday morning – to lunch with the *Nation* editors on Friday. I wonder what time on Friday you'll be in the Ritz Carlton. Ring me up at Seltzers at about eleven oclock, if you can, and we'll meet and have a little chat. Frieda may or may not come in to town. – I expect we shall return here Friday evening. You come out which day you like: and stay as long as you wish. Though I don't suppose we shall stay long now.

So ring me up at Seltzer's office on Friday either before 12.0 or after 3.0, and we'll make plans.

This address, it seems, if ever you wish to write, is

care Mr Hammerslaugh, Union Hill, *Dover*, New Jersey.

But nearest station from New York is *Morris Plains*.

You are having a quite ministerial time in the Capitol D.C.

au revoir   DHL (over)

[Frieda Lawrence begins]

Tuesday

Dear Bessie

We will love you to come on Monday – Can you only stay *one* night? Mrs Seltzer drives in on Monday morning, you might drive out with her when she takes Mr Seltzer to the station – It will be a very long drive for your brother, but I shall very much like to see him – It was *sad* you did not come to Mexico –

With love   Frieda

[Lawrence continues]

If we don't see you Friday, I'll leave word at Seltzer's office: and he comes out here every night, except Sat. and Sunday, when he's here all the time.

DHL

There is a phone in this cottage: *Dover* 699 F. 5.

2872. To Willard Johnson, [25? July 1923]
Text: MS YU; Unpublished.

care Seltzer. 5 West 50th St. *New York*
Wed.

Dear Spoodle

Your letter this evening – Hope Bynner's thing is really better – I never felt quite easy in my mind about it.

Am *very* sorry Scott is leaving the Arzap[alo]. Tell him from me.

We are in a farm-cottage the Seltzer's rented for us in New Jersey: very quiet, pretty, peaceful: quite alone: save Seltzer comes at evening. A horse and buggy: 4 miles from station, Morris Plains. I am busy correcting proofs: three books: much to do. More busy than happy. It's pretty, rural, remote, nice – but it doesn't make me feel happy. Desolate inside. – And New York – we were only there two[1] days – didnt make much impression on me so far. Sort of way outside me. – It's the *change*. Not adjusted yet.

Wasn't I rash to overdraw at Robles Gil's. Was very much surprised when I got their rather scared letter. I thought I'd left about 30 pesos: instead of which I'd overdrawn 'em. I sent them a cheque at once: expect they have it.

The journey in Mexico I really enjoyed: but not here in U.S. I didn't like New Orleans at all – dead, empty, much drearier than Guadalajara. And we had to come on by train – boats all filled with Californian tourists tripping east.

U. S. seems to me weary and rather dreary.

I'm not seeing anybody yet: feel I just can't face 'em.

The dollars for the typing.

F[rieda] still smoking Elegantes – thanking you.

Greet everybody from me. Tell Bynner to keep quiet inside. Tell all news.

D. H. Lawrence

[1] two] three

2873. To Benjamin Stern, [25 July 1923]
Text: American Book-Prices Current (1964), p. 830.

[care Seltzer, 5 West 50th St. New York City]

[25 July 1923]

[Lawrence requested 'that Thomas Seltzer see the agreement with Huebsch regarding "The Rainbow"'.][1]

2874. To Anna Jenkins, 26 July 1923
Text: MS WAPL; Priday, *Southerly*, xv (1954), 7.

care Seltzer. 5 West 50th St., New York City.

26 July 1923.

Dear Mrs Jenkins

We got your letter enclosing the one from Elder Walker today. I have meant to write you. We got back six days ago from Old Mexico – we went down there in March and had a house in Chapala, on Lake Chapala. I liked Mexico: find the U. S. A. rather wearing.

We think to come to London in August: then we shall see you. I haven't decided when we shall sail. At the minute we are in the country in New Jersey, and I am busy correcting proofs.

I hope you are feeling better. – I still hear from Mr Siebenhaar and even had a letter from Miss Skinner, who says she has sent me the MS. of a novel to read: though it hasn't come yet. – I was so sorry her mother died.

I shrink a little from coming back to England. Yet seriously, we intend to come in about three week's time. In England my agent's address will always get me:

care Curtis Brown, 6 Henrietta St, Covent Garden W. C. 2.

Greetings and au revoir from us both.

Yours Sincerely   D. H. Lawrence

---

[1] The agreement (in the possession of Viking Press), dated 14 June 1923, concerned Huebsch's right to publish *The Rainbow*. It named Stern as DHL's 'duly authorized representative' and it included 'Exhibit "A"' written in DHL's own hand:

25 June 1923. Chapala. Jalisco. Mexico.

To All Whom It May Concern

This is to certify that B. W. Huebsch. Inc. has up to January 1st. 1924 the sole and exclusive right to publish copies of "The Rainbow"; that I have not negotiated for or entered into any agreement with anybody else concerning its publication after January 1st. 1924; and that any announcement to the contrary is without authority and not in accordance with the facts.

D. H. Lawrence

2875. To Frederick Carter, 26 July 1923
Text: MS UT; Moore 748–9.

care Seltzer. 5. W. 50th St. New York.
26 July 1923

Dear Mr Carter

We are here near New York – in the country – The U. S. tries me.

I shall look for the MS. It interests me very much. If *only* it would be intelligible to the general public, Seltzer would do it. But as it stands, it would be useless to try to do it through a general publisher. You'd *have* to go to the people who do Meade[1] – in England – or the Theosophists, as you say.

After all, we shall never again know the heavens as we know the clock. And after all, the sum of all your work would be to translate so that the thing lives again. It's life that matters – and the big thing we've lost out of life needs to be recovered, livingly. I know all scientists and technical people have no patience with me: think I'm a fool not to be taken seriously except as a fiction-writer. Yet I know that no knowledge is knowledge unless it has its direct emotional-passional reference. Scientific truth is an illusion. And your macrocosm, perhaps, is only the skeleton of the old macrocosm, with the blood gone out. I don't believe the ancients were so *abstract* about it, *ever*.

We intend to come to England in August, and then if you don't come south I will come to Liverpool or somewhere there to talk this book – or this matter – over a bit, if you wish. My address in England:

Care Curtis Brown. 6. Henrietta St., Covent Garden. W.C.2.

Yours Sincerely   D. H. Lawrence

2876. To Curtis Brown, 26 July 1923
Text: MS UT; Unpublished.

Care Thomas Seltzer. 5. West 50th St. *New York*
26 July 1923

Dear Curtis Brown

I am sending by this mail corrected galleys – proofs – of *Kangaroo*. Seltzer never sent them to me – but I got them from his office as soon as I arrived in New York. – I have got also proofs of *Birds, Beasts and Flowers*: these I will send in a couple of days. Seltzer is leaving out *Tortoises*. Ask Secker what he wants to do.

Also I have got proofs of *Mastro-don Gesualdo*. Seltzer is publishing this in

---

[1] The reference is probably to L. T. (Elizabeth Thomasina) Meade (d. 1914), prolific Irish writer of stories for girls, whose publishers included Hodder and Stoughton, James Nisbet and J. F. Shaw, all of whom also published theological works.

September – he has made an arrangement to pay a small royalty to the heirs of Giovanni Verga. Could you not do the same – make the same arrangement. – I will send you duplicate proofs.

Seltzer intends *Kangaroo* for early September, and *BirdsBeasts* for the end of that month. He is publishing *Studies in Classic American Literature* about 15th August.

He will send you the eight necessary copies of each book he has out in advance of Secker.

We expect to be in London in August.

Yours Sincerely   D. H. Lawrence

2877. To Bessie Freeman, [30? July 1923]
Text: MS UNYB; Unpublished.

Union Hill, *Morris Plains.* N. J.
Monday

Dear Bessie Freeman

Got your note – You are leaving again so soon. We wanted you to come here. But we shall be here, I am almost sure, till about August 12th. Let us plan a few days together somewhere, when you get back from Washington. We must have a talk about Mexico and Palm Springs, and decide where we are going to spend the winter. I would come in to New York tomorrow, but feel still travel-battered – best wait a little while. – We are only an hour from town on the Lackawanna Railway – station *Morris Plains* – and you get a taxi up the hill to Hammerslaugh's house, – behind the millionaire Coffin's place. – Up Union Hill.

But let us do something nice for a day or two – You think of something.

Wiedersehen   D. H. Lawrence

[Frieda Lawrence begins]

Union Hill, Dover, New Jersey
Monday

Dear Bessie,

I wish we could have seen you to-day or to-morrow – the Seltzers say it's too *awful* to motor out – And *why* are you going away on Wednesday? Cant you come to-morrow and stay a night? It's too much for one day – I would so like to talk things over with you – Much love till we see you –

Frieda

2878. To Robert Mountsier, [1 August 1923]

Text: MS Smith; Postmark, Grand Central Sta AUG 2 1923; Unpublished.

care Seltzer, 5 W. 50th St., New York
Wed. 1st August

Dear M[ountsier]

I had your letter here – and all the Taos news. F[rieda] most shocked about the late Dr Woodman, who is not late at all:[1] – Mabel will hate Santa Fe – did Taos oust her?

We are in a cottage on the hills above Morris Plains in New Jersey, about 40 miles from New York. It's pretty, quite free – our own fields – horse and buggy. But I'm not smitten with it. The Seltzers come out at evening. – We were in New York only two days: and it only wearied me, without giving one any vivid impression of anything. But then we were tired from travelling. – We go in again tomorrow – and I am lunching with John Macy and another editor.[2] So far I didn't want to see a soul. – Have corrected proofs of *Kangaroo* and *Birds Beasts* and am doing *Mastro-don*. Much work, this last.

I don't think we shall stay long. We are due to go to England, but now the sailing comes near I feel I am balking it again. Can't get myself to go to Europe. – God knows why. But F. wants to go. Anyhow we shall go somewhere, soon – I won't stay here long. I'll let you know.

By the way did that MS. from Miss Skinner from Australia ever turn up?[3] I've seen nothing of it.

Seltzer's statement was again $4000–$4007, or somewhere there.

I think New Mexico is much nicer than New Jersey, anyhow.

Greetings from both   DHL

2879. To Amy Lowell, [3 August 1923]

Text: MS HU; Unpublished.

care Seltzer. 5 W. 50th St, New York
3 July 1923[4]

Dear Amy

We came in to town yesterday, and have your letter.

We neither of us want to go without seeing you. We should like to come for a couple of days. Probably we sail the 18th. – I am not sure. I balk going.

Write and tell me when we shall come – only not the next week-end – 11th

[1] Dr Isaac Woodman, father of Rachel Hawk.
[2] John Macy (1877–1932), literary editor of the *Nation* (1922–3); he reviewed *The Captain's Doll* (*Nation*, 6 June 1923) and *Studies in Classic American Literature* (*Nation*, 10 October 1923); and see also p. 318 n. 4. Oswald Garrison Villard (1872–1949), journalist, editor and owner of the *Nation* (1918–32).   [3] See p. 466 n. 4.
[4] DHL mistakenly dates this letter July instead of August; he was in Mexico until 13 July.

and 12th. And tell me a train from New York, will you: preferably after 10 a.m.
Because we are really staying in a Seltzer cottage in New Jersey, and have to
come in to town. Perhaps best write to the cottage – as Mr Seltzer doesn't
always come out with the letters.

    Mr Hammerslaugh's Cottage, Union Hill, *Dover*. New Jersey.

    Greet Mrs Russell from us both.

    Shall be glad to see you.

D. H. Lawrence

2880. To S. S. Koteliansky, [7 August 1923]
Text: MS BL; Postmark, New York AUG 8 1923; Zytaruk 256–7.

care Seltzer. 5 W. 50th St. New York.

7 August.

My dear Kot

    Have your second letter. I will write the *Dial* and ask them to let me have the
MS., in case they accept it.[1] – Isn't Thayer still in Europe?

    I feel I cant come yet to England – though I came here on purpose. But it's
no good, I shall have to put it off.

    Thank you so much for inviting us to the cave.

    Frieda intends to come. I think she will sail on the 18th to Southhampton. I
asked Mary Cannan to let you know if her flat is still available, in Queens
Gardens No 49. Mary herself is in Worcestershire. I think Frieda would stay a
week or two in the flat, then go to Germany.

    For my part, I shall go to Southern California, to the mountains – and
perhaps stay the winter, in which case F. will join me. We will see.

    Seltzer is publishing my translation of *Mastro-don Gesualdo* – Verga's novel
– in September.

    It's a pity one can't go ahead with the old thread of life. But I can't take it up
again this moment.

    I'll see about that MS.

DHL

2881. To Baroness Anna von Richthofen, 7 August 1923
Text: MS UCB; Frieda Lawrence 180.

care Seltzer. 5. West 50th St. New York City.

7 August 1923

Meine liebe Schwiegermutter

    Wir sind immer noch hier, in Amerika. Und ich finde, meine Seele kommt

---

[1] Maxim Gorky, *Reminiscences of Leonid Andreyev*, trans. Kot and Katherine Mansfield, was
later serialised in the *Dial* (June–August 1924). (See Letter 2894.)

so ungern nach Europa, sie ist wie Balaam's Esel, und *kann* nicht weiter fahren. Ich meine, ich komme nicht. – Die Frieda aber ja. Sie wird wahrscheinlich mit dem Schiff *Orbita* am 18n von New York nach Southampton, England, fortfahren. So ist sie am 25n in London: bleibt dort funfzehn oder zwanzig Tage: dann nach Baden.

Ich bleibe auf dieser Seite: gehe nach California, Los Angeles, wo wir Freunde haben. Und wenn es dort nett ist, kann die Frieda da kommen, in Oktober.

Ich weiss nicht wohl, warum ich nicht nach England gehen kann. Es kommt mir so eine Wehmut über der Sinne, als ich nur daran denke, dass ich glaube es wär besser hier zu bleiben, bis mein Gefühl verändert[1] ist.

Neu York habe ich nicht gern: eine grosse dumme Stadt, ohne Hintergrund oder Stimmung. Hier am Land ist es grün und ruhig. Aber gefällt mir besser Mexico.

Mit dem Herz hätte ich sehr gern kommen: mit Füssen auch, und Augen. Aber mit der Seele kann ich nicht.

Lebe wohl! Später wird der Esel fahren können.

DHL

[My dear Schwiegermutter

We are still here, in America. And I find my soul comes so unwillingly to Europe, it is like Balaam's ass, and *can't* travel any farther. I think I shan't come. – But Frieda, yes. She will probably sail with the ship *Orbita* on the 18th from New York to Southampton, England. So she will be in London on the 25th: stay there fifteen or twenty days: then to Baden.

I stay on this side: go to California, Los Angeles, where we have friends. And if it is nice there, Frieda can come there, in October.

I don't well know why I can't go to England. Such melancholy comes over my senses, when I only think of it, that I believe it would be better to stay here, till my feeling has changed. _

New York I don't care for: a great stupid city, without background or atmosphere. Here in the country it's green and peaceful. But I like Mexico better.

With the heart I should like very much to come: with feet too, and eyes. But with the soul I can't.

Fare well! Later on the ass will be able to travel.

DHL]

---

[1] verändert] ist

2882. To Amy Lowell, 7 August 1923
Text: MS HU; Moore, *Intelligent Heart* 320.

care Seltzer. 5 West 50th St. New York.

7 August 1923

Dear Amy

This to say perhaps you had better write to the New York address, as it is not very certain if the post will find us here in New Jersey.

I doubt if I shall get myself as far as England. Feel I dont want to go. But Frieda will sail on the 18th – and I shall sail somewhere or other.

Au revoir   D. H. Lawrence

2883. To John Middleton Murry, 7 August 1923
Text: MS NYPL; cited in Murry, *New Adelphi* 415.

care Seltzer. 5 W. 50th St. New York

7 August 1923

Dear Jack.

No, I don't feel we are enemies: why that? I was disappointed with the apologetic kind of appeal in *The Adelphi*: but you most obviously aren't my enemy in it. And anyhow you make a success of the thing: so what does it matter what I say.

I suppose I'll come back one day and stand on the old ground. But, as you say, not yet.

I wanted to send you that bull-fight beginning: but Seltzer didn't want it published, either here or in England, apart from the novel. I've been very busy doing proofs here: of *Kangaroo*, my novel: and *Birds Beasts and Flowers*: poems: and *Mastro-don Gesualdo* the Verga novel. I haven't arranged for the publication of any Verga in England. – Am glad you like 'St. Joseph's Ass.'[1] – I'll try and send you something for October – now I shall have a breathing space.

Frieda intends to come to England: thinks to sail on the *Orbita*,[2] Royal Mail Steam Packet Line, from New York the 18th of this month – to Southhampton. I wish you'd look after her a bit: would it be a nuisance? She will be all alone. I ought to come – but I can't. She thinks to stay in Mary Cannan's flat at 49 Queens Gardens W. 2. – if Mary continues in Worcestershire. – F. wants to see her children. And you know, wrong or not, I can't stomach the chasing of those Weekley children.[3] So I think I shall go to the mountains in southern California – and perhaps down into Sonora. I don't

---

[1] 'St Joseph's Ass', DHL's translation of a story by Verga, was published in *Adelphi*, i (September 1923), 284–97. (It was later collected as 'Story of the Saint Joseph's Ass' in *Little Novels of Sicily*.)   [2] *Orbita*] *Obita*
[3] Frieda's three children by her marriage to Professor Ernest Weekley were Charles Montague (1900–82), Elsa Agnes Frieda (1902–   ) and Barbara Joy (1904–   ).

care at all for these eastern states – and New York just means nothing to me. At the moment this so-called white civilisation makes me sicker than ever. I feel nothing but recoil from it. Now I've reached the Atlantic, and see Liberty clenching her fist in the harbour, I only want to go west, to the mountains and desert again. So there I am.

If you want a poem for the *Adelphi*, and Secker isn't ready with the publication[1] of *Birds Beasts and Flowers*, ask Curtis Brown for the MS. – or for a copy of the proofs. I expect Seltzer will have the book out about 20th Sept. Mary Cannan is at present at Holme Lea, Cheltenham Rd, Broadway, Worcestershire. I asked her to let Kot. know about her flat, if she'll be in it or not, and about the key.

I'll send you a copy of *Mastro-don Gesualdo*, when it's out.

DHL

2884. To Knud Merrild, 7 August 1923
Text: MS UT; Postmark, New York AUG 8 1923; Huxley 573–4.

care Seltzer. 5. W. 50th St., New York
7 August 1923

Dear Merrild

I have almost decided not to go to Europe. Frieda is sailing on the 18th to England. But I think I shall stay this side. I don't want to go: don't know why.

I think, when Frieda has gone, I shall come to Los Angeles. We might like to spend the winter at Palm Springs or among the hills. Or we might go again to Mexico. And I should like to see you and Götzsche and have a talk about the future. If there was nothing else to do, we might take a donkey and go packing among the mountains. Or we might find some boat, some sailing ship that would take us to the islands: you as sailors, myself as cook: nominal. Frieda, I suppose, will want to join me again at the end of October. Meanwhile we will have made some plan or other.

Probably I shall be in Los Angeles about the end of this month. Then we'll talk things over.

I care nothing for New York, and don't get much out of New Jersey.

Tell Götzsche; and think of something. – I wish we were rich enough to buy a little ship. I feel like that, now: like cruising the seas. I am a bit tired of the solid world. But perhaps it is quite nice to do as your engineer friend does,[2] and build an adobe house in the foot-hills.

Auf Wiedersehen   D. H. Lawrence

[1] publication] MS.
[2] Harry Roland Johnson (1880–1972), a consulting geologist, with whom Merrild and Götzsche were about to take up temporary residence while decorating his library (Merrild 309 ff). m. Olivia Rolfe (b. 1896).

2885. To Amy Lowell, [10 August 1923]
Text: MS HU; Unpublished.

New Jersey.
Friday

Dear Amy

I had already gone to sleep when you telephoned.

Frieda leaves next Saturday, and I the next week. She of course put off dentist till the last few days. So I don't see how we can come. Which is disappointing. – This was our free week. The next is a thousand and one things to do.

But we shall probably be in New York again soon. – Then we'll see you, surely. – I am sorry about this time. Greet Mrs Russell.

Yours ever.   D. H. Lawrence

2886. To S. S. Koteliansky, [13 August 1923]
Text: MS BL; Postmark, New York AUG 13 1923; Zytaruk 258.

[Thomas Seltzer, Inc. 5 West Fiftieth Street, New York][1]
13 Aug

Dear Kot

I'm not coming – not yet. Pazienza!

Frieda sails on the *Orbita* – Royal Mail Steam Packet Line, to Southhampton, on Saturday – She is due in Southhampton on the following Sat. night: 25th – or on Sunday 26th. I asked Murry to look after her all he could – and I ask you the same. Meet her at Waterloo if you can, will you. I'll ask her to wire.

I got your MS from the *Dial* today. They accept it, and I am going through it at once.

I think I shall go to California – perhaps sail the pacific ocean.

But one day I'll come back.

DHL

2887. To John Middleton Murry, 13 August 1923
Text: MS NYPL; cited in Murry, *New Adelphi* 415–16.

[Thomas Seltzer, Inc. 5 West Fiftieth Street, New York]
13 August 1923

Dear Jack

I have your letter – No, I'm not coming yet – suppose it isn't yet the right time. Let's wait a bit.

---

[1] DHL used Seltzer's headed notepaper here and for Letters 2887, 2897, 2898 and 2899.

I liked this month's *Adelphi* best. I like what you say about faith: One must have the faith to break an old faith.[1]

You are as bad as I am, rushing to extremes. I don't 'hate' the *Adelphi*, because the first number disappointed me and got me on the wrong side.

But let us wait and be a bit patient. – You know I'm not the calm sort.

I feel such a 'sadness', as Kot would say, about England and Europe, as if I'd swallowed a lump of lead. But let that digest away in my belly, and I'll be able to shake hands again. It's no good till I can come with a cheerful soul.

And America means nothing to me. – Yet I'm going right west again – I think to Los Angeles and into the mountains: perhaps to sail the Pacific. Do you remember our Islands, and ships! Ask the Lord to take away this heavy feeling in my belly, that I have when I think of England and home and my people: or even when I think of Fontana Vecchia.

I think you understand *Fantasia* and *Aaron* all right. It's I – because the sense of doom deepens inside me, at the thought of the old world which I loved – and the new world means nothing to me.

Frieda sails on Saturday on the *Orbita*, Royal Mail Steam Packet line, to Southhampton. She is due to arrive on the Sunday or Monday morning 26th or 27th August, – probably Sunday morning – She goes to Cherbourg first: the *Orbita*. I wish you would look after F. a bit. You know what a vague creature she is.

I suppose I'm the saddest, at *not* coming.

DHL

2888. To Witter Bynner, [14 August 1923]

Text: MS HU; Postmark, New York AUG 15 1923; Huxley 575.

care Seltzer. 5 West 50th St. New York.
14 August.

Dear Bynner

You may be home by now – and you may not. We are still here. Frieda sails on Saturday by the *Orbita* to Southhampton. I'm not going. – Where am I going? Ask me. – Perhaps to Los Angeles and then to the Islands, if I could find a sailing ship. Quién Sabe?

It's pleasant here – the trees and hills and stillness. But it is dim to me. Doesn't materialise. The same with New York: like a house of cards set up. I

---

[1] Murry printed chap. VIII of *Fantasia of the Unconscious*, using the title 'Education and Sex', in the *Adelphi*, i (July 1923), 123–36. This provoked a letter of protest from the Westminster Catholic Association which Murry answered in the August issue of the *Adelphi* (pp. 177–84), under the title 'Religion and Faith'. (During the course of his article Murry contrived to remark that DHL 'is become, since Katherine Mansfield's death, incomparably the most important writer of his generation'.)

like it best down at the Battery,[1] where the rag-tag lie on the grass. – Have met practically nobody: and the same thing, nothing comes through to me from them.

Tell Spoodle the *Horse* came, and his red letter.[2] The picture of the horse looks like a sobbing Ass. The inside quite amused me – of the *Horse*. A little more guts, a little less indigestion.

Your plays came too. I had read them long ago – it seems long – and forgotten the titles: also *Beloved Stranger*.[3] Many of these poems I really like.

It hasn't been hot here – quite pleasant. I wish things were real to me. I see the lake at Chapala, not the hills of Jersey – (New). And these people are just as you said of New England – quenched. I mean the natives. As for the trains full of business men –

Tell me what you are doing – I shall probably leave for somewhere next week. I've booked F's passage and she's setting off alone, quite perky. Sends you greetings.

D. H. Lawrence

2889. To Bessie Freeman, [14 August 1923]
Text: MS UNYB; Unpublished.

care Seltzer. 5 W. 50th, N. York
14 Aug

Dear Bessie Freeman

I sent you your sewing to 10 Saybrook St. Trust you got it.

Frieda sails on Saturday by the *Orbita* to Southampton. I may go next week right to Los Angeles. I shall see you when you come west.

I found your brother very interesting – he isn't like the other Americans I have met. But I believe too he'll have to take care of his nerves.

Hope you're having a good time.

Greetings from us both.

D. H. Lawrence

2890. To Earl Brewster, [14 August 1923]
Text: MS UT; Brewster 72.

care Seltzer. 5. W. 50th St. New York.
14 Aug.

Dear Earl

I can't write letters: no good. The day of my letters is over –

---

[1] The southern tip of Manhattan.   [2] *Laughing Horse.*
[3] Witter Bynner, *A Book of Plays* (New York, 1922); *The Beloved Stranger; two books of song and a divertisement for the unknown lover* (New York, 1919).

Frieda is sailing on Saturday by the *Orbita* to Southampton. I'm not going. I think I shall go to Los Angeles, and get a boat and sail to the Islands: meet Frieda somewhere at the end of October.

America makes me feel I haven't a word to say about anything. Not that I dislike it so badly – but it seems unreal and makes me feel more remote.

I don't think I will come to New Haven now. We'll meet somewhere else, when the wheel has spun a little further.

Tell Achsah I'm glad she enjoys herself. F. sends many greetings.

Yours ever   DHL

2891. To Catherine Carswell, 15 August 1923
Text: MS YU; Postmark, New York AUG 16 1923; cited Carswell 176, 177, 190.

care Seltzer. 5 West 50th St. New York
15 August 1923

Dear Catherine

I'm not coming to Europe after all. Find I just don't want to – not yet. Later.

Frieda sails on Saturday for Southampton by the *Orbita* – Royal Mail Steam Packet Line. She is due in Southampton on the 26th of this month: which is a Sunday. She will probably stay in Mary Cannan's flat at 49 Queens Gardens, Hyde Park – that is, if Mary Cannan is still away.

I wonder when you will be back in town. Look after F. a bit. – She will stay a month or so – then go to Germany – then come back here – or meet me wherever I am. I think I shall go to California, and either pack with a donkey in the mountains, or get some sailing ship to the Islands – if the last is possible. – Perhaps by autumn I'll decide to come to England – Who knows! At present I can't come.

Seltzer says he liked *Open the Door* very much: he says Harcourt Brace deliberately neglected the *Camomile* and let it die:[1] didn't even tread on it. If you have another novel, try Seltzer. – But why don't you write a volume of criticisms, like Duse one.[2] 'The World from a Woman's Window.' If you say what you absolutely sincerely feel, you'll make a good book.

Au revoir   D. H. Lawrence

---

[1] Harcourt, Brace and Company (New York) published Catherine Carswell's second novel in 1922.
[2] She had contributed a short piece on the famous Italian actress Eleonora Duse (1858–1924) to the *Adelphi*, i (August 1923), 238–41. Catherine Carswell and DHL shared a fascination with Duse's acting and tempestuous personality (cf. *Letters*, ii. 595).

2892. To Martin Secker, 15 August 1923
Text: MS UInd; Secker 53.

care Seltzer. 5 W. 50th. N. York

15 August 1923

Dear Secker

Here am I once more putting off sailing. At the moment I don't want to come to England. Think I shall go to California.

Seltzer fixes Sept 15th for *Kangaroo*: be sure you don't bring the book out *before* that date. *BirdsBeasts* the 18th Sept.

I am sending you a couple of good photographs that Seltzer had taken of me.[1]

My wife is coming to London for a visit – am not quite sure where she will stay, but Murry will have her address. She might call and see you.

I enclose list of copies of *Kangaroo* and *Fantasia* and *Birds Beasts*.[2] Be so good as to have these posted, will you?

I'll see you one day again.

Yrs   D. H. Lawrence

P. S. Don't post me any presentation copies at all, to America.

DHL

2893. To Curtis Brown, 15 August 1923
Text: MS UT; Unpublished.

care Seltzer. 5 West 50th St. New York.

15 August 1923

Dear Curtis Brown

I am after all putting off my sailing to England. I can't understand my own reluctance to come.

Will you please let me know Secker's dates for publication of *Kangaroo* and *BirdsBeasts*. Seltzer fixes *Kangaroo* for Sept. 15th. Be sure that Secker does *not* publish before that date. *BirdsBeasts* is due for the 18th.

My wife is coming to London – will be there by the 28th. I wish you would forward to her any letters that have arrived for me, as they will be appointments by friends in London. Address:

Care S. Koteliansky, *5. Acacia Rd. N. W. 8.*

– I think I shall go to California for the meanwhile: But please address me care of Seltzer. – I am sending also a big photograph of myself, which Seltzer had done.

Yours Sincerely   D. H. Lawrence

[1] DHL may have been responding to promptings from Curtis Brown who had been told by Secker (on 10 May) to ask DHL for copies of any photographs taken in New York: see p. 448 n. 2   [2] The list is missing.

2894. To S. S. Koteliansky, 17 August 1923
Text: MS BL; Postmark, New York AUG 17; Zytaruk 259.

[219 West 100th Street, New York][1]

17 August 1923

My dear Kot

We were on board the *Orbita* this morning. They say she will probably not get in till Tuesday morning – the 28th. Which is very slow. So I expect Frieda will leave Southampton the Tuesday afternoon – be in London by evening.

I went through your Gorky MS. and returned it to *Dial*. I made the English correct – and a little more flexible – but didn't change the style, since it was yours and Katharine's. But the first ten pages were a bit crude.

I do *not* like New York an empty place. I am going to California on Monday: care Knud Merrild, 628 W. Twenty-seventh St, *Los Angeles*, Cal. Then I'll see how I feel.

Trust all goes well.

DHL

Perhaps you will phone Cooks or the Royal Mail Steam Packet Co. and ask when the *Orbita* gets in.

2895. To Amy Lowell, [18 August 1923]
Text: MS HU; Damon 639–40.

N. Jersey.

Saturday evening 18 Aug

My dear Amy

I have just got back from seeing Frieda off on the steamer, and found your letter. – I'm sorry we are not seeing you. I wasn't very sure if you wanted to be troubled by visitors. I knew of course your health was not good.

But I have always a very warm memory of you in those days in England: the Berkeley, and when you came with Mrs Russell to that cottage.[2] – Tempi passati! Già troppo passato![3]

I ought to have gone to England. I wanted to go. But my inside self wouldn't let me. At the moment I just can't face my own country again. It makes me feel unhappy, like a terrible load.

But I don't care for New York. I feel the people one sees want to jeer at us. They come with a sort of pre-determination to jeer. – But that is literary.

---

[1] Here and for Letters 2900 and 2901 DHL used headed notepaper.

[2] DHL alludes to a dinner party given by Amy Lowell at the Berkeley Hotel, London, on 13 August 1914 (*Letters*, ii. 207 and n. 3). The cottage was in Chesham, Bucks., which DHL invited her to visit in late August 1914 (see ibid., ii. 209–10).

[3] 'Those past times! Already too long ago!'

I am going West again – to Los Angeles, and then, if I can get a sailing ship of some sort, out to sea. This New York leaves me with one great desire, to get away from people altogether. That is why I can't go to Europe: because of the many people, the many things I shall have to say, when my soul is mute towards almost everybody.

Seltzer is bringing out various books of mine, and I have asked him to send you a copy of each. – The poems, *Birds Beasts and Flowers*, should be done – published I mean – by Sept 20th. I'll ask Seltzer to send you an advance copy. But don't review it unless you *really* feel like it.

Thank you for the little cheque.[1] Sending these tiny sums is a nuisance to you; don't bother to do it, give the money to somebody who is poor.

Frieda wanted to see England again: it is four years since we were there. And her mother in Baden Baden. My heart goes like lead when I think of England or Germany. – I am thankful we are no longer poor, so that we can take our way across the world.

Either Frieda will come and join me somewhere west – perhaps in Mexico: or I shall go to her in Europe. In which latter case, I'll let you know in plenty of time. And then tell me if you really want me to come: if you feel equal to the effort of visitors. As for me, I never want to be a visitor for longer than two days. That is enough.

But we'll keep a bit of decent kindliness at the bottom of our hearts, as we had ten years ago. I'll never let the world bankrupt me *quite* in this.

Greet Mrs Russell – I hope you'll feel strong again.

D. H. Lawrence

I am leaving this cottage for good on Monday – expect to leave New York on Tuesday.

DHL

[1] See p. 96 n. 1. (The cheque was for $4.95.)

2896. To Robert Mountsier, [19 August 1923]
Text: MS Smith; Postmark, New York AUG 20 1923; Unpublished.

care Thomas Seltzer
Sunday
Dear M[ountsier]

Thank you for the Miss Skinner MS.

Frieda sailed yesterday – I funked going.

I am going west tomorrow – to Los Angeles – and then down to Lower California or else if I found a nice ship, to the Islands. After which I shall either go to Europe in October, or F. will come and join me.

No, my new novel has nothing whatsoever to do with Mabel, nor with Taos, nor with the United States at all. – Are you doing Taos as it is – *in puris naturalibus?*[1] That should be amusing. But guard your skin and your MS.

I'll let you know when I have an address.

DHL

2897. To Martin Secker, 20 August 1923
Text: MS UInd; Postmark, New York AUG 20 1923; Secker 53.

[Thomas Seltzer, Inc. 5 West Fiftieth Street, New York]
20 Aug 1923
Dear Secker

Please send me a copy of *Sea and Sardinia*. I have not seen your edition: you didn't send me a copy, though I asked you.

Seltzer has *Kangaroo* for Sept. 15th – and *BirdsBeasts* for October 1st. I don't want you to bring the book out before those[2] dates.

My wife sailed Saturday. If you see her, tell her anything you have to say to me.

Yrs   D. H. Lawrence

2898. To Bessie Freeman, [20 August 1923]
Text: MS UNYB; Postmark, New York AUG 20; cited in Moore, *Intelligent Heart* 320.

[Thomas Seltzer, Inc. 5 West Fiftieth Street, New York]
Monday morning
Dear Bessie Freeman

Just come in to New York – got your letter. Frieda sailed Saturday. I expect, either she'll be here again by October, or I shall be going to meet *her* somewhere.

---

[1] 'in all its nakedness?'   [2] those] that

I should like to stay a night in your Buffalo – the Buffalo also of Mabel and Nina.[1] Thank you very much for the hospitality. I should like to go with you to see Niagara, very much.

Today I am going to the dentist. If I get through with him, I shall leave New York tomorrow: if not, Wednesday. I shall send you a telegram. – Don't know if you'll get this letter.

Yes, your brother must be *made* to relax. He is too much in his head: he'll have a smash. Best if he could be sent to sea with people who absolutely *don't* talk and *don't* understand him in the least, when *he* talks. – I can see he has naturally a great charm and singleness.

au revoir   D. H. Lawrence

2899. To Curtis Brown, 20 August 1923
Text: MS UT; Unpublished.

[Thomas Seltzer, Inc. 5 West Fiftieth Street, New York]
20 August 1923

Dear Curtis Brown

I told you, I am not coming yet to England.

Please do see to it that Secker does *not* publish *Kangaroo* before 15th. September, and *BirdsBeasts and Flowers* not before 1st October. If there is any answer to this, please let me know at once.

Also let me know if you have arranged the *Kangaroo* rights with Australia. If you have not, then I will keep these rights myself.[2]

Seltzer is sending copies of *Studies in Classic American Literature* this week.

My wife sailed for London on Saturday. She might possibly call, to have a little chat with you, which she can report to me.

Yours   D. H. Lawrence

2900. To Adele Seltzer, [21 August 1923]
Text: MS UT; Lacy, *Seltzer* 102.

[219 West 100th Street, New York]
Tuesday night

Dear Adele

Well then, goodbye for the moment. We'll meet again before very long: and some time we'll make a bit of a life in unison. I'm not going to allow this world to have its own way entirely with us all. – 'So he said: Fight on! Fight on!'[3] Since we know we *can* make a life together, we won't break the thread of it.

---

[1] See pp. 331 n. 3 and 332 n. 4.   [2] See Letter 2795.
[3] Cf. 'Sir Andrew Barton' (*Oxford Book of Ballads*, ed. A. Quiller-Couch, 1910, p. 694), stanzas 64 and 65.

We'll keep an invisible thread holding us together. 'See if I am not Lord of the dark and moving hosts
    Before I die.'
    There's the world – and there's me and the ones who are with me. And we'll possess ourselves of the future, see if we don't.
    'Peace I leave you; my peace I give unto you –'[1]
    Greet Schnitz also Fritz.[2]

DHL

2901. To Adele Seltzer, [22 August 1923]
Text: MS UT; Lacy, *Seltzer* 103.

[219 West 100th Street, New York]
Wed. morning

Dear Adele
    Raining. Am just leaving.
    Enclosed the ticket for that dyed dress. You won't mind paying for it with Amy's cheque? And if F[rieda] writes she wants the dress, we can send it. Otherwise let it lie here – or let the Brewis' take it to England in October. They leave about mid October – the landlord said he would renew their lease for 3 years at same terms as present $1,450 a year. It's quite a nice flat in a modern building, with a sitting-room overlooking the river: gives a sense of space, which is good.
    Mrs Joseph Brewis, 640 Riverside Drive, end of 141st St.
If you think you might like it ring up Brewis at the Butterick building. But I dont suppose you want to change.
    au revoir
    je' m'en vais
    me ne vo
    salgo.
    jetzt geh'ich
    Adios!

DHL

2902. To Knud Merrild, [22 August 1923]
Text: MS UT; Postmark, Buffalo AUG 23 1923; Merrild 311.

Buffalo.
Wednesday evening 22 Aug

Dear Merrild
    I have got so far – am staying in Buffalo till Friday at Mrs Freemans. Shall

---

[1] John xiv. 27 ['. . . I leave with you, . . .'].   [2] Adele Seltzer's cats.

probably stay a day in Chicago, also – perhaps – in Salt Lake City. I will
telegraph the time I arrive. It will be about a week from now.

D. H. Lawrence

2903. To Thomas Seltzer, [25 August 1923]
Text: MS UT; Postmark, Niagara Falls, N.Y. AUG 25 1923; Lacy, *Seltzer* 105.

10 Saybrook St. Buffalo
Saturday

Dear Thomas

I am still here. Thank you for sending on cablegram and letter[1] – You did
right to open cablegram.

The queerest thing in the world, being in Buffalo and going round their
'blue blood.' It's almost like *Cranford*: more old-fashioned than anything still
surviving in Europe: and really a genuine nice feeling among them – and a
pathos. A mixture of *Virgins of the Rocks* and *Cranford* and *The Wide Wide
World.*[2]

I've not been to Niagara yet – am due to go today. Lunching out there with
Mabel Sterne's mother.[3] You would hardly know me, I am so well-behaved. A
perfect chameleon. But the same old sphinx of a me looking at the different
grimaces of the sphinx of life. I think I learn more about the old *genuine*
America here, than anywhere.

Well, now we know one another, so we can go on with our mutual burden
separately. I am glad to have stayed that month with you and Adele. I find a
real reassurance in it.

Damnation to have missed two trains.

It has been cold as hell here – bit warmer. This dree, dree[4] lake! The town is
like Manchester sixty years ago – or Nottingham – very easy and sort of nice
middle-class, BOURgeois.

Vamos! Vamonos![5]

DHL

---

[1] Missing, but see letter following.
[2] Novels by: Gabriele D'Annunzio (1863–1938), *The Virgins of the Rocks* (1895; 1899), trans.
Agatha Hughes, which DHL had read before December 1916 (see *Letters*, iii. 43); Elizabeth
Gaskell (1810–65), *Cranford* (1853), which DHL had known intimately since his youth (see
E. T. [Jessie Wood], *D. H. Lawrence: A Personal Record*, 1935, p. 102; *Letters*, iii. 227); and
Elizabeth Wetherell, pseud. of Susan B. Warner (1819–85), *The Wide, Wide World* (New York,
1851).   [3] Sara Cook Ganson.
[4] I.e. tedious, dreary (northern dialect).   [5] 'Let's go! Let's go!'

2904. To Margaret King, [25 August 1923]
Text: MS Needham; PC v. American Falls; Postmark, Niagara Falls, ONT. AUG 25 1923; Unpublished.

[Niagara Falls, Ontario]
25 Aug.

At Niagara today – had cable about the new baby – very glad.[1] Hope you have seen your Aunt Frieda.

Love   DHL

2905. To Thomas Seltzer, 27 August 1923
Text: MS UT; Lacy, *Seltzer* 106.

46 Lancaster Avenue, Buffalo. N. Y.
27 Aug. 1923.

Dear Seltzer
I wish you would send to Miss Mary Wilkeson, at the above address, a copy of *The Lost Girl* and of *The Captain's Doll*. And to
Mrs Effingham Burnett, Columbia Avenue, Wanakah, *Hamburg, N. Y., Erie County,*
a copy of *Aaron's Rod*. To the same address, to Mrs John Knox Freeman, a copy of *Women in Love*.
I am leaving tonight for Chicago. – Pax tecum.

DHL

2906. To Bessie Freeman, [28 August 1923]
Text: MS UNYB; Postmark, Omaha [. . .] 28[. . .]; Moore, *Intelligent Heart* 320.

[Los Angeles Limited, Chicago & North Western Ry][2]
Tuesday afternoon

Dear Bessie Freeman
Thank you so much for the four full days in Buffalo. I feel I had there a fuller glimpse into the real old U. S. than ever before. I was really interested, and the real Buffalos at home were much nicer than I had expected, knowing only those other two Buffalos in Taos.[3] Only Sarah M.[4] depressed me: the dead weight of her: and now, I also feel a bit sorry for her. – Why doesn't somebody write your *Cranford*? Buffalo is a sort of *Cranford*.
It rained and fogged in Chicago, and floods of muddy-flowing people oozed

---

[1] Ada Clarke's son, William Herbert Clarke, b. 17 August 1923.
[2] Here and for Letter 2907 DHL used headed notepaper.
[3] Mabel Luhan and Nina Witt.   [4] Unidentified.

thick in the canyon-beds of the streets. Yet it seemed to me more alive and more real than New York.

You were very kind to me and I am very grateful. It's like another little page in my history.

au revoir – à bientôt   D. H. Lawrence

Tell Margaret your sister that above all things she is to find her own peace within – at all costs to the outside circumstances.

DHL

2907. To Mary Wilkeson, [28 August 1923]
Text: MS UNYB; Postmark, Omaha [. . .] 28 1923; Unpublished.

[Los Angeles Limited, Chicago & North Western Ry]
Tuesday afternoon

Dear Mary Wilkeson

A thousand thanks to you for your hospitality – the toast and the four-poster and the little hostess. We had a good time – at least I did – cooking the bacon and discussing the ways of the nature of man. I shall see you again, I am sure, and we'll add a few new references to our note-book. – Bessie suggested the two books[1] – I hope they'll come and you won't be bored.

Pack the china carefully and take care of the silk rug, and remember that moth and rust doth corrupt.[2]

a riverderci   D. H. Lawrence

2908. To Henry Seidel Canby, [28 August 1923]
Text: MS Holahan; Unpublished.

care Thomas Seltzer
Tuesday

Dear Dr Canby[3]

Thank you for the books. I will see if I can make *Contemporary Verse* the point of departure for the critique you speak of.[4] *Pazienza!* Also I will read the Swedish Stories, and see if I can do a notice of them.[5] Mr Seltzer will send you back Miss Stern and Mr Aiken.[6] Let me have my way – and then if you don't want to publish what I say, I shan't mind in the least.

---

[1] See Letter 2905.   [2] Matthew vi. 19 (A.V.).
[3] Henry Seidel Canby (1878–1961), Ph.D., Yale, was the editor of the Literary Review in the *New York Evening Post*, 1920–4; he was formerly assistant editor of the *Yale Review* and was to become editor of the *Saturday Review of Literature*.
[4] Canby published DHL's review of *A Second Contemporary Verse Anthology* in the *New York Evening Post*, 29 September 1923 (reprinted in *Phoenix* 322–6).
[5] If DHL wrote a review it has not been identified.
[6] Canby had probably sent DHL the latest publications by Gladys Bronwyn Stern (1890–1973), novelist and short-story writer, and Conrad Aiken (1889–1973), American poet and novelist: *The Back Seat* (New York, 1923) and *The Pilgrimage of Festus* (New York, 1923), respectively.

I shall see you when I am back in New York – and then I shall at least be a bit older in America as well as years.

Yours Sincerely   D. H. Lawrence

2909. To Thomas Seltzer, [31 August 1923]
Text: MS UT; Postmark, Los Angeles AUG 31 1923; Lacy, *Seltzer* 107.

care Knud Merrild, 628 W. 27th St. Los Angeles
Friday. 30th[1]

Dear Thomas

I got here safely last night. Thank you for sending on F[rieda]'s cablegram. I do so wonder how she likes it. – The Danes met me at the station with that ancient Lizzie of Del Monte fame. They are working on a room at Santa Monica – 20 miles out.[2] Perhaps I shall go and stay in the hotel there for a week. But this address is good. – I want to do the article for Canby, and if I can, put together Miss Skinner's Australian novel – which is good, if only threaded. – The letters sent on, one I enclose – the other from Prince Bibesco wanting to see me.[3] Dont care for him much, but like her. – Merrild rather down in the mouth because he hasn't much success. Götzsche working at a job and not complaining. – I think of Birkindele, and wonder how you are getting on. Tell Adele I don't forget her. – Now I am here I feel like going back to Mexico – it seems realer to me than the US. – Let me know when the MS of 'Quetzalcoatl' is typed, and let me have a copy if you can before I start moving again. And tell me how you are and what is happening. I feel I have to keep an eye on everything, like the eye of God, for fear the devil pounces in.

Salud.   DHL

2910. To Mollie Skinner, 2 September 1923
Text: MS WAPL; Postmark, Santa Monica SEP 2; Huxley 577.

[The Miramar, Santa Monica, Cal][4]
2 Sept. 1923

Dear Miss Skinner

I have read 'The House of Ellis' carefully: such good stuff in it: but without unity or harmony.[5] I'm afraid as it stands you'd never find a publisher. Yet I hate to think of it all wasted. I like the quality of so much of it. But you have no constructive power. – If you like I will take it and re-cast it, and make a book of

---

[1] Merrild and Götzsche met DHL on his arrival in Los Angeles, 30 August 1923 (Merrild 312). Friday was 31 August.   [2] See p. 481 n. 2.
[3] Prince Antoine Bibesco (1878–1951), Rumanian diplomat. m. 1919, Elizabeth Asquith (1897–1945), Lady Cynthia Asquith's sister-in-law. For DHL's attitude to Bibesco see e.g. *Letters*, iii. 315–18.   [4] DHL used headed notepaper.   [5] See p. 466 n. 4.

it. In which case we should have to appear as collaborators, or assume a pseudonym. – If you give me a free hand, I'll see if I can't make a complete book out of it. If you'd rather your work remained untouched, I will show it to another publisher: but I am afraid there isn't much chance. You have a real gift – there is real quality in these scenes. But without form, like the world before creation.

I am in California – but don't suppose I shall stay long. Write me
care *Thomas Seltzer, 5. West 50th St., New York.*

If I get this book done, we'll publish it in the spring. – And if you agree to my re-casting this: then I wish you would take up that former novel of yours, about the girl and the convict – and break off where the three run away – keep the first part, and continue as a love story or romance, where the love of the girl is divided between the Irish convict and the young gentleman – make it a tragedy if you like – but let the theme be the conflict between the two *kinds* of love in the heart of the girl: her love for Peter (was that the young man's name?) – and her love for the Irish ex-convict.[1] See if you can't carry that out. – Because of course, as you have it, the convict is the more attractive of the two men, but the less amenable. – Only all that adventure in the N. W. is not very convincing. Keep the story near Perth – or Albany, if you can.

If you see Mr Siebenhaar tell him I have hopes of *Max Havelaar* for the spring of next year too.

Best wishes to you all at Leithdale.

Yours Very Sincerely   D. H. Lawrence
Address
Care Thomas Seltzer, 5. W. 50th St, New York

2911. To Margaret King, [12 September 1923]
Text: MS Needham; PC v. Echo Park in Midwinter, Los Angeles, Cal.; Postmark, Los Angeles SEP 12 1923; Unpublished.

[Los Angeles]
12 Sept.

I am back in Los Angeles – been away some days motoring – saw the total

---

[1] When he was in Australia DHL had seen the MS of what, when re-written, was to become Mollie Skinner's novel *Black Swans* (1925). In his 'Preface to *Black Swans*' (first published in *Phoenix II* 294–6) DHL recalled the novel in its unrevised state: 'When I saw it, it was about a girl, a convict [Tim Rafferty], and a Peter: Lettie, I think her name was, poised between the entirely praiseworthy Peter and the fascinating convict. But there the tale tumbled away into a sort of pirate-castaway-Swiss-Family-Robinson-Crusoe-Treasure-Island in the North West. This "adventure" part was rather pointless. I suggested to Miss Skinner that she work out the Peter-Lettie-Convict combine on ordinary terra firma.'

eclipse: it was very wonderful – I also saw those seven torpedo boats smashed on the rocks – a rather gruesome sight.[1] – I hope by now you have seen your Aunt Frieda and had a good time with her. I haven't yet heard from her, since her cable. I wonder too how your Aunt Ada is, and the new baby. What a world of changes. I don't know how long I shall stay here – not long – perhaps go down to Mexico.

DHL

2912. To Willard Johnson, [12 September 1923]
Text: MS YU; PC v. Palms and Flowers, Westlake Park, Los Angeles, Calif.; Postmark, Los Angeles SEP 13 1923; Huxley 578.

[Los Angeles]
12 Sept[2]

– Don't ask me for letters – no puedo mas.[3] – Am in Los Angeles – no fixed address – probably going Lower California, but it might be Pacific Isles – Frieda in England will join me when I get somewhere – saw eclipse yesterday – very impressive – also 7 destroyers on rocks – depressive – Los A silly – much motoring, me rather tired and vague with it – came via Salt Lake – Owe Bynner letter – will send address then – am on the move – just in from S[an]ta Barbara.

DHL

2913. To Frederick Carter, [15 September 1923]
Text: MS UT; Unpublished.

Los Angeles.
15 Sept.

Dear Mr Carter

I got the new MS. of the 'Dragon' from Seltzer today.[4] So long these things take! I am going through it carefully. I think you'll have to give me permission to punctuate a little more, and sometimes to re-arrange your words a trifle, where you are a bit obscure. Will you do this? Because I am going to do my best to get Seltzer to publish the book. And perhaps I will write an introduction. On Monday I will try to buy a satisfactory handbook to Astrology, to learn the

[1] Seven U.S. destroyers were wrecked in fog on 9 September at Honda Point, n. of Santa Barbara. (For an account of the outing involving DHL and others to see the eclipse see Nehls, ii. 257–9.)
[2] Although DHL mentions the eclipse as having occurred 'yesterday', it actually took place on Monday 10 September (cf. Letter 2913); his dating of the postcard is correct.
[3] 'I can't do any more.'   [4] See p. 365 n. 3.

rudiments at least of the art. Can you suggest me a book? And I must see if this town contains a planisphere.

I saw a very impressive eclipse of the sun last Monday. – My wife is in London – perhaps she has written to you. – Write care of Seltzer.

Yours Sincerely   D. H. Lawrence

I think I shall go down to Mexico again next week. Shall not stay here.

2914. To Bessie Freeman, [16 September 1923]

Text: MS UNYB; Postmark, Los Angeles SEP 17 1923; cited in Moore, *Intelligent Heart* 321.

care Knud Merrild. 628 W. 27th St. Los Angeles.

Sunday

Dear Bessie Freeman

Your note enclosing Mabel's telegram. I didn't realise you hadn't this address. Anyhow it's very impermanent. No, I don't trust Mabel's idea of paying her debts: I have *my* idea of what she owes me. As for a vendetta, I'm ready. To hell with her, anyhow. I'm through with her now.

Met Mr and Mrs Forsyth[1] – Mrs Forsyth cross with me for not using the Mexico letters of introduction. But we went to the circus together and had a good time – and tomorrow I'm going to dinner.

I'm on the point of going down to Mexico again – shall probably leave, via Nogales, about the 24th. But am not sure. Now I am so near, Mexico pulls me hard. – When shall you be in Palm Springs I wonder – I shall try to see you.

Don't be cross with me for not writing a letter. Sometimes I just can't do it.

Remember me warmly to Mary Wilkeson. I remember so well her serious eyes while I fried bacon. And I do hope your sister Margaret is a bit soothed inside.

I feel it's time you left Buffalo again.

Thank you for the letter of introduction to Mrs Eaton.[2] Heaven knows if I shall go.

I hope to see you.

D. H. Lawrence

2915. To S. S. Koteliansky, 17 September 1923

Text: MS BL; Moore 752–3.

Los Angeles.

17 Sept 1923

My dear Kot

Your letters came on here. Thank you so much for promising to look after Frieda. I hope she landed comfortably and is having a nice time.

[1] Unidentified.   [2] Unidentified.

I sent your word to Seltzer, about the *Adelphi*. But he's not very good at doing extraneous jobs like that.

Here I've been in California eighteen days. The time slips by quickly. – It is a loose, easy, rather foolish world here. But also, a great deal of falseness is also left out. – It's not so bad, in some ways. – But I think I shall go down to Mexico about this day week. I shall look once more for a little ranch. We might all meet there one day. Who knows. And it's not far from the Pacific, whoever wants to sail that sea.

I am sending F. two books: one is merely a copy of *Studies in Classic American Literature*, the other a novel by Will Comfort, a man here.[1] If Frieda is away, don't bother to send them on. If Seltzer didn't send you a copy of *Studies*, and if F. doesn't want this copy, take it. I ordered a copy sent to you.

It seems hard to me to imagine England. It's not very real to me. But I shall come back one day – if only for a time. When I am more decided about this side of the world: and this Pacific seaboard.

Am waiting for news from you all.

Grüsse   DHL

2916. To Alfred Stieglitz, 17 September 1923
Text: MS YU; Postmark, Los Angeles SEP 17 1923; Unpublished.

Los Angeles.

17 Sept 1923

Dear Mr Stieglitz,[2]

Thank you so much for your letter about *Studies in Classic American Literature*. I am so glad. I expected abuse, and I get, for the very first word, a real generous appreciation that I myself can appreciate. One gets so sick of being carped at with the inevitable 'But Mr Lawrence – ' – It is a perpetual puzzle to me, why the voice of America is absolutely silent nowadays: because Dr Sherman's and Sinclair Lewis'es aren't voices, only echoes or catch-words.[3] Where *is* the onward-striving America? – They seem neither to able to call nor to answer. And such a big country full of people. It beats me.

I am going down to Mexico again this week – to try that. And I am glad to take your letter along with me, in my mind.

Yours sincerely   D. H. Lawrence

---

[1] See p. 430 n. 2. Comfort published *The Public Square* (New York, 1923).

[2] Alfred Stieglitz (1864–1946), distinguished American photographer and editor of photographic journals, decisive in the development of photographic art. He founded 'Little Galleries of the Photo-Secession' (later known as '291'); he was famous for introducing America to modern native and European art. m. 1893, Emmeline Obermeyer; 1928, Georgia O'Keefe (1887–1986), American landscape painter. (See *Times* obituary, 17 July 1946.)

[3] See p. 355 n. 4. Sinclair Lewis produced no comparable study to Sherman's *Americans*. DHL must have had in mind Lewis's fiction such as *Main Street*, which he read in February 1922 (see Letter 2458 and n. 3), or *Babbitt* (New York, 1922).

2917. To John Middleton Murry, 17 September 1923
Text: MS NYPL; cited in Murry, *New Adelphi* 415.

Los Angeles.
17 Sept 1923

Dear Jack

I had your letter here – also the *Adelphi*. – I like your little attack on Mr Mortimer: very amusing.[1] *Do* attack them. Go for them amusingly like this. Satirise them to death. That's your job.

And gradually the *Adelphi* will get a concrete fortress-value, by slow building. Till now it has been a bit vague. Build a new place of skulls,[2] the skulls of the imbecile enemy. That's *very* necessary.

What made you put 'da' in Verga's name?[3] Alas, he is just Giovanni Verga: Let's hope nobody notices it.

I hope you got a copy of *Studies in Classic American Literature*. I think it will amuse you. Also *Kangaroo* and *Birds Beasts*. – I asked Seltzer to send you on an article I posted him, which the N[ew] Y[ork] *Nation* wanted – to send it you immediately it was typed – 'The Proper Study'.[4] I'm afraid I wrote it more with the *Adelphi* in mind than the *Nation*. – I begin to see the *Adelphi* building up like a little fortress. – That *Lady into Fox* stuff is pretty piffle – just playboy stuff.[5]

One has to be an absolute individual, separate as a seed fallen out of the pod. – Then a *volte face*, and a new start. Takes some risking. – This classiosity is bunkum, but still more, *cowardice*. Son todos acobardados.[6]

I think, this day week, I shall go down to Mexico. Perhaps I shall find a little ranch there. Put a new peg in the world, a new navel, a new centre. – Esperamos! We're hardly beginning yet.

America's awfully foolish and empty. But perhaps, if it went through a great convulsion, it would be the place.

Write care Seltzer. Wonder how Frieda likes London.

Saluti, DHL

---

[1] 'On Fear; and On Romanticism', *Adelphi*, i (September 1923), 269–77, in which Murry refers to Mr Mortimer, who wrote for the *New Statesman* and had described the *Adelphi* as 'the last stronghold of romanticism' (p. 273).   [2] Cf. Matthew xxvii. 33.

[3] In *Adelphi*, the authorship of 'St Joseph's Ass' was mistakenly attributed to Giovanni *da* Verga (see p. 480 n. 1).

[4] Murry printed the essay in *Adelphi*, i (December 1923), 584–90; it never appeared in the *Nation*. (See *Phoenix* 719–23.)

[5] In 'On Fear; and On Romanticism', Murry also referred to Mortimer's citation of the David Garnett novel, *Lady into Fox* (1923), being awarded the Hawthornden Prize, as proof that classicism was taking over literature (p. 272).   [6] 'They are all frightened.'

2918. To Thomas Seltzer, [22 September 1923]
Text: MS UT; Postmark, Los Angeles SEP 23 1923; Lacy, *Seltzer* 109–10.

Los Angeles.
Sat. 22 Sept.

Dear Thomas

Götzsche and I leave on Monday for Mexico: for Guaymas and Navojoa first. We are going down the West Coast, not as before. The railway only runs as far as Tepic.

F[rieda] doesn't seem to like England much. Here in California people live so much from the outside, it's almost fascinating. But a great bore. Drunk with trivial externalities: that is California.

I am getting a letter of credit from the Bank of California, so be *sure* and have money for me in the New York bank. Don't ever let me overdraw there, on your honour.

I wish I had more *respect* for the world and its people. One turns to the Lord Almighty and shuts ones eyes, people are such shells of emptiness.

I shall be glad to have news from you: how is your prosecution case?[1] I have been thinking of that. How is *Studies* doing, and *Kangaroo*, and when are *BirdsBeasts* and *Mastro-don* ready? Send me all news as soon as you can. – Say if you are buying or leasing Birkendale, if the well is still dry, if the lunatics got hydrophobia in the draught, if Schnitz is large, if still coy with Fritz. Adele's letter about the Crambseys[2] was so lugubrious! And the Hammerslaugh, how did he wind up? Like a twisted rat?

I wish very much I were at Birkindele with you and that dish-washing demon of an Adele this week-end, to see the sun go down and the moon over the Lassieless pasture, and say a few wise things and hear a few, after all this *senselessness* out here.

And yet there seems a *wee* bit of gruesomeness among those New Jersey hills. – I wonder what Adele is doing with her Robot.[3]

Sei mir gegrüsst   DHL

---

[1] The case against Seltzer for publishing offensive literature which had been dismissed on 12 September 1922 (see p. 292 n. 1) was revived by Judge John Ford of the New York State Supreme Court; Seltzer was indicted for publishing 'unclean' books on 18 July 1923. The jury exempted *Women in Love* from the case but found *A Young Girl's Diary* and *Casanova's Homecoming* objectionable. Seltzer was released on bail pending a new trial by jury. (See Lacy, *Seltzer* 189.)

[2] Unidentified.   [3] Unidentified.

2919. To Knud Merrild, [23 September 1923]
Text: MS UT; Merrild 329.

[Los Angeles]
Sunday night

Dear Merrild

We are staying till *Tuesday*, so will see you tomorrow, at Mrs Mott's probably.[1]

The railway – for Tuesday – is the Southern Pacific.

DHL

2920. To Margaret King, [24 September 1923]
Text: MS Needham; PC v. Ostrich with eggs; Postmark, [. . .]; Unpublished.

Los Angeles
24 Sept.

I am just going down into Mexico again – down the West Coast by rail. I think I would like to stay the winter down there. – I hope your Aunt F[rieda] had a nice visit and that everything goes well. I will send an address as soon as I get somewhere – I went to the ostrich farm here – many ostriches.

Love DHL

2921. To John Middleton Murry, 24 September 1923
Text: MS NYPL; Huxley 579.

Los Angeles.
24 Sept.1923

Dear Jack

I am setting off tomorrow with a Danish friend, down the West Coast of Mexico, to look again for a place to live. I hope I shall find it. If I do you must come – You will have seen Frieda quite often.[2] I'm afraid Europe won't make her any the happier. I expect she'll be setting off again for here, by the time you get this.

California is a queer place – in a way, it has turned its back on the world, and looks into the void Pacific. It is absolutely selfish, very empty, but not false, and at least, not full of false effort. I don't want to live here, but a stay here

---

[1] '"At Mrs Mott's"' meant a small lunch-room, a wooden shack on an empty lot, across the street, where we ate most of our meals. The Motts were a hard-working couple. She did the serving, he, Walter, Irish-Scotch, a World War veteran in the six-foot class, did the cooking. . . . They were nice people; Lawrence liked them' (Merrild 329–30). The postcards which (according to Merrild) DHL sent to the Motts from Mexico are missing; see also Letter 2931.

[2] Frieda Lawrence wrote to Adele Seltzer in September 1923 (Lacy, *Seltzer* 109): 'I go to Germany on the 28, Murry goes to Switzerland, we travel together via Paris.'

rather amuses me. It's sort of crazy-sensible. Just the moment: hardly as far ahead as *carpe diem*.

I'll send you an address as soon as I get one. I'm glad to be going south. America exhausts the springs of one's soul. – I suppose that's what it exists for. It lives to see all real spontaneity expire. – But anyhow it doesn't grind on an old nerve as Europe seems to.

Grüsse   DHL

2922. To Adele Seltzer, [24 September 1923]
Text: MS UT; PC v. Peacock; Postmark, Los Angeles SEP 24 1923; Lacy, *Seltzer* 110–11.

[Los Angeles]
Monday. 24 Sept.

Dear Adele
– I am setting off tomorrow with Götzsche down the west coast, by train, to Mexico again. I am glad to go. America drys up the natural springs of one's soul. But I've had quite a nice time here – people are very nice to me. – It's a very selfish place, Southern California, in a rather simple way. People care about *nothing* but just the moment. But also that can be pleasant. – I wonder very much if you have bought Birkindele, and if its well is dry. I knew it was getting low when I left. You must simply have had to *starve* the dishes, at washing-up time. – Götzsche is just posting the portrait of me. I like it. – And I posted Kath. Mansfield's last book.[1] I think it's a downright cheek to ask the public to buy that waste-paper basket. Also I posted in the parcel the first part of the *Boy in the Bush*[2] – the Western Australia novel. I think it's very amusing. Ask Thomas to have it typed out when there's time – I can understand better and better how *bored* you are by New York – even by a publishing business and books – even mine. I feel like that. Oh to get away from the world! Only to get away and be by oneself with the things that live. – I shall write at once from Mexico. I seem to hear little from anybody. Write in readiness.

DHL

2923. To Thomas Seltzer, [25 September 1923]
Text: MS UT; Postmark, [. . .] Cal. SEP 25[. . .]; Lacy, *Seltzer* 111.

Los Angeles.
25 Sept.

Dear Thomas
These are the two keys of the two trunks in your cellar. If Frieda comes she

---

[1] Murry brought out the volume, *The Dove's Nest and Other Stories* (June 1923), a posthumous collection of twenty-one stories fifteen of which were unfinished. See also Letter 2946.
[2] The first use by DHL of what proved to be the novel's title. He posted the first three notebooks of the autograph MS to Seltzer.

will want them: especially at a frontier. Perhaps best tie them on to one of the trunks.

Sorry to bother you.

DHL

2924. To Baroness Anna von Richthofen, [26 September 1923]
Text: MS UCLA; PC v. Mountains near Palm Springs; Postmark, Palm Springs SEP 27 [. . .]23; Unpublished.

Palm Springs
Mitwoch.

Ich bin schon wieder unterwegs. F[rieda] schreibt sie ist erkältet – hoffentlich geht es ihr wieder gut. Ich hatte deinen Brief – ach Schwiegermutter, mach du mich nicht traurig. Ich kann nicht um zu weinen kommen. Ich möchte dich sehen, aber lustig, – warten wir noch ein Weilchen. – Hier is Wüste, Hitze, Sonne, Cactus, und alles vergessen. Aber doch nicht ganz vergessen.

DHL

[I'm once again under way. F[rieda] writes she has a cold – hopefully she is all right again. I had your letter – oh Schwiegermutter, don't you make me sad. I can't come to weep. I would like to see you, but jolly, – let's wait a little while yet. – Here is desert, heat, sun, cactus, and all forgotten. But yet not quite forgotten.

DHL]

2925. To Bessie Freeman, [26 September 1923]
Text: MS UNYB; Postmark, Palm Springs SEP 27 1923; Nehls, ii. 260.

Palm Springs.
Wed 25 Sept[1]

Dear Bessie Freeman

Came here to see you, and you've not arrived yet. Too bad! I can't even lay hold of Mr Hicks. And the Inn is shut. Still, it's not bad here[2] – only rough. – I saw your house and Mrs Birge's. Your house has still a *great deal* to be done. It will be jolly out there when it's all ready. Götzsche and I walked up to the stream, and sat under a tree. Very peaceful after Los Angeles. – We are on our way to Mexico – down the West Coast. – I will let you know what we find. – I expect Frieda will be coming out soon – then I hope you will see her. – Her

---

[1] Wednesday was 26 September.
[2] DHL joins 'here' by a line to 'Hotel La Palma' written at the top of the page.

address: care Thomas Seltzer. Write to her. – Mr and Mrs Forsyth were awfully nice to me – I feel full of gratitude. – Oh also a man picked us up at Whitewater Station when we were stranded – no stage or anything – and brought us in. I think his name is MacMahon – Mac something – and he lives in the adobe house just beyond The Inn – towards your new house. If you recognise him from this description – and if you feel like it – thank him for me, will you. – Palm Springs is lovely and still and clear, after Los Angeles. But I have on me, now I am so near, the wanting to go to Mexico again. If I find a place, you must come and see us.

Remember me to Mrs Birge when she comes. I hope you left all well in Buffalo and Wanakah. – Tell Mary Wilkeson I met a Mrs Dr Burton from Carmel – She seemed a nice soul.[1] Also a girl who dances and a young husband who will write.

There is a wind, and it is lovely and cool here, for all the sun.

tanti saluti D. H. Lawrence

2926. To Knud Merrild, [26 September 1923]
Text: MS UT; PC v. [Desert view]; Postmark, Palm Springs SEP 27 1923; Merrild 330.

Palm Springs.

Wed

That was an absurd way to leave – but saying no goodbyes is supposed to mean meeting again soon. This is a pale whitish desert – a bit deathly. And no Bessie Freeman – but we saw her house. And after Los A[ngeles], I was very happy lying under a tree by a little stream all morning – no sound of trains in Grand Avenue. Hope Lizzie behaved.

Grüsse DHL

2927. To Witter Bynner, [5 October 1923]
Text: MS HU; Postmark, Navojoa 5 OCT 23; Huxley 581-2.

Navojoa. Sonora.

5 Oct.

Dear Bynner

Here I am wandering slowly and hotly with Götzsche down this west coast. Where F[rieda] is I don't know.

This west is much wilder, emptier, more hopeless than Chapala. It makes

---

[1] Jeanne Burton, née d'Orge, is one of only two 'local' persons who can be identified: she was the wife of Dr Alfred E. Burton, Dean of M. I. T. (Nehls, ii. 508). She had been one of the party which watched the eclipse on 12 September. For a reference to Mrs Birge see Luhan 118.

one feel the door is shut on one. There is a blazing sun, a vast hot sky, big lonely inhuman green hills and mountains, a flat blazing littoral with a few palms, sometimes a dark blue sea which is not quite of this earth – then little towns that seem to be slipping down an abyss – and the door of life shut on it all, only the sun burning, the clouds of birds passing, the zopilotes like flies, the lost lonely palm-trees, the deep dust of the roads, the donkeys moving in a gold-dust-cloud. In the mountains, lost, motionless silver-mines. Alamos a once lovely little town, lost, and slipping down the gulf in the mountains, forty miles up the awfullest road I've ever been bruised along. But somehow or other, you get there. And more wonderful, you get *out* again. – There seems a sentence of extinction written over it all. – In the middle of the little covered market at Alamos, between the meat and the vegetables, a dead dog lay stretched as if asleep. The meat vender said to the vegetable man: You'd better throw it out. The veg-man looked at the dead dog and saw no reason for throwing it out. So no doubt it still lies there. – We went also to haciendas – a cattle hacienda: wild, weird, brutal, with a devastating brutality: Many of the haciendas are in the hands of Chinese, who run about like vermin down this coast.

So there we are. I think, when we get to Mazatlan, we shall take the boat down to Manzanillo, and so to Guadalajara. It is better there. At least there is not a dead dog in mid-market.

Write me a line care Dr Purnell. – I am a bad correspondent.

Write to F. care Seltzer. She may be in America again by now.

There is a circus, and lions roaring all night.

This town is a busy new adobe nowhere under a flat sun of brass. The old town was washed out in 1915.

I have letters of introduction to people this way, and so see what it's like.

Greet the Spoodle. Tell him to send me a line. Don't take any notice of my intermittency.

D. H. Lawrence

2928. To Knud Merrild, [5 October 1923]
Text: MS UT; Postmark, [. . .]; Huxley 580–1.

Navojoa.
Friday 5th Oct

Dear Merrild

Well here we are, still grilling in the sun of Navojoa. We came down yesterday from Minas Nuevas, over a road *much* worse than any Del Monte roads, and forty miles of it. I am bruised wherever I look. – A circus follows us down the coast, and the lions roar all night. The turkeys put their heads through the door – the doors are just wooden gates – and gobble in the bedroom at dawn. The people in the street linger to look in and see how you're sleeping; The horse-riding lady from the circus has the next room, and stalks about with yards of bushy hair sticking out, rather fat inside a violent dressing gown. The hotel, being a hollow square, is as public as the street. – But we are going on today to Mazatlan, the port. On the whole, the west coast is a little *too* wild – nothing but wildness, as Götzsche says. One wants a bit of hopefulness. These wild lost places seem so hopeless. – But a man said he'd *give* me six or eight acres of land near Guaymas, near the sea, in a very wild, very strange and beautiful country, if I'd only build a house on the place. Queer country, with clouds of wild duck, and geese, and queer flocks of pelicans. But one feels so out of the world: like living on Mars. As if the human race wasn't real. – I don't know what effect it would have on one in the end. – G. is getting very red in the face with this fierce sun. He looks at these broken, lost, hopeless little towns in silent disgust. He speaks not one word of Spanish, and is altogether an onlooker.

I think from Mazatlan we shall take the steamer down to Manzanillo, and from Manzanillo go to Guadalajara. I wish you would forward the letters there:

c/o Dr G. Purnell, Galeana #150, *Guadalajara.* Jalisco, Mexico.

We may be there in a week's time.

At Minas Nuevas we did nothing but drink beer and whiskey cocktails. Los Angeles seems in another life-time. I feel as if I should wander over the brink of existence.

Remember me to the Böterns[1] and send their address and I will write them a letter and return *Mogens*.[2] Also greetings to Mrs Mott and Mr Mott: I hope they are flourishing. Write to Guad.

DHL

If you see Johnson tell him I will write him. I ordered a book for him and Mrs Johnson[3] – hope they came.

Tell the Bee I hope she's busy laying up honey of wisdom.[4]

DHL

[1] J. Winchell Böttern, a Danish painter, and his wife Anna (née Grabow), were friends of Merrild and Götzsche in Los Angeles (Merrild 304).

[2] An asterisk was added to this word and the following marginal note in another hand: 'is a book by the Danish author J. P. Jakobsen, – translated by Mrs Böttern'. The book was *Mogens, and Other Stories*, by Jens Peter Jacobsen (1847–85), trans. Anna Grabow (New York, 1921).

[3] See p. 481 n. 2.

[4] Olivia Johnson's younger sister, Beatrice Rolfe, was affectionately known as 'the Bee' (Merrild 309). She received a postcard from DHL, c. 6 October 1923 (see Letters 2931 and 2952); it has not survived (letter to David Farmer, 18 January 1977).

P. S. – Once we are in Guadalajara, then the best way for F[rieda] to come will be by sea to Vera Cruz from N. York, or straight down by Laredo. This railway has 100 mile gap near Tepic – of which you must ride 9 hrs on horse. Otherwise you take the steamer for a day, and get round that way. The best way down from *Los Angeles*, once we are south of Tepic, is to take the steamer direct to Manzanillo, then it's only about eight hours on the train to Guadalajara.

When I look at the ranches, I doubt very much whether I shall ever try to live on one for ever and a day. But very nice to stay the winter.

We went to a big wild cattle hacienda – they are strange, desolate, brutal places: beautiful enough, but weird and brutal. I doubt if one could bear it: or if one *wants* to bear it.

I shall be glad to get some news. You write to Frieda,care Thomas Seltzer. 5 W. 50th St. – I dont know where she is. And send me the letters.

Hope things are going well with you.

DHL

2929. Dr George Purnell, [5 October 1923]
Text: MS UT; Unpublished.

Navojoa, Son.
5 October.

Dear Dr Purnell

Well, Götzsche and I gradually work our way south. We've been into the mountains seeing people. This is a wild, weird, uncanny region, this west coast. It somehow chills my blood, in spite of the fiercely hot sun.

I'm going to take the train down to Mazatlan this afternoon. Have had enough of this for the moment. We shall stay a few days in Mazatlan, then either go on to Tepic, or straight by boat to Manzanillo. In the latter case you will see us in Guadalajara in about a week's time. I like Guad. and Chapala much better than here: so much more human and livable.

I've taken the liberty of having my letters forwarded to Galeana #150. I know you won't mind. Keep them for me, will you.

But I *must* find a place for the winter. I'd rather be out of Chapala, on the lake. Think of something for me if you can.

I think I shall stay at the Garcia hotel, if Scott is there.

Tell Idella we will talk *Palms* and everything when I come.[1]

I don't know precisely where Frieda is: perhaps back in America by now. I expect she'll join me as soon as I can get word to her.

[1] See p. 435 n. 2.

I look forward to seeing you again, you and Idella. And to Guadalajara and Chapala – they seem so friendly.

Mr Götzsche is a Danish painter a bit younger than I am – probably he'll stay the winter with us.

Best of wishes to you both.

D. H. Lawrence

2930. To Margaret King, [6 October 1923]
Text: MS Needham; Unpublished.

Hotel de France. Mazatlan.
6 October

Dear Peg,

This is the Pacific Coast, and terribly hot; we are sailing tomorrow – D. V. – for Manzanillo, and so to Guadalajara. Write me a line care Dr G. Purnell, Galeana #150. *Guadalajara*. Jalisco: or perhaps better care Thomas Seltzer. – The little bird is the last remains of the wonderful Aztec feather-work.[1] I hope it isn't all rubbed off by the time you get it. – There is no railway from here to the south: one must go by sea. This west coast feels very far from everywhere, too far, too much out of connection. I must come back a bit. – I shall have no letters till I get to Guadalajara. Hope you are all well and gay.

DHL

2931. To Knud Merrild, [6 October 1923]
Text: MS UT; Postmark, Mazatlan 7 OCT 23; Merrild 335.

Mazatlan.
6 Oct.

Dear Merrild –

Götzsche says you won't want one of these birds – but why not? Though it's a swallow with no message. – Give the cards to their owners will you: Mrs Bötern, Mrs Mott, and Miss Rolf. I will write a proper letter to Harry Johnson, from Guadalajara. – Send me the letters there. We shall be more in the world: this is too much outside: like being shut out of the back door. And so hot!! – But it's rather like one of your beloved Pacific Islands, the view of the bay with all its cocoa-nut palms. – If we have luck, we shall be in Guadalajara by next Thursday – this is Sunday: a day and two nights at sea. – Wonder if you're bathing with the Böterns today.

DHL

Götzsche says the birds are too sweet: but candy must be sweet: we can't always suck lemons.

---

[1] This letter is written on a note card decorated with a figure of a bird made with feathers by the Mexican natives. (DHL sent several such cards: see the letter following, Letter 2952 and Merrild 335.)

2932. To Olivia Rolfe Johnson, [6 October 1923]
Text: Letter from Olivia Rolfe Johnson to David Farmer, 16 February 1977; Unpublished.

[Hotel de France, Mazatlan, Mexico]
[6 October 1923]

['A delightful letter thanking us [Harry and Olivia Johnson] for his stay of two weeks and ending:'] I hope that we may meet again, it were a pity else.

2933. To Adele Seltzer, [9 October 1923]
Text: MS Pepper; Postmark, Mazatlan 10 OCT 23; Lacy, *Seltzer* 113–14.

Hotel de France. Mazatlan
9 Oct.

Dear Adele

Do a little thing for me – have a couple of books (not mine) sent to
Mrs Arnos J. Jaeger. Minas Nuevas, *Alamos*. Sonora. Mex.

She and her husband were awfully nice to us.[1] She is about 35, large, 4 children, likes 'humour', has a husband always running round busy all over the country, and her nearest neighbor is 45 miles over a road that is agony. So choose her something suitable: and put with my compliments. I really like the husband better, but he'll be much more flattered if she gets books. Send her something 'cheery.'

Poor Adele!

Can you imagine how the sun blazes here! That whole vast Pacific blazes back a light that is almost unearthly and quite inhuman.

There are nice Germans here[2] – and a very nice ranch we might winter on. Still might. Only the heat at this sea-level.

Tepic is 3000 ft up. – Poor Götzsche sweats like Niobe.[3] I am visibly thinner.

There is no railway on from Tepic, so we shall have to go by stage and a day on mules, across the barranca, if we are to get to Guadalajara.

There is a certain fascination also about this place. It's very like the South Sea Isles in quality: as remote and soft and sensuous also, with an awful naked sea-front with rocks with flying staircases and half-built houses and delapidation. – No money here. – And Cocoa-nut palms like snakes on end. But good cocos to drink. And a queer bay with tropical huts and natives very

---

[1] Probably the Swiss couple whose silver mine DHL and Götzsche visited for two days on their way south from Guaymas (Merrild 334, 336).
[2] Walther Melcher and Federico Unger (see Letter 2943).
[3] In Greek myth Niobe, inconsolable for the death of her children, continued to weep even though turned to stone after her own death. (For Götzsche's description of his condition, see Merrild 337.)

like islanders, soft, dark, some almost black, and handsome. That Pacific blue-black in the eyes and hair, fathomless, timeless. They don't know the meaning of time. – And they *can't* care. All the walls and nooks of our time-enclosure are down for them. Their eternity is so vast, they can't care at all. Their blue-black eyes.

I have learnt something from them. The vastness of Pacific time, unhistoried, undivided.

Cockroaches running on the floor full speed.

I think Frieda would like her countryman Melcher here.

Adios   DHL

2934. To Dr George Purnell, 10 October 1923
Text: MS UT; Unpublished.

Hotel Brandes. *Tepic*. Nayarit
10 October 1923

Dear Doctor Purnell

You see how far we've got – coming over the hills instead of by sea. I expect we shall leave here on Sunday and stage as far as Ixtlan: go forward on Monday on mules to Quemada: and arrive Guadalajara on Tuesday by the train from Quemada. That is of course if there are no floods of rain or anything untoward. – I look forward to seeing you and Idella again, and the friendly Guadalajara. Tell Mr Scott if you see him that if he is still at the Garcia we hope to stay with him. – I wonder what Chapala will be like with no Arzapalo Hotel and the President in residence.[1] Don't fancy it much that way. Perhaps you may have heard of a place for me. – Of course I have no news from anybody while I am travelling but I hope to find letters at your office. I hope you don't mind my having given your address. If I had been sure Scott was at the Garcia, I would have used that. But I'll see you are not inflicted long.

Then au revoir. I hope to find you all well and flourishing.

Yours Sincerely   D. H. Lawrence

2935. To Margaret King, [13 October 1923]
Text: MS Needham; PC v. [Plaza and Cathedral in Tepic]; Postmark, Tep[ic] 13 OCT 23; Unpublished.

Tepic. Nayarit.
13 Oct

I am going on tomorrow to Guadalajara – a day by motor over the mountains, a day by horse-back, and then we get the railway again. This is beautiful

[1] Álvaro Obregón: see p. 465 n. 1.

mountainous country, and very wild. – I have had no letters since leaving Los Angeles – hope to find mail in Guadalajara. We shall have been three weeks without hearing from anybody.

Love   DHL

2936. To Knud Merrild, [13 October 1923]
Text: MS UT; PC v. [Plaza and Cathedral in Tepic]; Postmark, Tepic [. . .] 23; Merrild 336.

Tepic. Nayarit
Sat. 13 October.

We set off in the morning in a Lizzie over the mountains for Ixtlan: on Monday horseback all day, to pick up the other end of the railway. We should be in Guadalajara on Tuesday, and I hope to find letters. It is cooler here – 3000 ft up – but still quite hot enough. G[ötzsche] wants to paint, but hasn't got any paper, and of course can't buy any. Remember us to everybody.

DHL

2937. To Earl Brewster, 17 October 1923
Text: MS UT; Brewster 73–4.

Hotel Garcia. *Guadalajara.* (Jalisco), Mexico
17 Oct 1923

Dear Earl

I got your letter and Achsah's – yours from the sea, Achsah's from Quai Voltaire[1] – today when we came down from the mountains to here – We came two days on horseback to here, and my knees are stiff.

I was glad to get your letter. I think it is as you say: the cycles are slowly revolving which will bring us together again, it may be before long. It is always my steady desire, that a few people of us who take life from the same source, should live in contact and spin new threads. Who knows – it might be quite soon. Let us watch for the day.

Frieda is in England (or Germany). She writes that England is best after all, and wants me to come back. But Mexico now is so beautiful, so blue with pure sunshine and enough coolness to make one feel strong, I am afraid of the old sky of Europe. – I *don't* care for the U.S.A. – I don't care for Mexico all down the West Coast, till you pass Tepic and the barranca: and then it has a definite fascination for me. It seems to me as if the gods were here. – I should like to stay the winter. And then in the spring, if so be I must come to Europe, Europe let it be. Else perhaps you might like to come here. It is 5000 ft. up, so the

---
[1] I.e. from Paris.

nights are never hot, even in summer. And there is a great beauty. – Yes, I should be happy if I could have a little ranch, and you and Achsah and the child a house two fields away, and perhaps other friends that one could ride over to, on horse-back, not far. I wish that would come true.

And I'm sure you're right, one must have negation as a base. Then a new thing.

Tell Achsah, I think Frieda feels about Europe as she does: except of course for the loving relations, F's being cis–Alpine and not trans. But I'll hang on here a bit longer, see if I can't make a little start.

Perhaps New York was a bit soon, to meet. And it gave me a revulsion, made me want to go to the uttermost ends of the earth. Now I feel better. Let us hope for the near future.

DHL

2938. To Catherine Carswell, 17 October 1923
Text: MS YU; Postmark, Guad[alajara] 18[. . .]; Carswell 189, 191.

> Hotel Garcia. (thinking of Holly Bush House)[1] *Guadalajara.*
> Jal. Mexico.
> 17 Oct. 1923

Dear Catherine

I had your note and am glad you liked *Kangaroo.* – I always order you a copy of all my books from Secker. If you don't get all, it's his fault.

Frieda says she likes England now, and it is my place, and I must come back. I wonder. We rode two days down the mountains, and got to Eztatlan. Mexico has a certain mystery of beauty for me, as if the gods were here. Now, in this October, the days are so pure and lovely, like an enchantment, as if some dark-faced gods were still young. I wish it could be that I *could* start a little centre – a ranch – where we could have our little adobe houses and make a life, and you could come with Don and John Patrick. It is always what I work for. But it must come from the inside, not from the will. And when it will be it will be, I suppose. It is queer, all the way down the Pacific Coast, I kept thinking: Best go back to England. – And then, once across the barranca from Ixtlan, it was here again, where the gods may sometimes be awful, but they are young, here in Mexico, in Jalisco, that I wanted to be. And there is room – room for all of us, if it could but be.

But let us watch. Things, when they come, come suddenly. – It may be my destiny is in Europe. Quien Sabe! If it is, I'll come back.

Hasta el dia![2]

DHL

[1] Cf. Letter 2897.   [2] 'Until the day!'

2939. To Mabel Dodge Luhan, 17 October 1923
Text: MS Brill; Luhan 118–19.

Hotel Garcia. *Guadalajara*. Jal.

17 October 1923

Dear Mabel

I got your letter here today – when I arrived from Tepic. – Yes, I was pretty angry. But now let us forget it. At least I will forget, forget the bad part. Because also I have some beautiful memories of Taos. That, perhaps, is what makes the sting burn longer. – As for reviling you, when I am angry I say what I feel. I hope you do the same. When John Evans went round saying: 'Mother had to ask the Lawrences to get out', then I felt there was nothing to do but to throw the knife back. But now enough. If it's *got* to be a battle of wills, I'll fight the devil himself, as long as the necessity lasts. But it's not my idea of life.

There, there's an end to the enmity, anyhow.

Frieda is in England, and wants me to go over there. But I don't want to, she'd better come here.

You have striven so hard, and so long, to *compel* life. Can't you now slowly change, and let life *slowly* drift into you. Surely it is even a greater mystery and preoccupation even than willing, to let the invisible life steal into you and slowly possess you. Not people, or things, or action, or even consciousness: but the slow invasion of you by the vast invisible god that lives in the ether. Once you know that, you will never feel 'out of work', as you say. And its only a change of direction. Instead of projecting your will into the ether of the invisible God, let the invisible God interpenetrate into you. – After all, it's not a mere question of washing dishes. It's the soul's own mystery. And one can make a great great change in all one's flow of life and living, from the power of output to the mystery of intake, without changing one's house or one's husband. 'Then shall thy peace be as a river.'[1] – And when it comes, like a river, then you won't feel out of work, or unliving.

People tell me you are divorcing Tony, and there is another young man, and so on. Probably it is not true. I hope it's not. I don't think it is.[2] Tony always has my respect and affection. And when I say in my book: 'one cannot go back'[3] – it is true, one cannot. But your marriage with Tony may even yet be the rounding of a great curve; since certainly he doesn't merely draw you back, but himself advances perhaps more than you advance, in the essential 'onwards.'

Yrs   D. H. Lawrence

[1] Isaiah xlviii. 18 ['Then had thy peace been as a river'].   [2] The rumour was untrue.
[3] In 'Herman Melville's "Typee" and "Omoo"', *Studies in Classic American Literature* (Seltzer, 1923), p. 201.

We rode over the mountains from Tepic and down the barranca and to Etzatlan, and I thought very much of how you and Tony taught F. and me to ride on Granfer and my little Zegua. For that and many things like that, believe me, I am grateful.

DHL

2940. To Willard Johnson, [18 October 1923]
Text: MS YU; Moore 758–9.

Hotel Garcia. Guadalajara
18 Oct.

Dear Spoodle

We got here yesterday, a bit weary, after that trip from Tepic. Rode all day on mules over the mts to La Quemada, Monday, and got there at night, to find railway washed out, no more trains, road also under water. Rose at 5.0 next day, once more muled it for six painful hours to Etzatlan, where, thank goodness, yesterday came a train. My thighs still feel stiff and heavy, but I liked it really. – The country is very lovely, full of flowers, flocks of birds, blue sky, a sort of spring-autumn. – Had supper at club with Dr P[urnell] and Id[ella]: the latter having bobbed her hair very short, looks little. Otherwise all same: club just the same: Dr Walker, the big dentist, the little Chink, flied chicken yessir – idem. Idella bemoaning your absence: quite cold about my coming, because I'm not you. – Glad I'm not, in that respect. Frieda seems to be loving England – wants me to go back – says my place is there – etc etc. I don't know. Now I'm here I feel like staying the winter at least. The country is quite lovely in the autumn. – I dont care much for the hotel. It's depressing. Don't suppose I shall stay long. Götzsche just came in to say he had to sit in a chair, the bed-bugs were so fierce. Scott is a Jonah. Had a letter from Mabel – a flag of peace. Bueno, que sea paz. Let it be peace. It may be she is another woman. Quien Sabe? as you so sagely remark. – I asked Seltzer to send you both *Kangaroo*. But he's a bit arbitrary, and sends if he thinks fit. – If the spirit condescends to move me, I'll do you a sketch. At present most of my consciousness is in my legs, and the rest, I suppose, is still in the mule saddle. – But I'd like to go on a ranch somewhere here for the winter. More mulc. – As for 'Quet[zalcoatl]', he'll have to wait for the same spirit. – Are you jealous of Clarence's curls,[1] of his comings-on, or only of his tabernacle in Mabel's alfalfa field? – Spoodle, querido, you must have several souls: one for Idella, par example, y otra para la pobre Margarita[2] – and who knows how many

---

[1] Clarence Thompson was a protégé of Mabel Luhan (see Luhan 115 ff.).

[2] 'Spoodle, dear chap . . . for example, and another for poor Margaret' (possibly Margaret Scott, Winfield Scott's daughter).

more, for how many more señorititas? I shall call you Spoodle Almadisimo, the most be-souled. – If you really want to go to N. York, ask Seltzer flat out if he can give you a bit of work. Ask him gently, and tell him you don't want *much* money.

Hasta otra vez.[1]   DHL

2941. To Thomas Seltzer, 18 October 1923
Text: MS UT; Postmark, Guad[alajara] 18 OCT 23; Lacy, *Seltzer* 114–15.

Hotel Garcia. *Guadalajara*. Jal.

18 Oct. 1923

Dear Thomas.

We got here yesterday – very lovely the towers of Guadalajara under the October sky. It was quite a trip from Tepic. We rode mule back from Ixtlan over the mountains and down the barranca to La Quemada: a beautiful ride over a very rocky road. Nine hours in the saddle. Got to la Quemada, the other end of the S. Pacific Ry, to find no train, a land-slide, the line slipped away. La Quemada a sort of railway-camp, for the new construction. A lot of ill-bred hounds who think they are engineers:[2] louts and canaille. The S. Pacific is American, and a hateful concern. I was glad to get off it. It trails a sort of blight all down the west coast. Really, Americanism is a disease or a vice or both. – We slept in a shed and rose at dawn, got more mules, and rode for six hours across to Etzatlan, the town on the Mex. National Railway. This upland country in Mexico has a certain splendid beauty, I like it very much. And I like so much the real Mexico again, where the Americans haven't canned all the life. At the depths of me, Thomas Tomasito, I hate the Americans. There is still some strange raw splendour in Mexico. And it is green and full of flowers now, yellow and pink.

I found various mail from you forwarded from Los Angeles. Macy is a dead fish, bientôt il sera pourri. Pour les autres, ils sont des poissons demi-morti.[3] It's no good, that world has got to perish. But we have got to put something through before it perishes. And we are doing it. It's a fight all the way. Tant mieux. Miserable Midianites, one has to bite slowly through their heart-strings.[4]

You say you put $500 to my account in the Metropolitan bank: I suppose you mean the National Chase. I must settle with Mountsier.

---

[1] 'Until next time.'   [2] engineers] mining
[3] 'very soon he will be rotten. As for the others, they are half-dead fish.' For Macy see p. 477 n. 2; see also Letter 2943.
[4] A nomadic people on whom Moses carried out divine vengeance (Numbers xxxi) and who were later defeated by Gideon (Judges vi–viii).

I have letters from Frieda, saying England is best after all, and wanting me to come back. But now I am here I would rather stay the winter, anyhow. I must finish 'Quetzalcoatl'. By the way, I want you to read that MS. and tell me just what you think. Because I must go all over it again, and am open to suggestions. This winter I must finish it. (Dear Adele, in parenthesis, I should like your opinion of 'Quetzalcoatl', if the sight of a MS. is not too nauseating to you.) I expect you got the MS. also of *The Boy in the Bush*. I want you to tell me about that. I think it would be best to publish it *before* 'Quetzalcoatl', and we must decide whether it is to be under my name and Miss Skinner's, or a nom de plume, or what. I think I shall go ahead with that, the *Boy*, to finish it before I try 'Quetzalcoatl' again, because this is much more important to me, my 'Quetzalcoatl'. *The Boy* might be popular – unless the ending is a bit startling – I sometimes feel that, when these two books are off my hands, I shall give up writing for a time – perhaps a few years. I get so tired of the continual feeling of canaillerie one gets from the public and from people. Toujours canaille. – As Adele says, let people cease to exist for one. They easily can – especially here. Meanwhile, adelante! Quasi consummatum est, Domine![1]

Adios   DHL

2942. To William Siebenhaar, 18 October 1923
Text: TMSC NWU; PC; Unpublished.

Guadalajara,
18 Oct. 1923.

I had your letter when I arrived here – very much amused by your bickerings with the professor.[2] My wife went to England from New York – and I didn't want to go. So I crossed to Los Angeles, stayed there a while, and came down the west coast, part of the way on mule-back. Aimard or not,[3] it is still very romantic. The p.c. is quite typical of this city – the second city in Mexico, Pearl of the West. I came back because I want to finish a Mexican novel I was doing in the spring. My wife urges me to go to Europe, but I hope instead she'll come here, at least for the winter. The Italian translation is out, and being very well reviewed.[4] I hope it goes well. It will then make way for Multatuli. I ordered a copy of *Kangaroo* for you – hope you got it. I have Miss

---

[1] 'forward! It's more or less finished, O Lord!'
[2] Most likely Walter Murdoch (1874–1970), foundation professor of English at the University of Western Australia, 1913–39; essayist and literary critic.
[3] Gustave Aimard. (See p. 449 n. 1.)
[4] *Mastro-don Gesualdo* had been published by Seltzer on 13 October 1923 (Roberts A28).

Skinner's MS. – putting in some work on it. It should make a very interesting book. Yes, I have the essay on *Havelaar* safely kept.[1] Pity Mrs. Siebenhaar can't meet my wife in England.

Best wishes   D. H. Lawrence

2943. To Thomas Seltzer, [20?–2 October 1923]
Text: MS UT; Postmark, Servicio 22 OCT [. . .]; Lacy, *Seltzer* 115–17.

Guadalajara. Jal. Mexico.
[20? October 1923]

Dear Thomas

Your letter with Macy's review of *Studies*[2] and with the review of *Mastro-don* came last night. These people have *no* guts. – I wrote Macy a little letter. Wish you saw it. It tickled me.

I send you the Cooper letter. These people are nothing but sieves for gnats. I shan't answer Cooper.[3]

I'll see if I can write a few little sketches for *Vanity Fair*. Don't worry about the price. – Do you know, I'd much rather be printed in *Vanity Fair* than in these old high-brow weak-gutted *Nations*.

I am dying to see *Mastro-don* and the *Poems*. But at the moment I don't mind if America doesn't like me, because I feel a great disgust for America. – Send me just *one* copy of each, by book post, care Dr Purnell. But don't send MS. yet.

Mabel Sterne (Mabel Lujan – or Luhan)[4] wrote that when she had heard how I reviled her, she was very angry: till at last it dawned on her that I was right, that her way of *will* was wrong. So she had given it up. But it left her feeling rather out of work.

Now I call that sporting. So of course I have also buried the hatchet. And am watching for the leopard to change her[5] spots.

F[rieda] seems to want me to go back. I might be driven to make a visit, if I could fix myself up a bit of a place here before I left. – I like being in Mexico. It gives one a certain strength and a power of mockery of all the Macyerie. – But I wouldn't mind going with you to England, for a visit – if I could fix up here. I'd like to travel with you over.

I wish you would send a copy of *Sea and Sardinia* to
Señor Don Walther Melcher. Casa Melcher, *Mazatlan*. Sinaloa. Mexico.

---

[1] See p. 240 n. 2.
[2] See p. 477 n. 2. (DHL's letter to Macy has not been found.)   [3] Unidentified.
[4] The spelling of the name was officially changed to Luhan, although at this time DHL may simply not have remembered which was correct.   [5] her] his

Also a copy of *Kangaroo* and a copy of *The Captains Doll* to
Señor Don Federico Unger, Casa Melcher – same address.
They are both Germans and very nice to me in Mazatlan.

Adele won't really be sorry to be in New York, when winter comes: and that
will be best for you both. By this time next year, she ought to be able to afford
herself a house with Schnitzes and even Robots if she wants 'em: and Lassies
that don't cough and are not aged in years, and rooms uncontaminated by
Hammerslachts.[1] Tout vient.

Did you get the Götzsche portrait of me? And did you like it?

Have you got the *Boy in the Bush* MS., with the book for Adele? Let me
know. – I mean the first half sent from Los Angeles.

I feel I want to go into the country soon.

DHL

Monday 22nd Oct

Dear Thomas

I have had no mail except the one letter from you and the one forwarded
from Curtis Brown – and the *Adelphi*. – Nothing from Frieda, so dont know
where she is. I went to Chapala for the day yesterday – the lake *so* beautiful.
And yet the lake I knew was gone – something gone, and it was alien to me. I
think I shall go to Europe soon – dont be surprised if you get a telegram saying
I am leaving. I might go direct – or might come to New York. I'll let you know.
Anyhow see you in England. If I don't come to New York you could bring the
trunks. Would you?

Tell F. if you have her address.

DHL

2944. To S. S. Koteliansky, 22 October 1923
Text: MS BL; Postmark, Servicio 22[. . .]; cited in Gransden 29.

Hotel Garcia. *Guadalajara*. Jalisco
22 October 1923

My dear Kot

There, now I've tried Mexico again. I was at Chapala for a day yesterday.
The lake lovelier than before – very lovely: but somehow gone alien to me.
And a sense of suspense, of waiting for something to happen – which
something I want to avoid.

I really think I shall come back to England now: in about a fortnight's time,
when I have arranged money and ships. I feel it is time I saw you all again: time

---

[1] I.e. Hammerslaughs.

to talk with you and Murry again, even if one only talks and goes away again. And I think I would stay in England – not go to Sicily for the winter.

It's some time since I got a letter from Frieda – my travelling. But wherever she is, let her know, will you – or Ill write her a note.

DHL

2945. To Baroness Anna von Richthofen, [22 October 1923]
Text: MS (Photocopy) UT; PC; Postmark, [. . .]; Unpublished.

Guadalajara.
22 Oct.

I was at Chapala yesterday – It felt strange to me, not the same place. – I think it really is time for me to come back to Europe. So I will get a ship and come in about a fortnight's time. I haven't heard lately from Frieda, but hope she won't start west.

DHL

2946. To John Middleton Murry, 25 October 1923
Text: MS NYPL; cited in Murry, *New Adelphi* 417.

Hotel Garcia. Guadalajara. Jal.
25 Oct. 1923

Dear Jack

I had your letter from Switzerland yesterday. From Frieda not a word – suppose Germany swallowed her.[1]

Yes, I think I shall come back now. I think I shall be back by the beginning of December. Work a while with you on the *Adelphi*. Then perhaps we'll set off to India – Quien sabe!

Anyhow, though England may lead the world again, as you say, she's got to find a way first. She's got to pick up a lost trail. And the end of the lost trail is here in Mexico. Aqui està. Yo lo digo.[2]

The Englishman, per se, is not enough. He has to modify himself to a distant end. He has to balance with something that is not himself. Con esto que aqui està.[3] But I will come back – I won't say home, it isn't home – for a time. When a rope is broken, it's no use tying a knot in one end. You have to tie both ends together. England is only one end of the broken rope. Hay otro. There's another. There's another end to the outreach. – One hand in space is not enough. It needs the other hand from the opposite end of space, to clasp and form the Bridge. The dark hand and the white.

[1] See p. 502 n. 2.   [2] 'It is here. I say it.'   [3] 'With this which is here.'

Pero todavia no. No alcanzan. Todavia no alcanzan. No tocan. Si debe esperar.[1]
'Learn to labour and to wait.'[2]
Muy bien. Vengo, y espero.
Vengo y espero.[3]

DHL

I got *Dove's Nest* here. Thank you very much. Poor Katharine, she is delicate and touching. – But not *Great*! Why say great?

2947. To Robert Mountsier, 25 October 1923

Text: MS Smith; Postmark, Guadalajara 25 OCT 23; Unpublished.

Hotel Garcia. Guadalajara (Jalisco)

25 October 1923

Dear M[ountsier]

I heard you were leaving Taos, so write to New York. Here am I in Guadalajara: came down the west coast, which is an out-of-the-world, forlorn, but quite beautiful trip, very hot. Frieda is in England – that is, if she's back there from Germany. She seems to have taken a great fancy to England, and wants to stay there. Doesn't want to come back to America or Mexico. – I really like Mexico. – But everybody urges me so hard to come home to England, that, since F. won't come here, I shall probably have to go quite soon now, even if I only stay a short while. Seltzer talks of going to London in November. But I think I shall sail straight from Vera Cruz to France. Am not sure. The statement you remember, was $4037.58, so I enclose cheque for $404. I suppose Seltzer has put at least $1000 of it to my credit. He wanted me to have a New York account, in the National Chase bank, as that was easier. But when I can get more money from him, I shall keep some in the Charleroi bank too. I believe I've only about $500 there now.

I had a friendly sort of bury-the-hatchet letter from Mabel: so buried it in a return letter.

I feel unsettled at the thought of going to England, instead of staying here. I was doing over Miss Skinner's West Australian MS. – quite interesting. Did you do your Taos book?[4] I hope Seltzer sends you copies of all 'works'. – I made the *BirdsBeasts* jacket, is it nice? Haven't seen it. – Where are you going next? – Write Care Seltzer, I may be gone – and I may not.

Yrs.   DHL

---

[1] 'But not yet. They do not reach. Not yet do they reach. They do not touch. One must wait.'
[2] Longfellow, 'A Psalm of Life' (1838), l. 36.
[3] 'Very well I come, and I wait. I come and I wait.'
[4] No book on Taos was published by Mountsier.

2948. To Adele Seltzer, 28 October 1923
Text: MS UT; Postmark, [. . .]; Lacy, *Seltzer* 117–18.

Hotel Garcia. Guadalajara. Jal.

28 Oct 1923

Dear Adele

I got your Symposium of Fritz Schnitz Thomas and Lawrence: and neither you nor Aline[1] able to tell t'other from which. Perhaps by now you have extricated me from the whirl of fluff etc in which Schnitz coruscates, and you can be a sensible woman once more. Anyhow I'm going to treat you as such.

Are you *really* cross about leaving Birkindele? Don't be. There was a bit of a shadow over it somewhere, and that shadow would have sunk in. I believe you have had the best out of Birkindele. Leave it now, to its owner and coffin and the Robot, and its own *rather* evil daimon. Labour and wait. You'll have a better place in the country than Birkindele, before long. Something more cheerful.

I am still here. Frieda writes she will not come back. 'The lady loves her will.' Muy bien, que la tenga.[2] Let her have it. – I suppose I shall go back to England. They all press me so hard. But I shan't hurry. There *is* something good about Mexico, something that opens again, at least in part, the flood-gates of ones soul. The U S A and the world shut the flood-gates of my soul tight. And here they begin to open, and the life flows, even if it flows in oneself alone. – But there is a sort of *basic* childishness about these people, that for me is the only manliness. When I say childishness, I only mean they don't superimpose ideas and ideals, but follow the stream of the blood. A certain innocence, even if sometimes evil. And a certain child-like patience and stoicism. – I like it really, our tough, dry, papier-mâché world recedes. – It's queer that F. hates it. – Sometimes I am driven to hating the white-white world, with its whiteness like a leprosy.

I suppose I shall go back some time in December, to see Murry and work on the *Adelphi* a bit. I think the *Adelphi* improves. I think I may put some of myself into it, for 1924, and see if anything results. F. declares England is still best. Murry declares England will again lead the world. But I myself know that England alone cannot. She must be juxtaposed with something that is in the dark volcanic blood of these people. One thing alone won't work: nor one spirit alone. It needs a polarity of two.

Send me a line care Dr G. Purnell. Galeana 150. Guadalajara.

Tell me: 1. Did you get Götzsche's painting of me – did you like it? (He loves this place, wants to paint it all.)

---

[1] Close friend of Adele Seltzer (see Lacy, *Seltzer* 232–3).   [2] 'Very well, let her have it.'

2. Did you read 'Quetzalcoatl'? Tell me what you think.

hasta otra vez   DHL

2949. To Thomas Seltzer, [28 October 1923]
Text: MS UT; Lacy, *Seltzer* 119.

care Dr G. Purnell. Galeana #150, Guadalajara, Jal
28 Oct

Dear Thomas

This is just a note. I think I shall stay on till mid-December here. Send me mail, and a copy of *BirdsBeasts* and *Mastro-don* each to above. Tell me:

1. Did you get Götzsche's portrait of me – did you like it?
2. Is 'Quetzalcoatl' typed? What you think of it. (But don't send it till I ask for it.)
3. Have you got *The Boy in the Bush* MS. If the office is busy, have it typed by a hired typist. I will pay it. Very soon I'll send you another booklet of it.[1] It's really good, and I want it out in the spring, before 'Quetzalcoatl': and I want Miss Skinner to see it before it comes out and to decide how – under what name or names, it shall appear.
4. If you go to England, will you take the two trunks from your basement? I sent you the keys. I suppose you have them. Take the trunks for Frieda. I will pay all costs. Forgive this bother.
5. I think I shall sail direct from Vera Cruz. I feel still a certain disgust for the U S A and New York.
6. I *don't* think I shall get to England till about January 1st – don't want to spend Christmas with my people. But if I change I'll let you know at once.

Write to me now, and tell me everything.

DHL

Don't be impatient with me for bothering you. – You might have somebody worse.

I paid Mountsier his $404. – Acabado![2]

2950. To Mollie Skinner, 1 November 1923
Text: MS WAPL; Huxley 584.

Hotel Garcia. Guadalajara. Jal. Mexico.
1st Nov. 1923

Dear Miss Skinner

I have been busy over your novel, as I travelled. The only thing was to write

---

[1] See p. 503 n. 2. [2] 'Done with!'

it all out again, following your MS. almost exactly, but giving a unity, a rhythm, and a little more psychic development than you had done. I have come now to Book IV. The end will have to be different, a good deal different. Of course I don't know how you feel about this. I hope to hear from you soon. But I think, now, the novel will be a good one. I have a very high regard for it myself. – The title, I thought, might be *The Boy in the Bush*. There have been so many 'Houses' in print.[1]

If possible, I should like to hear from you in time to arrange for publication in England and in America simultaneously in early April. As soon as ever I can, I will have a type-script copy sent to you, with your own MS. Your hero Jack is not quite so absolutely blameless an angel, according to me. You left the character psychologically at a standstill all the way: same boy at the beginning and the end. I have tried, taking your inner cue, to make a rather daring development, psychologically. You may disapprove.[2]

But I think it makes a very very interesting book. If you like, we will appear as collaborators – let the book come out in our joint names. Or we can have a single *nom de plume*. – And we can go halves in English and American royalties. – All, of course, if you approve: – Then of course I've got the publishers to consider. They will insist on their point of view.

I wanted my wife to come and spend the winter in Mexico. But she has gone to London and won't come back. She says England is best. So I shall have to go there. Write to me care Curtis Brown. 6 Henrietta St. Covent Garden. W.C.2.

My best wishes to you. I will order you a copy of *Kangaroo*.

Yours sincerely.   D. H. Lawrence

2951. To William Hawk, 2 November 1923
Text: MS UT; Postmark, Servicio [. . .] NOV 23; Unpublished.

Hotel Garcia. Guadalajara. Jal.
2 November 1923

Dear William

Seltzer sent on the little birth-card to me here. I am so glad you and Rachel have got a son.[3] Hope he's bonny, and you both are glad about him, and his stars are good. He'll be a real young Lobo life. – Think of that cold night in March, when we came back in detestable Lizzie from unspeakable Sunshine Valley, frozen: and all had to begin running to save the unannounced young

[1] See p. 466 n. 4.
[2] DHL doubtless expected disapproval: Jack Grant's story was adapted from the experiences of Mollie Skinner's brother, John ('Jack') (1870–1925), whom DHL had briefly met at Leithdale.
[3] Walton Hawk.

gentleman on his journey: the doctor swearing because you had been so bashful and never let on, not a syllable, to anybody. Well anyhow the cat – or the Lobo-kind – is out of the bag now! I suppose he gaily gurgles and yells in the cabin. And I suppose he is fair, like Rachel.

I came on here down the west coast with Götzsche – hot as hell on the coast yet. My wife insisted on going to London from New York. I didn't want to go just then. Now she won't come away, and cables me I must go there. Well, I suppose there's nothing else to do. I expect I shall be in England for Christmas. And Götzsche will go to his beloved Denmark. Every man to his own place.

By the way, I sent on the little card to Frieda.[1]

Many greetings to Rachel – with the cabin all smartened up, and a son, what more can she want? Kindest regards to your mother and father, and to Betty, who I hope is flourishing. Götzsche and I often talk about Del Monte. We have awfully pleasant memories of it. Surely I shall see it again one day.

Yours   D. H. Lawrence

2952. To Knud Merrild, 3 November 1923
Text: MS UT; Postmark, Ser[vicio] 3[. . .]; Merrild 345.

Hotel Garcia. Guadalajara. Jal.

3 November 1923

Dear Merrild

Your letter yesterday – and what a tale to tell! Setting yourself on fire, quitting your job, and altogether being irresponsible. Get someone to insure you against yourself.

The new Lizzie – but she's not a Lizzie, I suppose her name is Florodora – sounds very grand. I see you, a gentleman of leisure with a large hole burnt in your pants, driving majestically out on to Grand Avenue. For heaven's sake go gently.

The little picture looked quite smart in print.[2] I hope your next shot at Fame and Fortune will bring down both birds. Götzsche is busily covering canvas with people in hats.

I managed to get off the Tlaquepaque pots – the vases for G's various friends (also mine) – by express yesterday. The express I was only able to pay to Ciudad Juarez (the El Paso border). The agents are supposed to ship them over the frontier and on to you by express – this part you must pay on delivery,

---

[1] It has not survived.
[2] Merrild had joined an artists' group in Los Angeles and exhibited with them; two newspapers reproduced one of his paintings – 'the one Lawrence wanted to help me paint at the ranch' (Merrild 345) – and he had sent the clippings to DHL.

but it can't be much: just one box, not at all heavy. The agents are
Angeles y Velarde, Agentes Aduanales, *Ciudad Juarez* – Chihuahua.
If the box doesnt come, you might write and ask them. I sent Mrs Seltzer a
vase in a basket by the same shipment – for New York.

Götzsche will have told you that Frieda won't come back: not west any
more. I had a cable yesterday asking me to go to England. So there's nothing
for it but to go. And G. will try and get a cheap ship to Denmark, to look at
home once more. It seems to be the only thing he really wants to do. – So I
think we shall go on to Mexico City next week – this is Saturday – and look for
a ship.

These are great fiesta days here, very gay and full of peóns and the streets
full of stalls and vendors, mostly of toys. The midday is hot still – but evening
cool. I think Guadalajara is pleasant. In a way I am sorry to be going. But now
it seems inevitable that I must go back to England, and square up with that
once more.

Remember me to the Böterns: hope they are beginning to build their house.
They must call it Puppenheim, after the famous dolls that started their
fortune. Greet also the Motts – and the Johnsons. I wrote them a letter. – I
hope Miss Rolf got her little bird too.

Yours   D. H. Lawrence

2953. To Thomas Seltzer, 3 November 1923
Text: MS UT; Lacy, *Seltzer* 120–1.

Hotel Garcia. Guadalajara. Jal.

3 November 1923

Dear Thomas

I got the telegram yesterday: *Cable from Frieda Lawrence cone* was what it
said. I suppose F. cabled for me to come to England. *À la bonne heure*! – But I
intend to leave next week for Mexico City, and look for a ship. If I can I shall
find a cargo boat or cheaper boat because Götzsche wants to go home to
Denmark. It's the best for him too. – He is painting quite busily here.

Today I have got *Mastro-don* and *Birds-Beasts*. Both look very nice indeed,
especially *BirdsBeasts*. Isn't my jacket nice too?[1] I am pleased with that book.
The *canaille* of a public isn't worthy of it.

Yesterday I sent Adele a vase from the native Tlaquepaque factory just near
here. It is common earthenware, only cost three or four pesos, but very
interesting I think: perhaps more suited to an office than a home. I could only
send it by express in a basket: I paid the express as far as *Ciudad Juarez* – that is

---

[1] Seltzer published *Birds, Beasts and Flowers* on 9 October 1923; the dust jacket – almost certainly
designed by DHL himself – is reproduced in Lacy, *Seltzer* 123.

El Paso border – couldn't pay any more. I hope it'll come, and come unbroken, so you can see what it's like. It was to be shipped across the border by Angeles y Velarde. Agentes Aduanales, *Ciudad Juarez* (Chihuahua).

I am busy with the Australian novel. I told you I would like it to come in spring, if possible before 'Quetzalcoatl'. I wish, if you are coming to England, you would bring the MS with you. I think I'll take all this remainder and have it typed in London.

And do please take the trunks across the water if you go.

I hope very much to be in London when you come. Meet on my native soil.

Mexico is sunny and lovely. These are the fiesta days of Todos Santos and Todos Muertos. They make All Souls day a great feast: and sell toys of skeleton men on skeleton horses, skeletons in coffins, skeletons like jack-in-the-boxes – skeletons of marzipan – skeletons on bulls, skeleton bull-fighters fighting skeleton bulls. – Bones! And they seem fascinated. They all buy little toys. Galeana St is crowded – like a sort of Arabian Nights, booth, awnings, water-carriers, baloons, big hats, sarapes, candles, lanterns. Quite amusing, but un peu trop enfantil. *Hay voladeros!*[1]

I wish you'd send two copies of *Mastro-don*, and one copy each of *BirdsBeasts* and *Kangaroo* to:

Baningenieur V. Götzsche, *Gentofte*, Bregnevej. 5. Denmark.

Gotzsche wants them.

I am looking for a letter from you.

DHL

2954. To Mabel Dodge Luhan, 8 November 1923
Text: MS Brill; Luhan 120–1.

Hotel Garcia. Guadalajara. Jal.
8 Novem. 1923

Dear Mabel

I had your letter from California yesterday.

Don't trouble any more. Let the past die and be forgotten.

Don't trouble about the Indians. You can't 'save' them: and politics, no matter *what* politics, will only destroy them. I have said many times that you would destroy the Indians. In your lust even for a Saviour's power, you would just destroy them. The same with Collier. He will destroy them. It is his saviour's will to set the claws of his own white egoistic *benevolent* volition into them. Somewhere, the Indians know that you and Collier would, with your salvationist but poisonous white consciousness, destroy them. Remember,

---

[1] A reference to an Aztec fertility ritual performed at certain fiestas.

Jesus, and The Good, in our sense, in our mystic sense, not just the practical: Jesus, and The Good as you see it, are poison for the Indians. One feels it intensely here in Mexico. Their great Saviour Juarez did more to destroy them than all the centuries of Viceroys.[1] – Juarez was a pure Indian. – This is really a land of Indians: not merely a pueblo.

I tell you, leave the Indians to their own dark destiny. And leave *yourself* to the same.

I[2] shall not *write* that third book:[3] at least not for many years. It's got to be lived out: not thought out.

I also fight to put something through. But it is a long, slow, dark, almost invisible fight. Yet little by little I win. And unless there comes death, or the unforeseen bad, I shall win.

One day I will come to you and take your submission: when you are ready. Life made you what you are: I understood so much when I was in Buffalo and saw your mother. But life put into you also the germ of something which still you are not, and which you *cannot* be, of yourself, and if you go on in the same way. People, lawyers, politics, enemies, back-biters, friends and pseudo-friends: my dear, it is all chimaera and nothing. I will take a submission from you one day, since it is still yours to give. But apparently, not yet. – I was your enemy. But even saying things against you – and I only said, with emphasis and in many ways, that your will was evil masquerading as good, and I should still say that of your will: even as an enemy I never really forsook you. There, perhaps I have said too much. But don't think, even so, you can make a fool of me.

DHL

Frieda and everybody insist on my going to England. And I, I shall give in once more in the long fight. I may as well go and settle finally with England. But I shall not stay long. A short time only. And directly or indirectly I shall come back here, this side, Mexico. I fight against the other side: Europe and the white U. S. Before very long I hope to come and see you again.

DHL

I'll let you know when I go.

---

[1] Benito Juárez (1806–72), Mexican national hero. Fought in the civil war of 1858, elected president in 1861. Defeated Emperor Maximilian (1867) and was re-elected president in 1867 and 1871. Mexico had endured Viceroys since the Spanish Conquest (1519–21) until the early 19th century when it achieved independence.

[2] MS reads 'I.I'.

[3] Cf. Mabel Luhan's reminiscence: 'He said he wanted to write an American novel that would express the life, the spirit, of America and he wanted to write it around me – my life from the time I left New York to come out to New Mexico; my life, from civilisation to the bright, strange world of Taos; my renunciation of the sick old world of art and artists, for the pristine valley and the upland Indian lakes' (Luhan 52). DHL might be referring here to this third section.

2955. To Frieda Lawrence, 10 November 1923
Text: MS BL; [Spender], *Encounter*, i (December 1953), 33.

Hotel Garcia. *Guadalajara*. Jal
10 November 1923

We keep on trying for ships, but nothing so far. We should like to sail from Manzanillo through the Panama Canal: it still may be possible to find a tramp steamer. If not, we shall go to Mexico City and get the first regular boat that goes out of Vera Cruz, if that infernal port is open: if not, Tampico. I'm not keen on going to Tampico, because of the fever. And I feel I simply can't look at the U.S.A. again, just yet. – The quickest steamers are the Dutch and the Hamburg Amerika – they take three weeks to Southampton or Plymouth. Mexico is still very attractive and a very good place to live in: it is not tame. Sometimes here in Guadalajara one sees the wild Guichilote Indians, with their bows and arrows and hardly any clothing.[1] They look so queer, like animals from another world, in the plaza listening to the band. – We've had several thunder showers, but the sky is blue and bright again. I like the plains round Guadalajara, with the mountains here and there around. I like it better than the lake. The lake is too shut in. – The barranca also is very impressive – you never saw that. – I still wish I was staying the winter on a ranch somewhere not far from this city. I still don't believe in Europe, England, efforts, restfulness, *Adelphi*s or any of that. The egg is addled. But I'll come back to say how do you do! to it all. I am glad if you have a good time with your flat and your children. Don't bother about money – why should you. When I come we'll make a regular arrangement for you to have an income, if you wish. I told you the bank was to transfer another £100 to you. – I wonder if Seltzer is in England. I haven't heard a word from him or Adele for three weeks, so know no news. – The Australian novel is very nearly done.

tanti saluti   DHL

Enclose note from Mabel Luhan – she says she still has hopes we might live in contact. Quien sabe! Mañana es otro dia.[2]

2956. To Baroness Anna von Richthofen, 10 November 1923
Text: MS UT; Frieda Lawrence 158–9.

Hotel Garcia. Guadalajara. Jal. Mexico.
10 Novem. 1923

Meine liebe Schwiegermutter
    Ich hatte heut' abend zwei Briefe von Frieda aus Baden, mit Billet-doux-

[1] The Huichole Indians inhabited the states of Jalisco and Nayarit in Western Mexico.
[2] 'Who knows! Tomorrow is another day.'

chen von dir. Ja Schwiegermutter, ich glaube doch man muss siebzig Jahr
haben, vor man ganz voller Muth ist. Die Jungen sind nimmer mehr wie halb
voll. Auch die Frieda macht eine lange klagende Nase, und sagt sie schreibt an
der Mond. Guadalajara is gar keine Mondstadt, und ich bin ganz und gar auf
der Erde, mit festen Füssen.

Ich komme aber Zurück: warte nur auf einem Schiff. In Dezember werde
ich in England sein. Und im Frühjahr, wann die Primrosen – wie sagt man,
Primeln? – blühen, werde ich in Baden sein.

Die Zeit geht schnell und schneller vorbei. – Frieda schickte mir den Brief
von Hartmann von Richthofen. Es war nett. Aber die Frauen heute haben
immer mehr Muth wie die Männer. Kam auch ein Brief von Nusch: ein wenig
traurig, aber doch lebendig. In dem Frühjahr werde ich sie auch sehen. – Man
muss auf die Hände spucken und feste Griff[1] nehmen. Findst du nicht.

Ich war an dem Barranca – ein grosse grosse Schlucht (Ravine) – in den
heissen Quellen badend. Kam heim, und fand das ganzes Deutschland in
meinem Zimmer.

Ich habe es sehr gern hier. Ich weiss nicht wie, es gibt mir Kraft, dieses
schwarzes Land. Es ist voller Mannes-kraft – vielleicht nicht Frauenkraft –
aber es ist gut wie altes deutsches Helden-bier, für mich. Ach
Schwiegermutte, du bist nett und alt und verstehst wieder wie die erste
Jungfrau versteht, dass ein Mann muss mehr wie nett und gut sein, und dass
die Helden haben mehr wert, wie die Heiligen. Die Frieda versteht nicht, dass
heute ein Mann braucht Held zu sein, und mehr wie Ehemann. Ehemann ja,
auch. Aber mehr. Ich muss hin und her gehen, durch die Welt. Ich muss
Deutschland gegen Mexico, und Mexico gegen Deutschland balanciern
(balance). Ich komme nicht für die Ruhe. Der Teufel, der heilige Teufel hat ja
die Ruhe um den Hals. Ich weiss wohl, die muthvolle Alte versteht mir besser
wie die Junge: oder etwas von mir, versteht sie besser. Die F. muss immer
denken und schreiben und sagen und nachdenken, *wie* sie mich liebt. Es ist
eine dummheit. Ich bin doch kein Christus auf seinem Mutter's Schoss
liegend. Ich geh meinen Weg durch die Welt, und wenn die F. es[2] ein sehr
schweres Werk findet, mich zu lieben, denn, du lieber Gott, lass sie seine
Liebe zur Ruhe gehen, gib es Feiertage. Ach Schwiegermutter
Schwiegermutter, du verstehst, wie meine Mutter endlich verstand, das der
Mann braucht nicht, verlangt nicht die Liebe, von seiner Frau, aber Kraft,
Kraft, Kraft. Es ist Kampfen, kampfen, kampfen, und immer noch kampfen.
Und man braucht kraft und Muth und Waffen.Und die dumme Frau singt
immer Liebe! Liebe! Liebe! – und Liebesrechten! Frauenliebesrechten! Zum

---

[1] Griff] Halt   [2] es] findet

Teufel mit der Liebe. Gib mir Kraft, nur Schlachtkraft, Waffenkraft, Kampfenkraft. Gib mir dies, du Frau.

Ich weiss nicht ob mein Deutsch zu verstanden ist.

England ist so *ruhig*: schreibt Frieda. Schäm dich, dass du heute um die Ruhe fragt. Ich will keine Ruhe: ich geh die Welt kampfend herum. Pfui Pfui! In dem Grab find ich meine Ruhe. Erst lass mich kampfen und durchwinnen.

Doch doch, Schwiegermutter, mach mir ein Aikenstrauch – Eichenstrauch – (oak-wreath) – und bring die Stadt-Musik unter die Fenster, kommt der halb-Held heim.

DHL

Das Geld ist Weihnachtsgeld für dich und Else und Else's Kinder. Ich schicke etwas an Nusch für Hadu.

[My dear Schwiegermutter

I had this evening two letters from Frieda from Baden, with billet-doux-lets from you. Yes Schwiegermutter, I do believe one must be seventy years old before one is entirely full of courage. The young ones are never more than half full. Frieda too makes a long complaining face, and says she writes to the moon. Guadalajara is not at all a moon-city, and I am altogether on the earth, with firm feet.

But I'm coming back: only waiting for a ship. In December I will be in England. And in the spring, when the primroses – what does one say, Primeln? – bloom, I will be in Baden.

Time goes by fast and faster. – Frieda sent me the letter from Hartmann von Richthofen.[1] It was nice. But women today always have more courage than men. Came also a letter from Nusch: a little sad, but still lively. In the spring I will see her too. – One must spit on one's hands and take firm hold. Don't you think.

I was at the Barranca – a great great ravine – bathing in the hot springs. Came home, and found the whole of Germany in my room.

I like it very much here. I don't know how, it gives me strength, this black land. It is full of man-strength – perhaps not woman-strength – but it is good like old German hero-beer, for me. Oh Schwiegermutter, you are nice and old and understand again as the first virgin understands, that a man must be more than nice and good, and that heroes have more value than saints. Frieda doesn't understand that today a man needs to be a hero, and more than a husband. Husband yes, also. But more. I must go back and forth, through the world. I must balance Germany against Mexico, and Mexico against Germany. I do not come for peace. The devil, the holy devil himself has peace

[1] Hartmann (1878–1953) was Frieda's cousin: see *Letters*, iii. 314

round his neck. I know well, the courageous old one understands me better than the young one: or some of me, she understands better. F. must always think and write and say and ponder *how* she loves me. It's stupidity. I am after all no Christ lying on his mother's lap. I go my way through the world, and if F. finds it very hard work to love me, then, dear God, let her give her love a rest, give it a holiday. Oh Schwiegermutter Schwiegermutter, you understand, as my mother finally understood, that the man does not need, does not ask for love from his wife, but strength, strength, strength. It is fighting, fighting, fighting and still fighting. And one needs strength and courage and weapons. And the stupid woman always sings love! love! love! – and the rights of love! The rights of woman's love! To the devil with love. Give me strength, only battle-strength, weapon-strength, fighting-strength. Give me this, you woman.

I don't know if my German can be understood.

England is so *peaceful*: writes Frieda. Shame on you, that today you ask for peace. I want no peace: I go about the world fighting. Pfui Pfui! In the grave I will find my peace. First let me fight and win through.

Yes yes, Schwiegermutter, make me an oak-wreath and bring the town music under the windows, when the demi-hero comes home.

DHL

The money is Christmas money for you and Else and Else's children. I'm sending some to Nusch for Hadu.]

2957. To Rosalind Baynes, 10 November 1923
Text: MS BucU; Nehls, ii. 279.

Hotel Garcia. Guadalajara. Jal. Mexico.
10 Novem. 1923

Dear Rosalind

Your letter found me here – not Sicily. But Frieda is in England – she went from New York in August, and I turned west again. Now I am coming along: expect to be in London by the New Year – care S. Koteliansky. 5. Acacia Rd. London N.W.8. And before June I bet we shall be in Sicily – in Italy. And of course we should call in Florence if you were there. Koteliansky's address will find Frieda.

a rivederci.   D. H. Lawrence

2958. To Mollie Skinner, 15 November 1923
Text: MS WAPL; Huxley 585.

Hotel Garcia. Guadalajara. Jal. Mexico
15th Novem. 1923

Dear Miss Skinner

I finished the novel yesterday. I call it *The Boy in the Bush*. I think quite a lot of it. Today I am sending the MS. to my agent,

Curtis Brown, 6 Henrietta St, Covent Garden, London W. C. 2.
His cable address is Browncurt. London. Curtis Brown will have the MS typed, and the moment I get to London – I hope to be there by Christmas – I will go through it and have a copy sent to you.

Seltzer wants to do the book in New York in April: so that would mean Martin Secker bringing it out at the same time in London. Seltzer suggests my name and yours as joint authors.

I shall wait to hear from you.

Yours sincerely   D. H. Lawrence

2959. To Curtis Brown, 15 November 1923
Text: MS UT; Huxley 585–6.

Hotel Garcia. Guadalajara. Jal. Mexico
15 Novem. 1923

Dear Curtis Brown

I am sending you today the chief part of the MS. of a novel *The Boy in the Bush*. Seltzer has the first part: he is having it typed and will send it to you. Please have this MS. typed so that it can be ready when I get to England: and have *two* carbon copies made.

It is an Australian novel – A young woman in West Australia – Miss M. L. Skinner, *Darlington*. W. A. – showed me a MS. when I was there – it had good stuff in it. I suggested she did things to it. – Then in the early summer this year she sent me another MS. of a novel – I'll give it you when I come – and again the thing was a queer bewildered muddle. Because I liked the stuff of her book – She called it 'The House of Ellis' – and because I felt a good deal of sympathy for her, I tackled the thing, and wrote it all over afresh. And here it is. It's an interesting book. – She by the way published a sort of war novel *Letters of a V. A. D* – I think Heinemann.[1] Not bad. I don't know how she managed to keep it so sane. The later stuff is just muddled and a bit crazy.

I am going on to Mexico City in a couple of days time – and then, as soon as I get a ship, coming to England. So I ought to be in London by Christmas.

Seltzer by the way wants to publish this novel – *The Boy in the Bush* – in the spring, probably under my name and Miss Skinner's together. I want Miss Skinner, if possible, to see the MS before it is published. I wrote her two months ago.

I hope the MS arrives safely.

Yrs   D. H. Lawrence

---

[1] R. E. Leake [pseud.], *Letters of a V.A.D.* (1918) was published by Andrew Melrose.

2960. To Robert Mountsier, [16 November 1923]
Text: MS Smith; Unpublished.

Guadalajara. Jal

16 Novem

Dear M[ountsier]

Saw Mr Sass[1] in the Plaza yesterday – he said you were still in Taos. – I sent you a cheque for $404. to New York. 417 W. 118 – hope you have it. – We leave this afternoon for Mexico City – and as soon as I can get a steamer from Vera Cruz, we shall sail to Europe – Götzsche and I. He'll go to Denmark. Are you permanently at Taos?

Best wishes   DHL

2961. To Witter Bynner, 17 November 1923
Text: MS HU; Postmark, Mexico D. F. 17 NOV 1923; Huxley 586–7.

Hotel Monte Carlo. Av. Uruguay. Mexico D. F.

17 Nov. 1923

Dear Bynner

We got here this morning – hotel just the same, save fewer suck-men.[2] All enquiring for you and the thin one[3] – and for F[rieda]. But Mexico seems cold and dark after Jalisco. I like Jalisco very much – the plain round Guadalajara. It is Pacific Ocean influence, without the too-much softness. – I want to get a boat on, as soon as I can now, to England. God knows how long I shall stay there. This cold, gloomy morning in this city makes me think of it with repugnance. It was just nicely warm in Guadalajara. But we must bring penalties on ourselves.

Perhaps later we'll all meet and make a place in Jalisco: even Mabel Lujan. – It's terrible here, I can't speak Italian any more – only bad Spanish. – We had a flask of the *very* good chianti for lunch. Tonight we're going out to dinner with the Brit. Consul General at Tlalpam[4] – all in evening dress. How's that for committing suicide on the spot? My dinner jacket is so green with overripeness. – I'm going to look for Covarrubias.[5] – We ran across old Sass from Taos in Guadalajara plaza – like a lost chicken, and unable to get *any*

---

[1] An eccentric septuagenarian painter whom DHL and the two Danes had known in Taos; Merrild felt more kindly disposed towards him than did DHL (Merrild 266–70).

[2] Mexico was famous for hangers-on, beggars, would-be guides, people in general trying to make a peso off the foreigner.

[3] I.e. Spud Johnson.

[4] Götzsche reported that on 17 November he and DHL 'put on [their] best clothes' to dine with (Sir) Norman King (1880–1963), the British Consul-General in Mexico City, 1920–6. King was a painter and had 'a large rich home' in Tlalpam (Merrild 350).

[5] Miguel Covarrubias (1902–57), Mexican artist, part of the prototype for the young Mexican who conducted the tour of the frescoes in *The Plumed Serpent*. For an account of DHL's first meeting with Covarrubias, see Bynner 29–31.

word out.– I miss you at the corner table – miss everybody and everything here. Dont like it – want to get out quick. This city doesn't feel *right* – feels like a criminal plotting his next rather mean crime. Write to me care Seltzer. Tell Spoodle this is for him too. 'Una arancia, una banana, ò dolce de prugne?'[1] Mine's a banana.

Hasta luego DHL

2962. To Ada Clarke, [17 November 1923]
Text: MS Clarke; PC v. [Pyramid of the Sun at Teotihuacan]; Postmark, [. . .]; Unpublished.

[Hotel Monte Carlo, Av. Uruguay, Mexico D.F.]
17 Nov

– Am sailing from Vera Cruz on the 22nd – due to arrive Plymouth on Dec. 12th – so shall see you all before the New Year.

DHL

2963. To Emily King, [17 November 1923]
Text: MS Needham; PC v. [Carving of Quetzalcoatl at Teotihuacan]; Postmark, Mexico D. F. 19 NOV 23; Unpublished.

[Hotel Monte Carlo, Av. Uruguay, Mexico D.F.]
17 Nov.

Am sailing from Vera Cruz on 22nd – due to arrive Plymouth about 12th Dec – So shall see you soon.

DHL

2964. To Dr George Purnell, [17 November 1923]
Text: MS UT; Unpublished.

Hotel Monte Carlo. Av. Uruguay, Mexico D. F.
17 Nov.

Dear Dr Purnell

I hope you are safely and satisfactorily back by the time you get this. I was sorry really to go away and see no more of you: but with silver up your sleeve 'enough to put the house down the vein,' as Idella said, you weren't the same man.

We got here safe and sound. It's cold, dark, gloomy, and I don't like Mexico D. F. one bit. I shall get out as *soon* as possible. But now, oh hell!, they've suspended the sailing of the *Toledo* on the 22nd and probably we shall only be

[1] 'An orange, a banana, or a prune sweet?'

able to sail for New York by Ward Line on 29th. *Hell!!!* Damn Vera Cruz and all its True Crossians.

Tonight we're going – all in dinner suits – to dine with the Brit Consul Gen. in Tlalpam – with Colonel X and etc etc. How's that for rushing up the social ladder! – Am already quite tipsy with a flask of very good chianti. But I may as well begin to be a gentleman.

If you got home in time, you found Idella safe and sound and very chirpy. I left her such.

Thank you for all your kindness and hospitality – the tea that the tea egg laid, and the cruise and the tequila, the beans and the chayotes. We'll start our spreeing again later on.

Au revoir   D. H. Lawrence

2965. To Willard Johnson, [19 November 1923]
Text: MS YU; Huxley 587–8.

Hotel Montecarlo, Mexico
19 Nov.

Dear Spoodle

I am off to Europe – la mala suerte.[1] We sail, Götzsche and I, on the *Toledo*, from Vera Cruz, on Thursday – three days hence – and I get to Plymouth about 12th Decem, he gets to Hamburg two days later. – Well, I don't care, since I've got so far. This city is a bit nervy and not in good spirits, and cold. From the roof this morning, Ixtaccihuatl and Popo[cateptl] clear in snow.[2] The monkey, the parrot and the chihuahua dog gone: but the large husband and the wife with a nose, still living upstairs. Not many 'mariners' any more – more Mexicans, and less of a *Pirates of Penzance* atmosphere. Everything a bit heavier. They expect more revolution – Calles and De la Huerta[3] – probably a bad one. No business doing – and the common people a bit brutal. Oh heavenly bolshevism. Tell Bynner to come down and see heaven descend to earth with a red rag. I'm the bull. – But expected revolutions so often never revolve. I bought a serape in the Volador – dark brown with big white stripes and boca – eleven pesos. Shades of Hal![4] – As yet I've not been able to think of anything to make the horse laugh. Hope he's not sobbing his way into a new year.

---

[1] 'bad luck'.   [2] Two dormant volcanoes s. of Mexico City.
[3] Plutarco Elías Calles (1877–1945) and Adolfo de la Huerta. See p. 465 n. 1.
[4] Witter Bynner.

Dear Spoodle, I hope we shall all one day become quite nice people, and make a new spot on earth, more or less together. Meanwhile I wander on, till my ass shall bray that the angel says no further.[1] If yours is a *Laughing Horse*, mine is a slowly smiling donkey. Chi cammina, arriva. – Which is, Who goes, gets there. Anyhow I keep on going.

Dear Spoodle, I think of you often affectionately, whatever I may say. Also of Bynner. We'll meet again one of these bright mornings. I am sure Mexico will feel my tread once more – unless a bolshy bullet stops me.

a rivederci   DHL

address
>   care S. Koteliansky, 5. Acacia Road, London N. W. 8

2966. To Bessie Freeman, [19 November 1923]
Text: MS UNYB; Postmark; Mexico D.F. 20 NOV 1923; cited in Moore, *Intelligent Heart* 322.

Hotel Montecarlo, Mexico D.F.
19 Nov.

Dear Bessie Freeman

I have expected so often to hear from you – a word in answer to that lovely letter I left at Palm Springs. And I have to kick myself to realise that you won't write till I send an address. And now I'm going, I send it. I am sailing for England from Vera Cruz in three day's time.

I'm sorry to go, for many things. I still like Mexico exceedingly – especially the State of Jalisco. But Frieda wont come back – she wants to stop in England and everybody expects more revolution here. Mexico City is rather cold and a bit depressed and depressing, after the warm west. I am not sorry to go on.

Mabel and I have buried the hatchet. She wrote me a Peccavi, peccavi, c'est ma faute[2] letter. And I, I know there is something bigger in her than in most folks. So the hatchet is buried, and I'm planting a fig-seed over it.

I hope you and Mrs Birge and your brother are all happy at Palm Springs. As for poor wandering me, I lay my head first in one place then in another, but sleep quite soundly. Write me a word:
>   care S. Koteliansky, 5 Acacia Rd, London N. W. 8.

Greet your sister Mary. – I shall come west again soon, and shall see you.

au revoir   D. H. Lawrence

---

[1] See p. 177 and n. 3.   [2] 'I have sinned, I have sinned, it's my fault'.

2967. To Knud Merrild, [19 November 1923]
Text: MS UT; PC v. Goddess of Symbols; Postmark, Mexico D.F. 19 NOV 1923; Merrild 349.

Mexico DF
19 Nov.

We sail on the *Toledo* Hamburg-Amerika boat from Vera Cruz – I to England, G[ötzsche] to Hamburg. I am due in England about Decem 12th. Send me any letter, and write to me
      care S. Koteliansky, 5. Acacia Rd, London N. W. 8.
I shall see you again one day, am sure of that.

Wiedersehn   DHL

2968. To Idella Purnell, [19 November 1923]
Text: MS UT; Unpublished.

Hotel Monte Carlo. Mexico DF
19 Nov.

Dear Idella
    Don't like Mexico City: it's cold and *unsympatisch.*
    We sail on Thursday next by *Toledo* – I to Plymouth Götzsche to Hamburg. I ought to be in London by 14th Decem. Write me there –
    care S. Koteliansky, 5 Acacia Rd., St. Johns Wood. London N. W. 8.
Since we're going, best go quickly. But I like Jalisco – the plains round Guadalajara. Volverò.[1]
    We sail from Vera Cruz – hope the Bolshies won't eat us alive.
    Götzsche – or I, because he never does things – will send you the copy of *Sons and Lovers* from here.
    Hope you won't have to water the unwilling *Palms* with your tears.
    Remember me to Dr Purnell – I wish I was having a cup of tea and a drop of anise with him at this minute.

a rivederci   D. H. Lawrence

2969. To Mabel Dodge Luhan, 19 November 1923
Text: MS Brill; Luhan 121–2.

Hotel Monte Carlo. Av Uruguay, Mexico D. F.
19 Nov 1923

Dear Mabel
    I had your letter from Guadalajara this morning. – There, you have found your way, the first step. And I am finding mine. Taos was a last step to me too.

---

[1] 'I shall return' ['Volveré'].

On a good day we will meet again, and start afresh. – The end of the old is bitter, but there is the new for us.

I am sailing on the 22nd – in three days – from Vera Cruz to England. Write to me there

care S. Koteliansky, 5. Acacia Rd, St. Johns Wood, London N. W. 8.

I don't much want to go. But I suppose, at the moment, it is my destiny. But I shall come back. I like the west best.

Idella Purnell showed me your California poem.[1] I agree with you, Taos is far, far better than California. I like Jalisco very much. But Taos is about the best place in U.S.A. I believe that.

We'll go our separate ways, and see where they'll bring us. – Mine, I always think, holds the chance of my getting shot. Pues vedremos.[2] Anyhow we'll meet again and it will be different from what it was.

DHL

2970. To S. S. Koteliansky, [20 November 1923]
Text: MS BL; Postmark, Mexico D.F. 20 NOV 1923; cited in Gransden 29.

Mexico D. F.
20 Novem.

My dear Kot

I sent a wire to Seltzer yesterday to tell him I was sailing on the 22nd – two days hence – on the Hamburg-Amerika boat *Toledo* to Plymouth. She is due in Plymouth on the 11th. or 12th. of December – but she may be later. I sail from Vera Cruz, and touch at Havana, and at Vigo, Spain.

I am not very keen to come, but this time it is settled. I have bought my ticket and leave in the morning for Vera Cruz. Going out to dinner with English people here makes me already a bit weary with Europe. It is not, as you say, that I fight with shadows: but that I feel I don't belong. As for being angry, I am not angry unless someone annoys me. I've lost my faith in the old world. Murry says so confidently – The New will happen over here, certainly not in Mexico. – Quien sabe! I'll tell you better in six weeks time.

Pero vengo.[3] And I may be as glad to be back as Frieda appears to be. Anyhow I am glad to see you and pick up again the old connections.

Pues, hasta luego.[4]

DHL

I hope you don't get very tired of having F's letters and my letters forwarded to you.

---

[1] Probably 'Fairy-Tale' (see Luhan 137) which Idella Purnell published in *Palms*, Christmas 1923.   [2] 'Well we'll see' ['veremos'].
[3] 'But I am coming.'   [4] 'See you soon.'

2971. To Harriet Monroe, [20 November 1923]
Text: MS UChi; cited in Monroe, *Poetry*, xxxvi (May 1930), 92.

Mexico. D. F.
20 Novem.

Dear Harriett Monroe

I am sailing in two days time from Vera Cruz to England. In September I was in Chicago for a day: a queer big city with a sort of palpitation I couldn't quite understand. But I hope to come again soon, and to understand a little more.

Did you like *Birds Beasts and Flowers?* I promised you a signed copy, and I will send it you from London.

Idella Purnell was cross when I saw her in Guadalajara because I gave her[1] a poem which you had previously paid for. I hope you weren't cross too. I had completely forgotten.

Would it be a nuisance for you to send her a copy of the anthology in which the poem – 'Nostalgia' – appeared, and at the same time, if possible, the number of *Poetry* in which the thing first saw light?[2] You have her *Palms* address – Galeana #150, Guadalajara. And send the bill to me
care S. Koteliansky. 5. Acacia Rd, London N. W. 8.

I still am coming to Chicago – poco a poco. Am not very keen on going to Europe, if I must confess it.

D. H. Lawrence

2972. To Mabel Dodge Luhan, [20 November 1923]
Text: MS UT; cited in Luhan 122.

Mexico D F
20 Nov

Dear Mabel

I am just packing, to leave in the morning – your letter is here. – Yes, let us keep an invisible thread between us. Blessed are the pure in heart.[3] – And change – you will change, I am changing. Sometimes I too feel as if I should depart from this life and this world. One has had enough. But one must live through to win through, I know that. – Don't think of the *world* any more. Leave that to me, I am more cunning, and being alone, one must be a serpent as far as the world is concerned.[4] As for the fight – subtly and eternally I fight, till something breaks in me. You needn't fight. – Yes, I am glad if you will

---

[1] her] you
[2] 'Nostalgia' appeared in *Poetry*, xiii (February 1919) and in *Voices* (ed. Thomas Moult), July 1919 (see *Letters*, iii. 376 n. 4).
[3] Matthew v. 8.   [4] Cf. Matthew x. 16.

stand behind me, and I know it. I need someone to stand behind me, badly. – I don't want much to go to England – but suppose it is the next move in the battle which never ends and in which I never win. – But yes, I won with you. – Don't talk to the world: keep still towards people, or be very wary. And back me up, in silence – And leave the world to me. And know that with the world I must go as the serpent – if I am open they will destroy me. The serpent of the sun.

I don't think I shall stay long in Europe. Though I *might* come west via India. But I feel I belong here. – We might meet down here. This is the Indian *source*: this Aztec and Maya.[1]

Send me some strength then on my way. My need is perhaps greater than yours. Give me your strength, and I'll fight a way through – little by little. Don't you see I find it very hard.

DHL

I sent you the address
      care S. Koteliansky, 5 Acacia Rd, London N. W. 8.

2973. To Margaret King, [25 November 1923]

Text: MS Needham; PC v. Cuba, Climbing the Royal Palm; Postmark, Cuba [. . .]; Unpublished.

Havana. Cuba
Sunday 25 Nov.

Got so far on the journey – guess I shall be home before you have this.

DHL

2974. To Knud Merrild, [25 November 1923]

Text: MS UT; PC v. Habana, Nursing Goat; Postmark, Habana NOV 25 1923; Merrild 351.

Havana
– 25 Nov

Two days here – am already sick of ship – mixed German, Spanish, Danish, English – a nearly empty boat. G[ötzschc] at last happy.

DHL

---

[1] The Aztec people had an empire in the 15th and 16th centuries consisting of what is now central and southern Mexico. Their rule ended with the Spanish Conquest (1519–21) under Cortés. The Mayan people occupied southern Mexico and part of central America before the Spanish Conquest.

2975. To Baroness Anna von Richthofen, 14 December 1923
Text: MS UCB; Frieda Lawrence 181.

110 Heath St. Hampstead. London. N.W.3
14 Dec 1923

Meine Liebe Schwiegermutter

Da bin ich wieder. Frieda ist nett, aber England ist hässlich. Ich bin wie ein wildes Tier in einer Falle, so ist es dunkel und eingeschlossen hier, und nimmer zieht man freie Luft. Die Leute sind aber freundlich. Frieda hat eine nette wohnung – ich geh aber herum wie einer eingesperrte Coyote, und kann nicht ruhen. – Ich meine, wir gehen am Ende des Monat's nach Paris: und nachher nach Baden.

Hörst du mich heulen?

DHL

[My dear Schwiegermutter

Here I am again. Frieda is nice, but England is hateful. I am like a wild animal in a trap, so dark and closed-in it is here, and never does one draw free air. But the people are friendly. Frieda has a nice flat – but I go round like a caged coyote, and can't rest. I expect we shall go at the end of the month to Paris: and afterwards to Baden.

Do you hear me howling?

DHL]

2976. To Frederick Carter, [14 December 1923]
Text: MS UT; Unpublished.

110 Heath St. Hampstead, N.W.3
14 Dec.

Dear Frederick Carter

I am just back in London from Mexico – sailed straight from Vera Cruz to Plymouth. I think I shall go up to Derby next week to see my sister: and in that case I might run along to Liverpool – or Pontesbury[1] – and see you too. Let me know if you are at home.

Haven't got my breath yet, being back.

Yours Sincerely   D. H. Lawrence

2977. To Thomas Seltzer, [14 December 1923]
Text: MS UT; Postmark, Hampstead DEC 14 1923; Lacy, *Seltzer* 124.

110 Heath St. Hampstead, London N.W.3.
14 Dec.

Dear Thomas

Am here – loathe London – hate England – feel like an animal in a trap. It all seems so dead and dark and buried – even *buried*. I want to get back west –

---

[1] Pontesbury is 6 m. s.w. of Shrewsbury, Shropshire. Cf. Letter 2998.

Taos is heaven in comparison, even if Mexico for the time is impossible. It's good to see Frieda again, but then I can take her with me, out of this cold stew.

Shall see Curtis B[rown] tomorrow and get MSS. – I hope he has them all safe: will write you.

I hope business is good – there were slightly alarming reports here, from America. But I trust you to keep me informed. – Till tomorrow.

DHL

2978. To Curtis Brown, 14 December 1923
Text: MS UT; Unpublished.

110 Heath St. Hampstead, N.W.3.

14 Dec 1923

Dear Curtis Brown

So I am here. I shall probably call in at your office in the morning – Saturday – to have a talk with you. I hope you have that *Boy in the Bush* MS safe and ready for me to go through it. Seltzer says he sent on the first part. – If I didn't answer your last letters it was because they were returned here.

Tomorrow then.

D. H. Lawrence

2979. To Alfred Stieglitz, [17 December 1923]
Text: MS YU; Postmark, Hampstead, DEC 17 1923; Unpublished.

110 Heath St. Hampstead, London N.W.3.

17 Decem

Dear Alfred Stieglitz

Well I must say, it's nice to see somebody get a bit warm about my immortal works. I got back here from Mexico a few days ago, and found your letters. I feel even worse in London than you did in New York: not lonely, but buried alive, under the yellow air and the vast inertia. There is no Duse nor Meistersinger,[1] there are friends who somehow belong to a dead past in me, and I am rolling my eyes in the tomb. I'd rather be in New York, and I don't like New York either.

But I expect to be back in America in the spring. Then I should very much like to see your photographs, and the maker of them. And I should like to see Lake George, which I mixed up with Lake Champlain in my *Studies*, and got duly scolded for.[2]

Meanwhile I commend myself to the Herr Gott.

Yours   D. H. Lawrence

---

[1] See p. 485 n. 2. Meistersinger was a title taken by some burgher poets in Germany (14th–16th centuries) who tried to revive the national minstrelsy of the Minnesingers.

[2] In *Studies in Classic American Literature*, chap. v, 'Fenimore Cooper's Leatherstocking Tales', DHL confused the location of Cooperstown as well as the upstate New York settings of the Leatherstocking novels. The Stieglitz family had a summer home on Lake George.

2980. To Thomas Seltzer, [17 December 1923]
Text: MS UT; Postmark, Hampstead DEC 17 1923; Lacy, *Seltzer* 126.

110 Heath St. Hampstead, N W 3
17 Dec.

Dear Thomas

Have you sent the MSS of *Boy in the Bush* and 'Quetzalcoatl': neither is here. I had a thrilled letter from Miss Skinner, very pleased at our collaboration. She is nice. – I had a letter from Mountsier – 417 W. 115th St – thanking me for the $404.00 and saying would I deduct a $22 he owes me from the 'third and last payment.' How's that for cheek – when I just said the money I received in March and Sept 1923. Damn him. He'll get no third and last. He still warns me sententiously against you and myself. He's a fool. I'll have no more to do with him.

I'm in bed with a bad cold. I *loathe* every minute of it here. I expect to be in Paris before Jan 1st – then I want to go to Spain for a time – then back to America. I think by March we shall be coming west once more. I can't stand this side. Murry wants me to link up with him – he wants to travel with me! talks of India and the Ursprung[1] of the Aryan races. But hell can have the Aryan races, and India along with it.

God get me out of here.

You heard that Boni was here – and Knopf.[2] I don't believe there's any point in coming here.

Why didn't you write me a letter for my arrival? What's amiss with Adele, that there's no sound from her, not even thank you for Frieda's shawl or for the vase? I feel something's the matter – what is it? – Curtis urging me to have an American agent etc – God knows. I shall have to see about my income tax in the U.S.A. I suppose if I'm back in early March I can pay it myself. Let me know. And tell me what's wrong with you.

Don't bring those boxes of ours. I don't want em here, and I won't cart 'em round any more. I don't care what happens to them.

DHL

2981. To Idella Purnell, [17 December 1923]
Text: MS UT; Nehls, ii. 293.

110 Heath St. Hampstead. N. W. 3.
17 Dec

Dear Idella

Here I am – in bed with a bad cold – hate it. Just hate it all. It's like being in

---

[1] The source or origin.
[2] Alfred Abraham Knopf (1892–1984), American publisher. (See *Letters*, iii. 471 n. 1.)

the tomb. I expect to go to Paris in a fortnight – then to Spain[1] – and by March back to the American continent. Meanwhile it's dark, damp, dead, and sickly here. F[rieda] is well – and says she's prepared to come west. I swear at her for having brought me here.

I thought to have had a line from you. Did your father get back safe and sound and soon. And is all quiet in Guadalajara?

Let me know.

D. H. Lawrence

2982. To Mabel Dodge Luhan, [17 December 1923]
Text: MS Brill; Luhan 127–8.

110 Heath St. Hampstead. London N W 3
17 Decem

Dear Mabel

Here I am, already in bed with a bad cold. And I simply hate being here. I simply detest it. I shan't stay long: soon I shall go to Paris, and perhaps to Spain for a while: then back to America. I guess I shall be in America again by March. Then we'll see.

I have your story,[2] and two letters, here. The story is good. I shall ask Murry if he would like to print it in the *Adelphi*. This is a very crucial time for all of us. I feel if we can pull through to 1925, we have saved the situation. Meantime it's hell. England is a tomb to me, no more. – Yet perhaps it's as well I went away from that revolution in Mexico.

But I don't belong over here any more. It's like being among the dead of ones previous existence.

In spite of the bad time you are having, I feel that somewhere you are really happier, and feeling a bit free from the old compulsion. – I hope Tony doesn't get a hard life out of it all. I know he feels exiled. – The only way to help the Indians is to *leave 'em alone*. – We'll laugh last: and really laugh, not jeer. A test of the soul is its insouciance.

Meanwhile I am a diminished specimen, here. But I shall soon rise up again.

When are you going back to Taos? If we are back in America in March, shall we come and see you there? I want, when Mexico is quiet, to go down to Oaxaca. I don't suppose this 'revolution' will last long.

Never think of coming to Europe. – But Mexico is another matter.

F[rieda] is well and sends *saluti*.

DHL

[1] Spain] Rome
[2] A story about Mabel Luhan's friend, Francesca Alexander, who grew a wild olive tree in her roof garden on top of an old palace in Florence, from a plant given her by Ruskin. See Luhan 127.

2983. To Witter Bynner, [17 December 1923]
Text: MS HU; Postmark, Hampstead DEC 17 1923; Huxley 589.

110 Heath St. Hampstead, N W 3

17 Decem

Dear Bynner

Here I am. London – gloom – yellow air – bad cold – bed – old house – Morris wall-paper – visitors – English voices – tea in old cups – poor D.H.L. perfectly miserable, as if he was in his tomb.

You don't need his advice, so take it: *Never* come to Europe any more.

In a fortnight I intend to go to Paris – then to Spain – and in the early spring I hope to be back on the western continent. I wish I was in Santa Fe at this moment. As it is, for my sins, and Frieda's, I am in London. I only hope Mexico will stop revoluting.

De Profundis[1]   DHL

2984. To Mabel Dodge Luhan, [19 December 1923]
Text: MS Brill; Luhan 129–30.

110 Heath St. Hampstead, N W 3

19 Decem

Dear Mabel

My literary agent, Curtis Brown, has a son who has lung trouble, and who *perhaps* would like to come to New Mexico to get strong again – he's not very bad. He has a wife and *three* little girls: quite small.

Capt. M. L. Curtis Brown, Whitney Point, Broome Co., New York.

The question is, could he have a house at about $50. a month in Taos: he's got no money but what his father gives him. If you have anything to suggest, send him a line. If you don't want to let any of your houses – or can't – perhaps suggest another. But *don't* do anything unless you feel quite easy about it.

We seriously think of New Mexico in early spring: and Middleton Murry wants to come along – also, probably, Dorothy Brett, who paints, is deaf, forty, very nice, and daughter of Viscount Esher.[2]

I'm longing to get out of England.

DHL

---

[1] 'Out of the deep' (Psalm cxxx).
[2] Hon. Dorothy Eugenie Brett (1883–1977), artist, daughter of 2nd Viscount Esher, studied at the Slade School of Art and first met DHL in 1915. She was to return to USA with the Lawrences in March 1924. Author of *Lawrence and Brett: A Friendship* (Philadelphia, 1933). (See Irvine, Brett 1–116.)

2985. To Witter Bynner, [20 December 1923]
Text: MS HU; Postmark, Hampstead DEC 20 1923; cited in Huxley 589.

110 Heath St. Hampstead, N W 3
20 Decem.

Dear Bynner

My agent Curtis Brown has a son with lung trouble, and thinks he might get him to New Mexico. Money scarce. Said son has wife and three baby girls: don't know ages. Do you think he could find a house for $50 or $60 a month in Santa Fe. If you have wind of anything, send him a line:

Capt M. L. Curtis Brown, Whitney Point, Broome Co., New York.

Don't curse me for bothering you – you are nice about these things. Ask Alice Corbin to help you think of a place. Tell her I consider we never quarrelled in the least, therefore are friends. Also Frieda and I think of coming to New Mex. in early spring, on way to Old Mex. And Middleton Murry says he wants to come too – and probably another friend – How's that? – I wrote to you, *don't* come to Europe, it's awful. I hate being here – plainly – New Mexico is far far far better. Dead this side. Stay in N. M. – Greet Spoodle and the Alices, and be greeted by me and F. As I said to Spoodle, I get so cross with you for still being a democrat, but, hombre, there is the underlying affection.

DHL

2986. To Frederick Carter, [20 December 1923]
Text: MS UT; Unpublished.

110 Heath St. Hampstead, N.W.3
20 Dec.

Dear Frederick Carter

Of course I had to get a bad cold and get stuck in bed. I really hate it here.

I have to put off my going to see my people till next week. Is it the same to you if I come on then? I should come on from Derby – Midland – Then which way? – I suppose I'd come about Thursday or Friday. I want to talk about 'Dragon'. – Middleton Murry is reading it now.

Thank you for asking my wife. I was cross that she didn't answer your letter – but that's how she is.

Did you ever get *Kangaroo* or *Fantasia* or *Birds Beasts?* Let me know, and I'll get on Secker's track for not sending them. He's done the same to my other friends – just not sent.

All good wishes.   D. H. Lawrence

2987. To Knud Merrild, 20 December 1923
Text: MS UT; Postmark, Hampstead DEC 20 1923; Merrild 352.

110 Heath St. Hampstead. London N.W.3

20 Decem 1923

Dear Merrild

Well I've been here a week: don't like it a bit. It feels so heavy, so dead, with no answer in it. I feel I don't belong any more. I'd much rather be in Taos: even in Los Angeles.

I think very soon – by the New Year probably – we shall go to Paris – and then to Spain – And by March I hope to be coming west again. If Mexico is still revoluting, we may stay a time in New Mexico. I told you Mabel Sterne and I made friends again: but a different friendship from before, I assure you. – Murry and another friend want to come along, to make a home of a sort away in Mexico if possible. We'll see. I'll let you know when we move. Our old plans of having a ranch may still mature.

I've not yet heard from Götzsche – it is nine days since I left him on the ship in Plymouth – I wonder if Denmark depresses him as much as England does me.

Dont come to Europe – unless for a 'flying' visit. One doesn't belong any more.

There is snow – not much.

Save a bit of money to be free to go *somewhere* in the spring.

F[rieda] sends warm greetings, and we talk about last Christmas – before Archipenko was sculpted[1] – the frozen chickens hanging in the shed. Nice to remember.

au revoir   D. H. Lawrence

2988. To Martin Secker, [20 December 1923]
Text: MS UInd; Postmark, Hampstead DEC 20 1923; Secker 54.

110 Heath St. Hampstead, N W 3

Thursday. 20 Dec.

Dear Secker

I called on Saturday at your office – nobody there. And I've had such a bad cold: got out Tuesday and saw Curtis Brown, then no more. But I want to come tomorrow, Friday morning, about 10.30 or 11.0, to see you. We lunch later at Mary Cannan's. Remember to give me a copy of *BirdsBeasts* for her.

[1] Merrild elucidated the remark: 'Slaughtered, plucked chicken, [DHL] called, "before Archipenko" – prehistoric Archipenkos, and all kinds of variations, chicken and Archipenko became identical' (Merrild 355). (Alexander Archipenko (1887–1964), the Russian-born American sculptor – one of the most influential sculptors between the wars – had recently moved to USA from Paris.)

I was so sorry Mrs Secker was knocked up.[1] Frieda was so charmed with her.

Yrs   D. H. Lawrence

A friend of mine, Evelyn Lawford,[2] who came over from Mexico with me, will, I hope, call at your office in the morning about eleven, and I want you to give him from me a copy of *The Ladybird* and a copy of *Women in Love*.

2989. To Thomas Seltzer, 24 December 1923
Text: MS UT; Postmark, Hampstead DEC 24 1923; Lacy, *Seltzer* 127.

110 Heath St. Hampstead. N. W. 3.
24 Decem 1923

Dear Thomas

I haven't had a word from you since I am back.

I am still waiting for that MS of *Boy in the Bush*. I have all the typescript from Curtis Brown – am hung up for your part.

I saw Secker. He complained bitterly of your treatment of him over plates for *Sea and Sardinia*,[3] also of your refusal to answer him about *Mastro-don Gesualdo*. They urge me to let Curtis Brown act for me in New York, to simplify matters. Have you settled anything with Blackwell about *Mastrodon*?

I am doing a series of articles for the *Adelphi*. The February number will contain a very caustic article by me, against England: 'On Coming Home.' Also another article, the first of a series: 'On Being Religious.' – I want to write further 'On Being a Man' – and : 'On Writing a Book' – and 'On Reading a Book'. Probably I shall expand it to six essays.[4]

We happened to be talking about Magnus – Murry wants very much to see that *Memoir* of Maurice Magnus – he thinks he would like it very much, as a serial, in the *Adelphi*. Will you please post it to me, with Magnus' own MS. of the *Foreign Legion*, – to

care The *Adelphi*. 18 York Buildings. Adelphi W. C. 2.

I should be glad if you would post this at once.

I still think of going to Paris in January, and on to Spain. Then come to America and go west in early spring. I want to go back to Mexico when I can, and finish 'Quetzalcoatl'. Murry talks of coming with us: says he too wants to

---

[1] I.e. unwell.   [2] Unidentified.   [3] See p. 366 n. 1.
[4] Murry rejected 'On Coming Home'; its first complete publication was in *Phoenix II* 250–6. It was 'On Being Religious' which Murry published in February 1924; he also published 'On Human Destiny' (March 1924) and 'On Being a Man' (September 1924). 'On Writing a Book' and 'On Reading a Book' were perhaps combined in 'Books'. DHL MSS exist containing notes for an essay entitled 'On Being in Love' and three pages of an essay 'On Taking the Next Step' (Roberts E288.5 and E292.5).

break away. The idea is, if we get the *Adelphi* planted in America, after about six months or a year, to publish it from that side and get more American contributors: but to keep it if possible a little 'world' magazine. One can only try. – Dorothy Brett, an old friend, wants to come too. She is deaf – and paints pictures – and is a daughter of Viscount Esher.

I don't know if you still think of coming to England – as a place, it is dismal enough.

Best wishes to you and Adele for the New Year. I am a bit annoyed with you.

DHL

2990. To Robert Mountsier, 24 December 1923
Text: MS Smith; Postmark, Hampstead DEC 24 1923; Unpublished.

110 Heath St. Hampstead. N. W. 3.
24 Dec 1923

Dear M[ountsier]

Here I am back in London. It seems very dark, and one seems to creep under a paving-stone of a sky, like some insect in the damp. I don't like it at all. Also there seems a deadness everywhere, in the people, in everything. But that is probably only the change from the brightness of Mexico.

I don't intend to stay long. In January I think we shall go to Paris for a short time – and then to Spain – and in the early spring come again to America. I should like to go back to Mexico, if it will be quiet again.

I had your letter with the receipt for the dollars. You speak of a 'third and last payment'. I don't understand that. I thought I said clearly, a tenth of the money I received in spring and autumn, 1923, from Seltzer. That was what I meant. And that I have given you. So the matter is settled. – Never mind that odd twenty-two dollars from the journey.

I wonder what you will be doing in New York. Anyhow don't come to Europe. It seems to me unspeakably dreary.

Best wishes from Frieda and me for the New Year.

Yrs   D. H. Lawrence

2991. To S. S. Koteliansky, 25 December 1923
Text: MS BL; Gransden 29.

[110 Heath St. Hampstead, NW3]
Christmas 1923

Kot

Let the old warrior put his hat on and make ready.

DHL

2992. To John Middleton Murry, [c. 25 December 1923]
Text: MS NYPL; John Middleton Murry, *Son of Woman* (1931), facing p. 206.

[110 Heath St. Hampstead, NW3]
[c. 25 December 1923][1]

[1] Murry reproduced DHL's MS in *Son of Woman* and added: 'An enlarged impression of a seal given by D. H. Lawrence to the author at Christmas 1923, with the accompanying note.'

2993. To Emily King, [26 December 1923]
Text: MS Needham; PC v. Am Bildstöckl; Postmark, Hampstead DEC 27 1923;
Unpublished.

Hampstead.
Wednesday¹

I'm feeling my cold again – and here's snow – so I'd better put off my coming
for a day or two again – till Monday I think.

DHL

2994. To Ada Clarke, [26 December 1923]
Text: MS Clarke; PC v. Der Oberbauer; Postmark, Hampstead DEC 27 1923;
Unpublished.

Hampstead.
Wednesday²

I feel my cold again – don't feel quite well – and it's snowing – so I think I'd
better put off coming north until Monday.

DHL

2995. To Mabel Dodge Luhan, 27 December 1923
Text: MS Brill; Luhan 131–3.

110 Heath St. Hampstead, N.W.3.
27 Dec 1923

Dear Mabel
    Your letters come on safely – I think I have them all. Write whenever you
feel like it – I am glad to know you are with me. – It is hateful here in England,
so dark and stifling, and everyone and everything trying to drag one back.
They have no life of their own, and they want to drag one away from the life
one would³ make. I feel the English much more my enemies than the
Americans. I would really rather be in America. But anyhow or anywhere it is
an awful great struggle to keep one's spark alight and perhaps kindle something new. There doesn't seem really to be anybody. – I'm afraid I don't know
much about Wobblies or I.W.W.'s, about whom you ask me.⁴ I don't know
much about societies and groups anywhere: mistrust them when I do know
them.
    I am due to go to the Midlands to my people, but don't bring myself to set
out. I don't want to go. It's all the dead hand of the past, over here, infinitely

---

¹ Wednesday] Thursday   ² Wednesday] Thursday   ³ would] should
⁴ Industrial Workers of the World, whose members were called 'Wobblies', was a federation of
industrial unions founded in 1905 in Chicago for the purpose of overthrowing capitalism. The
IWW was responsible for sabotage as well as general strikes. By 1923 its strength had declined
as the result of government prosecution of its leaders.

heavy, and deadly determined to put one down. It won't succeed, but it's like struggling with the stone lid of the tomb.

I wonder why Seltzer has not written to me – for about six weeks I have nothing from him. I wonder if something has gone wrong with him or his business. Hope not, that would dish me in another direction.

When I can *really* break the clutch of the dead hand over here, so that its grip is broken in the world forever, I think I shall go to Paris. And I really hope to be in America by March: apparently Murry does want to come, but I don't altogether trust him. Can't rely on him *at all*.

Remember I am depending on your spirit at the back of me, over there – no matter what there is over here. I am glad when I hear you feel relieved of the old tension, and happy apart from taking thought. That is how it should be. Perhaps it is because you are learning to *give* your life into the creative future. For a woman, the greatest joy, I think, is to give her spirit and know it is not in vain, that the gift is needed. Which it is.

I shall tell you when we move. I wish it might be soon. How much I would rather be in Taos than here.

Remember me to Tony.

DHL

2996. To Martin Secker, [29 December 1923]
Text: MS UInd; Secker 55.

110 Heath St. Hampstead
Saturday

Dear Secker

I have kept on putting off my visit to the Midlands – now I have *definitely* promised to go for the New Year: so doubt I shan't be back by the 5th – but probably by the 7th. I will let you know.

If Evelyn Lawford calls at your office, give him the two books I spoke of, *Women in Love* and *Ladybird*.

Best wishes for the New Year.

Yrs   D. H. Lawrence

2997. To Frederick Carter, [31 December 1923]
Text: MS UT; PC; Postmark, Nottingham DEC 31 1923; cited in Moore, *Poste Restante.*

Nottingham.
31 Dec.

I am going on to Derby tomorrow, and shall come on to Shrewsbury on Wednesday or Thursday – I'll send a telegram for time of train.

D. H. Lawrence

2998. To Frederick Carter, [1 January 1924]
Text: MS UT; cited in Moore, *Poste Restante* 77.

Nottingham.

1st Jan.

Dear Frederick Carter

I shall leave Derby on Thursday morning at 9.5, Great Northern Ry, get to Stafford 10.55, and to Shrewsbury somewhere near midday – stupidly, I've lost your little paper of trains.

If it would be inconvenient to you, my coming on Thursday, send me a telegram to c/o Clarke, Grosvenor Rd, Ripley nr. Derby. Otherwise I shall turn up.

Don't bother meeting me, unless you have something else to go to Shrewsbury for. – You will know me by a red beard.

Good wishes for the New Year.

D. H. Lawrence

My wife didn't come north.

2999. To Frederick Carter and Mrs Carter, [6 January 1924]
Text: MS UT; cited in Moore, *Poste Restante* 77.

110 Heath St. Hampstead. N. W. 3.

Sunday

Dear Carter and Mrs Carter

Got back here very nicely yesterday evening – and glad I came to Pontesbury. My wife now wishes she had come too.

Here is the ten bob –

Do the little essay. Murry is an uncertain fish; but with him or in spite of him we must make something out of the future.

Don't think *too* much and tie yourself into knots (this to F. C.) And you, Madame, don't do too many good works, or they'll be on your own head.

Saluti   D. H. Lawrence

3000. To Willard Johnson, 9 January 1924
Text: MS YU; Unpublished.

110 Heath St. Hampstead, London N W 3

9 Jan 1924

Dear Spoodle

Your Christmas card portrait drawing not bad, but 'schweetened', as Götzsche would say: nose too small, forehead not bulby enough.

Still disliking it here.

Got your *Horse*.[1] Send you an article in shape of letter.[2] Do as you like with it, exactly. I think I'll try and send you a similar article each month.

We're due to go to Paris on 21st inst. but may be too floody there.

Still think of coming to America and New Mexico in early spring – March – with Murry and Brett and Frieda. What cher!

Greet Bynner – Alice Corbin, how is she?

Be greeted.

DHL

3001. To Mabel Dodge Luhan, 9 January 1924
Text: MS Brill; Luhan 134–5.

110 Heath St. Hampstead, N.W.3.
9 Jan 1924

Dear Mabel

You certainly are an egoist, and your letters are egoistic, as you say. Soon you must learn to forget yourself. You must learn *not to care*, not to think, and simply to laugh. Poco a poco.

I have heard enough about that place at Fontainebleau where Katharine Mansfield died to know it is a rotten, false, self-conscious place of people playing a sickly stunt.[3] One doesn't wonder about it *at all*. One knows. – Now call into action your common horse sense, of which you have your share, as I have mine, and use that. Don't go back on your common horse-sense. It is the centaur's way of knowledge. And if we come back into our own, we'll prance in as centaurs, sensible, a bit fierce, and amused. – I am sure seriousness is a disease, today. It's an awful disease in Murry. So long as there's a bit of a laugh going, things are all right. As soon as this infernal seriousness, like a greasy sea, heaves up, everything is lost. And it was so with us at Taos. If only we'd kept up an *honest* laugh. Not a dishonest laugh: but an honest laugh: then the vileness of 1923 need not have been. – Now it takes far more courage to dare not to care, and to dare to have a bit of a laugh at *everything*, than to wallow in the deepest seas of seriousness. The thing I admire most about you is your dauntlessness. Be dauntless in this, then, not any forced will of your own, nor any forced submission, but a certain *real* trust, and the courage *not to care*, and the power to laugh a bit. Do this and we'll have a good time among ourselves. One's got to put a new ripple in the ether. And one can do it only by *not* caring about any of the old things, by going beyond them all with amusement and a

---

[1] *Laughing Horse* (December 1923), which contained DHL's essay 'Au Revoir, U.S.A.'.
[2] 'Dear Old Horse. A London Letter', in *Laughing Horse* (May 1924).
[3] Mabel Luhan had asked DHL 'to find out about Gurdjieff and the Fontainebleau Institution, and this made him mad' (Luhan 134). See p. 375 n. 2.

bit of jolliness, and having a bit of stark trust inside oneself. Stark trust in a Lord we have no name for, and also stark trust in one another. Instead of a recklessness of defiance and mistrust, a recklessness of trust, like a naked knife.

I find that here in London they all *instinctively* hate me: much more so than in America. But that too, in the end, only makes me laugh. My Gods, like the great God Pan, have a bit of a natural grin on their face. Nous nous entendons.[1]

I am still planning to come west at the end of February or in March, with Frieda, Murry and Brett. I hope you are looking forward to it. But on your honour, Mabel, no seriousness. The seriousness of the great God Pan, who grins a bit, and when he gets driven too hard, goes fierce. You are one of the very few people in the world at the moment who are capable of this: this fierce recklessness, based on trust, like the recklessness of Pan: trusting deep down to the springs of nature, the sources: and then the laughter.

The old communion was in seriousness and earnestness. The new is in fierceness, daring, knife-like trust, and laughter. Bien entendu.

DHL

3002. To Frederick Carter, [11 January 1924]
Text: MS UT; Unpublished.

110 Heath St. N.W.3.
Friday 11 Jan.

Dear Carter

The essay and the woodcuts came yesterday. I think the essay is excellent. I made a few slight alterations only to your style, which is sometimes odd and obscure, as befits the magic art: and the title I think shall be 'The Ancient Science of Astrology'. It's too late, I'm sorry to say, for the February *Adelphi*, so it will have to go in the March number.[2] Meanwhile prepare a second essay, the same length, for April.

There is a great deal of beauty in the woodcuts: beautiful craftsmanship. You know I don't really like the Blakean attitude towards concrete things, particularly the nude. But the drawings are beautiful. Koteliansky has a scheme – you remember Kot is the busy bee of the *Adelphi*, Murry the sort of queen bee – to become a small publisher of special books. He thinks that by May he should have some five or six books ready: The Adelphi Press: with Murry and myself and Kot and two others all partners in the company. Now

---

[1] 'We understand one another.'
[2] 'The Ancient Science of Astrology' appeared in *Adelphi*, i (April 1924), 997–1005.

nothing of this is yet realised, so don't count on it. But it is likely. I think it would be good to publish the woodcuts. My idea is to have them loose in a folio. Kot would rather they were bound into a book with a few little essays pertinent to the drawings. What do you think? Let me know. If you want to write Koteliansky direct, he is

S. S. Koteliansky, Care *Adelphi*, 18 York Buildings, Adelphi. W. C. 2. If the Press gets going, we could do the 'Dragon' in autumn. – But prepare anyhow one or two little essays for the *Adelphi*, and if you wish these can go then into the book of drawings.

Actually a bit of sunshine! Makes me flutter my wings at once.

I will let you know my plans. Greet Mrs Carter.

Yrs   D. H. Lawrence

3003. To Mollie Skinner, 13 January 1924
Text: MS WAPL; Postmark, Hampstead JAN 13 1924; Moore 771–2.

care Curtis Brown. 6 Henrietta St, Covent Garden, London W.C.2.

13 Jan 1924

Dear Miss Skinner

I am back as you see in London. Two of your letters have followed me here – also Lord Strathspeys fume against *Kangaroo*.[1] Amusing. The reviews were very good here, especially in the *Times*.[2]

I have got the complete typescript of *The Boy in the Bush* now, and am going through it. It's awfully good, I like it immensely. I hope in about four day's time to post you the third of the typed copies. Will you go through it at once, and let me have *by return* any suggestions you can make. Be quick, and you'll be in time for the proofs, I hope. Seltzer wants to do the book in New York in April.

But friends of mine here – John Middleton Murry, and others, – want to set up as publishers, and would like to kick off with *The Boy in the Bush*. They might be ready for May. But I like to have the publication simultaneous in New York and London. If I don't keep *The Boy* for Murry, I shall let Secker have it, as he does my other books. – Curtis Brown, whose address I give, will draw up an agreement and send a copy to you to be signed. My idea is to

---

[1] Trevor Ogilvie-Grant of Grant, 4th Baron Strathspey (1879–1948), a New Zealander by birth. On 11 November 1923 the Perth *Sunday Times* carried a report of his view – based on a reading of some 'clippings' of passages from *Kangaroo* – of DHL's alleged hostility to Australia. He remarked on DHL's 'bad taste' and 'piffle', and concluded: 'this is a book which no one should read'.

[2] The reviewer in *TLS*, 20 September 1923, felt that DHL had 'never been more of an artist in vision and word' than in *Kangaroo* – 'a fine book: experimental, masterful, challenging' (Draper 216).

publish under both our names and go halves in the royalties. The preliminary expenses – such as this typing – are mine. Of course publishers are glad to get the MS – they pay us, not we them. But I don't think I'll ask for advance on royalties, unless you wish it. If you *do* wish it, write to Curtis Brown, and say you would like an advance of £25 or £30. Otherwise we get an account at the end of six months, and the money three months later.

I don't care for England – so dark, so wet, so dismal. I think we shall go to Paris next week, and in March back to America. You might, if you have time, send me a letter c/o Curtis Brown and another c/o Seltzer, 5 W. 50th St. New York, simultaneously.

I think very often of you and Miss Beakbane – I'd forgotten her *name*, but not her face – and of your brother, out there in W. Australia. I am sure I shall see you again. Hope Letty goes well.[1] Always write *what you want* to write. Did you mean a biography, or a novel, of the noble Lord.[2] – My wife will write to you.

                                            Yours   D. H. Lawrence

3004. To Martin Secker, [18 January 1924]
Text: MS UInd; Secker 54.

                                            110 Heath St. N. W. 3.
                                            Friday
Dear Secker
    We are going to Paris on Wednesday. Are you free on Monday? Shall we come to lunch with you then?

                                            D. H. Lawrence
    Am at the *Adelphi* for a few minutes – but got to go to Chelsea for tea – The girl will bring a note if you like.[3]

                                            DHL

3005. To Thomas Seltzer, 22 January 1924
Text: MS UT; Postmark, Hampstead JAN 23 1924; Lacy, *Seltzer* 128–9.

                                            110 Heath St. Hampstead, N W 3
                                            22 Jan 1924
Dear Thomas
    I had your cable last week, and answered Accept – the $5000 for film rights of *Women in Love.*[4]

---

[1] See p. 496 n. 1.
[2] Mollie Skinner was doing research for a biography of John Forrest (1847–1918), 1st Baron Forrest, P.C., Australian explorer and politician; Treasurer and Premier of Western Australia, 1890–1901; the first Australian politician to be raised to the peerage.
[3] DHL's letter was delivered to Secker by hand.
[4] The deal fell through (cf. Lacy, *Seltzer* 188).

They have been waiting very anxiously to hear from you about the *Adelphi*.

We leave for Paris in the morning – expect to be there about a fortnight, then to BadenBaden for about ten days. I think we[1] shall come to New York early in March, to pay my *income tax*. If I am not there in time, I shall trust you to pay it for me. The papers of last year are in that green *iron* trunk in your basement – and at the *end* of a green MS. book you'll find what figures I made for the early year. For the latter half of the year you have all the figures. I paid $70.00 tax – to the Inland Revenue Officer in Albuquerque, New Mexico, last year. This year it will be more.

I have had a great struggle getting *Boy in the Bush* done – you sent me only one copy. I had to have everything re-typed. And somehow everything seemed to be so confusing and difficult, I asked Curtis Brown to act for me in America through his New York branch. I have given him the MS. of *Boy in the Bush*, with instructions to try it for serial purpose – somewhat cut down. But of course he is to give you the MS for book publication at the earliest possible date. – He also will try to place a few articles for me. You are so frightfully busy, I can't bear to worry you any more. – Things will be just the same between us as before – only Curtis Brown will act for me. And whatever you really want, I will get him to comply with. I have told him that. We'll make an arrangement about the money when I see you. Meanwhile pay in what you can, will you, because I shall have to be spending American money to come across the Atlantic. – I shall try and be in New York by first week in March – pay my tax – and go west, to Santa Fe or Taos. Murry and Brett will either come along or follow a little later.– I'm sure you'll get on perfectly simply and well with Curtis Brown, and it'll be better if I don't have to think about it. – I very much want to come back and finish the Mexican novel for the autumn. Couldn't do it here. Besides I don't like it here.

Perhaps better address me care Curtis Brown, or else care S. Koteliansky. Send the Magnus *Memoir and* the Magnus MS. to Koteliansky at the *Adelphi*, when it's typed out, please.

We'll be able to talk everything over peacefully when I come. Greet Adele and thank her for her letter. It pours with rain here.

Wiedersehen.   D. H. Lawrence

3006. To Mabel Dodge Luhan, 22 January 1924
Text: MS Brill; Luhan 136.

110 Heath St. London N. W. 3.
22 Jan. 1924

Dear Mabel

We are leaving for Paris in the morning – stay there about a fortnight, then a

[1] we] I

while in Germany – and by early March I still hope to be in New York; and in New Mexico by end of that month.

I think I have had most of your letters – but none yet to say you have heard from me. And I sent a line as soon as I got here. Let us know your plans.

London, England wearies me inexpressibly – I cannot tell you how this winter in England wearies me, and the people. But it will finish.

Let's try and be really sensible when we meet again – and laugh and send most things to the devil. None of the strain of insistence. Why insist.

Yes, I liked 'Fairytale'.[1] And your poems do amuse me. But I'm not going to think of you as a writer. I'm not going to think of you even as a knower. You know and write whatever you feel like, of course. But the essential you, for me, doesn't know and could never write: the Eve who is voiceless like the serpent, yet communicates.

But let us above all things be able to laugh and not care, and not scheme and insist, and not, in a tight way, exclude. One can ignore so much, and it is so good. The last days of life are for living, not for knowing or insisting.

Poor old Tony, learning to read!

Let's have an open, careless heart.

DHL

3007. To Curtis Brown, [22? January 1924]
Text: MS UT; Unpublished.

110 Heath St. N. W. 3.
24 Jan 1924[2]

Dear Curtis Brown

After all I am sending you the Amer. copy of *The Boy in the Bush*. Murry has the copy for England.

This novel might serialise in America. They can cut it as they like for serialisation purposes. And Seltzer has the promise of it, for book publication. If it seems unlikely that the thing would serialise, let Seltzer have the MS *at once* for spring publication.

I enclose two letters and an article. There was a third letter from Alyse Gregory, of *The Dial*, asking for something to print.[3] I wish you would have that answered too.

D. H. Lawrence

---

[1] See p. 539 n. 1.
[2] By 24 January DHL was in Paris, and he wrote to Curtis Brown again from there (Letter 3015); this letter was probably written before he left London.
[3] Alyse Gregory (1884–1967), managing editor of the *Dial*, January 1924–April 1925.

3008. To Willard Johnson, [24 January 1924]
Text: MS YU; PC v. Paris – Le Panthéon; Postmark, Paris 25. I 1924; Unpublished.

[Hotel de Versailles, 60 Bvd Montparnasse, Paris]
24 Jan.

Out of London at last – much nicer here, though Paris seems quiet – and cold but sunny. Did you get the little article for the *Horse*? I ought to be doing you another. F[rieda] sends greetings.

DHL

3009. To Baroness Anna von Richthofen, 24 January 1924
Text: MS UCB; *Nur Der Wind* 183.

Hotel de Versailles, 60 Bvd Montparnasse, *Paris*
24 Jan. 1924

Meine liebe Schwiegermutter
    Gestern kamen wir hier. Paris ist doch netter wie London, nicht so dunkel-grau. Die Leute sind ganz freundlich.
    In zehn oder fünfzehn Tagen kommen wir zu Baden Baden, wenn alles fertig ist. Schreibe du an dieses Adresse.

Auf wiedersehen   D. H. Lawrence

[My dear Schwiegermutter
    Yesterday we came here. Paris really is nicer than London, not so dark-grey. The people are quite friendly.
    In ten or fifteen days we're coming to Baden Baden, when all is done. Write to this address.

Auf wiedersehen   D. H. Lawrence]

3010. To Catherine Carswell, [24 January 1924]
Text: MS YU; PC v. Paris – Petit Palais; Postmark, Paris 25. I 1924; cited in Carswell 215.

Hotel de Versailles, 60 Bvd Montparnasse
Thursday

We had an easy journey – Paris looking rather lovely in sunshine and frost – rather quiet, but really a beautiful city. We're both tired – almost stupified from London.

DHL

3011. To Hon. Dorothy Brett, [24 January 1924]
Text: MS UCin; PC v. Paris – La Place de la Concorde; Postmark, Paris 25 I 1924; Irvine, Brett 33.

Hotel de Versailles, 60 Bvd. Montparnasse
Thursday

Very nice here – Paris looking rather lovely in a sharp frost, with sunshine. Anyhow better than London.

DHL

3012. To Knud Merrild, [24 January 1924]
Text: MS UT; PC v. Paris – Le Grand Palais; Postmark, [Pari]s 25–1 24; Merrild 356.

Paris.
24 Jan.

Came here yesterday – am terribly sick of the dark dreary winter of this Europe – but Paris better than London – much best stay in California. I think we shall be back in New York by March – then probably to New Mexico.
F[rieda] sends greetings.

D. H. Lawrence

3013. To Adele Seltzer, [24 January 1924]
Text: MS UT; PC v. Paris – L'Hôtel de Ville; Postmark, Paris 25 I 1924; Lacy, *Seltzer* 129.

Hotel de Versailles. 60 Bvd Montparnasse, *Paris*.
24 Jan.

We came here yesterday – Paris looking very lovely still, in the winter sunshine and the frost. Frieda buying clothes. – I suppose we shall stay about two weeks, before going to BadenBaden.

DHL

3014. To Idella Purnell, [24 January 1924]
Text: MS UT; PC v. Paris – La Sainte-Chapelle; Postmark, Paris 25. I 1924; Nehls, ii. 321.

Paris.
24 Jan.

I haven't heard a word from you since I left Guadalajara – do hope you and Dr Purnell are all right. We have come to Paris for a while – but I think we shall go back to New York in March. I'd still rather be in Mexico.

D. H. Lawrence

Write
c/o Curtis Brown. 6 Henrietta St. London W. C. 2.

3015. To Curtis Brown, [24 January 1924]
Text: MS UT; Unpublished.

Hotel de Versailles, 60 Bvd. Montparnasse, Paris.

24 Jan

Dear Curtis Brown

This is the address for the moment – how many moments I can't say. Paris is nicer than London, anyhow.

I suppose Koteliansky left the MS. of *The Boy in the Bush* with you. I wish you – or your New York representative – would just send a line to Seltzer to say you have the MS (it's really his copy) and that you'll let him have it at the earliest opportunity. Open up a friendly connection with him. I have written to him.

Yrs   D. H. Lawrence

3016. To S. S. Koteliansky, [24 January 1924]
Text: MS BL; PC v. Paris – Avenue des Champs-Élysées; Postmark, Paris 25. I 1924; Zytaruk 263.

Hotel de Versailles, 60 Bvd. Montparnasse
[24 January 1924]

Had a good journey – Paris quite lovely, much nicer than London – and cold, but sunny.

DHL

3017. To Catherine Carswell, [25 January 1924]
Text: MS YU; cited in Carswell 214, 215.

Hotel Versailles, 60 Bvd. Montparnasse, Paris.

Friday

Dear Catherine

Today it is dark and raining, and very like London. There really isn't much point in coming here. It's the same thing with a small difference. And not really worth while taking the journey. Don't you come just now: it would only disappoint you. Myself, I'm just going to sleep a good bit, and let the days go by: and probably next week go to BadenBaden to get *that* over. – I somehow *can't* answer to Europe any more. Paris has great beauty – but all like a museum. And when one looks out of the Louvre windows, one wonders whether the museum is more inside or outside – whether all Paris, with its rue de la Paix and its Champs Elysée isn't also all just a sort of museum.

Don't be disappointed – it would only be a greater disappointment to spend your effort coming here, and to find nothing at the end of it. I'll help you to a *real* holiday in place of this –

Don't bother to put more stamps on the re-addressed letters – they don't need them. And the number is 60. I hope you won't have thousands of my letters to readdress.

I feel I shall be back soon, and we'll see you then.

DHL

3018. To Martin Secker, [25 January 1924]

Text: MS UTul; PC v. Paris – Le Dôme des Invalides; Unpublished.

Hotel Versailles, 60 Bvd Montparnasse
[25 January 1924][1]

Paris still looking lovely – but not much life, and a dark rainy day once more. Think we shall go to BadenBaden next week.

DHL

3019. To Catherine Carswell, [29 January 1924]

Text: MS YU; PC v. Paris – La Sainte-Chapelle [detail of the picture of Adam and Eve's expulsion from Paradise]; Postmark, Paris 29. I 1924; cited in Carswell 214, 215.

[Hotel de Versailles, 60 Bvd Montparnasse, Paris]
Tuesday

Had your second p.c. – am glad you don't feel really disappointed. Really, there is nothing at all to come for, except to look at buildings or shops. I'm trying to amuse myself writing stories.[2] Something real later on: that's what I feel. And save oneself up for it. Lie low. Here I merely lie low. We had one sunny day – now its dark like London.

DHL

3020. To Emily King, [29 January 1924]

Text: MS Needham; PC v. Notre-Dame de Paris, Détail de la façade Ouest; Postmark, Paris 29. I 1924; Unpublished.

Hotel Versailles, 60 Boulevard Montparnasse
Tuesday

Had a bit of sunshine here – then more darkness. Tell Peg to send me a line to say you're all well. How's the new house going?

DHL

[1] Dated with reference to the mention of a dark rainy day in the previous letter.
[2] Almost certainly 'Jimmy and the Desperate Woman' (see Carswell 215); probably 'The Last Laugh' (first called 'The Great Return') and 'The Border Line'.

3021. To Hon. Dorothy Brett, [29 January 1924]
Text: MS Forster; PC v. Paris. – La Sainte-Chapelle. Détail du Porche de la Loggia. Le Fruit Défendu; Postmark, Paris 29. I 1924; Unpublished.

Hotel Versailles – 60 Bvd Montparnasse
[29 January 1924]

Two apples – one each – bet she ate the pippin and give him the Keswick. How's the little Paradise – still perched on the roof of time? Touched up, or not?

Think we'll be here another week.

DHL

3022. To S. S. Koteliansky, [31 January 1924]
Text: MS BL; cited in Gransden 29.

Hotel de Versailles, 60 Bvd Montparnasse, Paris.
Thursday.

My dear Kot

I send back the proofs.[1]

I haven't heard from you or Murry, only a letter from Brett to say there is great gloom. Why be gloomy! Did the man not offer the money for the publishing scheme?[2] You've still got Schiff.[3]

I read his book – quite good in a rather awful way. Gives one a sense of depravity not faced out, back of it all.

Paris is rather nice – the French aren't at all villains, as far as I see them. I must say I like them. They are simpatico. I feel much better since I am here and away from London. I can't tell you how I loathe London and those six weeks.

Don't worry about things. All there is to do is to go ahead as far as you can with what you want to do, and not trouble further.

We think of going to BadenBaden next Wednesday – the 6th. – stay about two weeks – Then I'm not sure. If I can get out of going to New York so soon, I think we shall go to Arles and Avignon for a few weeks, come to London about 25 march, and sail at end of month. But I'm not sure of anything.

I was trying to write a couple of stories, keep myself going.

---

[1] Most likely the proofs of 'On Being Religious' (see p. 549 n. 4) being returned to Kot in his capacity as business-manager for *Adelphi*.

[2] Murry's friend, the poet Vivian Locke-Ellis, had put up £400 to launch the *Adelphi* (F. A. Lea, *The Life of John Middleton Murry*, 1959, p. 105).

[3] Sydney Schiff (1868–1944), novelist (pseud. Stephen Hudson) and wealthy literary patron. His book to which DHL refers may have been *Prince Hempseed* (1923); it could not have been *Tony* (as proposed in Moore 774) since that book was not published until March 1924.

Paris quite cold, but better than London: cleaner, not quite so dark –
Thank you so much for sending that history book to my niece. I'll pay when
I come back.

Do you want the Schiff book again?

I still have no word from Seltzer. Have you?

Greet Sonia and Grisha.

DHL

3023. To Baroness Anna von Richthofen, [31 January 1924]
Text: MS UTul; PC v. Notre-Dame de Paris. – Façade Ouest; Postmark, [. . .] 31–1 24;
Unpublished.

– 60 Bvd Montparnasse
31 Jan.

Kam deinen Brief – wir bleiben hier bis Mittwoch, 6 Februar – dann nach
Strasbourg – und kommen an Baden Freitag, 8n, um 2 uhr ungefähr,
nachmittags. Jetzt gibt's einen Zug von Strasbourg. Es ist nett hier – Leute gar
nicht schlimm. Die Frieda lässt sich Kleider machen. *Was sollen wir
mitbringen?* Schreib sofort.

DHL

[Came your letter – we stay here till Wednesday, 6th February – then to
Strasbourg – and arrive in Baden Friday, 8th, at 2 o'clock approximately,
P.M. Now there is a train from Strasbourg. It's nice here – people not bad at
all. Frieda is having herself some dresses made. *What shall we bring with us?*
Write immediately.

DHL]

3024. To Mollie Skinner, [31 January 1924]
Text: MS WAPL; PC v. Notre-Dame de Paris, Détail de la façade Ouest; Postmark, [. . .]
31–1 24; M.L. Skinner, *The Fifth Sparrow* (Sydney, 1972), p. 128.

Paris.
31 Jan.

I have your letter via Curtis Brown, and am returning it to him, so that he can
make the agreement. His cable address is *Browncurt, London.* Seltzers is
Letters, New York. Best do everything through Curtis Brown. I dont know
how long I shall stay in Europe: perhaps till end of March.

Hope the MS doesn't alarm you – don't let it, anyhow.

DHL

3025. To Willard Johnson, [1 February 1924]
Text: MS YU; PC v. Château de la Malmaison; Postmark, Paris 2. II 1924; Unpublished.

Paris.
1 Feby.

– Just got your brown letter from Colorado. Yes, I *liked* that *Horse*. Didnt I say so in that London Letter on Cheval that I sent you?[1] Did you get it? If there is time send me a typescript – to London – for revision. I sent you a Paris Letter too[2] – both to Santa Fe. The Paris Letter I definitely want to look over before you print it. Dont forget. – We think of going to BadenBaden on the 7th., for a couple of weeks or so. After that, vague. I haven't heard from Bynner or Idella at all: hope both are alive. Were at Malmaison today: O Amy's Poem![3]

DHL

[Frieda Lawrence begins]
I have a lovely tie for you.

F

3026. To Mark Gertler, [2 February 1924]
Text: MS SIU; PC v. Paris – Façade de Notre Dame; Postmark, Paris 2. II 1924; Unpublished.

Hotel de Versailles. 60 Bvd. Montparnasse
2 Feb.

[4]Paris isn't so bad – to me much nicer that London – so agreeably soulless. – Today we go to Fontainebleau – next week to Baden Baden. Beyond that, vague. – I hope you got your books and are well.

DHL

3027. To Bessie Freeman, [2 February 1924]
Text: MS UNYB; PC v. Paris – Le Carrousel; Postmark, Paris 2. II 1924; Unpublished.

Paris.
2 Feb.

Pleased to have a word from you and to know Palm Springs is jolly. Paris is not unpleasant either. We shall probably be in America in the spring.
See you then. F[rieda] sends love.

D. H. Lawrence

---

[1] See p. 555 n. 2.   [2] Published in *Laughing Horse*, April 1926.
[3] Amy Lowell's poem 'Malmaison', in *Men, Women and Ghosts* (New York, 1916). Josephine Bonaparte's château at Malmaison had become a museum.
[4] Mark Gertler (1892–1939), painter, friend of DHL's since 1914. See *Letters*, ii. 214.

3028. To John Middleton Murry, [2 February 1924]

Text: MS NYPL; PC v. Paris – Avenue du Bois de Boulogne; Postmark, Paris 2–2 1924;
Moore 774.

[Hotel de Versailles, 60 Bvd Montparnasse, Paris]
2 Feb.

– Keep myself amused here dodging round a bit and trying to write a story.
Went to Malmaison yesterday. N[apoleon] and Josephine were a bit common.
Today we're going to Fontainebleau. Think to leave for BadenBaden on 6th or
7th. Tell Brett I had her letter and will buy the little paints. Paris is still rather
simpatico to me, the light is paler than London but as for sun!

DHL

3029. To Frederick Carter, [2 February 1924]

Text: MS UT; PC v. Paris – Le Tour Eiffel; Postmark, Paris 2. II 1924; Unpublished.

Hotel Versailles. 60 Bvd Montparnasse
2 Feb.

Paris is still quite nice, though hardly gay. We leave on 6th or 7th for
BadenBaden. I'm still waiting for the sun to shine, not improving meanwhile
in temper.

How are you both?

D. H. Lawrence

3030. To Hon. Dorothy Brett, [4 February 1924]

Text: MS UCin; Irvine, Brett 33.

Hotel Versailles. 60 Bvd Montparnasse, Paris.
4 Feb.

Dear Brett

Amused to have your letter. I will get you the paints on the way back – think
I know the shop. We leave on Wednesday for Strasburg. I expect we shall be
back in Paris by the 23rd Feb: and in London by 1st March – unless we do
make a little trip to Arles or somewhere south, which I doubt. I think I shall
want, and need to be in New York by about 20th March. – Paris has been quite
entertaining for the two weeks: good food and wine, and everything very
cheap. But I think I am about ready to go. I wanted to make a trip to Chartres,
but we'll do that on the way back. I just gave a look at that Ouspensky place at
Fontainebleau[1] – talked to a man called Pinder:[2] seems a rotten place, to me.

---

[1] Peter Ouspensky (1878–1947), Russian mathematician, philosopher and journalist. He was
Gurdjieff's chief disciple, hence the association of his name with the Institute at Fontainebleau.
See p. 375 n. 2.

[2] F. S. Pinder, British intelligence agent and engineer, also associated with Gurdjieff (see John
Carswell, *Lives and Letters*, 1978, p. 171 n.).

The bulk of the members – or congregation – have gone to America to propagand and pick up dollars. Haven't had a line from Murry – expect he is glooming. What's the good of gloom, anyhow! – I think we'll stay in some little hotel down in London for the week we're back. Do you know of one? – F[rieda] burst out into garments, but *nerveuse* in spite of it all: or on account of it all. Write a line

care Frau Baronin von Richthofen, Ludwig-Wilhelmstift, Baden-Baden.

Shall we go on a one-class boat, rather slow. – the R. S. M. P. Line – or second on the *Leviathan* or one of the other big boats of the United States line? As for me, I don't care. Sail somewhere about March 10th. or 12th.

3031. To Robert Mountsier, [4 February 1924]
Text: MS Smith; PC v. Paris – L'Hôtel de Cluny; Postmark, Paris 4–2 24; Unpublished.

Paris.
4 Feby.

Been here a fortnight – going on to BadenBaden on Wednesday – or at least as far as Strasburg – Paris nicer than London, anyhow – but a European winter very dreary. Prefer Del Monte. I think we may be in New York by March 20th, to pay my income tax. We shall see you then, and talk things over. Send a line care Curtis Brown.

DHL

3032. To Thomas Seltzer, 4 February 1924
Text: MS UT; Postmark, Paris 4 II 1924; Lacy, *Seltzer* 129–30.

['Shakespeare and Company', Sylvia Beach, 12 Rue de l'Odéon, Paris]
4 Feb 1924

Dear Seltzer

I wish you would send a copy of my photograph to Miss Beach at this address.[1] This is quite a famous little modern library: sells my books.

We go on Wednesday to Strasburg for BadenBaden. Be *sure* to let me know about the income tax – I've only had one letter from you since I am in Europe.

une poignée   D. H. Lawrence

---

[1] Sylvia Woodbridge Beach (1887–1962), American publisher; from 1919–41 operated Shakespeare and Company, the celebrated Paris bookstore and publishing house (whose headed notepaper DHL used for this letter). Published Joyce's *Ulysses*.

3033. To Mabel Dodge Luhan, [4 February 1924]
Text: MS Brill; PC; Postmark, Paris 4–2 24; Unpublished.

Paris.
4 Feb.

Paris quite pleasant – very quiet – We go on at end of week to Germany. Wish it weren't winter for so long. How are you all?

DHL

3034. To S. S. Koteliansky, [5 February 1924]
Text: MS BL; PC v. Paris – Palais et Jardin du Luxembourg; Postmark, Paris 5. II 1924; Gransden 29.

[Hotel de Versailles, 60 Bvd. Montparnasse, Paris]
5 Feb

Leave in the morning for Strasburg – address
c/o Frau Baronin von Richthofen, Ludwig-Wilhelmstift, *Baden Baden*.
Am quite ready to be on the move again – Greet Sonia.

DHL

3035. To Catherine Carswell, [5 February 1924]
Text: MS YU; PC v. Paris, L'Arc de Triomphe du Carrousel; Postmark, Paris 5. II 1924; cited in Moore, *Poste Restante* 77.

[Hotel de Versailles, 60 Bvd Montparnasse, Paris]
5. Feb.

We go in the morning to Strasburg – then on to Baden-Baden – address
c/o Frau Baronin von Richthofen, Ludwig-Wilhelmstift.
Not sorry to be moving on, though the French are really quite nice.

DHL

3036. To Lady Cynthia Asquith, [5 February 1924]
Text: MS UT; Postmark, Paris 5. II 1924; Unpublished.

Hotel de Versailles, 60 Bvd Montparnasse, Paris.
5 Feb.

Your letter came on here. We leave in the morning for Baden Baden. But I expect we shall be in London in March, when we should both like very much to see you. Glad your news seems pretty good: measles better, pens flying, gay time.

au revoir   D. H. Lawrence

3037. To Curtis Brown, [5 February 1924]
Text: MS UT; PC v. Paris, Avenue de l'Opéra; Postmark, Paris 5. II 1924; Unpublished.

[Hotel de Versailles, 60 Bvd Montparnasse, Paris]
5 Feb

Leave in the morning – address
c/o Frau Baronin von Richthofen Ludwig-Wilhelmstift *Baden-Baden*
Germany.

Yrs   D. H. Lawrence

3038. To Catherine Carswell, [5 February 1924]
Text: MS YU; Unpublished.

Paris.
Tuesday night

Dear Catherine
Your p.c. just come. You might open the packets and see what's in 'em. If the one from Seltzer is a *Memoir* of Maurice Magnus by me, read it if you like, and ring up Koteliansky and give it him. He can fetch it. The others are from Mabel Sterne. If they're just MS. lump them together and post them MS to Baden – if anything else, just tell me.

We go in the morning.

I'm glad you didn't come here. There's really nothing to come for. Save oneself up for something better.

DHL

3039. To S. S. Koteliansky, [5 February 1924]
Text: MS BL; Postmark, Paris 6. II 1924; Moore 774.

Paris.
Tuesday night

Dear Kot
We go in the morning.

We met Lock Ellis tonight. I don't like him. I think he doesn't like you. I said two words to him only about the publishing scheme – then felt a certain contempt for him. Don't *ask* him again. Better Schiff. But think of something else.

A postcard from Cath Carswell that there is a registered parcel for me from Seltzer. It may be *Memoir* of Maurice Magnus. I asked her to open it and see, and if it is, to ring you up and you or Murry would call for it. You won't mind, will you.

That Lock Ellis is one of those birds I dont like.

DHL

3040. To John Middleton Murry, 7 February 1924
Text: MS NYPL; cited in Murry, *New Adelphi* 455.

per Adr. Frau von Richthofen, Ludwig-Wilhelmstift, BadenBaden.

7 Feb. 1924

Dear Jack

We've just got here – all snow on the Black Forest, but down in here only wet.

Europe gives me a Wehmut, I tell you.

We stay here two weeks – then back via Paris. I learnt in New York that the income tax must be paid by March 15th., and I still have no word from that miserable Seltzer.

I dont know if you really want to go to Taos. Mabel Luhan writes she is arranging for it. You seemed to me really very unsure. You resent, *au fond*, my going away from Europe. C'est mon affaire. Je m'en vais. But you, in this interval, decide for yourself, and purely for yourself. Don't think you are doing something for me. I don't want that. Move for yourself alone. Decide for yourself, in your backbone. I don't really want any allegiance or anything of that sort. I don't want any pact. I won't have anything of that sort. If you want to go to America, *bien.* Go without making me responsible.

But if you want to go with Frieda and me and Brett – encore *bien!* One can but try, and I'm willing. But a man like you, if he does anything in the name of, or for the sake of, or because of somebody else, is bound to turn like a crazy snake and bite himself and everybody, on account of it.

Let us clear away all nonsense. I don't *need* you. That is not true. I need nobody. Neither do you need me. If you pretend to need me, you will hate me for it.

Your articles in the *Adelphi* always annoy me. Why care so much about your own fishiness or fleshiness?[1] Why make it so important? Can't you focus yourself outside yourself? Not forever focussed on yourself, ad nauseum?

I met Lock Ellis. Didn't like him.

You know I don't care a single straw what you think of me. Realise that, once and for all. But when you get to twisting, I dislike you. – And I very much dislike any attempt at an intimacy like the one you had with Lock Ellis and others. When you start that, I only feel: For God's sake, let me get clear of him.

I don't care what you think of me, I don't care what you say of me, I don't even care what you do against me, as a writer. – Trust yourself, then you can expect me to trust you. – Leave off being emotional. Leave off twisting. Leave

---

[1] In his essay 'Heads or Tails' (*Adelphi*, February 1924), Murry described himself as a merman who seems to grow 'fishier and fishier' and will eventually become a fish 'as Mr. Lawrence says I ought to be' (p. 771), an allusion to DHL's essay 'The Proper Study' in *Adelphi*.

off having any emotions at all. You haven't any genuine ones, except a certain anger. Cut all that would-be sympathetic stuff out. Then know what you're after.

I tell you, if you want to go to America as an unemotional man making an adventure, bien, allons! If you want to twist yourself into more knots, don't go with me. That's all. I never had much patience, and I've none now.

DHL

3041. To Mabel Dodge Luhan, 7 February 1924
Text: MS Brill; Luhan 138–9.

care Frau Baronin von Richthofen, Ludwig-Wilhelmstift, *Baden-Baden*, Germany
7 Feby 1924

Dear Mabel

We have just come here – I find two letters from you.

It would be good if we could make a bit of a life at Taos. The only thing is to try. I think it would be a good idea to run the big house as a guest-house.[1] But henceforth in the world I count on nothing. Things will have to happen in their own way. No good trying to *make* anything. Yet of course one has to provide for the hour, even if one looks no further. So I think it quite a good idea to make the big house a guest house, and the rest of us dispose ourselves in the others. Frieda must write to you too. Which house would you choose for yourself?

We are due to stay here two weeks: then we go back to Paris and London. It may be necessary for me to be in New York by March 15th, to pay my income tax. If Seltzer will see that it is paid for me, we may not come until beginning of April.[2] – If we come early, we might come on to Mill Valley. Quien sabe!

Your long letter about extroverts and introverts. You know, those classifications mean so little to me. No classifications whatever mean much to me. But it seems to me, the life that rises from the blood itself is the life that is living, while the life that rises from the nerves and the brain is the life that is death. – As for washing windows – we called at that Fontainebleau place. The Russian there believes entirely in going against the grain.[3] He would make you wash windows and scrub floors eight hours a day, and the viler your temper the better he would find it for you. Get your energy out of reaction and out of resentment. The fine fury of resentment. His idea.

But as for me, I am no curer. At least I am not extrovert enough for that.

---

[1] See p. 442 n. 4.   [2] April] February   [3] See p. 568 n. 1.

Please yourself whether you wash windows or whether you don't. Myself, I don't care much for washing dishes or windows any more. But, in these cities, I would be very glad to be cutting down a tree and sawing it up, or cutting the ice in the stream, as in those months at Del Monte with the Danes.

I am awfully sorry about Granfer. And my little Zegua[1] – what a tartar she'll be by the time I see her again!

If being an introvert means always drawing in, in, in to yourself, and not going bravely out, and giving yourself, then for God's sake wash windows also and go out to them, if only savagely.

Que vamos hacer? Quien sabe![2]

DHL

Best write to London.

3042. To S. S. Koteliansky, [9 February 1924]
Text: MS BL; Postmark, Baden-Baden 9 2 24; Moore 777.

Ludwig Wilhelmstift, BadenBaden
9 Feb.

Dear Kot

I had a letter from Murry. He says he is putting £500 and you £200 to the publishing scheme. As soon as I can get to America and can see what I've got I will let you have the other £300. Meanwhile nothing from Seltzer, and the latest I learned in Paris was that income tax must be paid by March 15th.

Murry seems to have got another man up his sleeve. It means he'll fasten on to somebody else, and not come to Taos. Thank God for that. I don't want him, flatly. You keep him in London and do businesses with him.

Germany is queer – seems to be turning – as if she would make a great change, and become manly again, and a bit dangerous in a manly way. I hope so. Though everything is poorer, terrible poverty, even no tram-cars running, because they can't afford the fares, and the town dark at night, still there is a certain healthiness, more than in France, far more than in England, the old fierceness coming back.

We think of going to Munich for a few days.

If Murry talks to you about America at all, dissuade him from going, at least with me.

Greet Sonia and Grisha and Ghita.

DHL

---

[1] Granfer, the horse Frieda rode, had died (see Letter 3047). DHL rode Zegua (cf. Letter 2939).
[2] 'What are we going to do? Who knows!'

[Frieda Lawrence begins]
Lawrence quite cheerful here with my mother and sister! Good wishes for your happiness!!

F –

3043. To David Garnett, 9 February 1924
Text: MS NYPL; Postmark, Baden-Baden 9 2 24; Unpublished.

c/o Frau Baronin von Richthofen, Ludwig Wilhelmstift, *Baden Baden*
9 Feb 1924

Dear David

I expect I shall – we shall – be back in London in early March. Will let you know, and we'll fix a meeting.

Yes, use the 'Snake' if you wish, but please for formality's sake ask Secker.[1]

Glad you have a wife, a child, a novel, and renown to your name.[2]

Wiedersehen   D. H. Lawrence

3044. To Frederick Carter, 9 February 1924
Text: MS UT; Unpublished.

care Frau Baronin von Richthofen, Ludwig-Wilhelmstift, *Baden Baden*
9 Feb 1924

Dear Carter

I got the essay as we were leaving the hotel in Paris – haven't read it yet. Your letter came on here.

Koteliansky's publishing scheme seems in abeyance for the moment. Remains to see what he will devise.

The MS. of the 'Dragon'·I left with Murry, who was reading it. Would you mind writing to him to send it you, – at the *Adelphi*?

Here it is quite sunny, but cold, with snow on the Black Forest. Prices enormously high – Germany beginning to get her back up.

We're due to go on to Munich for a few days: then back here. I expect to be in England in early March, hope to see you then.

Greet you both.

D. H. Lawrence

---

[1] It is possible that Garnett wanted Francis Meynell and Vera Mendel to include 'Snake' in the 'Zoo' section of *The Week-End Book* which they were compiling (to be published by the Nonesuch Press on 26 June 1924). Since none of them appears to have sought Secker's permission, if this was Garnett's plan, it failed.

[2] Garnett's first son, Richard Garnett, b. 8 January 1923. David Garnett's novel, *Lady into Fox*, was awarded the Hawthornden and Tait Black prizes in 1923. (Cf. Letter 2917 and n. 5.)

3045. To Mabel Dodge Luhan, [9 February 1924]
Text: MS Brill; Luhan 140.

Baden Baden
9 Feb.

Dear Mabel

Now don't you keep on going on to me about introverts and extroverts and insides and outsides. It's all in the head, and no good will come out of the head. I can feel you going like a terrible clockwork when you write those letters.

And wash just a few windows and dishes, till you can do it rhythmically and with a grace. It's good for you. But no need to condemn yourself to any of those things. Only don't condemn yourself further to headwork. It's just *futile*.¹ You must learn to abstain from that vice of 'knowing', when knowing is mere nothingness, not even an end in itself, because there's no end to it, like a bottomless pit: which swallows every human relation. Worse than sensation.

I read *Demian* in Germany when it first came out, and have almost forgotten it. But the first part interested me. The last part I thought *sau dumm* with its Mother Eva who didn't know whether she was wife or mother or what.²

Germany is queer, though. Just changing, making a great change. Very interesting. Things might happen here, and people might be as one wants people to be.

We are going to Munich for a few days.

I rather hope Murry won't come to Taos. Don't trust him very well.

DHL

3046. To Martin Secker, 9 February 1924
Text: MS UInd; Postmark, [. . .]; Secker 55.

Ludwig Wilhelmstift, Baden Baden
9 Feb 1924

Dear Secker

Thank you for sending on the letters. Here's one of them – of course from America. But it might one day be useful.

Sunny and cold here, with snow on the Black Forest. Germany awfully poor: prices abominably high, and even no tram-cars running here, because folks can't afford them. The RentenMark is frightfully expensive:³ result, some 4,000,000 unemployed. So they say. – Nevertheless Germany is getting her back up: she's going to leave off looking round for help: she'll help herself again before long. Seems much more manly.

¹ The word is heavily underlined five times.
² Hermann Hesse, *Demian, Die Geschichte einer Jugend* [*Demian, A Story of Youth*] (Berlin, 1919). Demian's mother, Eva, has an ambiguous relationship with both her son and his friend, the narrator of the story.   ³ The new gold Mark.

We'll be going to Munich for a few days, then back here.
Grüsse from both.

D. H. Lawrence

3047. To Mabel Dodge Luhan, 10 February 1924
Text: MS UT; Moore 778–9.

Baden Baden.
10 Feb 1924

Dear Mabel

I will answer your introvert extrovert question, since evidently it is a problem to you.

One must be both. No doubt every individual is predominantly one. But we keep our sanity by being both. A *pure* introvert is insane and a destructive influence. So is a pure extrovert, like Lenin or Karl Marx or most Americans. You are too much an introvert. Then learn, and humbly learn to be sufficiently an extrovert, so that you may have a balance. Otherwise it's all no good. You've got to curb your introverted pride, first and foremost. One's pride should be in one's *wholeness*, not in an intensification of ones own partiality. You pride yourself on your intense power of *drawing-in* to yourself. But in the end, this power is your destruction. If you want to destroy yourself in this way, well and good. If you don't, you must quite humbly learn to go forth and give. Give even to the window that you polish. Give it its polish. *Serve* with the spirit and create or make with the body. Even make the window shine.

In all the four modes you've got to learn to serve, instead of[1] to demand and command and absorb. Tony's very helplessness made you serve him. But it is not only weakness you must serve. You should learn to be glad to serve strength. The new joy of that. Much deeper.

Don't you see, a pure introvert becomes at last purely conceited, out of gear with everything, and putting everything out of gear. Even Ghandi is that. It is all very well for bringing about a debâcle. If you want to bring about all the debâcle possible, be a pure introvert, like Ghandi or St. Francis. – Otherwise, learn the error and the hatefulness of pure introversion. Even repent.

There is necessary a balance. But you have gone so far to one side, it is *really* easier for you to go over the edge than to return. Collier is utterly out of balance.[2] The Santa Fe crowd is perhaps seeking a little balance, in its own way. Learn to modify yourself.

---

[1] instead of] not only   [2] See p. 332 n. 1.

Of course a pure extrovert is as hateful as a pure introvert. This purity is their horror. Like Lenin and maybe Ramsey MacDonald.[1]

DHL

The great sin is the trying to destroy the living balance. The Holy Ghost is the Balancer. And the sin against him is unpardonable, because, once finally destroy the balance, and your soul is broken, your being is inchoate.

If you can't handle the dishes gently and delicately when you wash up, more shame on you. If you see the 'innate depravity' of a cup and saucer, it lies in yourself.

The Fontainebleau place practices these things, but all by *will* and force, releasing energy by friction: You'd be *forced* to scrub floors. In my idea, you must *choose*, with your whole soul's consent, to do what you're going to do.

[Frieda Lawrence begins]

Baden-Baden
10. II 24.

Dear Mabel,

I want to be in Taos by the end of April – We never saw the spring there and I want to see that – and I dont see why with some good will on all sides we shouldnt live near each other; not quite à la Fontainebleau: a community *forced on* us from the *outside*, but we have all reached the same point as far as the world is concerned and we *must* go *on* further together; nobody else will – Personally I always feel happy these days – Lawrence also is happier here and in Paris, England is really like an unboiled pudding at present. It would be fun to stay at the ranch too a little while in the spring – And poor old Granpa dead, that grieves me – We *wont* have a friendship like Alice Corbin, 'small beer' wont do – You must have had a hard and lonely time, but it's good for one and you have Tony – It must be so difficult to understand each other you and Tony – *such* a gulf, it's wonderful really! I am looking forward to our new life! Your washing dishes and hating it made me laugh! You don't know how *lazy* I have been sometimes – Just as one feels!

All good to you,

Frieda

---

[1] James Ramsay MacDonald (1866–1937) became first Labour Prime Minister in Britain, in January 1924. (Cf. *Letters*, i. 3.)

3048. To Emily King, [11 February 1924]
Text: MS Needham; PC v. Baden-Baden – Markt und Neues Schloss; Postmark, Baden-
B[aden] 11 2[. .]; Unpublished.

> BadenBaden
> Monday

Bright frosty weather here – everything very dear, everybody very poor – even
no tram-cars running, people can't afford the fare. Yet the people seem more
alive. – We may go to Munich for a few days.

> DHL

3049. To Idella Purnell, [11 February 1924]
Text: MS UT; PC v. Baden-Baden – Altes Schloss; Postmark, Baden-Baden 11 2 24;
Nehls, ii. 322.

> *Baden Baden*
> 11 Feb.

I keep sending you a word, but get no sign from you – hope all is well. I hear of
you via Spoodle. – Germany cold and sunny and very poor. I remember how
Dr Purnell hates postcards – hope you don't.

> DHL

3050. To S. S. Koteliansky, 12 February 1924
Text: MS BL; Postmark, Baden-Baden 13 2. 24; Zytaruk 268.

> Ludwig-Wilhelmstift. BadenBaden
> 12 Feb. 1924

My dear Kot
    I have your letter. Very good, go ahead with the publishing scheme. I'll be
in London before long, and we can settle it all up. We are due to leave here on
the 20th – stay a few days in Paris – and be in London by about 26th. I have no
word at all from that dog of a Seltzer, so it looks as if I shall have to go quickly
to New York. God knows what he may be up to. – I haven't much money in
England, but there should be plenty in New York to make up all you want:
unless Seltzer has gone all wrong.
    Don't think about doing that Magnus MS. till we have talked it over. I
didn't want my memoir to be published apart from Magnus' own *Foreign
Legion* book. There doesn't seem any point in it.
    If we are only going to stay in London a week or so, we shall not go up to
Hampstead, but shall stay in some hotel down town. You might tell me if you
know a decent quiet place.
    This Europe still wearies me. I shall be glad to leave it.

> Wiedersehen   DHL

3051. To Catherine Carswell, 12 February 1924
Text: MS YU; Postmark, [. . .]; cited Carswell 216.

Ludwig Wilhelmstift – BadenBaden
12 Feb 1924

Dear Catherine

Thank you for sending on the MS. – I suppose the things from Mill Valley were the two letters you forwarded.[1]

Germany sunny but cold – very poor – even no trams – but the people getting their back up again.

We stay one more week here – then back to Paris to pick up our bags. Ought to be in London by 26th. – That hateful Seltzer writes never a word – looks as if he was up to tricks. I shall have to go quick to New York – So shall probably stay just a week in London. Do you know a quiet hotel somewhere in town? Don't tell anybody I'm coming. I don't want to see people.

Europe very wearying – and no point in travelling, at least in winter. Far better save one's energy at home.

wiedersehen   DHL

3052. To Hon. Dorothy Brett, 13 February 1924
Text: MS UCin; Postmark, Baden-Baden 14. 2 24; Irvine, Brett 34.

Ludwig-Wilhelmstift, BadenBaden
13 Feb 1924

Dear Brett

Your letter and Murry's this evening. Tell him not to bother to buy a new dark suit. And if he's not coming till first week in April, why bother with a new overcoat? Leave it till next year.

As for Frieda and her finery, it's not very fine, and she's already not thrilled by it any more. The old things are nicest. – My new and splendid brown shoes I have given away, because they pressed my heel, and I don't intend to have my heel bruised by a brown shoe, even if the serpent may bruise it.[2]

I am getting worried about that dog of a Seltzer: am afraid we shall have to rush off, first week in March. Thank you so much for saying you will let me know about an hotel. Look up the ships too. I think you will find that the one-class boats take three or even four days longer than the big boats, so perhaps we'd better go second on a big boat, for quickness. Somebody said the *United States Line* was cheapest, because they don't have drinks. I expect you will know. You must decide whether you will come with us, or with Murry at the end of the month. Perhaps better with us – and we can wait for him in New York or not far off. Ask your sister-in-law to advise you of an inexpensive hotel

---

[1] I.e. letters from Mabel Luhan.   [2] Cf. Genesis iii. 15.

in New York.[1] And if you go with us, you can arrange a visit to your millionaire relative in the interim of waiting for Murry. That is quite a good idea. – I wish we could get an apartment in New York for a little while – till we can move on. Or perhaps in the country near. I must see. I will also write about it.

I am feeling very weary of Europe. But the time is drawing very near, to go.

Perhaps better if Jack makes that little trip on the ocean alone. He *wants* to be alone for a bit.

We leave here on the 20th. for Paris – same address in Paris.

Let me know your decision.

DHL

3053. To John Middleton Murry, 13 February 1924
Text: MS NYPL; Huxley 595.

Ludwig-Wilhemstift, *Baden-Baden*
13 Feb. 1924.

Dear Jack

I wrote Kot about the money for the publishing scheme. Get the thing ready so we can fix it up before we go – before I go. I don't hear a word from Seltzer – he has only written once since I was in Mexico. I begin to feel a bit anxious. I expect I shall have to be in New York by about 10th March – so I shall be in London again by the end of this month at least. I think probably it's best to get that MS. finished with.[2] If we have to go a fortnight ahead, we can wait for you in New York. And Brett can go along with us if she likes.

Sometimes I really get discouraged: quite discouraged altogether.

We leave here on the 20th., for Paris.

It's a low-water mark.

But one must eschew emotions – they are a disease.

DHL

(a bad pen!)

3054. To Earl and Achsah Brewster, [13 February 1924]
Text: MS UT; Brewster 67–8.

care Frau Baronin v. Richthofen, Ludwig Wilhelmstift, *Baden Baden*.
Germany
13 Feb. 1923

Dear Brewster and Achsah

We were in Paris a while and Frieda talked so much of you. I'm sorry you were not there.

---

[1] Antoinette Heckscher Brett (d. 1965), daughter of the New York industrialist August Heckscher; m. 1911, Oliver Sylvain Baliol Brett (1881–1963), later 3rd Viscount Esher.
[2] Cf. Letter 3050.

Europe depresses me rather – and Germany is cold. I am like you now: I loathe a European winter, particularly here in the north.

It looks as if I shall have to get back to New York before March 15th – which also is rather a blow. I can't get any answer from Seltzer to my letters, nor whether he has paid in any of the money he owes me, nor whether he will send in my income tax for me, nothing. So I shall just have to go and see to it all. I intended going later, but not till warm weather was there. It's rather a bore.

I suppose we shall go west again, to New Mexico, and later down to Old Mexico. At the moment I don't feel like going east. I feel so strongly that all the oriental stuff is really played out, that the religions of the east have passed into that inevitable second phase, and become false religions, and people like Ghandi false prophets. Maybe later one will go. But not now.

Then again I really like Mexico and feel some hope there. If the revolution is over, we shall go back there – probably to Oaxaca. And if we manage to settle down at all, I hope you and Achsah and the child will come and see us. It is never cold – same latitude as Delhi, but high altitude.

I didn't go on with my psychologic books.[1] The response to them was so very stupid, in the world, best leave the rest unsaid. The next thing coming is another Australian book. When we were in West Australia a young woman showed me an MS. I said, why didn't she write a plain Australian book. A year later came the MS of the plain Australian book – and such a muddle and mess, but good stuff in it, very. So I just wrote the whole thing out again from end to end, added and took away, and it will come under our joint names. – *The Boy in the Bush* is the title. I like it. Hope you will.

Middleton Murry wants to come with us to America, but cant get away till April. We may have to wait for him in the east. I wonder where? – Can you recommend a quiet, not very expensive hotel in New York? Or we might try the country near. If you have a suggestion write to me:

Hotel Versailles. 60 Bvd Montparnasse, Paris. 6.

We shall be there on the 21st and stay a few days: then London, which I don't like.

I wish we could have met and had a talk. Damn Seltzer and all publishers. Frieda greets you.

DHL

---

[1] *Psychoanalysis and the Unconscious* and *Fantasia of the Unconscious*.

3055. To Frederick Carter, [14 February 1924]
Text: MS UT; PC v. Baden-Baden; Postmark, Baden-Baden 14.2.24; Unpublished.

Ludwig-Wilhelmstift. Baden Baden.
[14 February 1924]

Have you read *The Book of Revelation* – by John Oman – Cambridge University Press 7/6?[1] I should think his rearrangement would interest you – seems to me fairly sound. – We stay here another week, then back to Paris for a short time.
Greet Mrs Carter.

D. H. Lawrence

3056. To S. S. Koteliansky, [18 February 1924]
Text: MS BL; PC; Postmark, Baden-Baden 18 2. 24; Zytaruk 269.

Baden Baden
Monday

Thanks for sending letters. Haven't you had mine? I wrote by return – agreeing heartily. We leave Wednesday for Paris – expect to be in London by 26th at latest.
Pardon postcard. I am incorrigible.

DHL

3057. To Curtis Brown, 18 February 1924
Text: MS UT; Huxley 595–6.

Ludwig-Wilhelmstift, *Baden-Baden*
18 Feb. 1924 Monday

Dear Curtis Brown,
We leave here on Wednesday for Paris – stay there a few days – Hotel de Versailles, 60 Bvd. Montparnasse – and come on the 26th to London.
I shall have to go at once to New York, as I can't get any answer from Seltzer, whether he has put me any of the money he owes me into the bank, and whether he will pay my income tax. So I shall have to go myself. For six weeks I have had no word at all from Seltzer, in answer to my letters. I shall be

---

[1] John Wood Oman (1860–1939), *Book of Revelation; theory of the text* (Cambridge, 1923). Oman was a Presbyterian theologian at Westminster College, Cambridge.

thankful to hand over the business to your representative, once I am over there.

I will call in and see you as soon as I am back.

Yrs   D. H. Lawrence

Mrs Luhan writes that your son will probably go to Taos.

3058. To Mabel Dodge Luhan, [18 February 1924]

Text: MS Brill; PC v. Baden-Baden – Neues Schloss; Postmark, Baden-Baden 18 2 24; Unpublished.

Baden.

18 Feb.

A bunch of your letters just come on. I don't understand about the cable – everybody had my Paris address in London. I will write tomorrow, Frieda too. We go in two days to Paris – I still expect to be in New York by middle of March. It would be fun to motor from San Francisco – but we must not decide just yet. I think I'd rather have the two-story house – but it seems greedy. Anyhow we'll write tomorrow – this to catch post.

DHL

3059. To E. M. Forster, 19 February 1924

Text: MS KCC; cited in Paul Delany, *D. H. Lawrence's Nightmare* (New York, 1978), p. 57.

Baden Baden.

19 Feb 1924

Dear E M

Thank you for *Pharos and Pharillon*, which I have read.[1] Sad as ever, like a lost soul calling Ichabod.[2] But I prefer the sadness to the Stracheyism.[3] To me you are the last Englishman. And I am the one after that.

We leave here tomorrow – Gott sei dank. Paris for a few days. Then London for a few days. Then America again.

The milk's all spilt. One's got to look for another cow.

Hope to see you about the 28th.

DHL

---

[1] Forster's *Pharos and Pharillon* – a collection of articles based on his experiences in Egypt – was published by Leonard and Virginia Woolf, Hogarth Press, 1923.

[2] See 1 Samuel iv. 21. The name is usually translated to mean 'the glory has departed'.

[3] The witty, cynical irony associated with Lytton Strachey (1880–1932) in his *Eminent Victorians* (1918), etc. DHL's strong distaste for him was of long standing: see *Letters*, ii. 272, 315, 321.

3060. To John Middleton Murry, [19 February 1924]
Text: MS NYPL; Unpublished.

[Ludwig-Wilhelmstift, Baden Baden]
[19 February 1924][1]

I send you this little article on the California Indians by a Basque Spaniard anthropologist called Jaime de Angelo – Mabel Sterne sent it me.[2] I think it interesting – If you like to put some of it in the *Adelphi*, I should think there would be no objection – though better ask Mabel –

Mrs Mabel Luhan. Mill Valley. Marin County. California.
We've both got colds – curse this winter.

I send you a little review of Oman's book, which you print if you like or throw away if you like.[3]

Post this letter to Mrs Seltzer for me – I think it will be quicker.

Dont put my name on the review if you use it.

3061. To Mabel Dodge Luhan, [19 February 1924]
Text: MS Brill; Luhan 150–1.

Baden Baden.
19 Feb.

Dear Mabel

I can't answer about those diagrams and Jung introvert stuff[4] – it really means nothing to me. I don't really like the mental excitation of it all. Nor the sort of excitation that comes out of de Angulo's letter, and that business of Clarence and the puppy and the 'anima'.[5] It all seems to me a false working-up, and an inducement to hysteria and insanity. I know what lies back of it all: the same indecent desire to have everything in the *will* and the *head*. Life itself comes from elsewhere.

---

[1] On 18 February DHL received a number of letters from Mabel Luhan, which he acknowledged immediately (Letter 3058) promising to write again the following day. This letter to Murry (written on an envelope) with which he enclosed the article by Jaime de Angulo must have been written at about the same time.

[2] Mabel Luhan had recently made the acquaintance of Jaime de Angulo (1887–1950). He had worked with Jung in Zurich and it was from him that Mabel Luhan acquired the habit of seeing life in terms of extroverts and introverts (Luhan 138): cf. Letters 3041, 3045, 3047.

[3] Review of Oman's *Book of Revelation*, signed by 'L. H. Davidson', appeared in *Adelphi*, i (April 1924), 1011–13 (see p. 583 n. 1). See *Apocalypse*, ed. Mara Kalnins, pp. 41–2.

[4] Mabel Luhan referred to this material as 'the psychoanalytic rigamarole I had been sending him' (Luhan 150).

[5] Clarence Thompson had one of Mabel Luhan's puppies, which he called 'Anima'; he killed it accidentally. For de Angulo's interpretation of the relationship between the puppy and its owner, see Luhan 144–5.

As for inviting de Angulo to Taos, do as you like. It doesn't matter much, either way.

The little story of Tony is nice: but the road is more difficult than snow and ham.[1]

That *Men Beasts and Gods* seems to me a good deal faked.[2] Anyhow that oriental stuff is a fraud. The middle of Asia there is the old evil destructive centre, now about to rouse again and work on us – particularly Europe.

But we have no real faith unless we can see through all that stuff, and then ignore it. Also all this poking and prying into the Indians is a form of indecency.

I feel very unsure about everything – Taos and everything. Everything seems to take the wrong direction. Why do you send me those clock-face diagrams and ask me to draw you? Can't you see the effect that has on me – makes me just completely skeptical. – However, one just fatalistically makes a move – like Tony's going east.

By the middle of March I expect we shall be in New York – then we'll decide the next move. Frieda wants to come to Taos.

DHL

I read *Arabia Deserta* long ago – but shall like to read it again.[3]

3062. To Baroness Anna von Richthofen, [20 February 1924]
Text: MS UCB; PC v. Strasbourg – Un Nid de Cigognes; Postmark, Strasbourg [. . .]; Unpublished.

[Strasbourg]
Mittwoch abends

schon hier – essen in der Stadt, dann weiter – wir haben Betten im Schlafwagen
Grüsse Nusch.

DHL

[Wednesday evening

already here – dine in the city, then onwards – we've got beds in the sleeping-car.
Greet Nusch.

DHL]

[1] For Tony Luhan's story see Luhan 146–7.
[2] Ferdinand Antoni Ossendowski (1876–1944), *Beasts, Men and Gods* (New York, 1922).
[3] Charles Montagu Doughty (1843–1926), *Travels in Arabia Deserta* (1888). The book had been re-issued in 1921 with an introduction by T. E. Lawrence.

3063. To Hon. Dorothy Brett, [20 February 1924]
Text: MS UCin; PC v. Strasbourg – Nid de Cigognes; Postmark, [Strasb]ourg 20[. . .];
Irvine, Brett 35.

[Strasbourg]
Wed evening

eating here, then on through the night to Paris – Hotel de Versailles, 60 Bvd.
Montparnasse.
Send a line.

DHL

3064. To Baroness Anna von Richthofen, [20 February 1924]
Text: MS UCB; PC v. Strasbourg – Nid de Cigognes; Postmark, [. . .]; Unpublished.

Strassburg
– 9 Uhr Abends

Denke dir, der Bub vom Löwen ist zu spät mit dem Grossgepäck gekommen,
wir haben den Zug verloren, könnten erst an 2.0 Uhr abreisen – jetzt fahren
um 10.25 von hier, und reisen durch die Nacht. Ich aber habe Schlafwagen,
die andern sitzen im Coupé. Schlimm! Wir kommen aber wohl an.

DHL

[Just think, the boy from the Löwen came too late with the large luggage, we
missed the train, couldn't depart till 2.0 o'clock – now leave here at 10.25, and
travel through the night. But I have a sleeping-car, the others sit in the coupé.
Awful! But we will indeed arrive.

DHL]

3065. To S. S. Koteliansky, [21 February 1924]
Text: MS BL; PC v. Château de La Malmaison [Napoleon's Throne]; Postmark, [Par]is
21–2 24; Zytaruk 269.

Hotel de Versailles, 60 Bvd. Montparnasse, Paris 6.
Thursday.

Got back here this morning – stay probably till Tuesday, but will write. Had
your letter: nothing from Seltzer.

DHL

3066. To Baroness Anna von Richthofen, [21 February 1924]
Text: MS UT; PC v. Château de La Malmaison; Postmark, [. . .]21–2 24; Unpublished.

Hotel de Versailles. 60 Bvd Montparnasse
Donnerstag

Wir sind schon hier – um sechs Uhr angekommen – sehr kalt in Paris, aber kein Schnee.

Es was sehr nett bei dir in Baden: gute Erinnerüngen haben wir. Bleib du selig und gesund bis wir kommen, nächstes Jahr.

Grüsse DHL

Dies ist das Schloss von Josephine.

[We're already here – arrived at six o'clock – very cold in Paris, but no snow.

It was very nice with you in Baden: we have pleasant memories. You keep blissful and healthful till we come, next year.

Greetings DHL

This is Josephine's palace.]

3067. To Catherine Carswell, [21 February 1924]
Text: MS YU; PC v. Château de La Malmaison: Sous bois dans le Parc; Postmark, [Pa]ris 21–2 24; cited in Moore, *Poste Restante* 77.

Hotel de Versailles. 60 Bvd Montparnasse
Thursday

Just got back here – shall stay probably till Tuesday then London – still no word from Seltzer.

DHL

3068. To Thomas Seltzer, [21 February 1924]
Text: MS UT; Postmark, Paris 21–2 24; Lacy, *Seltzer* 130.

Hotel Versailles. 60 Bvd Montparnasse, *Paris 6.*
21 Feb.

Dear Thomas

We are back here from Baden Baden – still without having any word from you – which is almost mysterious. I intend to go to London on Tuesday, and sail about 5th March to New York, to be in time to pay my income tax and arrange with you and Curtis Brown in New York about the *Boy in the Bush.* Then once I am fixed up with Curtis Brown I needn't bother about the business end of our relationship any more.

I have been drawing cheques on the National Chase Bank: hope you have kept my account supplied. Also I wonder if you disposed of the film rights of *Women in Love*.[1]

But I suppose I shall know when I see you.

Yrs D. H. Lawrence

3069. To S. S. Koteliansky, [23 February 1924]

Text: MS BL; Zytaruk 270.

Paris
Saturday

Dear Kot

We arrive Victoria from Dover at 5.10 on Tuesday afternoon. I asked Brett to get us a room at Garlands hotel in Suffolk St – near National Gallery. *Adelphi* too close to Martin Secker. I asked Brett and Murry to meet us if they felt like it – you too if you feel like it. Anyhow let us all dine together, Garlands or elsewhere, Tuesday evening, and discuss everything.

Wiedersehen DHL

3070. To Baroness Anna von Richthofen, [23 February 1924]

Text: MS UCB; Frieda Lawrence 183–4.

Hotel de Versailles. 60. Bvd Montparnasse, Paris.
Samstag

Liebste Müttchen

Wir sitzen hier im Bett – haben kaffee getrunken – Uhr sagt 8.50 – und sehen die Leute und Wagen im Boulevard draussen vorbei gehen, in der Morgen Sonne. Die alten Frauen und Männer in dem hohen Haus gegenüber schütteln die Teppische von den Balkonen, und sind sehr putz-fleissig. Paris ist immer noch Paris.

Wir waren gestern an Versailles. Es ist aber dumm, so furchtbar gross und flach, viel zu gross für die Landschaft. Nein, so eine grössheit – oder Grösse – ist nur wie der aufgeblasenen, selbst-aufgeblasenen Frosch, der sich grösser als Natur machen will, und natürlich geht er Pop! So war der Roi Soleil: ein sehr künstliches Licht. Die Frieda furchtbar entäuscht uber den Petit Trianon von Marie Antoinette: ein Puppen Palast, und puppen Schweizer Dorf von der Bühne. Die arme Marie Antoinette, wollte so einfach sein und ganz Bauerin werden, mit ihrem Spielzeug Schweizerdorf und ihrem netten, etwas ordinären, oesterreichen blonden Gesicht. Entlich ward sie zu einfach, ohne Kopf. – Auf dem Grossen Kanal Schuhschlitterten die Leut', ein Paar Leut, klein und kalt und ohne Freude zwischen diesen gekämmten Bäumen

---

[1] Cf. Letter 3005 and n. 4.

die da stehen wie Haare mit Allee-scheiteln. – Und dies ist Grösse! Der Mench ist dumm. Natürlich geht der Frosch Pop!

Die Frieda hat sich zwei Hüte gekauft, und ist stolz – wir haben 20 von Nusch's dollars gewechselt, 23.60 francs dem Dollar: und haben ihr drei sehr schönen Blusen gekauft.

Morgen gehen wir an Chartres, den Dom zu sehen. Und das ist der letzte Ausflug. Dienstag reisen wir nach London.

So, Schwiegermutter, du weisst alles was wir machen, und reist dabei und damit. So ist das Leben. Wir können zusammengehen, trotz Trennung, und du kaunst reisen, reisen, trotz älte.

Salutations, Madame. DHL

[Dearest Little Mother

We sit here in bed – have drunk coffee – clock says 8.50 – and see the people and waggons in the boulevard outside going by, in the morning sun. The old women and men in the tall building across from us are shaking the carpets from the balconies, and are very diligent at cleaning. Paris is still Paris.

We were yesterday at Versailles. But it is stupid, so frightfully large and flat, much too large for the landscape. No, such a greatness – or size – is only like the puffed-up, self-puffed-up frog, who wants to make himself larger than nature, and naturally he goes Pop! So was the Roi Soleil: a very artificial light. Frieda frightfully disappointed at the Petit Trianon of Marie Antoinette: a doll's palace, and doll's Swiss village from the stage. Poor Marie Antoinette wanted to be so simple and to become a perfect peasant, with her toy Swiss village and her nice, somewhat common, Austrian blonde face. Finally she became too simple, without a head. – On the Grand Canal the people were skating, a couple of people, little and cold and without joy between these combed trees that stand there like hair with avenue-partings. And this is greatness! Man is stupid. Naturally the frog gocs Pop!

Frieda has bought herself two hats, and is proud – we changed 20 of Nusch's dollars, 23.60 francs to the dollar: and have bought her three very lovely blouses.

Tomorrow we're going to Chartres, to see the cathedral. And that is the last excursion. Tuesday we travel to London.

So, Schwiegermutter, you know all that we're doing, and travel beside us and with us. Such is life. We can go together, in spite of separation, and you can travel, travel, in spite of age.

Salutations, Madame. DHL]

3071. To Hon. Dorothy Brett, [23 February 1924]
Text: MS UCin; PC v. Château de La Malmaison, Le Premier Consul; Postmark, Paris
23–2 24; Irvine, Brett 35.

[Hotel de Versailles, 60 Bvd Montparnasse, Paris]
Saturday –

Many thanks for the letters – I think we'll stay in Garland's Hotel – arrive
Tuesday evening in London, but I'll write the hour. The strike seems to be
settled.¹ We'll have £7 for the mysterious purchase, each: at least I hope so. It
was very cold here yesterday – we were at Versailles – silly place. Tomorrow
Chartres – and that's the last.

au revoir   DHL

3072. To Curtis Brown, 23 February 1924
Text: MS UT; Huxley 596.

Hotel Versailles, 60 Bvd Montparnasse, Paris
23 Feb. 1924

Dear Curtis Brown
     Thank you for your letter. I shall come to London on Tuesday, and on
Wednesday or Thursday come in to see you. If you should happen to be away,
send me word
          care *The Adelphi*. 18 York Buildings, Adelphi.
     I shall have to go to New York to get that MS of the Mexican novel – and I
must go down to Mexico if I am to finish that book for autumn – so probably I
may as well go at once. But I'll talk it over with you.

Yrs   D. H. Lawrence

3073. To Ada Clarke, [23 February 1924]
Text: MS Clarke; PC v. Château de La Malmaison, Le Vestibule; Postmark, Paris 23–2 24;
Lawrence–Gelder 162–3.

Paris.
Saturday

I still don't hear anything from Seltzer, so shall probably come to London on
Tuesday. Were at Versailles yesterday – a silly big place – and bitter cold. But
sunny today.

DHL

¹ Dock workers accepted the proposed settlement on 24 February 1924.

3074. To Gerald Duckworth, 27 February 1924
Text: MS Heinemann; Unpublished.

Garlands Hotel, Suffolk St, Pall Mall. SW1
27 Feb. 1924

Dear Duckworth

I wish you would be so good, in the future, as to make all statements of royalties for my books, and pay all the money in to Curtis Brown, at 6 Henrietta St. I change my address so often, it will be much easier and safer so.

Yrs   D. H. Lawrence

3075. To Earl Brewster, [28 February 1924]
Text: MS UT; Brewster 69.

[Garland's Hotel, Suffolk Street, Pall Mall, S.W.1][1]
Thursday 28 Feb

Dear Earl

We are back in London. I had your letter in Paris – glad all goes well. I will go in to Martin Secker tomorrow and send you those two books of mine. – F[rieda] says she would love a picture from you and Achsah when we have a place. We expect to sail on March 8th for New York. I shall certainly send a note to Willa Cather; I should very much like to see her.[2] My address will be

care Curtis Brown, 116 West 39th St. New York.

Though I don't suppose we shall stay long. Thank you for the addresses you sent. – You are probably right about the Wisdom of the East. If it be not a millstone round our necks.

Greet Achsah and the child.

D. H. Lawrence

3076. To Hon. Dorothy Brett, [c. 28 February 1924]
Text: MS UCin; Unpublished.

[Garland's Hotel, Suffolk Street, Pall Mall, S.W.1]
[c. 28 February 1924]

Banker: ask him to transfer your allowance to a New York bank, from now until further advice: and please to send the name of the Banker in New York, and to give you a letter to him: enclose specimen signature.

---

[1]   For this letter and all letters following up to and including 3086, with the sole exceptions of 3080 and 3085, DHL used the hotel's headed notepaper.

[2]   Willa Cather (1876–1947), American novelist. According to Dorothy Brett (*Lawrence and Brett*, pp. 38–40) DHL contacted her in New York (she lived in Greenwich Village), and on 4 April 1924 he asked Seltzer to send copies of *Kangaroo* and *The Captain's Doll* to her.

Ask sister-in-law for addresses.

Ask father for a couple of letters of introduction.

Will the New York bank allow you to have a current account and a chequebook.

Say you think of sailing on March 8th.

3077. To Frederick Carter, 29 February 1924

Text: MS UT; cited in Moore, *Intelligent Heart* 323.

[Garland's Hotel, Suffolk Street, Pall Mall, S.W.1]

29 Feb 1924

Dear Carter

I think we sail next Wednesday for New York on the *Aquitania*. My publisher seems to be turning out queer, so I must hurry.

I was so disappointed when I found Murry had not put the Astrology article in the *Adelphi*. He says it is for April.[1] But he took it for March. Bah, one can't rely on him.

I feel very weary of Europe and its fidgettiness and its complications.

I will write you from New York. Address me there

Care Curtis Brown, 116 West 39th. St.

Greetings to you and to Mrs Carter.

D. H. Lawrence

3078. To Mabel Dodge Luhan, 29 February 1924

Text: MS Brill; Luhan 153.

[Garland's Hotel, Suffolk Street, Pall Mall, S.W.1]

29 Feb 1924

Dear Mabel

I think we shall sail on Wednesday, 5th March, on the *Aquitania*, arrive in New York by 12th March. Send us[2] a line there –

care Curtis Brown, 116 West 39th. St, New York.

I am still having trouble with Seltzer: do hope he's not letting me down altogether.

Dorothy Brett is coming with us: but Murry not yet.

I look forward to Taos again, to space and distance and not all these people.

Greet Tony – Frieda sends her excited greetings.

D. H. Lawrence

---

[1] See p. 556 n. 2.   [2] us] me

3079. To Martin Secker, [1 March 1924]
Text: MS UInd; Secker 56.

[Garland's Hotel, Suffolk Street, Pall Mall, S.W.1]
[1 March 1924][1]

Dear Secker
Many thanks. No news of the next generation?
The parcel
    c/o Frau von Richthofen, Ludwig Wilhelmstift, Baden Baden.
if it is too heavy, leave out the least bit of crape stuff, or something small.
DHL

3080. To Baroness Anna von Richthofen, [1 March 1924]
Text: MS UCB; PC v. Cunard R. M. S. *Aquitania*; Postmark, London Mar 1 1924;
Unpublished.

[Garland's Hotel, Suffolk Street, Pall Mall, S.W.1]
Samstag. –

Wir gehen Mittwoch, 5n Marz, von Southampton, auf diesem *Aquitania*: und
kommen 11n oder 12n März an New York. Der Schiff ist so gross – riesengross
– es kann nicht viel wackeln.
Heut schichen wir das Paket für Nusch.

DHL

[We leave Wednesday, 5th March, from Southampton, on this *Aquitania*: and
arrive 11th or 12th March in New York. The ship is so large – gigantic – it
can't rock much.
Today we are sending the parcel for Nusch.

DHL]

3081. To Bessie Freeman, 1 March 1924
Text: MS UNYB; Postmark, London MAR 1 1924; cited in Moore, *Intelligent Heart* 326,
328.

[Garland's Hotel, Suffolk Street, Pall Mall, S.W.1]
1 March 1924

Dear Bessie Freeman
    We got your letter in Paris. You sound as enterprising as ever: Baja
California and all.
    Thank goodness we are getting out of Europe. It is a weariness to me. I
prefer to be on the American Continent.
    We are sailing on Wednesday on the *Aquitania*. I've got to hurry to New

---

[1] Dated by reference to the parcel, intended for Frieda's sister, Nusch, which is also mentioned in
    the letter following, postmarked 1 March 1924.

York also to see what my publisher is up to: something unsatisfactory. I suppose we shall be there a week or ten days: then probably to Taos, as a jumping-off place. Of course I want to go back to Mexico, if it is quiet enough. I have a novel I want to finish down there. I don't know how long we shall stay in Taos – a week or two: nothing permanent.

I am glad that your sister Margaret is well off – now she can leave that cold lake and take her own way in life.[1] Is she well? She needed a release, too. Write

care Curtis Brown, 116 West 39th St, New York.

I hope we'll be able to do a riding trip, all of us together, one day.

au revoir   D. H. Lawrence

[Frieda Lawrence begins]
Dear Bessie Freeman,

I am glad to be going to America again – except for seeing my children and mother here, it's cold and dreary and sad! I do hope we shall have you with us some time soon somewhere! Your sister Margaret's legacy seems like a fairy story only fortunately a reality!

So till we meet again all good things!

Frieda

3082. To Emil Krug, 2 March 1924
Text: MS (Photocopy) HU; Unpublished.

[Garland's Hotel, Suffolk Street, Pall Mall, S.W.1]
2 March 1924

Dear Emil

This is to introduce an old friend of ours, Mr. Grisha Farbman, who will be passing through Berlin from Moscow. I want you to take him to see Nusch, of whom we have often talked together.

Greetings to you.

D. H. Lawrence

3083. To Witter Bynner, 3 March 1924
Text: MS HU; Postmark, London MAR 3 1924; Huxley 596–7.

[Garland's Hotel, Suffolk Street, Pall Mall, S.W.1]
3 March 1924

Dear Bynner

We had your letter yesterday: wondered often where you were. – No news from Spoodle yet.

[1] I.e leave Buffalo and the Lake Erie area.

We sail on Wednesday on the *Aquitania* for New York: arrive about March 12th. We shall stay a week or so – then come on to New Mexico. Seltzer has been behaving queerly, I must see to him. Dorothy Brett is coming with us – she is deaf – and a painter – and daughter of Viscount Esher. I think we shall stay a while in Taos. I want to go back to Mexico – particularly I want to go to Oaxaca. What do you think of that?

We look forward to seeing you, and to making plans. Thankful to be leaving Europe – were in Paris and Germany.

                                                    Au revoir   DHL

3084. To Mollie Skinner, 3 March 1924

Text: MS WAPL; Postmark, Lo[ndon] MAR 3 1924; M.L. Skinner, 'D.H. Lawrence and *The Boy in the Bush*', *Meanjin* ix (Summer 1950), 262.

                          [Garland's Hotel, Suffolk Street, Pall Mall, S.W.1]
                                                           3 March 1924

Dear Miss Skinner

The Boy in the Bush is in the printer's hands, both here and in New York. After all Martin Secker is publishing it here: and I am signing a contract for it, drawn up by Curtis Brown. The contract is made between me and the publisher, and I sign on your behalf: and Curtis Brown has an order to pay you one-half of all receipts in England and America, after, of course, his 10% agent's fee has been deducted. It is possible Martin Secker will pay about £100. in advance of royalties – in which case Curtis Brown will at once send you a cheque for £50 or thereabouts. I will have all statements of sales made to you as well as to me. Statements are made on June 30th and Decem. 31st. and *payments* are made on 1st Oct. and 1st May, each year. Curtis Brown is very strict in business, so you will be quite safe. Write to him and ask anything you want to know.

My wife and I are sailing in two days time on the *Aquitania* to New York. Address me there, always,

          c/o Curtis Brown – 116 West 39th St., New York City.
You see the agency operates in both cities.

I am very anxious the book should be a success, and that you should get some money as well as fame. Also I hope you are pleased with it. You may quarrel a bit with the last two chapters. But after all, if a man really has cared, and cares, for two women, why should he suddenly shelve either of them? It seems to me more immoral suddenly to drop all connection with one of them, than to wish to have the two.

Write to me to New York. I expect we shall go to New Mexico, and then down to Old Mexico. But letters will come on.

The book, unfortunately, has been delayed here, and Secker will probably not have it out till early June.[1] Seltzer in America will probably be sooner – May, or even end of April. We shall see. You can write to Curtis Brown both in London and New York (in N. Y. the manager is Mr. Barmby) for all information. I will see you get six presentation copies from Secker, and six from Seltzer.

I hope now I have thought of everything.

I am not sorry to go back to America: Europe seems to me weary and wearying.

Best wishes to you. My wife sends her regards and remembrances. One day we shall meet again, and laugh things over, I know.

> Yours Sincerely   D. H. Lawrence

[Frieda Lawrence begins]
Soon I will write you a really long letter! Meanwhile all good luck to the boy!

> Yours very sincerely   Frieda Lawrence

3085. To S. S. Koteliansky, [3 March 1924]
Text: MS BL; Zytaruk 271.

> [Garland's Hotel, Suffolk Street, Pall Mall, S.W.1]
> 3rd March.

Dear Kot

Will you please give the MS. of *Memoirs* of Maurice Magnus to Secker's man. Secker wants to read it because he knew the people.

> Yrs   D. H. Lawrence

3086. To Baroness Anna von Richthofen, 4 March 1924
Text: MS UT; Frieda Lawrence 182.

> [Garland's Hotel, Suffolk Street, Pall Mall, S.W.1]
> 4 März 1924

Meine liebe Schwiegermutter

Der letzte Tag in England. Wir ziehen morgen früh abkommen um 1/2 10 an Bord der *Aquitania*. Ich habe genug von London.

Das Paket für Nusch schicken wir heute: alles fertig. Und der Bank hat schon die vier Pfund für dich an Emil geschickt: thut es am 1n. jedes Monats.

---

[1] In fact Secker received the typescript of the novel on the same day that DHL wrote this letter and, in a letter to Curtis Brown, reasonably observed: 'I think I should like to read it before signing the contract' (Secker Letter-Book, UIll). Secker wrote again to Curtis Brown on 6 March about contractual details despite his feeling that 'this book cannot pretend to be an authentic Lawrence book'. He published the novel in August, Seltzer in September 1924.

Wir hatten gestern deinen kleinen Brief: zum Abschied und zum wiederbringen, wiederkommen.

Seltzer hat telegrafiert. Wahrscheinlich ist er immer noch da, und das Geld ist nicht verschwunden, aber er zahlt es nicht. Mein agent, Curtis Brown, sagt es ist gut dass ich hin gehe, der Seltzer spielt mit meinem Geld, in seinem Geschäft.

Schreibe mir:

    c/o Curtis Brown Ltd. 116 West 39th Street, New York City.

Die Brett geht mit: der Murry kommt nachher.

                    Wiedersehen Schwiegermutter   DHL

[My dear Schwiegermutter

The last day in England. We depart tomorrow – come at 9:30 on board the *Aquitania*. I have enough of London.

The parcel for Nusch we are sending today: all ready. And the bank has already sent the four pounds for you to Emil: does it on the 1st of each month.

We had yesterday your little letter: for departure and for bringing back, coming back.

Seltzer telegraphed. Probably he is still there, and the money has not disappeared, but he isn't paying it. My agent, Curtis Brown, says it is good that I go there, Seltzer is playing with my money, in his business.

Write to me:

    c/o Curtis Brown Ltd. 116 West 39th Street, New York City.

The Brett is going along: Murry is coming afterwards.

                    Wiedersehen Schwiegermutter   DHL]

3087. To Martin Secker, [4 March 1924]

Text: MS UInd; PC v. Château de La Malmaison – Salon de Reception; Postmark, Hampstead MAR 4 1924; Unpublished.

             [Garland's Hotel, Suffolk Street, Pall Mall, S.W.1]

                           Tuesday afternoon

Many thanks for sending off the parcel. – Do you mean the typescript of Magnus' own MS? That is in New York. I will have it sent to you as soon as I get there. – We leave at 7.25 in the morning. I'm sorry the next generation hasn't arrived before we go.[1]

                        Saluti   D. H. Lawrence

---

[1] Adrian Secker, b. 11 March 1924.

3088. To Hon. Dorothy Brett, [4 March 1924]
Text: MS UCin; PC; Postmark, [. . .]; Irvine, Brett 35.

[Garland's Hotel, Suffolk Street, Pall Mall, S.W.1]
Tuesday

Off in the morning – pity we didn't see you tonight. I have left paints and Barbottine¹ and crochet hook here – and some books for Gertler. Would you or he call for them. Am awfully sorry to trouble you. – I feel I'm taking the first step. So glad to get out.

DHL

3089. To Mark Gertler, [10–11 March 1924]
Text: MS SIU; Postmark, New York MAR 11 1924; Moore, *Intelligent Heart* 327.

[Cunard R.M.S. 'Aquitania']²
Monday 10 March

Dear Gertler

We come to New York tomorrow morning – a very quick run. It was quite warm till yesterday – we were in the Gulf Stream. Now we are off America there is a strong north wind, the sea smoking its spray, and dark grey waves, and this big ship rolling. But it doesn't upset us, except Frieda a bit. The unending motion irritates her. I rather like it. Brett of course is very happy and pleased with herself. Suddenly I saw her wearing a little blue brooch I recognised as having given to Ottoline years ago – a chalcedony stone. She says Ottoline flung it at her at the time of the row. I always liked that soft blue stone. Queer how things come back to you.

The boat is very comfortable – only rather too big – like living in a Town Hall. We have a little *Daily Mail* printed on board, but not much in it. One might suggest to Kot running an 'important' daily on a liner. It would *command* attention: everybody reads our *D. M.* down to the advertisements of hotels all over America. What an opportunity of making oneself heard! An opportunity wasted. – I left Kot with a sore head: but better that than a sore heart and spirit. It's no good, the Old Jehovah does *not* rule the world any more. He's quit. Send a line to Taos, New Mexico – I expect we'll be there in ten days time, or thereabouts. There's luncheon gong, thank God! Clocks go *back* an hour each day, and the mornings are endless. Remember me to Milne and Waterton.³

DHL

¹ Barbotine is a mixture of kaolin clay used for ornamenting pottery.
² Here and for the letter following DHL used the ship's headed notepaper.
³ Herbert J.M. Milne (1888–1965), member of British Museum staff; Waterton is unidentified.

Tuesday afternoon – Here we are in New York, in half a blizzard, snow and rain on a wild wind. Seltzer met us – not very reassuring – his business in low water.[1] Brett only bewildered now.

DHL

New York looks horrible this weather. Send a line – just
Taos. New Mexico, U S A.

3090. To John Middleton Murry, [10–11 March 1924]
Text: MS NYPL; cited in Murry, *New Adelphi* 455–6.

[Cunard R.M.S. 'Aquitania']
Monday 10 Mar

Dear Jack

We come to New York tomorrow. The sea is swinging and smoking now, in a cold wind since we came out of the Gulf Stream. But it has been a pleasant passage, and we have missed none of the meals. The boat is very comfortable, only too big – like being in a town. Very quick though – we make about 580 – or 585 sea miles a day: very good going. Brett is very happy – insatiably curious – teas with doctor etc: Frieda doesn't really like the sea – the motion. I like to feel myself travelling. And it's good to get away from the doom of Europe. – I'll add a word in New York.

Yrs DHL

Tuesday afternoon
landed at last, and got all the things through customs – such a fuss. Don't come in by New York if you can go to Galveston. And little ships are humanly much nicer than big ones. – The passport officials looked askance at Brett travelling alone – called her 'this girl.' I got so mad. Then they soon slowed down, quieted up sharp. The customs people were very nice – but oh, so long. – We struggled up to 100th St buried in luggage, in a taxi, in half a blizzard, snow and rain on a gale of N E wind. New York looking vile. Seltzer was at the wharf, though I hadn't told him I was coming. He'd got it from Curtis Brown. He looks very diminished, and him so small already. Apparently his business has gone very badly this winter, and he has sleepless nights. So, it seems, might I. My money is at present in thin air, but I believe it will materialise bit by bit. Damn it all and damn everything. But I don't care terribly. – Brett just bewildered.

DHL

---

[1] Seltzer's financial troubles (a loss of $7,000 the previous year) were aggravated by his being summoned to court in January over *Casanova's Homecoming* (see pp. 292 n. 1 and 501 n. 1; Lacy, *Seltzer* 191).

Write to
Taos, New Mexico, U S A.

We'll go next week. When you come, don't declare anything on your customs declaration paper – put 'Personal Effects and Clothing' – no more. Brett went and put paints, artists materials, *Banjolette*, and I had to wangle out of paying duty. But the Customs people are nice enough.

DHL

INDEX

No distinction is made between a reference in the text or in a footnote.
All titles of writings by Lawrence are gathered under his name.
For localities, public buildings, etc. in London, see the comprehensive entry under the place-name; all biblical references are collected under 'Bible'.
A bold numeral indicates a biographical entry in a footnote. '

Abraham, 90, 198
Achsah, *see* Brewster, A.
Ada, *see* Clarke, L. A.
Adams, Franklin P., 16
Adelaide, 10, 237–8, 241, 243, 249, 273
Adele, *see* Seltzer, A.
Adelphi (Adelphi Press, The), 15, 20, 298, 327, 432, 447–8, 454, 458, 462, 480–1, 483, 485, 499–500, 519–20, 522, 529, 545, 549–50, 556–9, 565, 572, 575, 585, 591, 593
Adelphi Press, The, *see Adelphi*
Aden, 204, 206, 208, 211
Adventures of Maya the Bee, The, see Bonsels, W.
Africa, 120, 122, 219, 239, 244
Aiken, Conrad, *The Pilgrimage of Festus*, 494
Aimard, Gustave, *see* Gloux, O.
Alain, *see* Insole, A.
Alamos, 506, 570
Alamosa, 338, 354
Alan, *see* Insole, A.
Albany (Western Australia), 496
Albuquerque, 559
Aldington, Richard **242**
Alexander, Arthur, **67**
Alexander, Francesca, 545
Alexander, John, 'An Antipodean Study of D. H. Lawrence'. 9–10
Alexandria, see Forster, E.
Alfred, *see* Weber, A.
Algiers, 127
Alice, *see* Henderson, A. C.
All Things are Possible, see Shestov, L.
Alpes Maritime, 299
Alpha, *see* Barlow, A.
Alps, 65
Amalfi, 97
America, 27, 29, 31, 40, 58, 73, 86, 95–7, 100, 103–4, 107–11, 113–14, 117–18, 120–1, 124, 127, 129–32, 135, 137–8, 141-2, 144, 148–51, 154, 157, 159–61, 164–6, 168–71, 173, 175–77, 180–2, 186, 190–2,

196–8, 200, 202, 207–8, 213, 219, 224–6, 229, 235, 242–51, 253, 257–9, 267–8, 270, 272–7, 280–4, 287, 290–1, 296, 299, 305, 307, 311–14, 325, 343, 349, 351–3, 359, 362, 364–5, 368, 372, 374, 387, 398, 415, 431, 443, 447, 451–2, 457–8, 470–1, 478–9, 483, 485–6, 492, 495, 499–500, 503, 506, 508, 518, 521, 524, 542–5, 549–50, 552–3, 556, 559–60, 567, 569, 573–4, 576, 582, 584, 594–5, 596, 597, 599
American Express, 39, 44, 75–6, 79
Amy, *see* Lowell, A.
Angeles y Velarde, 526–7
Angulo, Jaime de, 585–6
Anita, *see* Schreibershofen, A. von
Antarctic, 242
Anticoli, 52, 80, 111, 127, 138
'Antipodean Study of D. H. Lawrence, An', *see* Alexander, J.
Antipodes, 282, 283
Antoinette, Marie, 589–90
Apache country, 298, 300–3, 312
Apaches, 296–7, 303, 309, 313, 432
Apocalypse Unsealed, The, see Pryse, J.
Appenine mountains, 84
Aquitania, R. M. S., 20–1, 593–4, 596–9
Arabia, 212
Arabia Deserta, Travels in, see Doughty, C.
Arabian Nights, 7, 208–11, 213, 527
Arabian Sea, 208, 213
Aran Isles, 38
Archipenko, Alexander, **548**
Ardnaree (Kandy), 179–1, 186–7, 191–6, 198–9, 201, 207–8, 213–18, 221, 243, 266, 279
Argegno, 190, 195
Arizona, 142, 362
Ailes, **565**, 568
Arno river, 83–4
Arzapalo Hotel, 436, 473, 511
Ascona, 39
Asia, 586